BALANCHINE'S
Complete Stories
OF THE
Great Ballets

Also by George Balanchine and Francis Mason
101 STORIES OF THE GREAT BALLETS

BALANCHINE'S

Complete Stories

OF THE

Great Ballets

Revised and Enlarged Edition

BY GEORGE BALANCHINE
AND FRANCIS MASON

DOUBLEDAY & COMPANY, INC.
GARDEN CITY, NEW YORK

Dancing is an action, showing outwardly the spiritual movements which must agree with those measures and perfect accords of harmony which, through our hearing and with earthly joy, descend into one intellect, there to produce sweet movements which . . . endeavor to escape and reveal themselves in movement.

GUGLIELMO EBREO, "William the Jew of Pisaro,"
Italian Dancing Master of the Renaissance

Vainest endeavor, to try to document dance, the most ephemeral of the arts. Suppose that you find the bricks and boards, the levers and pulleys of a theatre intact, and that your lunatic friend who loves the archives helps locate sources from which the scenic decoration, musical orchestration and plot evolution of a famous, forgotten ballet could be reconstructed. Suppose further that you were extremely fortunate in your friend and his treasure hunt uncovered even a precise, pre-Laban notation that enabled one to teach each pas to contemporary dancers. Still . . . Reason . . . would tell you that the essential movement would be missing. The trappings would be there, but you would not see the "dance urge" Heine saw watching Carlotta Grisi, or recognize with Kleist dance mannerism as a dislocation of the soul from the central still point of movement to the trajectory. Remember how different La Sonnambula *seemed only a few years ago as* Night Shadow? *Today's dancers . . . attend that sort of party only in line of duty and then look obligingly uncomfortable. So you leave the past buried and go back to the new theatre to watch the business at hand, ballet as it is danced today—which is the living issue, not the death mask of ballet yesterday. You leave reluctantly; besides the ballet's immediate sensual beauty, and its brilliance in time and space as a medium of silent ideas, an urgent part of the reason you had worshiped it before all other arts was the simple wonder of seeing a human body moving in the same step for the same reason as did its predecessors a century or more ago.*

GEORGE JACKSON, "Notes Towards an Anti-History of Ballet in Vienna,"
in *Ballet Review*, 1967

Each fairy tale is a magic mirror which reflects some aspect of your inner world, and of the steps required by our evolution from immaturity to maturity.

BRUNO BETTELHEIM, The Meaning and Importance of Fairy Tales, 1976

To the Subscribers,
   those who come to the ballet today,
   know it and like it so much they will
   come also tomorrow

PREFACE

This book attempts to tell the stories of ballets of lasting importance in the history of the art and to provide a record of significant new work performed in the past twenty-five years—ballets that are still a part of the contemporary repertory or ballets that made an enduring impression at the time.

Ballets of lasting importance—and by that we mean ambition fulfilled—ballets like *La Sylphide, Giselle,* and *Swan Lake,* have held the stage for more than a hundred years; *La Fille Mal Gardée* for almost two hundred. The new ballets that we see nowadays with increasing frequency all aspire to the same longevity. While few succeed, many remain in the active repertory longer than is imagined. A great number, like *Petrouchka,* come and go; others disappear entirely. (That has happened, naturally, to some of my own ballets; there is no point in insisting on keeping what doesn't work; there is also no point in reviving what cannot be properly recalled.)

The new pieces of the modern repertory, and now fortunately there are many of them every year produced by the growing number of ballet companies, are all candidates for lasting value and inclusion in the quasi-permanent repertory. Hopefully, many described in this book will last. Those that have not done so since *Balanchine's New Complete Stories of the Great Ballets* in 1968 have given place here to new ballets. We have tried to keep the stories of ballets likely to be revived one day, or ballets of interest from the point of view of music, choreography, design, or performance. In 1954, when the first edition of this book appeared, 131 ballets were described. In 1968, 241 were described in the second edition. Now, minus some 40 from the latter, there are 404.

The ballet audience has grown tremendously in recent years. In 1965 it was estimated that one million people attended dance performances in the United States. In 1975 that figure was fifteen million. It has been projected to reach twenty-five million in the near future. I believe it.

New audiences for ballet, of course, are not created by new dances that have just a passing interest. What makes an audience, what makes a newcomer committed is a dance that will cause him to ask, "When can I see that *again?*" Those are the ballets we are all looking for.

I have watched ballet grow wonderfully. When we began work on the first edition of this book, New York was lucky to see two months of ballet, domestic and foreign combined, all year. In a recent season, it was possible to see in a single year more than ten months of ballet performances by native and foreign ensembles. The result has been a marvelous proliferation of new work performed by an ever increasing number of gifted dancers.

When Lincoln Kirstein and I began to work together and started the School of American Ballet in 1934, we knew that our dancers would one day be admired throughout the world. This happened much more rapidly than we imagined. Now, many schools associated with ballet companies throughout the country are turning out talented young dancers.

The same thing has happened in England, where Ninette de Valois founded her school the same year; the Royal Ballet is the result. Now the Royal Ballet and the New York City Ballet dance next door to each other in Lincoln Center. Both of us sell out. There is no end to what trained talent can give.

Audiences cannot be trained, of course, only advised a little—most of all advised to go to the ballet and to keep on going. It is the closest the observer can come to the steady training required of the dancer in order to create the performance that will captivate him.

Years ago maybe it was possible to go to the ballet regularly and not experience a great evening on every occasion; today, there are many great evenings. This book is designed to help find them and to give some preparation to those who do not trust their eyes and ears in the theatre first. Much as reading about ballet may be useful after enjoying performances, it will scarcely substitute for the initial excitement of seeing and hearing performance in the theatre. But if it leads to the theatre, we are pleased. Francis Mason and I have enjoyed working toward that possibility.

We wish to thank Harold Kuebler and Debra Groisser for prolonged editorial assistance and patience. I have other jobs to do and it has not been easy to give this one priority.

We often wonder what Lawrence Sherman and Marion Patton, our first editors, must think of how the book we first planned with them has grown. It is maybe like the Christmas tree in *The Nutcracker*.

GEORGE BALANCHINE

ACKNOWLEDGMENTS

Many have helped in the making of this book. First, those who made it possible to see the ballets described here—the press representatives of the ballet companies whose repertories we have made an effort to record. Second, the critics and other writers on dance whose work is often quoted in the text. When the first edition of this book was prepared in the early 1950s, the dance critics in the daily press in the United States could be counted on the fingers of one hand; now, with ballet and dance companies established in many cities or touring throughout the country, newspapers and magazines of repute have realized that they must have competent persons to write about them. (For the first time, in 1976, a Pulitzer Prize was awarded to a dance critic—to Alan Kriegsman of the Washington *Post*.) There has been a happy increase, too, in the number of dance magazines. What writers on dance have to say, in acute and informative reviews, is valuable not only as history but in giving here a round character to flat recollection.

The Dance Collection of the New York Public Library at Lincoln Center is the master source in the world, as I hope everyone now knows, for those who seek history and knowledge of the dance. It is also the liveliest archive in the world as it succeeds in holding for the future the most ephemeral of the arts. The Dictionary Catalogue of the Dance Collection, the major bibliography of all materials relating to dance, has recently been published in twelve large volumes. It is very simply a monumental dance index—a guide to who danced what when, in whose design, to what music, what was written about it, what the dancer recalled, perhaps, and what it looked like in photographs of the time or on film. The dancers, choreographers and designers, the collectors, historians, critics, and lovers of dance who have given to the Dance Collection over the years must take considerable pride in this rare jewel in the crown of the New York Public Library. What Genevieve Oswald, the Curator of the Collection, and her colleagues have done is not only to pin down the butterfly, but in many cases to make it fly again. For in the written and spoken word, in film, photographs, drawings, prints, the Collection is becoming increasingly valuable. Those who read these words and cherish their own collections and files of dance materials are urged to remember the Dance Collection's concern to keep such things permanent in a perishable world. The Collection is situated in the

New York Public Library's Museum and Library of the Performing Arts at Lincoln Center, 111 Amsterdam Avenue, New York 10023. Don't throw anything away!

We are deeply grateful to the critics and writers on dance whose work is quoted in this book: Jack Anderson of *Ballet Review, Dance Magazine,* and the *Dancing Times;* Barbara Archer of *The Record;* Robb Baker of *FM Guide;* Clive Barnes, dance and drama critic of the New York *Times;* Patricia Barnes of *Dance and Dancers;* Ann Barzell of *Dance News;* Byron Belt of the *Long Island Press;* Elena Bivona of *Ballet Review;* Alexander Bland of *The Observer;* Jane Boutwell of *The New Yorker;* Erik Bruhn for his essay "Beyond Technique" (*Dance Perspectives* 36); Richard Buckle of *The Sunday Times* (London), founder and editor of *Ballet;* Mary Clarke, editor of the *Dancing Times;* Selma Jeanne Cohen, founder and editor of *Dance Perspectives;* William Como, editor-in-chief of *Dance Magazine;* the filmmaker Gardner Compton in *Dance Magazine;* the art critic and collector Douglas Cooper in *Dance and Dancers;* the conductor and writer Robert Craft; Clement Crisp of the *Financial Times* (London); Arlene Croce, dance critic of *The New Yorker,* founder and editor of *Ballet Review,* correspondent of the *Dancing Times;* Edwin Denby, poet, critic (for the New York *Herald Tribune, Modern Music* and *Dance Magazine*), author of *Looking at the Dance* and *Dancers, Buildings and People in the Streets;* George Dorris of *Ballet Review;* John T. Elson of *Time* magazine; Janet Flanner of *The New Yorker,* author of *Paris Was Yesterday,* edited by Irving Drutman; Joseph Gale of the *Daily News;* Joseph Galeon of *Dance News;* Nancy Goldner, author of *The Stravinsky Festival of the New York City Ballet;* Robert Greskovic of *The Soho Weekly News* and *Ballet Review;* John Gruen in the New York *Times;* Henry Haslam in *Ballet Review;* Doris Hering of *Dance Magazine;* Frances Herridge, dance critic of the New York *Post;* Allen Hughes of the New York *Times;* Michael Iachetta of the *Daily News;* George Jackson of *Ballet Review* and *Dance News;* Robert Jacobson of *Cue;* Lydia Jaffe of *Dance Magazine;* Deborah Jowitt, dance critic of *The Village Voice* and author of *Dance Beat;* Oleg Kerensky of *The New Statesman,* author of *Pavlova* and *The World of Ballet;* Lincoln Kirstein for innumerable sources, most importantly *Movement and Metaphor: Four Centuries of Ballet, The New York City Ballet,* and *Nijinsky Dancing;* Anna Kisselgoff of the New York *Times;* Vera Krasovskaya, the Soviet critic; Alan M. Kriegsman of the *Washington Post;* Herbert Kupferberg of the *National Observer;* Jean Battey Lewis of the Washington *Post;* John Martin, the first dance critic of the New York *Times;* Jacqueline Maskey of *High Fidelity;* Nancy Mason of *Dance Magazine;* Olga Maynard of *Dance Magazine;* Don McDonagh of the New York *Times;* Bob Micklin of *Newsday;* James Monahan of the *Dancing Times* and *The Guardian;* Sam Norkin of the *Daily News;* Patrick O'Connor of the *Jersey Journal;* John Percival, dance critic of the *Times* (London) and *Dance and Dancers;* Richard Philp of *Dance Magazine;* Andrew Porter of *The New Yorker* and the *Financial Times* (London), author of *A*

Musical Season; Dame Marie Rambert, author of her autobiography *Quick-silver;* Alan Rich, music critic of *New York* magazine; Peter Rosenwald of the *Wall Street Journal;* Hubert Saal of *Newsweek;* Winthrop Sargeant of *The New Yorker;* Robert Sealey in *Ballet Review;* Marcia B. Siegel, dance critic of *The Hudson Review,* the *Soho Weekly News,* the Boston *Herald Examiner* and author of a collection of criticisms, *At the Vanishing Point;* Anna Greta Stahle of *Dance News;* Walter Terry, dean of American dance writers, dance critic for the New York *Herald Tribune* and *The Saturday Review;* Rose Anne Thom of *Dance Magazine;* Arthur Todd of *Dance Observer;* David Vaughan of *Ballet Review* and author of *Frederick Ashton and His Ballets* (1977); the late James Waring in *Ballet Review;* William Weaver of the *Herald Tribune;* Anne Marie Welsh of the Washington *Star;* Thomas Willis of the *Chicago Tribune;* and Peter Williams, founder and editor of *Dance and Dancers.*

For permission to quote from books, we wish to express thanks to George G. Harrap Co., Ltd., London, for an excerpt from *Frederick Ashton, a Choreographer and His Ballets* (1971); Horizon Press for *Dancers, Buildings and People in the Streets* by Edwin Denby (1965); Macmillan and Co., Ltd., for "The Bumboat Woman's Story," from *Bab Ballads* by Sir W. S. Gilbert; Pellegrini and Cudahy, Publishers, for *Looking at the Dance,* copyright 1949 by Edwin Denby; Random House, New York, and Faber and Faber, Ltd., for *The Age of Anxiety* by W. H. Auden; Saturday Review Press for *At the Vanishing Point: A Critic Looks at Dance* by Marcia B. Siegel, 1972; the late Igor Stravinsky for *Stravinsky: an Autobiography;* the late Carl Van Vechten for "The Russian Ballet and Nijinsky" from *Interpreters* by Carl Van Vechten.

The press and public relations representatives of ballet companies have responded generously to frequent requests. We are especially grateful to Charles France, Director of Publicity and Public Relations for American Ballet Theatre, Elena Gordon, Assistant to Charles France, and Joan Ehrlich-White, Virginia Hymes and Irene Shaw of that company; Tom Kerrigan of the Brooklyn Academy of Music; Isadora Bennett, Rima Corben and Robert Larkin of the City Center Joffrey Ballet; Dick Hendriks and Rima Corben of the Dutch National Ballet; Winnie Sampson of the Dance Theatre of Harlem; Judith Jedlicka of the Harkness Ballet; Sheila Porter, General Press Representative, Hurok Concerts and John Gingrich, Associate Press Representative; Virginia Donaldson, Press Representative of the New York City Ballet and her associates: Leslie Bailey, Linda Cioffoletti, Marie Gutscher, Clarence Hart and Larry Strichman; and Vivien Wallace of the Royal Opera House, Covent Garden, London.

We are deeply grateful to William Como, editor of *Dance Magazine,* for permission to reprint entire the long interview between Jerome Robbins and Edwin Denby on the subject of the ballet *Dances at a Gathering,* and the filmmaker Gardner Compton's article on Robert Joffrey's *Astarte.* Also valuable have been interviews by Jane Boutwell in *The New Yorker* with Maurice

Béjart, Leonard Bernstein and Jerome Robbins, and Kenneth MacMillan; in *Show* magazine with Rudolf Nureyev; and in *Dance and Dancers* with Eliot Feld. The invaluable books of Igor Stravinsky and Robert Craft and Eric Walter White's *Stravinsky: the Composer and his Works* (1966) have been consulted frequently. David Vaughan kindly permitted us to read part of the manuscript of his book of *Frederick Ashton and His Ballets* (Alfred A. Knopf, New York, 1977).

We wish to thank, too, the publishers of *Ballet Review*, Marcel Dekker, Inc., for permission to quote so frequently from the pages of that magazine.

For helpfulness and interest we should like particularly to thank Jane Allison of the Indianapolis *Star;* Frank Darvas; Darryl Dodson of American Ballet Theatre; Harvey Lichtenstein of the Brooklyn Academy of Music; Cora Cahan of the Eliot Feld Ballet; Richard Philp of *Dance Magazine;* Karel Shook of the Dance Theatre of Harlem; Betty Cage, Barbara Horgan, Edward Bigelow, Robert Cornell, Carole Deschamps and Mary Porter of the New York City Ballet; Nathalie Molostwoff and Elise Reiman of the School of American Ballet; Robert Irving, Music Director of the New York City Ballet; and the staff of the Dance Collection of the New York Public Library at Lincoln Center, especially Genevieve Oswald, Curator, Reynaldo Alejandro, Natalie Bassein, Paul Le-Paglia, Lacy McDearmon, Winifred Messe, Madeleine Nichols, Andrew Wentink, and Henry Wisneski.

Henry Wisneski's counsel and advice on the photographs in this volume were invaluable and we are much indebted to him. The arrangement and presentation of the photographs, so important in a book on ballet, have been done by Randall Mize, to whom we wish to express special appreciation.

Words are insufficient for the thanks we owe the photographers whose work appears in this book. Unlike the dance writer and critic, whose work exists in print and does not perish, the dance photographer takes thousands of valuable photographs, many of which never see the light of day and all too few of which are published. The photographers are the unsung heroes and heroines of ballet, recording its history in frozen moments of performance we strive to recall in words that only approximate reality.

We wish also to thank most warmly for editorial assistance throughout the book Shields Remine. Harold Grabau has prepared the final text in exemplary fashion.

FRANCIS MASON

CONTENTS

ILLUSTRATIONS

PART ONE

Stories of the Great Ballets

ABYSS

Music by Marga Richter. Choreography by Stuart Hodes. Costumes by André Delfau. First presented by the Harkness Ballet at the Casino, Cannes, France, February 21, 1956, with Lone Isaksen and Erik Bruhn in the principal roles.

Based on a story by Leonid Andreyev, *Abyss* shows what might happen when an innocent young couple encounter bestial forces. One of Russia's great writers whose work in many ways resembles that of Edgar Allan Poe, Andreyev relates in his story a disturbing incident that is presented here in dance terms. A young girl and boy, not yet old enough to be seriously in love but close since childhood and certain one day to marry, walk one day alone in the forest. There they are suddenly attacked by three menacing figures. The boy is powerless to protect the girl and she is carried off by two of the men. When the boy eventually finds her again, she is distraught and half out of her mind. He is about to leave her in horror at what the attackers have done. But he finds himself also curious and attracted. The abyss opens before him and he, too, seizes the girl.

ADAGIO HAMMERKLAVIER

Music by Beethoven. Choreography by Hans Van Manen. Set and costumes by Jean-Paul Vroom. Lighting by David K. H. Elliott. First presented by the Dutch National Ballet, October 4, 1973. First presented in the United States by the Pennsylvania Ballet.

Inspired by the choreographer's listening to a recording by Christoph Eschenbach of the Adagio from Beethoven's *Hammerklavier Sonata*, this is a dance ballet. Eschenbach's performance, especially slow in tempo, stretches the possibilities of playing pianissimo to its extreme. His recording is used to accompany *Adagio Hammerklavier*, a dance for a boy and a girl, accompanied by two other couples.

Writing of a performance by the Dutch National Ballet in Canada in 1975, the critic Rose Anne Thom said in *Dance Magazine* that a pas de deux by

Alexandra Radius and Hans Ebbelaar "communicated a sense of balance and
confidence that was reassuring not only technically, but emotionally . . . It
was the quiet understatement that made *Adagio* work . . ."

AFTER CORINTH

*Music by David Gagne. Choreography by Walter Raines. Scenery by Gary
Fails. First presented by the Dance Theatre of Harlem at the Uris Theatre,
New York, April 29, 1975, with Virginia Johnson, Melva Murray-White,
M. Elena Carter, and Roman Brooks.*

A new perspective on the story of Jason and Medea, *After Corinth* takes the
view that Jason's new wife, Glauce, victimizes his first, Medea. It will be
recalled that in the dominant classical version of this story in the Greek drama
of Euripides, Medea, enraged at Jason's desertion of her, devises the murder of
Glauce. Medea then murders her own children by Jason. The ballet imagines
that, after death, Jason and Medea return to earth and that Glauce is then seen
as the murderess.

AFTER EDEN

*Music by Lee Hoiby. Choreography by John Butler. Scenery by Rouben
Ter-Arutunian. First presented by the Harkness Ballet at the Broadway
Theatre, New York, November 9, 1967, with Lone Isaksen and Lawrence
Rhodes.*

After Eden is a dramatic ballet about Adam and Eve after the Fall and the ex-
pulsion from the Garden of Eden. It shows in dance terms, with no narration,
something of the agony, regret, defiance, and resignation of the two lovers as
they face the fate they had not imagined. In the process, their dependence on
each other varies and it is this that makes the drama of the piece: Will they,
after what they have come through, be able to stay together? At the start of
the dance they are united in their misery and therefore mutually dependent.
Later, realizing their new, appalling freedom, it seems briefly possible for them
to separate or to entertain that notion. But not for long, for they have survived
much and cannot go their separate ways. They are like magnets, alternately attracting and repulsing as they turn in different directions. In the end, they are
newly united and apparently resolved to encounter the future together.

    After Eden was revived by the City Center Joffrey Ballet, March 21, 1972,
with Starr Danias and Dennis Wayne. Writing of this revival in the New York
Times, the critic Anna Kisselgoff said that "Mr. Butler's symbolic images are
so strong and so psychologically apt that he succeeds almost beyond belief

in taking a specific emotional situation and generalizing it into a commentary
on the universal human condition . . . Mr. Wayne and Miss Danias give a
very strong performance . . . Miss Danias' Eve is fragile; she is much closer
to the state of innocence just left behind than her partner. Mr. Wayne's Adam
reacts through instinct, logically stressing the irrationality with which man
often reacts to a new situation."

THE AFTERNOON OF A FAUN

*Choreographic tableau in one act. Music by Claude Debussy. Choreography
by Vaslav Nijinsky. Scenery and costumes by Léon Bakst. First presented
by Diaghilev's Ballets Russes at the Théâtre du Châtelet, Paris, May 29,
1912, with Vaslav Nijinsky as the Faun. First presented in the United States
by Diaghilev's Ballets Russes at the Century Theatre, New York, January 17,
1916, with Leonide Massine as the Faun.*

The music for this ballet was written by Debussy as a *Prélude* to a poem by
Stéphane Mallarmé. Nijinsky's idea of portraying a languorous faun whose rest
is disturbed by beautiful nymphs is thus related to Debussy's inspiration.
Debussy wrote of his score: "The music of this prelude is a very free illustration to Stéphane Mallarmé's beautiful poem. It does not follow the poet's
conception exactly, but describes the successive scenes among which the
wishes and dreams of the Faun wander in the heat of the afternoon. Then,
tired of pursuing the fearful flight of the nymphs and naiads, he abandons
himself to a delightful sleep, full of visions finally realized, of full possession
amid universal nature."

When the curtain rises on the ballet we see a faun idling away a hot summer afternoon. He lies on a hillock, playing the flute and eating grapes. It is
apparent that his wants are simple and innocent. Dressed in light brown tights
dotted with brown patches below the waist, he seems to be half boy, half
animal.

A group of seven lovely nymphs on their way to bathe in a lake near by
enter the faun's domain. They move in a line, forming a likeness to a Greek
frieze, their bodies always turned to the audience, their faces always in profile.
The faun has never seen such beautiful creatures before and climbs down from
his hillock to observe the naiads with the golden hair and soft, gauze tunics
more closely. The nymphs, in turn, are astonished by this creature who seems
to be a handsome boy spotted like a goat with small horns growing from his
forehead. What can he be? they wonder. Soon, as the playful faun leaps about
them, the startled nymphs flee to the forest.

When they return, the faun tries to ingratiate himself with them. But still
the naiads are frightened, and again they run away. All except one. This
nymph is less embarrassed than her sisters and more anxious to discover the

faun's secret. The faun is emboldened to make playful amorous gestures. The nymph allows him to touch her; she seems to respond to him, but then she eludes his grasp. She is frightened and rushes off to join the others. As she leaves, a silken scarf from her garment falls to the ground.

The faun, no longer playful, is sad at her departure. He picks up her scarf and holds it as if it were a treasure. He returns to the hillock, holds the scarf in his hands as if it were a woman's face, and touches it tenderly. Now he lays the scarf down softly and as he caresses it, imagines it to be the naiad he frightened away. With his possession of the scarf, the faun is content with his afternoon revery. It is as if the nymphs had never appeared, as if he had dreamed of their presence and in his dream possessed utterly the most beautiful of them all.

NOTES   *The Afternoon of a Faun* was Vaslav Nijinsky's first ballet. In its choreography and in its dancing the work completely rejected traditional forms. It was not a ballet in the accepted sense; it was a "choreographic tableau," a moving frieze, a work to be seen only from the front, a two-dimensional ballet. In his imitation of Greek paintings, Nijinsky was faithful to the spirit and to the letter; the traditional movements of classical ballet were altogether rejected in favor of an angular rigidity that would make possible a new expressiveness for the dancer's body.

Since Nijinsky's first performances, many dancers have taken the leading role in *The Afternoon of a Faun*, among them Leonide Massine, Serge Lifar, David Lichine, Igor Youskevitch, Leon Danielian, and Jean Babilée. Dame Marie Rambert, who knew Nijinsky well, has written of his achievement in her autobiography *Quicksilver:* "One is often asked whether his jump was really as high as it is always described. To that I answer: 'I don't know how far from the ground it was, but I know it was near the stars.' Who would watch the floor when he danced? He transported you at once into higher spheres with the sheer ecstasy of his flight.

"The most absurd theories were put forward about his anatomy. People said that the bones in his feet were like a bird's—as though a bird flew because of its feet! But, in fact, he *did* have an exceptionally long Achilles' tendon which allowed him with his heels firmly on the ground and the back upright to bend the knees to the utmost before taking a spring, and he had powerful thighs. As to his famous posing in the air, he indeed created the illusion of it by the ecstasy of his expression at the apex of the leap, so that *this* unique moment penetrated into every spectator's consciousness, and seemed to last. His landing, from whatever height he jumped, was like a cat's. He had that unique touch of the foot on the ground which can only be compared to the pianist's touch of the fingers on the keys. It was as subtle and as varied.

"And then there was his unique interpretation. He wafted the perfume of the rose in *Spectre de la Rose;* he was the very spirit of Chopin in *Les*

Sylphides; he looked like a Hamlet in *Giselle;* his Petrouchka broke your heart with his sorrow, and his Faune had the real breath of antiquity.

"As to his choreography, I would not hesitate to affirm that it was he, more than anyone else, who revolutionized the classical ballet and was fifty years ahead of his time. Fokine was a logical development of Petipa, but Nijinsky introduced completely new principles. He produced three ballets in all: *l'Après-midi d'un Faune, Jeux,* and *Sacre du Printemps.* For each of them he established a basic position strictly adhered to all through the ballet. For *Faune* he took his inspiration from Greek vases and bas-reliefs. The body was facing front while the head and feet were always seen in profile. The deportment had to be classical, yet the head had independent movements not connected with deportment in the classical vocabulary, and so had the arms. It was an orchestration of the body, with each part playing a totally different melody. There was nothing you could do automatically. The walking was all done on one line parallel to the footlights, the whole foot on the ground. It was an incredibly difficult position to achieve, let alone use in walking, or changing direction, or combining with highly stylized arm movements. He did not explain why he wanted them thus, but he showed again and again the way they had to be done until he obtained a perfect copy of his own movement. His method of creation was diametrically opposed to Fokine's. Fokine always took the dancers into his confidence and allowed them, even encouraged them, to participate in the creation of a character. Not so Nijinsky. When once I was extolling the virtues of *Petrouchka* to him, saying it was Fokine's masterpiece, he said that it *was* so, as far as the three main characters went, but the crowd was treated too loosely, and everybody did what they wanted within the space indicated to them. Nijinsky on the contrary did not allow the slightest freedom of movement or gesture and exacted only a perfect copy. No wonder it took some 120 rehearsals for *l'Après-midi d'un Faune,* lasting about ten minutes, to be achieved as he wished, since not a single movement could be done spontaneously, each limb having to be studied separately. He required a perfect ballet technique and then broke it down consciously to his own purpose—and then it proved a masterpiece. Each nymph looked a goddess. Although they were incapable of understanding Nijinsky's intentions, the mere fact of faithfully copying his unique movements gave them the requisite style. He told them: no expression in the face, you must just be as though asleep with your eyes open—like statues.

"Once when a new girl had to learn Nijinsky's sister's part, in which the Nymph suddenly sees the Faune, turns away and walks off—he said to her: 'Why do you look so frightened?'

"She said she thought she was meant to be. Thereupon, quite in a rage, he said that the movement he gave her was all that was required of her, he was not interested in her personal feelings. And how right Nijinsky was for his particular choreography! It acquired an impersonal, remote character—just like the paintings on Greek vases or bas-reliefs—not that he ever attempted to copy any particular poses from these, but created them by the profoundest penetration into their very spirit. The walking was done not strictly to the music, but rather loosely as though walking 'through' the music."

In 1936 Edwin Denby reviewed a performance by David Lichine:

"The *Faun* is an astonishing work. After twenty-three years it is as direct and moving as though it had been invented yesterday. It gathers momentum from the first gesture to the last like an ideal short story. From this point of view of a story, the way the veil is introduced and re-emphasized by the nymph is a marvel of rightness. From the point of view of visual rhythm the repetition of the nymph's gesture of dismay is the perfection of timing. It is, of course, because so few gesture motifs are used that one can recognize each so plainly, but there is no feeling of poverty in this simplification. The rhythmic pattern in relation to the stage and to the music is so subtly graded that instead of monotony we get a steady increase in suspense, an increase in the eyes' perceptiveness, and a feeling of heroic style at the climax.

"It is true that most of the gestures used have prototypes in Greek reliefs and vase paintings, but, in addition to that intellectual association with adolescence, the fact is that when the body imitates these poses, the kind of tension resulting expresses exactly the emotion Nijinsky wants to express. Both their actual tension and their apparent remoteness, both their plastic clarity and their emphasis by negation on the center of the body (it is always strained between the feet in profile and the shoulders *en face*)—all these qualities lead up to the complete realization of the faun's last gesture. The poignancy of this moment lies partly in the complete change in the direction of tension, in the satisfying relief that results; and the substitution of a new tension (the incredible backbend) gives the work its balance. But besides, the eye has been educated to see the plastic beauty of this last pose, and the rhythmic sense to appreciate its noble deliberateness. That it is so intensely human a gesture, coming after a long preparation of understatement, gives it, in its cumulative assurance, the force of an illumination. This force of direct human statement, this faith in all of us, is the astonishing thing about the *Faun*. It is as rare in dancing as in the other arts. These last moments of the *Faun* do not need any critical defense. But they have been so talked about that I am trying to point out for intellectuals that they are not a sensational tag, but that the whole piece builds up to them, and reaches in them an extraordinary beauty.

"The De Basil company danced the *Faun* beautifully. Lichine in the title role excelled. It is a part that demands exceptional imagination as well as great plastic sense. And Lichine had besides these a fine simplicity."

Music by Claude Debussy. Choreography by Jerome Robbins. Set and lighting by Jean Rosenthal. Costumes by Irene Sharaff. First presented by the New York City Ballet at the City Center, New York, May 14, 1953, with Tanaquil LeClercq and Francisco Moncion.

Mallarmé's poem that inspired Debussy's music *Prélude à l'après-midi d'un Faune* describes the reveries of a faun and his real or imagined encounter with nymphs. In 1912 Nijinsky presented his famous ballet, drawing his ideas from both the music and the poem, among other sources. This *pas de deux* is a contemporary variation on those themes.

The scene is a room with a mirror, very much like a modern ballet studio with one wall a mirror so that dancers can watch themselves. The mirror wall is the imaginary wall toward the audience, so that when the dancers stare out at us they are really looking at their own reflections. The setting, with walls and ceiling of transparent cloth against a blue sky, seems to float in space; it is as remote and silent as the sylvan scene of Nijinsky's work. On the floor of the room a boy, naked to the waist, lies asleep. At the call of the music, he stirs, rolls over, arches his back, stretches like a cat. He sits up and stares out at us with such interest and objectivity that we know he appraises himself in the mirror. He stands, watching himself, adjusts his belt, poses to the sensuous music, gestures, then slowly somersaults and lies on the floor again, languorous and satisfied with himself. He falls asleep. A girl in white practice dress approaches the room. She pauses at the door, prepares her ballet shoes for the work to come and looks at the mirror. From the door she is drawn toward her image—and does not notice the boy. She has eyes only for her own reflection. She poses at the mirror, then kneels. She then begins to exercise at the *barre*. The boy wakens like a startled faun and watches her. She observes herself closely. When she comes to an open pose the boy steps in and lifts her up and away from the *barre*, as if she were coming up for air. The boy holds her in poses that please her image, both always looking into the mirror and never directly at each other. She likes the way she looks as he supports her, misses his hand at her waist when he is not there. She luxuriates for a moment, then stands and looks at the floor. He comes to her, his hands touch her hair, but she rises immediately into a formal *attitude*, rejecting any contact except what will make her more lovely to herself.

The enchanted boy, now watching only her in the mirror, lifts her now to his shoulder; she descends, her loose hair falling about her face. They separate then to opposite sides of the room, watching each other in the mirror. Their cool concentration on the invisible reflections before them is so intense that we know when one of them is watching the other. They approach each other slowly, reaching out. They stand side by side for a moment. The boy makes a circle of his arms and the girl slips through them, held there full length, swimming in the air. Then her body collapses as if a spell had been broken. She kneels on the floor, the boy beside her. He now looks at her directly while she still watches in the mirror. He leans toward her, his face comes close, he kisses her cheek. Her hand slowly moves up to her cheek. She stands and still looking straight ahead in the mirror, walks backward out of the room, her hand still at her face. He watches her in the mirror. She is gone. The boy lies down on the floor, pushes himself up on his arms and descends slowly again into sleep.

NOTES   Since this ballet was first performed, it has been danced throughout the United States and many countries overseas by the New York City Ballet, by the Royal Ballet, and by Jerome Robbins' Ballets: U.S.A. The latter performed it at the White House, April 11, 1962, following a state dinner given by President and Mrs. Kennedy for the Shah and Queen of Iran.

Soon after the first performance of *Afternoon of a Faun*, Doris Hering wrote in *Dance Magazine:* "*Afternoon of a Faun* is a work of great awareness and wry insight and one that shimmers with atmosphere from beginning to end . . .

"There is a wonderful sense of theatrical rightness in Mr. Robbins' choice of the antiseptic studio atmosphere for history of nascent love vying with narcissism—not only because dancers live in a world of mirrors, but because this particular format allowed him to concentrate on the rich mood relationship between the music and his own choreography. And instead of making a 'dance' in the formal sense of the word, he allowed the movement to flow out of the materials of the classroom, which are often more beautiful than their embellished stage versions. And he found two exceedingly sensitive performers in Francisco Moncion and Tanaquil LeClercq."

THE AGE OF ANXIETY

Dramatic ballet in six scenes. Music by Leonard Bernstein. Choreography by Jerome Robbins. Scenery by Oliver Smith. Costumes by Irene Sharaff. Lighting by Jean Rosenthal. First presented by the New York City Ballet at the City Center, New York, February 26, 1950, with Tanaquil LeClercq, Francisco Moncion, Todd Bolender, and Jerome Robbins in the principal roles.

Inspired by Leonard Bernstein's Second Symphony, *The Age of Anxiety,* and the poem by W. H. Auden on which this music is based, this ballet concerns the attempt four people make to find themselves. The ballet follows the sectional development of the poem and music.

THE PROLOGUE   The curtain rises on a scene that might be a public place in any part of a large modern city. A man enters on the left and walks slowly to the center of the stage. A girl appears on the right and walks toward him. Two men join the couple. All are strangers. The four figures stand opposite each other to form a small square, as if they were standing about a table. They sit together, become acquainted, discover mutual interests and a common problem, and with quiet, implicit understanding agree to set out on a journey together.

It is clear that each of these four people has something to fear. Their gestures and smallest movements are timorous and tentative. Because they do not know each other well, they seem always to be seeking something in their relationship to make it seem less odd that four strangers should meet and instantly, instinctively, feel a need to share each other's thoughts. Strangers they certainly are, but in their immediate awareness of a common problem their relation assumes an interested tenderness, a feeling of relief that companionship is still possible. All are humble in the face of this unstated problem, which seems at first to be loneliness. The journey they take together is a metaphor, a figure in dance terms, of the long exploratory conversation they begin to have in order to learn more of themselves and their age. The dance mirrors their talk.

THE SEVEN AGES The four characters show us the life of man from birth to death in a set of seven variations. In the first variation, one of the men learns to stand, to walk, to articulate. In the words of Auden's poem:

> Behold the infant, helpless in cradle and
> Righteous still, yet already there is
> Dread in his dreams at the deed of which
> He knows nothing but knows he can do,
> The gulf before him with guilt beyond,
> Whatever that is, whatever why
> Forbids his bound; till that ban tempts him;
> He jumps and is judged: he joins mankind . . .

The girl comes forward and dances the second age. Her movements are warm and open, joyously happy. The girl is not only conscious of herself, but conscious of life about her, and displays an eagerness to participate in that life: she sacrifices part of herself to the world.

In the third variation, the four strangers meet love—the inevitable consequence of knowing and discovering something outside the self. It is love on an elemental, physical level, the love of extreme youth that recalls Auden's lines:

> Since the neighbors did,
> With a multitude I made the long
> Visitor's voyage to Venus Island . . .

The fourth age shows us the plight of social man, man thrust into the world of ambitions. Here he becomes aware for the first time of what he must do to climb the road to his ideal, how this road sometimes diverges and how he is perhaps deceived about his goal. Here he faces the problem of realizing a dream in an apparently dreamless world: which fork in the road shall he choose?

Now, in the fifth age, the dancers find material success and discover the price paid to achieve it. Here we imagine very easily a great modern city where nature is entirely absent, where everything moves on a fixed schedule, and where citizens are mere readers of timetables, conforming religiously to the demands of a huge machine that they have no power to control.

The sixth age shows us a reaction to this superhuman condition—disillusionment, a brief effort to rise above it, a danced argument as to which is better: to give in to the determinism of the city or to fight against it fearlessly. The four strangers split into two groups and take these differing points of view. At the end, one of the dancers tires. His fist moves to his mouth to stifle a yawn. He sits, curled up like a child.

In the final age, man has abandoned hope, abandoned his rage at human error, and ceased to have any reason to act. The dancer walks slowly, is ignored by passers-by. He reaches out, collapses, and is carried off. Slowly a figure moves across the stage, dragging behind him a long piece of crepe. The end has come. Man is dead and no longer a member of the minority.

THE SEVEN STAGES   The four figures come together again. They stand in a close line and move together awkwardly, reaching out in unison toward an invisible goal. They separate and look about, then start on a dream journey to find happiness.

Four figures dressed exactly like them, but with masks covering their faces, enter. Lines of masked creatures file in and dance between the four characters and their doubles, who imitate precisely the movements of the four.

One by one, and with different partners, the four strive for a goal where they will have no doubts and feel secure. They wander in a maze, lose their way, lose each other, then meet again safely. Nothing definite has been gained, but together they have had a harrowing common experience. They repudiate their doubles, pushing them aside. Now the four not only subconsciously know each other very well, but they are friends, too.

THE DIRGE   The four friends fall flat on their faces as the All-Powerful Father enters. This father symbol is depicted as a huge figure on stilts, a tin man of faith. He beckons to them with mechanical movements and stalks forward. They take courage and touch him. Other people enter and pay homage to the Father. It is interesting that he moves awkwardly, that he requires the assistance of his disciples. He is not so much a religious as a political figure: a representation of power that exists not through his own will alone. He sits on the shoulders of the crowd. The girl dances before him ecstatically, fascinated with the new-found rapid grace in movement his presence gives her. She reaches out to him supplicatingly. The Father responds to her plea by falling over, collapsing. The four regard him as the god that failed.

THE MASQUE   The exhausted girl falls against one of the boys. There is silence for a moment. Then carefree music blares out. The music simulates jazz,

and the four characters cavort about the scene forgetting their problem in
playful versions of jive. But soon their vigorous efforts to be cheerful begin to
pall. One of them stops dancing and stomps in raging despair: it is the kind of
protest of the half-intoxicated, the man who knew that drink would solve nothing at all. The girl curls up on the ground.

EPILOGUE   One of the men seems to die. The girl and another man go to
him and help him. Now all four stand together as at the beginning of the
ballet. They kneel together, then rise. The girl reaches out to the men, as if she
wants to ask a final question the answer to which is very important to her. But
they all have such questions. Gradually they turn and walk toward the four
corners of the stage from which they came. Just before they exit, they turn and
bow slightly to each other in gratitude for the faith they have given each other
in the anxious age.

NOTES   W. H. Auden's *The Age of Anxiety: A Baroque Eclogue* was published in 1946. *The Age of Anxiety*, Leonard Bernstein's *Symphony No. 2 for
Piano and Orchestra*, on which the ballet was also based, was first performed
by the Boston Symphony Orchestra, Serge Koussevitzky conducting, on April
8, 1949. The composer was the piano soloist. At that time Bernstein offered a
description of his work and its source, the poem by Auden. "The essential line
of the poem (and of the music) is the record of our difficult and problematical
search for faith. In the end, two of the characters enunciate the recognition of
this faith—even a passive submission to it—at the same time revealing an inability to relate it personally in their daily lives, except through blind acceptance . . . If the charge of 'theatricality' in a symphonic work is a valid one, I
am willing to plead guilty. I have a deep suspicion that every work I write, for
whatever medium is really theatre music in some way . . ."*
   Jerome Robbins, who had collaborated with Bernstein on two ballets for
Ballet Theatre, *Fancy Free* (1944) and *Facsimile* (1946), was inspired by the
music to choreograph a new work, his second as Associate Artistic Director of
the New York City Ballet. Robbins has pointed out, however, that his ballet is
different from both the poem and the score: "It is a ritual in which four people exercise their illusions in their search for security. It is an attempt to see
what life is about."

AGON

*Music by Igor Stravinsky. Choreography by George Balanchine. Lighting by
Nananne Porcher. First presented by the New York City Ballet at the City
Center, New York, November 27, 1957, with Diana Adams, Melissa Hay-*

* Program notes of the Philharmonic-Symphony Society of New York, 1949–50.

*den, Barbara Walczak, Barbara Millberg, Todd Bolender, Roy Tobias,
Jonathan Watts, Arthur Mitchell, Roberta Lubell, Francia Russell, Dido
Sayers, and Ruth Sobotka.*

While the New York City Ballet has in its repertory many works by Igor
Stravinsky, *Agon* is the third Stravinsky ballet composed especially for our
company. Lincoln Kirstein and I had always wanted a new Stravinsky work to
follow *Orpheus,* and at first it seemed possible that this might be based on another Greek myth. We looked into a number of possibilities, but none of them
seemed to work out. We began nevertheless to discuss possibilities of a new
ballet with the composer. It was Stravinsky who hit upon the idea of a suite
of dances based on a seventeenth-century manual of French court dances—
sarabandes, gaillards, branles—he had recently come across. We all liked the
idea, especially as Kirstein and I recalled Stravinsky's other masterful treatment of polkas and other dance forms, including ragtime rhythms. The title of
the ballet, *Agon,* the Greek word for *contest, protagonist,* as well as *agony* or
struggle, was a happy inspiration of Stravinsky's. It was to be the only Greek
thing about the ballet, just as the dancing manual, the point of departure, was
to be the only French.

Stravinsky and I met to discuss details of the ballet. In addition to the court
dances, we decided to include the traditional classic ballet centerpiece, the *pas
de deux,* and other more familiar forms. Neither of us of course imagined that
we would be transcribing or duplicating old dances in either musical or dance
terms. History was only the takeoff point.

We discussed timing and decided that the whole ballet should last about
twenty minutes. Stravinsky always breaks things down to essentials. We talked
about how many minutes the first part should last, what to allow for the *pas de
deux* and the other dances. We narrowed the plan as specifically as possible.
To have all the time in the world means nothing to Stravinsky. "When I know
how long a piece must take, then it excites me." His house in California is
filled with beautiful clocks and watches, friends to his wish for precision, delicacy, refinement. We also discussed in general terms the character each dance
might have and possible tempos.

When we received the score I was excited and pleased and set to work at
once. Sounds like this had not been heard before. In his seventy-fifth year
Stravinsky had given us another masterpiece. For me, it was another enviable
chance to respond to the impulse his music gives so precisely and openly to
dance.

Music like Stravinsky's cannot be illustrated; one must try to find a visual
equivalent that is a complement rather than an illustration. And while the
score of *Agon* was invented for dancing, it was not simple to devise dances of
a comparable density, quality, metrical insistence, variety, formal mastery, or
symmetrical asymmetry. Just as a cabinetmaker must select his woods for the
particular job in hand—palisander, angelique, rosewood, briar, or pine—so a

ballet carpenter must find dominant quality of gesture, a strain or palette of consistent movement, an active scale of flowing patterns which reveals to the eye what Stravinsky tells the sensitized ear.

I was fascinated by the music, just as I had been fascinated and taught by Stravinsky's *Apollo* in the 1920s. As always in his ballet scores, the dance element of most force was the pulse. Here again his pulse built up a powerful motor drive so that when the end is reached we know, as with Mozart, that subject has been completely stated. Stravinsky's strict beat is authority over time, and I have always felt that a choreographer should place unlimited confidence in this control. For me at any rate, Stravinsky's rhythmic invention gives the greatest stimulus. A choreographer cannot invent rhythms, he can only reflect them in movement. The body is his medium and, unaided, the body will improvise for a little while. But the organizing of rhythm on a large scale is a sustained process, a function of the musical mind. To speak of carpentry again, planning a rhythm is like planning a house; it needs a structural operation.

As an organizer of rhythms, Stravinsky, I have always thought, has been more subtle and various than any single creator in history. What holds me always is the vitality in the substance of each measure. Each measure has its complete, almost personal life; it is a living unit. There are no blind spots. A pause, an empty space, is never empty space between indicated sounds. It is not just nothing. It acts as a carrying agent from the last sound to the next one. Life goes on within each silence.

Agon was written during the time of Stravinsky's growing interest in the music of Anton Webern and in twelve-tone music. He has said: "Portions of *Agon* contain three times as much music for the same clock length as some other pieces of mine." The score begins in an earlier style and then develops. The piece contains twelve pieces of music. It is a ballet for twelve dancers. It is all precise, like a machine, but a machine that thinks.

Like the score, the ballet is in three parts, performed without interruption. The first part consists of a *pas de quatre* for four boys, a double *pas de quatre* for eight girls and a triple *pas de quatre* for all twelve dancers. The curtain goes up before the music begins. There is no setting, only a plain backdrop. Four boys in practice clothes stand facing the back. They turn toward us quickly; as they step forward, the music begins, with a bright trumpet fanfare. The boys soon give way to eight girls. To a faster rhythm they, too, seem to be warming up. Then the boys come back and as the music, now a variation and development of the previous section, becomes more familiar and Stravinsky gives short solo passages to some of the principal instruments, the dancers stand in a state of readiness. Supported by the full confidence of the orchestra, all twelve dance.

There is another fanfare and three of the dancers, two girls and a boy, face us. They dance a *pas de trois*. The boy then dances a *sarabande*. Stravinsky's scoring is for solo violin, xylophone, tenor and bass trombone. This seems an odd combination on paper, but it is lovely in fact, and the contrast between the instruments is very interesting to the ear. The music changes then and we have the two girls dancing a *gaillard* featuring three flutes, chimes, mandolin, harp, and the lower strings in marvelous combinations. This gay dance with leaping steps merges into a coda for all three, as the boy comes back. The coda is the first piece in twelve-tone style and, now that our ears have been tuned in, we are ready for its complexities.

After a fanfare and a brief orchestral interlude again, the first *pas de trois* is replaced by another and the second part of the ballet begins with three *branles*. Descriptions of many old *branles* are available in dance histories, but my dances of course are improvisations. The two boys show off the girl, lifting her, balancing her, then she leaves.

Robert Craft says in his notes to the recording of *Agon* that Stravinsky saw an engraving in the old French manual depicting two trumpeters blowing accompaniment to a *branle simple* and that suggested the brilliant combination of those instruments for the next part, which is canon form. The two boys each take the part of one of the trumpets.

The *branle gai* is a solo for the girl, dominated by the rhythmic sound of castanets and the sort of dance style they suggest. The full orchestra then intervenes and the boys rejoin the girl for a final *branle double*.

Next comes the *pas de deux*, again after the fanfare and a short interlude. The music of the adagio is scored for strings, with a concertante part for the solo violin. There are variations for the boy, the music of which recalls the second *branle*, and the girl, and a coda. A brief quartet for mandolin, harp, violin, and cello is especially memorable in the score.

Four horns then recall the opening fanfare. The music for the first movement of the ballet is repeated and the piece ends as it began, with four boys dancing alone. They face the backdrop as the curtain falls.

In his book *Movement and Metaphor: Four Centuries of Ballet* (1970), Lincoln Kirstein, who commissioned *Agon* from Stravinsky for the New York City Ballet, has written interestingly about the background of the first production and given his impressions of the ballet. He writes that "the innovation of *Agon* lay in its naked strength, bare authority, and self-discipline in constructs of stressed extreme movement. Behind its active physical presence there was inherent a philosophy; *Agon* was by no means 'pure' ballet 'about' dancing only. It was an existential metaphor for tension and anxiety . . ."

Edwin Denby, the poet and critic, in *Dancers, Buildings and People in the Streets* (1965), fortunately now available in paperback, has written at length of "The Three Sides of *Agon*."

ALBORADA DEL GRACIOSO

Music by Maurice Ravel. Choreography by Jacques d'Amboise. Costumes by John Braden. Lighting by Ronald Bates. First presented at the New York City Ballet's Hommage à Ravel at the New York State Theatre, Lincoln Center, May 22, 1975, with Suzanne Farrell and Jacques d'Amboise in leading roles. Dedicated to Richard Boehm. Conducted by Robert Irving.

Ravel composed this piece of music as "an experiment in writing music that would sound improvised." Written first for the piano, and later orchestrated, it was originally part of a suite called *Miroirs* which consisted of pieces dedicated to five friends of the avant-garde, the "Apaches."

An *alborada* is an instrumental early Spanish folk form translatable as "dawn song" or "morning serenade." A *gracioso* is a comic or grotesque lover, perhaps like Don Quixote. Later, the *alborada* developed into a kind of dance especially popular in the Spanish province of Galicia near the Basque country of Ravel's ancestry. This is the structure upon which Jacques d'Amboise based his ballet.

Writing after its premiere the critic Herbert Kupferberg reported to *The National Observer* that this ballet is "Jacques d'Amboise's most notable achievement."

ALLEGRO BRILLANTE

Classic ballet. Music by Tchaikovsky. Choreography by George Balanchine. Costumes by Karinska. Lighting by Jean Rosenthal. First presented by the New York City Ballet at the City Center, New York, March 1, 1956, with Maria Tallchief and Nicholas Magallanes; Carolyn George, Barbara Fallis, Barbara Millberg, Barbara Walczak, Arthur Mitchell, Richard Rapp, Jonathan Watts, and Roland Vasquez.

Tchaikovsky's first piano concerto is played so often that many forget his other compositions for piano and orchestra. If my ballet to his second piano concerto, *Ballet Imperial*, has made that work better known, I am delighted. The music of his unfinished third piano concerto, Opus 75 in E Flat, has also seemed to me most appropriate for dancing. This was in fact the last music Tchaikovsky composed; he died less than a month after finishing the orchestration of the first movement, *Allegro Brillante*, on October 15, 1893. The composer had originally projected this music for use in a symphony, but after dismissing that idea, he rewrote the first movement for piano and orchestra and discarded the rest. As its marking suggests, the score is brisk and declarative but it is also deeply contemplative, I think.

The ballet is arranged for two principals and an ensemble. I had no narrative idea for the work, only wishing to have the dancers complement the music as best I could. The leading dancer of the work follows the piano in the cadenza, but her cavalier also has his important part, as do the supporting dancers, in conveying what I hope is the spirit of the work.

L'AMOUR ET SON AMOUR (Cupid and His Love)

Ballet in two scenes. Choreography by Jean Babilée. Music by César Franck. Settings and costumes by Jean Cocteau. First presented by Les Ballets des Champs-Élysées, at the Théâtre des Champs-Élysées, Paris, December 13, 1948, with Jean Babilée and Nathalie Philippart in the title roles. First presented in the United States by Ballet Theatre at the Metropolitan Opera House, New York, April 17, 1951, with Jean Babilée and Nathalie Philippart as Cupid and Psyche.

The story is told in mythology of Psyche, the daughter of a great king, who was so beautiful that the goddess of love became jealous of her. Wrathful Venus thereupon sent to earth her son, Cupid, to excite the girl with a passion for a hideous and hateful man, as a penalty for thus emulating the most beautiful of all the goddesses. Cupid came to Psyche to fulfill Venus' designs, but was so enchanted by the girl's loveliness that he fell in love with her. Secretly he came to earth every night to visit Psyche, taking leave of her before the break of day to conceal his identity, lest Venus discover his treachery in love.

Psyche's sisters knew of these visits and in their jealousy instilled doubts within the girl's heart: why should a lover conceal himself in the dark? The next night Psyche vowed to see her lover. As he slept, she lighted a lamp and saw the handsome god. But a drop of oil from the lamp fell on Cupid's shoulder, and he awoke to see her watching him. The youthful god rose up, told Psyche that her lack of faith had spoiled their love, and vanished into the night.

The desperate girl waited night after night, but her lover never returned. She went in search of him, beseeching the help of all the gods and goddesses. At last she came to the temple of Venus and humbly invoked her aid. The goddess swore vengeance and devised for Psyche a series of tasks she must accomplish before she could find her love. Venus' instructions were so difficult to carry out that Psyche almost died in her efforts to fulfill them. But Cupid, observing her plight, encouraged and aided his love from afar.

Venus became reconciled to the girl's beauty and no longer despised her. Psyche joined Cupid in the heavens, and the two lived happily ever after.

Psyche is the Greek word for soul, and the girl in this myth thus represents the human soul that strives and labors through insuperable difficulties to reach the supreme happiness of Olympus.

L'Amour et Son Amour does not recount the details of this story. Instead, the ballet strives to present the quality of the love that gave rise to the myth, to portray in movement the reunion of the god with the earth-bound girl and the attachment that made that reunion possible. The ballet carries a motto by Jean Cocteau: "Love has no explanation—do not seek a meaning in love's gestures." The music is César Franck's *Psyché* Suite.

The subdued music begins slowly. A drop curtain, white against a misty violet, depicts the profile of a youth whose eyes are directed toward a small opening in the painted frame that contains his image. The music heightens slightly and subsides again as the violet of the curtain changes to green. The curtain rises. A bright backdrop, painted in the sunny colors of the Mediterranean, pictures an imaginary map; it is framed by a Greek design. The scene is earth.

Psyche enters on the right. A flesh-color, skintight bodice reveals the beauty of her body. About her waist she wears a dark net skirt. Her long dark hair reaches to her shoulders. She moves slowly, almost listlessly. The graceful poses she assumes become an impressionistic rendering of the flow of the music. She moves as in a dream.

A man enters on the left, then another. The two approach Psyche, kiss her hands, and pay tribute to her beauty. They lift her gently, and the girl moves in mid-air between them. They hold her as she poses ethereally, like a drifting cloud. She stands alone for a moment, enchanted by some distant reality the men know nothing of. They come close to her again, and the three dance. The girl's arms stiffen. Holding her hands, one of her partners lifts her to the other. Psyche leads the dance with soft gestures, as if to instruct her admirers in the realm of her imagination. Her arms gesture with tender voluptuousness.

The men leave her, and Psyche stands alone, her arms at her sides. The music whirs to announce the arrival of seven zephyrs, who enter breathlessly. Their misty green gowns float in the air behind them. They surround Psyche in a wide semicircle. She responds to them with a gesture of sudden awakening. The zephyrs kneel and bow their heads, and Psyche dances alone. The zephyrs rise, and she dances among them, taking their hands as they weave in and out into a close circle that encloses her. Their hands flutter over Psyche's head to the accompaniment of the harp. Psyche falls back in the arms of one of the zephyrs. Another comes and lifts her legs, and three zephyrs carry her off toward Olympus. The other zephyrs fly into the twilight. The drop curtain falls.

After a brief interlude, the scene changes. Now we are high in the heavens. It is night. White lines sketch in the outlines of great constellations made by twinkling stars. The sky is warm, midnight blue. Psyche enters on the left. She marvels at the spacious beauty of the scene, its limitless starry light. The zephyrs stand behind her as she dances with them. Psyche senses that her dream is about to come true. The zephyrs rush her off.

Cupid leaps in, seemingly sustained in the air by the white wings he wears. He circles the stage in bold and daring flight. He becomes thoughtful and kneels. He looks toward the left and beckons with a noble godlike gesture toward the light. He leaves the scene. Just as he steps off, Psyche enters with the zephyrs; she moves in retarded, slow motion. The glow of the sky darkens. Psyche lies down. The stars black out.

Cupid appears in a circle of soft white light that seems to emanate from his person. He moves his arms slowly, as if he were pulling effortlessly invisible wires. Psyche attempts to rise. Cupid goes to her. Now she stands, holding onto his shoulder for support. The young god puts his arm about the girl's waist in recognition, and the two dance, softly and slowly, backward and forward. The music mounts to a crescendo. The two lovers kneel together. Cupid rises, turns with tremendous speed. Psyche imitates his movement. He holds out his arms, and the girl rushes toward him. He catches her foot in his hands and carries her back swiftly as she hovers over him.

Psyche steps down and poses against Cupid's back. He kneels, and the girl walks around him as he holds her hand. The music gradually loses its intensity. The two dance together gently. The light dims. Cupid holds up his left hand. The girl circles the stage and disappears. The light fades. Cupid stands in his domain, governing the light of the stars with his hands. The stars lose their luster; the circle of light about the god narrows to a pin point.

ANASTASIA

Scenario and choreography by Kenneth MacMillan. First performed in a one-act version by the Ballet of the Deutsche Oper, Berlin, June 25, 1967, with Lynn Seymour in the title role. Music by Bronislav Martinu (Symphonic Fantasy). Introductory score by the Studio for Electronic Music of the Berlin Technical University. Designed by Barry Kay. Film scenes from the Aero Film production From Tsar to Stalin. *Conducted by Ashley Lawrence. First given in three-act version by the Royal Ballet at the Royal Opera House, Covent Garden, London, July 22, 1971, with Lynn Seymour as* Anastasia, *Derek Rencher and Svetlana Beriosova as the* Tsar *and* Tsarina, *and Antoinette Sibley and Anthony Dowell as* Kschessinska *and her partner. Music for Acts One and Two by Peter Ilyich Tchaikovsky (Symphonies Nos. 1 and 3). Scenery and costumes by Barry Kay. First presented in the United States by the same ensemble with the same principals at the Metropolitan Opera House, New York, May 5, 1972.*

The nursery was the center of all Russia's troubles.
                                    SIR BERNARD PARES

Anastasia tells the story of the royal Russian princess who survived, some believe, the Bolshevik Revolution to live on and recall her past. Robert Massie in his book about the last Russian Tsar and his wife, *Nicholas and Alexandra*, quotes an older relative of the real Anastasia, who knew the child well, the Tsar's sister, Grand Duchess Olga: "My telling the truth simply does not help in the least, because the public simply wants to believe the mystery." This three-act ballet relates the young Anastasia's early life in the Russian imperial family and concludes with a scene in a Berlin hospital in 1920 where A Woman Who Believes She Is Anastasia looks back on her story. The same dancer depicts both. Through Anastasia's personal history the Russian past and cataclysmic public events are telescoped and recaptured.

Tsar Nicholas II came to the Russian throne in 1894 at the age of twenty-six. His wife, Alexandra, bore him four daughters—Olga, Tatiana, Marie, Anastasia—and one son, his first heir, the Tsarevitch Alexei, a hemophiliac. The Tsarina believed implicitly in the power of the Russian priest and mystic, Rasputin, to treat her son's bleeding.

The boy's tutor, the Swiss Pierre Gilliard, later wrote: "The illness of the Tsarevitch cast its shadow over the whole of the concluding period of Tsar Nicholas II's reign and alone can explain it. Without appearing to be, it was one of the main causes for his fall, for it made possible the phenomenon of Rasputin and resulted in the fatal isolation of the sovereigns who lived in a world apart, wholly absorbed in a tragic anxiety which had to be concealed from the world." And Alexander Kerensky, the Russian revolutionary leader removed by the Bolsheviks, declared: "Without Rasputin, there could have been no Lenin."

In March 1917 the Tsar abdicated as a result of the outbreak of revolutionary activity and, following the Bolshevik October Revolution that same year, the imperial family was imprisoned. On the night of July 16/17, 1918, the Tsar and his family were killed by Bolshevik forces at Ekaterinburg.

It was in 1920 that a woman patient in a Berlin hospital was recognized by some as one of the daughters of the Tsar. Since then this woman has endeavored to prove her identity as the Grand Duchess Anastasia.

ACT ONE: IN THE COUNTRYSIDE, AUGUST 1914 The imperial family is at a picnic in a birch grove by a lake with guests, who include the Tsarina's great friend Madame Vyrubova, Rasputin, and a group of naval officers. The party ends as the Tsar receives news of the outbreak of World War I.

The royal family is seen here to be a loving, close-knit group who have a congenial but necessarily distant relationship with the officers and courtiers who surround them. On this informal occasion, a picnic in the country, where the young can romp and play, where the Tsar can relax and take snapshots of his children, there is an illusion of tranquility broken only by the presence of young officers. Dominating the scene is the Tsarina's concern for her son and her faith in Rasputin's power to keep him from any dangerous accident. One of her relatives later recalled: "The Empress refused to surrender to fate. She talked incessantly of the ignorance of the physicians. She turned toward religion, and her prayers were tainted with a certain hysteria."

Anastasia, in a sailor blouse, enters on roller skates. She soon establishes a forthright, playful character, yet is considerate of others. She dances with three of the young officers who attend the family and, later, dances with her mother, who shows her the steps of an old Russian dance. When a telegram is brought to the Tsar and news of war breaks the calm, the soldiers and sailors in attendance begin to practice drills and maneuvers. The Tsar dances reassuringly with his wife, Rasputin leads them all in prayer, and there is a hope of victory. But one senses that it is a thin hope. The critic Peter Williams, remarking on the silver-birch setting of the scene, noted that some of the trees "have been cut down, with just their stumps showing, to suggest that the ballet opens where Chekhov's *Cherry Orchard* left off—a warning wind symbolic of the passing order."

ACT TWO: PETROGRAD, MARCH 1917 Despite rapidly growing unrest, the Tsar is giving a ball to celebrate the coming out of his youngest daughter, Anastasia. He has invited his favorite ballerina—with whom he had a liaison before his marriage—to dance for his guests. Anastasia is puzzled by the outburst of revolutionary activity.

The setting of the ballroom, like the first act, is circular in form, with a circular staircase descending like a vortex just off-center. Before the ballroom, however, an outside scene, with slogans and discontent in the streets, reminds us of unrest among the Russian people.

In the ballroom itself, which contrasts vividly with the poverty we have just seen, there are ceremonial dances for the Tsar, the royal family, and their guests. Anastasia, who has come of age, looks lovely and has a new maturity. The ballerina Mathilda Kschessinka, one of the great Russian ballerinas, first dancer of the Maryinsky Theatre for more than twenty-five years, enters and with her partner performs a *pas de deux* to the second movement of Tchaikovsky's symphony. Favorite of the Tsar before his accession to the throne and later the wife of the Grand Duke Andrei, the real Kschessinkaya in fact left Russia to live in Europe, where she danced triumphantly and taught for many years. Margot Fonteyn, and numerous other dancers were among her students. She died in Paris, in 1971, at the age of 99.

Later, when the ballerina has changed from her costume to a ball gown and joined the party, there is a *pas de quatre* in which she appears with the Tsar, the Tsarina, and Rasputin. Kschessinkaya's partner later joins in that dance, where old and new relationships excite the participants. The young Anastasia watches her parents and their friends and is bewildered; coming of age is more complicated than she has imagined if life, and love, are like that. An officer who tries to involve Anastasia herself is repulsed.

Now the action shifts back to the unrest in the streets of St. Petersburg.

Soon the populace and troops outside the palace interrupt the processions and formal dances of the ballroom. They invade the premises and the ball ends in disaster.

ACT THREE: SOME YEARS LATER   For the woman who believes she is Anastasia, past and present intermingle. She relives incidents from the years since the massacre of the Tsar and his family; her rescue by two brothers; the birth of her child; her marriage; the death of her husband; the disappearance of the child; her attempted suicide; the confrontation over the years with relatives of the imperial family who deny her identity as the Grand Duchess Anastasia.

The scene here is a Berlin hospital, where Anastasia sits on a white iron bed. She has recovered from a long period of unconsciousness and, reliving the past, is trying to find out who she is. Is she a plain person named Anna Anderson who has suffered simply a series of personal tragedies, or is she the Grand Duchess Anastasia who, in addition to personal misfortune, symbolizes another world? Filmed flashbacks of the past aid her memory of historic events, shown in newsreels and still photos, while her personal history and relationships are danced and depicted on stage. We see her rescue, the man who becomes her lover, their child, their happiness. This, too, is destroyed by another firing squad, for her husband is shot. She escapes yet again with his brother. Intermingled with the recapitulation of history and personal tragedy are confrontations the girl endures with members of the imperial family who refuse to recognize her as Anastasia. She herself, however, has no doubt; transcending all of her prolonged personal misfortune is her vivid recollection of the lovely past, when families might picnic under the silver birches and a young girl in a sailor suit might be so beloved by her parents that she would surely have a happy life. The ballet ends as we see Anastasia poised high at the foot of her hospital bed. The bed begins to move, coming toward us like an open royal limousine, it progresses; Anastasia, still and triumphant, receives silently the homage of the world.

Reflecting on Kenneth MacMillan's achievement in the three-act ballet form, Arlene Croce wrote in *The New Yorker* in 1974: "Of the three full-evening ballets MacMillan has produced so far, *Anastasia* seems to me the best, not so much because of what it achieves as because of what it attempts. In *Romeo*, MacMillan had before him both Leonid Lavrovsky's version for the Bolshoi and Cranko's for the Stuttgart; in *Manon* he is working à la Cranko. But in *Anastasia* he produced a personal fantasy about a global cataclysm entirely from nothing. I don't think he was being pretentious, and the insults that were showered upon him for missing the mark themselves missed the mark. MacMillan's taste, musical instinct, and technical skill place him first among those British and European choreographers whose careers began in the fifties."

APOLLO (Apollon Musagète)

> Ballet in two scenes. Music and book by Igor Stravinsky. Choreography by George Balanchine. Scenery and costumes by André Bauchant. First presented by Diaghilev's Ballets Russes at the Théâtre Sarah Bernhardt, Paris, June 12, 1928, with Serge Lifar as Apollo, Alice Nikitina as Terpsichore (Alexandra Danilova alternated with Nikitina in this role in the original production), Lubov Tchernicheva as Polyhymnia, and Felia Dubrovska as Calliope. First presented in the United States by the American Ballet at the Metropolitan Opera House, New York, April 27, 1937, with scenery and costumes by Stewart Chaney. Lew Christensen was Apollo; the three Muses were danced by Elise Reiman, Holly Howard, and Daphne Vane.

To the Greeks, the god Apollo was many things: he was the god of prophecy, the god who punished wrongdoers, the god who helped those in trouble, the god of vegetation and agriculture, and the god of song and music. Apollo received different epithets, different names, for each of his various powers. Because of his powers of song and music, he was also closely associated with the Muses, goddesses who represented the different arts and derived inspiration from Apollo's teaching. This ballet concerns itself with Apollo, leader of the Muses, the youthful god who has not yet attained the manifold powers for which he will afterward be renowned among men.

The three Muses of the ballet were selected for their appropriateness to the choreographic art. In the words of the composer, "Calliope personified poetry and its rhythm; Polyhymnia represents mime; Terpsichore, combining in herself both the rhythm and the eloquence of gesture, reveals dancing to the world and thus among the Muses takes the place of honor beside Apollo."*

The ballet begins with a brief prologue that depicts the birth of Apollo. Before the opening curtain, the string orchestra intimates the theme that will become identified with the god as the ballet progresses. This theme receives a rhythmic accompaniment from the lower strings, and the curtain rises.

The scene is Delos, an island in the Aegean Sea. It is night; stars twinkle in a dark blue sky. Back in the distance, in a shaft of light, Leto gives birth to the child whom the all-powerful Zeus has sired. She sits high on a barren rock and holds up her arms to the light. The music quickens, the woman buries her face in her hands, a hurried crescendo is cut off sharply, the strings are plucked, and Apollo is born. Leto disappears, and in the shaft of light at the base of the high rock stands the infant god, wrapped tightly in swaddling clothes. He hops forward stiffly to a swift, flowing melody.

* From Igor Stravinsky, An Autobiography, Simon and Schuster, Inc., New York, 1936.

Two handmaidens leap softly across the stage and come to Apollo. The new-born god falls back in their arms; his mouth moves in an inarticulate cry for help, and the two women begin to unwrap his swaddling clothes. They circle the god, unwinding the rich cloth, but before they can finish, Apollo spins sud-denly and frees himself of the garment and looks about the dark world, not seeing clearly, not knowing how to move. After this burst of energy, he is frightened. His head is crowned with golden vine leaves and his body is en-dowed by nature with sinuous strength, but the young god is bewildered.

The two handmaidens bring to him a lute, sign of his future greatness in music. Apollo does not know how to hold the instrument. They place it in his hands and stand behind him, reaching out their hands to pluck the strings. Apollo follows their example and finds the first clue to his immortality. There is a blackout.

The musical statement that marked Apollo's birth is repeated sonorously. When the lights come on again, the scene is brilliant, as if a flash of lightning had been sustained and permanently illuminated the world. Apollo, dressed now in a short gold tunic, stands in the center of the stage. To the music of a solo violin, he plays upon the lute. He whirls his arms around and around in a large circle over the strings, seeming to draw music from the instrument with his youthful strength. Other strings now accompany the solo violin softly. Apollo places the lute on the ground and dances alone. He reaches out to the lute for inspiration and moves tentatively, carefully, but with a new-found ease. Now that he has proved his potential grace in movement, Apollo picks up the lute again. He turns slowly in attitude, holding the lute before him. The solo violin concludes the theme.

Three Muses appear to Apollo, walking slowly and respectfully toward him from three corners of the stage. With a godlike gesture, the god welcomes them. The young goddesses bow to him, then in unison bend in low arabesques about the lute he holds high in his hands. They break this pose and stand together. The melody is strong yet moving, vigorous yet simple, like the youth-ful, inexperienced quality of the dance that now begins.

Apollo reaches out and, touching their hands gently, draws the Muses close to him. The three girls stand close together, one behind the other. Apollo takes their hands one by one. They pose in arabesque for an instant and move to the center of the stage. He motions two of the girls aside; Terpsichore, Muse of song and dance, falls back in his arms. He leaves her kneeling alone and, enclosing the other two girls in his arms, he lowers them slowly to the ground so that they also kneel.

Terpsichore rises and, dancing on point, slowly takes the hands of her sister Muses and encircles their kneeling figures. Now the three Muses stand again in a close line. The lower strings play the poignant theme with deep strength, and Apollo circles the stage in broad, free leaps as the girls move their arms in rhythm to the music.

The god returns to the Muses and supports each as she turns close to the ground. The girls form a line behind Apollo and move across the back of the stage, their bold, youthful figures imitating the dance of their leader. The girls pause and kneel, then rise at once. Apollo, arms outstretched, supports them as they hold hands and form a circular tableau.

When this tableau is broken, the Muses form a close line in front of Apollo. This line moves backward as one, the young god and goddesses shuffling awkwardly on their heels. The line comes to a rest. The three girls stand motionless; Apollo bends down and tenderly pushes them into motion with his shoulder. Led by Terpsichore, the Muses dance alone. The melody ends.

Apollo presents each of the Muses with the symbol appropriate to her art. To Calliope, Muse of poetry, he presents a tablet; to Polyhymnia, Muse of mime, a mask that symbolizes unearthly silence and the power of gesture; and to Terpsichore, Muse of dancing and song, he gives a lyre, the instrument that accompanies those arts. The Muses accept these gifts with delight and respect, form a line, and hop like pleased children to the side of the stage. Apollo commands the Muses to create and sits to watch what they will do.

Calliope comes forward with her tablet. She holds it out before her, then clutches it to her heart. Placing the tablet on the ground, she dances. The melody she moves to is based in form on the Alexandrine, the classical heroic measure of French poetry. Her dance is emotional, yet not weakly so; as she circles the stage before Apollo, her leg boldly sweeps the air before her. She is scribbling hastily on the palm of her hand when her dance nears its end, wondering if she has done well. She becomes a little sad, the music seems to cry out softly with her, and she goes to show Apollo what she has written. He does not approve.

Brilliant chords herald the dance of Polyhymnia, who soon puts her mask aside and dances rapidly to a sprightly, rhythmic melody. The girl holds her finger to her lips throughout the dance, as she tries to maintain the dignity of her mask, but her youthful enthusiasm gets the best of her: she forgets—as she responds to the happy, worldly music—and before she knows what has happened, her lips have moved and she has spoken. Terrified, she claps her hands over her mouth, punishing her own naughtiness, but Apollo sees what she has done and censures her.

Terpsichore comes forward and dances in profile with her lyre. She holds the instrument high above her head, her curved arms suggesting the shape of the lyre, and her feet pluck at the ground as if they played upon it. She moves adroitly and sharply, with assured grace; the gestures she makes with her arms as she poses in a series of balanced arabesques show us that her whole body is coordinated to beauty. The music she dances to is similar in melody to Calliope's, but the rhythm is different; like her dance, it is more pointed, less romantic. Of all the Muses, she alone dances perfectly, and Apollo commends her.

Now the young god dances alone. Majestic chords announce the theme of his variation. He reaches his arms up toward Olympus, leaps grandly into the air, then kneels. To the quiet rhythms of the music, Apollo performs with ideal perfection, setting an example to the Muses and reminding us that he himself has acquired the skill he demands of them.

As his dance ends, Apollo sits on the ground in a graceful, godlike pose. Terpsichore appears before him and touches his outstretched hand. The young goddess steps over his arm and bends low in extended arabesque beside him. Now the girl rises and sits on Apollo's knees. He holds his arm up to her, she takes it, and both rise to dance a muted *pas de deux*. The melody is softly lyrical, but at the same time strong; it depicts in sound an awakening of Olympian power and strength, beauty and grace.

Apollo supports Terpsichore in extended arabesque, lifts her daringly high so that her body curves back over his shoulder, holds her as she extends her legs and sinks on the ground to rise on point in graceful extensions. She pirouettes swiftly and sharply in his arms then entwines herself around Apollo. The music brightens, they separate, dancing playfully, then meet again. Both kneel. Apollo puts his head in Terpsichore's open hands. Now, at the end, she falls across Apollo's back as the god bends down to give the Muse a short swimming lesson as a reward for her beautiful dancing. Her arms push the air aside as if they were moving in the water. When Apollo rises, Terpsichore's body is curved against him.

Calliope and Polyhymnia rush in and join Apollo and Terpsichore in a joyous coda in which the Muses surround Apollo with their new-found pleasure in movement. The young god, in their midst, holds out his arms; two of the girls grab hold, and he swings them through the air. The quick grace of the Muses is accompanied by lively, shifting rhythms in the music that rushes to a finish. Apollo takes them by the hand and drives all three across the stage in a swift chariot race. As the music ends, Apollo stands alone. The three girls walk toward him together and in unison clap their palms. Apollo leans down and places his head against their hands.

From on high, Zeus calls his son Apollo home with mighty crescendos of sound. Apollo stands motionless, as if under a spell, listening. The three Muses sit upon the ground. Apollo walks slowly around them. As he stands in back of them and reaches out over them, the three girls lift their feet to meet his hand. Apollo blesses them with a noble gesture. The Muses reach their arms up, and Apollo lifts them up beside him. For a moment the arms of the four figures are entwined, then the three Muses pose in arabesque behind Apollo's profiled figure to form a tableau in which the goddesses are as one with him.

Now Apollo takes their hands and draws them like a chariot across the stage. He takes them to the foot of the high rock, then walks forward and begins to climb to the summit, pointing the way to Olympus. The Muses follow. The four figures are silhouetted against the sky, holding out their arms to the sun. Leto, Apollo's mother, falls back in the arms of his handmaidens as she reaches up to her son in farewell.

NOTES   *Apollo* is not the kind of ballet most people expect to see when they know its name. When the ballet was first performed, a French critic said that this was not Apollo at all, that the choreographer had cultivated the deliberately odd, that Apollo would never have done this, or this, or this, etc. When the critic was asked how he knew what Apollo would have done, he had no answer. He was thinking of some familiar statue of Apollo, the Apollo Belvedere perhaps, and imagined that a ballet about the god would personify sculptural representations. But *Apollon Musagète* is not Apollo Belvedere; he is the wild, half-human youth who acquires nobility through art.

Stravinsky's *Apollon Musagète* was originally commissioned by Elizabeth Sprague Coolidge and received its first performance at the Library of Congress in Washington on April 27, 1928, with choreography by Adolph Bolm, who danced the principal role. Ruth Page (Terpsichore), Elise Reiman (Calliope), and Berenice Holmes (Polyhymnia) were the three Muses. After this first performance, Stravinsky offered the score to Diaghilev, who assigned the ballet to me.

This was the second time I had worked closely with Stravinsky's music (*Le Rossignol* was a first attempt, an exercise set me by Diaghilev in 1925). *Apollo* was a collaboration. As I wrote in *Stravinsky in the Theatre,* "I look back upon the ballet as the turning point in my life. In its discipline and restraint, in its sustained oneness of tone and feeling, the score was a revelation. It seemed to tell me that I could, for the first time, dare not use all my ideas; that I, too, could eliminate. I began to see how I could clarify, by limiting, by reducing what seemed to be myriad possibilities to the one possibility that is inevitable.

"In studying the score, I first understood how gestures, like tones in music and shades in painting, have certain family relations. As groups they impose their own laws. The more conscious an artist is, the more he comes to understand these laws and to respond to them. Since working with Stravinsky on this ballet, I have developed my choreography inside the framework such relations suggest."

Stravinsky, in his 1936 *Autobiography,* notes that the invitation to compose a ballet for a contemporary music festival in Washington gave him an opportunity to carry out an idea that had long appealed to him, "to compose a ballet founded on moments or episodes in Greek mythology plastically interpreted by dancing of the so-called classical school . . . I had especially in my thoughts what is known as the 'white ballet,' in which to my mind the very essence of this art reveals itself in all its purity. I found that the absence of many-colored effects and of all superfluities produced a wonderful freshness. This inspired me to write of an analogous character. It seemed to me that diatonic composition was the most appropriate for this purpose, and the austerity of its style determined what my instrumental ensemble must be. I set aside the ordinary orchestra because of its heterogeneity . . . and chose strings.

"On June 12, 1928, I conducted the first production of *Apollo* . . . in Paris . . . George Balanchine, as ballet master, had arranged the dances exactly as I had wished—that is to say, in accordance with the classical school. From that point of view it was a complete success, and it was the first attempt to revive academic dancing in a work actually composed for the purpose. Balanchine . . . had designed for the choreography of *Apollo* groups, movements, and lines of great dignity and plastic elegance as inspired by the beauty of classical forms . . .

"As for the dancers, they were beyond all praise. The graceful Nikitina with her purity of line alternating with the enchanting Danilova in the role of Terpsichore; Tchernicheva and Dubrovska, those custodians of the best classical traditions; finally, Serge Lifar, then still quite young, conscientious, natural, spontaneous, and full of serious enthusiasm for his art—all these formed an unforgettable company."

The importance of *Apollo* to the history of ballet has been described by Lincoln Kirstein: "*Apollon Musagète* introduced to ballet in its time a spirit of traditional classicism absent since Petipa's last compositions almost thirty years before. It demonstrated that tradition is not merely an anchorage to which one returns after eccentric deviations but the very floor which supports the artist, enabling him securely to build upon it elements which may seem at first revolutionary, ugly, and new both to him and to his audience. *Apollon* has now lost for us the effects which offended, irritated, or merely amused an earlier public. We forget that much of the 'modernism' of adagio movement in our classic dance derives directly from *Apollon;* that many ways of lifting women, of turning close to the floor, of subtle syncopation in the use of *pointes,* of a single male dancer supporting three women, were unknown before *Apollon.* These innovations horrified many people at first, but they were so logical an extension of the pure line of Saint-Léon, Petipa, and Ivanov that they were almost immediately absorbed into the tradition of their craft.

"Glenway Wescott said that instead of *Apollo, Leader of the Muses,* the ballet should have been entitled *Apollo's Games with the Muses.* The mimed athletics, the strenuous atmosphere of violent physicality recall the nervousness of runners before a race. Each variation seems a training for the final translation to Olympus. In the chariot-race finale which evokes memories of the profiles on Roman coins and cameos and of the decathlon, visualized in the newly extended idiom of Russian ballet, a transformation of the Olympic games into contemporary dancing takes place. Of all Balanchine's works *Apollon* is the most significant historically, the most compact, the most influential . . ." (In "Balanchine Musagète," *Theatre Arts,* November 1947.)

North German Television in 1967 made a film of rehearsals and a performance of *Apollo.* A spoken commentary by John Drummond described the occasion, in which Stravinsky and I participated. The dancers were Jacques d'Amboise as Apollo, Suzanne Farrell as Terpsichore, Gloria Govrin as Calliope, and Patricia Neary as Polyhymnia.

APPARITIONS

Dramatic ballet in three scenes with prologue and epilogue. Music by Franz Liszt. Choreography by Frederick Ashton. Book by Constant Lambert. Scenery and costumes by Cecil Beaton. First presented by the Sadler's Wells Ballet at the Sadler's Wells Theatre, London, February 11, 1936, with Robert Helpmann as the Poet and Margot Fonteyn as the Woman in Ball Dress. First presented in the United States by the Sadler's Wells Ballet at the Metropolitan Opera House, New York, October 25, 1949, with the same principals.

The inspiration of a poet is the subject of this romantic ballet. Here the poet derives his work not from real life, or from anything connected with it, but from the realm of the fantastic imagination, from apparitions. The ballet thus depicts the poet as character rather than creator, as a victim of the apparitions he finds it necessary to invoke. The scenario of *Apparitions* was suggested by the synopsis Hector Berlioz wrote for his *Symphonie Fantastique*. The music, orchestrated by Gordon Jacob, was selected from the later works of Franz Liszt by Constant Lambert.

PROLOGUE   The curtain rises on a scene representing the poet's study. It is an immense, dark, high-ceilinged room with great leaded windows—the kind of room in which we think instantly of hidden shadows lurking in the corners. It is night. On the right, a lamp stands upon a desk. Seated at the desk is the poet. He is evidently engrossed in composition, for at first he does not look up. Soon, however, he rises and gestures impatiently. His poem is not progressing as he would wish; he seems to require a fresh stimulus to continue.

The poet is astonished as light appears outside the windows. He is amazed further when he observes in the window frames mysterious apparitions. There stands a beautiful young woman in a formal ball dress, there a handsome hussar, and there a monk. Immediately the poet is enamored of the woman, who smiles at him in recognition. He sees in her an idealized version of all women, a picture of the perfect romance, and for a few moments he imagines that he has the key to the end of the poem he has been writing. But the woman and the other figures disappear. He reaches out toward them, then turns and sits again at his desk. Now his inspiration is so intense that words will not come. His mind is preoccupied with the source of his inspiration rather than the lines she might assist him to create. His mind whirls with romance. He gives up in impatience, abandons the poem, and takes a potion to induce sleep. The curtain falls.

SCENE ONE: A BALLROOM   Now the scene shifts to the locale of the poet's dream. The curtain rises on a ballroom, where fashionable couples are dancing. The poet enters, observes the scene, and wishes to participate in the discreet gaiety, but the dancers look through him as if he were the empty air. At a pause in the dancing, the lovely woman in the ball dress enters the room. All the men—particularly a handsome, swashbuckling hussar—are deferential to her dark beauty and vie for her favor. The dancing recommences. In this new dance, the women change partners constantly, and suddenly the poet is holding in his arms the apparition that delights him. But she is unaware that she has seen him before and turns her head away to catch sight of the hussar. She leaves the scene when the hussar rejoins her, and soon the ballroom is empty. The poet, alone, despairs.

SCENE TWO: A SNOW-CLAD PLAIN   The dream changes, and the poet finds himself in the lonely winter forest. He longs for the reappearance of the woman, but imagines that she will again reject him. He hears bells in the distance, wonders what they are for, and dancers who wear skirts shaped like bells move around and around him, giving vivid expression to his romantic hallucination.

A funeral procession enters. Cloaked figures carry the body of the deceased on a bier. The poet is startled to see that the procession is led by the monk who appeared in the window of his study. Now he has seen again all three: the girl, the hussar, and the monk. Is this the end? What will happen? Will his dream be resolved?

He is drawn to the bier. Before the monk can prevent it, he snatches away the burial cloth and discovers the face of his beloved. Again he despairs. The monk reprimands him. The procession moves on. The poet falls to the ground to weep and to pray.

SCENE THREE: A CAVERN   The scene now is a dark, secluded cavern. Creatures in red costumes have gathered here to practice some secret, magical rite. The poet joins them, seems to be accepted among them, rejoices, then falls back aghast as he sees before him the creature of his imagination, her face defaced, grotesque, ugly. The poet disclaims responsibility for his dream and seeks to escape. The woman is now attracted to him and will not let him go. The poet faints. As he passes into deep unconsciousness, her face miraculously takes on its previous apparent beauty.

EPILOGUE   The final curtain rises on the poet's study. He is still asleep. Gradually he wakens. He cannot shake off his dream, and as he pieces it together, he sees the dream as a telling, romantic poem on his own pursuit of romanticism—a perpetual destruction of the self in the seeking of the unattainable. He kills himself.

The woman of his imagination enters and grieves. She turns her face away as cloaked figures take up the poet's body.

ARENA

Music by Morton Subotnick. Choreography by Glen Tetley. Lighting by John B. Read, executed by Gilbert V. Hemsley, Jr. First presented by the Netherlands Dance Theatre at the Royal Theatre, The Hague, February 4, 1969. First presented in the United States by the Stuttgart Ballet at the Metropolitan Opera House, Lincoln Center, New York, June 4, 1975, with Richard Cragun, Egon Madsen, and Dieter Ammann in leading roles.

When *Arena* was first danced, the choreographer has recalled, critics tried to read into it the Cretan myth of the Minotaur—doubtless because the composer of its electronic score, Morton Subotnick, had given his work the title *The Wild Bull.* "But I did not consciously intend any such meaning," Tetley has said. "The relationships that I tried to portray arose solely from the kinds of movement that I wanted to use, and from tensions implicit in the music. However, for the sake of those who find it hard to get by without some kind of 'plot,' let me essay the following interpretation: The ballet seems to me rather like a set of variations on the theme of might, dominance, pure power. When people are forced into close proximity, the mutual tensions can lead to an explosion of violence, which may manifest itself on either a physical or spiritual plane. These were the thoughts that had been suggested to me by the music."

The action of *Arena*, which is danced by six men, takes place in an undefined space from which there is apparently no clear escape. A struggle develops between two of the men; jealousy and love in varied ways are displayed until one of the major participants, in understandable rage, begins to throw chairs around the stage.

The dancer and writer James Waring reported to *Ballet Review* in 1971, after the ballet's premiere: "*Arena* is about self-doubt, and self-confidence, and their oscillation. The six men are gladiators of some sort, in a circus of the mind. Three of them function mostly as decor. Of the other three, Frans Vervenne (sometimes, Harmen Tromp) sleeps on a pile of nesting chairs. Hans Knill is a final challenger who overcomes the principal figure, Jon Benoit. The ballet unfolds in a series of physical challenges, alternating with periods of retreat."

ASTARTE

Created and choreographed by Robert Joffrey. Music performed by Chamberlain, conducted by Hub Miller. Commissioned score composed by Crome Syrcus. Lighting design and set by Thomas Skelton. Costumes by Hugh Sherrer. Film created and photographed by Gardner Compton. Produced by Midge Mackenzie. First presented by the City Center Joffrey Ballet at the City Center, New York, September 20, 1967, with Trinette Singleton and Maximiliano Zomosa.

Astarte, moon goddess of love and fertility, borrowed from the Babylonian-Assyrian Ishtar by the Greeks, is the heroine of this multimedia work. Astarte gave herself to all men, but was owned by none. She has been called the patron goddess of Women's Liberation, lover and destroyer, bestower of both life and death. The ballet that celebrates her powers uses music (an acid-rock score specially commissioned) amplified dramatically, lights (incandescent and strobe), film, and dance in the first combination of these elements in the theater of ballet. Techniques and impressions familiar in the discothèque are here, melded with dance to produce a dramatic *pas de deux* unlike any seen before.

What happens in general is simple. As the music starts full volume, the darkened theater is suddenly filled with varied kinds of light. A steadily blinking strobe stares out from the front of the stage so that no one in the audience can see for a moment of necessary adjustment; the stage itself begins to have some light on it, and searching spotlights are aimed at the audience, trying to find we know not what.

We soon find out. The backcloth of the setting on stage is a tightly stretched white cloth pulled in at the center like a belly button, and, against a drop farther back, a frantic film is being projected, of frantic birds and a hypnotic girl —the goddess Astarte. The seeking spotlights find a boy seated on the aisle in the audience as the eye of the goddess winks. He rises, transfixed by her glance, and slowly makes his way down the center aisle of the theater as we all watch. He crosses then to the right, toward steps to the stage, meanwhile looking at the stage at the goddess who has materialized before us. He goes up on stage and, standing there, still staring alone at the eyes of the goddess, begins to take off his clothes—all of them, down to his briefs, as her image looms huge above him on the screen. Soon his image, too, is seen to merge with hers. The rock singer has begun to sing, and the boy puts his clothes tenderly on the ground under the watching eye of the mysterious girl. He now goes to her, holding out his hands and, reaching her, molding them to her body. She steps forward then, and he begins to hold her in a dance that is anticipated, gesture by gesture, by the film that wraps around them and shows through them. The dance is slow, cool, collected, as the music blasts, and the boy and the goddess who controls him are in a different world, out of all contact with those who watch. There is no appeal here for attention to the spectator; there is only attention to each other, and the spectators are beyond reality. The boy in his dance worships the girl as he maneuvers her, lifts her, touches her. He attempts in mounting frenzy for a moment to control and subdue her as an erection rises in the stretched jersey of backcloth, and to kiss her. Then the music quietens. In the film we see his body branded with the impress of the goddess's as his passion is spent. She lets down her hair, and the dance of engulfment continues relentlessly, he, as always, powerless to resist her beauty and powerless, too, completely to claim her. He falls back, and, in the film, we see him somersault in pain and fall forward so that she in triumph can cause him to writhe at her feet.

She hovers over him as the rapid pulse of the strobe illumines them. She raises her leg over him, and the boy crouches there below her. Then, holding her above him, he rises and, before we realize it, he is carrying her and displaying her curved body aloft, as the filmed image has already anticipated, her legs locked about his head, his hands clasping her ankles. It is a posture of glory for the remote goddess and proud submission for the boy. He kneels at last so that she can step down. Before he realizes it, she is gone. The backdrop dissolves, and the boy walks back, back, through the back wall of the stage, where huge, high doors open for him, through the storage of scenery and props, to the exit to the street. These doors, too, open for him and, still transfixed by the goddess and his joy in her, he moves out into the light and traffic, perhaps to rejoin the world.

NOTES   Gardner Compton, who created the films for *Astarte*, has had some interesting things to say about its composition. Writing in *Dance Magazine*, he said: "The discothèque is the temple of electricity with its light shows, audio-visual devices such as film (which, in essence, is merely the reproduction of light), and other visual effects. In these new temples, some dance to electronic music while others sit in small groups on the floor watching the God Electricity (Light) perform on the walls and ceilings. The milieu of *Astarte* was precisely this new house of worship.

"One of the elements of this new creed is the use of multimedia devices to obtain involvement. *Astarte* sought to bridge the gap between the loose, unrefined area of the happening and a legitimate art form—in this case, ballet. What Robert Joffrey and I tried to avoid was the looseness of form characteristic of the happening. Our concept was more classical in nature. The choreographer was using movement in a magnificent sustained counterpoint to the amplified acid-rock music. It was the dancers who were receiving the audio massage, a massage that tuned them *out* on the world of the audience. In so doing we hoped that the fantasy of the film media combined with the reality of the dancers would tune *in* the audience on the ritualistic milieu of the discothèque.

"But *Astarte* was merely a beginning, a primer for what is to come. It is only one of the first steps in the direction of a totally involved multi-media theatre experience. And I believe this will be a vital concept of the whole.

"In order for choreo-cinema to be successful, there must be a perfect blending of these concepts to form one unified artistic viewpoint. . . . I remember Martha Graham giving an image in class that made first position a reality to me. The essence of that image was as follows: Your arms are carried from the back as though you are standing in a shower and the water is like energy draining down the arm and off the middle fingers of the hands. A cameraman should film a dancer so that the last object to leave the frame is that portion of the body that moves the energy from space to space. The camera itself should also move the energy from one space to another, or it is not contributing. Timing and framing are the essential tools of a dance cameraman. One must frame on space and let the dancer move into it. Space is the dancer's canvas, whether on stage or on film. Both space and movement, too, may have to be modified or distorted to make the choreo-cinema effective to an audience.

"The camera is the eye of the audience, the establisher of the involvement, the point of view, the movement. Why should the joy of movement be limited to the dancers? The members of the audience, too, can enjoy it, but only if the camera works for them. Thus if someone were to ask me the difference between a *pas de deux* on stage and a *pas de deux* on film I would answer as follows: A *pas de deux* on stage is a dance for two people (usually a boy and a girl), whereas a *pas de deux* on film is a dance for a boy, a girl, *and* camera. If cinematographic movement techniques are used successfully with dance, a successful marriage can result. One must wed the movement of one art to the movement of the other in order to achieve a true choreographic end.

"In *Astarte*, Robert Joffrey choreographed for the stage. What I filmed was Joffrey's choreography (even the abstract images are derived from images of the dancers themselves). However, I selected and chose for my camera, making the film very different from what the dancers were doing on stage. Often to reach a total choreographic concept, I borrowed the fugue form from music. I repeated themes in such a way that the movement would start with the live dancers and then be repeated and built through film, although the dancers on stage were then doing something altogether different. At other times the film would initiate the theme and then the dancers would echo it and build it to climax which the film would again pick up. . . ."*

AS TIME GOES BY

Music by Franz Josef Haydn. Choreography by Twyla Tharp. Lighting by Jennifer Tipton. Costumes by Chester Weinberg. Assistant to Miss Tharp: Harry Berg. First presented by the City Center Joffrey Ballet at the City Center, New York, October 24, 1973. Conducted by Seymour Lipkin.

As Time Goes By is a dance ballet to wonderful music by Haydn—the third and fourth movements of the *Symphony No. 45 in F-Sharp Minor*. Mozart once said, I think, that Haydn's music had given him immense amusement and also the deepest reflections. Mozart, as usual, was right. The music here is the famous *"Farewell" Symphony*, where the players get up and leave the stage one by one. What the choreographer does with that situation, and with other

* Reprinted by courtesy of *Dance Magazine*.

plots and developments of the music, is her own special business. The critic
Marcia B. Siegel described it for *Dance Magazine*: "Beatriz Rodriguez' opening solo in silence is allegro ballet laced with those odd dislocations of body
parts, those big transformations with smooth, almost lazy recoveries that we've
come to think of as Tharpian. As Haydn's minuet begins, five other dancers
join her and they slip through a long chain of decorous attitudes and preparations that melt or click into surprise partnerships. Haydn leaves the music
dangling on an unfinished cadence, and the dancers redeploy themselves to
begin The Four Finales, a glorious rout in which you can just pick out elements of various overworked dance endings, exits, and climaxes, all overlapped
and out of joint and meticulously mistimed. Finally, to Haydn's famous adagio,
where the musicians leave one by one, Larry Grenier spins out an extraordinary solo in one long, sinuous, self-involved phrase of movement, while the
stage fills with dancers and empties again. You can't remember where he came
from and you can't imagine where he'll stop. The curtain goes down while he's
still dancing.

"I'm not inclined to take the title of *As Time Goes By* too seriously—it
might have come about by accident. A harried person from the Joffrey publicity department runs into the studio a week before the première and pleads:
'Twyla, time is going by. The papers are screaming. We've got to have a title
for your ballet!' Without taking her eyes off the rehearsal, Tharp mutters:
'Okay, call it *As Time Goes By*. Now don't bother me.'

"However that was, the ballet seems more concerned with continuity than
with time itself. It shows us the bridges between things, the awkward foldings
that precede the beautiful unfoldings, the movements that connect rather than
the poses that separate. The beginning is the end is the beginning. Amen."

Arlene Croce, dance critic of *The New Yorker*, has written of Twyla Tharp's
work in the November 19, 1973, issue of that magazine:

"Twyla Tharp is the Nijinska of our time. *Deuce Coupe*, an unidealized portrait of American youth in the nineteen sixties, is her *Les Biches*, and *As Time
Goes By*, an abstract fantasy about individuals against the blank canvas of a
tribal society, is her *Les Noces*. Of course I'm generalizing, but not, I hope,
idly. *As Time Goes By*, created this season for the Joffrey Ballet and employing an all-Joffrey cast and Haydn music, is a study of classical dancing. Its
'tribal' ethos is that of young, hard-working New York-American dancers,
subspecies Joffrey, and its light-speckled fancies and serene inversions of classical principles are as far from the iron wit of *Les Noces* as the heterogeneous
home-style social dances of *Deuce Coupe* are from the monolithic encounters
of that Parisian salon in *Les Biches*. Nevertheless, the parallel persists between
Twyla Tharp and ballet's greatest woman choreographer. I think that, like
Nijinska's, Twyla Tharp's work exacts a primitive force of expression from its
subject, which is classical ballet. It seems to seek out first principles and turn
them over with curiosity, finding new excitement in what lies on the other side
of orthodoxy. And it gains a secondary kind of raw power from what seem de-

liberate lapses from ballet decorum and refinement. Sometimes, a classical step is resolved with a new twist; it forms itself and then re-forms itself backward. But sometimes the step isn't all there; it seems truncated or only half-quoted; the effect is of a surgical cut, a slash at the fat body of unusable style. The negations and distortions of Nijinska's choreography cut away rhetorical flab. The turned-in toes and obsessive stiff pointwork of *Les Noces* were a radical distortion, necessary if women's feet and not simply their points were to become significant once more on the stage. In much the same way, Twyla Tharp is moving toward a new quality of plain speech in classical choreography. At times, she seems to be on the verge of creating a new style, a new humanity, for classical-ballet dancers. If she doesn't go all the way to a full enunciation of that style, that is probably because the ballet is not long enough. Time, in this ballet, goes by much too fast.

"*As Time Goes By* is in four sections, quasi-dramatic in their progression. Beginning with the Individual, it moves on to the Group, then to the Mass, and finally back to the Individual. (These designations are my own; I prefer them to the unevocative titles in the program.) The opening solo is danced by Beatriz Rodriguez in silence. It is a concise statement of the material that will be developed, a ball of string that will be unwound. We see semaphore arms, snake hips, pirouettes stopped in mid-whirl, a paroxysm of flexions in *relevé*. Rodriguez, who looked childlike in *Deuce Coupe*, is transformed again. She is monumental, like a Nijinska iron woman. Three boys and two girls join her (Adix Carman, Henry Berg, William Whitener, Eileen Brady, and Pamela Nearhoof) and the music begins—the Minuet and Trio of Haydn's '*Farewell*' *Symphony*. The dance that accompanies it is not one dance but six—one for each member of the sextet. All six dances go on at the same time, now linking up, now separating, and the whole moving from one tight cellular cluster to another. This sextet, which builds up the fascination and the deadpan humor of a clockwork toy, is a classical arrangement of the Tharpian group dance and typically democratic. The multifocal viewpoint makes a special event of the partnering (which keeps changing hands). It also eliminates the conventional hierarchy of the ballet ensemble. No one here is a ballerina; anyone may partner or be partnered. The sextet builds up pressure, too. The little hexagonal unit seems to become more and more confining, but the sweet musicianship of the choreography keeps the scene clear, its density unharrowing.

"The music breaks off, and one of the girls does a little walk-around in silence as new dancers enter. The Presto movement of the symphony starts. Suddenly, the stage seems to expand to unbelievable size. Dancers pour on and spread out. The broadened pattern has released us, but the tempo has stepped up the pressure, and we redouble our concentration. Now, against a complex background of moving dancers, solo variations occur; one, for Nearhoof, is galvanically funny, though at this breathless speed the laughs can't keep up with the jokes. Nor can we keep up with the ballet. There is no time to ponder the new logic of the steps—new in the way they combine close musical fit with a 'natural' loose look suited to each individual dancer; there's just time enough to enjoy it. One would like the key to that new logic; what makes it work at this tempo? Whatever it is, the result is a hyperkinesthesia that takes hold of the audience and doesn't let up until, once more, Haydn waves his wand and the dancers stroll nonchalantly away.

"The end of the piece is as Haydn would have wished it. To the Adagio finale of the 'Farewell'—so called because the instrumentation thins out until only two violins are left—a dancer (Larry Grenier, whose attenuated lyrical style is itself a statement of slackening force) moves alone while others set about disappearing in a fashion that is unpredictable and sometimes chancy. A girl leaves, only to return a moment later. A boy lifts a girl off, turning her twice in the air, so another girl has to duck three times to avoid being hit. Ultimately, Grenier is *all* alone, having spun out the last thin skein of movement.

"*As Time Goes By* is not a pretentious enough ballet to make people feel that they have witnessed a heroic new undertaking in choreography. Its fifteen minutes are loaded with interest, but, like all of Twyla Tharp's work, the piece is peculiarly horizonless. Although each work she has made is self-contained and perfectly lucid in its own terms, each seems almost accidentally bound by the rise and fall of a curtain, and to be part of a larger continuity that exists out of time—out of the time, that is, of this ballet we have just seen. Somewhere, perhaps, there are unseen dancers unrolling the patterns and following up every implication, but we in the audience are spared their tortuous zeal. Twyla Tharp makes us feel that a ballet is nothing more than divisions of a choreographer's time. Although she understands cheap sensation and uses it well, there is no gloss, no appeal for attention, no careerism in her work. It's amusing to think of what a promoter like Diaghilev would have done with her. First, I think, he would retitle the sections of this ballet *Ariadne, Athens, The Labyrinth,* and *Theseus*. Cocteau would write the program notes and design the costumes. (The ones we have, by the Seventh Avenue designer Chester Weinberg, are examples of modest chic in shades of taupe.) Diaghilev would call the whole piece *The Minotaur*, because there's no Minotaur in it, and he would proclaim 'La Tharp' the herald of a new age. Which she is."*

AT MIDNIGHT

Music by Gustav Mahler. Choreography by Eliot Feld. Décor by Leonard Baskin. Costumes by Stanley Simmons. Lighting and scenic supervision by Jean Rosenthal. First presented by American Ballet Theatre at the New York State Theatre, Lincoln Center, December 1, 1967, with Bruce Marks, Christine Sarry, Terry Orr, Cynthia Gregory, and Eliot Feld in the principal roles. Sung by William Metcalf. Conducted by Kenneth Schermerhorn.

* "A Moment in Time," by Arlene Croce. Reprinted by permission; © 1973 The New Yorker Magazine, Inc.

Danced to four of the "Five Rückert Songs" of Mahler, lyrics arranged by the composer to poems by Friedrich Rückert, *At Midnight* is named for the first of those songs. But the ballet is not based on what the songs say. They are rather an accompaniment to a danced narrative that reflects the motto of the ballet, a quotation from Thomas Hardy: "In the ill-judged execution of the well-judged plan of things, the call seldom produced the comer, the man to love rarely coincides with the hour for loving. Nature does not often say 'See!' to her poor creature when seeing can lead to a happy doing or answer 'Here!' to a body's cry of 'Where?' till the hide-and-seek has become an irksome, outworn game."

The curtain rises on a dark stage. Illumined in the back is a painting of a face in torment surrounded by two ravens. We make out on stage toward the left a crouching group of men. A half-naked boy climbs onto their bent backs, lying there for support in an hour of need in the middle of the night. He stretches out and rolls off onto the floor as the baritone begins the song "At Midnight." The men cluster around the boy, covering his face with their hands. He is lifted high and then let down to dance alone. At the end, he leaps back into the arms of the men, where he first curls up, then stretches, his arms reaching out in an agony that has not gone away.

The backdrop changes to a painting of a figure crouching in despair. To the song "Ich atmet' einen Lindenduft" (I breathed a fragrance soft and sweet), a boy and girl, she in flowing yellow, he in gray, move in an intense yet lyric dance. Two extraordinary catches at the end of this buoyant *pas de deux* yield to a high lift, and the boy carries the girl away as she rides on his shoulder.

A boy, lost and never a part of a group of other boys and girls who dance happily and unaware about him, laments his loneliness and tries to imitate them. The music is the song "Ich bin der Welt abhanded gekommen."

The second song is now repeated. To its music, a girl joins the couple of the second song. There is no real communication between them, however, as she dances along and the couple, preoccupied, stands and sits together. They remain after the girl leaves and seem to waken from their reverie. Four other couples join them now, as do the lone girl of the last song and the boy of the third. Here, too, each of the single figures is so engrossed in trouble and separation that they have no eyes for each other. Amidst all these persons there is no new personal contact. They remain on stage as the song ends, alone as we first saw them.

NOTES   Anna Kisselgoff of the New York *Times* has called *At Midnight* a "landmark ballet, poetic in its depth but accessible to everyone on its theatric level." Reviewing the ballet in the *Dancing Times*, the critic P. W. Manchester wrote that Eliot Feld's "first ballet, *Harbinger*, premièred in the 1967 spring season, indicated that a new talent had arrived. *At Midnight* more than confirmed the promise of *Harbinger*. Feld has set it to four of Gustav Mahler's songs. The first one provides the title for the ballet and is also the finest part of the work. It is a study in man's aloneness. The choreography, marvelously interpreted by Bruce Marks, aches with the doubts and loneliness of the fears that come only in sleeplessness. The second song . . . is a *pas de deux* for young lovers, done with exquisite, unsentimental sweetness by Christine Sarry and Terry Orr. . . . *At Midnight* is both moving and masterly. And . . . Feld is entering on his career as a choreographer while he is also just beginning his best years as a dancer. . . . His closeness to his company as colleague as well as choreographer may well be a major factor in what everyone is hoping will truly be a new era for American Ballet Theatre, one in which it will at long last have its own choreographer, creating for its particular talents, moulding its special and unique style."

Writing of the première in the *Jersey Journal,* the critic Patrick O'Connor said: "It is a unique privilege to be present at the first presentation of a great American work of art. But that's what happened to me last night at the American Ballet Theatre. In truth, there's no such thing as an American work of art. There are only works of art sometimes, too rarely, I'm afraid, composed, put together, by an American. Last night it was *At Midnight* by Eliot Feld. I won't say choreographed. It seemed much more than a dance composition. Feld is involved in what Doris Humphrey once called the art of making dances.

"Movement is, of course, the essential element but so is the painter's brush, the dynamics of stillness, the sacrifice of the mass, the crucifixion, the resurrection, the healing power of love. The whole piece was bathed in love and so was the audience; they knew it, felt it and were grateful.

"It seems almost profane to talk about the dancing. It wasn't dancing; it was another kind of activity—exalted movement. Cynthia Gregory in pentecostal lavender made one weep, and Christine Sarry in pentecostal yellow sustains stillness miraculously. She also danced brilliantly. Bruce Marks—as the Christ figure?—gave a shattering performance. Feld the dancer served Feld the choreographer like a ministering angel. A rare privilege, an historic occasion, something to tell my grandchildren."

Reviewing a 1975 performance by the Eliot Feld Ballet with Lawrence Rhodes, the English critic John Percival wrote in *Dance and Dancers:* "Rhodes, perhaps the greatest of American male dancers today, for some reason has never settled down with one of the major companies, and nowadays combines membership in Feld's company and the Pennsylvania Ballet. He has a slight, supple physique and the ability to make every movement eloquent. *The Consort* shows him to be capable of a show-off solo, but a role like the central figure of *At Midnight* suits him even better . . . He gives it great bitterness."

AUREOLE

Music by George Frederick Handel. Choreography by Paul Taylor. Lighting by Thomas Skelton. First presented by the Paul Taylor Dance Company at Connecticut College, New London, Connecticut, August 4, 1962.

A dance work that has happily entered the repertory of the Royal Danish Ballet and been seen in presentations by Paul Taylor's ensemble with Rudolf Nureyev, *Aureole* has proved itself a most distinguished work in the contemporary repertoire. Paul Taylor, regarded by Clive Barnes as "one of the most talented and innovative choreographers this country has ever produced," has danced it with his own company at home and abroad. It was my pleasure some years ago to work with Paul Taylor in the New York City Ballet's *Episodes*.

Aureole is a dance for five—two boys and three girls. Its content is a most original response to Handel's lyric and expressive score (the *Concerto Grosso in G* and the fourth movement of *Alexander's Feast*).

BACH SONATA

Music by Johann Sebastian Bach. Choreography by Maurice Béjart. First presented by the Ballet of the Twentieth Century, 1970, with Suzanne Farrell and Jorge Donn. First presented in the United States by the same ensemble at the Brooklyn Academy of Music, New York, January 29, 1971, with the same principals.

A *pas de deux* set to Bach's *Sonata No. 5 for Violin and Harpsichord,* and designed to show the artistry of the two principals, *Bach Sonata* is not the usual display piece for the ballerina and her partner. Instead, it poses the problem of how an infatuated boy can encircle and win a girl who appears to be indifferent to everything he does.

LE BAISER DE LA FÉE (The Fairy's Kiss)

Ballet-allegory in four scenes. Music and book by Igor Stravinsky. Choreography by George Balanchine. Scenery and costumes by Alicia Halicka. First presented by the American Ballet at the Metropolitan Opera House, New York, April 27, 1937, with Gisella Caccialanza as the Bride, William Dollar as the Bridegroom, and Kathryn Mullowney as the Fairy.

Stravinsky dedicated this ballet "to the memory of Peter Tchaikovsky . . . It was his Muse (like our Fairy heroine) whose fatal kiss, imprinted at birth, made itself felt in all the work of that great artist, and eventually led him to immortality. Thereby does our ballet (with a similar tale) become an allegory." The story of the ballet is derived from a tale by Hans Christian Andersen—"The Ice Maiden." Stravinsky selected elements from this long and beautiful fairy tale to compose his scenario. Here, the Ice Maiden comes down from the sky to claim for her own a hapless youth. When he is a child, abandoned in the snow, the fairy kisses the boy coldly with a fatal kiss that seals his eternal devotion to her. The babe becomes a man and, with no recollection of the fairy's power over him, is engaged to be married. The Ice Maiden returns to fulfill the prophecy of her kiss and to carry him away to the ends of the earth.

FIRST TABLEAU: PROLOGUE—THE SNOWSTORM   The curtain rises soon after the orchestra has begun to play softly a lilting lullaby. The scene is deserted, barely lit. Snow begins to fall. A woman enters, carrying a child. She dances across the stage, her hood flowing behind her. She lifts the child in her arms lovingly and covers it with her cape. At first she does not appear to be alarmed at the snow, but the lullaby to which she dances changes to an ominous melody presaging a severe storm and the woman is frightened for her child. She covers it more carefully, holds it close to her breast, and continues on her way. Winds leap across the stage from right and left, passing close to her, then circling about her as if to enclose her with their freezing force. She cowers in terror. Myriad snowflakes enter behind her, hover over her, and leave her shivering on the ground. The piercing winds return, their frigid capes streaming from their shoulders; the snowflakes re-enter and surround the mother. She rises helplessly and attempts to flee, but the snowflakes divide into groups and block her escape. The music increases its ominous force. The snowflakes force her to the front and drown her with freezing snow. As the mother cowers beneath them, she thinks only of her child. She dies. The winds remove her body, and the child is abandoned to the snowflakes, who pass over the pathetic bundle as they vanish.

The winds pull in a swift white sleigh that brings onto the scene a beautiful fairy, the Ice Maiden. A spotlight catches her imposing figure. She stands in statuesque pose, holding high a wand of ice; her noble head is crowned with a star of white jewels; her dress is white, long, and full. She steps down from the sleigh, presents her wand to her escorts, and directs them away. Immediately she begins to dance. Each one of her open, flowing movements is imitated by a figure in black, who stands in the distance like a shadow to remind us that the beauty of the fairy is bewitching. The fairy dances close to the child. She stands over him; her flowing white dress seems to cover him as she turns brilliantly on point. She bends over the child, reaches out, draws him close to her face. She kisses him tenderly, yet coldly, and places the child on the ground. Now that she has sealed the fate of the helpless child, the fairy dances away slowly on point. Her shadow disappears with her.

The scene darkens. A peasant enters, carrying a lantern. He is followed by a group of mountain climbers, who help him as he seeks to recover the lost child. The music imitates their anxieties. At last one of the men sees the small bundle in the snow. The light is brought nearer, and the other men hold him as he reaches down and picks up the child while the orchestra sounds climactic chords of pathos. The scene blacks out as they hurry off.

SECOND TABLEAU: THE VILLAGE FESTIVAL   Twenty years have passed. Befriended by peasants, the child has grown up to become the most popular young man in the village. He is to be married soon to the miller's daughter.

After a brief orchestral interlude, the lights come up on a colorful mountain scene overhung with fir trees; snow-capped peaks are seen in the distance. Boys and girls of the village dressed in gay Swiss costumes stand in a wide circle dancing a folk measure to a rhythmic, holiday tune. A group of boys then move to the center, where they are surrounded by the smiling girls. They all gather behind the village bandsmen and parade around the stage.

A high-spirited boy carrying a gun runs into the crowd. This is the bridegroom. Everyone welcomes him, particularly the girls, and it is clear that he has the affections of them all. He dances forward with two of the girls to the light rhythm of the music, which soon becomes strong and robust. Everyone joins them in their youthful dance. When the dance is over, the young man calls one of his friends and directs him to shoot at a distant target. The boy aims and misses. Another boy tries and misses. The bridegroom seizes his gun, shoots, and hits the target, to the delight of the girls, who playfully congratulate him.

The bride enters, surrounded by six of her bridesmaids. She dances briefly before the company, and then the boy joins her for a happy duet that reflects their mutual joy. Several of the village girls start a yodeling contest, which is interrupted for a final festival dance by the bride, the bridegroom, and all their friends. The peasants encircle the bride and bridegroom and begin to leave the stage. The bride goes off with her friends. The boy seems to depart with the rest, but as the stage empties, we see that he has remained. He sits on the ground in quiet meditation. One of his friends tries to persuade him to continue with the celebration, but the boy refuses. He is alone.

On the right a beautiful gypsy enters. She is dressed in black and white. The boy does not notice her as he looks at the ground thoughtfully. The gypsy crosses the stage in a determined stride, her arms gripped at her sides. The jewel she wears on her forehead catches the light for an instant; her face is a frigid mask. It is the face of the Ice Maiden, who has disguised herself to discover the boy. She approaches him, circles him several times, as if to be sure of his identity, then sits down close beside him and looks up straight into his

face. The orchestra sounds a sharp chord; she grips his wrist fiercely and examines his open palm to foretell the fate she herself has planned for him.

The boy is completely passive to the strange gypsy fortuneteller. His body
falls back as she circles his hand before her savagely. She rises, throws his
hand away from her in a gesture of triumphant recognition, and dances before
him. The boy watches as she steps with fascinating, malevolent vigor, flinging
her loose black hair over her face. He responds to her exotic dynamism and
comes to her. He holds the gypsy obediently while she walks forward as if she
were driving her points into the ground. Now they cross the stage to the right,
the gypsy whirling rapidly, the boy following and falling at her feet as she extends her leg to lash the air above him. He rises to embrace her, but she
shoves him away contemptuously, then seizes him violently and passionately.
The boy is obedient to her every gesture as he realizes her power to fulfill his
fortune. She turns him around, stands in back of him, points her arm forward
over his shoulder, and pushes him in its direction. The boy does not resist; he
walks in a dream as the gypsy directs him toward his destiny. Blackout.

THIRD TABLEAU: INSIDE THE MILL A group of peasant girls are arranged in
an open triangular tableau as the lights illuminate the interior of the bride's
home. The rough wood walls are decorated with wreaths; candles hang low
from the ceiling; there are two large windows at the back. The scene is framed
with old Swiss lace. The day of the wedding is approaching, and all of the
bride's friends have gathered to prepare for the occasion. The peasant girls
dance gaily to a blithe melody, led by a girl in a bright yellow skirt, whose energy and enthusiasm are expressed in precise, rapid steps.

The bride enters and dances in front of the group. Dressed all in white, she
wears a small wreath of white flowers in her hair. The girls in back of her imitate her movements. The bride walks back to welcome her friends; some of
them form a circle around her. She bows, then bows to another group that surrounds her. She blows kisses to them all and exits.

The peasant girls dance again; the bride returns just before the music ends
and she stands in the center of a beautifully posed group her friends form
about her. The girls run off and leave the bride alone. The orchestra begins to
play quietly a lovely, sweeping melody. The bride circles the room, goes to the
window, looks out expectantly, but sees nothing. She is waiting for the bridegroom. She walks over to the other window, her back turned to the room. The
bridegroom enters. The bride does not see him. He circles the room looking for
her. She moves away from the window as if she felt his presence, but does not
find him, for the boy has walked behind her. Both stand in the center of the
room, their arms held out, seeking. Their backs almost touch and they move
away in opposite directions to circle the room again. The boy kneels. The girl
sees him, runs up behind him softly, and leans over his shoulder to welcome
him playfully. He rises. Their *pas de deux* begins.

The couple cross the front of the stage together, extending their arms to the side in rhythm to the flow of the music. The bride falls back in the boy's arms. The music changes, as a clarinet states the theme of their adagio. The boy holds the girl about the waist as she dances quickly but softly, like a sylph. He lifts her as they move together, and her points continue their dance in the air. The bride kneels and watches the boy dance. Then both circle the stage. The girl beckons to him and whispers something. They stand together in the center of the stage. They bow low to each other. The boy holds out his hand and, as the orchestra states the climax of the theme, the girl takes his hand and poses in a low, deep arabesque. She rises and falls back against his arm. He raises her off the floor with low lifts in which the girl bends her knees softly. He holds her under her arms, and the girl sits on his knee, smiling happily, her legs extended before her.

The bridegroom stands aside and watches the girl dance alone to a fresh, piquant theme. She dances flirtatiously, flouncing her skirt high. She mimes her intense happiness, feigning intoxication from her joy. The black shadow of the Ice Maiden suddenly appears before her and points menacingly. The boy does not see the apparition, who disappears before the girl has rushed backward into his arms. The bride looks toward the vanished shadow and moves her hand in front of her face in innocent, unbelieving astonishment.

A pounding drum announces a sharp, accelerating dance melody. The peasant girls re-enter to take up its rhythm, and the bride and bridegroom leave the stage. The bridegroom returns to dance a short, brilliant variation. He is followed by the bride, who comes down the stage diagonally, dancing smartly on one point, extending her other leg straight out to the side with every step. She finishes her dance with a series of rapid turns that delight the whole company, then runs across the stage at full speed toward the bridegroom, who catches her daringly in midair.

The couple leave the stage to the dancing peasants for a moment, then return to join them in a final ensemble. At its conclusion one of the girls brings out the bride's veil and throws it playfully over her head. The girls gather about the bride and separate the two lovers. The bride leaves the stage with her playful friends. The bridegroom remains alone. The light dims.

The bridegroom turns rapidly; as he comes out of his spin, he sees on the right a girl dressed in white, her head and shoulders covered with a long white veil. As he recognizes his fiancée, he seems also to be remembering slowly and with effort that he must have known her like this always—tall, beautiful, and in white. He moves toward her, fascinated by his illusory recollection and the new loveliness she has for him. The girl does not move; she remains motionless, drawing the boy toward her with mysterious and bewitching magnetism. He stands in front of her, reaches around her strongly, and holds her tightly by the waist, his face buried in the frigid whiteness of her veil. Thus holding her, he lifts her feet off the floor; her body arches back, and he carries her walking slowly backward. Now the orchestra states fully but quietly the melody of

Tchaikovsky's "None But the Lonely Heart," which was suggested softly at the beginning of the scene.

The boy lets the girl down gently and falls helpless against her. His limp body falls to the floor at her feet. The girl bows over him, opens her arms wide, takes his hand, and pulls him up as she circles about him. They move a short distance together; then the boy kneels. He stretches his arms back; the girl takes his hands. He crawls forward. The girl stands against his back, her body in arabesque, her face falling over against his. Her white veil envelops his face in a glacier of tenderness. The tragic melody, now at its height, accompanies them as they move across the stage.

The boy falls forward on the ground. The girl bends down and covers him with her veil. He rises under it, throws the veil back over her head, and stands transfixed as he beholds her face—the face of the Ice Maiden and gypsy in one. The Ice Maiden stands regally as we saw her in the first scene, her lovely, noble head crowned with a star of shimmering crystals. The boy backs away from her in terror at his recognition, then draws close to her again in helpless, passionate longing. He rests his head on her breast. The Ice Maiden stands rigid, head back, her arms stretched out behind her. Slowly she lifts her arms and touches the boy's head with a retarded and considered gesture that seems to freeze the gentleness of her touch and turn him to ice. Now she moves her hand down the boy's trembling arm, takes his hand, and leads him away. The scene blacks out.

FOURTH TABLEAU: EPILOGUE   The lights come up on the same scene. The bride enters the room, searching for her fiancé. She circles the stage, looks out of the windows from which she has so often seen him come to the mill. He is nowhere to be found. She waves her veil over her head sadly and begins to despair. Then suddenly, in the back, the wall of the room disappears and the bride beholds in the sky a scene that makes her tremble. High up, far away in the distance, the Ice Maiden sits in the cold blue winter sky holding out her arms to the bridegroom, who strives to reach her. He stretches out his arms to the magical fairy, who seems to enfold him. They rise together in the sky. The bride kneels and, weeping, waves her wedding veil in farewell.

NOTES   At the end of 1927, when he was finishing the music of *Apollo*, Igor Stravinsky was asked by Madame Ida Rubinstein to compose a ballet for her. Bronislava Nijinska was to be the choreographer, Alexandre Benois the designer. Stravinsky writes, in his autobiography: "The idea was that I should compose something inspired by the music of Tchaikovsky. My well-known fondness for this composer, and, still more, the fact that November, 1928, the time fixed for the performance, would mark the thirty-fifth anniversary of his death, induced me to accept the offer. It would give me an opportunity of paying my heartfelt homage to Tchaikovsky's wonderful talent.

"As I was free to choose both the subject and scenario of the ballet, I began to search for them, in view of the characteristic trend of Tchaikovsky's music, in the literature of the nineteenth century. With that aim, I turned to a great poet with a gentle, sensitive soul whose imaginative mind was wonderfully akin to that of the musician. I refer to Hans Christian Andersen, with whom in this respect Tchaikovsky had so much in common. To recall *The Sleeping Beauty, The Nutcracker, Swan Lake, Pique Dame,* and many pieces of his symphonic work is enough to show the extent of his fondness for the fantastic.

"In turning over the pages of Andersen, with which I was fairly familiar, I came across a story which I had completely forgotten that struck me as being the very thing for the idea which I wanted to express. It was the very beautiful story known to us as the 'Ice Maiden.' I chose that as my theme and worked out the story on the following lines. A fairy imprints her magic kiss on a child at birth and parts it from its mother. Twenty years later, when the youth has attained the very zenith of his good fortune, she repeats the fatal kiss and carries him off to live in supreme happiness with her ever afterwards. As my object was to commemorate the work of Tchaikovsky, this subject seemed to me to be particularly appropriate as an allegory, the Muse having similarly branded Tchaikovsky with her fatal kiss, and the magic imprint has made itself felt in all the musical creations of this great artist.

"Although I gave full liberty to painter and choreographer in the staging of my composition, my innermost desire was that it should be presented in classical form, after the manner of *Apollo.* I pictured all the fantastic roles as danced in white ballet-skirts, and the rustic scenes as taking place in a Swiss landscape . . ."

The ballet was performed for the first time November 27, 1928, at the Opéra, Paris, with the composer conducting. It was performed in other European capitals and, in 1933, at the Colón Theatre in Buenos Aires. November 26, 1935, Frederick Ashton choreographed a new version of the ballet for the Sadler's Wells Ballet. This version, designed by Sophie Fedorovitch, featured Pearl Argyle, Harold Turner, and Margot Fonteyn—her first created role. Frederick Ashton, interestingly enough, had danced in the original Nijinska production. I staged the ballet in 1937 for the American Ballet's Stravinsky Festival in New York.

Certain parts of the story of the ballet are hard to make clear on the stage. At the beginning of the Second Tableau, for example, how is the audience to know that the bridegroom is the child of the Prologue? Believing that everything must be clear on the stage, I have tried to indicate this in a number of ways in different revivals of the ballet, as I have also endeavored to make it obvious that the gypsy is, in reality, the fairy disguised. The finale of the ballet also presents a mechanical difficulty. Ideally, the ending should have a magical effect: the fairy should appear to be suspended and the bridegroom, just below her, must seem to be swimming through space, as it were, to reach her. The Ice Maiden drags the boy down into the lake with her, and in recent revivals I have tried to indicate that the two figures are moving together in the water, but limited audience visibility of the back of the stage has prevented this plan from attaining real success. There is no question but that the final Tableau requires a stage high and deep for the achievement of full illusion.

The Fairy's Kiss has been revived twice by the Ballet Russe de Monte Carlo: on April 10, 1940, at the Metropolitan Opera House, with a cast headed by Alexandra Danilova as the bride, André Eglevsky as the bridegroom, and Mia Slavenska as the fairy; and on February 17, 1946, at the City Center, New York, with Alexandra Danilova, Frederic Franklin, and Maria Tallchief. It was staged for the Opéra, Paris, July 2, 1947, when Tamara Toumanova, Alexandre Kaliujny, and Maria Tallchief took the principal roles. At its revival by the New York City Ballet November 28, 1950, the leading roles were danced by Tanaquil LeClercq, Nicholas Magallanes, and Maria Tallchief.

Although his version of the ballet is unfortunately unknown in the United States, Sir Frederick Ashton choreographed *Le Baiser de la Fée* for the Sadler's Wells Ballet at the Sadler's Wells Theatre, London, November 26, 1935. The production was designed by Sophie Fedorovitch and the leading dancers were Pearl Argyle, Margot Fonteyn, and Harold Turner. An excerpt from this ballet, a *pas de deux*, was performed at the Royal Opera House, Covent Garden, in July 1970, at the Gala Performance in Ashton's honor.

The Royal Ballet revived *Le Baiser de la Fée* in a new version by Kenneth MacMillan at the Royal Opera House, Covent Garden, April 12, 1960, with Svetlana Beriosova, Donald MacLeary, and Lynn Seymour in the principal roles. This production, designed by Kenneth Rowell, was introduced to the United States by the Royal Ballet at the Metropolitan Opera House, New York, September 27, 1960, with the same principals.

In 1972, for the New York City Ballet's Stravinsky Festival, our celebration of the composer's ninetieth birthday, I arranged new dances for music from this ballet under the title *Divertimento from Le Baiser de la Fée*. This was based on Stravinsky's symphonic suite from the ballet, which uses just under half the score and which he called *Divertimento*. The dances were new ones, though some remembered gestures and movements were retained as I wished. The piece was presented without a setting and without a story line, as a dance ballet, for the first time on June 21, 1972, at the New York State Theatre, with lighting by Ronald Bates. Robert Irving was the conductor and the leading roles were danced by Patricia McBride, Helgi Tomasson, Bettijane Sills and Carol Sumner.

Writing about the staging of the *Divertimento* for the Stravinsky Festival in *The Nation*, Nancy Goldner said: "One of my favorite moments was a sequence of jumps for Helgi Tomasson in the *Divertimento from Le Baiser de la Fée*. All the sequence amounted to was a variation on something very commonplace: a preparatory sliding step with a little spring in it, called a *glissade*, followed by a moving jump in which one leg is thrown forward and the other backward. Usually, after the *glissade* the weight is on the front foot. This gives the dancer the momentum to jump off the floor on the front foot, with the back one swinging forward and up into the jump. His back is straight and he faces the line of direction. But that is not what Balanchine had Tomasson do. Instead of springing naturally off the front foot, he jumps off the back foot. Instead of facing the line of direction, his whole body is almost at right angles to it. He does these jumps in a circle, leading with the 'wrong' foot and at the 'wrong' angle. The effect is that of a car skidding around a corner on its outside wheels. Tomasson was so skimming and elegant in this unnatural deployment of momentum and balance that he seemed like those flying saucers that reportedly can veer at a right angle without slowing down."

The critic Anna Kisselgoff, reviewing a performance in the New York *Times* in 1974, said: "In Helgi Tomasson, the New York City Ballet has one of the best classical male dancers in the world today. No wonder then that George Balanchine chose him as the dancer upon whom to create one of the most unusual and poetic male solos in the Balanchine repertory.

"Saturday night at the New York State Theater, Mr. Tomasson's special combination of elegance and virtuosity was evident again in that solo, in the short ballet entitled *Divertimento from 'Le Baiser de la Fée,'* choreographed by Mr. Balanchine for the 1972 Stravinsky Festival . . . Perhaps it might be wiser to forget the now-discarded story line for the first Balanchine version of *The Fairy's Kiss* (the ballet's English title), and to view the current divertissement as a plotless pure-dance excerpt. Yet the fact that Stravinsky's original scenario had a hero and not a heroine as the protagonist might help explain why the choreography for the male dancer tends to overshadow the ballerina's.

"In this bright, joyful and tender *pas de deux,* backed by an ensemble, Mr. Balanchine has reserved the most inventive sequences for Mr. Tomasson. The man's variation, with its unexpected changes of direction, suggestions of swoons and a series of jumps followed by falls to the knee, appears totally original. In the coda, the extraordinary way Mr. Tomasson seems to be off balance when he is not is a tribute to both the imagination of the choreographer and the rock-firm technique of the dancer. At the same time, Mr. Tomasson is one of dance's most finished classic stylists."

Music by Igor Stravinsky and Peter Ilyich Tchaikovsky. Choreography and book by John Neumeier. Costumes and sets by Jürgen Rose. Lighting by Jennifer Tipton. First presented by the Frankfurt Ballet in 1974. First presented in the United States by American Ballet Theatre at the New York State Theatre, Lincoln Center, in 1975.

The choreographer John Neumeier has devised a new libretto, with a flashback technique, for his ballet on this theme. In addition to Stravinsky's score he uses two short works of Tchaikovsky in his score: the "Feuillet d'Album," Op. 19,

No. 3, and "None But the Lonely Heart," Op. 6, No. 6—a principal element, of course, in Stravinsky's.

The action of the ballet follows this libretto:

PROLOGUE: THE WEDDING CELEBRATION   The marriage of Rudi and Babette is being celebrated at a party with their friends. Among the guests is a stranger who sings a lovely, melancholy song, at the end of which she gives Rudi a kiss. Her song, and the kiss, awaken in him the memory of an old desire, as intangible but as haunting as perfume. With the memory, Rudi feels an inexpressible yearning, disturbing the happiness he hopes to find with Babette.

SCENE ONE: REMEMBRANCE (BALLET BLANC)   Rudi's *Sehnsucht* (his subconscious yearning self) takes him back to his childhood and the memory of an experience. In a clear, white world, Rudi, as the child he once was, is entranced by the vision of beautiful dancing creatures. One of these, the most dazzling of all, gives the boy a kiss, then disappears among the others. Rudi searches in vain for her, in an agony of love and longing that will haunt his life.

SCENE TWO: THE WEDDING CELEBRATION CONTINUES   Rudi realizes that the mysterious singer is the same beautiful creature from the pure, white world of his childhood for whom he has searched his entire life. Rudi's longing once more takes him in search of her.

SCENE THREE: IN THE GARDEN   Stealing away from the party, Babette finds Rudi in the garden, where she again expresses her love for him. They are interrupted by the departing guests, making their adieux. Together again, Rudi turns to Babette, feeling in her presence the strength of a love great enough to overcome his yearning for the unattainable. Reassured, Babette re-enters the house to prepare herself for their wedding night.

SCENE FOUR: TOWARD ETERNITY   Alone in the garden, Rudi's *Sehnsucht* grows stronger and stronger, overpowering Rudi's will . . . It compels him to obey the unearthly summons of the Fairy. Rudi goes in quest of his glorious tormentress, leaving Babette to wait in vain for his return.

BALLADE

Dramatic ballet in one act. Music by Claude Debussy. Choreography by Jerome Robbins. Scenery and costumes by Boris Aronson. Costumes executed by Karinska. Lighting by Jean Rosenthal. First presented by the New York City Ballet at the City Center, New York, February 14, 1952, with

Tanaquil LeClercq, Janet Reed, Nora Kaye, Roy Tobias, Robert Barnett, Louis Johnson, John Mandia, and Brooks Jackson.

This ballet's program note reminds us that a *ballade* (or *ballad*) is "a musical composition of poetic character . . . a dancing song, a poem of unknown authorship which recounts a legendary or traditional event and passes from one generation to another." The legendary or traditional event in the ballet is enacted by the legendary and traditional characters Harlequin, Columbine, and Pierrot, who find themselves in a band of other, more modern, theatrical characters. The music for *Ballade* is Debussy's flute solo *Syrinx* and the same composer's *Six Antique Epigraphs,* orchestrated by Ernest Ansermet.

Snow is falling on a quiet scene as the curtain rises. Seven people lie asleep in chairs that are grouped about the stage. In the back is a drop curtain that depicts the sun and moon surrounded by clouds of ice. The people take no notice of the snow; their bodies lie limply in the chairs, and they seem like so many rag dolls.

To the quiet music of a flute, a strolling musician enters, carrying balloons. The snow stops falling. Slowly he goes to each of the chairs and at each one he leaves a balloon. When he has distributed balloons to all seven, he watches as the hands that hold them are drawn mysteriously upward. Gradually all the figures waken and rise toward their balloons. They bow to the strolling player and look up at the balloons he has left them as he leaves the scene.

One of the girls steps out. She is dressed in Harlequin's traditional costume of varicolored diamond patches. Slowly she turns; the others move the chairs back and run about the stage with their balloons. Now they tie the balloons to the chairs and come forward to dance in a semicircle.

The rest of the group retire as three boys dance forward rapidly and, like clowns and tumbling artists, execute a rushing, circusy number. When they finish, the girl dressed as Harlequin comes forward. She reaches down, takes her foot in her hand, brings it around behind her back, and turns. Now she somersaults and her movements take on an angular quality. As the music becomes faster, she leaps wildly, circles the stage, revolves in bouncing turns, and goes back to her chair.

A girl in pink, her cheeks spotted with circles of bright red rouge, begins to dance. This is Columbine. A boy, also dressed in pink, kisses her hand. He kneels before her as she begins to dance to quick, subtle music. The girl is indifferent to the boy and wanders almost accidentally into his arms. He tries to get some reaction as he declares his love, but the girl, like a rag doll, looks at him stupidly. Finally he embraces her and kisses her throat. The girl reaches into her dress to find her heart and brings out a handful of sawdust. The astonished youth retires, and the girl sits on the floor at the left.

Now a girl representing Pierrot takes the center of the stage briefly. The melody sounds hauntingly. Pierrot collapses and dies. Two boys take up her

loose, disjointed body and carry her. The others grieve. Pierrot is given a
balloon and slowly she rises. She wonders at the balloon's magical force in
bringing her to life again. The strange figures watch breathlessly as she ponders this mystery and makes a decision. The music stops. Pierrot stares up at
the balloon, then deliberately allows it to slip through her fingers. In stunned
silence her fellow actors imagine that she has sacrificed her life. Everyone
watches as the balloon disappears overhead.

Forgetful of Pierrot's sacrifice, the whole troupe dances a happy ensemble.
Suddenly the lights begin to go down. The strolling musician returns, and the
players return to their chairs. As he takes their balloons away, each collapses
and becomes lifeless again. The strolling musician stares at Pierrot, who stands
alone without a balloon. Slowly he leaves the scene. Pierrot looks after him for
a moment, then goes to each of the chairs, trying to waken their occupants.
She cannot stir them. Snow begins to fall again, and the curtain descends as
Pierrot, sad that she alone possesses a life outside the magic of the theatre,
stares off into the distance.

BALLET IMPERIAL (TCHAIKOVSKY CONCERTO NO. 2)

*Classic ballet in three movements. Music by Peter Ilyich Tchaikovsky. Chor-
eography by George Balanchine. Setting and costumes by Mstislav Doboujinsky. First presented by the American Ballet at the Hunter College Playhouse, New York, May 27, 1941, with Marie-Jeanne, Gisella Caccialanza,
and William Dollar in the principal roles. Revived by the Ballet Russe de
Monte Carlo at the City Center, New York, February 20, 1945, with Mary
Ellen Moylan, Maria Tallchief, and Nicholas Magallanes in the leading roles.
Revived by the Sadler's Wells Ballet at the Royal Opera House, London,
April 5, 1950, with scenery and costumes by Eugene Berman and a cast
headed by Margot Fonteyn, Michael Somes, and Beryl Grey. Revived by
the Ballet of La Scala, Milan, with scenery and costumes by Eugene Berman, March 25, 1952, with Olga Amati, Gilda Maiocchi, and Giulio Peru-
gini in the principal roles.*

Great ballets of the past are directly associated with great composers of the
past. *The Sleeping Beauty,* the masterwork of the great nineteenth-century
choreographer Marius Petipa, survives not only for its dancing, but also for its
music. Petipa created more than sixty full-length ballets during a half century
of work as ballet master at the Imperial Russian Theatre. Few of these works
are performed today. This is not because the dancing in these ballets was not
good; it is because their music was not good enough to inspire the dancing to
new heights. Audiences have wished to forget the bad music and, consequently, the dances that went with it.

Since the death of Petipa, in 1910, much has happened to the classical dancing he developed into so high a form in his famous ballets. The basic vocabulary is the same, but we have added new words, new phrases; classical dancing today is much more difficult, more complex, more intricate, more demanding. Oftentimes people are inclined to think that the great dancers of the past were incomparable and that dancers today are as nothing beside them. This is not true. The great dancers of the past were incomparable for what they did. Today we do something else.

Ballet Imperial is a contemporary tribute to Petipa, "the father of the classic ballet," and to Tchaikovsky, his greatest composer. The ballet is set to Tchaikovsky's *Piano Concerto No. 2 in G.* It is a dance ballet and has no story.

FIRST MOVEMENT: ALLEGRO BRILLANTE   The orchestra and piano introduce the opening theme, a brilliant and noble melody. The piano develops this theme alone, and a quick rush on the strings signals the second theme. The curtain rises. Eight couples in classical costume stand in a diagonal, the boys facing the girls some distance apart. They begin to dance. The stage frame is draped with blue velvet trimmed with ermine. We are in the room of a palace. In contrast to this sumptuous warmth, in the distance there is a view of the snow-covered Fortress of Peter and Paul. The royal gates that direct our eyes to this view are embellished with the imperial eagle. The dancing is quick and formal, bright and dignified.

Eight girls join the eight couples, and after them comes a soloist, a beautiful young girl who prepares the stage for the ballerina. The ballerina enters, dances to a piano cadenza, and by her loveliness in performance convinces us that we are watching a queen among dancers. At first she dances alone, finishing her variation in open rapid turns that encircle the stage. The music is softer, has now a stately romantic quality, and the ballerina dances with a cavalier. Now the ballerina and the *corps de ballet* leave the stage and the soloist performs a *pas de trois* with two boys. The second theme has returned with the same signal from the strings, it has merged with the first, and the music gathers to a flourishing finish. The ballerina and the *corps de ballet* dance to this music with young, regal splendor, and the movement is over.

SECOND MOVEMENT: ANDANTE NON TROPPO   After a brief introduction, the piano plays alone the principal theme. This is music of sentiment, pathos, and high feeling—slow, almost retarded, in its romantic commitment. A solo violin plays the theme accompanied by the piano. The ballerina enters with her cavalier. Eight girls form a maze through which the ballerina and her partner move. Now she and her partner are lovers. They appear to be happy, but then the man pleads with her intently and we understand that their love is not perfect. But soon the ballerina responds to her lover's plea and dances with tender intimacy. The *corps de ballet* dance protectingly around the couple and lead them gently into the wings.

THIRD MOVEMENT: ALLEGRO CON FUOCO The music is gay and assertive with a fiery brightness and crispness. The ballerina is carried in high on the shoulders of her partner. He sets her down softly, and she dances with ravishing quickness to the brilliant music. She and her partner leave the stage for a moment to the *corps de ballet*, but return again and again to lead the dancing. The ballerina's partner dances a variation, the soloist is seen briefly leading the crowded stage of dancers, and the ballerina comes back to finish with her court the final, electric flourish of ensemble movement.

NOTES *Ballet Imperial* has been danced by a number of companies in recent years. The Royal Ballet mounted a new version, in a setting by Carl Toms, October 18, 1963, and the New York City Ballet on May 19, 1964, presented its own production, staged by Frederic Franklin. Its scenery by Rouben Ter-Arutunian and costumes by Karinska suggests the splendors of the Imperial capital in Russia, Peter the Great's "Window on the West," the city of canals and painted stucco that recalls the heroic grandeur of Italy. In the background, across the broad Neva River, framed by the rostral columns celebrating Russian naval supremacy, is the lancet spire of the Peter-Paul fortress. The azure draperies reflect the color of the Maryinsky Theatre of Opera and Ballet for which Tchaikovsky composed his great theatrical scores.

On January 12, 1973, with its name changed to *Tchaikovsky Concerto No. 2*, the ballet was presented in a new version by the New York City Ballet at the New York State Theatre, Lincoln Center. Patricia McBride, Peter Martins, and Colleen Neary were the principals. The setting was a plain cyclorama and the costumes much simplified. So also was the Second Movement, where the pantomime of the cavalier was eliminated. I made these changes because the times have changed since the ballet was first done. Our audiences these days don't require elaborate costumes and decoration in a ballet, and rightly so. We see dancing better than we used to and prefer to see it directly, unencumbered. The music and the dancing themselves are enough here, I hope, to form illusions that scenery and costumes only made specific.

BALLET SCHOOL

Music by Liadvov, Shostakovich, and Glazunov. Choreography by Asaf Messerer. First presented by the Bolshoi Ballet at the Metropolitan Opera House, New York, September 17, 1962.

This work originated from a collection of dances presented by pupils of the Bolshoi Ballet School upon their graduation. It shows in compressed form the years of training and work required to become a classical dancer. The ballet was made by the ballet master at the Bolshoi, Asaf Messerer, who has said of his work: "I endeavored to show to the audiences the richness of the Russian classical school and give some insight into the training of its dancers—from the initial steps of the child pupils to the mature masters of ballet. I tried to avoid brilliance of technique as an end in itself and did not wish to turn the performance into a mere display of the skill of the soloists. I aimed also at introducing to the public many of our promising and gifted dancers. Thus, not only such stars as Maya Plisetskaya and Fadeyechev dance in it, but some of the younger members of the company, among them Nina Sorokina, Natalia Bessmertnova, and Mikhail Lavrovsky."

Before the leaps and the pirouettes lie long hours of systematic practice at the *barre*. Before the child is given exercises in the center of the classroom, she must be taught the five basic positions at the *barre*. *Rond de jambe, arabesque, grands battements*, each *pas* is learned under the discerning and exacting eye of the ballet master. The children learn the small leaps, the *changement de pieds*, the *entrechats*. And finally in *adagios* and *pas de deux* they are able to demonstrate such taxing exercises as the *grande fouettée*. Groups of male dancers leap across the stage. To the familiar strains of Glazunov's music the *jetté* is displayed.

UNE BARQUE SUR L'OCÉAN

Music by Maurice Ravel. Choreography by Jerome Robbins. Costumes by Parmelee Welles. Lighting by Ronald Bates. First presented at the New York City Ballet's Hommage à Ravel at the New York State Theatre, Lincoln Center, May 29, 1975, with Victor Castelli, Daniel Duell, Laurence Matthews, Jay Jolley, and Noland T'Sani.

A dance for five boys dressed in white and blue who move against a vibrant sea color in the background, this ballet responds to the music without specific narrative. The boys move like waves and eddies or submarine currents, reacting to water and wind, the forces and whims of nature.

Reflecting the work of Impressionist painters, Ravel, like Debussy, was interested in water movement: its perpetual shifts and shimmering colors. By orchestrating *Une Barque*, as Lincoln Kirstein has written, Ravel enlarged his theme so that "as the music gathers resonance the arpeggios grow to sweeping splashes of harp and the whole orchestra seems to vibrate as much with color and with physical motion of the waves." Jerome Robbins, I have heard, calls his ballet *Sailing*.

BARTÓK NO. 3

Music by Béla Bartók. Choreography by John Clifford. Costumes by Ardith Haddow. Lighting by Ronald Bates. First presented by Los Angeles Ballet Theatre, March 27, 1974.

This is a dance ballet to Bartók's last work, the *Piano Concerto No. 3*. There are three movements, the first led by three girls with accompanying corps de ballet, the second a romantic *pas de deux* supported by six girls, the finale an ensemble for the entire group.

When *Bartók No. 3* was danced in New York, by the New York City Ballet (May 23, 1974), Bob Micklin of *Newsday* wrote that he liked Clifford's ballet "very much. It is the best work he's done to date."

LA BAYADÈRE

Ballet in four acts. Music by Ludwig Minkus. Book by S. N. Khudekov. Choreography by Marius Petipa. First presented at the Maryinsky Theatre, St. Petersburg, February 4, 1877. First presented (Act IV) in the United States by the Kirov Ballet at the Metropolitan Opera House, New York, September 14, 1961, with Kaleria Fedicheva as Nikiya, and Sergei Vikulov as Solor.

The libretto for this ballet, which is still active in the Soviet repertory, tells the story of a hapless Indian bayadère—a temple dancer—named Nikiya. The bayadère is loved but badly treated by Solor, a young warrior who breaks his pledge to her and marries another. Nikiya is poisoned by a confidante of her rival and dies. In the final act, the repentant Solor dreams that he seeks his beloved in the "Kingdom of the Shades." Though, like Orpheus and Albrecht, he finds her, she eludes him, despite his pledge that he will never forsake her again.

But the important thing about Act IV of *Bayadère* is not the story but the dancing. What happens is that the wraithlike inhabitants of the "Kingdom of the Shades" descend upon the stage down a long ramp at the back, parallel to the audience, all in profile in *arabesque penché* at each step. There are thirty-six Shades. These and their ensuing steps, while basically simple for dancers to perform, so direct the attention by their repetition that an otherworldliness results. Next there is a *pas de trois* for three of the Shades, followed by variations for each. Solor now dances a variation that reasserts his humanity in this atmosphere of immortals. The *pas de deux* between the two lovers ties them together as it were by a long diaphanous scarf. As Nikiya holds one end of the scarf with one hand, Solor at the other end supports her in a series of turns that is rivaled only by the lifts in the final act of *Giselle* for an expression of close spirituality.

NOTES Rudolf Nureyev's fine production of *La Bayadère* for the Royal Ballet has become well-known in the United States. Another production, by Natalia Makarova, was presented in July 1974 by American Ballet Theatre. Arlene Croce wrote in *The New Yorker:* "It is an astounding success—more evidence that self-exiled Russian stars have as much to give as to gain in the West. *La Bayadère* (short for *La Bayadère*, Act IV: The Kingdom of the Shades) is an old Petipa classic of which most Westerners were unaware until the Kirov Ballet toured it in 1961. When Rudolf Nureyev, who defected on that same tour, produced it two years later for the Royal Ballet, it seemed that a miracle of transposition had taken place. Makarova has wrought an even greater miracle. She's not only reproduced a masterpiece of choreography, she's taken Ballet Theatre's corps and recharged it from top to bottom.

"The process of transformation is as yet incomplete, but never in my experience had the company danced a classical piece in so strict a style, on so broad a scale, and with such clarity of rhythm. Without these qualities, *La Bayadère* wouldn't be fun—it wouldn't even be *La Bayadère*—and what's *most* fun about this production is that every girl on the stage seems to be aware of the sensational progress she's making. . . . What matters . . . is that the motor impulse is there, solidly pumping energy into the right channels.

"Makarova's direction has been faithful and revealing. That motor impulse is basic to Petipa's exposition of movement flowing clean from its source. It flows from the simple to the complex, but we are always aware of its source, deep in the dancer's back, and of its vibration as it carries in widening arcs around the auditorium. This is dancing to be felt as well as seen, and Petipa gives it a long time to creep under our skins. Like a patient drillmaster, he opens the piece with a single, two-phrase theme in adagio tempo (arabesque, cambré port de bras), repeated over and over until all the dancers have filed onto the stage. Then, at the same tempo, with the dancers facing us in columns, he produces a set of mild variations, expanding the profile of the opening image from two dimensions to three. Positions are developed naturally through the body's leverage—weight, counterweight. Diagonals are firmly expressed. Returning to profile, the columns divide and flutter one by one to the rear. The final pose is of two long columns facing the wings with annunciatory arms. Now, to a collection of beer-garden tunes (the composer is Ludwig Minkus), Petipa sets dances for five soloists—a ballerina, a danseur, and three principal Shades—while behind them the vast, tireless corps responds in echoes, diverges, vanishes, regathers into garlands, into gateways, tosses, and freezes. The choreography is considered to be the first expression of grand-scale symphonism in dance, predating by seventeen years Ivanov's masterly designs for the definitive *Swan Lake*. But our first reaction is not to how old it looks but to how modern. Actually, the only word for this old-new choreography is immemorial. *La Bayadère* (1877) looks like the first ballet ever made: like man's—or, rather, woman's—first imprint in space and time.

"The subject of 'The Kingdom of the Shades' is not really death, although everybody in it except the hero is dead. It's Elysian bliss, and its setting is eternity. The long, slow repeated-arabesque sequence creates the impression of a grand crescendo that seems to annihilate all time. No reason it could not go on forever. And in the adagio drill that follows, the steps are so few and their content is so exposed that we think we'll remember them always—just like dancers, who *have* remembered them for a hundred years and for who knows how long before Petipa commemorated them in this ballet. Ballets, passed down the generations like legends, acquire a patina of ritualism, but *La Bayadère is* a ritual, a poem about dancing and memory and time. Each dance seems to add something new to the previous one, like a language being learned. The ballet grows heavy with this knowledge, which at the beginning had been only a primordial utterance, and in the coda it fairly bursts with articulate splendor. My favorite moment comes in the final waltz, when the three principal Shades are doing relevé-passé, relevé-attitude cambré to a rocking rhythm, and the corps, seeing this, rush to join them in the repeat. They—the corps—remember those cambré positions from their big dance.

"It's the corps' ballet—a fact the management should recognize by allowing a company call after, as well as before, the soloists have taken their bows. But the soloists in the performance I saw—Cynthia Gregory, Ivan Nagy, Karena Brock, Deborah Dobson, and Martine van Hamel—deserved their applause. Gregory was at her greatest. She took her grand port de bras the way it was meant to be taken—straight up out of the floor and through the body. Van Hamel, who may be the most talented of the company's younger ballerinas, did her variation the hard way by not coming off point until she was well up and into arabesque, and the excessively slow tempo made it even harder. Nagy has a way of filling a role superlatively without actually doing the steps. In his variation, he gathered himself powerfully and unfurled something that started like double assemblés and ended halfway to double sauts de basque. In the *pas de deux* with the veil, he didn't parallel the ballerina's steps and poses— but this is one of the differences between Makarova's staging and Nureyev's. Another difference is that she doesn't stroke the upbeat, or break the path of a gesture in order to point it. The way these two have staged the piece corresponds to their styles as performers—hers, musically more fluid; his, more emphatic. Also, her arabesques are not penchées, the solos are arranged in a different order, and she ends the ballet with the corps stretched along the floor in a semicircle rather than backbent in a sunburst. I prefer the Royal Ballet's orchestration, with its drumrolls and its protracted climax that accompanies the sunburst, and I think I prefer the sunburst, but apart from those things there's little to choose between these productions. They're both marvellous. Marcos Paredes' costumes for Ballet Theatre are in the Victorian style traditional to this ballet, and I liked his headdresses for the women—beaded circlets à la Anna Pavlova."*

In *Baryshnikov at Work*, the dancer Mikhail Baryshnikov calls *La Bayadère* "one of the great, if not the greatest, classical works in the history of ballet. It

* From "Makarova's Miracle" by Arlene Croce. Reprinted by permission; © 1974 The New Yorker Magazine, Inc.

is Petipa's idea of life in the beyond . . . Poetically, it is unmatched in the classical repertory."

LE BEAU DANUBE

Ballet in one act. Music by Johann Strauss. Choreography by Leonide Massine. Scenery and costumes by V. and E. Polunin, after Constantin Guys. Costumes by Comte Étienne de Beaumont. Book by Leonide Massine. First presented in a two-act version by Comte Étienne de Beaumont's Soirée de Paris, Paris, May 17, 1924, with Lydia Lopokova as the Street Dancer. First presented in the final one-act version by the Ballet Russe de Monte Carlo at the Théâtre de Monte Carlo, April 15, 1933, with Alexandra Danilova as the Street Dancer, Leonide Massine as the Hussar, Tatiana Riabouchinska as the Daughter, Irina Baronova as the First Hand, and David Lichine as the King of the Dandies. First presented in the United States by the Ballet Russe de Monte Carlo at the St. James Theatre, New York, December 22, 1933, with the same principals.

This famous character ballet takes place in a public park, the Prater, in old Vienna. Nowadays we are somewhat used to ballets that are set in parks—where policemen romance with governesses, where children rollick and get into mischief, and where the perennial gigolo tries to interest the young, innocent girl. These are all adaptations of *Le Beau Danube* (*The Beautiful Danube*) and a tribute to its popularity. Roger Désormière arranged and orchestrated the pieces by Johann Strauss that make up the ballet's score.

The curtain rises on a charming wooded park in Vienna. It is Sunday afternoon, about a hundred years ago. A gardener is tidying up the grounds, a young artist is painting at an easel; we hear the sound of a Strauss waltz and we believe the pretty picture we see on the stage. Strollers soon enter and enjoy the beauty of the scene: a family with two daughters, ladies of the town, seamstresses and dandies.

The artist is attracted to the first hand, the seamstress, and flirts with her as he sketches her portrait. The girl is pleased with the artist until the King of the Dandies rushes in and whisks her away from him.

Now a dashing hussar, in immaculate uniform, promenades with one of the daughters of the family. He is deferential to her family and is apparently formally engaged to her, for when he dances a mazurka with the girl their romance appears to be permanently happy. They leave the scene hand in hand.

A small band of street entertainers enter and set up to amuse the crowd that has gathered. The manager of the troupe points with pride to his principal artiste, a dancer, and the beautiful girl begins a lively solo that thrills the crowd. The manager and an athlete with bulging muscles join her; the dance becomes hilarious and everyone applauds them.

The hussar and his fiancée stroll back into the park at this point, and the hussar is embarrassed to see his past catch up with him. The street dancer instantly claims him as a former devoted lover and, to his fiancée's horror, pretends that the hussar has deserted her! The poor girl swoons during this scene of simulated jealousy and her family escort her out of the park, vowing vengeance on the ne'er-do-well hussar. The street dancer, not to be outdone by her rival, pretends to swoon also.

The hussar is distressed at what has happened, but he could hardly control the whims of the street dancer and there is nothing else for him but to take up with her again! The crowd wanders off and they are alone. The first familiar bars of the *Blue Danube* Waltz are heard. The hussar is moved to dance; quietly and slowly the music accompanies his recollection of his romance with the dancer, and he opens his arms to her. He waits, not moving. She too remembers. She feels false jealousy no longer, and they begin to dance, their initial restrained steps building gradually to an ebullient and joyful whirling with the persistent swell of the waltz.

But just as the former lovers seem to be reunited, the hussar's fiancée returns. She has run off from her raging family and insists on claiming the hussar: after all, she loves him. Why should she give him up so easily? The hussar, who has never seen such determination in a woman, is charmed by her completely and again forgets the street dancer. The *Blue Danube* has ended.

The young girl's family race in and try to separate their daughter from the fickle hussar, but the younger daughter steps in, cajoles and persuades, and tears turn to laughter. The hussar is properly deferential again to his fiancée's family; the father blesses the handsome couple; and the crowd in the park dance in celebration of the happy resolve. The street dancer, too, congratulates them with a final display of high-spirited dancing, and the charming park becomes a place where nothing unpleasant can ever happen.

BEAUTY AND THE BEAST

> *Dramatic ballet in two scenes. Music by Maurice Ravel. Choreography by John Cranko. Scenery and costumes by Margaret Kaye. First presented by the Sadler's Wells Theatre Ballet at the Sadler's Wells Theatre, London, December 20, 1949, with Patricia Miller as* Beauty *and David Poole as the* Beast. *First presented in the United States by the Sadler's Wells Theatre Ballet at the Denver Auditorium, Denver, Colorado, November 14, 1951, with the same cast.*

Ravel's *Mother Goose* Suite is made up of five movements, each based on a famous fairy story. The familiar tale of "Beauty and the Beast" inspired the fourth movement of the suite, but the English choreographer John Cranko has been inspired to use this dramatic theme as an accompaniment to almost all of Ravel's score.* The ballet is an intimate drama, actually a long *pas de deux* for the two principal characters.

The curtain rises soon after the music has begun. The scene is the forest where the beast is king. The light, almost transparent, cloth on which the trees of the forest are painted is cut into strips, giving a jungle effect. The light is dim. The beast reclines alone in the forest. He seems to be sleeping; he wakens and rubs his eyes with his long, clawlike hands. Then we see that he is weeping. His whole body shakes with violent sobbing.

Behind him, a beautiful young girl enters the forest. The beast does not see her, and the girl, unaware that she has happened upon a dangerous wood, moves in and out among the trees. The beast rises, sensing a strange presence. He wishes to welcome the girl, but knows he will frighten her. As her back is turned, he reaches out to her plaintively. The girl moves off into the forest, and the beast follows her. She begins to feel that she is not alone.

The ragged trees rise, and the scene changes to another part of the forest. Here in the center of the jungle is a dark clearing. A little light penetrates the darkness through an entrance formed by curving trees. Here the girl enters. Now she is thoroughly lost and frightened and she does a little dance to allay her fear—a kind of whistling-in-the-dark variation. Gradually she tires and sits down to rest. Soon she falls to the ground and sleeps.

Light begins to fill the jungle through the grottolike entrance formed by the trees. The girl wakens and looks about. She observes birds in the trees, dances happily, gesturing lovingly to the surrounding forest. She approaches one of the trees to pick fruit. As she takes the fruit, she sees that it is held in the hairy paws of the beast, who has been observing her secretly.

The girl faints. The beast picks her up and holds her carefully. The girl sobs in his arms and releases herself. She attempts to flee the forest, but at the entrance, branches of trees reach out to restrain her. The door of the cage has been shut, and the girl looks at the beast in terror.

The beast tries to convince her that he means no harm. Gently he kneels before her and holds out a red flower. Again the girl wishes to escape. The beast grovels on the ground, then crawls helplessly. He drops the flower and begins to cry. The girl goes over to him, but she is still too frightened to indicate her pity. She turns to run through the entrance, where the confining branches have disappeared. She passes through, out into the light, but her hand still holds the side of the entrance: she is uncertain and returns.

She dances back into the jungle. Now she is completely unafraid. She stands over the beast and helps him rise. He lifts her high in his arms and holds her so that she almost stands above him. The girl reaches down and holds his face

* The section *"Laideronette, Impératrice des Pagodas"* is omitted in the ballet.

in her hands. The music rushes magically; the beast releases her; and we see that his face is no longer the fierce mask of a ferocious beast, but the face of a handsome young man. The girl caresses his face, and the two lovers dance a flowing *pas de deux* in which the changed beast holds the girl secure as her feet gently touch the ground. At the end, the lovers reach out to each other and the curtain falls.

BHAKTI

Based on a Hindu theme and musical setting. Choreography by Maurice Béjart. Costumes by Germinal Casado. First presented by the Ballet of the Twentieth Century in 1968. First presented in the United States by the same ensemble at the Brooklyn Academy of Music, New York, January 25, 1971.

A Hindu love poem in dance, *Bhakti* is a ballet in three parts. The themes of those parts have been described by their creator, Maurice Béjart: "It is through love that the worshiper identifies with the divinity; and each time he relives the legend of his god, who is himself only one of the faces of the supreme and nameless reality." The three parts of the work are *pas de deux* between certain girls and their heroes:

RAMA an incarnation of Vishnu. His love affair with Sita, symbol of purity, is related in the celebrated Hindu epic *Ramayana*. This poem forms the basis of every classical dance or theatrical production in India.

KRISHNA another incarnation of Vishnu. He is the God of Youth and Beauty, the divine Player of the Flute whose affairs with the shepherdesses and the lovely Radha are sung in the *Gita Govinda*. He is also the teacher par excellence, and it is he who speaks in the *Bhagavad-Gita*, one of the most important books of all.

SHIVA the third person in the Hindu Trinity (*Trimurti*): Brahma, Vishnu, Shiva. As the "Destroyer," he kills illusion and personality. God of the Dance, his wife Shakti pursues the vital energy that flows from and returns to him, immobile, yet forever in motion.

Introduced by three young men, the ballet proceeds to representations of these gods and their ladies, each supported by appropriate ensembles.

LES BICHES

Ballet in one act. Music by Francis Poulenc. Choreography by Bronislava Nijinska. Scenery and costumes by Marie Laurencin. First presented by

Diaghilev's Ballets Russes at the Théâtre de Monte Carlo, January 6, 1924, with a cast that included Vera Nemtchinova and Anatole Vilzak, Alexandra Danilova, Bronislava Nijinska, Felia Dubrovska, Ninette de Valois, Alice Nikitina, Lubov Tchernicheva, Nicholas Zverev, and Leon Woicikowski. First presented in the United States by the Marquis de Cuevas' Grand Ballet at the Century Theatre, New York, November 13, 1950, with a cast headed by Marjorie Tallchief, George Skibine, and Olga Adabache.

Two ballet companies have preferred to call this ballet *The House Party* and *The Gazelles.** It is certainly about a house party. There is a hostess, a woman considerably older than her youthful guests; she seeks to form an attachment with one of the young men at her party. The relations of some of her guests are similarly romantic. The ballet thus has a romantic theme rather than a specific plot; the characters are dancers. The ballet is in eight parts, corresponding to the divisions of the score: "Rondo," "*Chanson dansée*," "Adagietto," "*Jeux*," "Rag Mazurka," "Andantino," "*Chanson dansée*," "Finale."

Before the curtain rises, the orchestra plays a short introduction; slow at first, the music becomes smartly quick and pulsating and reminds us of the vitality of youth. The curtain rises on an enormous room that bears the mark of the fashionable interior decorator. Painted blue curtains at the back enclose a window. A large blue couch stands at the rear. Twelve girls enter and dance pertly to the rhythm of the music. Their long, cool pink dresses whirl about them in innocent contrast to the sophistication of their steps. The girls kneel, rise, circle on point, bend back seductively, and choose partners as the music hastens to a brisk finish. They run off in gushing, schoolgirl fashion.

Three boys in bathing trunks enter to the strong, choppy beat of the "*Chanson dansée*." They dance in a line; their movements are assertive and angular. They thrust out their chests and display their biceps in a dance that stylizes athleticism. The two boys on the side imitate the turns of the dancer in the center. They kneel. The twelve girls run in. The boys continue their dance for the girls' benefit, while the girls try to attract them. They surround each of the three boys, then stand in a semicircle behind them. The boys kneel before the girls, but seem to be disinterested.

A girl dressed like a page boy in white tights, blue tunic, and white gloves enters on the right and interrupts the scene. She crosses the stage on point, holding her hand up stiffly, as if she were on some secret errand. She takes no notice of the guests, but the boys are fascinated. The girl leaves and, abandoning all hope of winning the boys, four of the girls flounce away and arrange themselves decorously on the sofa. The others continue their flirtation with the boys, who abandon them again when the girl enters as before. One of the youths is attracted to her; she dances off, and the flighty girls take up with the

* Literally, *les biches* means *the hinds*, but colloquially it also means simply *girls*, or *young ladies*.

other two boys. The strange girl recrosses the room, but pauses this time to dance briefly. Her hands are joined and she holds out her arms as she poses; her movements are softly angular. Two of the boys have gone off with the girls in pink, and one of the boys watches the girl in blue as she dances alone, apparently oblivious of his presence. He comes up behind her as she finishes her variation, comes close and holds her arms; the two exit together.

The two boys return with the girls and begin a rollicking game. The boys slide the couch forward. They stand on it, lifting the girls over it; then the girls dance across the couch one by one and hop off the arm onto the floor. The boys walk off. The sofa is turned with its back to the front, and the girls hide behind it as the girl in blue re-enters with her partner. They dance briefly and exit when they see they are being watched. The boys come back to find the girls. They move the couch back near the window, and all leave the stage.

A woman in an elaborate yellow dress enters and crosses the stage with mannered steps. This is the hostess. She brandishes a long cigarette holder pointedly, as if she were posing for a stilted advertisement, and at the same time nervously belies her pose by playing with her long pearl necklace. Her hands are constantly in motion; she cannot remain still for an instant. Her dance is the dance of a woman who can never imagine herself alone; it is the perpetual and desperate performance of a woman who has to be seen to appreciate herself. No one interrupts her parody of a youthful dance, and she stops. She arranges herself languidly on the couch.

The two young men enter suddenly. They dance proudly, asserting their masculine strength. They approach the hostess, stomping their feet. She is delighted and joins them in a dance to the "Rag Mazurka." Vigorous at first, their *pas de trois* slows down. The hostess is enamored of both her partners. Both boys offer their arms. She doesn't know which to choose. She takes a chance and breaks free. Both boys follow her off.

The girl in blue meets her partner in the center of the stage for a *pas de deux* to the "Andantino." Their gestures and steps are strangely discontinuous; they move, pause, move again—formal, but intimate. Their dance ends as the boy holds the girl straight in his arms; then, with an intricate twist of both their bodies, the girl is poised high on his shoulder. They leave the stage.

To a sprightly tune two young girls enter and dance a lively duet in which each tries to outdo the other in expressing their attachment. Their dance becomes secretive when they imagine they are not alone. They blush and exit hurriedly.

In different groups that turn rapidly as they cross the stage, the entire ensemble gradually returns for the finale—first the girls, then the boys, followed by the hostess and the girl in blue. All romantic attachments seem to be forgotten as the ensemble joins together for a final fling.

NOTES   One of the popular ballets of the Diaghilev era, *Les Biches* is regarded by its choreographer as the modern equivalent of *Les Sylphides*. It has been revived since its first production by the Markova-Dolin Ballet, when Alicia Markova danced the part of the girl in blue and Anton Dolin danced her partner; and by the Grand Ballet of the Marquis de Cuevas, where the production met with critical and popular approval, both in Europe and New York.

The composer, Francis Poulenc, noted in the English magazine *Ballet* (Volume 2, No. 4) that *Les Biches* "is a ballet in which you may see nothing at all or into which you may read the worst . . . In this ballet, as in certain of Watteau's pictures, there is an atmosphere of wantonness which you sense if you are corrupted but which an innocent-minded girl would not be conscious of."

Nijinska revived *Les Biches* for the Royal Ballet December 2, 1964, with Svetlana Beriosova, Georgina Parkinson, David Blair, Keith Rosson, Robert Mead, Maryon Lane, and Merle Park in leading roles. This revival was first presented in the United States at the Metropolitan Opera House by the Royal Ballet the following spring.

THE BIG CITY

Music by Alexander Tansman. Book and choreography by Kurt Jooss. First presented by the Jooss Ballet at the Opera House, Cologne, November 21, 1932. Costumes and lighting by Hermann Markard. First presented in the United States by the City Center Joffrey Ballet at the City Center, New York, February 28, 1975. Staged by Anna Markard. Costumes and lighting by Hermann Markard, re-created by Ray Diffen and Jennifer Tipton. Pianists: Stanley Babin and Mary Roark. Conducted by Sung Kwak.

The Big City was originally presented just four months after Kurt Jooss' masterwork, *The Green Table*, had won first prize in an international dance competition. Although the ballet is often described as the first dance composition to deal with social criticism, Jooss maintains that this was not his intention. He has described the work as an "attempt to portray the loneliness of city people by means of dramatic dance." He was inspired by the "bustle of city life, backyard gloom and the glamour of dance halls." The Joffrey Ballet version, taken from the final 1935 version, was staged by Jooss' daughter, Anna Markard.

The action of the ballet is compressed into three graphic scenes accompanied by music (Tansman's *Sonatine Transatlantique*) that recalls the time of Europe's first appreciation of *le jazz hot*. The plot: "In the hurrying throng of a continental city are seen a young Girl and a young Workman, her sweetheart, homeward bound after the day's work. A Libertine, in search of new conquests, follows the young Girl to her home. Dazzled by the promise of adventure, she fares forth on his arm to the dance halls, where disillusion awaits her."

Writing of the American revival of *The Big City* in *The Village Voice*, the critic Deborah Jowitt said that "the life of this city is a bitter cartoon of what we can imagine life in a German city at the edge of World War II to have been like." . . . What makes the ballet absorbing and moving is not the sad little plot or the social message, but the delicate way Jooss was able to suggest characters, social backgrounds, occupations of people through the ways he made them move. What he gives you in many cases seem like rapid sketches of something he means to develop later—but what sketches!"

Interviewed in the New York *Times* by Anna Kisselgoff at the time of the Joffrey revival, Kurt Jooss said that *The Big City* "must be seen now as a period piece of the nineteen-twenties . . . I am not a social-protest choreographer . . . I consider myself a choreographer first."

BILLY THE KID

Ballet in one act. Music by Aaron Copland. Choreography by Eugene Loring. Book by Lincoln Kirstein. Scenery and costumes by Jared French. First presented by Ballet Caravan at the Chicago Opera House, Chicago, October 16, 1938, with Eugene Loring as Billy, *Marie-Jeanne as the* Mother *and* Sweetheart, *Lew Christensen as* Pat Garrett, *and Todd Bolender as* Alias.

The story of Billy the Kid is already a legend in America, a part of the larger legend we know as the Opening of the West. The facts known about him—that his real name was William H. Bonney; that he was born in New York City in 1859; was taken to Kansas when he was three; killed his first man in Silver City, New Mexico, when he was twelve; and by the time he was hunted down and shot, at the age of twenty-one, had killed a man for every year of his life— these facts remind us of a gangster movie. But actually these facts do not tell us the whole story of the Kid. They do not tell us that, although Billy the Kid was regarded as the most dangerous desperado of his time, he was loved and admired as much as he was feared, and that the Far West after the Civil War was a place where these emotions could interchange and resolve—to make of his life the heroic myth it has since become. This ballet is not, therefore, a simple biography of a wild West killer: it is the story of the life of Billy the Kid as it became a part of the life of his time.

PROLOGUE The first, slow notes of the music are subdued and eerie, like sounds in the wilderness at night. The curtain rises. Across the front of the stage a spotlight shines, making a path of brilliant orange light. The rest of the stage is suffused in a semidark glow, as if bathed in the light of the golden sun. An arid khaki-colored desert and tall, branching cacti are seen in the distance. From the right, a man dressed in a cowboy outfit steps boldly into the path of light. Later we shall learn that this is Pat Garrett, the sometime friend

Anna Pavlova in *La Fille Mal Gardée*. Dance Collection, N.Y.P.L. at Lincoln Center, Astor, Lenox and Tilden Foundations.

Tamara Karsavina and Vaslav Nijinsky in *Le Spectre de la Rose*. Dance Collection, N.Y.P.L.

Clockwise from top left: Vaslav Nijinsky in *Giselle, Scheberazade, Jeux*, and *Afternoon of a Faun*. All photos from the Roger Pryor Dodge Dance Collection, New York Public Library.

Galina Ulanova in *Romeo and Juliet*. Collection of Rosemary Winckley.

Galina Ulanova in *Swan Lake*. Collection of Rosemary Winckley.

Alicia Markova and André Eglevsky in *The Nutcracker*. Photo by Maurice Seymour, from the Dance Collection, N.Y.P.L.

Alicia Markova in *Giselle*. Photo by Fred Fehl.

Alexandra Danilova and Frederic Franklin in *The Nutcracker*.

Alicia Alonso and Igor Youskevitch in *Giselle*. Photo by Fred Fehl.

of Billy the Kid who becomes sheriff and kills him. But at the moment he is simply any American pioneer, moving westward toward the blaze of the setting sun. He moves stiffly, with determination; for each step forward he will take none back. Then his progress becomes a dance, the movements of which remind us of the frontiersman's work: he circles his arm high over his head to lasso invisible cattle; he pulls back roughly on invisible reins to halt a covered wagon, then drives the horses on with a lash of a whip; he kneels motionless, gun pointed, to catch the imaginary Indian. The music gains in strength with his vigorous movements. It becomes stronger still, as Garrett is followed by another man and a woman. The man copies every one of his leader's gestures, while the woman sets a dance pattern for the pioneer mother who rocks her children to sleep even when danger surrounds her. Other couples enter, and the orchestra builds gradually to sound a mighty processional as the pioneer figures follow their leader in this formalized march to the West. Now Garrett thrusts his arms forward, pushing back the frontier. He faces directly into the light. He pirouettes rapidly, spine in the air, and repeats these movements as all the men in the caravan follow his lead. All the dancers catch the full vitality of the music, which itself pushes forward to a resistless, persistent climax. Then, at its fullest volume, the music is cut off sharply. There is a blackout.

STREET SCENE   When the lights come up again, the backdrop still depicts, as it will continue to do, the same arid desert, but before the curtain move a group of particular characters—not pioneers simply—who place this episode in the hot and sunny main street of an early Western town, just north of the border. Woodwinds play an old Western tune that the rest of the orchestra takes up gaily and playfully. A smiling, sinuous Mexican in a wide-brimmed hat struts about, pawing the street with his boots like a tame but unbridled stallion. Pioneer women, dressed for the town in close-fitting bonnets, pass him by, their arms crooked to carry invisible burdens. The Mexican ignores them. Cowboys ride across the scene, spurring on the imaginary horses they straddle. Three dancing girls enter, their hands on their tightly corseted hips in an impudent attitude. Two women look them up and down and, noting their high-buttoned gold shoes and garish red tights, turn up their noses in disapproval, sniff at the air, and walk away. Eight cowboys ride on, and there is a short rodeo. At the end three of them stop and take up with the dance-hall girls. A group of lovely Mexican girls come onto the scene, and now the street seethes with activity. The people stand about, some talking, some flirting, others going about their private business.

Then suddenly the music is quiet. An oboe sounds a theme, and on the left a small, attractive woman comes in. She is dressed in city clothes and is clearly a stranger to the community. A big, gangling boy, dressed only in overalls and a straw hat, hangs onto her skirts, and they move through the crowd. This is Billy the Kid. The boy looks about and appears to want to stop, but his mother walks on ahead and they exit. The Mexican and the four Mexican girls dance together briefly, and then the Kid and his mother return. This time the Kid shows off his strength by softly lifting his mother around for several measures. She pushes his cheek to tell him how silly he is, and he turns his face away, blushing, but he persists at the game and the two waltz off.

Meanwhile something has happened to the crowd. They stand closely packed together, watching an argument between the Mexican and a man in red. The argument becomes a fight. They hit each other in slow motion, neither falling. The music accompanies their blows with retarded rhythm that increases in volume and speed as the fight becomes serious. The people in the crowd begin to sense that they should stand back. Now, as a trumpet sounds the theme militantly, the Kid enters with his mother. Both of them are fascinated by the brawl and stand on the fringe of the crowd. Just as they join the group, the Mexican pulls a gun. The man in red turns quickly to defend himself and steps against the crowd, right next to Billy and his mother. The Mexican fires. He misses. Billy's mother doubles up in agony. She falls against her son, who stands transfixed, staring straight ahead, not comprehending. She grasps his arm, slides down slowly to the ground, and dies. The people are horrified, but they, too, are motionless. They remain still and shocked as the Kid shakes off his dream, grabs a knife, and dashes over to the Mexican. Billy kills him with one quick stab in the back. He topples over. Everyone steps back, unbelieving. Billy looks about wildly, wondering where to go. Pat Garrett steps in to help him, but the Kid ignores him and runs off. Already he has chosen his way.

One of the men stoops to pick up the body of the Kid's mother, and the whole crowd leans over in unison, expressing the common grief. Another man kneels down beside the dead Mexican, throws him over his shoulder, and carries him off. But the Mexican will reappear. He becomes Alias, a character of many disguises who haunts the Kid constantly throughout his life and finally helps to kill him.

The crowd begins to disperse. Couples walk away, shaking their heads, still stunned by the two murders. But instead of leaving the stage, they mill about, circling slowly, and we see after a few minutes that perhaps they are not the same men and women who saw Billy the Kid's first crime. The men lift their women affectionately, just as Billy lifted his mother, but everyone is wary and suspicious. The people have changed. They have grown older and, as we have been watching them, years have passed in the street. Finally, one by one, the couples leave and the stage is empty.

THE DESERT The Kid enters in the back. He is no longer a child. He is dressed in black and white striped riding breeches, boots, a wide-brimmed hat; there is a skull on his shirt pocket. He dances alone. In this dance we understand a little of how the Kid has grown up. The proud pose that begins and ends the dance is confidently self-assertive, and in between the Kid performs a series of difficult movements with ferocity rather than grace. He stomps loudly with his heavy boots, circles an imaginary foe with his gun ready to fire, spins swiftly in the air, lands, and kicks out at his victim. He is going through the only vocabulary he possesses, and we realize that all of his life, every waking moment, is a practiced preparation for the next time he will have to kill. His dance gesture for shooting is a quick aim at the target, then a spin in the air that matches the speed of a bullet, and finally a vicious kick. It is the gesture of a man who hates his dead foe and the whole world. And there follows inevitably the same pose of self-assertion. Never does this man doubt that he has done the right thing, never has he supposed himself guilty of a crime. Shooting happens to be his way of living: a murder is just like lighting a cigarette.

As the Kid nears the end of his soliloquy, he is interrupted by the arrival of a small posse. Three men canter across the stage in formation, circle, and try to close in on the Kid. He hides. Then he aims, spins, and kicks. The leader of the three men falls dead. The Kid prances slowly and softly, then draws himself up to his full height and stands triumphant. The scene blacks out.

A spotlight at the front of the stage comes on. Sitting close to the footlights, around a campfire, the Kid and Pat Garrett are playing cards. Garrett is now sheriff, but still a friend to the Kid. The light from the fire makes enormous silhouettes of their figures against the backdrop. The orchestra plays a quiet, wistful melody. The Kid shuffles the cards and deals. The two men draw their cards. A man and two cowgirls, all friends of Billy, approach the fire. The man stoops down to watch the card game. Garrett is distracted for an instant, but turns back to find the Kid cheating. He protests. The Kid is patient with him at first, denies cheating, and attempts to humor him. Pat continues to protest, but when he sees that the Kid will not accept his friendship, will not even admit to overt cheating, he rides off into the night. Billy's three friends gather about the fire and take up the cards while the Kid stands aside. His rage mounts. Pat has got the better of him. He stomps angrily, regretting that he did not kill his friend. The group at the fire turn and stare at him; they are frightened at what he may do. But the Kid does not have time to act. Shooting is heard in the distance, and before he can flee, the stage fills with people. The drums boom with gunfire as Pat Garrett leads a posse on in pursuit of the Kid. Billy moves to defend himself, shoots wildly as his friends gather about him and his attackers fall on their faces to protect themselves. A fierce gun battle ensues, during which the Kid continues to shoot out indiscriminately at all comers. He and his friends are hemmed in by two lines of gunfire. They are all killed except Billy. As he is about to fire another round, he trips over the body of one of his own men. Two men move in to hold him. One of them is Alias. The Kid kills Alias. The other is Pat Garrett. Pat is quick: he sticks a gun in the Kid's back and rides him off to jail. The Kid does not seem to care in the least.

The posse that has helped capture Billy—cowgirls and cowboys—now join together to celebrate and dance joyfully. In the midst of their frolic, the Kid's sweetheart, a beautiful Mexican girl, walks in and tries to find her lover. No one pays any attention to her. She leaves the scene disconsolate. The celebration is blacked out.

THE JAIL   Billy stands on one foot, shuffling cards. Naked above the waist, he wears a kerchief about his neck, arm bands, and black riding togs over white tights. His jailer, Alias, stands at his side, ready to receive his cards. Billy bides his time, shuffles the cards slowly, and shifts to the other leg. The jailer grows impatient and turns away for an instant. Billy moves openly to grab his gun, as if the jailer expected him to. The jailer, of course, sees the move but ignores it. He suggests that it is all part of the game and that Billy won't do anything wrong. He walks away. The Kid sneaks up on him softly and this time does grab his gun. The jailer turns back, expecting the Kid to hand it over. The Kid laughs. He kills the jailer and stands again triumphant. Blackout.

THE DESERT   The Kid gallops across the stage to his hide-out. He disappears. A posse follows, but they are unable to pick up the trail. Billy enters again, screened by two Mexican girls, who stand between him and the posse. Alias, now disguised as an Indian guide, leads him away. The Kid arrives at a quiet spot, and Alias leaves him. Pat Garrett and his riders pass by, but see nothing. Billy takes his hat off and undresses to go to sleep. He is so tired he seems to be asleep already. He crouches on the ground to the right and stacks his clothes automatically, as if in a dream. His sweetheart enters on the left, behind his back. She dances on point, formally. He does not turn and see her, but looks up, seeing her in his mind's eye. He looks back down at his clothes. The girl touches his shoulder and poses briefly. He stirs, first swings his right leg out and back from his crouching position—a movement in stylized keeping with the girl's remote intimacy. She stands close beside him, but he is never aware of her real presence. He rises, stretches; the girl holds onto him and poses again beautifully, and they begin a short *pas de deux* to a sensuous waltz. He lifts her gently and swings her body slowly, not looking at her at all; he might be dancing with any girl and she with any man. Almost immediately he abandons her and goes back to stretch out to sleep. The girl dances off as quietly as she came, with no protest. The dream is over.

Pat Garrett, led by Alias, comes in and watches Billy asleep. Billy has not heard them, but wakes up as if warned by something. He reaches for his gun, holds it ready. The night is black: he sees nothing. For an instant he is afraid. Garrett and Alias stand stock-still, holding their breath. Billy calls out "¿Quien es?" ("Who is it?"), his voice hoarse with fear. There is no answer. He waits. Still no sound. He laughs to himself, silently. To reassure himself, he laughs harder; his body shakes with laughter. He stops, takes out a cigarette, strikes a match, and illuminates his face for a flickering moment. Garrett fires. Billy falls. He is dead.

Long-robed Mexican women enter and stand over his body. They pass by slowly, mourning, to music of lamentation, and the light fades.

EPILOGUE   The setting sun shines across the stage, and Pat Garrett walks in boldly, as he did at the beginning of the ballet, leading a host of pioneers. All march facing west, then turn back east, then west again, as the music impels them forward.

BIOSFERA

> *Music by Marlos Nobre. Choreography by Arthur Mitchell. Scenery and costumes by Fred Barry. First presented by the Dance Theatre of Harlem at the ANTA Theatre, New York, March 10, 1971.*

Biosfera is a dramatic *pas de deux,* not the usual display piece for two dancers but an opportunity for the two artists to become involved in a situation beyond themselves. The curtain rises on a dark stage where we gradually make out a girl and a boy, posed on platforms at opposite sides of the scene. The girl is dressed all in white, he in black. They leave their platforms to dance in a spotlight in the center. The music is lightly electronic, mysterious. The dance has a kind of detached romanticism about it. At the end, the girl and the boy return to the platforms at either side of the stage.

Reviewing *Biosfera* in the New York *Times* in March 1971, Clive Barnes said of the dancers: "Sheila Rohan is the girl, dancing with a crisp clarity, and the man is the distinguished and elegant Walter Raines, who at one point has to stand on his hands for what seems like two minutes . . . Mr. Mitchell has gotten himself the makings of a first-rate American classic ballet company."

BIRTHDAY OFFERING

> *Music by Alexander Glazunov. Choreography by Frederick Ashton. Costumes by André Levasseur. First presented at the Royal Opera House, Covent Garden, London, by the Sadler's Wells Ballet on May 5, 1956, with Margot Fonteyn, Beryl Grey, Violetta Elvin, Nadia Nerina, Rowena Jackson, Svetlana Beriosova, Elaine Fifield; Michael Somes, Alexander Grant, Brian Shaw, Philip Chatfield, David Blair, Desmond Doyle, and Bryan Ashbridge in the principal roles. First presented in the United States by the same company at the Metropolitan Opera House, New York, September 11, 1957.*

Birthday Offering was the Sadler's Wells Ballet's danced celebration of its twenty-fifth anniversary. Set to music from Glazunov's *The Seasons, Ruses d'amour,* and other works, as arranged by Robert Irving, the ballet displayed the special gifts of the first dancers of the company and was a tribute to the tradition and practice that had made the ensemble famous. That *Birthday Offering* is more than a *pièce d'occasion* was suggested by a revival in 1960 when it was danced by young aspiring ballerinas. Mary Clarke wrote in *The Dancing Times:* "This quality of youth and freshness gave the ballet a different kind of charm. Choreographically, it is a wonder. Each of the solos is a small masterpiece and the flow and patterns of the ensemble work are marvelously smooth yet delicate. Ashton here, in a Maryinsky mood, proved himself to be the equal of Petipa."

The score was taken from the following compositions of Glazunov: Entrée: *Valse de Concert, No. 1;* Grand Adagio: *Scènes de Ballet;* Fifield's Variation: *Scènes de Ballet;* Jackson's Variation: Winter (*Les Saisons*); Beriosova's Variation: Winter (*Les Saisons*); Grey's Variation: Summer (*Les Saisons*); Fonteyn's Variation: *Ruses d'amour.*

BLUEBEARD

Comic ballet in two prologues, four scenes, and three interludes. Music by Jacques Offenbach. Choreography by Michel Fokine. Book by Michel Fokine. Scenery and costumes by Marcel Vertès. First presented by Ballet Theatre at the Palacio de Bellas Artes, Mexico City, Mexico, October 27, 1941, with a cast headed by Anton Dolin as Bluebeard, Alicia Markova as Hermilia, Irina Baronova as Boulotte, Ian Gibson as Prince Sapphire, Antony Tudor as King Bobiche, Lucia Chase as Queen Clementine, Miriam Golden, Jeannette Lauret, Nora Kaye, Rosella Hightower, and Maria Karnilova as Wives of Bluebeard, and Dimitri Romanov, Donald Saddler, Annabelle Lyon, Jerome Robbins, and Hugh Laing as the Queen's Lovers. First presented in the United States by Ballet Theatre at the Forty-fourth Street Theatre, New York, November 12, 1941, with the same principals.

Bluebeard is a comedy with a double plot. Its characters are everywhere at once, and if you don't have a clear idea of who they are and what they're up to, the ballet doesn't turn out to be as funny as it might be. The music, arranged and orchestrated by Antal Dorati, is taken from Offenbach's operetta *Barbe-Bleue* and other scores by that composer. The time is the beginning of the sixteenth century; the place is the mythical kingdom of King Bobiche.

FIRST PROLOGUE   There is a rousing, thumping overture. The curtain rises. King Bobiche, a tottering old man in purple robes and ruby crown, enters the scene carrying an infant. This is his daughter, Hermilia, who must be exiled because she is not a son. The old king doesn't know quite how to go about this, but he is determined that the child's birth shall be kept secret. Count Oscar, his chancellor, brings on a basket. The dejected monarch secures a necklace

about the child's throat to identify her royal lineage; the two men place her
carefully into the basket and sneak off to set her adrift in the river. Blackout.

SECOND PROLOGUE   Count Bluebeard sticks his head through the curtains
and steps out quickly. He tweaks his beard, rolls his eyes, smacks his thigh,
and appears to be a real devil of a fellow. He embraces a girl who comes along
and kisses her so passionately that she collapses. This is his first wife. The
same thing happens to two other maidens. A fourth girl is so overcome by the
mere sight of Bluebeard that she falls in a trance before he can grab her. The
fifth wife drinks with her husband. When she dies of the poison prepared by
Bluebeard's henchman, Popoloni, Bluebeard stands over her body with an
eager and how-was-that-for-killing-them-off leer.

ACT ONE: THE PALACE OF KING BOBICHE   The drop curtain rises on a medieval castle. Huge battlements rise up in the distance. It is night, some eighteen
years after King Bobiche cast his daughter into the stream. On the right is a
garden bench.

Queen Clementine dances in, followed by a page of the court. The page immediately begins to make love to the queen on the garden bench. The queen
does not seem to care in the least. Bobiche interrupts them, parts the two
lovers as if he'd spent his life dealing with his wife's infidelities, and then
storms about with pretentious jealousy.

The queen pleads with him, but the king is adamant and orders that the
page be hanged. When the poor lad is dragged off by the king's soldiers, the
king chases his queen about the garden. They disappear for a moment. By the
time the queen returns, two more suitors, dashing Spaniards with castanets
and guitars, are ready to pay court to her. She is enchanted and watches with
pleasure as the two men draw swords and fight for her affection. The two men
readily see, however, that the queen is generous and can love them both. They
put down their swords and alternately she kisses them as she joins them in a
pas de trois.

Again the king interrupts and again we have tears, royal insistence, and an
order for two more executions. This process goes on until five of the queen's
many lovers have been caught in the act and sent off to be hanged. But still
the king is not satisfied. He can certainly not expect his wife to love him and
his mind goes back to the daughter he might have loved so much. He turns his
back on the queen and weeps. He must get his daughter back, if by some miracle she is still alive!

The king orders his chancellor to search every corner of the kingdom for
Hermilia and then condescendingly takes the hand of the queen. Members of
the court kneel as the royal pair leave the garden. The drop curtain falls.

FIRST INTERLUDE: A CITY STREET   On his way to carry out the king's order,
Count Oscar encounters the lovers of the queen, who are being led by their ex-

ecutioner to the gallows. He takes pity on them and inquires if they have any money. Luckily, they have. Good old Oscar empties their pockets and pardons them. The five men dance for joy while the chancellor counts his money.

ACT TWO: THE COUNTRYSIDE   With a roll of the drums, the curtain rises on a bright scene in the country. Scarecrows look out over the wheat fields in the distance, and the sun shines with an intense, glowing yellow. Peasant girls and boys dance together happily, circling and forming a chain, moving in vigorous, youthful harmony. One of the girls we notice right away because she is the prettiest of them all and because everyone seems to admire her. This is Floretta, in reality Hermilia, the daughter of King Bobiche. As if this weren't enough, the shepherd with whom she dances a romantic *pas de deux* is actually no shepherd at all but Prince Sapphire!

As Floretta sits on her shepherd's knee, a stunning blond girl comes in and berates the shepherd. She brags of her jealousy in a big emotional display, stamps her foot at Floretta, and the two lovers fly from her rage. Boulotte follows them.

Popoloni, the old alchemist who has helped Bluebeard kill off his wives, comes onto the scene. He tells the peasant girls that Bluebeard needs a new wife and that he will choose one of them for his bride. Bluebeard follows him almost immediately in an absurd chariot, and the girls quake at the sight of him. A few of the more courageous girls surround him, while others manage to form a line. Bluebeard looks the girls over one by one as if he were examining fresh meat. He doesn't like what he sees and pouts. As all the girls circle him, Boulotte re-enters. Bluebeard is just another man to her. She smacks him on the back, tweaks his beard, and treats him as if he were a rough and ready peasant. Ready Bluebeard obviously is: no woman has been so bold with him in years. He dances with her and soon proposes. Boulotte instantly consents, and Bluebeard carries her to his chariot. All wave as they exit.

Now the two plots of the ballet cross. Count Oscar, the chancellor, enters with one of the king's men. He is searching for the king's lost daughter. Popoloni engages Oscar in conversation, and as they talk, Floretta and her shepherd pass by. The shepherd bids the girl a hurried good-by as soon as he sees the count, who would expose his disguise. Count Oscar approaches her, asks politely to see her necklace, and Floretta is revealed as Princess Hermilia! Floretta fears that her shepherd might not love a Princess and wants to make sure of his affections. But, of course, Prince Sapphire is off sulking with similar thoughts. The drop curtain falls.

SECOND INTERLUDE   Bluebeard and Boulotte are racing across the stage to celebrate their marriage when their chariot passes Count Oscar and Hermilia. The fickle Bluebeard eyes the princess, and already he has had enough of the bouncing blonde. He must marry her, he decides, and vows to set a new plot in motion.

ACT THREE: A CELLAR IN BLUEBEARD'S CASTLE   The scene is dark as a dungeon. This is the laboratory of the alchemist Popoloni. On the left, at a table, chemicals burst into flame as he mixes them together. He chuckles to himself, delighted that his master has given him a new project. On the right are five vaults, each bearing the name of one of Bluebeard's dead wives! A sixth grave, as yet uncovered, is ready to receive another wife.

Bluebeard stalks in to give Popoloni his final orders: Boulotte must die! Boulotte enters and slaps him on the back. Bluebeard, out of all patience, tells Popoloni to be hasty. Boulotte takes one look at the five graves and clasps Bluebeard frantically in her arms. He pushes her off and Boulotte rolls about on the floor in despair. She rises and hangs on Bluebeard's neck, pleading with him to save her. "No!" he answers, and leaves her alone with her poisoner.

Boulotte goes over to Popoloni and tries to flirt with him. But the old man pushes her off his knee and tells her to leave off. He tells her that he has something for her and bids her drink from two goblets. Boulotte looks toward the open grave and refuses to drink. When Popoloni turns his back for a moment, she picks up a goblet from his table and drinks that one, instead. Poor girl, all the goblets are filled with the same poison! She falls to the floor.

Popoloni pretends grief; he is joined in his sorrow by Bluebeard, whose body shakes with sobs. He kneels beside his beloved and then, suddenly, he is up dancing as if he is absolutely delighted! He leaps over the body and dashes off in pursuit of the Princess Hermilia.

Old Popoloni's grief turns out to be genuine. He takes a feather, touches it to Boulotte's face, and she is alive again. Then, at a clap of his hands, all the graves open and we see that all the other wives have been similarly brought back to life by the alchemist. Bluebeard's first five wives surround Boulotte and pay tribute to the kindly Popoloni in a happy dance. The scene blacks out.

THIRD INTERLUDE   Bluebeard, too, has his qualms. The ghosts of his murdered wives circle around him as he recalls his crimes. For a moment, he is sorry.

ACT FOUR: THE COURT OF KING BOBICHE   King Bobiche leads his queen to their great, ermine-draped throne, and both prepare to welcome the Princess Hermilia to her true home. They embrace their daughter, who is strangely unhappy. They find out why when the king proposes that she marry a prince named Sapphire. Hermilia doesn't want a prince; she wants her shepherd. She storms about the court, refusing to consent to her father's wish. In despair, the king calls for Prince Sapphire, and when he appears, Hermilia cannot believe her eyes. Everyone rejoices.

But not for long. Bluebeard, no longer remorseful, is determined to wed Hermilia. He dashes in and flourishes his sword. The king is terrified and hides behind the throne. Prince Sapphire, the only fearless member of the court, suggests a duel. They begin to spar with their swords. Bluebeard tricks the prince

and stabs him in the back. Bluebeard chuckles as his rival falls dead. Hermilia
mourns her lover while the heartless Bluebeard wipes his sword and turns to
her. Now, indeed, she must marry him!

Popoloni enters the court leading five masked women. Bluebeard is so busy
sitting in Hermilia's lap that he doesn't pay much attention. Poor Hermilia can
do nothing but cry. When Bluebeard looks up, the five women unmask: he
sees all his dead wives! He leaps high into the air and runs for his life. The
wives close in and beat him soundly. He frees himself and threatens Popoloni.
But he observes that one of his former wives was really worth saving, after all.
He drops the sword and goes to embrace her.

But King Bobiche has other ideas. The queen's five lovers have returned
from the dead, too, and something must be done quickly: so he pairs them off
with Bluebeard's wives. Old Popoloni recalls Prince Sapphire to life, and
Hermilia is happy. The royal couple parade with Bluebeard and Boulotte,
trumpets blare, Boulotte whirls around and around and around, and the colorful assembly of courtiers and peasantry rejoice.

BOURNONVILLE DIVERTISSEMENTS

*Music by various composers indicated below. Choreography by Auguste
Bournonville. Staged by Stanley Williams. Costumes by Ben Benson, after
the original designs. Lighting by Ronald Bates. First presented by the New
York City Ballet at the New York State Theatre, Lincoln Center, February
3, 1977, with Nichol Hlinka and Daniel Duell; Patricia McBride and Helgi
Tomasson; Merrill Ashley, Robert Weiss and Kyra Nicholas; Suzanne Far-
rell and Peter Martins; Colleen Neary, Adam Luders, Victor Castelli, Muriel
Aasen, Wilhelmina Frankfurt, Heather Watts and Bart Cook.*

I hope that by this time everyone knows the Danish ballet is built on a technique established in the nineteenth century by the great August Bournonville
(1805–79), himself a remarkable dancer and choreographer, creator of many
lasting works in the repertory of the Royal Danish Ballet. Bournonville was a
pupil of Auguste Vestris, the first universally renowned male dancer in Europe,
and brought superb technique to Denmark which he afterward modified in his
own way. We see the result of his teaching in every ballet the Danes dance
and whenever Danes dance. I have known and respected Bournonville's work
ever since I worked at the Royal Danish Theatre in 1929 as guest choreographer.

Stanley Williams of our School of American Ballet is a much respected authority on Bournonville and we thought it would be good for our dancers, and
for our audiences, to come to know well some of Bournonville's finest dances.
Stanley Williams then put together a most entertaining ballet.

The ballet is in five parts, the first the *Ballabile* from the first act of *Napoli*,

1842, Bournonville's masterwork, with music by Paulli. Next, the *Pas de Deux*
from Act I of *Kermesse in Bruges*, 1851, with music by Paulli. The third dance
is a *Pas de Trois* from *La Ventana*, 1854, with music by Lumbye. The two
concluding pieces are the famous *Pas de Deux* from *Flower Festival in Genzano*, 1858, with music by Helsted, and the *Pas de Sept* from *A Folk Tale*,
1854.

As Svend Kragh-Jacobsen observed in our program at the New York City
Ballet, these five pieces made up a well-varied program with which to present
Denmark's grand old master to a new audience.

BOURRÉE FANTASQUE

*Classical ballet in three parts. Music by Emmanuel Chabrier. Choreography
by George Balanchine. Costumes by Karinska. Lighting by Jean Rosenthal.
First presented by the New York City Ballet at the City Center, New York,
December 1, 1949, with Tanaquil LeClercq and Jerome Robbins, Maria
Tallchief and Nicholas Magallanes, Janet Reed and Herbert Bliss as the
principals.*

This dance spectacle in three movements has no story, but each of the three
parts has its own special character and quality of motion to match the buoyant
pieces by Chabrier that make up the ballet's score. Each movement of the
ballet is danced by a different *premier danseur* as principals. The "Joyous
March" that serves as the overture sets a festival pace for the proceedings:
loud, cheerful chords, crashing cymbals, and themes so blatantly vivacious that
our senses are prepared for the high-spirited geniality with which the ballet
both begins and ends.

BOURRÉE FANTASQUE   The curtain rises just before the overture finishes its
final crescendo. Transparent white gauze curtains are draped across a blue
background, and from the ceiling of the stage hang three black chandeliers,
each holding differently colored candles. To the extreme right, standing in a
straight line at right angles to the footlights, are four couples waiting for their
cue. They are dressed in smart, crisp black; the girls fan themselves with small
black fans. The sprightly music begins. The couples join arms and dance
across the stage with jaunty, playful steps. The boys encourage the girls, who
turn rapidly as their movements become more complicated. Four girls enter at
the back; the couples stand back on either side as the newcomers move downstage, dancing in unison a series of bright, high steps. All the dancers are
manifestly enjoying themselves immensely as they execute the precise, sparkling routine, yet they all maintain a firm, dead-pan expression, which makes
their dancing absurdly comic. The boys leave their partners and pull the girls
into their line. Everyone bows low.

A tall girl and a boy much shorter run out onto the stage and dance together briskly. The girl wears flowers high in her hair and fans her face impatiently. They stop suddenly; the music hesitates. The girl turns her back on the boy and looks down at her fan, which clearly amuses her more than he does. The boy tries to make a graceful pose and grabs hold of the ballerina's waist for support. She looks down at him with bored contempt; apparently he will think anything funny. He puts out his leg and looks on incredulously as the ballerina steps across it with little, mincing steps. He smiles at her gratefully; every one of her gestures is marvelous to him. She collapses in his arms and dances frantically. She holds her leg high, and he obligingly supports it under the knee. He stoops down close to the floor to watch her feet closely. The ballerina is determined to exploit his patience at every opportunity and when the boy supports her in attitude, she throws her leg up behind him and kicks him in the back of the head. The boy continues, however, to fancy that she is perfection itself. He moves to sit down, but the ballerina jumps into his lap before he reaches the floor. He tries to engage her flirtatiously, but she will have none of it; he nods his head beseechingly, but she shakes her head insistently. They rise and exit with a flourish.

The eight girls and four boys dance briefly. Like the ballerina's partner, the boys crawl on the floor to admire the girls' dancing feet. Then they move between the two rows of girls and join them in witty steps to the staccato verve of the music.

The ballerina and her partner return and enliven the fun to a high pitch of merriment. The boy holds the ballerina about the waist and squats low behind her as she hops toward the back on one point. Then he joins the other four boys in a dance that becomes intensely brisk. The ballerina fans herself calmly. The girls come forward and rejoin the boys, and the ballerina's partner twirls her about. He catches her in a tight embrace, but she bends her body back, trying to escape. He attempts to put his arms around her neck, but she holds his hands; their arms tangle hopelessly. The two move close to the footlights and forget all classical pretensions as they turn swiftly around and around on one foot, like circus performers. They both stop this exhibition simultaneously and join the group in a final round of merriment that ends abruptly on a note of rampant gaiety.

PRELUDE The gauze curtains are pulled slightly higher over the empty stage. Eight girls enter from the wings and cross the stage fleetingly, softly, devising a fragile, romantic mood to the new sensuous melody. They arrange themselves in two striking poses about their leaders. A lovely girl walks out slowly from the back. She is looking for someone; she approaches like a sleepwalker and notices no one. A boy emerges from the opposite side. He, too, moves as if he were in a dream. The boy and the girl wander in different directions, weaving in and out among the other dancers as if caught in a labyrinth that will never lead them to each other. Each appears to sense the other's presence, but as they pass closely, their hands almost touching, their reverie does not allow them to see and after a pause they continue on their search.

At last the boy discovers the girl. Her back is turned to him. He places his hand on her shoulder; at his touch she poses gracefully. The boy takes his supporting hand away; the girl stands motionless on point for an instant until he has moved in front of her. She places her arms on his shoulders, and the boy assists her as she displays her comeliness in open turns that cause her black dress to flow about her. Their contact is intimate but also remote, warm yet formal; they recognize each other only in the perfection with which they dance together. She falls back in his arms.

The boy turns briefly to support two of the other girls, but returns to the ballerina. She pirouettes rapidly with her arms high over her head; the boy catches her still turning figure and circles with her. He lifts her tenderly. Momentarily, he is separated from the ballerina and the other girls group themselves around him. He kneels and they cover his head with their arms possessively so that he does not see his lover approach him. She moves away listlessly, returns, retires, then moves back toward him determinedly, in a running leap. The boy looks up and catches her falling body tenderly as the other girls back away. He lifts the ballerina high, and they move forward diagonally across the stage, two girls following along closely, their arms stretched up to clasp the ballerina's outstretched hands. The other girls move by in the opposite direction, passing under their arms swiftly and creating an impression of effortless speed. Now the boy moves backward with the ballerina and the group moves forward beneath her. He lifts her down and for an instant he loses her. The sumptuous music nears its fullest statement as he finds her again. He holds her hand, she rises on point and extends her leg slowly but firmly. Her extended point seems to pierce the richness of the melody.

With an elegant flourish, the ballerina bends low before the boy in a formal gesture of gratitude and acceptance. She rises to turn rapidly in attitude; the boy steps forward quickly and catches her about the waist as she turns full circle. The movement is repeated several times, after which the lovers stand close together, her head on his shoulder. They move apart; the girls glide in between them, forming the same intricate pattern that separated them at the beginning. They look about, seeking, wandering in and out; they pass, pause, but do not find. Both walk off as they came, preoccupied with their private dreams. The others dance slowly into the wings.

FÊTE POLONAISE To the tune of a lively fanfare, a girl and a boy run out onto the stage. The boy kneels, takes the girl's hand, and holds her secure as she races around him. They are followed by three couples, who repeat this routine while the orchestra hurries its preface to the principal theme. Two other couples join the group. These two girls place their hands on their hips and look out into the audience with the gay impudence of chorines. A loud

beat is sounded on the drum, and the exhilarating polonaise begins as the two
girls are thrown high by their partners.

The other couples join the dance; the boys kneel around the girls in a circle
and with a whipping motion encourage their cavorting. Directly all the
dancers have caught the vivacity of the music, the ballerina enters to make the
scene more animated still. Her grace and high good humor infect the dancing
with fresh lightness. She seems astonishingly light as her partner swings her
high about him. Finally, he catches her in a breath-taking leap and the two
exit.

There are now eight couples on the stage, who dance together briefly before
the ballerina and her partner return. This time the boy swings the ballerina
about him on one arm; her legs beat together in midair. The girls circle them;
the ballerina is turned rapidly by her partner as the girls dance around them;
then she kneels. She leaves the stage, and the romantic ballerina of the prelude
enters with her group of dancers. Soon all three ballerinas and their partners
are assembled with the entire *corps de ballet*. The *corps de ballet* form con-
centric circles about the romantic ballerina, who is lifted high above them, and
for a few moments the entire scene whirls with movement as each circle of
dancers runs around and around.

All the boys dance a short routine with boundless energy, and the three
ballerinas come to the front of the stage with their partners. Now it is almost
like a competition between them. The ballerinas gather with their different
groups. They take turns leading the groups of eight girls across the stage
diagonally with broad, running jumps. The groups crisscross in midstage as the
music nears a climax of jubilation. Then all the ensemble is reunited for the
height of the festivity. Their ensembles are grouped behind the three ballerinas in a spectacular pose as the music ends and the curtain falls.

LA BOUTIQUE FANTASQUE (The Fantastic Toyshop)

*Ballet in one act. Music by Gioacchino Rossini, arranged and orchestrated
by Ottorino Respighi. Choreography by Leonide Massine. Scenery and costumes by André Derain. First presented by Diaghilev's Ballets Russes at
the Alhambra Theatre, London, June 5, 1919, with Enrico Cecchetti as
the Shopkeeper, Lydia Lopokova and Leonide Massine as the Cancan Dancers, and a cast that included Lydia Sokolova, Leon Woicikowski, Stanislas
Idzikowski, Vera Nemtchinova, Lubov Tchernicheva, and Serge Grigoriev.
First presented in the United States by the Ballet Russe de Monte Carlo at
the Majestic Theatre, New York, March 20, 1935, with a cast that included
Alexandra Danilova and Leonide Massine (Cancan Dancers), Eugenia Del-
arova, Tamara Grigorieva, Nina Verachinina, Yurek Shabelevsky, Roland
Guérard, David Lichine, and Serge Grigoriev.*

Like *Coppélia, La Boutique Fantasque* is based on the charm of the mechanical doll. Here, in a great fantastic toyshop in southern France, dolls from all over the world entertain customers from all over the world, who have come to see the detailed and charming workmanship of a master dollmaker. The time is the 1860s.

At the rise of the curtain, the sunny shop is empty. It has been closed for lunch. The shopkeeper and his helper return and open the doors for business. While they are busy preparing for their work, a dirty little boy comes in and attempts to steal gold lace from one of the shopkeeper's prize dolls. The thief is apprehended and, fleeing, bumps into two prospective customers, an English old maid and her companion.

The old maids want to see the best dolls and when the shopkeeper has shown them the mechanical peasant dolls on display, they ask to see more. New customers, an American family with two children, charge in. The family know the English ladies and after all the customers have exchanged greetings, the American turns to the shopkeeper and asks to see his dolls.

The shopkeeper obsequiously consents, and two tarantella dancers are wheeled in. When the customers have examined them, the two dolls, an Italian girl and her sweetheart, break into an animated tarantella to the lively accompaniment of rattling tambourines. Then, as if their mechanism had run down, the dancers collapse.

Next there is a mazurka, danced by dolls representing the Queen of Clubs, the Queen of Hearts, the King of Diamonds, and the King of Spades.

A Russian couple enter with their four children. The English ladies resent the intrusion of these foreigners and take their leave.

The next set of dolls displayed by the shopkeeper represent a snob and a melon hawker, a combination of the rich and the poor. The snob bustles about busily while the melon hawker slices a melon and presents it to him. Then the melon hawker shines the shoes of the snob, who trips over the hawker, only to rise again in a mechanical miracle.

The customers are now convinced that they are seeing a great and marvelous entertainment. Their mutual enthusiasm makes them all friendly and they watch with delight as more dolls perform.

Five Cossack dolls led by a chief perform a rapid dance next. Then the chief Cossack is joined by a Cossack girl doll, who kisses him while the soldiers snap to attention. The porters of the fantastic toyshop drill the Cossacks off.

Now two dancing poodles display their skill by walking on their hind legs. The female dog tries to attract the male dog by her cavortings and the male dog, in his enthusiasm for her dancing, rushes around and around her. The American couple are shocked at this amorous display and blindfold their children.

The shopkeeper now informs his prospective customers that they are about to see the most ingenious dolls of all: the cancan dancers. The couple who are wheeled in dance with such gusto that all the spectators are bound to agree.

As the girl doll abandons herself in the cancan, her partner is so delighted that he performs marvelous gravity-defying tricks.

Now both families who have been watching the dolls want to buy the can-can dancers. The American children like the male doll best, the Russians the girl. Their fathers talk to the shopkeeper, agree to pay his price, and leave, saying that they will call for the dolls in the morning.

Night has fallen. The shopkeeper and his assistants lock up and leave.

Now that they are alone, all the dolls in the shop emerge from their boxes and become more animated than ever. They are very happy to be dancing so freely, but they are also sad. The cancan dancers are to be separated tomor-row. The two lovers dance together for what seems to be the last time, and the other dolls dance about them, celebrating their love. At the end of the revels there is a general cakewalk, danced by all the dolls.

When morning comes and the shop is reopened, all appears to be as it was the night before. But when the American and Russian families call to pick up the dolls they have engaged to buy, something is amiss: the cancan dancers have disappeared from their boxes! The children howl, the fathers berate the shopkeeper, and the mothers rage. The shopkeeper and his assistants are beaten, and the whole toyshop is attacked by the disappointed customers.

Just when it seems likely that the irate foreigners will destroy the shop com-pletely, the toy dolls come to the rescue. The poodles attack the Russian mother; her husband and children are set upon by the card toys; and the Americans are routed by kicking ballet-dancer dolls. Finally the Cossacks drive the customers from the shop.

Unbelieving, the Americans and Russians stand outside and look back through the window. They see all the dolls in the shop dancing together a bril-liant ensemble, a final happy dance. The shopkeeper and the cancan dancers shake hands. All the dolls rejoice that the two lovers are still together.

BRAHMS QUINTET

Music by Johannes Brahms. Choreography by Dennis Nahat. Costumes by Willa Kim. Lighting by Nananne Porcher. First presented by American Bal-let Theatre at the Brooklyn Academy of Music, New York, December 1969, with Cynthia Gregory, Ivan Nagy, Mimi Paul, Gayle Young, Naomi Sorkin, Ian Horvath, Eleanor D'Antuono, and Terry Orr as principals.

This dance ballet to a masterpiece by Brahms uses the score for its narrative. The music critic Donald F. Tovey referred to the Brahms *Quintet in G Major, Op. 111,* as "an immensely powerful outburst of high spirits. . . . The first movement seems unlimited in its capacity for expansion. The adagio . . . is one of Brahms's tragic utterances. Its tempo is slower than that of any other piece of classical music since Beethoven's C Minor Concerto." Tovey found the third movement to be an "exquisite plaintive little scherzo and trio" and the finale "vigorous. . . . At the end its coda breaks away into a completely new dance tune, the phrases of which reel down in bacchanalian irregularity to explain themselves with impudent assurance as connected with the main theme by ties as intimate as a borrowed visiting card." (From *Cobbet's Cyclopedic Survey of Chamber Music*, 1963.)

Reviewing the ballet for the Washington *Post*, the critic Jean Battey Lewis said that "Nahat's *Brahms Quintet* is one of those flowing, floating dance works so appealing to us these days. It has a lovely, curving wind-swept quality and an abstraction that still celebrates the affection between the dancers."

BRAHMS-SCHOENBERG QUARTET

Music by Johannes Brahms, orchestrated by Arnold Schoenberg. Choreography by George Balanchine. Scenery by Peter Harvey. Costumes by Karinska. First presented by the New York City Ballet at the New York State Theatre April 19, 1966, with Melissa Hayden and André Prokovsky, Patricia McBride and Conrad Ludlow, Allegra Kent and Edward Villella, and Suzanne Farrell and Jacques d'Amboise in leading roles.

In talking about music that is good for dancing I have often said that most string quartets are not suitable—they are too long, they are full of repeats, and of course they are meant for smaller audiences. This quartet of Brahms, the *Piano Quartet in G minor, Opus 25*, I have always liked a great deal but it never occurred to me to use it for a ballet until Robert Craft told me about Schoenberg's orchestration.

This undertaking was of course most unusual for Schoenberg. But in a letter to Dr. Alfred Frankenstein, Schoenberg gave his reasons: "1. I love the piece. 2. It is seldom played. 3. It is always very badly played, as the better the pianist, the louder he plays and one hears nothing of the strings. I wanted for once to hear everything and this I have achieved."

I liked hearing everything too, and wanted to see the piece danced. The result is a dance ballet, with only a musical narrative. The movements are marked *Allegro, Allegro ma non troppo, Andante*, and *Rondo alla Zingarese: Presto*.

BROUILLARDS

Music by Claude Debussy. Choreography by John Cranko. First presented by the Württemberg State Ballet at the Opera House, Stuttgart, March 8, 1970. First presented in the United States by the same ensemble (the Stuttgart Ballet) at the Metropolitan Opera House, New York, April 30, 1971.

Nine piano preludes by Claude Debussy are the inspiration for *Brouillards* ("Mist"). The choreographer, John Cranko, said: "Mist, snow, heather and sails are the transient pictures in Debussy's music: the mist dissolves, the snow melts away, the heather fades, and the sails grow slack—leaving behind remembrance and regret only because of their beauty. Every day passes away— like all human relations." While thus a ballet without a narrative, *Brouillards* may be said to have a mood plot set to music.

The piano begins and the curtain rises on a dark scene where we gradually discern a chain of dancers in white. They swirl and gather in the center, undulate in the mist, separate, return and cluster. A girl and three boys, to the music of *La Puerta del Vino* ("The Gate of Wine"), perform a bright dance in which, first riding on the back of one, then dancing an adagio with another, and finally turning to respond to the third, the girl shows that she likes all three. The boys leave her, sulking, at the end.

To *Voiles* ("Sails"), a girl and boy dance, responding to the music with daring lifts, slides, and turns, he going in one direction with the wind, as it were, she in another. Next, a *Cakewalk*, a comic turn to quick, witty music for three boys. *Bruyères* ("Heather"), which follows, is a dance for a boy who is enamored of a sleeping beauty who lies nearby on a bench. He kneels at her feet, kisses her, dances for her, but she does not respond. When, finally, he shakes her in exasperation, she rises and coolly walks away.

Two girls dance to the music of *The Fairies Are Exquisite Dancers* and make of it a joyful competition of held poses and leaps. To *Dead Leaves* there is another *pas de deux*, a passionate adagio. *Homage to S. Pickwick, Esq.* is a tribute to John Bull, armed with bowler hat and umbrella, by six boys who kid him and rag him until he collapses. They cover him up, the bowler on the umbrella remaining as a kind of gravestone.

Footsteps in the Snow is for a girl and two boys, both of whom seem to follow in pursuit of the girl, and the *Finale*, again, is an ensemble piece, the group of dancers filling the surface of the stage with swirling mist.

BUGAKU

> *Music by Toshiro Mayuzumi. Choreography by George Balanchine. Scenery and lighting by David Hays. Costumes by Karinska. First presented by the New York City Ballet at the City Center, New York, March 30, 1963, with Allegra Kent and Edward Villella in the leading roles.*

Over the years the New York City Ballet has had a happy association with Japan. The company danced there in 1958, and in 1959 the musicians and dancers maintained by the Imperial Household known as *Gagaku* came to the United States and appeared with great success on the regular programs of the New York City Ballet. The *Gagaku* is the oldest dance company in the world,

with an uninterrupted tradition of repertory and performance extending almost
a hundred years. Having heard the *Gagaku* and seen their fine dancers with so
much pleasure, I asked the gifted young Japanese composer Toshiro Mayuzumi to write the music for a ballet. The work was commissioned by Mrs. Norman LaSalle. Our idea was that the piece would be in the style of Japanese
court music (*Bugaku*), but for Western orchestration.

Mayuzumi's score I liked very much when we received it. Just as the composer had transposed the Japanese court music into a Western vocabulary, I
attempted in the dances to transpose the classic Western academic ballet into
a style suggested by the music.

The setting is a severely simple arena-like stage typical of formal Japanese
presentations. The costumes are a free fantasy on traditional Japanese court
dress. The dance is in three main parts. At the beginning, before any dancers
appear, the ear takes in the strange sounds of the orchestral introduction. Five
girls enter and dance with grave formality, following the lead of a girl in a
rose-petal skirt. They are joined by five boys, who file on to the vigorous sound
of drums. Later, these couples return in ceremonial robes to escort the boy and
girl who have led them. The diaphanous ceremonial robes of the girl flow
behind her as the boy lifts her in a dance of praise. But love here is as ritualistic as the setting. The attendants remove the ceremonial robes of the couple.
They continue their dance, now unencumbered by the costumes. Their dance
is a *pas de deux* of discovery. After the adagio, the girl dances joyously, then
the boy, but then the music slows down. The attendants return to dress them
again in their robes and there is a stately procession at the end of which all
kneel.

THE CAGE

*Ballet in one act. Music by Igor Stravinsky (Concerto Grosso in D for
Strings). Choreography by Jerome Robbins. Costumes by Ruth Sobotka.
Lighting by Jean Rosenthal. First presented by the New York City Ballet
at the City Center, New York, June 10, 1951, with Nora Kaye as the Novice,
Yvonne Mounsey as the Queen, and Nicholas Magallanes and Michael
Maule as the Intruders.*

This ballet is a dramatic demonstration of a phenomenon common to insect
and animal life and to Western mythology too: the phenomenon of the female
considering the male as prey. The mantis devours her partner after mating; the
spider kills the male unless he attacks first; and the Amazons, in Greek mythology, were a cult of warlike females who did not associate with men, except for
procreation. The Amazons despised their male children and maimed or destroyed them. Woman was sufficient; Man was accidental. *The Cage* shows us
such a tribe of women.

Before the ballet begins, the auditorium is completely dark. The footlights come up before the curtain, then go out; the lights in the orchestra are extinguished. There is no music. The curtain rises. The light is obscure and misty, but we see hanging over the stage a tangle of multicolored strands, like the web of some huge spider. Mysteriously, as if it were a living thing, the web rises, stretches, and hangs over the floor. On the left stand a group of female figures arranged in a tight tableau; they are clustered together like bees in a hive.

The music begins with three notes sounded sharply on the strings. The women stir. In the center of the group sits the queen of the tribe. The lights come up gradually. A still, shrouded creature is drawn out from between the queen's legs; the novice has been born. The queen strips the confining membrane from the novice's body. The new member of the tribe crouches slightly. Her body is marked with endless, tangled viscera. Her face is still covered. She is motionless. The queen stands behind her, extending her arms grotesquely, seeming to enclose the novice with her long talons.

The orchestra begins a vibrant march. The twelve members of the tribe turn their backs, rise on point, and commence a grotesque ceremonial dance. As their bodies turn, we see that their backs are insectlike: strands reach out from their black spines to cover their backs, and they seem to resemble scuttling beetles. The queen leaves the novice and dances among the tribe. The women circle her and bow low obediently as she dances. The novice remains inert.

Now two of the women go to the novice and drag her to the center, before the queen. The queen tears off the membrane covering her face. The novice's hands reach up to protect her eyes from the sudden light. Her face is a mask; her hair, dark and wet, clings to her head. The queen is well pleased at her ugliness. The birth rite is over; the queen and her creatures leave to watch the novice from the surrounding darkness. Just as she departs, the queen touches the novice's dark head in blessing.

The melody changes; the music slows in tempo. The novice's untrained limbs do not yet know how to move and she squats alone. She tests her arms and legs, pushes her body up on them, rises on point. Her gestures are sudden and sharp, her body angularly contorted. Her fingers are clawing and knifelike blades cutting at the air tentatively; her arms are sinuous, serpentine. She walks with knees open and bent, arms ready to enlace her prey.

The music breaks into a loud, rapidly rhythmic burst of sound. A man rushes in and seizes the novice by the waist. She twists away in revulsion. The intruder attempts to pull her close to him and falls to the ground. The novice falls upon him, and they roll over together. The exhausted intruder lies quiet as the novice rises and steps upon his chest with the sharp point of her foot. Now she straddles his body, grabs his head between her legs, clenches her fists, tightens and twists her body, and cracks his neck with her knees. He is dead.

The music quietens. The novice kicks the body over on its face. As the orchestra resumes the opening march, she dances alone, her knees rising high, driving her feet hard against the ground. Her head is thrown back and her mouth hangs open in a shriek of triumph.

The queen leads the tribe back to the novice. The hideous women stalk into the light, surround the novice, and congratulate her. She has met the test, her instinct has obeyed the law of the tribe: she has killed her first male. The novice kicks at his body contemptuously, and he is dragged off.

The queen embraces the novice. Other women in the tribe pair off and rest together. The women are content with their own society and relax without fear of intrusion. Then the music sounds a warning. The couples separate. The light dims. The queen signals the others to hasten away. The novice, suddenly afraid, is running off after them as her swift body is caught up in the arms of a dark, handsome intruder. Her legs try to kick her body free as he holds her, but she cannot loosen his grasp. The warning in the music ceases; the melody flows yieldingly. The novice is now unsure. Gradually she succumbs to the superior strength of the intruder and dances with him a romantic love duet. He holds her on his knee, and she sharpens her claws together, not for battle now, but for love. Their bodies separate and their fingers approach and entwine like bristling antennae. She tries to make herself graceful as she dances and falls back into the intruder's arms. He catches her body between his legs; her face turns up toward his, and their arms embrace in a cocoon. The novice's feet beat at the floor as the intruder becomes her lover.

The lights go down for a moment. The music whirrs ominously. The frightened intruder moves and the woman falls to the ground. The two lovers cower together, trying to conceal each other in the darkness, as the queen and the tribe enter. Then, as the intruder sees the women who would claim the novice, he revolts and pushes the woman, now hideous to him, into the arms of her Amazon queen.

This is what the tribe have waited for. The queen directs her creatures to attack the intruder as the novice is held secure. The women climb upon the intruder like ants on a stick of candy. He is released briefly and rolls helpless on the ground. The novice's native instinct begins to return. She falls upon him, straddles him, and slides her body over the passive male. She squats guiltily as the women seize him and carry him aloft. The queen orders her fellow creatures to carry the novice on their shoulders and hold her poised above him. The novice's claws are straight and sharp for the kill. She aims carefully and deliberately and slashes.

The body of the intruder lies again on the ground. The hungry women crawl over him, devouring his limbs. The novice strangles him between her knees. His body curls for a moment, then straightens. He is dead. His body is rolled across the stage. The victorious women leap over it as they dance triumphantly.

The novice cleans her talons. The queen joins her to accept her as a true member of the tribe. The two grotesque figures whirl together, then stand motionless, their deformed bodies dominating the dark cage. The music stops. The great spidery web loosens and falls about them to the ground.

NOTES When *The Cage* was presented during the New York City Ballet's Stravinsky Festival in June 1972, the critic Sam Norkin wrote in the *Daily News:* "A hit since its premiere 21 years ago, this ballet is a 16-minute spellbinder . . . The driving music that accompanies the ballet was danced sensationally by Melissa Hayden as the novice. Here was a great ballerina in full mastery of her role. Gloria Govrin and Nicholas Magallanes were convincing in their roles as the queen and intruder respectively."

CAKEWALK

Ballet in three parts. Music adapted and orchestrated by Hershy Kay after music by Louis Moreau Gottschalk. Choreography by Ruthanna Boris. Scenery and costume by Robert Drew. Lighting by Jean Rosenthal. First presented by the New York City Ballet at the City Center, New York, June 12, 1951, with a cast headed by Janet Reed, Patricia Wilde, Yvonne Mounsey, Herbert Bliss, Frank Hobi, Tanaquil LeClercq, and Beatrice Tompkins.

Cakewalk is an American ballet based on the minstrel shows. The great era of the minstrel show began to end toward the turn of the century, but this ballet reminds us of why this form of entertainment, native to America, was once so universally popular: like the original, it has humor, sentiment, magic, and liveliness. *Cakewalk*, being a ballet, doesn't have the two sets of bones, the two banjos, the two tambourines, and the singers that every real minstrel show used to have. These musical elements are taken care of by the orchestra, which plays in special arrangements a group of pieces and songs by Louis Moreau Gottschalk, the American composer and pianist whose music was so popular among original minstrel show artists: such works as "Bamboula," "Maiden's Blush," and "Won't You Buy My Pretty Flowers?" On stage, the dancers imitate the conventional minstrel show turns in dance terms that combine folk dancing with an enlivened classical technique. Like all proper minstrel shows, *Cakewalk* is divided into three parts.

PART ONE The orchestra strikes up a loud, ebullient overture. The curtain rises. At extreme left and right are entrance doors on to the stage. In the back hangs a drop curtain that shows a huge Mississippi side-wheeler plying up the stream. Already, before the dancers appear, we have a vivid sense of the atmosphere in which the original minstrel show flourished.

One by one, the performers make their entrance to begin the "Grand Introductory Walkaround." They strut across the stage rapidly, led by the interlocutor, giving us a hint of the novelties to come. Finally, when all have disappeared in the door at the left, the drop curtain rises and we see the stage set for the minstrel show. In the back stands a long platform with ramps leading forward down to the stage. Gold chairs and torches are lined up on stage and platform. The "Grand Introductory March" reaches a climax of happy anticipation, and the artists—the center performers, the semicircle, the auxiliary ladies and gentlemen, and the two end men—move to their seats. A tambourine claps for order as all sit down at the interlocutor's signal.

The interlocutor leads forward a dainty girl, whose old-fashioned curls and somber countenance presage a dance of great seriousness. The orchestra sounds the first notes of a "Pathetic Ballad" in slow waltz time; the girl moves forward on point and renders a dance of absurd tragedy. She is all alone; the four boys who dance with their partners in a semicircle around her will not pay any attention to her. She is doomed to be a perpetual wallflower. Yet all the time the girl maintains in her steps and gestures an indifference to ordinary mortals that exposes her addiction to pathos. She loves to be sad, and sad in the grand manner. She clasps her hands and raises them in supplication; she kneels, begging for help in her distress; she turns beseechingly to the happy couples for succor. No one will help her! The girl raises a pointed hand to her temples and fires. The saccharine music expires, and the unfortunate creature is free to be happy again. She takes her seat, rises disconsolately to the audience applause, and sits down again, her eyes downcast.

The interlocutor, his black cane in hand, comes forward and performs "Sleight of Feet," a rhythmic jumping specialty that makes him a magician in movement. He tries to attract our attention to his hands, his coattails, and his cane as his feet perform quick marvels. The end men run forward with a chair, and he falls back, exhausted by triumph.

The interlocutor is followed by the two end men, one short, the other tall, who rise from their places at each end of the line and dance "Perpendicular Points." This number displays their adroit sharpness in dancing almost continually on their toes to curtly paced music that would trip them up if it could. Their long swallow-tailed coats bounce in the air as their points hit every beat of the music. As their number ends, they rush over to the left and end up sitting in the lap of the surprised interlocutor.

The lights go down. A bright spotlight catches a girl in a shining red dress who rushes out and dances a vigorous "Freebee" to a fresh, rousing theme. All the performers clap their hands in rhythm to the music; the girl dances faster; the whole troupe catches the contagious liveliness of her movement and the members come forward to join her. They parade across the platform as the girl in red is lifted high between two boys and carried around the stage. But the instant her feet touch the floor, she is on fire again with movement and leads all in a jumping, turning ensemble that increases in speed and dizziness. All fall flat on the floor, exhausted.

PART TWO   The dancers rise and carry out the chairs and benches. The drop curtain falls, and some of the performers come forward and sit to watch the show themselves. The stage is now empty and dark. The music warns of mysterious events. Three capes—red, green, and purple—seem to move across the stage unsupported, sweeping the air before them. Then the capes are dropped and we see that they are worn by Louis, the Illusionist, and his two assistants, Moreau and Lessau—the interlocutor and the two end men in disguise.

Louis and his two assistants make magic signs, gather close in a line, their capes before them. The drop curtain rises. The three cloaked figures slide off into the wings, miraculously leaving before us, in the center of the stage, the goddess Venus, gamboling on the green with three Graces. When they have danced their bit, the magician and his helpers return. They enclose the four mythical figures in their capes and they disappear.

Next Louis brings forth a wild pony, transmigrated from its native hills. The wild pony, danced by the leader of the frenzied "Freebee," cavorts and bucks about her unnatural surroundings with stubborn, bold abandon. The magician tries to tame her, pulling the reins taut, but the pony's mane switches the trainer's face and he at last releases her.

Tinkling music is heard. Perched on a seat hung with flowers, Hortense, Queen of the Swamp Lilies, swings into view and off again. Her garlanded swing brings her back, however, and she is lifted down to earth by Harolde, the young poet, who joins her in a *pas de deux*. To the music of a solo violin and the harp, the idealized lovers dance with considered, prolonged languor, never hurrying, never reaching their goal.

PART THREE   The lights come up. The magician has materialized his last illusion and he and his assistants leave the scene stealthily, their cloaks wrapped about them. The orchestra begins a catchy march, and all the participants parade the stage in a spirited, strutting, gala cakewalk that moves rapidly to a boisterous, rollicking conclusion. All the dancers wave responsive greetings to the audience as the curtain falls.

CAPRICCIO ESPAÑOL

Ballet in one act. Music by Nikolai Rimsky-Korsakov. Choreography by Leonide Massine, with the collaboration of Argentinita. Book by Leonide Massine. Scenery and costumes by Mariano Andreù. First presented by the Ballet Russe de Monte Carlo at the Théâtre de Monte Carlo, May 4, 1939, with a cast that included Argentinita, Alexandra Danilova, Michel Panaieff, and Leonide Massine. First presented in the United States by the Ballet Russe de Monte Carlo at the Metropolitan Opera House, New York, October 27, 1939, with Mia Slavenska, Alexandra Danilova, André Eglevsky, and Leonide Massine in the leading roles.

Capriccio Español is a ballet about Spain, rather than a Spanish ballet. Just as Spanish dance themes provided Rimsky-Korsakov with melodies for a bright and colorful orchestration, the choreography here uses Spanish dance steps to create a romantic and colorful representation that some of us might imagine to be Spain. The ballet, therefore, has no particular story to tell; instead, it tries through a series of dances to create an atmosphere, a feeling that something real has been touched.

The ballet begins with a dance called the alborada, a morning serenade. We find ourselves in the public square of a small Spanish town whose inhabitants are preparing for a festival. The music is almost uncontrolled in its loud, blaring enthusiasm. Boys of the village dance with wild abandon to this music. Soon they are joined by a group of girls. But instead of choosing the boys for their partners, the girls turn to the elders of the village and dance with them playfully and charmingly. The girls are aware that only these older men, who have seen so many beautiful women in their lives, have a real and knowing appreciation of their loveliness, and the older men, in turn, are charmed by the fact that the girls know this. The music is quieter, occasionally bursting into crescendos, as it varies the more gentle secondary theme.

The turbulent first movement is now repeated, and the boys again take up their dance. There is a roll on the drum, which the brasses build into a fanfare, and a stunning gypsy comes into the square. This is the fortuneteller. She begins to dance, enchanting all the village with her fiery, sinuous movements. A gypsylike melody inserts itself between solos for various instruments as the fortuneteller continues to hold everyone's attention. She is joined by a partner and in the rapid stampings, quick whirls, and persistent rhythms of their dance, the bodies seem to make the whole square vibrate. The strings are plucked like guitars, and the couple bring their duet to a close with a fandango.

Another couple come forward and, in the midst of the excited crowd, now overflowing with the spirit of the festival, this peasant boy and girl lead all the natives in a tempestuous ensemble. The fortuneteller returns with her partner to join the peasant couple as the festival reaches a peak of excitement. All the people have now forgotten that they are moving in a dance, for their dancing derives from a holiday impulse that makes everything but dashing and turning movement impossible. Inspired by the dazzling display of the two lead couples, the villagers become intoxicated with joy at their own brilliant facility and dance with their leaders a final, uproarious ensemble as the opening theme of the ballet triumphantly returns.

CAPRICHOS

Ballet in four episodes. Choreography by Herbert Ross. Music by Béla Bartók. Costumes by Helene Pons. First presented by the Choreographers'

Workshop at the Hunter Playhouse, New York, January 29, 1950. Presented by Ballet Theatre at the Center Theatre, New York, April 26, 1950, with Charlyne Baker, Jenny Workman, Nana Gollner, John Kriza, Ruth Ann Koesun, and Mary Burr as the principals.

This ballet derives its inspiration from the comments the Spanish artist Goya made on a series of his etchings. The choreographer has taken four of these comments and visualized opinion. The ballet is performed to Béla Bartók's *Contrasts for Piano, Clarinet, and Violin*. A blue backdrop is the only scenery.

There are two girls on stage as the curtain rises. They are dressed in brief white nightgowns. They wear black crucifixes about their necks and long black gloves. Goya's comment is: "These good girls have seats enough and nothing to do with them better than carry them on their heads." The girls are not good at all. Their principal pleasure consists in pulling their dresses up to their necks as often as possible. They carry two stools and try to amuse themselves by playing with them as they cavort about the stage. Finally the girls realize that they are boring themselves to death. One stands holding a stool on her head; the other falls to the ground in an idiotic posture.

"No one ever escapes who wants to be caught" is Goya's second comment. The two girls remain on stage to watch. One fans her dress back and forth to cool her body; the other relaxes with her head in her hand. A woman in black enters, her head concealed by a blue shawl. She is followed by two men in cloaks. The woman moves over to the two girls, who observe her with preoccupied, gum-chewing expressions. The woman begins to dance. The men close in. She pretends to detest them and to want to be alone. The men are delighted by the pretense at resistance and allow her to fascinate them. They move in and caress her boldly, and the three dance together, the woman clapping her hands with simulated Spanish pleasure. The two men lift her up to their shoulders, then each holds her and swings her body around and around. As one of the men embraces her, the other picks up her feet. They lay the woman on the ground. Now something has happened that the two girls can understand; they move over to the woman. The men walk away. The girls frolic about the stage. The woman rises and disappears, her blue shawl whirling with her movement.

The girls are dejected again. A young widower enters. He mourns his dead wife and holds his hand before his eyes as he sees the lascivious girls. He moves over toward them, his face determined to be sad. Then he goes to the back of the stage and stands close to the wings. He holds out his arms in supplication. Suddenly, as if he were holding out his arms to catch a potato sack, his dead wife falls into his arms. Her body is limp, absolutely lifeless. The man kneels. He attempts to bring his love to life, but her loose body resists his efforts. If he does not hold her, the girl falls over on her face. The young man gets a little annoyed and tries to dance with his rag doll of a wife. He is forced to push her legs ahead of him. Now he is embarrassed. He shows the girls that his wife really is dead. There is no use pretending. Goya's comment is: "If he were more gallant and less of a bore, she would come to life again." He carries his wife off.

The color of the backdrop changes to a bright green. The two girls rise from their siesta as four hooded figures enter slowly, carrying long brooms of straw. The girls are suddenly respectful in the presence of these mysterious, religious men. Two of the men carry a plank; a woman sits upon it, resigned to her fate. ". . . They are determined to kill this saintly woman. After judgment has been pronounced against her, she is dragged through the streets in triumph. She has indeed deserved a triumph, but if they do it to shame her, they are wasting their time. No one can make her ashamed who has nothing to be ashamed of . . ."

The triumphal procession is over. The men stand the plank upright and fix its base in the ground. The girls stand on their stools at the back to see better. The saintly woman is tied to the plank. Red light appears at her feet, and from the movement of her toes it is apparent that she is uncomfortable. She tries to escape the licking flames by lifting one tortured foot, then another away from the fire. One by one, the four men toss their brooms of straw at her feet. The woman trembles all over. The light on the backdrop becomes brilliantly red. With a hideous gesture, the woman at the stake claws at her flesh, seeming to pull it up over her face like a mask. One of the men stands behind the stake and extends his arms straight out, sanctifying the project. The woman's body falls forward. Her bonds still hold her to the stake. Everyone is still but the two girls, who move about slowly. One finally rests on her stool and amuses herself alone. The other girl, on the right, imitates crudely the sufferings of the saintly woman. The curtain falls. A voice says, *"El sueño de la razón produce monstruos"* ("The dream of reason produces monsters").

CAPRIOL SUITE

Ballet in one act. Music by Peter Warlock. Choreography by Frederick Ashton. Scenery and costumes by William Chappell. First presented by the Marie Rambert Dancers at the Lyric Theatre, Hammersmith, London, February 25, 1930. First presented in the United States by the Sadler's Wells Theatre Ballet at the War Memorial Opera House, San Francisco, California, December 5, 1951, with a cast that included Patricia Miller, Donald Britton, and David Poole.

This entertainment ballet is a twentieth-century version of dances that were popular four hundred years ago. In 1588, the Frenchman Thoinot Arbeau set down in writing a record of sixteenth-century dances with the music that accompanied them. This book, called *Orchesographie* (writing dancing), appeared seven years after the presentation of the first modern ballet, the first ballet to unify in one entertaining spectacle the theatrical elements that had amused the courts of Europe for many centuries.

Arbeau's book is a dialogue, in the classical manner. He and a novice at the dance, a young man named Capriol, talk about dancing—how it came to be so popular among mankind, the different kinds of contemporary dancing, and the proper music to accompany the different forms. Peter Warlock, the English composer, arranged a number of the tunes set forth by Arbeau in an orchestral suite, and Frederick Ashton, in turn, devised the appropriate sixteenth-century dances as described by Arbeau to young Capriol.

The curtain rises and the orchestra begins a sprightly tune. The setting is simple and formal: a low stone railing topped with urns curves about the back of the stage. The back cloth is light green. Two couples dressed in the six-teenth-century French fashion perform a basse danse, a light but dignified measure. When they finish, the lights dim and two boys lead on a girl dressed in a long skirt. The orchestra plays a stately pavane, and the girl begins to dance between her escorts. Soon she pauses and sits on the knee of one of the boys. He presents a red rose to her. She sweetly refuses to accept it and when the other boy offers her a scroll, upon which he has written a poem to her, she will have none of him. She rises, and the boys stand on each side of her con-templating the gifts she has rejected.

The lights brighten, and to gay, bouncing music a girl and a boy dance a tordion, a court dance that is nevertheless playful and uninhibited in enthusi-asm. The dancers who performed the pavane watch the dancing couple. An-other girl enters. When the tordion finishes, those two couples come forward. The dancing, which has mostly been confined to the floor, now rises as the boys perform *pieds en l'air* to entertain the girls. When the dance is over, the boys kneel and the girls fall back over their shoulders. They leave the stage.

The music becomes bright and brisk. Four boys jump out onto the stage and dance a mattachins, a vigorous sword dance. Three of the boys lift the victor high over their heads as this dance ends. Gradually all the dancers return and perform different versions of the branle, a sixteenth-century court dance so popular that there were different versions for different age groups. The music increases in gaiety. The more ebullient dancers enclose in a moving circle the more stately couples, and the curtain falls.

CARACOLE (*see* DIVERTIMENTO NO. 15)

CARD GAME (Jeu de Cartes)

> *Ballet in three deals. Music by Igor Stravinsky. Choreography by George Balanchine. Book by Igor Stravinsky, with the collaboration of M. Malaieff.*

Scenery and costumes by Irene Sharaff. First presented by the American Ballet at the Metropolitan Opera House, New York, April 27, 1937.

The characters in this ballet represent the cards in poker hands. There are twenty-six cards for the whole ballet, representing portions of the four suits, plus the joker. Fifteen of these cards—one always the joker—are dealt out to make up three separate hands of poker for each of the three scenes in the ballet. The ballet is prefaced by this translation from a poem by La Fontaine:

One should ever struggle against wrongdoers.
Peace, I grant, is perfect in its way,
But what purpose does it serve
With enemies who do not keep faith?

FIRST DEAL The orchestra plays a sonorous and playful march. The curtain rises on an empty stage. The scene is enclosed in a green felt façade. A great crystal candelabra stands at the left, representing one corner of a card table. The green tabletop stretches back up against the backdrop, where another candelabra is suspended at the opposite corner of the table; the stage thus becomes the table itself.

Fifteen dancers trip out from the right and form in a line straight across the stage. All hold large yellow-striped cards before them, concealing their identity. The joker is among them. Easily identified by his yellow costume striped with bright orange and his silly fool's cap, he steps out of line and runs about, trying to find the best hand. The cards turn and move close together in a shuffling movement. Then the hands are dealt out by an invisible player. The first five cards on the left jump out of line over to the left; the remaining cards form hands at the center and on the right. All the characters still hold the cards before them, but the joker can be distinguished in the hand on the left.

The hand on the right throw the placards over their heads to reveal themselves as the Ace and Queen of Hearts, the Queen of Clubs, the Jack of Spades, and the Jack of Diamonds—a two-pair hand. All the cards are easily identifiable in their resplendent costumes. The Ace of Hearts, his head covered like some medieval armored knight, flourishes his powerless sword in the air, and the smiling Queen of Hearts is surrounded by her dancing partners. The cards fall back in line and bow to the hand at the left.

The second hand turns out to be two kings and two eights—with the joker, a full house. The four cards and the joker step out proudly, the joker flagrantly boasting about the two kings. Now the members of the back hand throw off their placards. The joker holds his nose in contempt as he sees a pair of sevens, but he is stunned along with everyone else as they see three aces with the two sevens—another full house, which beats the joker's hand unaided! The joker comes forward, laughing hilariously to music that accompanies his dance. He grips his sides and bends over as he laughs. His loose, disjointed figure cavorts about the stage in short, jerky steps, running to the left, then to the right. He pirouettes like a top and circles the stage in wide, distorted leaps, turns in the air, slaps the table with his hands, and exits. The three hands spread out and close. All the cards choose partners and slowly dance off. The last couples to leave the stage are the two disconsolate kings with their two eights hanging limply on their arms.

SECOND DEAL   The introductory march to the ballet heralds the second scene. A new line of cards run out from the left, holding up before them large blue-striped placards. They form in a line down the center of the table, shuffle, and form three hands as before. From the hand at the left two jacks step out and dance. They bow and scrape before the three kings in their hand, carrying their trains and saluting them endlessly to a comic martial tune. They fall back into line and bow ceremoniously to the right after they have danced a courtly measure.

The Queen of Hearts steps out of the second hand, bounces in royal attitude, and dances a sprightly variation to a vivacious tune while throwing kisses gaily to everyone. She resumes her place, and the Queen of Clubs emerges and dances alone. She spins rapidly with her arms extended and as the whirring tune finishes, she stands with her hands on her hips while the Queen of Diamonds performs a difficult series of steps to a fresh melody. The Queen of Spades follows her, and then all four queens stand and watch the Jack of Hearts, their one remaining card, perform his variation. He bows to the queens; they all dance together and resume their places. They gesture toward the hand arranged in the center. Four aces and the ubiquitous joker come forward, the joker walking arrogantly, congratulating himself on the good luck he brings. But his hand has won the deal on its own merit, without his help.

The joker dances with the four queens as all the other cards leave the stage. He pulls them around in a line as he kisses the hand of the Queen of Hearts, then tags onto the end of the line. The joker stands in the middle of the line and dances lackadaisically with the queens, amusing himself at their silly posturings and leading them in a dance that burlesques their charm. Finally he pushes them all into the wings.

THIRD DEAL   The same march begins the third deal. A line of cards, their identities concealed as before, file out from the right; the cards are dealt into three hands. The hand on the left—a flush of Hearts, the five, six, seven, eight, and nine—walk to the front and dance pertly but modestly. They retire, and the joker dances forward with the hand on the right—the seven, eight, nine, and ten of Spades—with the joker, a higher flush than the first hand. The joker tries to play off his Spades against the Hearts, but the first hand moves away to stand in front of the final hand, which is still unrevealed. The joker and his Spades form a huddle to decide on the best method of play, then the five cards form a line, with the joker at the end. He bumps the girls forward and dances with them playfully as the orchestra mimics a bright melody of Rossini's.

The Hearts move forward; the joker and his Spades run back to see the final hand and stand aghast as they behold a royal flush: the ten, Jack, Queen, King, and Ace of Hearts! The joker grips his head in despair: he can laugh no longer when the joke is on him. He falls on his back, the music laughs at him, he rolls over and crawls off.

The royal flush marches forward to a delightful tune. The jack holds up his hand, trumpeting their arrival; the king and queen raise their hands in greeting and congratulate each other that the royal family is reunited. The queen jumps and everyone jumps. All the cards in the three deals gather behind them. They blow kisses to all her family and everyone else in sight and they all bow to her in mock humility. The other cards come to shake the hands of the lucky hand, and the king and queen welcome them. The king orders all the Hearts in the deck to come forward with the royalty. The other suits form lines behind the Hearts and all dance a courtly measure to the king's command. The deck of cards form a tableau about the queen. She is lifted high above them; the surrounding multitude fall forward in obeisance to her; and as the lights go out, all the cards are seen scrambled together in the middle of the table, shuffled together for a new game.

NOTES   *Card Game* was the first collaboration between Stravinsky and myself in the United States. In 1936, when Lincoln Kirstein and I decided upon a Stravinsky Festival for the American Ballet, we wanted to present a new Stravinsky ballet. We wrote to Stravinsky in Paris, commissioning him to write a new ballet. We told him to write anything he wanted. He decided on a dance with playing-card characters, a poker-game ballet.

Soon after the score arrived in New York and I had begun rehearsals on the new ballet, Stravinsky himself arrived. As always, the ballet was a collaboration. Lincoln Kirstein has noted that Stravinsky possesses "the profound stage instinct of an amateur of the dance, the 'amateur' whose attitude is so professional that it seems merely an accident that he is not himself a dancer."

In *Card Game*, Stravinsky and I attempted to show that the highest cards—the kings, queens, and jacks—in reality have nothing on the other side. They are big people, but they can easily be beaten by small cards. Seemingly powerful figures, they are actually mere silhouettes.

Card Game was revived by the Ballet Russe de Monte Carlo at the Fifty-first Street Theatre, New York, October 14, 1940, with Frederic Franklin as the joker and a cast that included Alexandra Danilova, Nathalie Krassovska, Alicia Markova, André Eglevsky, and Igor Youskevitch. In the most recent revival by the New York City Ballet (first performance February 15, 1951), Todd Bolender and Janet Reed have danced the joker and leading parts have been danced by Janet Reed, Patricia Wilde, Doris Breckenridge, Jillana, Francisco Moncion, Frank Hobi, Michael Maule, and others.

Another version of Stravinsky's score was choreographed in 1945 by Janine Charrat and had its first performance by the Ballets des Champs-Élysées in Paris, with Jean Babilée as the joker.

John Cranko's production of *Jeu de Cartes* was first presented at the Württemberg State Theatre, Stuttgart, January 22, 1965, with scenery and costumes by Dorothee Zippel and lighting by Gilbert V. Hemsley, Jr. The ballet, introduced to the United States by the Stuttgart Ballet at the Metropolitan Opera House, New York, June 17, 1969, has been staged by the City Center Joffrey Ballet.

CARMEN

Dramatic ballet in five scenes inspired by the opera by Meilhac and Halévy. Music by Georges Bizet. Choreography by Roland Petit. Scenery and costumes by Antoine Clavé. First presented by Les Ballets de Paris de Roland Petit at the Prince's Theatre, London, February 21, 1949, with Renée Jeanmaire and Roland Petit in the principal roles. First presented in the United States by Les Ballets de Paris at the Winter Garden, New York, October 6, 1949, with the same principals.

SCENE ONE: A PUBLIC SQUARE IN SEVILLE   What seems to be a building with an outside staircase stands at the back of the square, and from it a long clothesline hung with multicolored garments suggests that it is a cheap public square. Three men play at cards on a plank that has been set up between two high ladders. Couples mill about the square in a casual and desultory manner, smoking, dancing occasionally with simulated high spirits, but in general implying that if they wait about long enough, something important may happen. They are not disappointed. Upstairs in the building someone is making a ruckus. Everyone listens attentively. Down the stairs runs an unfortunate girl who is clearly having difficulty with her pursuer. We understand why when we see that her pursuer is Carmen.

Everyone in the public square knows Carmen, every woman and especially every man. By experience and reputation fierce in love, Carmen is also fierce in jealousy, and although no one knows or cares what she is fighting with this other girl about, all the people in the square assume that the fight is worth watching. They take sides. Between two groups who egg them on, Carmen and the girl scratch each other and tear each other's hair out and kick each other around. The crowd is delighted with their ferocity and cheers spitfire Carmen when she succeeds in throwing her opponent to the ground. Just as they begin to express their enthusiasm for her victory, Don José, cape flying, enters on the run. Everybody seems to know him, too.

Don José is an official of some sort, a man from another part of the town, perhaps a policeman in mufti. He does not approve of what is going on and tries to break up the crowd. He takes pity on the prostrate girl, but then he sees her conqueror. The music sounds an ominous theme; the drum beats warningly. Don José is transfixed, immediately attracted to Carmen, as all the men seem to have been. He takes in her long and supple body, her boyish bob, her defiant eyes, her wide red mouth that seems a brilliant slash across her white round face, and doesn't know what to do. Then he remembers his duty. He seizes Carmen by the shoulder, coldly, officially, to admonish her. Carmen responds by glaring up at him and yanking down her blouse to expose the voluptuousness of her other shoulder. Don José is confused. Instead of arresting her, he allows Carmen to make a rendezvous with him. He dashes off, and the spectators nod to themselves knowingly.

SCENE TWO: A TAVERN   The stage is dark as the curtain rises on the second scene. Gradually a line of paper lanterns light up across the scene, and behind the lanterns is a tavern: tables and chairs, a bar in the back, and steps leading to an upstairs room. A number of steady customers are disposed about the tavern. A couple are making love, indifferent to their surroundings, and other habitués sit on the wooden chairs in an attitude of boredom. Some of them get up and start a kind of dance—wiggling and stomping and turning cart wheels and revolving the chairs on one leg—signifying their willingness to make the evening a deliberate, if not a spontaneous, success. Back near the bar, a man cloaked in black dozes.

Don José enters the room. He enters it just as he entered the public square: officiously, disapprovingly. But in the tavern, he senses that this will not be tolerated. After all, he has come on his own account, not on any official business, and everyone happens to know his particular business. And so, he joins the steady customers to prove that he is a regular fellow. He dances all by himself to prove also that he is a dashing fellow, while the crowd stands back and sings to the rhythm of his stomping the "Habañera." Although this song, with its warnings of rebellious love that can never be tamed, accompanies Don José's solo, he is sensitive only to its rhythms, which the spectators accentuate with militant clapping of hands. Don José is thinking of his meeting with Carmen.

Carmen has apparently been hiding behind the bar all this time. Suddenly, we see her sitting on top of it. Two gallants lift her down, and she commences a dance of her own. She carries a small black fan, which she holds close to her breasts. Her naked shoulders and her hair are covered with shiny spangles that fall from her body as she turns in powerful spins. Carmen's dance has more dash and strength than Don José's, and everyone watches her long legs as she traverses the tavern with steps that reveal her character as an untamable lover. Don José observes her more intently than the rest. At the end of her dance, Carmen kneels at his feet, her arms open in a gesture of welcome that is both public and intimate.

Don José goes to her. Carmen pretends that she is indifferent and fans herself nonchalantly. A pickpocket tries to rob Don José, but he brushes him aside. He picks Carmen up, holding her knee in his arm. He carries her closely, possessively, as if she had never been carried by a man before. He turns and carries her upstairs; Carmen relaxes in his arms.

When the two lovers have disappeared, two men and a girl begin a tempestuous dance that attracts all the customers. All join in the dance and whip themselves into a frenzy of happiness. Carmen's rendezvous has been a success, Don José has been seduced, and there is cause for rejoicing: they need fear officials no more. Carmen and Don José run down the stairs and lead the dance. The crowd fall on their knees around the lovers and beat the floor to the hysterical rhythm of their feet. At the climax of the music, Don José enfolds Carmen in his cape and runs off with her.

SCENE THREE: CARMEN'S ROOM; IT IS THE MORNING AFTER   Don José pulls back the yellow curtains that conceal the boudoir from the audience, and bright sunlight from an open window fills the room. Carmen lies on a disordered iron bed, sucking a plum. She rises lazily, stretches, and slowly goes into a dance. Don José pours water in a basin, washes his hands, dries them on the curtains, and seems not to notice the increasing sensuous pleasure Carmen derives from her own seductiveness. He sits and watches her disinterestedly. She caresses her body, her hands moving from her hair over her face to her shoulders, her breasts and her thighs, and up again to her face. Don José shows no signs of interest and, tired of self-love, Carmen turns away with disgust toward the balcony outside the window. The noise of the street attracts her. Instantly, Don José is on his feet. Really, he isn't tired at all. He wishes her to stay! Carmen moves to leave the room, but Don José pulls her back. Carmen, however, will be detained only by love. The lovers kiss and begin a dance together.

Don José lifts Carmen up to his shoulder, then holds her as her body comes down full length in his arms. Carmen's interest in him is renewed and gradually she compels Don José to share her passion. His body falls back to the floor and he braces himself on his arms and legs as Carmen poses aggressively above him, her knee resting between his. Carmen's breathing is now as lusty as her movements, and Don José responds fully. The climax of her passion approaches. She lies upon him. Don José raises his knees, and Carmen's legs stretch out straight from her curved body in an attitude of diving. The tenseness in their bodies relaxes as the music ends and the two lovers lie exhausted.

Barely has their passion subsided than three of Carmen's friends enter to persuade them to come out into the street. The friends whisper secretively to Carmen, and she motions to Don José to follow them. Now he will follow her anywhere.

SCENE FOUR: A STREET IN SEVILLE   It is night again. The scene is abandoned. Old cart wheels stacked against posts constitute the only scenery. Carmen and Don José, followed by her friends, walk on carefully, not wishing to be overheard. Cloaks disguise their identity. There is a brief conference. They are giving Don José his final instructions. Carmen puts a dagger in his hand. He listens and nods; the others leave and he is alone. The orchestra again sounds the theme that marked the first, fateful meeting of Carmen and Don José, and the drum now beats the rhythm of death. Don José stomps his feet in unison with the drum and waits. On the right, a man in a purple cloak enters. Don José seems to recognize him, stands motionless as he passes, then throws himself upon him. He stabs the man in the back. The man falls flat on his face. Don José reaches for his purse. Carmen and her bandit friends run out from hiding, grab for the money, and run off. Don José kicks the body over and follows them.

SCENE FIVE: IN FRONT OF THE PLAZA DE TOROS   Now that Don José has become a part of Carmen's life and has made the ultimate sacrifice and killed for her, Carmen begins to lose interest in him. She must always be taming someone to her will; once they have given in, she must seek new conquests. At the beginning of the fifth scene a crowd of lovely girls dressed colorfully but formally stand outside the arena, the Plaza de Toros, waiting for the bullfight to start—but waiting, too, for the arrival of the handsome toreador. The toreador, brought in on the shoulders of his admirers, gets down smartly and welcomes the greetings of the girls. As he flirts with them, he notices Carmen standing away from the crowd. She stares at him. She wears a veil, and the toreador prefers her indifference to the open affection of the young ladies. Don José enters and observes this silent exchange between Carmen and the toreador. The bullfight is about to begin; the toreador turns away from Carmen regretfully, and the crowd follows him into the arena. Carmen starts to join them.

Don José rushes up to her, tears off her veil, and grasps her throat in a passion of jealousy. He holds her face between his hands, and Carmen defies him. They separate, take positions at either side of the stage, and stand for a moment facing each other with so deep an anger that they become animal in their hatred. One of them must tame the other. The drum sounds slowly in a staccato beat; spotlights magnify and double the shadows of Carmen and Don José against the side of the arena. They approach and separate in a manner very similar to the fight in progress inside the ring, daring each other on, determined that one of them shall die. The drum beats faster and louder; Carmen circles Don José. He pulls out the dagger, rushes her quickly, and stabs her in the heart. He holds her about the waist as her body writhes back. She reaches up a trembling arm and caresses the face of her lover. She can stand no longer. Don José holds her to him still, and her legs vibrate with her heart's last beat. She falls limp. The music sounds brilliantly. Hats are thrown in from the arena. The fight has been won. The love has been lost.

Ballet in two acts. Music: a Bizet collage by Wolfgang Fortner in collaboration with Wilifried Steinbrenner. Choreography by John Cranko. Scenery and costumes by Jacques Dupont. Lighting by Gilbert V. Hemsley, Jr. First presented by the Stuttgart Ballet at the Württemberg State Theatre, Stuttgart, February 28, 1971, with Marcia Haydée, Egon Madsen, and Richard Cragun in the principal roles. First presented in the United States by the same ensemble at the Metropolitan Opera House, New York, April 28, 1971, with the same principals.

The ballet, in seven scenes, conveys in dance terms the plot of Bizet's opera. The locale is Spain, about 1820. The first scene takes place in a cigarette factory where Carmen, a beautiful, sultry girl who works there, has an argument with the woman in charge and scratches a cross on her back. She is arrested by a sergeant, Don José, a country boy who is immediately attracted to her. In the next scene, at the barracks jail, Carmen gets Don José to free her. He is stripped of his rank and jailed. In Scene Three, at a gap in the town wall of Seville, Carmen persuades Don José, who is on guard, to let the smuggler band to which she belongs pass out of the city. Don José follows them. In the final scene of the first act, in the gypsy camp of the smugglers, there is a love scene between Carmen and Don José. Soldiers arrive to arrest Don José, who has deserted. He stabs the officer in charge.

Act Two of the ballet opens at an inn on the beach. Here Carmen dresses for her dance and sends Don José away on an errand. The toreador arrives with a group of friends and is fascinated by Carmen. Don José returns and is fiercely jealous. The desert region is the next scene, where Carmen's fate is revealed to her in a game of cards. Don José feels that he is losing her. A traveling Englishman is robbed and killed by the smugglers. Now an outlaw and a murderer, hunted by soldiers, nearly rejected by Carmen, Don José becomes desperate as he watches Carmen leave on the arm of the torero. In the final scene, outside the arena in Seville, Carmen accompanies the torero to the bullfight. She sees Don José there and has a presentiment of her fate. After the corrida has begun and they are alone, Don José pleads with her to come back to him. Knowing her fate, she still refuses. Don José stabs her.

CARMEN SUITE

Music by Rodion Shchedrin. Choreography by Alberto Alonso. First presented by the Bolshoi Ballet at the Bolshoi Theatre, Moscow, in 1967, with Maya Plisetskaya in the leading role. First presented in the United States by the same ensemble at the Metropolitan Opera House, New York, 1974.

The first ballet to be choreographed especially for the celebrated Soviet ballerina Maya Plisetskaya, *Carmen Suite* presents the familiar story of Mérimée's novella as a mortal combat in a simulated bullring. It emphasizes character rather than plot. While we see Carmen, Don José, and the toreador assume their expected roles, the ballet is dominated throughout by Fate in the form of a bull. A huge head of a bull painted on a backdrop high over the arena dominates the decor. The program says: "Carmen is a beautiful woman who is free, true to herself, and completely honest. Don José lies, and thus he loses her. The Bull represents Fate. Therefore Carmen and the Bull die at the same time because she and her Fate are one." The final *pas de deux*, a danced contest between Carmen and Don José, is a simulated bullfight in which the ballerina assumes the combined roles of heroine and Fate in the form of a bull.

CARMINA BURANA

Music by Carl Orff. Choreography by John Butler. First presented by the New York City Opera at the City Center, New York, September 24, 1959, with Carmen de Lavallade, Veronika Mlakar, Scott Douglas, and Glen Tetley in the principal roles.

Carmina Burana, a choral theater piece based on poems discovered in the library of an ancient Bavarian monastery, is a secular rather than a sacred work. The thirteenth-century poems and songs composed by minstrels and monks who had freed themselves of monastic discipline were set by Carl Orff to vigorous, compelling music. The chorus of monk-clad singers stands at both sides of the stage.

The ballet, which begins after the First Chorus, is an abstract landscape of movement, not a realistic retelling of the poems. The Prologue regrets the ever-changing fate of man, first riding the Wheel of Fortune with success, then ground under by it. The first part relates the joys of spring. The second celebrates the pleasures, extravagances, and despairs of tavern life. The third part is a series of love poems. The Epilogue returns to the plaintive bemoaning of the ruthless Wheel of Fate.

Leopold Stokowski, a champion of the score, characterized it as "a synthesis of beauty of melodic line, remarkable rhythmic variations; lusty vitality; immense range of mood, humor, frenzy; folk-like simplicity, satire, mystery, spontaneous eloquence and tranquility . . ."

Fernand Nault created a *Carmina Burana* for the Colorado Concert Ballet in Denver, in 1962. This version, with decor by Robert Prevost, was presented by Les Grands Ballets Canadiens at the Salle Wilfred Pelletier, Montreal, June 24, 1967.

Writing of the first presentation of John Butler's ballet, the critic Arthur Todd in *Dance Observer* said that "All of the movement for the four dance principals is composed in honor of eroticism . . . Most notable of the four is Scott Douglas, notable heretofore chiefly for his classical balletic style."

CARNAVAL

Romantic ballet in one act. Music by Robert Schumann. Choreography by
Michel Fokine. Scenery and costumes by Léon Bakst. Book by Michel
Fokine. First presented at Pavlova Hall, St. Petersburg, 1910, with Tamara
Karsavina as Columbine, *Vera Fokina as* Chiarina, *Ludmilla Shollar as*
Estrella, *Bronislava Nijinska as* Papillon, *Leonide Leontiev as* Harlequin,
Vsevolod Meyerhold as Pierrot, *Enrico Cecchetti as* Pantalon, *and Joseph*
Kchessinsky as Florestan. *First presented in Western Europe by Diaghilev's*
Ballets Russes at the Théâtre National de l'Opéra, Paris, June 4, 1910, with
the same principals except for the following substitutions: Vaslav Nijinsky
as Harlequin, *Adolph Bolm as* Pierrot, *and Ivan Kussov as* Florestan. *First*
presented in the United States by Diaghilev's Ballets Russes at the Century
Theatre, New York, January 1916.

First performed as a *divertissement* for a benefit in St. Petersburg, *Carnaval*
was later revived and presented in Paris by Diaghilev. It became one of the
most popular ballets in his repertory and one of the most popular works in the
repertories of ballet companies that have since performed it, though it must be
admitted that contemporary revivals have hardly retained the spirit of the
original. The music is an orchestration of Schumann's *Carnaval* Suite for piano.
The principal characters—Pierrot, Columbine, etc., are drawn from the *commedia dell' arte,* the popular early Italian street comedies.

The scene is an antechamber to a ballroom. At the rise of the curtain, we
are introduced to the atmosphere of the ball that is taking place in the next
room. Girls run by, pursued by their escorts. Dancing couples from the ball
take refuge in the empty spaces of the anteroom and waltz. Chiarina and Estrella, two charming girls, enter with their partners. Two lovers kiss in passing
and return to the ball.

Pierrot, the sad clown, pokes his head into the room. He steps into the room
carefully, lest anyone hear or see him, his long, loose sleeves flapping dejectedly at his sides. He moves with slow melancholy; he seems to be saying that
he is the only one in the world who will not dance and enjoy himself at the
ball. Aware of his ugliness and awkwardness, he is filled with self-pity.

Harlequin bounces in, notes the melancholy Pierrot, and taunts him for not
joining in the fun the music calls for. Unmercifully the energetic Harlequin
pokes at the helpless clown, who falls to the floor. The irrepressible Harlequin
leaves him in disgust.

Couples from the ball dance through the anteroom again. Pierrot looks at
them and takes himself off before he can be chided once more.

Now the romantic poet Eusebius enters. He sits on a settee and wistfully
contemplates a vision he has of an ideal lady. The lady materializes in the

form of Chiarina, who gives him a rose. Estrella, ambitious and flirtatious, enters pursued by the eager Florestan, who beseeches her to grant him the favor of some small attention. Estrella pretends to disapprove of his advances, but then links her arm in his; the two exit for a dance.

Eusebius and Chiarina dance, or rather Chiarina dances and Eusebius observes her with adoring eyes. They leave the scene together.

Papillon, a girl whose varied, busy movements suggest a perpetual giddiness, rushes in. Pierrot discreetly follows her, hoping to make a conquest at last. He watches her from behind a settee, then bounds out into the room to catch her. When poor Pierrot thinks he has finally found a partner, Papillon escapes his grasp and leaves. The helpless clown is alone again.

Now there is an interval of dancing by Chiarina and two of her girl friends, who are masked. Florestan, still in pursuit of the coquettish Estrella, comes into the room. The girls playfully try to detain him, but the determined youth flees.

Columbine, gay and flirtatious, enters with Harlequin. They play together amorously. Though she seems to like him very much, the girl refuses Harlequin's invitation to elope. Their rendezvous is interrupted by the foppish Pantalon, who sits on a settee and reads with relish a note. Columbine goes to the back of the settee and puts her hands over Pantalon's eyes, while Harlequin snatches the note away from the intruder.

Pantalon, who was only reading the note to attract attention, tries to ingratiate himself with Columbine, who toys with him amusingly and then suggests that he join her and Harlequin in a *pas de trois*. At the end of the dance, she and Harlequin send Pantalon on his way.

Harlequin sits on the floor and indicates to Columbine that his heart lies at her feet. The fickle girl goes to the settee, where Harlequin sits adoringly in front of her.

The dancers return and, observing Harlequin and Columbine, congratulate them on their love. Columbine is suddenly nice to everyone. She comforts the pompous Pantalon and permits poor Pierrot to kiss her hand. All join in a happy dance.

The joviality is cut short by a crowd of busybodies, proper people who think that the people in the anteroom are not behaving with decorum. The gay dancers mock them and shove them about until they take flight. In the melee, the trickster Harlequin sees that Pierrot and Pantalon are pushed together. Before the two can separate themselves, Harlequin has tied Pierrot's long sleeves together around Pantalon. While Pantalon tries to release his bonds, all the other dancers gather about Columbine and Harlequin to form an admiring tableau.

CELEBRATION

Ballet by Jerome Robbins. Music and choreography as specified below.
Scenery by Rouben Ter-Arutunian. First presented by the Festival of Two
Worlds at the Teatro Nuovo, Spoleto, Italy, July, 1973, with Antoinette
Sibley and Anthony Dowell (England), Violette Verdy and Jean-Pierre
Bonnefous (France), Carla Fracci and Paolo Bortoluzzi (Italy), Patricia
McBride and Helgi Tomasson (United States), and Malika Sabirova and
Muzafar Bourkhanov (Soviet Union).

Subtitled "The Art of the *Pas de Deux*," *Celebration* combined in a few historic performances classical *pas de deux* of the past with contemporary dance.
The basic idea was to show the classic *pas de deux* in all its glamor but to
show, too, the depth of feeling of contemporary ballet duets. The original intention was for *Celebration* to begin with a brief talk and demonstration of the
art of the *pas de deux* by Anton Dolin, the famed partner of many ballerinas.
Jerome Robbins decided instead to introduce his ballet himself, saying simply
that it would be a "celebration of dancing by dancers."

The dancers are five couples from England, France, Italy, the United States,
and the Soviet Union. Heralds carrying flags introduce the action. All five
dancers enter to a fanfare and dance to the music of a Tchaikovsky waltz.
Then one by one, the couples performed some of the great *pas de deux*. First,
Sabirova and Bourkhanov in *The Corsair Pas de Deux,* then Fracci and
Bortoluzzi in the love duet from *La Sylphide,* the oldest work of the evening.
A *grand pas classique* for Verdy and Bonnefous came next, followed by Robbins's own *Afternoon of a Faun* by McBride and Tomasson. The *grand pas de
deux* from the final act of *The Sleeping Beauty* by Sibley and Dowell con-
cluded the first act of the presentation.

The second part consisted of the Balanchine *Tchaikovsky Pas de Deux*
(McBride and Tomasson), the Ashton *Pas de Deux* from *Thaïs* (Sibley and
Dowell), the Petipa/Minkus display piece from *Don Quixote* (Sabirova and
Bourkhanov), Robbins's new *Bagatelles* to music from Beethoven (Verdy and
Bonnefous), and the celebrated final *pas de deux* from the Mérante/Delibes
Coppélia.

The finale was an arrangement by Jerome Robbins for all five couples of the
Ivanov adagio from *Swan Lake,* Act Two.

NOTES   Robbins's *Bagatelles,* called then simply *A Beethoven Pas de Deux,*
had been performed initially at a preview in New York, May 16, 1973,
at the New York City Ballet's Annual Spring Gala. It was danced by Violette
Verdy and Jean-Pierre Bonnefous to *Four Bagatelles* of Beethoven, played by
the pianist Jerry Zimmerman: Nos. 4, 5, and 2 from *Opus 33* and No. 4 from

Opus 126. The costumes were by Florence Klotz and the lighting by Ronald Bates.

Reporting to the New York *Times,* the critic John Gruen wrote of the première of *Celebration* at the Spoleto Festival: "Bringing together five celebrated ballet couples (by no means an easy feat), and devising a work that would focus on international ballet styles, Robbins made clear both his magnetism as one of the world's great choreographers and his deep love of classical traditions."

The Ashton *pas de deux,* to the Meditation from the opera *Thaïs* by Jules Massenet, was first performed by Antoinette Sibley and Anthony Dowell at a gala ballet performance at the Adelphi Theatre, London, March 21, 1971. The critic Peter Williams wrote about the performance in *Dance and Dancers* magazine: Ashton "has created one of those oriental dream sequences that so reflect the whole mood of occidental awakening to the orient of the mid-nineteenth century. At least I imagine that Sibley must have been a dream figure, since she first appears with a light veil over her face as she approaches the kneeling Dowell. Everything about this dance evoked Pavlova, whom Ashton adored without reservation and whom he delighted in imitating until once, while staying at a country house, he seriously damaged his foot in an impromptu performance of *The Dying Swan.* But although the accident put a stop to any further imitations, Pavlova continued to cast a loving shadow over his life. This new *pas de deux* is all drifting and swooning and some fiendishly difficult lifts which have to look as though she is a wraith, and in which Dowell managed to make Sibley look as though she was. . . . It was lovely, and they were lovely, and to those that remembered, it must have brought on waves of nostalgia for Pavlova with Mordkin. . . ."

Writing after the first repertory performance of *Four Bagatelles* by the New York City Ballet, January 10, 1974, with Gelsey Kirkland and Jean-Pierre Bonnefous, Anna Kisselgoff said in the New York *Times:* "The very structure of *Four Bagatelles* follows the conventional sequence of the nineteenth-century classic *pas de deux:* adagio, variation for the man, then the woman, coda. In the first part, Mr. Robbins throws out almost subliminal quotes from three styles. A fleeting reminder of Denmark's Bournonville school, as in *Flower Festival at Genzano,* occurs in the beginning with the girl's *penchées arabesques,* head tilting and the man's leaps. Later, as Miss Kirkland slowly extends her leg to the side from on-toe position, while Mr. Bonnefous supports her in an image directly culled from the *grand pas de deux* of *The Sleeping Beauty,* there is a flashing allusion to the Russian style of Petipa.

"The adagio ends with Miss Kirkland down on one knee and Mr. Bonnefous behind her, in a reversal of the traditional pose that closes the adagio of Act Two of *Giselle*—a nod toward French Romantic ballet.

"These are, of course, whiffs of history wafting through a contemporary work, and the allusions are absent from the solos. Mr. Bonnefous's variation has folk touches that are echoed in the coda and some interesting experiments in phrasing. It is a tricky solo, somewhat short on transitional steps, and Mr. Bonnefous could not quite conceal the effort involved. Miss Kirkland, obviously most suited to the Robbins choreography, danced with brilliant technique and demure appeal. Mr. Zimmerman played with his customary excellence."

CELLO CONCERTO

Music by Antonio Vivaldi. Choreography by Gerald Arpino. Lighting design by Thomas Skelton. First presented by the City Center Joffrey Ballet at the City Center, New York, September 6, 1967. Cellist: Nellis De Lay. Conducted by Seymour Lipkin.

A dance ballet to Vivaldi's *Concerto for Cello, Strings, and Continuo in E Minor,* this is Gerald Arpino's second work to the music of Vivaldi for the City Center Joffrey Ballet. It is in four movements.

While an ensemble figures at the beginning of the first movement, it is in fact dominated by the adagio *pas de deux* of the girl and boy who finish it. The second movement, brisk in style, is again an ensemble, led at first by a girl who performs a brilliant variation.

The third, quiet, movement is danced by two couples, who perform two adagios to the lyric score; the girls are lifted high into the wings at its close.

Bright again in tempo and atmosphere, the final movement features brisk variations by a boy and his girl against the animation of the ten supporting dancers.

CHABRIESQUE

Music by Emmanuel Chabrier. Choreography by Gerald Arpino. First presented by the City Center Joffrey Ballet at the City Center, New York, February 1, 1972.

A dance ballet to Chabrier's *Trois Valses Romantiques, Souvenirs de Munich,* and *Cortège Burlesque, Chabriesque* is arranged for fourteen dancers. Writing of the ballet's performance in Chicago, the critic Ann Barzell said in *Dance News:* "*Chabriesque* is a classical suite in the high key of exhilarating virtuosity to which Arpino stretches his most virtuosic dancers. The choreographer delights in spaciousness and his fourteen dancers are seldom on stage all at the same time. His designs are not group tableaux, but groups flowing in ever-changing patterns. Arpino's inventiveness is boundless as he finds new ways to fly and whirl, to lift a partner or catch her coming or flipping from on high. There are new combinations of steps, new interweavings and through it all he maintains a style, romantic in mood and airy in movement. The girls wear white leotards with a cloud of sequin-spattered tulle for skirts. The men are in dark-blue tights and shirts.

"No matter how many unique roles dancers star in they feel the need to appear in what is nearest to them, the basic classicism of the daily class. So, it is understandable that Christian Holder has a pivotal role in *Chabriesque,* perhaps to prove that serenity of classicism is in his range. He danced with exemplary style, partnering the excellent Pamela Johnson. Starr Danias and Glenn White were notable throughout and after one stunning *pas de deux* set audiences cheering into the next dance. Francesca Corkle, recovering from an injury, brought her special bounce to several dances partnered by Scott Barnard, always excitingly precise."

CHACONNE

Music by Christoph Willibald Gluck. Choreography by George Balanchine. Lighting by Ronald Bates. First presented by the New York City Ballet at the New York State Theatre, Lincoln Center, January 22, 1976, with Suzanne Farrell and Peter Martins in the leading roles. Conducted by Robert Irving.

It is no secret that I have loved Gluck's music for *Orpheus and Eurydice* almost all my life. Soon after I came to America, when Lincoln Kirstein and I took our new, young American Ballet to the Metropolitan Opera, I did a ballet to all of his music for the opera. The opera became, in fact, a ballet, with the dancers taking the stage and the singers performing with the orchestra from the pit. That production, designed by Pavel Tchelitchew with settings and costumes we could never produce today, is part of history. My next involvement with *Orpheus* was with Stravinsky, with whom I did the ballet of that name in 1948. But I returned to Gluck and his opera in Hamburg, in November 1963, when Rolf Liebermann of the Hamburg Opera kindly invited me to stage the work there. To conclude the production of the opera, which was brilliantly designed by Rouben Ter-Arutunian in a high baroque style of extraordinary extravagance, I had an opportunity again to do dances to Gluck's music. I repeated them in 1973, after Liebermann moved to the Paris Opéra and invited me to produce *Orpheus* there, too. The present ballet is an adaptation of what was first done for Hamburg, plus the introductory *pas de deux.* Brigitte Thom, who danced in the Hamburg production, helped me to revive it.

The chaconne of the title of course refers to an old-style dance, now centuries old, but it also was the popular name for ballet music used to end an opera. Basically, the ballet is a set of two *pas de deux* with other *divertissements*—a duet, a trio, a dance for five, with an ensemble. There is no story.

Listen to the music first, if you can. Words you might try to use to describe it—mysterious, reflective, contemplative, plaintive, noble, etc.—are not enough for Gluck's lyric masterpiece.

The critic George Jackson has written: "Vainest endeavor, to try to document dance, the most ephemeral of the arts."

CHANSONS MADÉCASSES

Music by Maurice Ravel. Choreography by Jerome Robbins. First presented at the New York City Ballet's Hommage à Ravel at the New York State Theatre, Lincoln Center, May 28, 1975, with Patricia McBride and Helgi Tomasson, Debra Austin and Hermes Conde. Conductor: Robert Irving.

The music here is three songs for soprano, piano, flute, and cello. The work was commissioned by Elizabeth Sprague Coolidge of Washington, D.C., and first performed in 1926. Ravel used poems by the Creole poet Evariste-Désiré de Parny, who lived in India and collected folk songs of Madagascar: "which may give an idea of their customs and habits. They possess no verse; their poetry is nothing but an elaborate prose. Their music is simple, gentle and always melancholy."

Ravel once said he believed this music introduces a "new element, dramatic —indeed, erotic, resulting from the subject matter of Parny's poems."

Jerome Robbins set the three songs in an individual way. The first is a love song; the second, where the action of the ballet principally focuses, expresses doubts about the white man and his role in Madagascar's past; and the third song depicts a hero husband lying in the heat of the shady tree, wondering what's for dinner.

CHECKMATE

Dramatic ballet in one scene with prologue. Music by Arthur Bliss. Choreography by Ninette de Valois. Scenery and costumes by E. McKnight Kauffer. First presented by the Sadler's Wells Ballet at the Théâtre des Champs-Élysées, Paris, June 15, 1937, with June Brae as the Black Queen, Robert Helpmann as the Red King, Pamela May as the Red Queen, Harold Turner and William Chappell as the Red Knights, Richard Ellis and Michael Somes as the Black Knights, Frederick Ashton and Alan Carter as the Two Players, and a cast that included Margot Fonteyn and Leslie Edwards. First presented in England by the Sadler's Wells Ballet at the Sadler's Wells Theatre, October 5, 1937, with the same principals. First presented in the United States by the Sadler's Wells Ballet at the Metropolitan Opera House, New York, November 2, 1949, with Beryl Grey as the Black Queen, Leslie Ed-

wards as the Red King, *Gerd Larsen as the* Red Queen, *Alexis Rassine and John Field as the* Red Knights, *Kenneth Melville and Philip Chatfield as the* Black Knights, *and a cast that included Pauline Clayden, Rosemary Lindsay, Rowena Jackson, Kenneth MacMillan, and John Cranko.*

Checkmate is an allegory, a story of the battle between love and death told in terms of a chess game. It is apparent from the beginning who will win, but the contest, with its determined conflicting forces, creates a dramatic situation that often precludes prediction and the spectator, like the quiet chess player, finds himself deliberating the outcome.

The terms of the allegory are introduced in a prologue. The music is ominous, doomful, without relief in its projection of the battle to come. The curtain rises on a chess game. Two players in armor, Love and Death, sit opposite each other at a small table in the center of the stage. The chess game begins as Love makes a move. Death watches, deliberates, and moves his skeletonlike hand over the table. He moves. Love tries to analyze the situation, will not move again as he sees that the situation is hopeless: it is checkmate and there has not been any game at all. Blackout.

A backdrop rises, and we see that the stage is covered with black and white squares, as on a chessboard. The red chessmen enter and begin to take their places on the board. First come the eight pawns, danced by girls, gay and lighthearted pages to the royalty to come. The two red knights march in from opposite sides of the board and practice their fierce skill in combat. Two black knights, sent by the enemy to report on the strength of the other side, herald the entry of the black queen, whose omnipotence over all the pieces on the board is soon apparent. She beats off one of the red knights who will not submit to her attractions. To make himself attractive to her, the other red knight dances a vigorous mazurka. When he finishes, she rewards him with a red rose —Death's symbol of the blood she will spill before she is through. The pawns leave the board, followed by the conquering black queen and the black knights. In their absence, one of the red knights dances the praises of the black queen. Two red bishops parade in ceremoniously, followed by two red castles. Finally the red king and queen enter. Both knights salute them. The red king, old and doddering, can hardly make his way about the board and it is clear he can win nothing, while the queen is anything but a matriarch. The red pieces are now all in place, and the game begins in earnest.

The black queen leads the onslaught. The red king tries to maneuver his forces to prevent a frontal attack, but the black queen sees an opening and dashes through the enemy line. Even the two red bishops cannot hold off the black pieces. The red queen begs for mercy for her king, but the relentless black queen delivers her into the hands of her two knights.

The red knight, who imagined himself powerful in love, even with the black queen, attempts to rally his king's forces. For a time the contest is equal, for the knight's love of his king appears to be a match for his passion for the

enemy queen. But when he must choose, when he has the chance to slay the
queen, when she is kneeling helpless before him, he naturally hesitates. The
black queen laughs in his face and cuts him down. The red king despairs.
Death enters. The body of the defeated red knight is held high by the red
pieces, and Death leads the cortege off the board.

The red king has been abandoned; he is alone on the board with the black
queen. She toys with him like a snake. He cannot escape: wherever he turns, a
new black piece appears to block his path. He makes a pathetic figure—but
then, from the beginning he has seemed weak and powerless—and the black
queen's game with him becomes a protracted mercenary exhibition of power.
She looks at him as if wondering whether the game were worth winning after
all, he being such a contemptible creature. He is backed into his throne. Now,
with nothing to lose, the king fights back with vigor for a brief moment. The
black queen admires his mettle so much that she condescends to kill him. It is
checkmate indeed.

CHOPINIANA (see LES SYLPHIDES)

CHORAL VARIATIONS ON BACH'S "VOM HIMMEL HOCH"

*Music by Igor Stravinsky. Choreography by George Balanchine. Scenery by
Rouben Ter-Arutunian. Lighting by Ronald Bates. First presented by the
New York City Ballet at the Stravinsky Festival, 1972, at the New York
State Theatre, Lincoln Center, June 25, 1972, with Karin von Aroldingen,
Melissa Hayden, Sara Leland, Violette Verdy, Anthony Blum, and Peter
Martins in the principal roles.*

The Christmas hymn *"Vom Himmel Hoch Da Komm' Ich Her"* is familiar
today as it was in Bach's own time. Its inspiriting music derived from a time
during the Reformation when popular feeling gained an ascendancy in church
music, and even today it is possible to find reflected in its melody an open,
confident, but at the same time tender conviction to match the words:

Vom Himmel hoch da komm' ich her,	From heaven high I come to you,
Ich bring' euch gute neue Mähr.	I bring you tidings good and new,
Der guten Mähr bring' ich so viel,	Good tidings of great joy I bring:
Davon ich sing'n und sagen will.	Thereof will I both say and sing.

In 1747, Bach wrote canonic variations on the hymn for two-manual organ
and pedals as a submission to a learned society. In 1955, Stravinsky began to
compose instrumental and choral variations on Bach's masterwork. The score,

for mixed chorus and orchestra, was dedicated to Robert Craft, who conducted its first performance at Ojai, California, May 27, 1956.

I myself first learned about the music from Stravinsky when he was working on the first two variations in New York at the end of 1955. When we were planning the Stravinsky Festival at the New York City Ballet after the composer's death, in 1971, one of the first works that I wanted very much to include was this one. Robert Irving conducted the first performance at the last night of the festival.

Those who will want to know more about the music will wish to read Robert Craft's exposition for Stravinsky's own recording of the work. As for the ballet, it is very simple.

There are five variations in the score. Brass proclaims the melody of the hymn as twelve young girls dance. All wear white. The background is a high chevron of white and brass rods, an imaginative simulation of pipes of the baroque organ.

In the four variations that follow, one is led by a ballerina and eight girls; another by four couples in which a *pas de deux* figures; another by a girl and boy against a background of twelve boys; and a finale with four *pas de trois* and eight girls, ending with the entire group of forty-six dancers. All forty-six dancers are on stage throughout the ballet, those not participating in the action standing aside.

It is boring, I think, to describe in any kind of detail what appears on the stage in a ballet that has only the music as its subject. What matters is the music itself and the more we can all be familiar with it, the better we are, both before seeing and afterward, too. This score is such an especially beautiful one that I hope you will hearken to it, but as always it is perhaps best to like it first without caring to, without preparation. I mean, many of the loveliest works of art are surprises we enjoy because we like them themselves, not because others alert us to them. Which is, of course, the point of the open mind, the open ear, the open eye!

CHOREOGRAPHIC OFFERING

Music by Johann Sebastian Bach. Choreography by Ballet of the Twentieth Century. First presented by that ensemble at the Brooklyn Academy of Music, New York, January 25, 1971.

The Artistic Director of the Ballet of the Twentieth Century, Maurice Béjart, has written in his *Notebook* about the philosophy behind this and other works by his company:

"Dancer-Choreographer collaboration / Choreography, like love, is done in pairs / In a choreographic work, the dancer is more important than the choreography, for it is the dancer who is author of the work; the choreographer

merely fits it together / To the extent that the choreographer strives to understand the shape, rhythm and will of the body one may create a work that appears original. The dancer's body, which is the interpretator, is always right.
When I say body, I mean the whole intuitive and spontaneous being, and not
the mind of the dancer. The dancer should be carefully observed, not only for
the steps he makes, which he believes favor him, but because, despite what he
says or thinks, his whole being is impelled to express itself in that very particular way / By listening to both the music of the bodies and that of the musical
work, one could very well create a work. But taken on the whole, the work is
not one's own, since it exists only because of its parts: the music and dancer /
After all is said and done, the important thing is that something happens, re-
gardless of who creates it / The dance is visual music."

The music for *Choreographic Offering* consists of eight canons from Bach's
Musical Offering, orchestrated by Münchinger, with percussion episodes. Bach
composed his work on a theme by King Frederick of Prussia. For almost a full
hour, the regal theme supports a prodigious suite of canons, which imitate the
theme, fugues and sonatas. Béjart's ballet, choreographed by his dancers, uses
as its theme an adagio exercise used by the great Italian dancer and ballet
master Enrico Cecchetti (1850–1928), teacher to pre-eminent Russian
dancers. Béjart writes: "Within the eight central canons of the work there is a
development which takes the form of a musical discourse; a countersubject,
which is developed by the dancers and the percussion, follows; the theme
meshes with a classic dance motif, modifying, supplementing and parodying it.
These two basic elements seem to struggle to dominate the work, which appears about to fall apart. 'Life' enters and supplies a conclusion. This ballet has
no other meaning, no other purpose, than to present, or to 'offer' the public the
quality called 'Twentieth Century Ballet.'"

Following Béjart's scenario, the theme is danced by a boy, classically
presented, but at once there is an "anti-theme" by another boy, who dances in
a completely contemporary way, in vivid contrast, to the music of drums,
chimes, and an "Iguanaphone." The ballet is full of surprises, seemingly improvised by the dancers, although there are the expected sequences in canon,
with couples repeating dances by their predecessors. The contrast between the
old and the new would appear to be the point, plus a useful and novel way to
introduce a ballet company to a new public who might wonder what it represents.

Interviewed in *The New Yorker* magazine (February 6, 1971), the choreographer said of *Choreographic Offering:* "It's a discourse between the two main
elements in my work—classical ballet, which is choreographed to Bach's *Musical Offering,* and modern dance, which appears during percussion passages, to
interrupt and parody the traditional steps. There is a struggle between the two
styles but we don't resolve it. We end with a young girl holding out a rose to
the audience. That's our way of saying, 'In New York, you have the best chor-

Lynn Seymour in *Homage to Isadora*. Photo by Beverley Gallegos.

Natalia Makarova and Anthony Dowell in *Swan Lake*. Photo by MIRA, courtesy of Hurok Concerts.

Svetlana Beriosova and Derek Rencher in *Enigma Variations*.
Photo by MIRA, courtesy Hurok Concerts.

Antoinette Sibley and Anthony Dowell in *The Sleeping Beauty*. Photo by Anthony Crickmay.

eographers and dancers, so we don't dare offer you a finished ballet. Come to your own conclusions.'"

CINDERELLA

Ballet in three acts and seven scenes. Music by Sergei Prokofiev. Choreography by Rotislav Zakharov. Libretto by Nikolai Volkov. First presented by the Bolshoi Ballet at the Bolshoi Theatre, Moscow, November 15, 1945, with Olga Lepeshinskaya in the title role. Designed by Pyotr Williams. Presented in a new version with choreography by Konstantin Sergeyev at the Kirov State Theatre of Opera and Ballet, Leningrad, April 8, 1946, with Natalia Dudinskaya in the title role. A new production, revised by Sergeyev, was presented at the Kirov Theatre, July 13, 1964, with Irina Kolpakova. Designer: Tatiana Bruni. This production was first presented in the United States by the Kirov Ballet at the Metropolitan Opera House, New York, September 11, 1964, with Irina Kolpakova and Yuri Soloviev.

Prokofiev wrote that he conceived of *Cinderella* "as a classical ballet with variations, adagios, *pas de deux*, etc. I see Cinderella not only as a fairy-tale character but also as a real person, feeling, experiencing, and moving among us." The Russian composer began work on the score in 1940, but because of other commitments during World War II did not finish the orchestration until 1944.

ACT ONE: A ROOM IN CINDERELLA'S HOUSE   It is evening and Cinderella's stepsisters—Krivlyaka (Affected) and Zlyuka (Furious)—are embroidering a silk scarf while their mother dotingly looks on. Cinderella sits alone at the fireplace, polishing a pot. The two sisters begin to quarrel over the scarf; their tempers are so bad that the mother can resolve the fight only by cutting the scarf in two. They now tease Cinderella, whom no one, not even her loving father, will defend. When they leave her alone finally, she sets about her routine of cleaning up the room. She finds a piece of the scarf and, forgetting herself, dances. But a mirror brings her back to reality; she sees her miserable dress and realizes that such a scarf is not for her. Her sadness induces memories of her beloved mother; she shuns the portrait of her cruel stepmother and tries to cover it with a curtain.

Her father returns and wants to comfort Cinderella. She sits on his knee and cries. But he fears his wife more than he loves his daughter, and, observing the covered portrait of his spouse, is apprehensive. Meanwhile, Zlyuka and Krivlyaka, who have been watching, alert their mother, who rushes in in a rage. She attacks her husband and taunts Cinderella mercilessly, finally collapsing in a fit of anger.

A beggarwoman appears, asking for alms. While the stepmother and the two sisters want to chase the woman away, and the father is too frightened to do anything, Cinderella turns and gives her a piece of bread.

Now preparations begin for the gala ball to which the family—all except Cinderella—have been invited. Dressmaker, hairdresser, dancing master, and musicians come to prepare the ladies. When everything is ready, they all depart for the castle, and Cinderella is alone.

Wishing also to be at the ball, Cinderella lets herself be carried away by unattainable dreams. She curtsies, as if before the prince himself. Suddenly the old beggarwoman appears again, but this time as Cinderella's fairy godmother. She promises to make the girl's dreams come true in gratitude for Cinderella's kindness. The fairy presents the girl with a pair of crystal slippers and orders four fairies representing the seasons of the year to prepare and dress Cinderella for the ball. The fairy of Spring brings her a gossamer dress, light as a cloud; Summer brings lovely roses; Autumn a splendid cloak glowing like the sun; and Winter diamonds and jewels, glistening like icicles. Dressed and ready now for the ball, Cinderella is truly a princess out of a fairy tale.

Before she leaves for the castle, however, the fairy godmother warns her that she must return home exactly at twelve o'clock, or she will turn back into her original state forever. She will be reminded of the approach of midnight by twelve dwarfs whom the fairy godmother will cause to emerge from the ancient clock at the castle. The fairy godmother wishes her godspeed and leaves, as a golden coach magically appears before Cinderella to take her to the ball.

ACT TWO: THE BALL AT THE PRINCE'S CASTLE   While waiting for their host to appear, the splendidly dressed ladies and gentlemen dance a stately measure. The stepmother and her two daughters arrive and, grotesquely imitating the manners of their betters, attract considerable attention. Two men are finally persuaded to ask the two sisters to dance.

The prince appears, greets his guests, and ascends the throne. As the ball continues, a new strain of enchanting music is heard, and, accompanied by attendants, a lovely young girl enters. The prince cannot take his eyes off her, and asks her to dance. The court is curious about her identity. No one, not even her own family and least of all the ugly stepsisters, realizes that the beautiful guest is Cinderella.

When Arab boys present Cinderella with three oranges, she is so moved by the envious glances of Krivlyaka and Zlyuka that she gives the fruit to them. The prince and Cinderella are then briefly alone. They have both fallen in love at first sight and dance together to declare their love.

When the guests return, the court festivities continue. But at the height of the celebration, before she has even contemplated that such an evening should ever end, the clock strikes twelve. True to the fairy godmother's word, twelve dwarfs emerge from the clock. Cinderella, terrified, flees the castle. The prince runs after her. The prediction of the fairy godmother is fulfilled: Cinderella is again as she first was, and only the crystal slippers remain from her ball dress.

She loses one slipper as she dashes home, and the prince, as he pursues her, finds it. He comforts himself that to find the girl all he has to do is find the owner of the slipper!

ACT THREE, SCENE ONE: COURTYARD OF THE CASTLE   In an effort to find the maker of the shoe, the prince summons cobblers throughout the kingdom. No one can name the shoemaker and the prince decides to set out himself on his search for his beloved.

ACT THREE, SCENE TWO   The prince searches far and wide, and every lovely girl in the land weeps that the slipper will not fit. The prince remains determined to find his true love.

ACT THREE, SCENE THREE: A ROOM IN CINDERELLA'S HOUSE   Cinderella sleeps, pressing the remaining slipper to her breast. The slipper falls to the floor. Waking up the next morning, she recalls the splendid ball and her meeting with the prince. She decides that it must all have been a dream. But in the course of going about her daily chores, she finds the glass slipper. So it was not a dream after all! She cannot believe it.

The stepsisters come and relate the fine time they had at the ball, how popular they were, and how a princess gave them oranges.

Noise from the street heralds the arrival of the prince, who is going from house to house in search of the unknown beauty. When he enters, both stepsisters try in vain to force their feet into the shoe, and even their mother tries her luck. Then the prince notices Cinderella standing in the corner. She is so stunned by her lover's presence that she does not know what to do. She becomes so confused that she drops the other slipper. There is now no doubt as to who she is! Her fairy godmother appears and blesses Cinderella and her prince.

ACT THREE, SCENE FOUR: A FLOWERING GARDEN   Cinderella and the prince have found each other. They celebrate their reunion and live happily ever after.

Ballet in three acts. Music by Sergei Prokofiev. Choreography by Frederick Ashton. Scenery and costumes by Jean-Denis Malclès. First presented by the Sadler's Wells Ballet at the Royal Opera House, Covent Garden, London, December 23, 1948, with Moira Shearer as Cinderella, Michael Somes as the Prince, Robert Helpmann and Frederick Ashton as Cinderella's Stepsisters, Pamela May as the Ragged Fairy Godmother, Nadia Nerina, Violetta Elvin, Pauline Clayden, and Beryl Grey as the Fairies, and Alexander Grant as the Jester. First presented in the United States by the Sadler's Wells

Ballet at the Metropolitan Opera House, New York, October 18, 1949, with Margot Fonteyn as Cinderella *and the same principals.*

Cinderella is a story everybody knows and in the past it has attracted a great number of choreographers—French, Russian, and English. This particular ballet on the story, however, is important for a special reason: it is the first classic English ballet in three acts, the first full-length English work in the style and manner of the great nineteenth-century classics. But *Cinderella* is entertaining as well as important. Here the familiar tale is embellished with dramatic and comic differences, with *divertissements*, and with the grace and warmth of the grand academic style.

ACT ONE: A ROOM IN THE HOUSE OF CINDERELLA'S FATHER   The curtain rises on a somber scene. Cinderella crouches on the hearth of a high stone fireplace on the right. On the left, at a plain table, her father sits reading. Near him sit Cinderella's two stepsisters, busily sewing a scarf. They are elderly and hideous, and there is an obvious tension in the room. Cinderella is sitting by the fireplace because she is not allowed to sit anywhere else. Dressed in worn, unbecoming brown, she makes a pathetic figure. The light shines on her face and, despite her sadness, we note that she is beautiful. The music is quiet but expectant; strings are plucked rapidly to sound curiously like the clicking of knitting needles.

The stepsisters, old maids that they are, have been invited to a ball this very night and they work at their sewing with some haste. They finish the scarf and begin to fight about who shall wear it. Cinderella glances at them as if their bickering were all too familiar: in this house there is either quarreling or silence. But she is afraid to interfere. She is no longer the daughter of the house but its servant. The daughters of her father's second wife now rule the house, and she, like her father, can exist only by conforming to their wishes.

The father tries to calm his stepdaughters, but abandons hope when they ignore him. Each tugs at her end of the scarf, and it is torn in two. The stepsisters leave the room, still quarreling, and he follows after them despondently. Cinderella is alone. She takes up a broom and moves wistfully about the room, posing gracefully. She is thinking of happier days, when her mother was alive and there was love for her to respond to. She picks up a piece of the scarf her stepsisters have left behind and puts it around her shoulders: now she is a lady, the lady her mother would have wanted her to be. She takes a candlestick from the table, crosses the darkened room, lights the candle at the fireplace, and holds it high to look upon her mother's portrait, which hangs above the mantel. The father returns, sees his daughter's despair, and attempts to cheer her. But he, too, is sad. The ugly stepsisters come in and reprimand him for keeping Cinderella from her housework. They warn the girl to return to her cleaning.

The orchestra sounds a new, magical melody. The stepsisters hear it, too.

Cinderella looks up expectantly, and into the room hobbles a hunchbacked woman in rags. Her face is grotesque, her rags are filthy, but Cinderella seems to welcome her. The old hag begs for money, and the two stepsisters go into a tizzy of silly fear, running away to the other side of the room. Cinderella would like to comfort the old hag, but she knows that she has nothing to give. When the woman begs from her, Cinderella can only give her a bit of bread. The elder stepsister is annoyed at this generosity and threatens the woman. But, like an omen fulfilled, she is suddenly seized with a toothache and flees back to her sister. As Cinderella watches, wishing she could help more, the old hag glances at her gratefully and gently and disappears.

No sooner has the father reminded his two stepdaughters that they must begin to dress for the ball, than purveyors arrive—a tailor, dressmakers, a shoemaker, a jeweler, a hairdresser, a dancing master, each taking advantage of the sisters' new-found popularity to sell all their wares and talents. The old women are delighted at this attention, costly as it may be, and titter constantly like debutantes. Soon they are decked out in extravagant dresses. At this point the dancing master reminds them of the courtly steps in which they must be perfect. The women practice their bows and try to dance, as two violinists play a gavotte. The elder stepsister, old as she is, manages to execute the gavotte more or less to the dancing master's satisfaction, while the meek, shy sister despairs of learning. The dancing master sees that neither will ever learn and finally pretends that both are perfect.

The time of the ball is drawing near, and the stepsisters hurry with their makeup, primping extravagantly, as if all the powder and rouge in the world would reduce their ugliness. Their coach is announced, there is a final flurry of activity, and the sisters, absurdly proud in their bearing, depart.

Again Cinderella is alone. She looks into the fire. The women did not even bother to say good night to her. She wonders what the ball will be like, what any ball is like. She dances again with the broom, holding it before her as if she were not waltzing alone, and moves happily about the room, imagining herself at the ball. Soon she sees how silly she is being, puts the broom down, and goes back to sit at the hearth.

The harp is plucked gently, and again the eerie, high, piercing cry that heralded the arrival of the old beggarwoman causes Cinderella to look up and smile. The music is magical, like the loveliness of a dream; it grows in volume as the lower strings sound a full, promising melody. The room in which Cinderella sits seems to disappear, its walls vanishing. The old woman stands in the center of the room. She looks at Cinderella, and then something more extraordinary happens. In a flash, the old hag is transformed into a lovely, kind fairy: the ragged cretin becomes a beautiful creature dressed in a shimmering gown.

Cinderella cannot believe her eyes and when her fairy godmother tells her that she must prepare for the ball, that now, really, she *is* going to the ball, the lonely girl almost cries with happiness. The fairy godmother waves her wand, calling forth four fairies to dress Cinderella for the ball.

First comes the fairy Spring, then the fairies Summer, Autumn, and Winter. One by one, the fairies each dance a variation. After each one appears, the accompanying backdrop vanishes and Cinderella's room stretches back into the distance farther and farther. The scenery is transformed completely for each fairy, changing in color from green to icy blue, in surroundings from abundant garlands to a pinnacle of ice, and the fairies and their attendants are dressed charmingly in the habits of their seasons.

Cinderella sits on the floor at the feet of her fairy godmother, taking in the full magic of her great powers. Now she understands. The fairy godmother tells her to bring a pumpkin. Before the girl's astonished eyes, she changes the pumpkin into a magnificent coach. Cinderella is surrounded by the fairies, who present gifts to her and dress her for the ball. Almost at their touch, the lonely girl becomes as beautiful as a fairy tale princess, dressed splendidly in white and gold, wearing a crown and a long, flowing cape with a high pearl collar that encloses her shining face.

Her godmother tells Cinderella not to delay, that a newfound happiness awaits her at the ball. But she warns the girl that she must leave the ball before the clock strikes twelve. If she remains after midnight, the magic will vanish as mysteriously as it came and she will be just a lonely girl again, dressed in shabby clothes. Cinderella promises that she will not tarry and bows to her in gratitude. The fairies and a multitude of stars surround Cinderella as she goes to her coach and proceeds to the ball.

ACT TWO: A BALL AT THE PALACE   The ball has already begun when the curtain rises. Members of the court are dancing a formal measure in a ballroom that has been set up in the palace garden. Two great trees and their overhanging branches enclose the festive scene. To the left and right, spectators watch the ball in low stage boxes. In the back, on either side of a flight of low steps, are two high elegant structures, pavilions set up especially for the ball. On the ground floor of these pavilions we can see other guests amusing themselves. Farther back, by the light of a distant chandelier, we can make out a splendid formal garden. At the top of the steps is the prince's throne. The prince has not yet arrived, and the court jester sits on the royal stool.

Cinderella's stepsisters make an absurdly grand entry in keeping with the elegance they have assumed for the occasion. Cinderella's father accompanies them and is made visibly ill at ease by their pretensions. The older sister is determined to enjoy herself and acts unimpressed by the beauty of the palace garden: it is all her due, designed for her enjoyment, and she imagines herself attractive. The younger sister is more honest and cannot so easily disguise the fact that all this elegance is strange to her. She tugs plaintively at her sister's dress and wants to go home. She is, of course, refused and resolves to see the evening out only when a courtier begins to pay her some attention, thus reviving her spirits. She is disenchanted when her jealous sister takes her suitor away.

Now, as another courtly dance commences, the two sisters have a chance to perform the measures the dancing master taught them. The older sister watches with disgust as the younger dances. She starts out well, and for a moment we think she is really going to make it, but her steps become tentative and it is apparent that she's forgotten every step she knows. The older sister laughs, executes the dance with grotesque accuracy, and then, to show off, tries to balance on one foot. The younger sister is terrified, and, of course, the show-off begins to topple over. The jester catches her as she stumbles about trying to keep from falling flat on her face.

Four friends of the prince enter and prepare the guests for the arrival of their host. The handsome prince enters with a regal but lively flourish, and all the guests bow to him. The two sisters attempt to make their reverence so that the prince will take particular notice of them, but he does not even glance at them. The prince's companions dance a *pas de quatre*, which is followed by another general dance by the court.

One guest has not yet arrived. The light, mysterious music that heralded the first appearance of Cinderella's ragged fairy godmother interrupts the court music, and everyone pauses. The jester, at the prince's order, goes to welcome the newcomer in the garden. The twelve girls representing stars and the four fairies with their pages enter at the rear, and the court wonders what to expect with such an elaborate preparation. All look toward the entrance to the ballroom as the prince awaits the guest. Finally the royal coach of Cinderella draws up to the garden gate. The girl steps out, and all are dazzled by her natural beauty and the loveliness of her costume. The prince, who is immediately charmed, takes Cinderella's hand and leads her forward. Two pages hold Cinderella's train while the stars and fairies kneel about their mistress. Wishing to discover more about this ravishing girl, the prince escorts her for a walk through the palace grounds.

The other guests, who have watched the entrance of Cinderella from the boxes at the sides of the ballroom, now mingle on the dance floor and begin a masked dance. The ugly stepsisters, of course, have not recognized Cinderella and accept her simply as visiting royalty. Soon the prince returns alone and dances a variation, after which he leaves the scene. Now Cinderella dances and in her movements she conveys the youthful and tender joy she feels at the ball. It is as if she belonged there, for she is unembarrassed and confident in her natural graciousness.

The two sisters, alone for a moment, spend their time gossiping about the unattractive girl who has gained the prince's favor. The two lovers return. The harp is plucked against a deep, flowing melody, and they begin a *pas de deux*. The dance is soft and considerate, yet strong in its regal elegance and the personal elegance of the handsome young pair. The prince kneels before Cinderella as their dance finishes. She responds to his love by dancing a variation that reflects her new-found pleasure in loving and being loved. She is so happy that she has no memory of her misery at home; she pirouettes rapidly, and her two stepsisters are a million miles away.

A Negro page brings to the prince an orange on a silver tray. This is the most highly prized fruit in all the kingdom and the finest gift he can give Cinderella. She accepts it graciously. Then the prince turns to the ugly stepsisters and bestows an orange on each of them. Instantly they begin to quarrel about whose orange is larger, and the dominating sister snatches the choice one away from the timid creature.

Cinderella and the prince lead the court in an ensemble dance. The music is a bright, sparkling waltz that gradually gains in sonorous force, and all the guests are caught up in the spirit of romance. Suddenly—as the waltz gains relentless force, cymbals shimmer, and we hear the loud ticking of a clock—a flourish of trumpets announces the approach of midnight. The cymbals crash, to warn Cinderella that she must hasten. The girl rushes from the prince's arms. He watches, astonished, as she tries to make her way through the crowded guests to the gate. The girl is desperate lest her secret be discovered. When she arrives at the gate, midnight has come. Her beautiful dress becomes her ragged work clothes, and she flees into the night, leaving behind one of her slippers. The prince cannot understand; he looks after her as the orchestra restates the theme of their *pas de deux* and the curtain falls.

ACT THREE, SCENE ONE: AFTER THE BALL   When the curtain rises on the first scene, again Cinderella is seen sitting by the fire in her father's house, just as she was at the entrance of the fairy godmother. She is asleep. She wakens, looks about, and thinks she has dreamed of the ball. Only the slipper she finds hidden in her apron convinces her that she really was there, that there was a handsome prince, and that he did love her. She dances again with the broom, reflecting in her steps her unhappiness before the ball, her recollection of her first love, and her resignation to her everyday life.

Her sisters return. They are so tired that they don't even wish to gossip until they have undressed and cast off the weight of their excessive finery. They sigh as they remove their shoes from their swollen feet. But soon they are taunting Cinderella with tall tales about the ball, the prince, and his attentions to them. They toy with the oranges he gave them, and Cinderella is thinking too much of what the ball was really like to care much about their prattling.

The women hear a disturbance in the street. Townswomen rush in and excitedly announce that a royal procession is waking everyone up, that the prince, enamored of a girl he cannot find, is determined to discover the owner of a shoe left behind at the ball. He vows that he will marry the girl whom the shoe fits.

The sisters are apprehensive lest the prince visit their house when they are not fully dressed and scurry about putting on their formal gowns and their tight shoes again. The prince enters with the jester and an entourage. He holds

Cinderella's lost slipper in his hand and declares that the woman it fits shall become his wife. He does not notice the girl in rags who crouches at the fire. The stepsisters do obeisance before the prince, who responds to them so graciously that they imagine one of them might be the chosen one. First, the shy stepsister tries on the shoe. She knows it is silly to pretend that it will fit and gives up wistfully. The other sister is delighted at her failure, but has no more luck herself, despite much straining and pinching in an effort to force her foot into the shoe.

When it is apparent that she, too, is a misfit, Cinderella helps her pull the shoe off. As the girl kneels before her sister, the other slipper falls from her apron pocket. The prince sees it and asks the girl if she will try on the shoe. Her stepsisters rail at her, but the prince insists. The shoe fits perfectly. At first the sisters cannot believe it, but when the prince announces that Cinderella will be his bride, they attempt in several reverential gestures to make up for the years of misery they have caused the girl. Cinderella understands them, pities them, and touches them lovingly as they bow before her. The prince and Cinderella embrace. The fairy godmother appears and raises her wand.

ACT THREE, SCENE TWO: AN ENCHANTED GARDEN   The scene is transformed. We find ourselves in a magical place, a colorful garden where the light seems to sparkle. There a great boat awaits the arrival of the lovers. The prince's friends and the fairies dance together, and Cinderella and the prince enter. Six of the stars surround them as they dance, the fairies pose gracefully with their cavaliers, and the music sounds soaringly the theme of ideal romance that marked the couple's first recognition of love. The fairy godmother and all the magical creatures wish the lovers godspeed, and they step into the waiting ship. The surging music falls off into soft measures that predict eternal joy. The prince holds Cinderella in his arms as they sail off on a happy voyage that will never end.

Yet another important version of this ballet came into the American repertory in 1970:

> Music by Sergei Prokofiev. Staged and choreographed by Ben Stevenson. Scenery by Edward Haynes. Costumes by Norman McDowell. First presented by the National Ballet at the Lisner Auditorium, Washington, D.C., April 24, 1970.

The synopsis of this version of the ballet is close to others, but has some important differences:

ACT ONE   Cinderella's father watches his two stepdaughters embroidering scarves to be worn to a ball given that evening by the prince. The cruel stepdaughters tease their stepfather with the scarves. Cinderella enters and stops them. The stepsisters are furious and order Cinderella to clean the kitchen as they drag their father from the room. Her only friend now seems to be the broom.

Cinderella, remembering a picture of her mother, takes it from its hiding place and sits gazing at it. Her father enters and is overcome with remorse when he sees how much Cinderella resembles his first loving wife. She tries to comfort him when the stepsisters enter and are enraged to see Cinderella in her father's arms. They pull them apart and snatch the picture away. Suddenly the door opens and an old beggarwoman enters. The stepsisters decide to give her the picture, but the old woman sees the resemblance between the picture and Cinderella and returns it to Cinderella. Cinderella gives the old woman her last crust of bread.

The dressmaker and the wigmaker arrive to ready the stepsisters for the ball. A dancing master also arrives with the impossible task of teaching the stepsisters how to dance. Cinderella is alone again, pretending she is at the ball, and dances with the broom, then bursts into tears realizing it is only a daydream. The old beggar returns and much to Cinderella's amazement is transformed into a beautiful fairy godmother. The kitchen changes into a magic glade with dragonflies swooping among the trees. The fairy godmother asks Cinderella to find a pumpkin and four lizards and gives them to one of the dragonflies, who darts off into the trees. The fairy godmother gives a pair of glass slippers to Cinderella. The fairies of Spring, Summer, Autumn, and Winter arrive and dance for Cinderella, changing the seasons as they do. Cinderella's rags become a beautiful dress. The fairy godmother shows Cinderella a magic clock and warns her that at midnight her magic clothes will turn again into rags. The fairy godmother changes the pumpkin and lizards into a coach and horses and Cinderella drives to the ball like a princess.

ACT TWO   A jester greets the guests as they arrive in the ballroom. The guests are amazed when the ugly stepsisters arrive. The prince enters, and he too is amused by the sight of the sisters; however, he asks them each in turn to dance with him to the amazement of the crowd. Cinderella arrives in her coach, and the prince falls in love with her at first sight. He offers his guests oranges, as they are the very rarest fruit in the land. One of the sisters is left without an orange; Cinderella sees this and gives up her own. The stepsister accepts without recognizing Cinderella.

While the prince and Cinderella are dancing together, the clock strikes midnight and Cinderella's beautiful clothes turn to rags. The prince rushes after her to find only one of her glass slippers on the stairs.

ACT THREE   Cinderella waits among the cinders in the kitchen thinking the ball only a dream until she finds the other glass slipper in her pocket. She quickly hides it as the ugly sisters arrive. They show Cinderella the oranges they received from the prince. Suddenly the jester enters the room, heralding the arrival of the prince and two of his friends who have with them the glass slipper. The stepsisters vainly try to squeeze their big feet into the tiny slipper. The prince sees Cinderella sitting by the fire and asks her father if she may try it. As Cinderella gets up from the stool, she drops the other glass slipper. The prince is overjoyed! The stepsisters beg Cinderella's forgiveness and the fairy godmother arrives, accompanied by the fairies of the seasons.

The prince returns the glass slippers to them and the kitchen once again changes into a magic glade. Cinderella and her prince dance a romantic *pas de deux*, and at its conclusion, the guests arrive for the coronation of Cinderella, the cruelly mistreated girl who rose from the cinders to a royal throne.

NOTES   Reviewing this production of *Cinderella* in the British magazine, *Ballet Today*, Kay Rinfrette wrote: "Ashton's *Cinderella* for the Royal Ballet influenced Stevenson's ballet in several aspects. Like Ashton, Stevenson employs the English pantomime tradition by having the stepsisters played *en travesti*, and he excludes the stepmother who usually appears in Russian productions. Also, Stevenson omits the prince's search around the world. Unlike Ashton, Stevenson changes the sequence of musical numbers in the ballroom scene to give the *grand pas de deux* a traditional, formal structure. (The adagio is followed by the man's, then the ballerina's variation.) The choreography, especially effective in solos and group work, and character development are Stevenson's exciting, original conceptions (with only a few distant reverberations of some Ashton choreography).

"The choreographic structure of the ballet—Stevenson's use of thematic materials—is magnificent. Two primary movement themes (motifs), used separately and in combination, are introduced in the four-seasons sequence in Act One: (1) sudden or unexpected changes in direction of movement, and (2) traveling lifts which give an impression of weightlessness. The feeling of lightness created in this sequence emphasizes a fairy-tale quality and contrasts to the heaviness of the previous fireside scene (the cumbersome, heavy awkwardness of the stepsisters, the figurative 'burden' falling on Cinderella's shoulders).

"Specifically, the thematic movements include the 'dragonflies' transporting the fairy godmother in multiple traveling lifts with quick changes of direction —at one point she is carried back and forth across the stage three times without pause—and the sudden direction changes in the solos for Spring and Autumn. The same movement themes appear in the ballroom scene, especially in the *corps de ballet* work: many lovely lifts in unexpected directions, often backwards; at the waltz's climax, the girls, arching their backs, fall forward sequentially into their partners' arms, only to be weightlessly lifted and wafted away. The ballroom grand adagio, with its many extend traveling lifts (in fact, some lifts looked awkward and unnecessarily difficult), is also a part of weightless fantasy—the ballerina is swept away by the fairy-tale grandeur both literally and figuratively.

"The adagio in the last act is less involved with fantasy, closer to a real-life love relationship. This meaning is underscored by the choreography which includes thematic elements but in different combinations: there are fewer lifts, more *terre à terre* work, including swift runs with sudden direction changes, as if the lovers were blown by the wind. Structurally, this adagio is the climax of the ballet, combining and reconciling the literary themes of fantasy versus reality and the choreographic motifs of floating lightness versus heaviness or a sense of weight. In the final coronation scene, heavy-looking imperial crowns are placed on the heads of Cinderella and the prince—the fantasy (lightness) becomes a reality (weight).

"Character and dancing aspects are well balanced in this production, meaning that the stepsisters do not monopolize the show. Their hilarious antics are most clever in sequences with the dancing master and at the ball when they 'send-up' ballet steps—such as one sister holding an *attitude* for several seconds and then collapsing in a heap. The polarization of characters is clearly established in the beginning, when the stepsisters angrily snatch away from Cinderella a painting of her mother, and when Cinderella is kind to the old hag visitor (fairy godmother in disguise). The father, depicted as a multiple-henpecked man unable to cope, is a kind of transition figure between the 'good' Cinderella and the 'evil' stepsisters. Even minor characters are sharply drawn—the snobbish, prim dancing master and the eccentric, dissatisfied wigmaker."

Reviewing this new production of *Cinderella* in the New York *Times*, the critic Clive Barnes wrote: "The result is most pleasing. This is a good *Cinderella*. The settings by Edward Haynes and the costumes by Norman McDowell are simple but elegant, and Mr. Stevenson's unaffectedly classical choreography is a model of good taste.

"This is a formidable undertaking for a small company—it does not have so many dancers as the City Center Joffrey Ballet—and it survived grandly. Mr. Stevenson's choreography is strongly influenced by Frederick Ashton—Mr. Stevenson being a former member of the Royal Ballet—yet not slavishly so. Often he has gone to some lengths to be different from the Ashton version of the score, and his concept is always attractive.

"It is the kind of choreography that suits dancers—graceful and understated. He is not afraid of virtuosity, and certainly Mr. Stevenson has made more demands upon these Washington dancers than any previous choreographer. He cannot prevent the first scene of Cinderella and her sisters from appearing prosey—it always does in any production—but he does give his two lovers the most intricately stylish *pas de deux*.

"The dancing was splendid. Mr. Stevenson has mounted his ballet on two couples, Gaye Fulton and Desmond Kelly, and Marilyn Burr and Ivan Nagy. At the performance I saw it was given by Miss Fulton and Mr. Kelly.

"Miss Fulton, a delicate figurine of a princess in hiding, made an enchanting Cinderella, and Mr. Kelly, elegant and assertive, was the most perfect of Princes.

"Another young man of more than usual promise is Kirk Peterson, from the Harkness Youth Company, who was dancing the Jester. He had a brilliant technique and was very cleverly used by Mr. Stevenson. I also admired the roistering humor of Frederic Franklin (the company's director) and Larry Long as the Ugly Sisters, and the style of Judith Rhodes and Christine Knoblauch among the fairies. But the entire company extended and excelled itself."

CIRCLES

Music by Luciano Berio. Choreography by Glen Tetley. Decor and costumes by Nadine Baylis. First presented by the Netherlands Dance Theatre at the Royal Theatre, The Hague, March 5, 1968. First presented by the same ensemble at the City Center, New York, April 19, 1968.

This dance ballet uses the Luciano Berio score *Circles* for female voice, harp, and two percussion. The score's libretto is three poems by e. e. cummings (*Numbers 25, 76,* and *22*). The ballet is for six dancers, all of whom appear at the beginning of the piece, moving, exercising, warming up in silence. A boy and girl separate themselves from the group and, to the first of the three songs, dance together. Another *pas de deux* accompanies the second song while the third is more of an ensemble that recalls what has gone before.

Reviewing the ballet after its American premiere, Clive Barnes said in the New York *Times:* "Mr. Tetley's *Circles* is a lovely work. It is curious—perhaps shameful—that while Mr. Tetley has an enormous reputation in the Netherlands and England, in his native land he goes as a prophet if not unhonored at least remarkably unrecognized . . .

"The dancing flickers, ebbs and flows in all directions at the happily wayward command of the music. The six dancers interweave their patterns with a kind of creative expertise, certain in its technique yet diffident in its artistic assurance. The impression is of golden people dancing in a golden landscape, yet a gold not without the threat of devaluation and a landscape not without the danger of erosion. Nothing here is quite so certain as the actual dancing—what lies behind could be another story."

CIRCUS POLKA

Music by Igor Stravinsky. Choreography by Jerome Robbins. First presented by the New York City Ballet at the Stravinsky Festival, 1972, at the New York State Theatre, Lincoln Center, June 23, 1972.

Stravinsky's *Circus Polka* was composed precisely for the circus—for the Ringling Brothers, Barnum and Bailey Circus in 1942. The circus impresarios wanted to do a ballet for elephants. They asked me to arrange the dance and told me I could choose the composer. Who else but Stravinsky? I telephoned him, not giving away the whole story. "What kind of music?" he asked. "A polka," I said. "For whom?" he wanted to know. "Elephants." "How old?" "Young!" "Okay, if they are very young, I'll do it." What he did served its purpose very well, and our ballet for *Fifty Elephants and Fifty Beautiful Girls*, staged by John Murray Anderson, with costumes by Norman Bel Geddes, and Vera Zorina riding at the head of the troupe at the first performances, was done no less than 425 times.

Jerome Robbins in his ballet took an entirely new direction, and the work was one of the happiest inventions during our Stravinsky Festival at the New York State Theatre in 1972. Robbins chose for his cast young girls from the School of American Ballet and put them, the youngest first, through their paces. As ringmaster of the troupe, in formal top hat and swallow-tail coat, he led forty-eight of our talented children to Stravinsky's brisk measures. At the end, at his direction, the children formed the Stravinsky initials, *I. S.*, with periods. The ballet was such a hit that the whole piece had to be repeated at once.

CLOCKWISE

Music by Jean Françaix. Choreography by Bruce Marks. Costumes by Stanley Simmons. Lighting by Jules Fisher. First presented by the American Ballet Company at the Brooklyn Academy of Music, New York, October 24, 1970, with Karen Kelly, Christine Kono, Elizabeth Lee, Christine Sarry, Cristina Stirling, Larry Grenier, Edward Henkel, Daniel Levans, Richard Munro, John Sowinski, Kenneth Hughes, Kerry Williams, Olga Janke and Eve Wallstrum.

This first ballet by a premier danseur of American Ballet Theatre is a dance work arranged to a composition about a clock of flowers, by the French contemporary Françaix. The piece is in seven parts, as is the ballet, where different combinations of dancers suggest the fleeting passage of time. A central *pas de deux*, to a pensive romantic melody, suggests permanent affection, too, but that soon yields to convivial ensemble, and the work ends as it began, with a simulation of a clock.

NOTES   The critic Clive Barnes, in the New York *Times*, said that Bruce Marks "has produced a graceful, charming work . . . that bodes well for his future as a choreographer. This elegant first ballet . . . was neatly danced, with Christine Kono, Christine Sarry, Daniel Levins, Elizabeth Lee and John Sowinski all to the fore."

THE CLOWNS

Music by Hershy Kay. Choreography by Gerald Arpino. Costumes by Edith Lutyens Bel Geddes. Lighting by Tom Skelton. Assistant to Mr. Arpino: James Howell. First presented by the City Center Joffrey Ballet at the City Center, New York, February 28, 1968, with Robert Blankshine, Frank Bays, Erika Goodman and Maximiliano Zomosa in principal roles. Special effects by Vernon Lobb and Kip Coburn. Conducted by Hershy Kay.

The Clowns is a dramatic metaphor about life as it is lived by those perennial reflectors of the human spirit—the floppy white clowns of the *commedia dell' arte.* The piece begins with a bang, as if all the world had exploded, and a lone clown, battered and bruised, appears to be the only remnant of civilization. But he is not quite alone, for bodies begin to fall out of the sky like hail, bodies of fellow clowns. Mournfully but doggedly determined and not stopping to grieve, the survivor piles them all up into a kind of pyre. But mysteriously, at least one of them is alive, for a girl emerges to join the clown. The two clowns dance together joyously. Their dance is a dance of renewal and liveliness and the life is contagious: before we know it, the whole pile of bodies is revived and the clown tribe lives again.

Not content, however, with renewal and resumption of their old funny and antic roles, the clowns now reveal their human side, too. They begin to plot against each other and to employ weapons—big balloons that seem to envelop the opposition. The original survivor, however much he tries not to get involved in this dark side of human nature, is soon caught up in it, too. The fellows he has helped revive turn hostile and he is the victim. In retaliation, he brings in the biggest balloon imaginable, a huge, long cylinder that becomes a transparent tunnel. What this instrument soon becomes is a clown catcher and all the opposition are entrapped in it, beating against its walls, helpless to get out. They can *see* out and the walls of the prison are soft but they cannot penetrate them. They are all sucked down into it. Except for one. The first survivor, who again survives.

LE COMBAT (*see* THE DUEL)

CON AMORE

Classic ballet in three scenes. Music by Gioacchino Rossini. Choreography by Lew Christensen. Libretto by James Graham-Luhan. Scenery and costumes by James Bodrero. Scenery executed by James Martin. First presented by the San Francisco Ballet, March 10, 1953, at the War Memorial Opera

*House, San Francisco, with Sally Bailey, Nancy Johnson, and Leon Dan-
ielian in the principal roles. Presented by the New York City Ballet at the
City Center, New York, June 9, 1953, with a cast headed by Sally Bailey,
Nancy Johnson, Herbert Bliss, and Jacques d'Amboise.*

Con Amore is a ballet about love as it was frequently depicted in nineteenth-
century European engravings. It is about love as it was regarded a hundred
years ago and about love as it is frequently still regarded today. The ballet is
in three scenes, each of which has for its music an overture by Rossini: the
overtures to *La Gazza Ladra, Il Signor Bruschino,* and *La Scala di Seta.*

SCENE ONE: THE AMAZONS AND THE BANDIT   After a musical introduction,
the curtain rises on a stylized rustic scene. Here a company of Amazons, handsome and robust girls in smart military uniforms, are drilling under the command of their captain and her lieutenants. The girls move briskly and sharply,
and it is apparent from their severe military bearing that they have never
known love and wouldn't even entertain the idea of it. They are perfectly
happy watching their beautiful captain as she sets an example of the brilliant
skill in dancing and drill that they themselves hope to attain.

Love, however, asserts itself. A bandit invades the wood and dances among
them. The girls treat the handsome intruder with disdain at first, but his uncontrolled gaiety and charm eventually pierce their hearts. But the vagabond
bandit will have none of them. He will not be tied down by love and spurns
their affections. He even dares to resist the charms of the lovely captain. At this
point the perennial wrath of woman scorned holds the bandit at bay. The Amazons aim their muskets at him and he kneels before them, helpless. Blackout.

SCENE TWO: THE HUSBAND'S RETURN   After a short musical interlude, the
curtain rises on the boudoir of a fashionable lady. She is alone in the room and
is obviously preparing for a tryst. This turns out to be a series of trysts. The
lady's husband is away at the moment, and all of her suitors have chosen this
night to visit her.

First, a man about town knocks at her door. The lady admits him. The man
attempts to embrace her, but the lady eludes him. It is clear, however, that she
does not wish to elude him long. But before she can succumb, there is another
knock at the door. The man about town hastily conceals himself, and the lady
admits a sailor, who relentlessly chases her about her apartment, breathing lustily. He has almost worn down the lady when there is still another knock. The
lady hides the sailor in her closet and admits a young student. This lad, instead of being eager for the lady's affections, finds her charms distasteful. She
is obliged to make the advances, which the young man, knees quivering, just
manages to escape. The man about town and the sailor, who have been
watching all this, emerge from their hiding place to berate the student and resume their attack. There is another knock at the door. The lady's husband

enters. He sees his wife with the three men and stares at them with his mouth open in astonishment. Blackout.

SCENE THREE: A TRIUMPH OF LOVE   In the final scene, we return to the finale of Scene One, where the bandit still kneels at the mercy of the angry Amazons. Amore (Cupid) enters in a chariot and with her skill attempts to remedy the situation. Hardly has she begun to do so than we are again presented with the dilemma of the finale of Scene Two. What is Amore going to do with all these men who seem to be in love with the same woman? But Amore solves everything. She draws her bow; her arrows pierce the hearts of all the men. As the curtain falls, the bandit, smitten finally with love for the Amazon captain, holds her in his arms; the lady is reunited with her husband; the man about town and the sailor embrace the Amazon lieutenants; and the timorous student, struck by love at last, rushes to claim Amore herself.

THE CONCERT

A charade in one act. Music by Frédéric Chopin. Choreography by Jerome Robbins. Costumes by Irene Sharaff. First presented by the New York City Ballet March 6, 1956, at the City Center, New York, with Tanaquil LeClercq and Robert Barnett in principal roles.

Jerome Robbins subtitles this ballet "The Perils of Everybody" and writes in a program note: "One of the pleasures of attending a concert is the freedom to lose oneself in listening to the music. Quite often, unconsciously, mental pictures and images form; and the patterns and paths of these reveries are influenced by the music itself, or its program notes, or by the personal dreams, problems, and fantasies of the listener. Chopin's music in particular has been subject to fanciful 'program' names such as the Butterfly Étude, the Minute Waltz, the Raindrop Prelude, etc."

During the overture to the ballet, we look at an amusing drop curtain, by Saul Steinberg, depicting the interior of an old-fashioned concert hall. When the curtain rises, a pianist crosses the stage, dusts the piano, and slumps down in meditation. Finally, he begins to play, and the audience begins to arrive, each carrying a folding chair: a man in a scarf who sits and meditates seriously, then two girls who clearly disturb him, then a girl in a huge wide-brimmed hat. She is so enthralled by the music that she snuggles right up to the piano and embraces it. A very serious student indeed follows, and then a husband and wife and a man on tiptoe. An usher tries to straighten out a mix-up over seats. When everyone is quieted down a bit, their fantasies begin to take over.

The husband envisages the murder of his wife and dreams of her substitute nearby. As the pianist pounds out a Mazurka, he sees himself as a brave hussar carrying off his beloved. His beloved, meanwhile, only wants to be a poor butterfly and acts that way. The wife intervenes, the poor girl is put down, and her husband is compelled to back down.

These are but some of the jokes that are played and acted out by these people to Chopin's music. To reveal all of them is to miss the fun of seeing the ballet, called by Patricia Barnes, in *Dance and Dancers,* "dance's funniest creation."

NOTES *The Concert* was extensively revised for Jerome Robbins's Ballets U.S.A. presentation at the Spoleto Festival June 8, 1958, with settings by Saul Steinberg that were used in the New York City Ballet revival (first presented December 2, 1971, at the New York State Theatre with Sara Leland, Francisco Moncion, Bettijane Sills, Shaun O'Brien, Robert Weiss, Bart Cook, Stephen Caras, Gloriann Hicks, Delia Peters, and Christine Redpath in principal roles. Jerry Zimmerman was the pianist).

The Concert was mounted for the Royal Ballet at the Royal Opera House, Covent Garden, London, on March 4, 1975, with frontcloths designed by Edward Gorey. Principal roles were taken by Lynn Seymour, Michael Coleman, and Georgina Parkinson. Writing in *Dance and Dancers* magazine, the English music critic Noël Goodwin said: "When I first saw *The Concert* in the inaugural Festival of Two Worlds at Spoleto in 1958, I ventured the opinion that this was one of the few deliberately comic ballets which could round off a program without anticlimax . . . Let me now amend that in the light of later experience and its welcome addition to the Royal repertory: *The Concert* is one of the few successful comic ballets on any count, and one that I still find the most hilarious I have ever seen."

CONCERTO

Music by Dimitri Shostakovich. Choreography by Kenneth MacMillan. First presented at the Deutsche Oper, West Berlin, November 30, 1966. First presented in the United States by American Ballet Theatre at the New York State Theatre, New York, May 18, 1967, with Eleanor D'Antuono and Scott Douglas, Toni Lander and Bruce Marks, and Cynthia Gregory in the principal roles. Decor and costumes after designs by Jürgen Rose. Lighting by Jean Rosenthal.

This is a dance ballet arranged to Shostakovich's *Concerto No. 2 for Piano and Orchestra.* Its plot is the music. The choreographer has said: "I just listen and listen and dig into the music. I don't do any actual preliminary work at home like some other choreographers, and so it can be a tricky business. Every choreographer has his own method of working, but I invent my ballets directly, in the rehearsal room. When there, I again listen to the music, this time with the dancers, and then start experimenting and inventing."

The first movement is led by a brightly dancing girl and boy, the second is dominated by a serious dance for two lovers, while the third is led by a charming girl. The mood and temper of the dances reflect a vision of the music.

The British critic Clement Crisp has written that *Concerto* has "a fresh, 'open' style that matches the exhilarating textures of the score with complete assurance."

CONCERTO BAROCCO

Classic ballet in three movements. Music by Johann Sebastian Bach. Choreography by George Balanchine. Scenery and costumes by Eugene Berman. First presented by the American Ballet at the Theatre of Hunter College, New York, May 29, 1940, with Marie-Jeanne, Mary Jane Shea, and William Dollar in the principal roles.

The only preparation possible for this ballet is a knowledge of its music, for *Concerto Barocco* has no "subject matter" beyond the score to which it is danced and the particular dancers who execute it. Set to Bach's *Concerto in D minor for Two Violins,* the ballet tries to interest the audience only by its dancing, its treatment of the music, just as Baroque art and architecture interested people not because of their subjects but because of the decorative treatment that embellished those subjects.

Bach's great concerto can stand alone. Some people then wonder, why arrange a ballet to such music? Why not arrange ballets to music that is more dependent, music that dancing can "fill out"? The answer is that bad music often inspires bad dancing, bad choreography. It is not an accident that the dance masterpieces of Saint-Léon, Petipa, and Fokine all have scores that are also masterworks. *Coppélia, The Sleeping Beauty,* and *Petrouchka,* with their scores by Delibes, Tchaikovsky, and Stravinsky, suggested to each one of these choreographers an advance in the development of ballet.

Choosing pieces of music for dancing is a matter for the individual choreographer. A choreographer disinterested in classical dancing will not care to use scores by Bach and Mozart except for theatrical sensational reasons; he will select music more to his immediate purpose. But if the dance designer sees in the development of classical dancing a counterpart in the development of music and has studied them both, he will derive continual inspiration from great scores. He will also be careful, as he acts on this inspiration, not to interpret the music beyond its proper limits, not to stretch the music to accommodate a literary idea, for instance. If the score is a truly great one, suitable for dancing, he will not have need of such devices and can present his impression in terms of pure dance.

FIRST MOVEMENT: VIVACE The curtain rises. The music begins. There are eight girls on stage. Dancing variously as one group, as two groups, and in duets, the girls correspond to the music the orchestra plays, but not in any strict or literal sense; they do not mirror the music, rather they move in accordance with its length, the space between its beginning and end being filled by a dance picture of the music. Just as the portrait is different from the news photograph, so the dance picture tries to tell something independent of an exact, bar-by-bar, rhythm-by-rhythm, mirror image of the music.

As the two violins take up their parts in the music, two soloists enter. Singly, together, and with the *corps de ballet*, they become a part of the dance orchestration. They support each other as the music of one violin entwines the other; they depict and develop dance themes that recur with the repetition and development of themes in the orchestra.

SECOND MOVEMENT: LARGO MA NON TANTO Now the soloists leave the stage. The orchestra sounds the touching, lyrical melody. One of the soloists returns, accompanied by a male partner, who lifts her softly and slowly, turns her as the *corps de ballet* bend low before her, and leads her in and out of a maze formed by the *corps*. The music is tender, but it possesses a warm nobility and strength that the ballerina's partner allows her to imitate as its development proceeds. When the music gathers toward a full statement and the theme repeats again and again, climbing with each repetition to a climactic rest, the ballerina's partner lifts her without pause high over his head, over and over again, to the accumulating sound. Then, toward the end of the movement, the boy slides the girl low across the floor in three daring movements. The ballerina rises each time in an open pose that reflects the strength underlying the lyricism of the theme.

THIRD MOVEMENT: ALLEGRO The music is now quickly rhythmic. All ten dancers seem to respond to it spontaneously, marking the beat of the music with soft, light jumps, crisp arm gestures, and syncopated groupings. As the joyous music ends, all the dancers kneel.

CONCERTO FOR JAZZ BAND AND ORCHESTRA

Music by Rolf Liebermann. Choreography by Arthur Mitchell and George Balanchine. Lighting by Ronald Bates. Conducted by Robert Irving. First presented by the New York City Ballet at the New York State Theatre, Lincoln Center, May 7, 1971, with dancers from the Dance Theatre of Harlem and the New York City Ballet.

This ballet, which received its one and only performance at a special gala occasion, will never be done again in all probability but is worth remembering and recording. It was a wonderful thing for me to collaborate on the choreography with Arthur Mitchell, who had become, in the New York City Ballet, our first black *premier danseur*, the first black first dancer in *any* major ballet company.

In 1968, at the time of the assassination of Martin Luther King, Jr., I did a memorial ballet, for one performance, to Stravinsky's *Requiem Canticles*. Arthur Mitchell, at that time disturbed by King's death and its meaning, determined that he would make it possible for other blacks to become fine dancers. The Dance Theatre of Harlem, and its associated school which he subsequently founded, is one of the great breakthroughs in the arts in America. To work with his dancers and our own on one ballet was, therefore, a special pleasure.

The music for the ballet, by the distinguished impresario and musician Rolf Liebermann, alternates a big jazz band (Doc Severinsen and the *Tonight Show* Orchestra) with a symphony ensemble. It is in six parts: *Introduction and Jump, Scherzo I, Blues, Scherzo II, Boogie Woogie,* and *Interludium.* Those who saw the ballet that night seemed to enjoy it very much and to appreciate the special quality of the occasion. It made me, personally, as it did Lincoln Kirstein, prouder than ever to be an occupant of the New York State Theatre.

CONCERTO FOR PIANO AND WINDS

Music by Igor Stravinsky. Choreography by John Taras. Costumes by Rouben Ter-Arutunian. Lighting by Ronald Bates. Pianist: Gordon Boelzner. Conducted by Robert Irving. First presented by the New York City Ballet at the Stravinsky Festival, 1972, at the New York State Theatre, Lincoln Center, June 20, 1972, with Bruce Wells in the leading role.

This wonderful score by Stravinsky, too seldom heard in the concert hall, has been used twice by John Taras for ballet. His first version, *Arcade*, was done for the New York City Ballet at the City Center, New York, March 28, 1963, with Suzanne Farrell and Arthur Mitchell in the leading roles. His second ballet to this music was presented during the Stravinsky Festival at the New York City Ballet in June 1972.

The ballet starts shortly after the orchestra begins, the curtain rising on fourteen boys, all in red costume. Different groupings take up the accent of the music, precise and percussive, as the piano, like a percussive instrument, plays a toccata-like theme. There are no strings in this orchestra, we remember, as the definitive gesture and movement point to vital and supple action rather than reaction.

The second movement, which is very slow and pulsating, has an entirely different character. The stage darkens and three spotlights point to three boys kneeling. They rise slowly in answer to the music, as do the lights, and in poses and groupings complement the piano and wind instruments' accompaniment. At the end, they again kneel in the dark.

Under bright lights, the dancers to the music perform a variety of brisk response that includes references back to the first part, a fugue, and a lively finale.

CONCERTO FOR TWO SOLO PIANOS

> Music by Igor Stravinsky. Choreography by Richard Tanner. Costumes by Stanley Simmons. First presented by the New York City Ballet at the New York State Theatre, Lincoln Center, January 21, 1971, with Gelsey Kirkland and John Clifford, Colleen Neary and James Bogan, and David Richardson as principals.

This work, the first by Richard Tanner for our repertory, was later performed at the New York City Ballet's Stravinsky Festival, on February 23, 1972. Stravinsky's music had its first performance in 1935, with the composer and his son Soulima as soloists. The concerto is in four movements: 1. Con moto, 2. Notturno—Adagietto, 3. Quattro variazioni, and 4. Preludio and Fuga; the ballet follows this same pattern, basing its movement on the score's development. The plot of the music is the ballet's narrative.

One of the remarkable aspects of the score, as Eric Walter White notes in his indispensable volume on Stravinsky, is its second movement, the Nocturne —"a slow movement of exquisite tenderness and feeling, closely related in style to the slow movements of the Piano Sonata and the Capriccio."

CONCERTO GROSSO

> Music by George Frederick Handel. Choreography by Charles Czarny. Costumes by Joop Stovkis. First presented by the Netherlands Dance Theatre at the Circustheatre, Scheveningen, Holland, January 29, 1971. First presented in the United States by the same ensemble at the Brooklyn Academy of Music, New York, April 1, 1972.

Handel's music for the Concerto Grosso No. 5 and the Allegro from the Concerto Grosso No. 12 accompany this dance ballet based on gymnastics and athletics. The first part, begun by four boys in gym suits, is a warm-up for exercises and games to come. Four girls join them. The second part, Obligatory Exercise, is for three dancers. In Shadow Boxing, in silence, eight dancers wearing red mittens fight with each other in a gentle way. Following a sequence for skating, a line is drawn on stage to represent a tightrope, on which the dancers balance and perform. Next, in bright striped costumes of red and white, two boys play at soccer, each embodying opposing sides. All four couples join together again for the finale, a *Karate Minuet*.

CONCERTO IN G

> *Music by Maurice Ravel. Choreography by Jerome Robbins. Sets and costumes by Rouben Ter-Arutunian. Lighting by Ronald Bates. First presented by the New York City Ballet at the Hommage à Ravel at the New York State Theatre, Lincoln Center, May 14, 1975, with Suzanne Farrell and Peter Martins as principals. Conducted by Manuel Rosenthal.*

One of the real hits of the New York City Ballet's Ravel festival in 1975, *Concerto in G* is danced to music that has an association with the United States. Ravel, at the peak of his fame and popularity, had just returned from a triumphant American tour when he began work on the piece. His hope was to compose a work that he could play himself, in order to fulfill the many requests that had accumulated for personal appearances. In the end he asked Marguerite Long, an old friend, to play as he conducted. Together they performed the concerto to great acclaim throughout Europe.

Janet Flanner attended the first performance and reported, under her pen name "Genêt," enthusiastically to *The New Yorker*, as Irving Drutman has recalled in *Paris Was Yesterday, 1925–39* (The Viking Press, New York, 1972).

Robbins's ballet to the *Concerto in G* is a dance piece without a story. There are three movements. While the first and third parts of the ballet, like the music, respond to jazz influences, a central sinuous adagio for the two principals creates an enduring impression.

Frances Herridge in the New York *Post* called *Concerto in G* "another gem for the repertory in a class with Robbins's *Dances at a Gathering*."

Writing in *Dance and Dancers* magazine, the critic Patricia Barnes wrote that Robbins's "opening and closing movements, inventive, fresh and lively, used the ensemble of boys and girls with a vitality that earlier characterized his *Interplay* and in its jazz-tinctured rhythms showed Robbins in his very best Broadway mood; but it was the adagio movement for Suzanne Farrell and Peter Martins that was the work's real heart. Robbins has used Farrell's exquisite body to fabulous effect, exploiting her length of limb, her whole-hearted approach to dancing, in a pas de deux of genuine tenderness. The blend of daring lifts, swoops and swirls is contrasted with wonderfully effective little pauses, moments of telling stillness."

THE CONSORT

Music by Dowland, Neusidler, Morley, and anonymous composers. Orches-
trated by Christopher Keene. Choreography by Eliot Feld. Costumes by
Stanley Simmons. Lighting by Jules Fisher. First presented by the American
Ballet Company at the Brooklyn Academy of Music, New York, October
24, 1970, with Marilyn D'Honau, Christine Kono, Elizabeth Lee, Olga
Janke, Cristina Stirling, Larry Grenier, Kenneth Hughes, Daniel Levans,
Richard Munro, and John Sowinski.

Seventeenth-century music, mostly English, with some bawdy German songs
for salt, provides the musical base for this dance ballet, orchestrated by the
then musical director of the American Ballet Company, Christopher Keene.
There is no plot here, and at first it appears that we shall be watching simply a
stately but vigorous period piece, expressive of the Elizabethan age. But a curious thing happens. The long, formal dresses of the girls yield to short shifts,
and before we know what has happened, the boys are whirling them about,
courtiers have become peasants and, perhaps, themselves. While the stylization
of the dances suggests a time long ago, the best of the orchestration and its demanding rhythms suggest the music of our own time, too, which is reflected in
a rustic dance difference. Set for ten dancers, there are combinations of ensembles, boys and girls alone as well as *pas de deux* and solos, that merge the two
styles of dancing.

NOTES   Writing about *The Consort* in the *Village Voice,* the critic Deborah
Jowitt said: "The first part of *The Consort* is courtly, restrained, with that
faint undercurrent of unpleasantness that you feel in a real pavane. Within the
elaborate ritual, everyone is sizing up his partner and engaging in an almost
invisible thrusting and parrying. Feld keeps the feeling of social dance; many
instances of couples doing unison movement based—very remotely—on period
dances. There are a few interludes that are more irregular. For example,
there's an interesting bit in which Olga Janke dances very slowly and mini-
mally, involved with her own skirt and a path that she is not quite progressing
along, while John Sowinski keeps circling her lightly, but not lightheartedly—
doing some of the subtly complex Feld steps that Sowinski performs with such
luminous intelligence. They are aware and yet not aware of each other, and
you are not quite sure which is the moth and which the star.

"As the court section ends, some of the women begin to help each other un-
dress on stage. Quietly and naturally, they remove headdresses, take off
boleros, loop their skirts up to above their knees. Daniel Levans examines and
strokes his feathered cap for quite a time before tossing it into the wings.
Again there is something faintly sinister in the air. When all the dancers are

ready, the peasant section begins and begins mildly, with some of the same steps from the court part. You almost feel that these could be the same aristocrats playing at being peasants. Yet the stage gets more crowded (five couples as opposed to the three who began the piece), the dancers' bodies begin to look more weighty and sprawling, the harp (Keene's lute surrogate) is less noticeable, and the brasses begin to bray. These are still social dances, but with a coarseness and an increasingly ribald air. Two men do a fast rowdy dance, each with two girls, to Hans Neusidler's marvelously strange "Der Juden Tanz." *The Consort* ends with a debauch—the men wobbling like scarecrows, clutching the women to them; just drunk enough to be singlemindedly lecherous and with enough control left to do something about it. As the curtain comes down, the women have their legs about the men's waists and are being tossed and worried at. It reminded me of one of those Breughel scenes: you feel that because most of the time the peasants must have worked so hard, their appetites for play and drunken oblivion must have been immense, simple, and quickly sated."

COPPÉLIA (The Girl with Enamel Eyes)

Classic ballet in three acts. Music by Léo Delibes. Choreography by Arthur Saint-Léon. Book by Charles Nuitter and Arthur Saint-Léon, after a story by E. T. A. Hoffmann. First presented at the Théâtre Impérial de l'Opéra, Paris, May 25, 1870, with Giuseppina Bozacchi as Swanilda and Eugenie Fiocre as Franz. First presented in the United States by the American Opera at the Metropolitan Opera House, New York, March 11, 1887, with Marie Giuri and Felicita Carozzi in the leading roles. First presented in England at the Empire Theatre, London, May 14, 1906, with Adeline Genée as Swanilda.

Just as *Giselle* is ballet's great tragedy, so *Coppélia* is its great comedy. Both ballets are love stories and both have their roots in real life as well as in fantasy. In *Giselle* there are ghosts to test the quality of the hero's love for the heroine, and in *Coppélia* there is another romantic device by which the heroine makes sure of her lover's devotion. This device is the beautiful, lifeless doll, whose quiet, mechanical beauty contrasts with the charming liveliness of the real-life heroine. Because the hero in *Giselle* can only meet his lost love briefly in fantasy, and thereafter she is lost to reality, the ending of the ballet is tragic. But in *Coppélia* the inadequacy of the fantastic wax doll leads the hero back to his real love, and the ending is happy. And where Albrecht in *Giselle* learns an unhappy lesson from which he will never completely recover, Franz in *Coppélia* learns a lesson that makes his life happy forever after.

ACT ONE: THE SQUARE A spacious overture sets the tone for the whole ballet. The music begins with a melody of quiet dignity, first stated by the horns, then swept up by the strings. A muffled drum sounds, and the mood changes spontaneously to open gaiety as the orchestra plays a spirited robust mazurka. At its conclusion, the curtain rises.

The scene is a square in any small town in Central Europe; the time is a sunny afternoon several hundred years ago. A small house in the back faces the audience; on the side, a higher dwelling with a balcony projecting from the second floor dominates the street. Other buildings cluster about the square in a pleasantly haphazard fashion. All the façades are clean and painted in bright colors, and the walls and roofs seen in the background confirm our impression of an old village whose charm has not been worn away by changing times. The square is empty. An old man, bent with age, hobbles out of the door of the house on the right. This is Dr. Coppélius, the town's most mysterious citizen. He is said to dabble in alchemy and magic, but no one knows precisely what he does. Coppélius looks up at the balcony of his house, and we see that a lovely young girl is sitting there, reading a book. She is hidden a little from the full light of the sun, is wholly preoccupied with her reading, and takes no notice of the old doctor. Coppélius points up at the studious girl, rubs his hands with satisfaction as if he were a delighted chaperone, and re-enters his house.

The door of the little house in the back opens in a moment, and Swanilda emerges. She is dressed in bright colors particularly becoming to her dark beauty. From her movements we know almost immediately that she is very young and very much in love. The music to which she dances is piquant in the unembarrassed fullness of its melody, and Swanilda dances to it with obvious pleasure at some inner happiness. She walks rapidly on point, looking about the square anxiously to see that she is alone. She is expecting someone, but has some business of her own to attend to first. She glances up at the balcony of the large house and sees there the charming young girl, just as attractive as she is. The girl is intensely occupied and, holding the book rigidly before her, she does not look down to see Swanilda waving to her. Swanilda is annoyed. First of all she is annoyed because the girl is clearly snubbing her, but she is chagrined mostly because she has noticed that Franz, her fiancé, has also waved at this strange girl and has never mentioned it to her. Everyone calls the girl Coppélia. She is said to be the old man's daughter, but Coppélius has never appeared with her in the streets of the town and their relationship is just as unfathomable as Coppélius himself. Swanilda imitates her, holding an imaginary book before her. Then she bows low to Coppélia, in mock ceremony. Still the girl will not notice her. Swanilda stamps her foot in annoyance and dances briefly. She does not understand why Coppélia sits there reading on such a beautiful day and suspects she might be in a trance. On the other hand, she might be waiting for Franz! Swanilda approaches the house to see the girl more closely, shakes her fists at her, but quickly turns away as she hears Franz coming down the street. She is carefully hidden by the time he enters and she observes him secretly.

Franz is a high-spirited young peasant dressed in country costume. Like Swanilda, Franz is open and carefree by nature, but his heartiness masks a certain conceit: he seems not to have a care in the world and would not think it odd if every girl in the village adored him as much as Swanilda does. He does not go directly to Swanilda's door, but strides over to the house of Coppélius. After making sure that he isn't being watched, he glances up at the balcony. He waves to Coppélia flirtatiously, but also casually, as if he were in the habit of greeting her every time he passed. He points to Swanilda's door and remembers his love for her in the midst of this new infatuation. He clearly enjoys not knowing which lovely girl to choose. He clutches his heart as he looks up at Coppélia, then blows a kiss to her. Swanilda's worst suspicions of Franz's fickleness seem to be justified. Her suspicions become fears when Coppélia looks up from her book and waves back to Franz. Neither she nor Franz can see that behind the girl Coppélius stands concealed. He watches the flirtation with obvious disapproval, steps forward quickly, and closes the window curtains in Coppélia's face. Franz is abashed by this sudden disappearance of his new love. He is so distressed that he doesn't notice Swanilda, who has come into the square and stands right behind him. Swanilda refuses to attract his attention when he won't even turn away from the balcony; she walks off.

Now Franz consoles himself by remembering his rendezvous with Swanilda. But he does not have time to reach her door before Swanilda returns, bringing a beautiful butterfly she has just caught.

Franz takes the butterfly from her and pins it to his shirt. To Swanilda, this harmless gesture is a stab at her own broken heart. She bursts into tears and angrily accuses Franz of being unfaithful to her. He demurs, but she has no patience with his offhand answers and suggests that they come to him just as readily as his flirtations. Now that he sees how serious she is, Franz sincerely denies that he loves anyone else. But Swanilda is firm in her disbelief; she will not listen. Now Franz begins to lose his temper: how can she fail, he wonders, to see that he loves only her? Swanilda leaves the square, and Franz hails a party of peasants, their friends, who are unaware of the tension between the two lovers. They dance the rollicking mazurka that the orchestra first played in the overture, and when Swanilda joins them, her anxieties are momentarily dispelled. But she is determined to keep clear of Franz and, even at the sacrifice of her happiness, will accept no explanations.

The dancing of the peasants halts as the burgomaster enters the square. Everyone stands aside to make room for him and listens attentively as he tells them that on the next day the village will receive a great new bell for the town clock as a gift from the lord of the manor and that they must prepare themselves for the celebration attendant upon the ceremonies. The peasants are delighted at the idea of an unexpected festival. Their pleasure is so great that they do not pay much attention to strange noises emanating from the house of Coppélius.

The burgomaster goes on to say that the gracious lord will present handsome dowries to the girls who marry on the festival day. Several couples look at each other expectantly, but Swanilda is unmoved. Franz watches her closely. The burgomaster turns and asks her if she will be wed tomorrow. Unwilling to expose her broken heart to her friends and perhaps still hoping that she may be wrong about Franz's love, Swanilda resorts to fate and takes up an ear of wheat which the burgomaster offers her and shakes it near her ear, looking at her fiancé. The custom is—if she hears anything, her lover "loves her true"; if the wheat is silent, her lover "loves her not." Franz supports Swanilda in lovely deep poses as she bends low to listen to the wheat. Swanilda hears nothing. Franz, who thinks this pretense is silly, also hears nothing. She beckons to a friend and shakes the wheat again. The friend claims there is a sound, but Swanilda will not believe it. She throws the straw to the ground and announces that she and Franz are no longer engaged. Franz stalks away in disgust at the ways of women, while Swanilda joins her friends to dance a bright, gay tune as if nothing had happened to disturb their good time. A drum roll sounds, and Swanilda's friends dance a czardas, a Hungarian folk dance that starts out with slow, formal dignity and then increases in both speed and humor to become delirious with joy. The light grows darker and the group soon disbands. The stage is empty as night falls.

The door to Coppélius's house opens, and the wizened old man totters out. He pulls out a large key, locks the door, tries it several times, puts his key away, pats his pocket, and proceeds slowly across the square, leaning heavily on his cane. Obviously reluctant at leaving his house, Coppélius is easily frightened by a band of pranksters who rail at him good-humoredly, dance about him, and boisterously try to overcome his reluctance to join in. He loses his temper, which only encourages the fun. As they push him about, Coppélius drops his key. The villagers do not notice this and soon leave him. He shuffles across the street on his errand, shaking his head at their impertinence.

Swanilda and a group of her friends pass him as they enter on their way to supper. Swanilda is delighted to find that he has lost his key. She looks back toward Coppélius, who has now disappeared, and then at his house. Her friends easily persuade Swanilda to try the key in Coppélius's door. At last she will discover the illusive Coppélia alone! She goes to the door, fits the key to the lock, and signals pleadingly to her friends to follow. She steps in. She backs out hurriedly, frightened at her own audacity and the dark interior. Her friends line up behind her in single file, trembling with fear, and one by one they enter the house.

The square is deserted for a moment, then Franz comes in, armed with a ladder. The petulant youth is determined to have his love acknowledged by Coppélia, now that Swanilda has renounced him, and he places the ladder against the house. He is climbing up to a window when Coppélius, who has finally missed his key, rushes in to look for it. He apprehends Franz, attacks him with his walking stick, and chases him off. He then continues to search for the key. When he fails to find it and discovers that his door is wide open, he throws up his hands in despair and with great agitation runs into the house. The persistent Franz re-enters, places his ladder again, and climbs toward the mysterious Coppélia. The curtain falls.

ACT TWO: COPPÉLIUS'S HOUSE   The scene is a large room with dark walls. There is a large window at the back, and on the left is a curtained enclosure. Curious immobile figures, staring straight ahead, sit and stand about the stage in fixed attitudes, each as if cut off in the middle of a gesture. But there is not time to observe them before Swanilda and her friends walk in on tiptoe. The girls take in the weird room and are clearly sorry that they have let Swanilda talk them into coming. A small light throws their shadows against the walls, and they retreat into the center of the room. More curious than afraid, but still treading softly, Swanilda roams about looking at the woodenlike characters.

They seem to be dolls, but they are all life-sized and the suspended gestures in which they are fixed are alarmingly human. On the right, seated on a cushion, sits a tall Chinaman dressed in a richly embroidered native costume. A one-man band in resplendent parade dress stands with arm out, ready to strike the huge drum he carries. An astronomer in long black robes and a high, peaked hat, a poised juggler in the middle of one of his tricks, a Harlequin in typical diamond-patched costume, and a king holding scepter in hand—all these characters occupy Coppélius's room as if it were their home. [In the Sadler's Wells Theatre Ballet production, the figures are a Chinaman, a Crusader, Pierrot, an astrologer, and an Oriental dancer.] They are all individuals, each seems to exist apart from the others, yet to Swanilda and her friends the silent, still figures have no animate existence at all and resemble nothing so much as oversized dolls. Still, the girls are terrified by the darkness and the strange silence. Swanilda is instinctively moved to investigate the curtained alcove, for nowhere does she see Coppélia. She goes over, starts to peep through the curtain, and then runs back to her friends. Her knees are trembling so much that one of the girls holds her shaking legs. The girls force Swanilda to return to the curtain, and this time she is a little bolder. She looks behind the curtain, runs back to her friends, and gestures with automatic movements to music that might accompany the dance of a mechanical toy! Coppélia is a doll! One of the girls accidentally collides with the sitting Chinaman, and the interlopers are aghast as the Chinaman throws out his arms like an automaton, wags his head knowingly, and does a little rhythm act. The terrified girls approach him carefully, but the Chinaman does not change his position. He is a doll, too, but a wonderful mechanical doll, so close to reality that the girls have never imagined his like before. They stare rapturously at his jerky, automatic gestures, laugh delightedly, and search for the hidden clockwork that makes him move. They find nothing. The music peters out. The doll stops as he began.

Swanilda and her friends examine the doll Coppélia. Swanilda reaches out tentatively and touches her. Coppélia is cold as ice, utterly lifeless, a wax doll like all the rest! Swanilda takes her book away, and the frozen girl sits as before, her stilted hands grasping nothing. Swanilda can make neither head nor tail of the book and turns back to be absolutely certain that the lovely girl will not look up and wave to her, as she did to Franz. She leans over to feel her heart. She feels nothing. Sure now that the charming creature of whom she was so jealous is merely an absurd doll, Swanilda gathers her friends about her and laughs with glee at the prospect of Franz paying court to her.

All the girls are tremendously relieved that they have no one to fear in the empty house and prankishly run to each one of the dolls. They wind the dolls up, and soon all the mechanical creatures are in motion. The one-man band plays his music, the juggler commences his act, the astronomer lifts a telescope to his eye—and the fascinated girls can't decide which they like best. They are so enchanted by the dolls that they do not hear Coppélius enter. The music imitates his fierce anger.

He runs in, cape flying behind him, speechless with rage. He shakes his stick at the intruders and rushes about to catch them. All the girls retreat toward the door—all of them except Swanilda, who sneaks into Coppélia's booth while the toymaker shakes his stick at her fleeing friends and pulls the curtains closed. Coppélius comes back into the room and makes straight for the curtains to see if the girls have harmed his most cherished creation. A window opens at the back, and Coppélius stops. Another intruder! He stands close against the back wall, ready to pounce on the stranger. Franz climbs into the room. Coppélius waits patiently until the youth cannot return to the window and then sets upon him. Franz pleads that he means no harm, that he has entered merely to see the girl he loves, and that he will die unless he talks with her.

Gradually Coppélius realizes that Franz is quite serious and he ceases to threaten him. He wants to hear more and astonishes Franz by becoming quite friendly. Coppélius insists that he stay, telling him that his daughter will be in very shortly, and invites the unbelieving youth to sit down and have a drink. When the drink is poured, Franz has no more apprehension and accepts it with relish. The toymaker chatters constantly, pretends to drink too, and Franz —gloriously happy now that he has neared his goal—fails to see that Coppélius is providing him with one drink after another. He tries to describe the beauties of Coppélia to the old man with drunken gestures, and his host nods repeatedly in agreement as Franz's intoxication is increased by a potion he has poured into the drink. Franz's head falls back against the chair, his arms hang limp in sleep, and in this room filled with dolls he is almost like a doll himself.

Coppélius checks to be sure that he is unconscious and wrings his hands in glee in anticipation of his next move. He takes out a huge leather volume, puts it down on the floor, and hurriedly leafs through the pages looking for a secret formula he has never used before. He finds it, leaps up, looks back at Franz, and approaches the drawn curtains of Coppélia's closet. He yanks back the curtains, peers in, and examines carefully every feature of Coppélia's face and dress. The clever Swanilda no longer resembles herself as she sits rigidly in Coppélia's costume, holding up her little book. Coppélius goes behind her chair and wheels Swanilda into the middle of the room as the orchestra sounds a beautiful melody on piercing, muted strings. He glances down at the book and makes magical gestures in Swanilda's face. Swanilda does not blink. Now the toymaker runs over to Franz and, moving his hands down the youth's body from head to foot, seems to pull the power of life from him like a magnet. Coppélius holds the life force tight in his hands and goes back to the doll, whom he tries to endow with this potency. He consults the book again and repeats the ritual. To his astonishment and happiness, Swanilda tosses away the book, and Coppélius believes his wooden doll has actually come to life.

Swanilda's arms move stiffly as the music mimics the mechanics of her strength. She raises her head and stands up, her body still bent over in a sitting position. The delighted Coppélius straightens her up, and she stands still for a moment. Her face is expressionless. Then she begins to try out her arms and legs, pushing her feet out before her in a simulated walk. Coppélia's master encourages Swanilda's every step with more incantations; the girl is excited at her success in deceiving him. She looks over at Franz and can hardly wait until he wakens. Meanwhile she lets Coppélius imagine that he alone is responsible for her new-found vitality. Her stance is rigid and her face assumes an equally artificial smile. At Coppélius's command, her legs move less mechanically, and soon she is dancing to a light, sparkling waltz, perfecting her steps as she circles about. Now that he has taught her to dance, the toymaker wishes her to continue showing off his magical powers. The doll smiles ingratiatingly, but instead of dancing she walks about the room, as if she were exploring it for the first time. She goes over to Franz, shakes him, sees the discarded wine mug, and raises it to her lips. Coppélius snatches it from her in the nick of time. He is beginning to find out that this live doll can be as exasperating as any young girl.

Swanilda keeps up her fun with him, but still maintains her mechanical characteristics. Like a child, she pretends in each one of her tricks merely to be doing what her teacher has told her to do in the first place. The tormented Coppélius beseeches her to dance again; she stares at him dumbly. Finally, to keep her out of any more mischief, he distracts her by placing a black mantilla about her shoulders. Swanilda responds instantly by dancing a bolero. The music is subdued, but the girl intensifies the impassioned Spanish dance as the tempo mounts. Coppélius now supposes that there is nothing he cannot make her do; he experiments further by investing the doll with a Scottish plaid. Sure enough, as the orchestra pipes a sprightly jig, she follows its rhythms like a good Scottish lass. At the end of this dance, however, Swanilda has had enough. She kicks the pages of his magic book and runs berserk about the room.

She tries to awaken Franz from his stupor. Coppélius, fraught with anxiety lest she harm herself as well as the other dolls, finally succeeds in grabbing her. He sets her down hard on her chair, shakes his finger in her face, and rolls the chair back into the curtained alcove. Franz stirs, stretches, and looks about. Coppélius allows him no time for questions and tells him to get out. Franz leaves eagerly, climbing back out of the window. Swanilda, no longer a doll, pushes the curtains aside and dashes about the room knocking over every one of Coppélius's precious toys except the king, who stands in ridiculous majesty over the chaotic scene. Then, all too lifelike, Swanilda escapes through the door to catch up with Franz.

The shocked Coppélius cannot believe his eyes. He pulls back the curtains, and there, thrown across her chair, he sees the naked, limp body of his beloved Coppélia.

ACT THREE: THE WEDDING   The festival day has arrived, and all the villagers have gathered in the sun on the manor house lawn to take part in the celebration. The town's new bell has been blessed, and the lord of the manor awaits the presentation of dowries to those who will marry on the holiday. Swanilda, radiant in her wedding costume, and Franz, also in formal array, approach the lord with the other couples. Franz cannot take his eyes off Swanilda, who has taught him the lesson he unconsciously yearned to know. He knows now that, as his wife, she will be to him all women—all the other girls the beautiful Coppélia represented. The assembled villagers share the exuberant joy of Franz and Swanilda. The lord of the manor congratulates them and presents the dowries.

The irate and pathetic Coppélius marches in and upsets the happy throng by reminding them of the damage he has sustained. Coppélius is so intent on securing compensation, rather than explanations and apologies, that the crowd does not sympathize with him readily. The only one who sympathizes is Swanilda, who steps forward understandingly and offers him her dowry. The sullen Coppélius is about to take it, but the lord of the manor motions Swanilda away and rewards the toymaker with a bag of gold. The old man leaves the scene, wondering whether it will ever be possible for him to create a doll as lovable as his ill-fated Coppélia.

The pageant of the day now commences. The peasants dance the familiar "Dance of the Hours," in which the arrangement of the performers imitates the progress of the hours around an enormous clock as the hurdy-gurdy music tinkles the time away. The twelve girls form a circle like the face of an enormous clock, kneel toward the center, and one by one rise, pirouette, and kneel again, telling the time away.

Soft woodwinds herald the arrival of Dawn, danced by a lovely young girl. Her dance, with the music, is at first slow and tentative, like the gradual approach of light; then her body responds to bright wakening music and she celebrates the rising sun.

Now Prayer—a demure girl who clasps her hands before her and turns slowly in deep arabesques—delights the villagers. She kneels as the harp ends the music for her dance.

A peasant couple perform a vigorous betrothal dance to rhythmic, piping music. They bow to the lord of the manor, and all await the arrival of the bride and groom.

Franz bows and holds out his hand to Swanilda. Together they dance a moving adagio to a deep melody from the strings. Franz carries Swanilda high on his shoulder, sets her down gently, and the girl kneels before him. She rises on point, pirouettes swiftly in his arms, is lifted again, released, and caught as her lover holds her across his knee. He turns her in arabesque, and the dance that symbolizes their reconciliation and pledged happiness comes to an end. Their dance together and the variation each now performs alone reveal the youthful strength and tenderness each possesses for the other. When they have finished, all the villagers join the smiling couple in a fast, constantly accelerating dance in which the whole company becomes a part of the breathless happiness reflected in the shining faces of Swanilda and Franz.

American Ballet Theatre revived *Coppélia*, in a new production by Enrique Martinez, during their 1968 season at the Brooklyn Academy of Music in New York. Carla Fracci and Erik Bruhn danced the first performance. Others dancing the principal roles were Cynthia Gregory and Gayle Young, Alexandra Radius and Ted Kivitt, and Eleanor D'Antuono and Ivan Nagy. When she joined the company, Natalia Makarova danced the role of Swanilda.

In 1974 I decided that we should stage *Coppélia* at the New York City Ballet (we needed another evening-long ballet) and asked the ballerina and teacher Alexandra Danilova, celebrated for many years for her Swanilda, to collaborate with me on the choreography. Rouben Ter-Arutunian designed the scenery and costumes, which were executed by Karinska. The ballet was first presented by the company July 17, 1974 at the Saratoga Performing Arts Center, the New York City Ballet's summer home at Saratoga Springs, New York.

Coppélia was first danced, of course, in France. It was introduced in Russia in 1884, with Marius Petipa's own version of Saint-Léon's original choreography. I remember very well performances by the Russian Imperial Ballet of *Coppélia* and as a member of the company danced in the mazurka. (It is said that the czardas and the mazurka were first introduced into ballet in *Coppélia* and, from then on, divertissements based on national and folk dances became very popular in ballet.)

I have often said that Delibes is one of my favorite composers for dance. In our new *Coppélia*, we used the entire score of the three-act version. The first dance drama of really uniform excellence deserves no less! No part of the ballet is subordinate to any other; most important of all, ballet music in

Coppélia participates in the dance drama as never before, Delibes' charming, melodic music assisting the plot and unifying the music and dance. As we know, Tchaikovsky was directly inspired by Delibes' scores to write his own ballet music. Delibes is the first great ballet composer; Tchaikovsky and Stravinsky are his successors.

The first American performance of *Coppélia,* though greeted with applause by press and public in 1887, was not as memorable as a later one, when Anna Pavlova, making her début in the United States, appeared as Swanilda at the Metropolitan Opera House, New York, February 28, 1910.

Most major ballet companies round the world dance *Coppélia* and many distinguished dancers have performed its leading roles. The Ballet Russe de Monte Carlo staged the ballet for Alexandra Danilova who was identified with it for many years. The noted dance critic and poet Edwin Denby called her "the most wonderful *Coppélia* heroine in the world." Madame Danilova now teaches at the School of American Ballet in New York, where we began our work on our production.

Writing of the first performances at Saratoga, the critic Arlene Croce said in *The New Yorker:*

"In the New York City Ballet's new *Coppélia,* which had its première at the company's summer home in Saratoga, Patricia McBride gives a great and a great *big* performance—big in scale as well as spirit. The role comes as a climax to the present and most exciting phase of her career. The scale on which she has been dancing this year is a new development in her style, and to reach it she hasn't sacrificed any of her speed or sharp-edged rhythm or subtlety of intonation. And although the role of Swanilda gives her plenty of unaccustomed material (such as extended pantomime), she sweeps through it without ever once looking like anyone but herself. She persuades you that Swanilda is Patricia McBride and always has been. This is a remarkable triumph for an artist whom the world knows as the flag-bearer of the New York City Ballet, the embodiment of its egoless-star ethic. McBride is fundamentally inscrutable. She doesn't exist outside her roles, and when you try to place her among her peers in world ballet—Gregory and Sibley and Makarova and the other great Russians whose names mean more to the public than McBride's does—her image dissolves in a succession of ballets: *Donizetti Variations, Rubies, La Valse, Brahms-Schoenberg Quartet, Who Cares?, Dances at a Gathering, Harlequinade.* McBride doesn't throw us cues to let us know how we ought to take her; she doesn't comment, doesn't cast herself as an observer of life. All she knows about life she seems to have learned through dancing, and all she has to tell she tells through dancing. How durable a bond of communication this is she proves once again in *Coppélia,* and in the very first moments.

"Swanilda's *valse lente* is the opening dance. By custom, it's a straight classical solo, and it gives us the ballerina in full flight almost as soon as the curtain has gone up. But in the New York City Ballet version McBride runs down to the footlights and, on the first notes of the waltz, addresses the audience in a passage of mime. 'This one up there,' she says, pointing to Coppélia on her balcony, 'she sits and reads all day long. That one, who lives over there, is in love with her, but she never notices him. Me, I just play.' And she plays (dances), first for her own pleasure, then for Coppélia's, with enticing steps that seem to say, 'Come down and play with me. See how nicely I play.' The structure of the waltz is mime, dance, dance-mime; in one stroke the means by which the story of *Coppélia* will be told are laid before us, and the fact that it's all done to an unvarying waltz rhythm lets us see easily how these different effects—of a mime gesture or a dance movement or a dance movement that functions as a mime gesture—depend for their force and clarity on having a different relation to an over-all rhythm. 'Mime' time is not 'dance' time, and each has to be established to musical time in a different way. This isn't as elementary as it sounds. The big catch in keeping the time values disparate is that the rhythm which connects them may disintegrate, and the worst danger of *that* is that the dancer will seem to be switching personalities on us, much as if she were a singer whose speaking voice didn't resemble the voice she sang with. (A lot of the modern distrust of mime comes from the schizoid effect of miscalculated rhythm.) In McBride's variation, and through her whole radiant performance, she plays excitingly close to the danger point. But the values of dance and mime, distinct in their time sense, are equalized in their scale—the largest scale that one could hope to see. So the meanings that are conveyed by all these sharply differentiated rhythms are always absolutely clear; they fly at you and away, or loom and settle, but there's no break in her consistency. She 'reads' at every moment. She is a character. McBride has never struck me as a particularly strong actress, and her method baffled me for years. How else, if not by acting, could she have made her character in 'La Valse' so vivid—a character unlike anyone else's who does the part? But for McBride acting is not the key; dancing is. And now that she's become so grand I don't see how anyone could miss that. She is a great dancer and a great star.

"The new production of *Coppélia,* staged by George Balanchine and Alexandra Danilova, is a combination of old and new choreography, the old being a first and second act built largely around the excellent 'after-Petipa' version in which Danilova used to star for the Ballet Russe de Monte Carlo, and the new being a glittering Act III, all of it Balanchine's except for the grand adagio and the ballerina's variation, which belong to Danilova-Petipa. Balanchine's dances are not uniformly masterpieces, but, taken all together, they ought to extend the life of this ballet another hundred years. In their unique blend of light irony and ingenuousness, they are a mirror of the music—serious music that was not meant to be taken too seriously.

"For his third act, Delibes envisioned a village wedding, with the villagers putting on an allegorical pageant of man's works and days. Most productions get through Dawn and Prayer and then give up in confusion, either reassigning the rest of the music (Work, Hymen, Discord and War) or dropping it altogether. Balanchine uses all the music Delibes wrote, and he does not mistake its spirit. His choreography really does present a plausible (though not a real-istic) village pageant stuck together with metallic threads and parchment and candle wax, but noble nonetheless, with an anti-grand-manner grandeur. The Waltz of the Hours, that sublime gushing fountain of melody, is danced by twenty-four grinning little girls in gold tunics, who line the path of the soloist, Marnee Morris, and form choral borders for the solos that follow: Dawn (Mer-rill Ashley), Prayer (Christine Redpath), and Work, or La Fileuse, here called Spinner (Susan Hendl). The entrance of these three graces—posed motionless as beauty queens in a carriage that circles the stage twice—is one of the most piercing visions in the ballet. And the solos for Ashley and Hendl are outstand-ing—complete summations of their gifts. There's a dance for Four Jesterettes in padded motley sewn with bells. (In the Monte Carlo production, this entrée—originally Hymen—was called Follies, which seems more to the allegorical point than Jesterettes.) Discord and War is a romp for boys and girls in horned helmets, a flourish of capes and spears waved as idly as pickett signs—a witty number, shakily danced. Then, after the bridal *pas de deux*, comes an exhilarating finale, with climax piled on smashing climax. Best of all is the ballerina's fish dive into her partner's arms, instantly followed by the only thing that could top it—the return of the twenty-four golden tinies cakewalking on in a wide curve, with Morris in the lead tearing off *piqué-fouetté* turns.

"Balanchine's hand is evident elsewhere in the production, too—in that first-act entrance of Swanilda, and in the Mazurka and Czardas, which surely have never before been so thick and bushy with (musical) repeats, so fertile with invention. Their one weakness is that they are isolated from the action and don't serve any purpose. But the weakness is very likely not a permanent one. This is not a finished production, and by the time it reaches New York, in No-vember, Balanchine is sure to have taken over more of it—filling up gaps in the staging, refurbishing or replacing some of the less effective old dances, and straightening out a few discrepancies, such as the sudden, unmotivated shift to a sunnier mood that follows Swanilda's solemn ear-of-wheat dance. Possibly he'll find more for the hero to do, too. At present, Franz has only one dance—an interpolation in the third act which old-timers will recognize as Eglevsky's variation from the *Sylvia Pas de Deux*. It's nice to have this great solo back again, especially as danced by Helgi Tomasson, but Tomasson, who is a charming Franz, doesn't get a chance to display his true dance power until the finale. I hope, too, that a way can be found to make the meaning of the ear-of-wheat episode (a direct descendant of the petal-plucking scene in *Giselle*) at least as clear to a modern audience as it is in the Ballet Theatre version.

"The part of the ballet that is, right now, just about perfect is the second act. Here, again, Balanchine has obviously been at work; you can almost feel him assuming command of the action the moment Coppélius enters his work-shop to find it overrun by Swanilda and her friends. Coppélius is Shaun O'Brien, giving the performance of his career. He is not a buffoon, and Swanilda is not a zany. He's a misanthrope, a tyrant, believably a genius who can create dolls everyone thinks are alive. She is a shrewd, fearless girl who grows into womanhood by accepting as her responsibility the destruction of Coppélius. She must break his power over gullible, romantic Franz, who has chosen the perfect woman, the doll Coppélia, over the natural woman, herself. The conflict between idealism and realism, or art and life, is embedded in the libretto of *Coppélia*, and Coppélius's passion is in the music. I enjoy burlesque versions of the second act (and in this tradition there's no Swanilda more enjoyable than that gifted zany Makarova), but the heart of the music isn't in them. Balanchine's Coppélius is kin to other Balanchine artist-heroes—not only Drosselmeier of *The Nutcracker* but Don Quixote and Orpheus and the Poet of *La Sonnàmbula*. And when he raises Swanilda-Coppélia onto her points and she remains locked there, upright or jackknifed over them, he's the strangest of all alchemists, seeking to transform his beloved twice over: doll into woman, woman into ballerina. Swanilda must become as totally manipulatable, totally perfectible, as a Balanchine ballerina. She must be a work of art, and then burst out of her mold. I once saw a brilliantly horrifying performance given by the Royal Danish Ballet, in which Solveig Østergaard and Frank Schaufuss confronted each other as monsters equal in might if not in cunning. But there was nothing in it like Shaun O'Brien's 'speech' to McBride, conveyed in a paroxysm of joy: 'I have made you and you are beautiful.'

"Rouben Ter-Arutunian's costumes are attractive, and his scenery is modest and quite pretty in several styles. Act I is like a child's pop-up picture book, with exaggerated perspectives. Act II, a cutaway of Coppélius's lab, ranges from Ensor to Burchfield, but the backcloth for Act III looked sketchily realized. A number of bells hanging above the stage (the pageant celebrates, along with everything else, a *fête de carillons*) bear the monograms of those associated with the original production—the choreographer, Arthur Saint-Léon; the librettist, Charles Nuitter; and E. T. A. Hoffmann, whose tale of Coppélius inspired the ballet—and those responsible for the present one. The largest bell, for which I forgive this somewhat presumptuous idea, is inscribed 'J'étais créé par Léo Delibes, 25 Mai 1870.' It is Coppélia herself who speaks. G.B., for George Balanchine, happen to be the initials also of Giuseppina Bozzacchi, who has no bell of her own. She was sixteen when she made her début at the Paris Opéra, appearing as the first Swanilda. Giuseppina took Paris by storm. Then Discord and War came in earnest. Six months later, in the siege during the Franco-Prussian War, she died of smallpox on the morning of her seventeenth birthday."*

In February 1975 Erik Bruhn, Resident Producer of the National Ballet of Canada, mounted for that company a new production of *Coppélia* which Clive Barnes in the New York *Times* (March 2, 1975) described as "unusual in its style and manner." This *Coppélia* was first presented in the United States by

---

* "I Have Made You and You Are Beautiful" by Arlene Croce. Reprinted by permission; © 1974 The New Yorker Magazine, Inc.

the same ensemble at the Metropolitan Opera House, New York, July 24, 1975, with Veronica Tennant, Rudolf Nureyev and Jacques Gorrissen as the principals.

Reviewing a performance in January 1975 of *Coppélia*, the critic Robert Greskovic wrote in *The Soho Weekly News:* "Swanilda, the lead in Balanchine/Danilova's *Coppélia*, was made on McBride. At this matinee she was sensational. The lusciously brocade layers of her dancing and the free, spunky spirit of her manner make hers the yardstick of interpretation for this role. McBride's physical response to the role's musical and choreographic demands is immediate and enchanting. She's the 'favorite daughter' of the village by virtue of the mental and physical prowess she brings to her almost constant presence in all three acts. Her mime, simple and clear with opera-house scale, is melded, like her dancing, with spontaneity, giving a fully articulated account of the music. McBride doesn't now act and then dance her characterization—she is always this Swanilda.

"Her large dark eyes create a focus that comments on her dancing. She *takes* everyone in, onstage and off, as she 'tells and shows' us what she's up to. Her strong and accentuated arm and leg joints stretch, curl and angle her limbs in a constant state of flirtatious flux. She elaborates her story as she responds to her music. As McBride's *batterie* cuts the air along a diagonal line, she proudly rivets her attention to the precise and generous activity of her feet. As she maintains her place to execute a series of multiple and varied turns, she sparkles, glances up and out; each time her head snaps around, she reverberates another wave of ecstatic after-energy.

"By the time she's dancing in celebration as the guest of honor at 'The Festival of the Bells' (Act III), she's fully matured. She doesn't rest on her laurels, her dancing scatters them in the wind of her joyous triumph. The conflict of her emotions in Act I and the calculation of her scheme in Act II are clearly behind her, here she's free and riding the crest of her popularity. This role is richly designed with some of Balanchine's finest dancing ideas, and McBride's pungent glamour and full-range dance power yield a Swanilda who is at home and home free."

LE CORSAIRE

Music by Adolphe Adam. Choreography by Mazilier. Scenery by Desplechin, Cambon, Thierry, and Martin. First presented at the Théâtre Impérial de l'Opéra, Paris, January 23, 1856, with Carolina Rosati, Mlle. Couqui, and Segarellu in the leading roles.

Based on Byron's poem, *Le Corsaire* was originally a three-act ballet that served as a useful vehicle for ballerinas such as Taglioni, Pavlova, and Karsavina. It was long in the repertory of the Russian theatres. Over the years, the work was much revised, with new music by Minkus and Drigo as well as new choreography by Marius Petipa and Vakhtang Chabukiani. A *pas de deux* from the complete ballet has frequently been performed by Soviet companies and by the Royal Ballet. Chabukiani's version, after Petipa, was first performed in the United States at Madison Square Garden by soloists of the Mali Opera Theatre, Leningrad, in July 1959. Margot Fonteyn and Rudolf Nureyev introduced the work to London at the Royal Opera House, Covent Garden, November 3, 1962.

In her *Autobiography* (1976), Margot Fonteyn describes the first performance of the *Corsaire pas de deux* with Rudolf Nureyev in New York in 1964. The applause lasted at least twenty minutes. "No one has ever danced *Corsaire* like Rudolf, and it is permissible in this case to use the adjective 'sublime.'"

When the Dance Theatre of Harlem took its version (by co-director Karel Shook) of the *Corsaire pas de deux* to London for a season at the Sadler's Wells Theatre in 1974, Peter Williams wrote in *Dance and Dancers* of the performance by Paul Russell and Laura Brown: "Russell gave one of the most exuberantly extrovert performances I have ever seen in this showy pas de deux. Looking for all the world like the Gold Slave from *Scheherazade* (naked torso, glittering baggy pants and bandeau round the brow), he bounds about, ripples his muscles, dives into head-to-floor back-bends in a manner which I feel Fokine originally intended for his Slave . . . Laura Brown had a few tricks in store, particularly in a dazzling manège of turns and a remarkable extension . . . At every performance I saw, this duet justifiably brought the house down in a manner I have seldom known in Rosebery Avenue."

In a long essay on the Dance Theatre of Harlem in *Ballet Review*, in 1974, the critic Robert Greskovic commented on this ballet:

"Shook's restaging is splendid. Laura Brown's princess manner is delicate enough to convey her character and strong enough to configure her choreography. The most finished of her 'finished' manners are showcased here. She projects smiles and knowingly wondrous eyes that gleam their brightest satisfaction at the top of her balances, lifts and posé arabesques. Her ear-high développé à la seconde reaches its height quickly as she holds a sharp steady balance. Her manège of: piqué turn, piqué (changing arms), piqué again, and fouetté turn in the coda is a clearly spotted and securely jumped ride around the world. In Russell's extraordinary, steady one-handed lifts, she's relaxed and regal.

"The delicacy and finesse of her performance is a perfect counterbalance and motivation for Russell's pirate. Paul Russell is Le Corsaire—Russian, French, exotic and proud, with a touch of American athleticism. The only other American dancers I've seen who succeeded in impersonating this swashbuckling bandit have been John Prinz and Edward Villella. Prinz ultimately failed by his lack of technical control and I've seen Villella only on television, but Russell is completely alive and breathing, full on stage. His rush-on entrance is immediately authoritative. His alert, darting eyes are seeing his space before they're looking for a partner. He takes us all in before he takes flight. His enthusiasm and freedom on stage suggest someone who's been on the seas for months and this is his first return to solid earth. He's found one of earth's treasures, and, as Brown enters, rises through ¾ point and folds himself to the ground in a sinking révérence. He approaches her and handles her with wondering care. The mechanics of the partnering gain drama from Russell's dazzling concentration. He must handle this beauty, now. He must lift her, he must catch her, he wants to hold her. He makes his job his passionate desire. And when he's alone and in his variations he's wanting to celebrate. When he takes his first attitude balance atop strong ¾ point, he dégagés back for a spinning cocked-leg double tour, landing on one knee with the other leg extended; then whips around a twisting sous-sus turn to stand full height again. These sous-sus turns with his hands on his shoulders are lusciously plastic in the smooth, changing tilt his shoulders take to propel his turn and stop it at an opposite angle to its beginning. Shook has set a clearly musical series of emboîtés en tournant that travel into preparation for the long spine-tingling axis of Russell's double tours. Coming out of even chaîné turns there is a tour that folds kneeling to the floor and unfolds instantaneously as, with a brazen slap of one hand to his stage, Russell springs to arabesque posé on ¾ point, perfectly placed, leanly arced—like an arrow's vibrating contact with the bull's-eye of a target. This is no formidable youthful debut as Le Corsaire, it's an electrifying (by any standards) triumph of theater."

CORTÈGE BURLESQUE

Music by Emmanuel Chabrier, orchestrated by Hershy Kay. Choreography by Eliot Feld. Decor by Robert Munford. Costumes by Stanley Simmons. Lighting by Jules Fisher. First presented by the American Ballet Company at the Festival of Two Worlds, Spoleto, Italy, June 27, 1969, with Christine Sarry and John Sowinski. First presented in the United States by that ensemble at the Brooklyn Academy of Music, New York, October 21, 1969, with the same dancers. Conductor: Christopher Keene.

A *divertissement* to Chabrier's *Cortège Burlesque* and *Souvenirs de Munich*, arranged for orchestra, this ballet featured the dancing of the two principals of the new American Ballet Company, Christine Sarry and John Sowinski, when the group made its debut. The *pas de deux* is danced against a fantastic backdrop that recalls the circus, its animals and amusements. The dance reflects the circus atmosphere as the boy and girl dance their bouncing display piece in open competition, the boy supporting the girl but acting, too, very much the soloist who won't be upstaged by any ballerina, however famous.

Not as often as he can help it, that is, which isn't much, for the girl takes over the scene steadily, yielding only to real perseverance from her partner.

NOTES Reviewing the ballet in *Dance and Dancers*, Patricia Barnes wrote that "*Cortège Burlesque* is one of those ballets that laughs at itself while exploiting the technical skill of its dancers. Sarry was a joy . . . and in the New York performances the two dancers really went to town, sending up the manners and egos of ballerinas and their partners with wit and some bold, assertive dancing. The piece is enhanced by yet another excellent backdrop by Robert Munford, portraying a circus atmosphere precisely right for its purpose."

CORTÈGE HONGROIS

Music by Alexander Glazunov. Choreography by George Balanchine. Decor and costumes by Rouben Ter-Arutunian. Lighting by Ronald Bates. First presented by the New York City Ballet at the New York State Theatre, Lincoln Center, May 16, 1973, with Melissa Hayden and Jacques d'Amboise, Karin von Aroldingen and Jean-Pierre Bonnefous in the leading roles. Conducted by Robert Irving.

I did this ballet for Melissa Hayden, who had been dancing with our company twenty-four years—when she decided in 1973 to retire. "Why not stop before you begin making excuses?" she said. "Why not stop when you're still enjoying everything?" The idea behind the ballet was simply to give Melissa Hayden yet another opportunity to enjoy herself and give our audiences pleasure.

The music is a collection of pieces by Glazunov (1865–1936), best-known for his ballet *Raymonda*. The finale of the ballet features a *pas classique hongrois*, where Hungarian gesture and dance are combined with the academic classic dance.

There is no story to *Cortège Hongrois*: it is simply, as its name suggests, a procession of dances in the Hungarian manner. There is a grand promenade at the start, which introduces two sets of dancers—first a group in colorful peasant costume, and then a group of courtiers led by the ballerina and her cavalier. The scene is a large formal ballroom.

Four of the courtly couples begin a dance in which others join. Next, eight couples, to a plaintive melody, dance a supported adagio.

In vivid contrast, the peasants, led by a vigorous couple, dance a czardas, a Hungarian folk dance of perennial popularity. Four of the courtly girls follow, for a whirring, accelerating *pas de quatre*.

Variations for some of the courtiers are now presented; first one for a girl, another for four of the boys, a third for another girl, and the finale, what we have been waiting for, a *pas de deux* for the leading courtly couple. Dressed in white embellished with gold and wearing a crown, the ballerina performs in the grand manner, dancing with her partner to a deep, stirring melody that gradually builds. There are variations for the two dancers, hers a character dance with much folk gesture. The courtiers rejoin the royal couple; the peasants come, too, to participate in the festivities, and there is a flourishing finish.

Finally, the two groups combine in a folk dance, heels and spurs clicking, and that seems to be the end. But there is another promenade, the lights go down, and only on the ballerina does the spotlight shine. A crown of lights illumines the stage and all kneel, acknowledging her radiance.

NOTES   At the time of the ballet's premiere, when ballerina Melissa Hayden was presented by Mayor Lindsay with the Handel Medallion, New York City's highest cultural award, Lincoln Kirstein wrote of her career in the New York City Ballet's program: "If one had to define one essential gift with which a dancer needs to be endowed, there might be a rush of answers. A beautiful body, grace of line, graciousness of spirit, joy in the work, ability to please, unswerving integrity, relentless ambition towards some abstract perfection. Certainly all these factors determine a dancer's character, and every element exists in some combination within the performing artist's presence. These factors and elements are never evenly, nor even justly distributed. The first lesson dancers approaching any wisdom about themselves learn is how little they can depend on any single attribute or even combination of a few of them.

"Perhaps the most essential gift donated by those forces who care for careers, cosmically or supernaturally, is an ability to animate, magnetize and dominate those factors which one likes least in oneself. The mirror is the first to tell us no one is perfect, but there is always a terrible temptation to whittle down our notions of perfection in order to accommodate what we imagine our mirrors reflect. Dancers are accustomed to look to their mirror for correction, criticism and even comfort from their earliest days in a classroom. Strong dancers never succumb to the blindness of narcissism. Dancers are not narcissistic; their selves are their material. These must be kept under constant scrutiny; their own eyes and minds are finally their closest friend and severest critic. The best performers know themselves better than anyone else. Whatever face they may put upon their image, they know exactly what face, best face and worst fits them.

"This kind of realism is not easily endured. In the best sense, it becomes a method, an analytical attitude towards performance. It is a strict school, a stoic attitude, but it has advantages. It permits survival. Of all the dancers with whom I've had the honor and pleasure of working, Melissa Hayden has been strongest and lasted longest. In the twenty-two years that she has been associated with Balanchine and myself, there has been no one whose strength surpassed hers. This is not alone in muscle, although one can mark little deterioration in her fantastic energy since the first season we danced at Covent Garden in 1950. To say that she has never missed a performance is less important than to realize that no single performance has ever been below her extraordinary level of efficiency. Whether or not the audience recognized it, her steely spine and wiry resilience, even under the attack of cruel strain or sprain, gives stamina to colleagues who know only too well what pain and strain are.

"Melissa has been the nearest thing to a 'star' in our starless company. We have never encouraged stardom on programs, posters or publicity; managers can't make stars; the public does. There has been a good deal of unobservant cant about a creature vulgarly entitled 'the Balanchine dancer.' When one takes the trouble to inspect the personnel of our company as it is now constituted, one can easily mark the corporeal distinction between Gelsey Kirkland and Gloria Govrin, between Peter Martins and John Clifford, between Karin von Aroldingen and Helgi Tomasson. Melissa Hayden was never a Balanchine-dancer, but she supported his repertory for over twenty years. In consideration of his much bruited intolerance or prejudice, this must mean something; Milly must have been doing something right.

"What she has given, and still victoriously gives, is a sense of security, a conviction that she knows what she's doing, how it should be done, and to what complete degree of energetic expenditure she can do it. The ballet, like *bel canto* voice production, is an area of extreme virtuosity; remove the element of physical electricity and acrobatics, the hazards of the arena overcome, and you delete most public curiosity. Ballet is a spectator sport; its very economics depend on mass appeal. For more than a century, whatever its association with kings and queens, courts lost or in decline, it is the big opera-house public that has justified its expense and problems. Intellectuals may analyze their pleasure, but it is fortunately not left to their tender mercies. Melissa Hayden is and has been a popular figure; she pleases, satisfies, thrills and amuses a big public which may make no very delicate judgment, but which in its instinct can not be fooled into thinking that boredom or dissatisfaction with emptiness is entertaining or instructive.

"From her own account, she has been dancing for forty years in schools and on stages, all over the world. Mathematically, considering the hours of practice, rehearsal, performance—plus a private life with a family, children and friends—this is staggering. Less accident-prone than almost any professional, she has probably made more appearances before a public than any other performer of the period. Her pleasure in performance has been so complete that it has been transmitted to her muscular organism like some blessed sun lamp, to keep her fit in spite of any mischance or fatigue.

"To stop dancing, to abandon the habit of a lifetime, to foreswear performance in a frame that has become familiar as one's bed and breakfast, is not the worst thing that can happen to a dancer. When the decision is made, as in the case with Melissa, there is the new adventure of energy reapplied. Her energy is no less; it will simply be channelled otherwise. Anyone who has heard her demonstrate in lectures knows that charm is a weak word for her didactic method. She has been a crusader for ballet as a language and a skill and now

she will direct her experience, taste and information towards a wholly new
audience—that of potential students, scholars and enthusiasts. The husbanding
of energy that has been her greatest gift permits no waste of effort. Hysteria is
an artificial additive that lack of control sometimes substitutes for temperament. Hysteria is not part of her nature, since she has always been a realist
and she realizes, from observation of colleagues less fortunate than she, that
irrational indulgence costs mind and muscle of which no one has too much to
spare. Her warmth is humane; she has had her fair portion of the world's grief.
She has not been given everything she may have desired or even deserved.
However, in situations in which she has found herself, and indeed in which
she has chosen to find herself content, she did better than most."

DANCES AT A GATHERING

*Music by Frédéric Chopin. Choreography by Jerome Robbins. Costumes
by Joe Eula. Lighting by Thomas Skelton. First presented by the New York
City Ballet at the New York State Theatre, Lincoln Center, May 8, 1969.
Pianist: Gordon Boelzner. Dancers: Allegra Kent, Sara Leland, Kay Mazzo,
Patricia McBride, Violette Verdy, Anthony Blum, John Clifford, Robert
Maiorano, John Prinz, and Edward Villella. Dedicated to the memory of
Jean Rosenthal.*

Dances at a Gathering is a ballet for ten dancers to piano pieces by Chopin.
Five girls and five boys dance in an open space as a pianist plays to the left of
the stage. He plays mazurkas, waltzes, études, a scherzo, and a nocturne—
eighteen pieces in all—as the dancers, distinguished in the program by the
color of their costumes, respond to the music.

The curtain goes up on a bare stage with a background of blue sky and
amorphous clouds; we are outdoors in a clearing, a field, a meadow, a grove. A
boy enters on the right, informally dressed in open white shirt, brown tights,
and boots. He walks slowly, quietly looking the place over, glancing up at the
sky, thinking. Then he is lifting his arm and his walk becomes a stride, a
dance, as the piano begins, *Mazurka, Opus 63, No. 3.* His dance reflects a
pleasure in being where he is on a day like this. As the music ends, he leaves,
meditating.

A girl and a boy enter and dance to the *Waltz, Opus 69, No. 2,* moving arm
in arm, at first a bit tentatively as if nothing will come of it, but the music
changes all that as they follow its flow in lifts, leaps, and a rushing exit with
the girl poised high on the boy's shoulder. Another girl and boy come in and
dance a little more formally, responding to the character of the *Mazurka, Opus
33, No. 3,* with arm gestures, too. But they, too, get carried away with the
music and she, too, is lifted off in a rushing conclusion.

A girl enters alone and dances fast to the staccato beat of a new, more demanding *Mazurka, Opus 6, No. 4*. She is still on stage as the next part begins.

Six dancers in different groupings respond to the music of four fresh *Mazurkas, Opus 7, Nos. 5* and *4, Opus 24, No. 2* and *Opus 6, No. 2*. There are two boys, dancing back to back in a kind of jig, one of the boys interested in one girl, who watches, the other in another. And not the same ones they were dancing with earlier. Rhapsodic as particular partnerships become, in the group commitments dissolve with no regrets and everyone begins again. In the dancing and watching of dances, in the joining in, partnerships shift. The dances become full of character and there is a feeling that we are in real Mazurka country as gesture identifies with music and place. There are friendships between the girls, too, and both boys and girls play at posing each other in groups for photographs.

Now to the *Waltz, Opus 42*, a girl and boy try to outdo each other in speed and virtuosity, each showing off to the other, he cartwheeling to victory, all of it a serious but affectionate competition. She touches his hand and he lifts her up to his shoulder, wrapping her about his head closely as they leave.

Three girls dance the *Waltz, Opus 34, No. 2*, entering in a dim light, strolling, doing solos, then all three dancing together. A boy comes to lift one girl away. They dance together as the other two watch. These two look into the distance. Then as quietly as he came the boy is gone, leaving his girl kneeling. She rises to join her two friends, they pose in a group, then separate with separate dreams, only to join arms and leave together.

The lights come up and two boys compete now to the music of *Mazurka, Opus 56, No. 2*, each trying to outdo the other, throwing each other about, making dramatic exits backward.

As the lights fade, a girl enters to dance thoughtfully alone to the *Étude, Opus 25, No. 4*.

To the big *Fourth Waltz, Opus 34, No. 1*, six couples dance, responding dramatically to the pulse of the music. There is an exhilarating series of slides and lifts, at the end of which the boys line up to pass the girls down a diagonal line, lifting them so that the next boy lifts them higher still to the demanding rush of the piano.

Now in dimmer light come a boy and girl. She clearly likes him and tries to make it clearer. He leaves her but another boy enters. She dances all around him, surrounding him with attention but he ignores her and goes off. With a third boy she has the same result, but more amused than despairing, she flicks her wrist and goes off.

Next a *pas de deux* to the *Étude, Opus 25, No. 5*, then a fast solo for a boy to the *Étude, Opus 10, No. 2*. The *Scherzo, Opus 20, No. 1* involves six dancers in dramatic declarations, fulfillments, and disappointments. As the three girls fall back in the boys' arms, they are a bit embarrassed and leave in a rush.

For the final piece, the *Nocturne, Opus 15, No. 1* and its slow melody, the lights come down. Gradually all ten dancers appear, singly and in couples, together now for the first time. One of them, the boy who began the dances at this gathering, touches the ground of the place. They all look at him and then up at the sky, which they watch intently. They pair off then and walk away. All move forward as the music dramatizes their situation. Then they look to the ground and raising their arms start a dance that does not develop. They go to the back of the stage, the boys to one side, the girls on another, and bow. The curtain falls.

NOTES *Dances at a Gathering* came about in an interesting way. "I started out to do a *pas de deux* for Eddie Villella and Pat McBride," Jerome Robbins told Hubert Saal of *Newsweek*. "Then I got turned on by the music. It all started to pour out as if some valve inside me had opened up and the purity of working with dancers took over. I had to find the form. Usually I work with a structured music, as in Stravinsky's *Les Noces*, where the literary material is built in. In this case I took whatever appealed to me and let it happen, trusting it. It's nice to work loosely and intuitively."

Shortly before the première, Robbins said to Clive Barnes of the New York *Times*, "I'm doing a fairly classical ballet to very old-fashioned and romantic music, but there is a point to it. In a way it is a revolt from the faddism of today. In the period since my last ballet (*Les Noces*, 1965), I have been around looking at dance—seeing a lot of the stuff at Judson Church and the rest of the avant-garde. And I find myself feeling just what is the matter with connecting, what's the matter with love, what's the matter with celebrating positive things? Why, I asked myself, does everything have to be separated and alienated so that there is this almost constant push to disconnect? The strange thing is that the young people are for love. Is that bad?"

Shortly after the première of *Dances at a Gathering*, Robbins was interviewed for *Dance Magazine* by the critic Edwin Denby. The complete text of the article, reprinted by courtesy of *Dance Magazine*, follows: "Robbins's *Dances at a Gathering* is a great success both with dance fans and the general public. And it is a beautiful piece. But it wasn't planned as a sure-fire piece—it wasn't planned at all beforehand and began by chance, as Robbins explains in the interview (taped shortly after the official première) which appears on the pages that follow.

"The ballet is set to Chopin piano pieces and the program lists ten dancers but tells you little more. The curtain goes up in silence on an empty stage. It looks enormous. The back is all sky—some kind of changeable late afternoon in summer. Both sides of the stage are black. Forestage right, a man enters slowly, deep in thought. He is wearing a loose white shirt, brown tights and boots. He turns to the sky and walks slowly away from you toward center stage. You think of a man alone in a meadow. As he walks you notice the odd tilt of his head—like a man listening, inside himself. In the silence the piano begins as if he were remembering the music. He marks a dance step, he sketches a mazurka gesture, with a kind of pensive vigor he begins to improvise and now he is dancing marvelously and, in a burst of freedom, he is running all over the meadow at its edge. Suddenly he subsides and, more mysterious than ever, glides into the woods and is gone. Upstage a girl and boy enter. At once they are off full speed in a double improvisation, a complexly fragmented waltz, the number Robbins speaks of as the 'wind dance.'

"As one dance succeeds another—the ballet lasts about an hour—you are fascinated by the variety and freshness of invention, the range of feeling, and by the irresistibly beautiful music which the dance lets you hear distinctly—its mystery too. You see each dancer dance marvelously and you also see each one as a fascinating individual—complex, alone, and with any of the others, individually most sensitive and generous in their relationships. The music and the dance seem to be inventing each other. For a dance fan, the fluid shifts of momentum are a special delight. For the general theater public, Robbins's genius in focusing on a decisive momentary movement—almost like a zoom lens—makes vivid the special quality of each dance, and all the charming jokes.

"But it is a strange ballet.

"Our talk began before the tape machine arrived. Robbins had been telling me how the ballet developed. He had been asked whether he would care to do a piece for the 25th Anniversary City Center Gala, May 8. Delighted by the way Patricia McBride and Edward Villella had been dancing *The Afternoon of a Faun,* he thought he would like to do a *pas de deux* for them—perhaps to Chopin music—and he accepted. As he listened to records and became more and more interested in the possibilities—it occurred to him to add two more couples—and he began rehearsal. In the course of rehearsals, however, all the six dancers he had chosen were not always free, so he went on choreographing with four others, using those who happened to be free. Gradually he made more and more dances, but without a definite plan for the whole piece. When about two-thirds of the ballet was done, he invited Balanchine (who had just returned from Europe) to rehearsal. At the end of it he turned to Mr. B and said, 'Don't you think it's a bit long?' Mr. B answered, 'More. Make more!' He did.

"Robbins said to me, 'As you see, there are still never more than six dancers dancing at once.' He told me that as the dances and relationships kept coming out of the different pieces of music and the particular dancers available, he began to feel that they were all connected by some underlying sense of community (he said, laughing, 'Maybe just because they were dancers') and by a sense of open air and sunlight and sudden nostalgia perhaps.

"We spoke of one of the many lovely lifts—this one at the end of Eddie's *pas de deux* with Pat where it looks as though he were lifting a sack onto his shoulder and, up on his shoulder, the sack suddenly changes into a beautiful mermaid. Robbins explained how it came out of a sudden metamorphosis in the music. And he illustrated how the lift is done.

"We were talking of Villella's gesture of touching the floor in the final minutes of the ballet, and Robbins mentioned that he was perhaps thinking of the dancers' world—the floor below, the space around and above. I was saying that I liked that gesture better the second time I saw it because it was slower and I wondered if he (Robbins) had changed it. At that point the tape begins:

"ROBBINS No, that's just a very subtle thing of acting and where the human being is at the time. I think two weeks ago at the preview, Eddie was under more difficulties and pressures—down more—and perhaps that made the difference.

"I think the ballet will seem different in almost every performance, not vastly, but shades like those you saw, they will happen, depending on the dancers. You said it, I remember, way back—the dancers read (in a review) what the ballet is about, then they change because now they *know* it (they know it in words)—before they just *did* it. And that can happen—there was a modesty and a sort of not knowing in the first showing. They may start to think now that maybe they should do it more like what everyone says it is. I don't know what to do about that except to ask them not to.

"I always tell them to do it for themselves, and to think of 'marking' it— Don't think of doing it full out.

"DENBY Well, that's another quality the ballet has. I was very happy to see that with Eddie, who is used to 'doing it full out'—he does that very beautifully, it's not vulgar selling at all—he's not forcing it. But the inner business he also does very well—in *Giselle*. He's remarkable, you know, wonderful.

"ROBBINS I like watching ballets, anyway, best of all at rehearsals when a dancer is just working for himself, really just working. They are beautiful to watch then. I love to watch George's (Balanchine) work that way. Just love to.

"DENBY How beautiful everything is before it gets its name. Did I hear you say that Melissa (Hayden) will be covering Violette (Verdy)?

"ROBBINS Yes, I think she'll be marvelous.

"DENBY And so is Verdy. Someone told me that you're working to add a much longer number for her. So I said, 'Oh, wonderful.'

"ROBBINS I haven't been around ballet for so long, I forget how scuttle-butty it gets around here. If you say to someone, 'I want to work with you tomorrow,' the next day someone asks you, 'Are you doing a new ballet?' It already has gotten that big.

"But it was nice working with them. I did enjoy it very much. Patty McBride, I just *love* working with her.

"DENBY Yes, she's remarkable. . . . And I am very happy about what you did with Bob Maiorano. Because this year he's suddenly become a very good dancer wherever I look at him. He was beginning last year and, all of a sudden, there he is—now you can really see it.

"ROBBINS Yes.

"DENBY He has a marvelous Italian beauty of gesture. Maybe he was afraid of it all this time. The arm is so heavy the way he moves it. But the weight is right for all of them—the boys especially.

Tanaquil LeClercq and Francisco Moncion in *Afternoon of a Faun*. Photo by Fred'k Melton.

Nora Kaye in *Pillar of Fire*. Photo by Fred Fehl.

Janet Reed and Jerome Robbins in *Fancy Free*. Photo by Fred Fehl.

Jerome Robbins in *Prodigal Son*. Photo by George Platt Lynes, from the Dance Collection, N.Y.P.L.

Erik Bruhn in *The Nutcracker*. Photo by Fred Fehl.

Cynthia Gregory and Ivan Nagy in *Giselle*. Photo by Louis Péres.

Fernando Bujones in *Le Corsaire*. Photo by Martha Swope.

Martine van Hamel in *The Sleeping Beauty*. Photo by Martha Swope.

Daniel Levans in *Billy the Kid*. Photo by Jack Mitchell.

"ROBBINS Bobby Weiss, have you seen him? In one of the performances he is going to do Johnnie Clifford's part.

"DENBY He was wonderful in a school performance last year, too. Especially in the end of *Sylphides,* when he lost his nervousness in the finale. He looks as though he were not letting go as much as is his nature.

"ROBBINS He is beautiful when he lets go. In rehearsal, I just made him go.

"DENBY Clifford was remarkable too; he is so positively there. But it's not so simple. There is also something private about it. And Tony's (Blum) great—so much livelier than he's been . . . often.

"ROBBINS That's the fun of having another choreographer work with the dancers. Like in Ballet Theatre, Eliot Feld was doing a ballet, and I looked at his dancers and thought, Now, those are people I bypassed, but he saw something in them and brought out another whole aspect of them. It's always charming. But every choreographer—Agnes (de Mille) has people she works with I can't see—people I work with that she can't see. That's nice for the dancers, isn't it?

"DENBY And for the choreographers if you are going to travel around. You should try out your dances on the Russians. I'm sure they would like to have a dance of yours, they like to gather things—archives in their minds. It would be so much fun.

"ROBBINS I'm going to Russia. I *would* like to see if I can get it either to the Bolshoi or Kirov. I would like to see them dance this. I really would. It might finally turn out to be a peasant parody, you never know (*laughter*)—that folk part of it—I was surprised.

"DENBY I was surprised that people made so much of it, because the dancers are always so elegant. They might be landowners, if they were anybody in Europe.

"ROBBINS At first I also thought they were very elegant people, maybe at a picnic, maybe doing something—their own thing.

"And also to me—and this I'm very careful about—I don't want it to be a big thing—but the boys and the whole period are very hippie-ish.

"DENBY At first you had the beards, I was quite pleased with that.

"ROBBINS The boys still had them at rehearsal because of the long lay-off. Tony had long hair and a moustache and John Prinz had long hair and a beard and it was marvelous looking. It really affected what I was doing. I liked the boots—and the sketches are much more hippie than they appear on stage, in the sense of belts and open blouses for the boys and long hair and ballooning sleeves. There is something in the nature of knowing who they are and having love and confidence in them.

"DENBY Competence? . . .

"ROBBINS Confidence—which I feel is in the work, finally. Loving confidence in themselves and in the other people.

"DENBY That is in there very strongly.

"ROBBINS   It has some strangenesses in it too, I'm sure, but I can't yet quite see it. Every now and then I look at a step and think that is a very odd step. There is a strange step that Eddie does in his solo—he should play with it the way one does this (*hand gesture*).

"DENBY   There was an eight-year-old Negro boy in the street and he was running; he suddenly started throwing his feet around—with such pleasure.

"ROBBINS   I saw something nice in the park. Near Sheep Meadow there was a black boy and a white boy, both happened to be wearing blue. The black boy had a blue sweat shirt and the white boy had a blue sweater and open collar. They were running toward each other and it was more than a game. They ran and reached out hands. Not just shook hands, because that's what it was about, but they took hands and swung around each other with their heads thrown back with laughter. And then let go and embraced each other. Oh, it was so beautiful, I was thrilled by it. There was so much rapture and ecstasy and friendliness and openness about it. Then they quieted down and began talking, (*laughs*).

"DENBY   There are things in the ballet that are a bit gruesome. And, you know, very interesting.

"ROBBINS   Gruesome?

"DENBY   It's partly in the lifts, partly sometimes in the way the boys treat a girl.

"ROBBINS   Well, opening night there was an accident. I want to be sure you know that it was an accident. There was a place where Sally (Sara Leland) was being swung around and they fell off the lift and it turned into a—it looked like she was in outer space—like she'd been released from a capsule. She was just swirling around. Horrifying for a moment. But there are?—I don't know, I can't tell.

"DENBY   It's definitely in the music. It's much stranger than one. . . .

"ROBBINS   Yes, than one thinks.

"DENBY   Than one is supposed to think.

"ROBBINS   There's a nocturne. I began late listening to one nocturne—it was like opening a door into a room and the people are in the *midst* of a conversation. I mean, there's no introduction, no preface; it's like a cut in a film; it's almost like Chopin had finished the previous nocturne, finished it properly, and there was a fade-out. And suddenly (*clap*) you're on somebody's face who's talking. But in the middle of a sentence! You don't even get 'and then,' it's right in the middle of a word and he's very strange, really quite strange. He knew a lot, I think. Much more than I thought before I began. It was fascinating that way—just like some connection happened between all those sounds that he thought of, and where I was at.

"DENBY   The movement through a piece is always so interesting, and that you catch so well and do so many things with.

"ROBBINS   I listened to a lot of recordings, different people playing the same piece. I used mostly Rubinstein and Novaes and some Brailowsky. I lis-

tened to some of the Dinu Lipatti. Then it was enough for me and after that I
knew I would start to get confused. There are hardly any liberties taken at all
—I would say none. Only one where at the end of Eddie's first dance it's
marked *fortissimo*—da da da *whoosh*—I don't even know if it's Chopin's indication—I choreographed it that way—and Eddie was gone, *whoosh*. I didn't like
it, it was a little obvious, like I was trying for a hand and the piece was trying
for a hand, I thought there was something else there, so I took it on retard and
soft, and let him take that poetic thing he does there. The dancers are beautiful.

"DENBY   Gordon (Boelzner) plays it very well because he also plays it for
movement, without those extra questions of pianism.

"ROBBINS   There are no sentimentalities.

"DENBY   If you were listening to the music at a concert you might want
more nuances, but this way you don't because the dancers are doing it, the
nuances.

"ROBBINS   And he's tireless, that boy. It's fantastic. He plays it all day long,
and does the other rehearsals, too. Some of those pieces are killers. I suddenly
thought, Look at a Chopin concerto—they play a piece and go off and rest.
They do maybe half an hour or twenty minutes and go and have a fifteen-
minute intermission. But he's tearing off those *Études* written for these two
fingers. You know about the one Eddie dances to—the little fast one—sort of
chromatically going up and down the scale? Well, Chopin devised it to give
these two fingers which are the weakest, a workout.

"DENBY   I am so glad you didn't orchestrate it. Not that it would be possible, but there's that temptation.

"ROBBINS   I got worried for a while before we got it down on the big piano
because it began to sound very hollow to me. And I thought, Well when people come to this big theatre and they have just seen a big ballet with a lot of
marvelous sounds, the piano is going to sound like a little rehearsal piano. But
it doesn't, where it is. It seems it fills the house and sustains—a good combination, I think, between what you are seeing and what you hear.

"DENBY   It isn't miked?

"ROBBINS   No, not at all!

"DENBY   And you're so glad to see him, too. I wondered whether he can see
the dancers.

"ROBBINS   Most of them, but not the ones on the side of the stage he is on.
But there is a place where we have a mirror—rigged way up high on the wings
so that if he looks up he can see someone come in for just a cue. And I thought
Tom Skelton did a very good job in a very little time. He did the lighting.

"DENBY   Some of it looks ominous, sometimes. I mean weather. It changes.
I suppose you wanted that too. I liked it.

"ROBBINS   I didn't mean it to look ominous, but I suppose that vast sky, it
is almost like nature changing on you. You're a little worried about what is

going to happen next, it doesn't matter if it goes up or down. It's just that it changes. Everything changes.

"I didn't know it was going to be that long a ballet or what it was going to be. I originally thought, we'll do it using the wings and the cyclorama because it's just going to be a *pas de deux*. But by the time it was all done, I thought, Wow, who should do a set? Is it Jane Freilicher, or is it one of those watery sort of places, or is it—? Now I'm used to the way it is. I don't know if I want a set, or anything softer around the edges. That's a very hard line, those black wings. But once it starts, I don't suppose you are particularly aware of it any more.

"DENBY When you watch you realize that there are woods there, and you're in a meadow and there are trees.

"ROBBINS Isn't that funny, odd how that all got evoked. My names for the dances themselves, for instance, the second dance for John Prinz and Allegra (Kent), I call it 'wind waltz' because to me they are like two things that are on the wind that catch up with each other. There is something about air—breezes which are clawing them and pushing them almost like two kites. And 'walk waltz' or 'the three girls' to me is somehow in the woods. On a Chekhov evening. It just is. I can't see it any other way. It has that quality.

"DENBY The whole piece is a Chekhov piece. There are so many things suggested and not explained. The business of looking around at the end is the trickiest. I didn't like it at all the first time. Yesterday I didn't mind it so much. It is like looking at an airplane, I think of missiles and war.

"ROBBINS They must do it very softly. That is almost one of the hardest parts to be able to do. It is very hard for them just to walk on and be confident and just raise their heads or eyes and look at something without starting to make it dramatic. I keep telling them, 'Relax, don't be sad, don't get upset, just see it, just whatever you want to pick, just see. It's a cloud passing, if you want. Take it easy on it, don't get gloomy.'

"DENBY It's because they all do it together.

"ROBBINS Together—right—they all follow one thing. And that upset you? You thought it was airplanes and missiles?

"DENBY The atom bomb comes in and everything else. The sort of thing about Hitler attacking Poland. Your mind gets full of ideas that you don't want, that don't have anything to do with the piece.

"ROBBINS If I had to talk about it all, I would say that they are looking at —all right—clouds on the horizon which possibly could be threatening, but then that's life, so afterwards you just pick up and go right on again. It doesn't destroy them. They don't lament. They accept.

"DENBY That's what I told myself. It must be that they are looking at clouds—clouds rarely go that fast, but it might be a storm coming up and they're wondering if it's going to happen.

"ROBBINS That section, it was the last piece I did, though. I spent about two weeks after I finished the bulk of the choreography—it was almost all done about two weeks before the eighth of May. But that last two weeks I spent in arranging, trying to get the right order. Not only who danced what, but also that sense of something happening—making the dances have some continuity, some structure, whether I knew specifically what it was or not. At one point I had the scherzo finishing the ballet and the grand waltz opening it. All different sorts of ways. It was just—it was a marvelous sort of puzzle. Here I have all these people and these situations and I know they belong to each other—now let me see how. It was almost like rearranging *things*. And suddenly a picture was there. I am surprised by a lot of it. I am very surprised by the reaction to it. I didn't expect it at all. Something is there that I didn't know I was doing.

"DENBY   The reaction?

"ROBBINS   To the ballet.

"DENBY   That everybody liked it so much.

"ROBBINS   So much. The questions you are asking me about it seem to—I was originally going to call it *Some Dances*. That's all they are, just a series of dances. But something else takes over.

"DENBY   I don't know that the title is exactly the best.

"ROBBINS   It's a hard one to find. I was going to say *Dances: Chopin, In Open Air*, but that isn't the right title. In French *Quelques Danses* is nice, but in English *Some Dances* is sort of flat. If you say *Eighteen Dances* or *Nineteen Dances*, it divides them into compartments.

"DENBY   And it's of no consequence. Once you see the piece, you figure it is a piece. That end is quite prepared for all along when it happens. You really didn't want a big dance at the end. Since they are walking so much anyway, it is natural to make the end out of that.

"ROBBINS   Also the end of it had to come out of the scherzo, that very restless piece which ends with them all sort of *whoosh* running out—disappearing like cinders falling out into the night, and it couldn't end there, either. That's not the end of it, that's not how I feel about these people—that they went *whoosh* and disappeared. They are still here and they still move like dancers. They are a community. They take—what's the Italian word?—'a *passegiata*'—they take a stroll, like in an Italian town, around the town's square at sundown. They may have felt a threat, but they don't panic, they stay.

"I was very touched by Maria (Talchief) last night. She was moved by the ballet, and I suddenly realized how much it meant to me that she *was* and that it pleased her, because she is such an image in my mind of what a dancer should be, and I can't think of her as a cinder which went *whoosh* and was gone.

"So coming back after the scherzo to the stage and the floor that we dance on, and putting your hand on it—if it's the earth or a ballet dancer's relationship to a wood floor—*that* somehow is the ending I knew I had to get to somewhere. Very little of this was conscious, Edwin. I don't like to make theory afterwards. I'm just trying to get at it—there may be seven other reasons I'm not mentioning, well, you understand.

"DENBY   I don't want to pull it out of you—

"ROBBINS   Well, besides, you have your thoughts about it anyway.

"DENBY   Of course. Everyone is very happy that you've done a ballet again.

"ROBBINS   So am I.

"DENBY   And the dancers are happy. And it's nice you want to do some more.

"ROBBINS   I'm surprised. I didn't know which I would do or how I would do. It's almost like an artist who has not been drawing for a long time. I didn't know how my hand would be. And I was so surprised that the dances began to come out and began to come out so gushing, in a way. And I worked in a way I hadn't worked before. Whether I knew the details or not, I pushed through to the end of the dance. I sort of knew where it was going, and then I'd go back and clean it up and fill it up. Quite often the dancers weren't even sure how they got through the steps to the next step. But they went with me. Well, what I started to say was that I was pleased to be choreographing again and to have it coming out, and it's given me a sort—it's unplugged something. And I want to do a lot of ballets. I want to go on and see if I can work a little bit more the way I've worked this time—that sort of trusting the intuition more than self-controlling the intuition. I'd like to see what happens with some other kind of music now. That music I feel I am very identified with and always have been. It may go all the way back to my sister's dancing days as a Duncan dancer. I think a lot of that's in there.

"DENBY   I imagined you and your sister at the piano—you were seven or eight. The first thing that came from it was *The Concert* which, the first time, I was quite offended by.

"ROBBINS   (*laughs*) I made up for that.

"DENBY   I miss it now. I'd love to see it. But your jokes this time are adorable.

"ROBBINS   I love them in the section where they're posing, just love them. . . . I had a researcher call me from a magazine to ask me some questions. The first one was something very close to this: 'Where do you place your newest ballet in the mainstream of the trend of abstract dancing today?' (*laughter*) I've also been asked, 'What is the relationship between *Les Sylphides* and your ballet?' Well, I guess we used the same composer.

"DENBY   Did you use any of the same pieces?

"ROBBINS   No, I didn't, except one, the adage that Tony and Pat do, the third dance. Evidently, that music was used as the man's variation at one point, which I didn't know. It's a lovely piece.

"DENBY   You told me that you are going to do another Chopin ballet.

"ROBBINS   I've finished one nocturne and I've about three-quarters of another one, and I have an idea for a third. I've started them and want to see how they come out. One for Millie, one for Allegra, and I think one for Kay Mazzo.

"DENBY   She's beautiful.

"ROBBINS   Isn't she lovely?

"DENBY   Sally is wonderful. She gets more and more of that giving-without-thinking.

"ROBBINS   She has a kind of toughness, not tough as much as a practical quality. But then I'll say something and can see in her eyes that she's suddenly grasped it, and you can see it explode inside her—such joy.

"DENBY   The dance of the girls comes off so wonderfully. Allegra is wonderful all through.

"ROBBINS   That's the way about all of them. At so many rehearsals, they didn't dance all out. They sort of walked. That's how I got Eddie to do that first variation the first night. He came into rehearsal and had to save himself for the performance and just marked through it. I ran back and said, 'Now, that's what I want.' The same with Allegra—when she marks something, she shows you what it is. I don't think they realize how trained they are—so clear. Like someone with a great voice who can whisper and you hear it. And that's what you see. And that's what they do.

"DENBY   They are so completely clear, it's extraordinary how clear they are because whatever is passing through is never a blur or an uncertainty or a conventionalism.

"[Postscript from Robbins to Denby (sent the following day from Stockholm where Robbins was supervising final rehearsals of *Les Noces* for its June 6 première with the Royal Swedish Ballet. He went from there to Moscow to attend, by invitation of the U.S.S.R., its International Ballet Competition.)]

May 27, 1969

"Dear Edwin:

"Something bothered me terribly after we met—one of your remarks about the people looking up and watching something cross the sky at the end of the ballet. You said something about planes—A bomb—war today, etc., and it jarred me very much. I couldn't figure out 'the why' right away—but then I did on the trip over. First of all I feel you are imposing a terribly out-of-context meaning to what they are seeing. The ballet stays and exists in the time of the music and its work. Nothing is out of it, I believe; all gestures and moods, steps, etc. are part of the fabric of the music's time and its meanings to me. I couldn't think of planes—A bomb, etc. Only clouds—and the flights of birds—sunsets and leaves falling—and they, the people's reactions are all very underplayed, very willing to meet whatever threat is *in the music.*

"Well, those people knew their disasters—felt them, maybe felt that at a certain time their being would come to an end—but they faced it as a part of living.

"I hadn't thought of *all* of this when I did it. All I knew is that they weren't afraid, had no self-pity, and stayed—didn't leave.

"And I do feel that last piece is the logical end of the whole ballet. To me it is very much the only possible result of all that's come before.

". . . Stockholm is lovely, limpid skies at midnight—looking clear and blue as a New York fall—It was so good to see you—J"

Dances at a Gathering has been acclaimed in the United States and in London, where it was first performed by the Royal Ballet, October 19, 1970. Marcia Marks in *Dance Magazine* found it "the most significant work for many a season. For Robbins, it is the most spontaneous outpouring of sheer creative force in his balletic career, and for the dancers, it is an unexpected revelation." Patricia Barnes in *Dance and Dancers* magazine said, "*Dances at a Gathering* is, by general consent, a masterpiece. . . . It has been interpreted by different people in different ways, but all seem agreed on one aspect. This is a ballet about people, recognizable human beings rather than mere ciphers. There is no story, but a strong mood and atmosphere are present. There are ten dancers, five boys and five girls—they could be Americans, Poles, Danes or Russians. Their nationality is unimportant. What is significant in the fluent, utterly captivating series of dances is a love of humanity, an observation and understanding that is remarkably conveyed by the dancers involved. It seems impossible to leave the theatre having seen *Dances at a Gathering* and not feel one's soul uplifted."

In London, where the first performance was danced by Rudolf Nureyev, Monica Mason, Antoinette Sibley, Anthony Dowell, Laura Connor, Ann Jenner, David Wall, Lynn Seymour, Michael Coleman, and Jonathan Kelly, the editor of the *Dancing Times,* Mary Clarke, wrote: "Genius is a word to be used sparingly in the small artistic world of ballet but genius is the only word for Jerome Robbins, as choreographer and man of the theatre. . . . It may sound exaggerated to say that this ballet, just about people dancing, is profoundly moving but it is true. There is more dancing than in some three-act ballets and certainly more emotion because it is happening here and now. It is an hour of delight and if you catch it on a program with Ashton's *Enigma Variations* or *The Dream,* your faith in ballet will be restored. The Press has been unanimous in praise. I echo Clement Crisp of *The Financial Times:* it is a ballet 'that will enrich our lives for years to come.'"

In 1972, Jerome Robbins wrote to *Ballet Review* the following letter, which is of general interest:

To the Editor:
    For the record, would you please print in large, emphatic and capital letters the following:

THERE ARE NO STORIES TO ANY OF THE DANCES IN DANCES AT A GATHERING. THERE ARE NO PLOTS AND NO ROLES. THE DANCERS ARE THEMSELVES DANCING WITH EACH OTHER TO THAT MUSIC IN THAT SPACE.

Thank you very much.

New York, N.Y.

Jerome Robbins.

The pianist Gordon Boelzner, interviewed by Arlene Croce and George Dorris in *Ballet Review* (Vol. 3, No. 4.), has many interesting comments on *Dances at a Gathering, In the Night* and *Who Cares?*

DANSES CONCERTANTES

Classic ballet in five parts. Music by Igor Stravinsky. Choreography by George Balanchine. Scenery and costumes by Eugene Berman. First presented by the Ballet Russe de Monte Carlo at the City Center, New York, September 10, 1944, with a cast headed by Alexandra Danilova and Leon Danielian.

Stravinsky's *Danses Concertantes* was first performed as a concert piece, but the composer had conceived the work with the choreographer and had intended his score to be used in the theatre. When the work was first played (1942), it was apparent that the music embodied dancing—not only dance rhythms, but specific poses and gestures for a group of dancers—so that to hear *Danses Concertantes* was also to visualize a ballet. The plot of the ballet *Danses Concertantes* is the plot of the score: "Introductory March," "Pas d'Action," "Four Variations on a Theme," "Pas de deux," and "Concluding March."

The curtain rises on a handsome, ornate drop curtain. Between two high columns draped in rich cloth, the legend of the ballet is sketched out and we read the name of the ballet, its composer, choreographer, and designer. The orchestra commences a rhythmic, witty march. The dancers, in bright costumes, parade before the curtain at the music's command. There are fourteen of them—eight girls, four boys, and the *premier danseur* and the ballerina, who enter toward the end of the march and finish it with a flourish.

The drop curtain rises. The ballerina dances before the *corps de ballet*, which is arranged in four groups, in each of which a boy partners two girls. The colorful, spangled figures of the dancers are outlined boldly against the dark back cloth. The ballerina dances with sweet, lyric grace, but also with humor, for the music contrives to interrupt and cut short its soft melody with sharp accents in surprising places. You get the impression that you might get from reading a lyric poem whose lines are sometimes truncated in the middle of words but nevertheless flow on to graceful conclusion.

The majestic opening of this second section is heard again, and the full orchestra plays a lively, precisely accented conclusion that merges directly into a new theme that is quiet, tender, and romantic. The ballerina has left the stage, and each of the four groups of dancers comes forward and dances a *pas de trois* to variations on the theme.

The first and second variations are rigorous in rhythm, and the musical phrases seem to balance about a center, as the two girls cluster and move away from the boy. The third variation, Andantino, is softer, more wistful; the fourth, happy and boisterous.

The dancers now leave the stage to the ballerina and her partner, who dance a *pas de deux*. The dancers are almost personified in the music, which demands at first beauty in slowness, then a quiet, pointed wit that ascends to an elevated, noble manner. The *pas de deux* ends on a note of tenderness.

All the dancers return. The opening march is resumed, and the entire group dances to its buoyant rhythm. The music ends sharply and unexpectedly. All rush forward and bow low to the audience as the curtain falls behind them.

NOTES   Frederic Franklin later took the role first danced by Leon Danielian. Maria Tallchief, Ruthanna Boris, and Mary Ellen Moylan were among the dancers in the first performance.

In 1972, for the Stravinsky Festival at the New York City Ballet, which we planned in order to celebrate the composer's ninetieth birthday, I did a new version of *Danses Concertantes*. It was not only that I did not remember what I had done the first time; it was that I wanted, with the new dancers I was working with, to do something different.

It often happens: we forget. I don't think that is so bad when we have in the present so much to do! How in the world is it possible—really for me, it is not—to create a ballet first done many years ago, with young dancers who are very different? Writers think with words; I think with bodies and the ballets I work on necessarily have a great deal to do with the here and now, not a recollection or a notation or someone's idea of accuracy of the past. That is perhaps a proper function in a ballet company for some ballet masters, to reconstruct, but it is not for me; I am too busy making for now. I think ballet is now. I remember saying to an interviewer, Louis Botto, as we were preparing for the Stravinsky Festival, precisely this—that ballet is about people who are now, not about what will be. Because as you don't have these bodies to work with, it's already finished. This is not a question of what the story is, or what the costumes are, or preserving the ballet of 1972 for future generations. I'm staging ballets for today's bodies. For people who are here now. And you admire the way he or she looks and how they move. It's this person today—not just *anybody*.

And so I enjoyed very much doing *Danses Concertantes* again.

The outline of the ballet is just as it was in the first version, but the details are radically different. The first performance of the new *Danses Concertantes*, by the New York City Ballet at the New York State Theatre, was danced by Linda Yourth and John Clifford, with a group of twelve dancers. The orchestra was conducted by Robert Irving. Scenery and costumes, as before, were by Eugene Berman.

DANTE SONATA

Dramatic ballet in one act. Music by Franz Liszt. Choreography by Frederick Ashton. Scenery and costumes by Sophie Fedorovitch. First presented by the Sadler's Wells Ballet at the Sadler's Wells Theatre, London, January 23, 1940, with Margot Fonteyn and Robert Helpmann among the principal dancers. First presented in the United States by the Sadler's Wells Ballet at the Metropolitan Opera House, New York, September 23, 1950, with Margot Fonteyn, Moira Shearer, and Michael Somes among the principals.

This ballet is based on appreciations of Dante's *Divine Comedy* by the poet Victor Hugo and the composer Franz Liszt. Liszt used Hugo's poem "After a Reading of Dante" as an eloquent statement of his own appreciation of that poet and wrote a composition for piano on its theme. This ballet, like Liszt's music, depicts an embattled conflict between the forces of good and the forces of evil.

The curtain rises on a decorative backdrop that indicates with a few white lines the fiery fumes of purgatory hovering above parallel lines reminiscent of ascending steps. There are two groups of people in the ballet: the Children of Light and the Children of Darkness. The former are dressed in innocent white, most of the latter in black. Black, shining snakes coil about the bodies of the two principal Children of Darkness, a man and a woman.

The Children of Light, apparently those who have understood their sins and repented, dance joyfully alone. Soon they are invaded by the Children of Darkness. The evil men and women attack the purified ones with determined concupiscence. The Children of Light try to beat them back, but some are seduced.

The Children of Light move flowingly, without suddenness, while their opposites fill the stage with violence. The efforts of the innocent to save themselves, to prevent any one of their number from yielding to this violence, enforce a constant tension. But finally their resistance is in vain: physically they become slaves to the powers of evil.

The Children of Darkness are not enlightened by their triumph and regard it with displeasure even as it is achieved. The curtain falls as the leaders of the Children of Light and the Children of Darkness, on opposite sides of the stage, are held up by their fellows in simulated crucifixion, their limbs twitching with agony.

DAPHNIS AND CHLOË

Dramatic ballet in three scenes. Music by Maurice Ravel. Choreography by Michel Fokine. Book by Michel Fokine. Scenery and costumes by Léon

Bakst. First presented by Diaghilev's Ballets Russes at the Théâtre du Châtelet, Paris, June 8, 1912, with Tamara Karsavina as Chloë, Vaslav Nijinsky as Daphnis, and Adolph Bolm as Dorkon. Revived, with choreography by Catherine Littlefield, for the Philadelphia Ballet, 1937. Revived, with choreography by Frederick Ashton, by the Sadler's Wells Ballet at the Royal Opera House, Covent Garden, London, April 5, 1951. Scenery and costumes by John Craxton. Margot Fonteyn, Michael Somes, Violetta Elvin, John Field, and Alexander Grant danced the principal roles. This is the version described below.

The two orchestral suites *Daphnis and Chloë,* now so familiar to us, are derived from an original ballet score designed for this ancient tale of youthful romance. Actually, two suites Ravel made of this music were performed in concert form before the ballet was produced. *Suite No. 1*—"Nocturne," "Interlude," and "Warriors' Dance"—begins at the end of Scene One of the ballet, after Daphnis has collapsed, and concludes with the end of the general dance of the pirates in Scene Two. *Suite No. 2*—"Daybreak," "Pantomime," and "General Dance"—is the music for the whole of Scene Three.

In its outlines, *Daphnis and Chloë* is not radically different from many ballets with stories that relate the love of young people who are finally reunited after some difficulty, some obstruction, has seemed to rule out a happy ending. This is naturally the way of ballet stories, as it is with all fiction, for unless there is some kind of obstruction, we are not apt to have a story: love, alone, is not enough. But it is the different quality of the love—the difference in the affection of Tristram for Iseult in *Picnic at Tintagel,* of Franz for Swanilda in *Coppélia,* of Amyntas for Sylvia in *Sylvia,* and in the way these lovers react to any interference—that make all these stories interesting. If we care about the kind of affection these lovers have for each other, what their gestures are, and how they look together, we are apt to be disturbed if any obstruction is put in their way and we are delighted at the end if the lovers seem to be happy and forgetful in their understanding of what has come between them. The two lovers in the story *Daphnis and Chloë* are very young; they are youthful innocents. We are made to see this and resent immediately the interference they endure. We are happy at the end because their initial innocence is not seriously violated: they still love, but with a difference that will make them happier.

SCENE ONE: A SACRED GROVE   On this day young people of a Mediterranean isle are paying tribute to the god Pan and his nymphs, whose grotto stands at the left. Daphnis, the handsome shepherd, and Chloë, the girl he has loved all his life, are among the worshipers. Their affection has become so accepted by the other young people that some of the maidens don't seriously believe in it. Still hoping that Daphnis will notice one of them, the maidens join him in a dance. Chloë reacts with appropriate jealousy and does not repulse the ad-

vances of another shepherd, Dorkon. All this is in the spirit of fun; the lovers
have taken a vow to be faithful to each other, and their friends are amusing
themselves a little because of the seriousness of the romance. Dorkon, however, is serious too, and Daphnis tells him to leave his girl alone. But Dorkon is
not to be easily routed. Daphnis becomes angry, and his friends try to make
light of the situation by suggesting that the two begin a dancing contest for
Chloë's favor.

Dorkon's dance is as crude and awkward as his advances toward Chloë have
been, and Daphnis, in a splendid dance with his shepherd's crook, easily de-
feats him. Chloë rewards Daphnis with a kiss, Dorkon departs, and her friends
take Chloë away.

Daphnis is alone. He lies down on the ground and daydreams of his perfect
love. He has almost fallen off to sleep when he is joined by the temptress
Lykanion. Daphnis is indifferent to her beauty, but strangely attracted also.
Lykanion is sure of her knowledge of love, and the inexperienced youth is disturbed. But Lykanion is too anxious to instruct Daphnis. He senses instinctively the evil in her advances and dismisses her.

Now the youth is roused by a battle cry. A band of pirates have invaded the
island, and the natives have risen in arms against them. The defenseless girls
seek the safety of Pan's grotto, but the pirates, disrespectful of the god, pursue
them. Bryaxis, leader of the pirates, captures Chloë and carries her off swiftly
before Daphnis can act. Daphnis cannot understand how this has happened.
He despairs and rails at the power of gods who would permit her abduction.

The music is quiet and mysterious. Suddenly one of the stone nymphs of the
grotto comes to life in a magical blaze of light. As the chorus begins to chant
along with the music, this girl and two other nymphs begin to dance. Daphnis
does not see them. Now they go to him, rouse him, and lead him before the
grotto of Pan. At the nymphs' call, an image of the god fills the sky. Daphnis
prays that the powerful god will restore Chloë to him.

SCENE TWO: THE PIRATES' HIDE-OUT   On the shore of another island, the pirates are celebrating their victory at night. They dance joyfully and divide
among themselves the day's profits. Chloë, her wrists bound together with
rope, is brought in, and Bryaxis, the pirate captain, commands her to dance.
The helpless girl is afraid to refuse, but soon, as she dances, she lifts her
bound wrists in supplication, begging to be released. Bryaxis only laughs at
her. The terrified girl trembles at the thought of intimacy with such a man.
Bryaxis is about to approach her when the seacoast is suddenly illuminated by
brilliant, flashing light. The pirates cower at this miracle and stare, astonished,
as the great god Pan appears in a vision. He orders the pirates to free Chloë.
The brigands flee to the hills.

SCENE THREE: ANOTHER PART OF THE SACRED GROVE   The orchestra is silent
as the curtain rises. Daphnis, lying alone, grieves over Chloë's loss. Gradually

the music imitates the sounds of the breaking day; the sun rises. Fellow shepherds come seeking Daphnis. But he does not wish to join them; only by praying to the god may he help his love to be rescued. Chloë's friends appear and
tell him that she has returned. The ecstatic Daphnis searches for her. At first
sight of Daphnis, Chloë runs into his arms, and the two lovers rejoice.

Lammon, an old shepherd, tells Daphnis that his prayers have indeed been
answered but that Pan acted in his favor because of the god's memory of his
own love for the Syrinx. Daphnis and Chloë, in their gratitude for Pan's inter-
vention, re-enact the god's romance for their friends. Daphnis, as Pan, vainly
pursues the lovely nymph, who flees from him. He pleads with her, but she
will not acknowledge him. She hides and, at Pan's persistence, casts herself
into a brook and drowns. The god takes a reed from the brook and makes of it
a flute, which he names for Syrinx. He plays upon the flute. At its sound, Chloë
begins to dance with tenderness and joy.

The ensemble joins the two lovers in a final general dance that celebrates
their reunion and their lasting love.

NOTES   Serge Diaghilev commissioned Ravel to compose a ballet in one act
on the story of Daphnis and Chloë. The work was to be performed in 1911,
and during the ensuing delay, Ravel arranged two suites from his score, both
of which were performed in the concert hall before the ballet's first performance. The ballet at last saw the stage June 8, 1912, with Tamara Karsavina
and Vaslav Nijinsky in the title roles. Fokine, the choreographer, had had in
mind a ballet on the Daphnis and Chloë legend for eight years. In 1904, in St.
Petersburg, he had submitted a scenario for such a work to the director of the
Imperial Theatre, along with a preface that detailed the reforms to be embodied in his work, reforms that he regarded as crucial for the art of ballet:
"The dance need not be a mere *divertissement*, introduced into the pantomime.
In the ballet the whole meaning of the story can be expressed by the dance.
Above all, dancing should be interpretive. It should not degenerate into mere
gymnastics. It should, in fact, be the plastic word. The dance should explain
the spirit of the actors in the spectacle. More than that, it should express the
whole epoch to which the subject of the ballet belongs . . . The ballet must no
longer be made up of 'numbers,' 'entries,' etc. It must show artistic unity of
conception . . . a unity which is made up of the three elements—music, painting, and plastic art . . . The great, the outstanding feature of the new ballet
. . . shall be but one thing—the aspiration for beauty . . ."

But the reforms suggested in Fokine's manifesto were largely ignored and
his project for a ballet was refused. Part of his original scenario was staged for
the Diaghilev Ballets Russes after many of his reforms had been realized, in
Les Sylphides, Firebird, and *Petrouchka.*

This production of *Daphnis and Chloë* was a considerable success. Tamara
Karsavina, who created the part of Chloë, has written that the ballet was, to

her mind, Fokine's masterpiece. "In it, Fokine explored to the full the recesses
of neo-Greek choreography as originally revived by Isadora Duncan."

Successful as it was, however, the production of *Daphnis and Chloë* created
a quarrel between the choreographer and the impresario. Fokine had difficulty
obtaining adequate rehearsal time and new costumes for his new ballet, and
since Nijinsky, in his staging of *The Afternoon of a Faun*, was being rewarded
with both, the older choreographer felt slighted. Soon after, he left the Diaghilev company for two years.

The *Daphnis and Chloë* of Catherine Littlefield, pioneer in American ballet,
was a completely new choreographic venture, first produced in 1937 for her
Philadelphia Ballet.

Two new productions of *Daphnis and Chloë* were given in New York in
1975. The first, with choreography by John Taras, costumes and production by
Joe Eula, and lighting by Ronald Bates, was part of the New York City Ballet's
Hommage à Ravel and received its first performance at the New York State
Theatre, Lincoln Center, New York, on May 22, with Robert Irving conducting. Peter Martins, Nina Fedorova, Karin von Aroldingen and Peter Schaufuss
were the principals.

The second new production, choreographed by Glen Tetley for the Stuttgart
Ballet and first presented at the Württemberg State Theatre, Stuttgart, May
17, 1975, with scenery and costumes by Willa Kim and lighting by John B.
Read, was first presented by the same ensemble in the United States at the
Metropolitan Opera House, Lincoln Center, on June 12, 1975 (lighting exe-
cuted by Gilbert V. Hemsley, Jr.), with Stewart Kershaw conducting the or-
chestra and chorus. Richard Cragun, Marcia Haydée, Birgit Keil, and Egon
Madsen were the principals.

DARK ELEGIES

*Music by Gustav Mahler. Choreography by Antony Tudor. Scenery and
costumes by Nadia Benois. First produced by the Ballet Rambert at the
Duchess Theatre, London, February 19, 1937, with Maude Lloyd, Antony
Tudor, Walter Gore, John Byron, Agnes de Mille, Hugh Laing, Daphne
Gow, Ann Gee, Patricia Clogstoun, Beryl Kay, and Celia Franca. First pre-
sented in the United States by Ballet Theatre at the Center Theatre, New
York, January 24, 1940, with scenery and costumes by Raymond Sovey
after the Benois originals. The principal dancers were Nina Stroganova,
Miriam Golden, Antony Tudor, Hugh Laing, Lucia Chase, and Dimitri
Romanoff.*

Dark Elegies is a dance ballet to the *Kindertotenlieder* (Songs of Childhood
Death) of Mahler. The singer on stage tells of the grief of a father over the
death of his children. The setting is somber, rough, jagged, with lowering

clouds over water and mountains and trees that seem to have been lashed relentlessly by the wind. As the music laments, a small group of villagers begin to dance. Their grief over a disaster that has befallen them all is communal and also private. We do not know what the tragedy is, there are no specifics, but with the expression and gesture of the dancers, we have no need. Their movement universalizes the particulars of Mahler's songs and we watch, as at a religious rite, the unfolding of desperate grief to mourning, to resignation and perhaps hope.

Dame Marie Rambert, in whose ballet company this ballet was created, has recalled in her biography *Quicksilver*: "Tudor told me he was anxious to do a ballet to Mahler's *Kindertotenlieder*. He had already suggested it two years before, but at that time I did not think he was mature enough to tackle such a tragic subject. I had also been perturbed by the main idea of a disaster that would kill all the children and leave the parents alive. I kept reasoning with Tudor that except for the Massacre of the Innocents such a special calamity had never happened and would seem *too* contrived. But now in 1937 he seemed very sure of the way to treat it. I asked him to show me one finished song and realized how profound the choreography was. He had seen at an exhibition of Nadia Benois a landscape which he was sure would be the right setting, and when I saw the painting I agreed with him. So we invited her to design the scenery and the costumes, which she did perfectly. The ballet was not purely realistic. It had lovely words and music, and the dances were classical for the soloists and in folk-dance style for the ensemble. Yet he managed to keep the style homogeneous.

"He called this ballet *Dark Elegies*. It was in two scenes: 1. Bereavement; 2. Resignation. It was like a mourning ritual accompanied by a singer on the stage. Singly or in groups, the bereaved parents express their sorrow in a slow dance at having lost their children when their village was stricken by calamity. They try not to show their pain, but it breaks through at moments. All was said in classical language, and this severe form made the expression more poignant when despair burst through it.

"When we performed this ballet in 1966 to a new young public, many of them thought that it was all about the Aberfan Disaster, to such a degree had the most unforeseen of calamities happened in reality.

"*Dark Elegies* was Tudor's masterpiece and has remained the greatest tragic ballet of the English repertoire so far.

"In addition to our own dancers he used a guest dancer, the American Agnes de Mille, a most remarkable artist."

Agnes de Mille's own recollections of *Dark Elegies* are recorded in a long interview with the critic Clive Barnes (see his book *Inside American Ballet Theatre*, 1977).

NOTE   *Dark Elegies* has been in the active repertory of the Ballet Rambert since it was first performed. It is now danced by the National Ballet of Canada and other companies. Jerome Robbins has said: "Fokine inspired me as a performer; he made me feel I could really dance. Tudor didn't; he made it complicated. He brought psychological motivation into ballet; he conveyed through movement emotions that could not be put into words. And he had the courage to persevere along this line in the face of adverse criticism. But he did wonderful things in pure dance, as well. *Gala Performance* and *Dark Elegies* stand alone, and I think they will last longest because they are more formal in structure . . . Tudor had a great influence on my early work and a great influence on all contemporary ballet."*

LES DEMOISELLES DE LA NUIT (The Ladies of Midnight)

Dramatic ballet in three scenes. Music by Jean Françaix. Choreography by Roland Petit. Book by Jean Anouilh. Settings and costumes by Léonor Fini. First presented by Les Ballets de Paris at the Théâtre Marigny, Paris, May 21, 1948, with Margot Fonteyn, Roland Petit, and Gordon Hamilton in the leading roles. First presented in the United States by Ballet Theatre at the Metropolitan Opera House, New York, April 13, 1951, with Colette Marchand, John Kriza, and Eric Braun.

This ballet rightly assumes that when a young man marries a cat, things are going to be pretty difficult around the house. How the young man meets the cat, how he is enamored of her feline grace, how his love transforms her for a time into a beautiful young girl, and how, despite his love, his wife is unable to conquer an irresistible inclination to scamper on the rooftops, the ballet chooses to relate in three scenes.

SCENE ONE: A HOUSE IN THE COUNTRY Low, moaning music is heard from the orchestra as a brief overture begins. The curtain rises. The scene is a large, high room whose walls are papered with yellowing, peeling newspapers. Cats sit about the room in relaxed attitudes: some polishing their nails, some resting against a ladder. A black kitten reclines on a white couch at the right. On the wall, partially obscured by a wispy rag, hangs a portrait of a big, beautiful white cat. A doorway in the center is hung with tattered and torn cloth; innumerable cats must have sharpened their claws on it.

A young musician enters. He pushes aside the dusty drapes and steps carefully into the room. He has been invited to this house in the country to play at a wedding and is astonished to see that no ordinary preparations for such an occasion have been made. He observes the curious cats and walks over to the portrait. He turns in the air in surprise at what he sees there. The entire house is occupied by cats!

* From "Antony Tudor" by Selma Jeanne Cohen, in *Dance Perspectives 18*, 1963.

Two black-and-white cats in handsome livery, pages to the household, dart out and grab the musician's hat. The tempo becomes brisk. The light brightens. He chases after them unsuccessfully. The black cat rises from the couch; she and three of the kittens surround the musician. The cats dance about the boy, scratching at his face. The black cat curls up at his feet. He dances for a short time with the kittens. They leave. Agatha, the beautiful white cat at whose portrait the musician has marveled, enters quickly, expectantly. Agatha is the bride of the month. The cat baron who rules over the house marries one of his harem every month, and it is Agatha's wedding that the musician has been invited to attend. Tall and graceful, with long, lithe legs, she immediately attracts the young man. She is dressed in white, with short gloves; a blue ribbon is tied about her throat. The music changes; an oboe plays a wistful, yet playful, melody to the accompaniment of plucked strings.

Agatha begins to dance. The musician watches, fascinated. The music becomes rhythmic. He compares the cat to her portrait. He goes up to Agatha. She circles him on point, and the strings commence a flowing theme. The boy turns swiftly and kneels at her feet. Now he rises and holds her close. The cat responds experimentally. Gradually Agatha becomes as interested in the musician as he is in her. He lifts, holds, and embraces her for a duet that lasts five minutes. The music whines plaintively. The other cats look on with horror. What will the cat baron do? They attack the boy and try to pull him away, but Agatha climbs up on his back. Cymbals and brass simulate the contest. The boy embraces the cat. The music is silent for a moment.

The cat baron enters, his fur bristling. A lovely black cat, whose costume is embellished with the skeleton of a fish, separates the lovers rudely. She is evidently the cat baron's principal aide. Footlights throw the shadows of the two lovers and the jealous cat baron against the back wall. The baron dances in gleeful anticipation of his wedding. Agatha dances with him, not unwilling at first, but she breaks away and gestures to the boy, who stands on the opposite side of the stage, holding out his arms to her plaintively. She goes to the boy. The cat baron pulls them apart and dances furiously. He threatens the musician with his long claws.

The black cat takes Agatha's hand and pulls her toward the baron. A white veil is thrown over the bride's head before she can protest. Daringly she pulls it off and rejoins the boy. The cat baron makes a last effort to dominate her passions. The pages hold the cat couple high on their shoulders in a wedding parade. But Agatha falls down into the musician's arms. The desperate cats scuttle off. Suddenly Agatha is no longer a kitten; her face is the face of a beautiful girl.

SCENE TWO: AT HOME   The orchestra plays a protracted interlude of hurried music. The curtain rises on a boudoir scene. A white bed canopied in white gauze stands on the left. At the right is a large window, looking out on to a dark-blue night. A bird cage stands near the window. Agatha, in a becoming white costume, her light hair shining, stands alongside her new husband. They embrace. The girl goes over to the bird cage, takes out a bluebird, fondles it, and dances as she holds it before her. The boy sits at the foot of the bed and watches her adoringly. Odd, this passion of hers for birds.

He rises, stands by the window, then goes over to the right wall. As he steps back into the room, the cat baron follows him closely. Agatha is agitated. Her lover tries to throw the intruder out, but the baron is so delighted to see his sometime fiancée again, even if she is a real girl now, that he forces her to dance with him. When the boy separates them, the cat jumps up onto his back and scratches at him fiercely. Both claim Agatha. Finally the musician succeeds in throwing the baron out.

Agatha seems to be grateful. To a quiet, deep melody, she stands behind the boy and wraps her arms about his neck. They begin to dance. In the midst of their *pas de deux*, the girl's limbs seem to quicken. The boy takes her to the bed. There he lifts her high on his shoulder. He lets her down slowly, and the girl's body curves backward. He rocks her back and forth, his knee a fulcrum to her seesawing body. The boy falls back, exhausted. Agatha falls over his knees.

Prolonged, mournful cat calls are heard. Agatha raises her head. The sounds persist. As she moves off the bed onto the floor, a cymbal crashes. Her movements are catlike. She looks back at her lover, despairs, and climbs out the window. The musician awakens. The orchestra plays the haunting music of the ballet's overture. Where has Agatha gone? Out on the roof again, presumably. He takes a candle and follows her.

SCENE THREE: THE ROOFTOPS   The theme of the overture persists throughout the interval. The scene, as the curtain rises, is a red rooftop against a blue sky. Four dormer windows penetrate the roof from within. There is a gutter at the front. Agatha and the cat baron stand poised against two of the windows. They run to each other and embrace in the gutter. The musician climbs onto the roof through the window at the left. Other cats crawl over the roof and stand ready to attack him behind the window. They pounce on him. The boy falls. Agatha and the cat baron lead a train of cats over the roof, in and out among the windows. The boy tries to follow and slides into the gutter. When he rises, the cats gather behind each of the windows and menace him as he tries to gain the top of the roof. He holds Agatha desperately for a brief moment. The cat baron pulls her away and leads her to the peak of the roof. There the other cats place her on the baron's back. He races down toward the gutter. Agatha falls. The musician has been slapping about in the gutter like a fish fresh out of water. He squirms over to the girl. He sits up. Agatha poses against him; then both fall back. Their bodies arch away from each other, their hands and feet joined. They move close and lift their legs so that their toes touch. The boy dies. The girl looks down at him and dies. Their heads fall

back and their arms dangle over the edge of the roof. Their curious love is
happy in death.

NOTES   After its performance by Ballet Theatre, *Les Demoiselles de la Nuit*
was called by John Martin of the New York *Times* "in many ways the best of
Petit's ballets to be seen in this country. Though it has his characteristically
theatrical approach, it has also much more of a choreographic basis than any
of his other pieces." Petit had originally planned to include this ballet in the
repertory of his own Ballets de Paris during one of its New York seasons, but
had been unable to do so. Colette Marchand had succeeded Margot Fonteyn
in performances of the principal role in Paris when the ballet was first produced; in New York, Marchand repeated her earlier success. The ballet has
been considerably revised since its first American performance. Mary Ellen
Moylan has danced Agatha with both critical and popular approval.

DESIGNS WITH STRINGS

*Music by Peter Ilyich Tchaikovsky. Choreography by John Taras. First pre-
sented by the Metropolitan Ballet at Wimbledon, England, February 6,
1948. First presented in the United States by Ballet Theatre at the Center
Theatre, New York, April 25, 1950, with costumes by Irene Sharaff.*

Designs with Strings is a dance ballet to the second movement of Tchaikovsky's *Trio in A minor*, arranged for piano and string orchestra. Instead of a
story it has a mood, a character that arises from the dancing. There is no scenery; all the dancers wear simple black classical costumes and it is only in
what they dance that they become individuals rather than performers.

The piano plays the stately, sentimental opening theme. There are six
dancers—two boys and four girls. When the curtain rises, they are grouped together and stand motionless in silhouette against a plain backdrop. Their arms
are extended slightly as they stand together; all the dancers appear to have a
common relation and when they respond to the music and begin to move
slowly in and out among themselves, they create an impression of unwinding
of latent, quiescent energy.

The lights come up, the full string orchestra takes up the theme, and three
of the dancers leave the stage. The remaining three, a boy and two girls, dance
softly to the music. Their movement, like the melody, is romantic—a little sad,
a little wistful. Their three companions return and circle the stage rapidly, as if
to show that there is happiness in romance also. All six dance together briefly,
and suddenly the melody quickens and the music becomes tinkling and light
and gay. The dancers duplicate this change of pace and temper with whirling
acceleration and with steps that are sharply fast and precise.

At the climax of this openly joyous sequence, the dancers leave the stage and a girl dances with a boy alone. The theme changes for this *pas de deux,* which is not at first so much romantic as it is matter-of-fact. But the dancing soon alters this, and we see as they move together that the girl and the boy are surprised and pleased to be by themselves, apart from the group. He lifts her off into the wings on the left; the first theme returns accompanied by a newly accented rhythm. Three girls rush out and dance brightly for a moment, to break the romantic spell, and leave the stage.

Another theme, noble and lowing, is heard on muted strings. The ballerina returns with two boys, who support her in a short dance. The wistfulness and playfulness have disappeared; the ballerina and her partners display a proud, youthful dignity. The new-found dignity breaks into pathos, however, upon the return of the other dancers. The six try to dance together as before, first the girls, then the boys. The first theme is heard again, poignantly on piercing strings. The ballerina separates herself from the group, and a boy supports her in a series of slow, extended movements across the stage. The other dancers move forward and separate them. The girl runs to the boy, seeming to plead with him and to claim him. But when she places her arms on his shoulders, he slips away from her and goes to rejoin the others. Slowly the girl follows him. The lights go down. The dancers stand as they were at the beginning, their figures silhouetted in a close group that seems now inseparable.

DEUCE COUPE

Music by the Beach Boys. Choreography by Twyla Tharp. Setting by United Graffiti Artists. Costumes by Scott Barrie. Lighting by Jennifer Tipton. First presented by the City Center Joffrey Ballet at the City Center, New York, March 1, 1973, with Erika Goodman, Twyla Tharp, and dancers from the Joffrey Ballet and the Twyla Tharp Company.

Described as a juxtaposition of classical ballet and choreography based on social dances of the 1960s, *Deuce Coupe* was the first major work to be staged with an important ballet company by the modern dancer and choreographer Twyla Tharp, who appeared in the piece with members of her company. The title refers both to an automobile and to the piece *Little Deuce Coupe* by the Beach Boys, the rock group whose music, on tape, is featured in the ballet. Another major feature of the ballet is the setting—a background of three high strips of translucent paper (at first they look like windows we can't see out of) that a group of young people gradually fill with graffiti. As they inscribe the long sheets of paper, the paper is rolled up until the full height of the stage reflects their handiwork.

What happens on stage can be simply suggested but inadequately described. While a ballet dancer, Erika Goodman, performs an alphabetical but not-so-straightforward rendition of steps from the classical ballet dictionary, beginning with *Ailes de pigeon*, the rest of the dancers, in various combinations and permutations, perform dances both ancient and modern.

There are nineteen dances: *Matrix I, Ailes de pigeon* through *Attitude,* for the ballerina type and a couple; *Little Deuce Coupe, Balancé* through *Ballon,* with eighteen dancers and the persistent ballet performer; *Honda I, Balloné battu* through *déboulés,* for a *pas de trois* and the ballet girl; *Honda II, Changement de pieds* through *Dégagé à la quatrième devant en l'air,* for a couple and the girl; *Devoted to You, Dégagé en tournant* through *Failli,* for two couples and the girl; *How She Boogalooed It, Faux* through *Manège,* for the girl and a large ensemble; *Matrix II, Pas de basque sur les pointes* through *Pas de chat,* for the girl and six; *Alley Oop, Pas de cheval* through *Répétition,* for the girl plus eight; *Take a Load Off Your Feet, Retire* through *Sissone Tombée,* for three girls and two boys; *Long Tall Texan, Six* through *Suite,* for three girls; *Papa ooh Mau Mau,* for six; *Catch a Wave,* for five; *Got to Know the Woman, Temps de cuisse* through *temps lié,* for two girls; *Matrix III, Temps lié grand* through *Voyage,* for the ballet girl; *Don't Go Near the Water,* for six girls; *Matrix IV,* for a girl and boy; *Mama Says—"Eat a Lot, Never Be Lazy,"* for five boys and a girl; *Wouldn't It Be Nice,* for ten; and *Cuddle Up,* a finale for the whole company.

NOTE   Writing on the première in the *Daily News,* the critic Joseph Gale said that *Deuce Coupe* "is all the sadness, joy, cynicism and flavor of the beat generation . . . and the ballet is a smash.

"It is never less than exciting in crazy whorls of frenzied choreography that races, expires, picks up, jets ahead, pauses, and finally lays itself bare in unshed tears of last hopes.

"Through it all, there is the shining thread that holds it together and is the ballet's signature. That is Erika Goodman, unruffled and serene, who goes through a fair lexicon of classical dance, from *ailes de pigeon* through *pas de cheval,* while the world breaks up around her. She is the symbolic glory and salvation, the one who, after all else has failed, proffers hope in the palm of her outstretched hand. . . .

"There is also the schizoid passion of Miss Tharp's own dancing and, too, the United Graffiti Artists, who scrawl up a wall with the best decor of the season."

See comments on *As Time Goes By,* another Twyla Tharp ballet, for other views of this choreographer.

In the City Center Joffrey Ballet's spring season, 1975, the ballet became *Deuce Coupe II,* with the removal of Twyla Tharp's own dancers from the ensemble, a revision of the dances, and a new backdrop. Writing in *New York* magazine, the critic Alan Rich said that "the new work creates its own joy. Its scenario is entirely new; instead of being a work about pure dance, with its central soloist re-enacting the classic steps in alphabetical order, it is now a work about style. It spends its 40-or-so minutes as a steady wash, its pop steps

from early on slowly oozing into romantic elegance as its dancers learn to un-
bend their knees and walk upon earth as adults. It is also, therefore, about
growing up. Its music track, still a pastiche of the Beach Boys's greatest hits, is
stronger, more poignant, altogether splendid."

DIM LUSTRE

> Music by Richard Strauss. Choreography by Antony Tudor. Scenery and
> costumes by Motley. First presented by Ballet Theatre at the Metropolitan
> Opera House, New York, October 20, 1943, with Nora Kaye and Hugh
> Laing in the leading roles.

The dancer Hugh Laing has defined the theme of this ballet to Richard
Strauss's *Burleske in D minor* for piano and orchestra: "Two people find they
have been caught up with memories, not with each other, and they part." The
scene is a ballroom. The atmosphere is heavy with recollection of another era.
There a couple are attracted to each other and dance. He kisses her on the
shoulder, she recalls the past, the action freezes, there is a blackout, and a girl
dancing a reflection of the lady relives her first innocent romance with a young
boy. When the young boy kisses her on the shoulder, the past dissolves and
the present dance resumes. Now the man is reminded suddenly by a tap on
the shoulder of a time spent with three coquettish girls. The action dissolves
again into the past and we see his double relive the earlier time (which was
the one he loved?). This emerges again into the present at the tap of a shoulder. Other memories converge upon the dance of the couple, there are flashbacks of a girl with an unforgettable perfume, of a man with a white tie. In
the end, the lovers part, aware that what attracts them to each other is not
themselves so much as pieces of the past. They cannot make for themselves a
new memory.

 Dim Lustre was revived by the New York City Ballet on May 26, 1964,
with costumes, scenery, and lighting by Beni Montressor. Patricia McBride
and Edward Villella danced the principal roles.

DIVERTIMENTO NO. 15

> Music by Wolfgang Amadeus Mozart. Choreography by George Balanchine.
> Costumes by Karinska. Scenery by David Hays. First presented by the New
> York City Ballet at the American Shakespeare Festival Theatre, Stratford,
> Connecticut, May 31, 1956, with Tanaquil LeClercq, Diana Adams, Patricia
> Wilde, Melissa Hayden, Allegra Kent, Nicholas Magallanes, Herbert Bliss,
> and Roy Tobias in principal roles.

This ballet is a complete reworking of *Caracole*, a ballet to the same music, Mozart's *Divertimento No. 15 in B flat major (K. 287)*, that was first presented by the New York City Ballet in 1952. Although *Caracole* had real success when it was first done, we did not dance it for several years and when the dancers and I began to work on a revival in 1956, we found we could remember very little of the original. So many new ballets had intervened that I had to start work all over again! That was not altogether a misfortune, for this score is one I admire most in the world.

Mozart wrote the *Divertimento* when he was twenty-one. He composed many similar works, pieces designed for special social occasions, large garden parties, carnivals, balls. All of these pieces were written to divert and charm audiences that expected to be entertained. Very often people danced to them. This particular divertimento is probably the finest ever written.

The ballet follows the different movements of the score. There is no story. It is designed for five principal girls, three boys, and a *corps de ballet* of eight girls. First movement—Allegro. Second—Andante Grazioso—Theme and Variations. Third—Minuet. Fourth—Andante. Fifth—Allegro Molto—Andante.

The ballet was danced for the first time at the bicentennial celebration of Mozart's birth that Lincoln Kirstein arranged at the American Shakespeare Festival Theatre. It then became a part of the repertory of the New York City Ballet.

DONIZETTI VARIATIONS

Music by Gaetano Donizetti. Choreography by George Balanchine. Costumes by Karinska. Lighting by David Hays. First presented by the New York City Ballet at the City Center, New York, November 16, 1960, with Melissa Hayden and Jonathan Watts in the leading roles.

This is a dance ballet, pure and simple, to some pleasant music by Donizetti. It was originally produced as part of "Salute to Italy," a dance program at the New York City Ballet honoring the one-hundredth anniversary of the formation of the Italian state. The program was planned around works with music by Italian composers, beginning with *Con Amore* (Rossini) and continuing with *Monumentum* (Stravinsky/Gesualdo) and *La Sonnambula* (Bellini). To contrast with the seriousness of these last two, we needed another, cheerful and sunny work. We found just what we wanted in music from a little-performed opera by Donizetti, *Don Sebastian*. The ballet features a central *pas de deux* for a ballerina and her partner—entrée, adagio, two variations and coda, plus variations and ensembles for the corps of six girls and three boys.

DON JUAN

Ballet by John Neumeier. Music by Christoph Willibald Gluck and Tomás Luis de Victoria. Choreography and staging by John Neumeier. Decor and costumes by Filippo Sanjust. Text by Max Frisch, translated by John Neumeier. Narrated by Sir Ralph Richardson. First presented in New York by the National Ballet of Canada at the Metropolitan Opera House, Lincoln Center, April 26, 1974, with Rudolf Nureyev in the leading role.

The romantic hero Don Juan is no stranger to ballet. Gluck's great music, so important for its time, is thought to be the first truly dramatic score for dance, designed to conform to a projected scheme of character, time, place, and situation. The first choreographer for the score was Angiolini (Vienna, 1761). Michel Fokine staged it for René Blum's Ballet Russe in London in 1936, with Anatole Vilzak as the hero and André Eglevsky as the Jester. Sir Frederick Ashton also choreographed a *Don Juan*, but to the score of Richard Strauss. This production, with Robert Helpmann, Margot Fonteyn, and Moira Shearer, was staged by the Sadler's Wells Ballet in London in 1948. Its theme was "The love that caught strange light from Death's own eyes," taken from Gautier's poem *"La Morte Amoureuse,"* and Ashton depicted the hero pursuing many loves but discovering that Death is his true beloved.

John Neumeier's ballet pursues a similar conception in a dramatic narrative accompanied not only by Gluck's music but also by the *Requiem Mass* of Victoria. Like a contemporary film, the ballet cuts back and forth in theme and music in such a way as to suggest motivations and insights the choreographer wishes to bring out, interweaving solemnity and celebration, action and passion, love and death. The context of the narrative is the familiar aftermath of Don Juan's murder of the father of a girl he has seduced.

When the curtain rises we discern behind a scrim a Lady in White. She is watched by a man who stands with his back to us, a mysterious creature in a long black cloak and black hat. It is November 2, the Day of the Dead in the Spanish calendar. A funeral procession passes. Commander Don Gonzalo de Ulloa is being carried to his grave, mourned by his daughter Doña Ana. After the bier has passed, the man in black reveals himself as Don Juan Tenorio, her father's killer. Doña Ana, still beguiled by the Don, is heartbroken as he rebuffs her. The Don proceeds to a banquet, accompanied by his servant and collaborator Catalinon.

In the next scene, a huge ballroom, Catalinon engages a troupe of dancers to present, in a series of *divertissements*, the amorous adventures of his master. Catalinon himself assumes the role of the legendary seducer, Don Juan. The Don and the ladies of the party watch with amusement as a placard announces the theme of the play, "Don Juan and the Ladies," which is enacted on a small stage at the back of the hall. There the Don is observed in successful pursuit of three girls. Next, in the scene "Don Juan Serenades Doña Ana," we flash-back to his conquest of that lady, whose fierce passion soon exhausts him. When her father enters unexpectedly, sword in hand, a duel ensues. After he has killed her father, Don Juan wipes his sword on Doña Ana's skirt.

Now the Lady in White appears, but only to Don Juan, who reaches out to her. They dance, he fascinated by her blond coolness, in a duet in which she rejects him. She seems to be leading him away in a direction he cannot deter-mine. For the first time, a woman has not succumbed to his charm. Mysteri-ously, she disappears and there is no one in his arms. In one of the moments of silence in the ballet, the hero composes himself. A voice says, "Don Juan is a narcissist who loves only himself . . . He is not a lover, he remains alone . . . Disguising his true self, Don Juan is his role."

Then the music resumes and Catalinon is organizing things again, this time with "A Peasant Wedding," where the rustic lovers dance a *pas de deux*. Watching the dance and eying the peasant girl, Don Juan, to reassure himself after the incident with the Lady in White, determines to seduce her. In the midst of the Don's conquest of the girl, Doña Ana enters and watches. She knows everything that is happening at once but is so in thrall to the Don that it does not seem to matter. The Don amuses himself by playing the two ladies against each other.

As a climax to his satirical presentation, Catalinon and the dancers present "The Damnation of Don Juan," which develops into an orgy involving all the guests.

Don Juan leaves the party, pursuing the Lady in White. He passes a proces-sion of mourners carrying the empty bier. Doña Ana is there, weeping. Gradu-ally he realizes that this is his own funeral cortege. As the Lady in White now beckons to him, he recognizes her as the Angel of Death.

Clive Barnes wrote in the New York *Times* after the New York premiere that "Mr. Nureyev is superb as Don Juan—from the nervous, preening way he pats his hair, to his smiling yet supercilious disdain, to his slightly nervous pride . . . The entire portrayal, morose, disenchanted and just a little foolish, is remarkable.

"The ballet shows the National Ballet of Canada at its very best and the whole performance could not have been bettered."

DON QUIXOTE

Ballet in four acts, eight scenes, and a prologue. Music by L. Minkus. Chore-ography by Marius Petipa. First presented by the Bolshoi Theatre, Moscow, December 26, 1869. First presented in the United States by the Bolshoi Ballet at the Metropolitan Opera House, New York, April 21, 1966, with Petipa's choreography revised by Aleksandr Gorsky and Rostislav Zakharov.

Scenery and costumes by Vadim Rindin. Maya Plisetskaya appeared as Kitri, *Vladimir Tikhonov as* Basil the barber, *Pyotr Khomutuv as* Don Quixote, *and Nikolai Samokhvalov as* Sancho Panza.

Miguel Cervantes's masterpiece *Don Quixote* has a long ballet history. Beginning with a danced version by Noverre in the mid-eighteenth century, the story has attracted dancers and choreographers many times. The two principal versions of Cervantes's novel are described below.

PROLOGUE: DON QUIXOTE'S STUDY   Don Quixote's servants, anxious about his growing obsession with ancient chivalry, are seen trying to throw his books away. He enters, reading, and sits at his table. He rejoices in heroic tales of brave knights and beautiful ladies. In a vision, he beholds the lady of his dreams, Dulcinea. Sancho Panza enters, pursued by angry shopkeepers from whom he has stolen a goose. The Don rescues him, appoints him his squire, and sets out on his adventures.

ACT ONE: THE SQUARE IN BARCELONA   Basil, a barber, is in love with the innkeeper's daughter, Kitri, but her mother wishes her to marry Gamache, a foppish nobleman. Don Quixote arrives with Sancho. The Don assumes that the inn is a famous castle. Sancho is teased by the townsfolk and tossed in a blanket. Don Quixote rescues him. Don Quixote now sees the beautiful Kitri. He is bewitched and acclaims her as his Dulcinea.

ACT TWO, SCENE ONE: INSIDE THE INN   Kitri's mother, still determined to marry her daughter to the nobleman, so distresses Basil that he pretends to stab himself. As he lies dying, he begs Kitri's parents to unite them.

ACT TWO, SCENE TWO: A GYPSY ENCAMPMENT   Gypsies and strolling players, alerted to the imminent arrival of Don Quixote and Sancho, prepare to trick the knight. Don Quixote enters and pays homage to their leader as king. The leader then calls for dances to begin. This is followed by a command performance of the puppet theater. Watching the play, Don Quixote mistakes the heroine for Dulcinea, sees her under attack, and rises to assault the puppet stage. Pursuing her further to windmills nearby, he imagines Dulcinea is being concealed. Mistaking the windmills for menacing giants, he tilts at them, only to be caught up in one of the wings and tossed in the air. Sancho revives and comforts him.

ACT THREE, SCENE ONE: A FOREST   The Don and Sancho lie down to rest in a wood. But still stunned from his fight with the windmill, the Don is troubled by fantastic dreams where he sees himself a knight in shining armor surrounded by lovely ladies.

ACT FOUR: PROLOGUE Hunting horns proclaim the arrival of the Duke of Barcelona, who has heard about Don Quixote and wishes to see the curious knight himself. He awakens the Don and invites him to accompany a *fiesta*. The Duke then persuades Basil to dress up and pretend to be a Knight Errant to play a trick on Don Quixote.

ACT FIVE: THE MAIN SQUARE OF BARCELONA It is *fiesta* time. The Duke and the Duchess and the Don watch the dancing. Suddenly the Don thinks that he recognizes his Dulcinea in a girl carried on by mysterious figures guarded by a strange knight. The Knight challenges the Don to a duel and the old man is soon vanquished. His opponent, removing his disguise, reveals himself as Basil the barber. The Don is so crestfallen by this trickery that the Duke and Duchess have pity and comfort him. Kitri and Basil then celebrate their betrothal in a *grand pas de deux*. Don Quixote realizes that he has not yet found his Dulcinea and with Sancho sets off for more adventures.

NOTES This *Don Quixote* includes the *grand pas de deux* that is often presented independently in various versions on ballet programs. The part of Kitri has been performed over the years by many famous ballerinas, Pavlova and Karsavina among them. Pavlova produced a shortened version of the ballet for her tours. Rudolf Nureyev produced his version of the Petipa ballet for the Vienna State Opera on December 1, 1966, himself appearing as *Basil* with Ully Wuehrer as *Kitri*, Michael Birkmeyer as *Don Quixote*, and Konstantin Zajetz as *Sancho Panza*.

In 1970, Nureyev staged his version of the ballet with the Australian Ballet in a production designed by Barry Kay. This production was first presented in the United States by the Australian Ballet in San Francisco, January 4, 1971. In 1972, Nureyev and Robert Helpmann made a film of this production.

Interviewed by Laura Bell for *Show* magazine in 1971 about certain aspects of his production of *Don Quixote*, Nureyev commented about the duel between the Don and his foppish rival Don Gamache: "The duel is mine but the stabbing is all in the original Petipa, and in the book. There, you may remember, it is even broader. Basilio has a bladder of sheep's blood hidden under his arm and when he stabs it, blood spurts everywhere. I decided this was going a bit far in literalness, and it would be messy. The duel, though, was originally between the knight and the heroine's father, an innkeeper. But I think it proper Don Quixote should fight his own kind, not a commoner, so I have him fight Don Gamache, who, in the bargain, is wearing the proper white gauntlets to throw down. I try all through to keep the six main characters together, playing off each other, as in *commedia dell'arte*—you can even match up characters. Quixote is Pantalon, Kitri is Columbine; Basilio, Pierrot, and so on. I wanted the story not to be about Don Quixote but about how people react to him, how they take advantage of him and devise ways to mock and laugh at him. Yet they go crazy doing this, they are as fanatic as the knight is.

"And Don Quixote himself . . . At first, I hated him quite a lot. I didn't understand for a long time. I was on the side of the people. To me he was just a clown. And then I read the book! There is so much there, but in a ballet you can only skim the surface. I tried to put in a lot of things I felt about the book, like impressions of the Callot lithographs, but you daren't put too much comment in. It really is largely a lot of dances and great zest and comic spirit . . . and yet, everybody seems to think of this ballet as kind of foolish.

"I can't take any credit for these productions which I do only to provide another vehicle for myself and to preserve what is left of Petipa. With *Don Quixote* I wanted a comic part and since no choreographer has ever offered me one, I did this. With original choreography you have to sit down and think and spend a lot of time. I do *not* like improvisations. If you want to create a ballet, you have to have a certain point of view, something you want to say, not just steps or variations that just 'come' to you. And even with *Raymonda* and *Don Quixote*, they took a lot of working out and research. Perhaps in time . . ."

A film of Nureyev's production of *Don Quixote* was made in Australia in 1972 with the Australian Ballet. Codirected by Nureyev and Sir Robert Helpmann, the film starred Lucette Aldous as Kitri-Dulcinea and Nureyev as Basilio. It was first presented in the United States, November 1, 1973, at a Gala Benefit for the Dance Collection of the New York Public Library.

Ballet in three acts. Music by Nicolas Nabokov. Choreography by George Balanchine. Scenery, costumes, and lighting by Esteban Francés. Assistant to Mr. Francés: Peter Harvey. Costumes executed by Karinska. First presented by the New York City Ballet at the New York State Theatre, May 27, 1965, with George Balanchine as Don Quixote, *Suzanne Farrell as* Dulcinea, *Deni Lamont as* Sancho Panza, *and the entire company.*

I first read Cervantes in Russian, but I have read parts of *Don Quixote* many times since, in English and French as well. The idea of doing a ballet about the Don has always seemed to me natural and inevitable, something I would want to do whenever time and opportunity came. Other ballets to *Don Quixote* I had perhaps seen but scarcely remembered. The Petipa ballet, with music by Minkus, was in the repertory of the Maryinsky when I was a boy (I danced in this production in 1916, when I was twelve), but it was not a serious work and not one of my favorites. Twenty years ago I discovered that my friend the composer Nicolas Nabokov had a similar enthusiasm for *Don Quixote*. He had written an orchestral suite on the Don and Dulcinea which I liked. We then spoke of doing a full-scale ballet on the subject one day, but it was some years before this came about. We began to work out a scenario in detail. We did several scenarios, in fact, arriving at a final one in June 1964. Throughout the composition of the score we were in frequent communication and saw each other as often as possible to discuss the music and the action. As a musician with a deep knowledge of ballet, Nabokov knew what he was getting into. Three-act ballets are difficult compositions. Nabokov's score has everything, it *has* to have everything to do its job properly, for music written to accompany a danced narrative with *divertissements* cannot preserve the unities designed for the concert hall. Nabokov worked within three traditions, the musical one, the ballet tradition, and the dramatic. His score in essence amounts to symphonic dance variations.

The action of the ballet follows closely the scenario Nabokov and I worked out together.

The form the novel took for us naturally does not follow the sequence of the book, but I must say we never had any difficulty in our ideas. The problem was always what we had to cut and put aside. Don Quixote's anguished search for human perfectibility, the intricate shifts from fantasy to reality that take place in his mind, are vividly expressed through his adventures and the dream of the Lady Dulcinea, who appears in many guises to him. Guises these always are—the Magdalen, the Virgin Mary, the Shepherdess Marcela, the Lady of the Silver Moon—and although he gives his whole life for her, he never really sees her. He is, if you like, a kind of secular saint whom no one believes in. Finally, his death brings him face to face with himself, seemingly defeated, but having lived as he believed.

PROLOGUE: DON QUIXOTE'S STUDY   Don Quixote sits alone and reads his books about chivalry. He searches through them for the answers to his dreams of knight errantry. He falls off to sleep. A mist covers the stage and strange figures from his dream take over the scene: a girl seems to materialize right out of the pages of a book; a dragon appears. The Don rescues the girl. He rests. A young girl, a maidservant, enters and washes his feet, drying them with her hair. He kisses her forehead and she leaves and Don Quixote rises.

Sancho Panza enters carrying the Don's clothes, does a pratfall but quickly rises to dress his master. The Don, with sword held high, follows the girl toward the brilliant sun she has let into the room. This is the only sun he will see. As Cervantes said, "Misfortunes always pursue men of talent." Don Quixote's study is now transformed, becoming:

ACT ONE, SCENE ONE: LA MANCHA   Don Quixote stands alone surrounded by earth and sky. Windmills in the distance. In the piercing light of midday there appears to him a vision of the Madonna, a girl with a resplendent headdress standing on a cart much as if a statue of the Virgin being carried in a village procession has suddenly come to life. It is the servant girl of the Prologue. He kneels before the vision, takes the oath of a knight, and receives the Madonna's blessing.

Don Quixote encounters a child being beaten by a man. He challenges the man and chases him off. The rescued child runs away, mocking the Don. Next he comes upon a group of prisoners being led in chains. He attacks the jailers

and frees the men, who thereupon set upon the Don and Sancho and give
them a good trouncing.

ACT ONE, SCENE TWO: A VILLAGE SQUARE   There are folk dances in front of
an inn. Sancho runs out, pursued by guards and fishwives from whom he has
stolen a huge fish. He is caught, beaten up, and tossed in a blanket. Don Quixote appears on his horse, dismounts and liberates Sancho. Sancho kneels at his
feet, weeping. The Innkeeper brings food and the Don comforts Sancho. A
cortege enters. A poet is being mourned. A beautiful country girl, Marcela, is
seized and accused of causing his death. We see that she is the same girl as in
the first scenes, dressed now as a shepherdess with a long crook. She is grateful to the Don and dances. In Cervantes, she explains that she is not to be
blamed for the poet's death: "If every beauty inspired love and won hearts,
men's fancy would become vague and bewildered and not know where to stop,
for as beauty is infinite, desire must likewise be infinite. If this is so, as I believe it to be, why do you ask me to surrender my will under pressure for no
other reason than that you say you love me? For beauty in a modest woman is
like distant fire or a sharp sword; the one does not burn, the other does not cut
the man who does not go near it. Now if modesty is one of the virtues and the
fairest ornament of the body and the soul, why must the woman who is loved
for her beauty lose it to gratify the desires of a man who, for his pleasure
alone, tries with all his strength and ingenuity to rob her of it? I was born free,
and to live free I chose the solitude of the fields. The trees of those mountains
are my companions; with the trees and the brooks I share my thoughts and my
beauty. I am the hidden fire and the distant sword . . ."

Now a puppeteer comes into the courtyard with his cart and arranges his
puppet show. In the midst of the show Don Quixote becomes indignant about
what he sees. Here again is the tiny blond heroine who emerged from his
books. To him, she is Dulcinea and when he sees her being persecuted by
Saracens, he charges the puppet show with his sword. The puppet theater falls
down on his head. Just then, to solemn music, heralds announce the arrival of
the Duke and Duchess of the region. The Duchess observes the wreckage of
the theater and orders it cleared out. She congratulates the Don on his victorious adventure with the puppet. Supported by Sancho, Don Quixote kneels before her. Recognizing him from Cervantes's book, the Duchess gives him wine
and invites him to come to the castle. He is lifted onto his horse, Sancho
mounts the donkey, and the villagers wave them farewell.

ACT TWO: THE PALACE   The curtain rises on the sumptuous ballroom of the
Duke's palace. Don Quixote enters with the Duchess, who places him to her
right as she sits on the throne. He stands by her side like a true gentleman.
Courtiers enter and as they bow to the royal couple, they also pay mocking
deference to Don Quixote, sensing the joke the Duchess is playing on the
knight. The courtiers and their ladies now dance a stylized courtly ballet: first,

a sarabande by the entire assembly, then a series of danced *divertissements: a
danza della Cacia*, a *pas de deux Mauresque*, a *Courante Sicilienne*, a *Rigaudon Flamenco*, and a *ritournel*. Now eight masked men enter. The Duchess
whispers to the Duke. All salute as Don Quixote escorts the Duchess down to
the dance floor to dance a *pavane*. The court has decided to end the charade
they have been playing with the Don. Sancho senses this and tries to take the
Don away, but the courtiers close in on them. They are blindfolded, tickled by
ladies' fans, pricked by swords. A wooden horse is brought in, they are placed
on it, fireworks are set off in its tail and at the explosion Don Quixote and
Sancho fall to the ground, where they are beaten. There then appears to Don
Quixote a vision of Dulcinea. The whole court freezes like waxworks. She gestures to him, seems to be calling to him to renew his adventures. He lays his
sword at her feet and kneels before her. Dulcinea helps him up and just as
Don Quixote is about to follow her, a masked lady approaches and beards him
with whipped cream, a final mockery. He ignores her scorn and in a trance
stumbles after Dulcinea to start again on his quest.

ACT THREE, SCENE ONE: A GARDEN OF THE PALACE   The Don and Sancho
enter. They lie down to rest under an old oak tree. He sleeps and begins to
dream. Masked courtiers arrive and cover him with a fishing net. Dulcinea appears. In his dream he sees a ballet in the Elysian fields. In the midst of the
dancing is the Lady of the Silver Moon in whom is embodied "all the impossible and chimerical attributes of beauty which poets give to their ladies." There
follows a classical *pas d'action*, consisting of a set of four variations, a *pas de
deux* and a coda. Dulcinea is challenged by a girl in black, the Night Spirit,
reminiscent of the Duchess, and tormented by the magician Merlin. She goes
to Don Quixote, and he rouses himself to help her. As he does so, dragging the
net behind him, the magic landscape of his dream vanishes. He is alone on an
empty field with mills turning their big wheels in the wind and seeming to
move ominously toward him and Dulcinea.

ACT THREE, SCENE TWO   A huge giant bears down on Don Quixote as high
as a windmill. The Don attacks him but his long lance is caught in a sail of the
windmill and he is tossed high into the air and falls back to earth. Sancho runs
to him and binds his head. Strange creatures cross the stage; like pigs they
swarm all over the place. Now four courtiers of the Duchess disguised in
masks bring in a wooden cage. Don Quixote crawls into it like a wounded dog.
Weeping, Sancho follows, holding his master's sword.

ACT THREE, SCENE THREE: DON QUIXOTE'S STUDY   To a *pavane funèbre* the
Don is carried to his home. He is taken from the cage and undressed for bed.
He asks for the last rites of the Church. In his delirium he sees a procession of
Bishops, Cardinals, monks, earls, and dukes, all hooded figures, march in to a
Gloria. His books are burned by these Inquisitors. Then, in another vision, he

sees again the vision with which his adventures began, the Madonna of the cart, the lovely blond girl with a halo. He reaches out to her yearningly, rises high in his bed as if by a miracle, she looks at him, then vanishes. The hooded figures are grouped around his bed as in the painting of the burial of the Count d'Orgaz by El Greco. But in a changing light, they are changed into the simple people of his village, the serving girl, the priest, Sancho. He recognizes them, blesses them, and dies quietly as the first lights of dawn come through the open window. The servant girl makes a cross of two sticks, places it on his body, and kneels to weep at his side. ". . . If he like a madman lived, at least he like a wise man died," said Cervantes.

NOTES   My interest in Don Quixote has always been in the hero's finding an ideal, something to live for and sacrifice for and serve. Every man has a Don Quixote in him. Every man wants an inspiration. For the Don it was Dulcinea, a woman he sought in many guises. I myself think that the same is true in life, that everything a man does he does for his ideal woman. You live only one life and you believe in something and I believe in that.

For criticism of this ballet, readers may wish to consult "The Story of 'Don Quixote'" by Elena Bivona in Ballet Review, Vol. 2, No. 2; and Andrew Porter's review of the 1973 performances of the ballet in The New Yorker, reprinted in his book A Musical Season.

The composer Nicolas Nabokov contributed to the January 1973 edition of the New York City Ballet program Playbill an entertaining and informative essay about his career and our collaboration on this ballet. His autobiography Bagazh, like his earlier book of recollections, Old Friends and New Music, is a fascinating account of his remarkable career.

DOUGLA

Music by Geoffrey Holder, arranged by Tania Leon. Choreography by Geoffrey Holder. Scenery and costumes by Geoffrey Holder. First presented by the Dance Theatre of Harlem at the ANTA Theatre, New York, April 20, 1974.

Dougla is a colorful, exotic dance ballet about an Asian and African marriage— a mix of Hindu and African ritual set to drumming music. The theme is: "Where Twains meet, where Hindu and African tangle, their offspring are called Dougla."

There are five parts to the ballet: "Dougla People," "Woman in Green," "Pas de Deux," "Women in Black," and "Acrobats," with the full company again on stage for a "Dougla People" finale.

When the Dance Theatre of Harlem conquered London in their first appearances there in 1974, the critic Peter Williams wrote in Dance and Dancers magazine: "What was shown during the season was quite enough to prove Arthur Mitchell's point which is that black dancers *can* take their rightful place in all areas of dance; it also proved what an incredible feat it was to have achieved all this in five years."

THE DREAM

Ballet in one act. Music by Felix Mendelssohn, arranged by John Lanchbery. Choreography by Frederick Ashton. Scenery by Henry Bardon. Costumes by David Walker. Lighting by William Bundy. First presented by the Royal Ballet at the Royal Opera House, Covent Garden, April 2, 1964, with Antoinette Sibley as Titania, Anthony Dowell as Oberon, Keith Martin as Puck, Alexander Grant as Bottom, Carole Needham as Helena, Vergie Derman as Hermia, David Drew as Demetrius, Derek Rencher as Lysander, and Alan Bauch as the Changeling Indian Boy. First presented in the United States by the Royal Ballet at the Metropolitan Opera House, New York, April 30, 1965, with the same cast, with Rennie Dilena as the Changeling Indian Boy. *

Frederick Ashton arranged his ballet to *A Midsummer Night's Dream* for the Royal Ballet's observance of the four-hundredth anniversary of Shakespeare's birth. Based on Shakespeare's play, using Mendelssohn's music, the ballet tells the magical story of the quarrel between the King and Queen of Fairyland and its outcome.

The King and Queen, Oberon and Titania, quarrel over the Changeling Indian Boy. Whom shall he belong to? Oberon sends his sprite Puck through the forest to pluck a strange flower, the juice of which when dropped in the eyes during sleep brings love for the first living thing seen on waking. Oberon plans to use this drug to spite Titania. Into the forest meanwhile have strayed a happy pair of lovers, Lysander and Hermia, and their unhappy friends Helena and Demetrius. Helena's desire for Demetrius is unrequited, for he mistakenly desires Hermia. Oberon has watched these mortals, and when Puck returns with the magic flower he sends him with the potion to charm Demetrius into love with Helena.

Now Oberon drops some of the charm into his Queen's eyes and causes her to be awakened by a rustic called Bottom on whom the returning Puck, to heighten his master's revenge, has fixed an ass's head. On waking, Titania at once falls in love with Bottom the Ass, but Puck, for all his cleverness, has complicated the affairs of the other, mortal lovers by charming the wrong man, Lysander, into love with Helena. Oberon commands Puck to create a fog, under cover of which all that is awry is magically put right. Titania, released

* See also A MIDSUMMER NIGHT'S DREAM.

from her spell, is reconciled to her master and the mortal lovers are happily paired off. Bottom, restored to human form but with dreamlike memories of what lately happened to him, goes on his puzzled way.

NOTES *The Dream* was staged by John Hart for the City Center Joffrey Ballet in 1973. The first performance, at the Wolf Trap Performing Arts Center in Virginia, near Washington, D.C., August 9, featured Rebecca Wright, Burton Taylor, Russell Sultzbach, Larry Grenier, Alaine Haubert, Charthel Arthur, Robert Talmage, Robert Thomas, Richard Coleman, Robert Estner, Phillip Hoffman, Jeffrey Hughes, Ted Nelson, Donna Cowen, Denise Jackson, Eileen Brady, Diane Orio, and Vinod Sahl. Writing of this production after its first New York performance (October 9, 1973), Clive Barnes said in the New York *Times:* "Ever since Ashton created *The Dream* for Britain's Royal Ballet nearly ten years ago, it has been one of that company's special treasures. This new production, authoritatively staged by John Hart, is a charmer, full of the original's mixture of Shakespeare, poetry, Mendelssohn, moonshine and fun. It is an extraordinarily English ballet, but the New York dancers have adopted it for their own.

"The costumes, fanciful and glamorous, are the same as David Walker designed for the original production, but Mr. Walker has devised a completely new setting to replace the earlier scenery by Henry Bardon. The setting, a sylvan glade, looks appropriately Victorian, but does not have the full romantic exuberance of the Royal Ballet's first staging. Yet what is more important is the style of the dancing, and here the Joffrey company does splendidly.

"Rebecca Wright made a Titania of glistening eyes and the most entrancing delicate footwork. It was a performance of gossamer and thistledown. As Oberon, Burton Taylor—making his welcome return to the stage after nearly two years off through injury—danced cleanly and forcefully. His presence was admirable, his partnering secure and his elegance always completely natural."

DRUMS, DREAMS AND BANJOS

Music by Stephen Foster; variations and orchestrations by Peter Link. Choreography by Gerald Arpino. Set by Rouben Ter-Arutunian. Costumes by Stanley Simmons. Lighting by Thomas Skelton. Vocalist: Charles Leighton. First presented by the City Center Joffrey Ballet at the City Center, New York, October 9, 1975, with a cast headed by Charthel Arthur and Dermot Burke. Conductor: Seymour Lipkin.

"He set a nation singing," wrote Harold Vincent Milligan in his biography of Stephen Foster; *Drums, Dreams and Banjos* is the Joffrey Ballet's bicentennial tribute. In 1951, President Truman issued a proclamation designating January 13, 1952, and each succeeding January 13 throughout the years as Stephen

Foster Memorial Day, calling upon all to observe that occasion with appropriate ceremonies, pilgrimages to the shrines of this beloved composer, and
musical programs featuring his compositions. Gerald Arpino's ballet celebrates
the Stephen Foster achievement, expressing in both dance and music the sentiment as well as the energy and ebullience of his work.

A Joint Resolution of the House of Representatives some years ago referred
to Foster and his work as "a national expression of democracy through his clear
and simple embodiment of American tradition" and called him the "father
of American folk music and the true interpreter of the fundamental spirit of
music."

Recalling as it does the charms of an earlier America, Foster's music has extraordinary appeal. Born in Pittsburgh on the fiftieth anniversary of the Declaration of Independence, Foster lived to hear his music flourish throughout the
land. His infectious songs, introduced by such groups as the Christy Minstrels,
quickly became a part of our heritage. They were sung by pioneers on the long
trek westward, hummed by harvesters in the fields and by workers laying the
first railroad lines. The forty-niners whistled "Oh! Susanna" while prospecting
for gold in California; his songs were favorites of soldiers on both sides during
the Civil War.

Besides his own large body of work, Foster arranged the songs of some of
the great European contemporaries—Bellini, Donizetti, Strauss—for inclusion in
his anthology *The Social Orchestra*. One of the aims of that successful volume
was to "improve the taste of the community for social music."

The Stephen Foster songs that are danced to in the ballet are "Angelina
Baker," "Old Folks at Home," "Oh! Boys Carry Me 'Long," "Nelly Bly,"
"Farewell My Lilly Dear," "Plantation Jig," "Open Thy Lattice, Love," "Ana-
dolia," "Some Folks," "I Will Be True to Thee," "Ah, May the Red Rose Live
Alway," "Eulalie," "Oh! Susanna," "Camptown Races," "Jeannie with the
Light Brown Hair," "Old Black Joe," "Ring de Banjo," "My Old Kentucky
Home," "Beautiful Dreamer," "Soiree Polka," and "Tioga Waltz." Taken from
The Social Orchestra are "Oh! Summer Night" by Donizetti and a waltz by
Strauss.

The dance and dramatic action of the stage panorama to the vivid score that
was arranged to this memorable music reminds us not only of the familiar
tunes but the times they were created in and the times they have lived
through. As such, it reminds us of years of war as well as peace, years that
Foster has made memorable.

THE DUEL (Le Combat)

*Ballet in one act. Music by Raffaello de Banfield. Choreography by William
Dollar. Costumes by Robert Stevenson. Lighting by Jean Rosenthal. First
presented by the New York City Ballet Company at the City Center, New*

*York, February 24, 1950, with Melissa Hayden and William Dollar, Val
Buttignol, Walter Georgov, Shaun O'Brien. This ballet is an extensive revision of the same choreographer's Le Combat, which was performed for
the first time in the United States by Les Ballets de Paris at the Winter Garden, New York, October 6, 1949.*

This short, dramatic ballet tells the story of the brave Christian warrior
Tancred and the pagan girl Clorinda: how they meet, fall in love, separate,
and meet again for a final, fatal encounter. A low beating of the drum and
subdued fanfares—heard as if from some distant battlefield—introduce the
warlike rhythms that dominate the ballet.

The curtain rises on a scene that might represent any barren field. Rocks are
clustered on the left, there are no trees, and a bright sky exposes the wasteland. Four Crusaders stand poised for action against any intruder. All are armored and wear high-plumed helmets with visors that conceal their faces. One
of them, the warrior in red, is the leader, Tancred. They begin to dance, holding out their arms to control invisible reins, jumping and turning, practicing
their skills in battle. They are all obedient to Tancred's command.

A strange warrior enters and approaches. The four Crusaders stand in line,
ready to attack. The stranger is dressed in black. This is Clorinda, the beautiful Saracen. From her golden helmet streams a green scarf lined with red. Her
movements are direct and unafraid; she is not in the least terrified of the
enemy. She comes nearer to the group. The men stand motionless until finally
the daring Clorinda challenges one of the Crusaders. He moves out of line and
engages her in battle; the other men observe their code of honor by refusing to
assist him. The two warriors rush each other swiftly, jumping high as they pass
back and forth. Clorinda gains the upper hand and wounds her opponent mor-
tally; and he falls over on his face. She dances around his body on firm points,
her head held high. During the duel, her helmet had fallen off, and the long
black hair that hangs down to her shoulders accentuates her proud beauty.
Tancred walks toward her, obviously moved both by her bravery and her loveliness. He takes off his helmet and bows in tribute. Clorinda does not respond.
She leaves the scene. Blackout.

Tancred enters alone. He dances, to reveal his superior strength and agility
as a prince of warriors, and exits. Clorinda follows him. Now she is dressed in
full battle array, with a visored helmet topped with a black plume. She leaps
around the stage lightly, glorying in her own adroitness. Suddenly she stops;
she senses danger. Two Christian warriors appear before her. She leaps into
the air as they rush by closely, trying to enclose her. The drum beats in staccato rhythm. Clorinda does not hesitate in her attack, and soon the Crusaders
weary of their effort to maneuver her into a dangerous position. She drives
them off.

Clorinda relaxes for a moment and briefly shows herself to be a beautiful
and pathetic girl, exhausted by the strenuousness of war. She holds her hand

up beseechingly and opens her arms wide, as if she were praying for relief
from the life she has chosen. She holds her head in her hands despairingly for
an instant, but then she is alert again, listening for anyone who might be
watching her. She crosses the stage slowly in an arrogant posture. A drum
beats, loudly and suddenly. Clorinda leaps off.

Tancred enters, seeking out the enemy. He follows Clorinda. She reenters
the field, the Crusader close behind. Neither recognizes the other. They begin
to fight, standing close together at first, then separating to each side of the
stage, then approaching each other warily. Tancred supports Clorinda and
turns her as she assumes first a tight, aggressive pose, then an open arabesque.
Now the duel becomes earnest as the two adversaries dodge and jump aside
from their strong thrusts. Clorinda wounds Tancred, but this only encourages
the Crusader. He stabs the girl as they engage in close contest. She falters in
pain. They separate, preparing for the finish. They approach slowly. The girl
falls. Tancred stands back. She pulls off her helmet. He sees her face; his own
face is shocked with recognition. He holds out his hands helplessly, then takes
off his own helmet and goes to her. He lifts her to him, and in her agony and
love Clorinda's body curls in his arms. Tancred stands and pulls Clorinda up.
She leans against him, her head on his shoulder, and he turns her in arabesque. Her movements are now automatic. She seems not to have the strength
to move at all, and yet she wishes to reassure Tancred of her own love. But she
is tired. He carries her in his arms; her body stiffens, her legs beat in a final
spasm, and she is dead. Tancred places her body on the ground softly and
stands over her. As he grieves, he remembers the long battle he has just begun.
He picks her up and carries her off.

DUMBARTON OAKS (A Little Musical)

*Music by Igor Stravinsky. Choreography by Jerome Robbins. Costumes by
Patricia Zipprodt. Lighting by Ronald Bates. First presented by the New
York City Ballet at the New York State Theatre, Lincoln Center, June 23,
1972, with Allegra Kent and Anthony Blum in the leading roles.*

Dumbarton Oaks is the name of a nice old house in Washington, D.C., with
magnificent gardens. Actually, all the house is not old, only a bit of it, but
there have been important additions (the place houses a superb museum of
pre-Columbian sculpture, a center for Byzantine studies, and a great library).
Mr. and Mrs. Robert Woods Bliss, who bought this property and endowed it,
were wonderful patrons of the arts for Washington and for the nation. In 1937
they commissioned Stravinsky to write a piece for their thirtieth wedding anniversary. The first performance was led by Nadia Boulanger at Dumbarton
Oaks, May 8, 1938, and Stravinsky's *Concerto in E Flat* for chamber orchestra
has been named for the place ever since.

The score is in three movements. The instruments of the chamber orchestra are treated as solo instruments and there is much variety in what Eric Walter White calls a work that "is gay and exhilarating in its effect."

The ballet is a dance to this music, with a theme. The theme is a recollection of time past, perhaps the 1920s, when a house like Dumbarton Oaks enjoyed a new lease on its lively history. The setting is wicker chairs, garden trellises with Japanese lanterns, and a tennis court in the background.

The piece begins with an ensemble of six couples, boys and girls in various combinations, who wear typical sporting dress of the 1920s (headbands for the girls, etc.). As they leave, a couple keen on tennis come into the picture. They put aside their tennis rackets and dance a vivacious *pas de deux,* syncopated and responsive to the music of the score's *Allegretto.* What starts out to be, at one point, sentimental, in the love duet returns to the flirtatious. From a recumbent posture, the girl picks up her tennis racket again and, as if a match were ended, shakes hands with her partner. Serious though it has seemed to be, the game is still the thing.

In the last movement, marked by Stravinsky *Con moto,* six boys tap-dance to a march with six girls. The lead boy then rushes in, finds the lead girl, and together they and the ensemble conclude a brisk finale to a *Fugato* climax.

NOTES   It is of interest that during the composition of this work, Stravinsky studied and played Bach regularly. He was greatly attracted, he writes in *Themes and Episodes,* to the Brandenburg Concertos, especially the third, "which I have also conducted. The first theme of my concerto is, of course, very much like Bach's in that work, and so is my instrumentation—the three violins and three violas, both frequently *divisi a tre,* though not chordally as in Bach. I do not think, however, that Bach would have begrudged me the loan of these ideas and materials, as borrowing in this way was something he liked to do himself."

The original costumes for this work were abandoned soon after its first performances during the New York City Ballet's Stravinsky Festival. It has been performed since in practice clothes.

Reviewing the ballet's entry into the regular repertory of the New York City Ballet, February 9, 1973, Clive Barnes wrote in the New York *Times:*

"On Friday night the New York City Ballet at the New York State Theatre gave everyone a surprise. A small surprise, but a surprise. It was the first repertory performance of Jerome Robbins's ballet *Dumbarton Oaks.* When this was originally given last summer at the Stravinsky Festival, it had an anyone-for-tennis setting. Now the work has been transposed to the ballet studio. Tennis rackets are out, and toe shoes are in.

"This strong but lighthearted work has taken the transposition well. The setting, which had a definite air of improvisation to it, could be improved and should be, for this is a most agreeable work. There is a playful flirtatiousness to the choreography, which is perfectly apt for this breezy, jazz-tinctured score. The ballet was fluently danced by a cast led by Allegra Kent and, dancing the role for the first time, Jean-Pierre Bonnefous."

DUO CONCERTANTE

Music by Igor Stravinsky. Choreography by George Balanchine. First presented by the New York City Ballet at the Stravinsky Festival, 1972, at the New York State Theatre, Lincoln Center, June 22, 1972, with Kay Mazzo and Peter Martins as the dancers, Lamar Alsop and Gordon Boelzner as the musicians. Lighting by Ronald Bates.

This work for violin and piano was composed by Stravinsky in the early thirties. It is a short piece in five movements and a marvelously lyrical one in several of its parts. It is not surprising that the composition of the *Duo Concertante* was associated in Stravinsky's mind with a book on the classical poet Petrarch by his friend Cingria, which appeared about the time he was writing this music. Stravinsky in one of his recollections quotes this passage from Cingria: "Lyricism cannot exist without rules, and it is essential that they should be strict. Otherwise there is only a faculty for lyricism, and that exists everywhere. What does not exist everywhere is lyrical expression and composition. To achieve that, a craftsman's skill is necessary and that must be learned."

This is exactly a thought I have tried so unsuccessfully to say myself on a number of occasions and it is wonderful to find it so finely expressed in connection with a composition I so much admire.

I am trying to recall the first time I heard the *Duo Concertante*. It was, I think, in France in a performance by Samuel Dushkin, the violinist, and the composer himself, both of whom in the early thirties toured Europe performing Stravinsky's music. It has always been a favorite of mine and when we were planning the Stravinsky Festival at the New York City Ballet, I decided to make a ballet to the music.

The less I say about the ballet, the more I think you may enjoy watching it. It is nothing very unusual, only two dancers, a girl and a boy, standing on stage next to a piano, where the two musicians begin to play. The dancers listen intently; we listen to them. The music for piano and violin is questioning at first, then declarative, open; it then tightens in rhythm and assertiveness of melody. Before we know it, the dancers are moving to the music. Sometimes they stop to listen. The second movement, Ecloque I, begins with a jocular tune and develops into a brisk dialogue between the two instruments. In Ecloque II, the violin takes the lead and in a slowly paced cadenza sings an idyll. For the fourth movement, there is a vigorous and lively Gigue. The stage darkens for the finale, the Dithyramb. Eric Walter White calls this a "noble rhapsody . . . a movement of grave beauty. The high-pitched violin part leads the piano into an increasingly elaborate passage. . . . The effect is that of an exalted threnody." The stage darkens for this music, one spotlight shining on the two musicians, another on the two dancers. The lights close down about the artists as the music ends.

A girl and a boy, a piano and violin. Perhaps, as Lincoln Kirstein says, that is what ballet is all about.

NOTES   Reviewing this ballet in *The Nation*, Nancy Goldner wrote: "*Duo Concertante*, for piano and violin, is one of the most beautiful duets Balanchine has ever done. As a metaphor on the idea that the festival celebrates music, Mazzo and Martins listen to the musicians, who are on the stage, almost as much as they dance. Watching them listen is a theatrical experience in itself. Their faces speak a multitude of unknown thoughts, but the intensity and sweet concentration with which they listen suggest that the notes are running through their bodies. Finally, they are moved to dance. At first they stick closely to the music's beat, almost 'conducting' it with arms and legs; torsos are still.

"Becoming more free, the dance turns into a melting duet, each phrase winding down on slightly bent knees, as in a whisper. They dance with seeming spontaneity. Even when Balanchine arranges an unusual means of partnering—as when Martins scoops her from the floor holding only the underside of her thigh—the movement spins off them with utter simplicity and naturalness. In other sections, they occasionally stop dancing to listen. At those times, Martins firmly takes hold of her hand or slips his arm around her waist. She is shy, but the music pleases her and so does he. She does not move away. They listen in repose, arm in arm. In the last part, the stage darkens except for a white spotlight. She places her arm in the light and raises it above her head. No longer is it her arm; it exists independently, like a segment of a statue. He kisses the back of her hand, a supplicant at the throne of beauty. She is now a goddess-ballerina; he, her servant. She steps out of the light. He steps into it. Not finding her, he leaves. She returns. He kisses her hand again. The jump from intimate hand-holding to ceremonial hand-kissing is theatrically daring. It is also inevitable, and those who cannot accept the leap or the brazen display of sentiment cannot ultimately accept one of the underlying themes of Balanchine's work. In his most noble ballets, he elevates the dancer into an image of love, a Muse-ballerina who inspires but is unreachable. And so this ending is an apotheosis of Balanchine's art."

DYBBUK VARIATIONS

Music by Leonard Bernstein. Choreography by Jerome Robbins. Scenery by Rouben Ter-Arutunian. Costumes by Patricia Zipprodt. Lighting by Jennifer Tipton. First presented by the New York City Ballet at the New York State

Theatre, Lincoln Center, May 15, 1974, with Patricia McBride and Helgi Tomasson as the principals and a cast headed by Bart Cook, Victor Castelli, Tracy Bennett, Hermes Conde, Daniel Duell, Stephen Caras, Nolan T'Sani, Peter Naumann, Muriel Aasen, and Stephanie Saland. Conducted by Leonard Bernstein. Baritone: David Johnson. Bass: John Ostendorf.

The composer Leonard Bernstein and the choreographer Jerome Robbins first conceived of the idea of a ballet to the dybbuk theme in 1944, at the time of their first brilliant collaboration, *Fancy-Free*. A dybbuk, in Central-European Jewish folklore, is a dead but restless spirit that enters and persists in the body of a living person. The possessed body acts and speaks with the voice and behavior of the dead one. The most famous treatment of the theme is the play by S. Ansky, *The Dybbuk*, renowned in its original Yiddish version and through many subsequent international productions, among them the Habimah presentation in New York in the 1940s. The restless spirit dominates the action.

Jerome Robbins has said that the ballet is not a retelling of Ansky's play, "but uses it only as a point of departure for a series of related dances concerning rituals and hallucinations which are present in the dark magico-religious ambience of the play and in the obsessions of its characters."

An understanding of the play is useful background to the ballet. It tells the story: In friendship, two young men pledge that their children will wed each other, should one have a son and the other a daughter. The friends part and go out into the world, where each marries and has a child, boy and girl, as hoped for. Chanon and Leah meet when grown and, unaware of their parents' commitment, fall in love. But because Leah is from a wealthy family and Chanon is a poor but devoutly orthodox theological student, their love is undeclared. Chanon is also regarded as a wanderer and seeker of truths that are perhaps best always hidden.

Leah's father arranges a suitable match for her; Chanon desperately turns to the Kabbala, book of mystic wisdom and dark magic. (This text, developed by rabbis from about the seventh to the eighteenth centuries, was based on a mystical technique of interpreting Scripture; by this method the initiated were empowered to foretell the future and penetrate sacred mysteries.) He seeks in the Kabbala for a way in which to win Leah for himself. As a last resort, he invokes the powerful but dangerous other-worldly formulae of ancient usage. At the supreme moment of discovering the secret words that unleash the dark forces, he is overwhelmed by the enormity of it, faints and dies.

At Leah's wedding, Chanon returns to her as a dybbuk and, claiming her as his rightful bride, clings to his beloved. Finally, through prescriptive counterrituals instituted by elders of the religious community, Chanon is placed under formal ecclesiastical curse and the dybbuk is expelled. Leah, unable to survive without her predestined bridegroom, dies to join him.

Throughout the Ansky play, a supernatural being called "The Messenger" is an omniscient and prophetic witness to each evolving phase of the drama.

The action of the ballet is divided into eleven parts: 1) IN THE HOLY PLACE: Variations for Seven Men; 2) THE PLEDGE: Male duet; two couples; three couples; 3) ANGELIC MESSENGERS: Variations for three men; 4) THE DREAM: *Pas de deux;* 5) INVOCATION OF THE KABBALA: the quest for secret powers; VARIATIONS: a. Solo with six men; b.c.d.e. Soli; f. Solo with six men; 6) PASSAGE; 7) MAIDEN'S DANCE; 8) TRANSITION; 9) POSSESSION: *Pas de deux:* allegro, adagio; 10) EXORCISM: Entire cast; 11) REPRISE AND CODA.

NOTES   Talking with *The New Yorker* about the ballet shortly before its première, the composer, Leonard Bernstein, described how he and Jerome Robbins had approached the dybbuk legend. "Ansky's story is a kind of ghetto version of *The Ring of the Nibelung.* Greed versus love. A compact that is broken. Two young men pledge that their children will marry, but one of them eventually disregards the oath because he wants a wealthy husband for his daughter, Leah. Chanon, the son of the other man, becomes a wandering scholar, a very *farbrente* Talmudist, and a Cabalist. He comes to this little town, sees Leah, and, even though he doesn't know about the pledge, falls in love and desperately tries to find Cabalistic ways of winning her. In (one) dance . . . Chanon calls on the dark powers to help him, and at the moment of revelation he dies, because no human vessel can contain that much fire and knowledge and survive. His soul becomes a dybbuk and finds its resting place in the body of his beloved. And when the rabbi exorcises the dybbuk from her body, Leah joins him in oblivion.

". . . You have to remember that this is a story about ghetto people who have nowhere to go, no professions they can be in, no place in the world except the isolated provincial town in which they live. They are forced in on themselves, and they turn to their Torah and live their whole lives in terms of that. And they get to such a point of intensity, of concern, of concentration on their relationship with God that they come to believe the whole universe depends on it. That is the reason behind all the diagrams, the mysticisms, and the calculations. Where else could these people look except to heaven? Jerry suggested a marvellous line for the program note. He said that this ballet deals with the visions, hallucinations, and magical religious manifestations of an oppressed people. And that's exactly it. All they had for centuries was a book with the words of God."*

Writing after the première of *Dybbuk Variations* in *Newsweek,* the critic Hubert Saal said: "Robbins's ballet does not tell the detailed story . . . of S. Ansky's 1914 play, a classic of the Yiddish theatre . . . but extracts highlights of the drama, making a superdrama of such abstractions as the conflict between light and dark, the individual and society, love and law. Sometimes what occupies a long scene in the play takes a moment in dance—and vice versa. In

* From "Possession" by Jane Boutwell in "The Talk of the Town." Reprinted by permission; © 1974 The New Yorker Magazine, Inc.

reorganizing what Ansky called a 'realistic play about mystic people,' Robbins and Bernstein have created a work that is theatrical without being showy, stylized without being stilted and Hebraic without being parochial.

"The eleven scenes, starkly and effectively designed by Rouben Ter-Arutunian, begin with the important mood setter, the dance of the seven elders, who with pious grace assume the shape of a Menorah, the Jewish candelabrum. Throughout the ballet they act as an irresistible force in their faith and fanaticism, embodying the inexorable power of Jehovah's Law and of social custom. Among the most dramatic scenes are the brilliant, complex variations for Chanon and his fellow scholars, who vainly try to dissuade him from the cabalistic investigation that ends in his death. Of all the dance sequences, perhaps the most satisfying is the long *pas de deux* in which the dybbuk takes possession of Leah. Their agitated bodies, trying to adjust to the violent collision of two souls, gradually fuse into one, through their love for each other.

"The climax is spine-tingling, with some magical stagecraft, as the exorcising elders force Chanon to leave the body of Leah and she abandons her own flesh to join him as pure spirit in the hereafter. As this Jewish Romeo and Juliet, the brilliant Helgi Tomasson and the radiant Patricia McBride dance with fire and tenderness.

"No one could have provided Robbins with a more resilient musical floor than Bernstein, who has remained in close touch musically with his Jewish origins. His first symphony, the 'Jeremiah,' was dedicated to his father, a noted Talmudic scholar, and his third symphony is called 'Kaddish.' With obvious eagerness, Bernstein has seized this opportunity to invent music with old-fashioned Hebrew lilt and cadence, an intonation that is part laughter, part tears, and a range from simple folk tunes to complex inversions of tone rows. . . .

"Robbins and Bernstein, two 55-year-old partners and friends, are complementary opposites. . . . Robbins emphasized that the new work 'is a ballet, not a play. It says things that the play doesn't. There are whole areas in the play that are non-verbal.' Bernstein was amazed by the performance of the New York City Ballet Orchestra. 'They're fantastic,' he exclaimed, 'the most wonderful theatre orchestra in the world.'

"Both men remembered the time 30 years ago when the idea for *Dybbuk Variations* came to them—standing on the stage of the old Metropolitan Opera House after the triumph of *Fancy Free*. 'I love the dark, lyric quality of Ansky's play,' says Robbins. 'The astonishing faith. Of all kinds.' Two years ago they isolated themselves in Jamaica and devoted a concentrated three weeks to finding an approach that lay between Robbins's feeling for the abstract and Bernstein's for the concrete drama. 'After that,' Bernstein says, 'I just wrote music and played it for Jerry and he would say that excites me or it doesn't.'

"Earlier Robbins had said, 'Choosing the *Dybbuk* had nothing to do with my being Jewish.' Now Bernstein said, 'In a larger sense what success we've had is based on our experience of Jewishness. Isn't that right, Jerry?' Robbins paused and said, 'I don't know,' and then smiled and added: 'But we are what we are and that feeds into it."

THE DYING SWAN (Le Cygne)

Music by Camille Saint-Saëns. Choreography by Michel Fokine. First produced at a concert in the Nobleman's Hall, St. Petersburg, Russia, in 1905, with Anna Pavlova. First presented in the United States at the Metropolitan Opera House, New York, March 18, 1910, by Anna Pavlova.

Perhaps the most famous of all dramatic solos for the ballerina, *The Dying Swan* shows the last minutes in the life of a stricken swan. Slowly, trembling, trying to hold on to life for a brief last flight but then giving up, she dies. It only takes about two minutes to perform. When Pavlova first danced it at the Metropolitan, Carl Van Vechten wrote that it was "the most exquisite specimen of her art which she has yet given to the public."

The choreographer, Michel Fokine, recalled that the dance was composed in a few minutes. One day Pavlova came and asked him to do a solo for her for a concert being given by artists from the chorus of the Imperial Opera. She had just become a ballerina at the Maryinsky Theatre. Fokine was at that time a mandolin enthusiast and had been playing at home—to the piano accompaniment of one of his friends—Saint-Saëns' *Swan*. He said right then, "What about Saint-Saëns' *Swan?*" She immediately realized, Fokine wrote, that a swan would be a most suitable role for her. "As I looked upon the thin, brittle-like Pavlova, I thought—she is just made for the *Swan*." A rehearsal was arranged and the dance completed very quickly. "It was almost an improvisation. I danced in front of her, she directly behind me. Then she danced and I walked alongside her, curving her arms and correcting details of poses.

"Prior to this composition, I was accused of barefooted tendencies and of rejecting toe dancing in general. *The Dying Swan* was my answer to such criticism. This dance became the symbol of the New Russian Ballet. It was a combination of masterful technique with expressiveness. It was like a proof that the dance could and should satisfy not only the eye, but through the medium of the eye should penetrate into the soul" (*Dance Magazine*, August 1931).

In 1934 in Paris, Fokine told Arnold Haskell (see his *Balletomania*): "Small work as it is, and known and applauded all over the world, it was 'revolutionary' then, and illustrated admirably the transition between the old and the new, for here I make use of the technique of the old dance and the traditional costume, and a highly developed technique is necessary, but the purpose of the dance is not to display that technique but to create the symbol of the everlasting struggle in this life and all that is mortal. It is a dance of the whole

body and not of the limbs only; it appeals not merely to the eye but to the
emotions and the imagination."

The French critic André Levinson has written of *Le Cygne:* "Arms folded,
on tiptoe, she dreamily and slowly circles the stage. By even, gliding motions
of the hands, returning to the background from whence she emerged, she
seems to strive toward the horizon, as though a moment more and she will fly—
exploring the confines of space with her soul. The tension gradually relaxes
and she sinks to earth, arms waving faintly as in pain. Then faltering with irregular steps toward the edge of the stage—leg bones aquiver like the strings of
a harp—by one swift forward-gliding motion of the right foot to earth, she
sinks on the left knee—the aerial creature struggling against earthly bonds; and
there, transfixed by pain, she dies."

The dancer and teacher Hilda Butsova, who became Pavlova's leading
dancer (1912–25) in the company that toured the world, has recalled with
Marian Horosko in *Dance Magazine* the joy and hardships of those days: "It
was not that she wanted to make money or had a big ego. She wanted people
to see dance. . . . It was Anna Pavlova, and no one else, who opened the
world to ballet. It was she who did the back-breaking work of pioneering. It
was Pavlova who found and cultivated audiences for contemporary ballet companies. Her service to ballet is priceless. No other single human being did
more for ballet than she. To all the millions of people for whom she danced,
she brought a little of herself; she brought a little happiness to them all. Her
genius was as intangible as the legacy she left behind. What remains of
Pavlova today is not a movement in the art, not a tendency, not even a series
of dances. It is something far more concrete, but possibly far more valuable:
inspiration."

EARLY SONGS

*Music by Richard Strauss. Choreography by Eliot Feld. Costumes by Stan-
ley Simmons. Lighting by Jules Fisher. First presented by the American
Ballet Company at the Brooklyn Academy of Music, New York, April 5,
1970. Soprano: Eileen Shelle. Baritone: Steven Kimbrough. Pianist: Gladys
Celeste Mercader.*

Early Songs is a dance ballet arranged to fourteen songs by Richard Strauss,
songs of the composer's youth, when he wrote with fervor and passion to accompany poems he admired about love, dreams, separation, longing, despair,
night. *Early Songs* can be said to be about love and the way different young
couples are involved in it, how they show it, hide it, seek it, find it, languish in
it, rejoice in it. There is no story, only the dance and gestural images we seek
on stage. Sometimes they are reflective of the music; sometimes they suggest
things beyond the music.

The music is sung by a soprano and a baritone, accompanied by the piano. The words are not directly relevant to the danced picture which is best seen beyond words, in the theater. Successful dance ballets are the hardest things in the world to describe outside their own language!

The ballet is in fourteen parts that flow together, accompanying the Strauss songs. While an understanding of the words of the songs, which are sung in German, is certainly not essential to enjoyment of the dances, you may wish to listen to recordings before coming to the theater.

The curtain rises in silence on two boys and a girl. The music is quiet as the baritone starts to sing of meadows at twilight and the pursuit of a beautiful woman "Dream at Twilight." As the song continues in that vein, rising slowly in intensity, one of the boys, in green, responds to the girl and the others among the couples who materialize about him. He would be with them, but is not, as they come and go. He is left, seeking but not finding, but not absolutely forlorn; after all, they have not rejected him: perhaps it is the other way round.

To the tempo of the rapid "Serenade," sung by the baritone, the boy dances with a girl quick in movement and flirtatiousness. He kneels at her feet and they dance together. Her legs tremble at the beauty of it. Two other couples, the girls responding similarly to the romantic ambience, appear to attend them; the boy then lifts the girl to his shoulder and takes her off into the wings. It is not surprising that the song should invoke the nightingale dreaming of kisses and a rose that, in the morning, should remember and shine with the recollection of the night.

Four couples dance pensively to a poem about "The Star." Next, in the fourth dance, again a *pas de deux* ("Tomorrow"), a young couple move quietly together as the soprano sings of a tomorrow that will unite happy persons, who will look into each other's eyes with muted recognition of their joy. Gently, the boy carries the girl off into the wings.

The baritone sings now a bright tune ("To What End, Maiden?") in which he wonders amusingly at the deceitfulness of a young maiden. There is a dance for three couples, then just one, where the boy seems to question the girl and to find her wonderful at the same time.

"Strolling at Night" follows, under a silvery moon, where an enraptured couple dance of their intense happiness. He falls at her feet. Now, two boys and a girl, hand in hand, dance to a song ("Beautiful, Yet Cold"); the soprano sings about the beautiful but cold stars of heaven that cannot compare to the eyes of the beloved.

Next, a girl moves toward dancing couples, seeming to see a vision of her own ideal and truly finding him in her thoughts, if not in reality ("Rest, My Soul"). The girl in lonely torment is joined by a boy who makes an effort to make her forget. Gentle at first, he fails to comfort her and then almost forces her to forget. She is then in torment, held by him agonizingly and turning her face from him. They leave, her arms folded and her hands curled over her face.

Bright light comes up and five couples rush on to celebrate with the baritone the coming of spring ("Sir Spring"). Next, a boy alone dances, introspectively and thoughtful ("All My Thoughts"). Then he faces three girls. He tries to lead them in a dance ("Ah, Woe Is Me, Unhappy Man!"), partnering them one after another, but does not succeed. He is alone again at the end.

A radiant couple swirl to a song by the baritone about the uselessness of descriptions of his beloved ("Nothing"). What do we know about the sun, the giver of life and light?

Two other lovers dance their joy as the soprano recalls the magic of the time they first looked into each other's eyes and love showered down on them ("Ever Since Your Eyes"). The girl leans against the boy as the lights dim. He touches her hand. Other lovers join them as the song speaks of night, which may steal one's love away ("Night").

NOTES   Writing about *Early Songs* in the New York *Times*, the critic Clive Barnes said that the ballet "is a picture of a world lost, a world full of gentle nuance, of literary feeling, of a rapture impassioned by the poetry of poetry rather than the poetry of life. Love is pure here, and its heartbeat is a kind of exquisite stylization of lust. It is the end of a civilization, and empty-handed cavaliers bearing silver roses are about to be everywhere. . . . It is a fantastically beautiful work; it lilts, it rises, it flies like a kite above our all-too-average dance works. . . . Feld offers a choreographic viewpoint that extends our view of the dance."

Walter Terry wrote in *The Saturday Review:* "*Early Songs,* tastefully costumed by Stanley Simmons and sensitively lit by Jules Fisher, is a work of superior craftsmanship choreographically, but more, it is an art experience that lifts the spirit. At its première, it was faultlessly danced by its cast of thirteen, including Feld himself, (Christine) Sarry, Elizabeth Lee, John Sowinski, and Richard Munro among the most impressive."

ECCENTRIQUE

Music by Igor Stravinsky. Choreography by Eliot Feld. Scenery by Oliver Smith. Costumes by Frank Thompson. Lighting by Jennifer Tipton. First presented by American Ballet Theatre at the City Center, New York, January 18, 1972, with Elizabeth Lee, Christine Sarry, and John Sowinski in leading roles.

This is a dance ballet to two works by Stravinsky—the *Four Studies for Orchestra* (1928) and the *Orchestral Suites 1 and 2* (1917–25). The first part of the ballet is for a group of girls and a leading dancer; the second, in a setting inspired by the image of Harlequin, is for a boy and girl and accompanying corps de ballet.

ECHOING OF TRUMPETS

Music by Bohuslav Martinů. Choreography by Antony Tudor. Scenery by Birger Bergling. First presented by the Royal Swedish Ballet at the Royal Opera House, Stockholm, September 28, 1963. First presented in the United States by the Metropolitan Opera Ballet at the Metropolitan Opera House, New York, March 27, 1966.

The theme of *Echoing of Trumpets* is closely related to another composition by Martinů, *Memorial to Lidice*, but the choreographer, Antony Tudor, was not aware of this until later. He chose instead Martinů's *Symphonic Fantasies Symphony No. 6* for his ballet about domination and war, about humanity under the heel of the conqueror.

The action takes place in an occupied village that has been ravaged by war. There the women whose husbands have been killed are in immediate conflict with the invaders. They are violated and killed. A refugee returning to the village to see his sweetheart is caught and killed. The girl dances a lament with her dead lover.

Many have seen in this ballet resemblances to the destruction of Lidice by the Nazis. The choreographer has denied that this is the theme of his work. "Perhaps it's more about how people always seem to want to dominate people. Everyone knows that's a stupid thing to do. Yet they keep on doing it. They never stop torturing each other with a kind of mild viciousness."

ELITE SYNCOPATIONS

Music by Scott Joplin and others. Choreography by Kenneth MacMillan. Costumes by Ian Spurling. First presented by the Royal Ballet at the Royal Opera House, Covent Garden, London, October 7, 1974, with Merle Park, David Wall, Monica Mason, Michael Colman, Jennifer Penney, Carl Myers, Vergie Derman, Wayne Sleep, Wayne Eagling, Jennifer Jackson, Judith Hower, David Drew, and David Adams in leading roles. First presented in the United States by the same ensemble April 27, 1976, at the Metropolitan Opera House, New York.

This is a dance ballet to Scott Joplin's music. The pieces that are illustrated by dance are the *Sunflower Slow Drag, Elite Syncopations, The Cascades, Hothouse Rag, Calliope Rag, Ragtime Nightingale, The Golden Hours, Stop-time*

Rag, *The Alaskan Rag, Bethena*—a Concert Waltz, *Friday Night,* and *Cataract Rag.*

EMBRACE TIGER AND RETURN TO MOUNTAIN

Music by Morton Subotnick. Choreography by Glen Tetley. Decor by Nadine Baylis. First presented in the United States by the Royal Swedish Ballet at the City Center, New York, November 21, 1974.

Fourteen centuries ago, the Chinese developed a system of calisthenics and shadowboxing called T'ai-Chi. The object in T'ai-Chi is to empty out all extraneous thoughts in order to gain an intense inner concentration. Today in China and on Taiwan persons gather in parks every morning to do these thirty-seven exercises. In the West, too, T'ai-Chi has become extremely popular with persons who seek a thoughtful but not exhausting form of exercise. The names of the thirty-seven exercises typify the action so that participants will remember the sequence. The seventeenth exercise is called Embrace Tiger and Return to Mountain. It is this that the choreographer Glen Tetley has seized upon in order to evolve a work that fuses Eastern and Western attitudes to movement. It is danced to an electronic score by Morton Subotnick and performed on a mirrored floor that adds a further dimension to the visual impression of the piece. What the dancers do is not determined by a story. The stances they take, the gestures they make, and the steps they perform suggest variations on exercise (for combat?), shadowboxing (illusions?), tracking (prey?), and hunting.

Embrace Tiger is also part of the repertoire of the Eliot Feld Ballet.

L'ENFANT ET LES SORTILÈGES (The Spellbound Child)

Lyric fantasy in two parts based on a poem by Colette. Music by Maurice Ravel. Choreography by George Balanchine. First presented by Raoul Gunsbourg at the Théâtre de Monte Carlo, March 21, 1925. Conducted by Victor de Sabata. First presented in New York by Ballet Society at the Central High School of Needle Trades, November 20, 1946. Costumes and scenery by Aline Bernstein. Conducted by Leon Barzin. The Child: Joseph Connolly. Presented in a third version by the New York City Ballet at the Hommage à Ravel, May 14, 1975, at the New York State Theatre, Lincoln Center. Costumes and sets by Kermit Love; supervising designer, David Mitchell. Orchestra, singers, and chorus conducted by Manuel Rosenthal. The Child: Paul Offenkranz.

"The essence of Ravel's genius is found in this sympathetic and somewhat sentimental masterpiece," writes the musician Arbie Orenstein in *Ravel: Man and Music* (1975). I very much agree, as will probably be clear from the number of times I have worked on this opera-ballet! The title has been variously translated—everything from *Dreams of a Naughty Boy* to *The Spellbound Child*, but I have preferred to stay with the original. Which is where I began, having worked on the first production with Ravel. The composer has always meant a great deal to me.

Ravel, who was fond of George Gershwin's music, wrote that *L'Enfant et les Sortilèges* "was composed in the spirit of an American musical comedy." The hero of the piece, a young boy, both sings and dances. He is about six or seven years old. Colette's text sets the scene in a country house in a room looking out on a garden. There are a large Armchair, a tall Grandfather's Clock, a round squirrel cage by the window, a boiling kettle in the fireplace, and a purring Cat. It is afternoon.

The boy is supposed to be studying, but he is bored and would rather do anything else. His Mother comes in and scolds him but he sticks out his tongue at her. For punishment, she gives him bitter tea and dry bread and says he has to stay alone until dinner. Alone, the boy stamps his foot and shouts that he hates everyone and will be as naughty as he likes. Proving it, he breaks the teapot and Cups, tries to torture the squirrel, pulls the Cat's tail, overturns the kettle, rips the wallpaper, stops the Clock and tears up his schoolbooks. He declares that he may be naughty but he is also free!

What he has also done, however, is to free the room and the objects in it. Animated by his naughtiness, they all begin to come to life and to sing and dance. First the Armchair, then the Grandfather's Clock, then the Teacups followed by the figures on the wallpaper, Shepherds and Shepherdesses. A Princess emerges from one of his schoolbooks, complaining, "Now that you have torn up the story, what will happen to me?" He vows to protect her from evil enchantment but she disappears. As he despairs, other books come to life and the Child is suddenly faced with arithmetic and other problems! This is followed by a duet for two Cats, who retreat into the garden. The boy follows them.

Now the room disappears, the walls giving way, and the boy is alone in the garden with the Cats. There the music of Dragonflies, Moths, Bats, Frogs, and rustling Trees greets him. Much as he wants to join in the enchanted world of the lively garden, he sees that they delight in their freedom and in their love for each other. He realizes that they are forgetting him; he cries, "I'm alone! . . . Mother!"

In chorus the Animals turn on the boy, attacking him as the naughty lad who had always tormented them. They are so anxious to strike him and to get in the first blow that they begin to fight each other. In the process a small Squirrel is wounded. He goes to the Child, crying in pain. The boy puts a bandage on him. The Animals observe this and are astonished at his kindness. They cannot believe it. Then they observe that they have hurt the boy, too.

As they wonder what to do they recall that he was calling someone. Who? Mother! They encircle the hurt Child and all call "Mother! Mother!" Then, getting no response, they take him to his nest. Dawn begins to rise. Proclaiming the boy to be good and kind and their friend, they leave him as he reaches out for home and his Mother.

ENIGMA VARIATIONS

Music by Edward Elgar. Choreography by Frederick Ashton. Scenery and costumes by Julia Trevelyan Oman. First presented by the Royal Ballet at the Royal Opera House, Covent Garden, London, October 25, 1968, with Derek Rencher, Svetlana Beriosova, Stanley Holden, Brian Shaw, Alexander Grant, Robert Mead, Vyvyan Lorrayne, Anthony Dowell, Georgina Parkinson, Desmond Doyle, Antoinette Sibley, Wayne Sleep, Leslie Edwards, and Deanne Bergsma in the principal roles. First presented in the United States by the same ensemble, with the same cast, at the Metropolitan Opera House, Lincoln Center, April 22, 1969. Conducted by John Lanchbery.

Subtitled, in the composer's words, "My Friends Pictured Within," *Enigma Variations* is a dance portrait of the artist among friends and family in Victorian England. The ballet is based on its score, which characterized thirteen friends and relations "who were there," and a fourteenth, "absent on a sea voyage" at the time, who remains the "enigma."

Describing one aspect of his composition, Elgar said it was "written at a time when friends were dubious and generally discouraging as to the composer's musical future." The action of the ballet, which is set in an English country house in the Cotswolds in 1898, occurs at a point when the composer needed friends most. It follows very closely the true story that Elgar had sent the completed score of his *Variations* to the celebrated Viennese conductor Richter, in the hope of interesting him in the work. Elgar's various friends, who visit him during the trying period of his awaiting a reply, pass an afternoon in the customary, relaxed pursuits of a Victorian autumn day. Only his wife, a constant source of inspiration and encouragement throughout his life, understands and watches over him to offer comfort. One by one the friends enter the action, identifying their separate personalities with each danced variation to the music Elgar wrote to characterize them. A chamber-music comrade, an amateur cellist, a tricycle-riding crony, a contemplative scholar, a romantic young girl, a gracious and sedate lady, and an eccentric dog lover all pass in review. Those closest to him, his wife and his friend "Nimrod" (who also knew the conductor Richter), continually reflect their understanding and the significance of the anxious waiting period. From time to time, Lady Mary Lygnon appears and reappears as a mysterious background figure, symbolic of the enigma of the long anticipated reply. At the end of the ballet, a telegram arrives for "Nimrod" from Richter, announcing that he will indeed conduct the first performance of *Enigma Variations.*

NOTES Unanimously regarded as a masterpiece when it was first presented in England, the ballet was called by John Percival, in the *Times,* "a rare and moving expression of the quality of friendship." It received wide acclaim after its U.S. première. Writing in the *Village Voice,* the critic Deborah Jowitt said: ". . . I am astonished at its power to move me. The key—or one of them—to the enigma of the ballet's beauty is the nostalgia inherent in certain things. Lorca once wrote that a flock of sheep bears nostalgia about with it; it need not matter whether one has longings at all relevant to a flock of sheep. I don't think that one needs to have known era, place, or people involved in Ashton's ballet to be beguiled.

"The setting is Elgar's house in Worcestershire in the late years of Victoria's reign and of the nineteenth century. Everything about the ballet has an air of lateness: the composer's lateness in achieving recognition, the ripe late-Romantic music, the autumn garden, the amber of the sunlight. Julia Trevelyan Oman's set and costumes are carefully and poetically authentic. It's the kind of set I loved as a child—so super-real that it's hard to believe that there actually is a backstage area and not just more lawns and paths. There is a brick entrance, a cutaway view of an interior stairway, hammocks, bicycles, trees from which occasional yellow leaves float. Those friends of Elgar's cryptically enshrined in the musical variations are conveniently brought together. . . . They wander about . . . each emerging to do his (or her) variation and then strolling off. At the end a telegram is brought. . . . Elgar's friends rejoice in his good fortune.

"I see most clearly in this ballet what Ashtonophiles rave about. He is best at being quiet; his effects are modest, unflamboyant, but extremely sensitive to the nuances of character. . . . Sometimes he creates character through rhythm and through subtle gestural grafts onto the ballet vocabulary. Other times . . . he suggests eccentricities by requiring an eccentric manner of performing straightforward classical steps. He has a fine way with small understated lifts that seem to come with no preparation; the girl's feet make shy conversational steps barely off the ground. There are several of these in the bittersweet duet for Elgar and a very young girl (beautifully done by Derek Rencher and Antoinette Sibley), and in one of more promise of fulfillment between Matthew Arnold's son and Isabel Fitton (Robert Mead and Vyvyan Lorrayne). I especially liked two delightfully brusque, erratic solos performed by Alexander Grant and Anthony Dowell; some affectionate conjugal passages between Elgar and his wife (Svetlana Beriosova); and a dignified . . . touching duet between Elgar and a friend (Desmond Doyle) to the famous *Nimrod* variation."

In a long essay on the work of Frederick Ashton in *Ballet Review* (Vol. 3, No. 4), the critic Jack Anderson has written:

"Man is capable of being better: he can dream, he can work, he can try harder. Such assumptions may seem old-fashioned and unduly optimistic. But they have not yet been proven totally wrong, and I can conceive of no satisfactory social relationships without them.

"One of Ashton's most unusual ballets on these themes is *Enigma Variations*. Formally, *Enigma* is daring—much more so than many ballets which ostentatiously proclaim their originality. For one thing, it is filled with "nondance." Elgar studies a manuscript. Two eccentrics ride bicycles. Lady Elgar examines a score. Nevinson yawns. Elgar and Jaeger gesticulate as though actually conversing in the "Nimrod" variation, which concludes with the men and Lady Elgar walking, arms linked, backs to the audience. The telegraph boy is tipped and the ballet ends with the taking of a photograph. Amidst these gestures—distillations of character traits akin to those Ashton uses in his comedies—passages of heightened movement occur like surges of feeling, as in "Nimrod" where the weighted stride of "real" walking gives way to low lifts and the long, eloquent line of classical ballet, only to subside back into walking. A master of choreographic repose, Ashton knows when not to move a dancer. In the passages for Elgar and his wife a movement is usually allowed to come to rest before a new movement begins, which makes these actions seem to arise from deep founts of emotion.

"The ballet is a quiet ode to friendship, to people one loves. The characters are not necessarily Elgar's friends as they were historically, they are his friends as he might have remembered them—an altogether different matter, since we glorify their virtues and convert their failings into eccentricities. And we see all in the light of affection.

"The hero is a successful artist. What an unlikely subject for a ballet! For, as Ashton shows, artistic creation is untheatrical—a matter of solitude, work, and worry, interspersed with conversations with neighbors and confidences shared with wife and friends. Elgar is often alone. But his work and solitude are not in vain. The telegram from Richter arrives. A party is held and friends take photographs. And tomorrow the new work begins.

"Art. Friendship. Meaningful work. Graciousness. Tranquility. These are some of the things Ashton's ballets celebrate."

In a long interview with Don McDonagh in *Ballet Review* (Vol. 3, No. 4), Frederick Ashton was asked if he had a preference for works with a narrative continuity or works that are lyrical abstract statements.

"A: No, it depends on the music. For instance in *Enigma Variations* I could have taken the music and done a series of dances. But this somehow didn't appeal to me. Then I hit upon the idea of using the actual people who were written about musically and this began to fascinate me. I did a lot of study on them and read biographies to try and get under the skin of it. When Elgar's daughter, who is now a very old lady, came to see it she said, 'I don't understand how you did it because they were exactly like that.' And she said, 'I never liked any of them except Troyte.'

"McD: There is very little dancing by Elgar himself and yet he is apparent everywhere. Just his presence as he stands upstage is very important. It focuses the piece.

"A: He needs to be that kind of solid character. I started by making him dance more but it seemed wrong, so I cut it out. Even when he does a few steps it kind of jars on me. When he and Jaeger have the conversation they're supposed to have had, about Beethoven's quartets, they do a bit of dancing there, and I tried to do it like question and answer. Even that I kept to minimal dancing."

David Vaughan's complete account of the creation of *Enigma Variations* in the book *Frederick Ashton and His Ballets* is strongly recommended.

EPILOGUE

Music by Gustav Mahler. Choreography by John Neumeier. Costumes by Mitchell. Lighting by Nananne Porcher. First presented by American Ballet Theatre at the New York State Theatre, Lincoln Center, New York, July 9, 1975, with Natalia Makarova and Erik Bruhn. Conducted by David Gilbert. Dedicated to Vera Volkova.

Epilogue, as the title suggests, is a dance narrative supplementing an earlier dramatic action. What that action was is never made clear. What is clear, as the curtain rises, is that there has been Trouble in the autumnal years. There is as yet no music. A spotlight shines from above and in it brown leaves can be seen to fall to the ground. A girl crouches. A man stands nearby. There appears to be no communication between them; but then the visible tension suggests these two know each other, are lovers in fact, and have had a serious quarrel that disallows contact. They want to make it up, but how? They bow to each other in curious ways, without acknowledgment. Then, as the man stands with his back to the girl, she goes to him, standing close. The music starts: the *Adagietto* of Mahler's *Symphony No. 5*. The dance now recapitulates the Effort at Reunion, the Difficulty in Giving In, Making Allowances, Permitting Forgiveness. Yet tensions persist. Long dances by each display varying degrees of anguish and being wronged; sometimes neither sees what the other suffers. Toward the end, in capitulation, the man falls at the girl's feet. She touches his head. As she falls back in his arms, the leaves again descend.

EPISODES

Music by Anton Webern. Choreography by Martha Graham and George Balanchine. Scenery and lighting by David Hays. Costumes by Karinska.

*First presented by the New York City Ballet at the City Center, New York,
May 14, 1959. Episodes I, with choreography by Martha Graham, was
danced by Miss Graham, Bertram Ross, Sallie Wilson, Helen McGehee,
Ethel Winter, Linda Hodes, Akiko Kanda, Richard Kuch, Dan Wagoner,
David Wood, Kenneth Peterson, James Gardner, and Robert Powell. Episodes II was danced by a cast headed by Violette Verdy and Jonathan Watts,
Diana Adams and Jacques d'Amboise, Paul Taylor, Melissa Hayden, and
Francisco Moncion.*

In the 1950s Stravinsky began to tell me about the music of Anton Webern,
the Austrian composer (1883–1945). Stravinsky called him a great composer
and was so enthusiastic that I thought he must be very good indeed, although
I was not then much interested in atonal music, except maybe Schoenberg's.
To me, Schoenberg was the Einstein of twelve-tone music; I didn't see how he
could be surpassed. But within the next few years, Robert Craft, Stravinsky's
friend, recorded all of Webern's work. Everyone who cares about music must
always be grateful to him. I listened to everything and liked it. The songs were
the best of all, but they were written to be listened to. The orchestral music,
however, fills air like molecules: it is written for atmosphere. The first time I
heard it, I knew it could be danced to.

To understand Webern better, I transcribed several of the instrumental
pieces for piano and played them over and over. The music seemed to me like
Mozart and Stravinsky, music that can be danced to because it leaves the mind
free to *see* the dancing. In listening to composers like Beethoven and Brahms
every listener has his own ideas, paints his own picture of what the music represents. Beethoven did not have this in mind, I am sure, but he does seem to
be painting a picture and people like to put themselves in that picture. Now
how can I, a choreographer, try to squeeze a dancing body into a picture that
already exists in someone's mind? It simply won't work. But it will with
Webern. This kind of music, which Mozart and Stravinsky have also written, is
like a rose—you can admire it deeply but you cannot inject your personal feelings into it.

Lincoln Kirstein shared my interest and admiration for Webern and we
thought we should try to do dances to all of the orchestral pieces. They are not
many and last altogether less than an hour. We decided to invite Martha
Graham to collaborate on the undertaking and she happily agreed. We accordingly divided the scores and got to work. Miss Graham did her dance on a
theme of Mary Queen of Scots while I began to do a ballet without a story.
Miss Graham's part of *Episodes* has unfortunately not been seen for some
years. It is our hope that one day it will be danced again.

EPISODES I   The music is the *Passacaglia, Opus 1*, and the *Six Pieces for Orchestra, Opus 6*, both composed in 1909 before Webern had used Schoenberg's idea of the twelve-tone row. The dance is based on the final moments of

Mary Queen of Scots. It recapitulates her last thoughts as she mounts the scaffold.

The setting is austere, a black platform across the back of the stage with steps on both sides approaching it; in the center of the platform stands a black box and a high halberd-like heraldic device. The music begins with an ominous plucking of strings. Mary, in black, stands below, tense. Her stiff dress seems both to armor and to imprison her. Suddenly high on the platform, she is free of it, stepping out as a young girl in white to meet her lover Bothwell. She comes down again and her black dress remains standing like an empty cage, on the platform accusing her worldliness. She rejects the crown-craving Bothwell, the love of her life, and is in torment.

Four girls now dress Mary in blood red and she begins her long contest with Queen Elizabeth of England. The music shifts to the *Six Pieces for Orchestra*. The black box on the platform becomes a throne. Elizabeth sits there in burnished gold. She descends. The two queens play a fateful game of tennis, a formal court tennis.

As Elizabeth wins, she is lifted high. Mary then sits for a moment on the throne. But now the throne is the scaffold. Mary kneels before it, the tall halberd, now an ax, turns in the air and a bright red light illumines her cast-off queenly garb.

EPISODES II   The music for this part of the ballet, which, like the first part, can stand alone, consists of Webern's other orchestral works.

To the *Symphony, Opus 21*, there is an ensemble. The curtain rises before the music begins. Four couples stand on stage. As the music starts, dryly and carefully, the boys touch the girls on the shoulder; they join hands then, pose briefly, and begin to move together. One couple leads the others but soon, just as the instrumentation shifts and develops, the other pairs react to the music differently. The dance is about the music; it is meant to look that way. Stravinsky has said that nothing in contemporary music has haunted him more than the coda of this symphony.

The second part, to the *Five Pieces, Opus 10*, is a *pas de deux*. The lights dim to darkness. Two figures emerge in spotlights, a boy dressed in jet black, a girl in white. She moves toward him slowly. He catches her, her body collapses over his arm and stays there, bent over, as he moves away. He leaves her there, then goes to find her again. Schoenberg said of Webern's music that it expresses an entire novel in a gesture, a joy in a breath. Although I did not know he had said that when I was working on this ballet, I believed it myself.

Some people watching this part of the ballet in the theatre laugh a little. That is, here at home, not on our tours of Europe or Russia. I sometimes think Americans feel obliged to laugh too much when there is not any reason to.

The third part, to the *Concerto, Opus 24*, is again a *pas de deux* for another couple, with four girls accompanying them. The boy moves the girl as the composer moves his instruments. Speaking of some of Webern's music, Robert

Craft says that "at first the listener might be reminded of a switchboard sporadically lighting up, but the plot of wires between the lights is what must be illuminated." Which is what I try to do.

The Variations for Orchestra, Opus 30. The original production of *Episodes* continued at this point with a dance performed by Paul Taylor, then appearing as a guest artist with our company. Just as Sallie Wilson from the New York City Ballet appeared in Miss Graham's part of *Episodes,* Mr. Taylor appeared in mine. The piece consists of a theme and six variations. Webern wrote of the *Variations:* "The motivic development uses much crab-wise movement with augmentation and diminution . . . By changing the center of gravitation within the two forms by augmentation and diminution the character and meter of the piece is constantly changing . . ."

The final part of *Episodes* is performed to Webern's tribute to Bach, the *Ricercata for Six Voices from Bach's Musical Offering.* The dances here, as elsewhere in this work, praise the music. The further Webern goes, the more active and lean the music becomes. The energy it has is that of free polyphonic voices, each equally individual and expressive. They keep shifting in balance and so do the dances. In Virgil Thomson's phrase, the music turns out to be "a dialect of Bach."

EPITAPH

Music by György Ligeti (Atmosphères *and* Volumina). *Choreography by Rudi van Dantzig. Scenery and costumes by Toer van Schayk. First presented by the Dutch National Ballet, June 25, 1969, in Amsterdam, Holland. First presented in the United States by the same ensemble at the Minskoff Theatre, New York, November 9, 1976.*

The Dutch critic Luuk Utrecht has rightly observed that *Epitaph* is "a gloomy comment on the life of man, like an inscription on a tomb." Love and death govern the action and there is never any doubt that the latter will win out. Two brides in spotless white symbolize, according to the choreographer, Rudi van Dantzig, "the illusions and ideals after which mankind always strives; sometimes unattainable, then senseless or cruel, sometimes ridiculous and often so overwhelming that generations sacrifice themselves or are offered to them." The two boys who devote themselves to the two brides perish, dancers are encased in black boxes and to the sound of a roaring organ all the ensemble collapses in a heap. The brides tidily close them all up in a box and kneel to weep at the loss.

L'ESTRO ARMONICO (Cycle of Harmony)

*Music by Antonio Vivaldi. Choreography by John Cranko. First presented
by the Stuttgart Ballet at the Württemberg State Theatre, Stuttgart, Germany, April 27, 1963. First presented in the United States by the Stuttgart
Ballet at the Metropolitan Opera House, New York, May 30, 1973.*

L'Estro Armonico ("Cycle of Harmony") is a dance ballet to three concerti by
Antonio Vivaldi, arranged by Kurt-Heinz Stolze, the *Concerto in A Major*, the
Concerto in A Minor, and the *Concerto in D Major*. The choreographer, John
Cranko, said of his ballet that it "uses a selection from the twelve concertos of
Vivaldi. Personally I should have liked to choreograph all twelve, but to avoid
boring the public I have chosen three. These concertos have been choreographically linked: the themes propounded in the first two concertos have been
taken up and developed in the third." A woman is the center of the ballet, the
male soloists supporting and revolving about her.

THE ETERNAL IDOL

*Music by Frédéric Chopin. Choreography by Michael Smuin. First pre-
sented by American Ballet Theatre at the Brooklyn Academy of Music, December 4, 1969, with Cynthia Gregory and Ivan Nagy.*

A romantic narrative ballet, *The Eternal Idol* is appropriately set to the
Larghetto of Chopin's *Concerto No. 2 in F Minor*. The theme and inspiration
for the ballet is Rodin's famous sculpture "The Eternal Idol," where a boy
kneels at a girl's feet and rests his head on her breast. The ballet begins that
way, reminding us of the pose of the sculpture. It then explores in a *pas de
deux* for the lovers the beginnings and growth of their love for each other. As
the critic Walter Terry has noted, the ballet evokes such images as Bernard
Champigneulle speaks of in his book *Rodin*: ". . . Songs and sighs of love,
cries of pleasure and pain, cries of pain and pleasure mingled, the eternal call
of woman, the call of man . . . all found expression in Rodin."

ÉTUDES

*Music by Knudager Riisager (after Czerny). Choreography by Harald
Lander. Scenery by Erik Nordgreen. First presented by the Royal Danish
Ballet at the Royal Theatre, Copenhagen, January 15, 1948. First presented
in the United States by the American Ballet Theatre at the Metropolitan*

Opera House, New York, October 15, 1961, with Toni Lander, Royes Fernandez, and Bruce Marks in the leading roles. Scenery and costumes by Rolf Gerard.

This ballet is the choreographer's tribute to the dancer and may perhaps be considered as a representation of the work that must be accomplished by young dancers throughout the long and difficult preparatory years. We see in the ballet the first elementary exercises at the *barre* by young pupils, then work in the center of the stage, away from the *barre,* followed by a *pas de trois,* a *pas de deux,* a *pas de quatre,* a *pas de six,* and ensemble work. At the end of the ballet, the soloists display their skill individually and collectively.

EUGENE ONEGIN

Ballet in three acts and six scenes after Alexander Pushkin. Music by Peter Ilyich Tchaikovsky, arranged and orchestrated by Kurt-Heinz Stolze. Choreography by John Cranko. Scenery and costumes by Jürgen Rose. First presented by the Stuttgart Ballet at the Württemberg State Theatre, Stuttgart, Germany, April 13, 1965, with Marcia Haydée and Heinz Clauss in the principal roles. First presented in the United States by the same ensemble at the Metropolitan Opera House, Lincoln Center, New York, June 10, 1969.

The ballet tells the story of Pushkin's great poem. The music, by Tchaikovsky, is not from that composer's opera *Eugene Onegin,* but has been arranged from his lesser-known compositions.

How is it possible for me to speak of Pushkin's poem *Eugene Onegin* without emotion? It is like asking an Englishman to speak of Shakespeare without emotion. Alexander Pushkin produced the first great Russian poem, or "free novel" in verse, in *Eugene Onegin* (1823–30). His work is the beginning of greatness of the Russian language. There are problems about the translation of *Eugene Onegin* into English. Many have tried to render the poem into English. Vladimir Nabokov's complete version is the best we have, but for the reader with no Russian, it is difficult to explain the poem's greatness. For it is not what we think of as an epic or a huge, classic poem. It is a story, first of all, a work in poetry in a language that was unknown before, a language that became with Pushkin the Russian language of literacy and spoken liveliness. At any rate, John Cranko chose to make a ballet of this narrative, having known it as a poem, and also as an opera in Tchaikovsky's profound version. He arranged his ballet not to the music of Tchaikovsky's opera, but to other work by Tchaikovsky researched, arranged, and orchestrated by Kurt-Heinz Stolze.

Interviewed by *The New Yorker,* Cranko spoke of his ballet: "'I see *Onegin* as a myth in the same way that Charlie Chaplin is a myth. . . . Myths always have double meanings, and in this sense Chaplin is both funny and terrifying. Onegin is a young man who has everything—good looks, money, charm—and yet he adds up to nothing. Which makes *him* terrifying. His problem is a very contemporary one—lack of recognition. Then, of course, the plot of the Pushkin poem is balletic—explainable in three different dance styles. The first act is a youthful peasant dance, the second is a bourgeois party, the third is an elegant St. Petersburg ball. And like a thread going through the labyrinth you have your soloists, with their problems, their stories.'

"Mr. Cranko . . . added that when he choreographed a ballet he tried to create visual images that speak for themselves. 'A diamond has no color, but it takes light, and when you look at it you see red, blue, green, and yellow,' he said. 'A ballet image should be like a diamond. No meaning. No color. But hard, not sloppy. I have a specific feeling which maybe I can only shape for myself. So the ultimate definition of the images comes from the eyes of the public, not from my eyes.'"

A synopsis of the ballet follows:

ACT ONE, SCENE 1: MADAME LARINA'S GARDEN Madame Larina, Olga, and the nurse are finishing the party dresses and gossiping about Tatiana's coming birthday festivities. Madame Larina speculates on the future and reminisces about her own lost beauty and youth. Girls from the neighborhood arrive, their greetings and chatter are interrupted by gunshots.

Lensky, a young poet, engaged to Olga, arrives and tells them there is no cause for alarm; he was hunting with a friend from St. Petersburg. He introduces Onegin, who, bored with the city, has come to see if the country can offer him any distraction. Tatiana, full of youthful and romantic fantasies, falls in love with the elegant stranger, so different from the country people she knows. Onegin, on the other hand, sees only a coltish country girl who reads too many romantic novels.

ACT ONE, SCENE 2: TATIANA'S BEDROOM Tatiana, her imagination aflame with impetuous first love, dreams of Onegin and writes him a passionate love letter which she gives the nurse to deliver.

ACT TWO, SCENE 1: TATIANA'S BIRTHDAY The provincial gentry have come to celebrate Tatiana's birthday. They gossip about Lensky's infatuation with Olga and whisper prophecies of a dawning romance between Tatiana and the newcomer. Onegin finds the company boring. Stifling his yawns, he finds it difficult to be civil to them: Furthermore, he is irritated by Tatiana's letter which he regards merely as an outburst of adolescent love. In a quiet moment, he seeks out Tatiana and, telling her that he cannot love her, tears up her letter. Tatiana's distress, instead of awaking pity, merely increases his irritation.

Prince Gremin, a distant relative, appears. He is in love with Tatiana, and

Madame Larina hopes for a brilliant match; but Tatiana, troubled with her own heart, hardly notices her kindly and elderly relative.

Onegin, in his boredom, decides to provoke Lensky by flirting with Olga who lightheartedly joins in the teasing. But Lensky takes the matter with passionate seriousness. He challenges Onegin to a duel.

ACT TWO, SCENE 2: THE DUEL Tatiana and Olga try to reason with Lensky, but his high romantic ideals are shattered by the betrayal of his friend and the fickleness of his beloved; he insists that the duel take place. Onegin kills his friend and for the first time his cold heart is moved by the horror of his deed. Tatiana realizes that her love was an illusion, and that Onegin is self-centered and empty.

ACT THREE, SCENE 1: ST. PETERSBURG Years later, Onegin, having traveled the world in an attempt to escape from his own futility, returns to St. Petersburg where he is received at a ball in the palace of Prince Gremin. Gremin has recently married, and Onegin is astonished to recognize in the stately and elegant young princess, Tatiana, the uninteresting little country girl whom he once turned away. The enormity of his mistake and loss engulfs him. His life now seems even more aimless and empty.

ACT THREE, SCENE 2: TATIANA'S BOUDOIR Tatiana reads a letter from Onegin which reveals his love. Suddenly he stands before her, impatient to know her answer. Tatiana sorrowfully tells him that although she still feels her passionate love of girlhood for him, she is now a woman, and that she could never find happiness or respect with him. She orders him to leave her forever.

NOTES The critic Walter Terry, reviewing a performance of *Eugene Onegin* in New York in 1971, wrote in *The Saturday Review:* "How Cranko tells a story in dance! He is a theater man through and through, as was his illustrious predecessor of two centuries ago in Stuttgart, Jean-Georges Noverre, whose revolutionary esthetics carried the ballet away from mere steps to *ballet d'action*—that is to say, to dramatic ballet, to movement with dramatic meanings.

"Cranko's *Onegin* has its virtuosic steppings—the cross-stage leaps by the company at the close of Act One, Scene 1, or the great pinwheel pattern in the ballroom scene—but of equal importance are the acted, not danced, duel and death scene that takes place way at the back of the stage (the late Doris Humphrey, among the great choreographers of our age, once stated that tragedy worked best in upstage remoteness and that comedy was for downstage familiarity), the finale in which the heroine stands alone center stage, and the remarkable mirror dance that combines acting and dancing as Tatiana literally draws her dream lover from the image in her mind and has him step from behind her own reflection in the mirror and into her arms.

". . . Marcia Haydée was Tatiana, a role identified with her very special artistry as both an actress and a dancer, and Heinz Clauss was Onegin, stern, strong, remote yet romantic. . . ."

EVENING DIALOGUES

Music by Schumann. Choreography by Jonathan Watts. First presented by the Joffrey City Center Ballet at the City Center, New York, October 22, 1974, with Francesca Corkle, Beatriz Rodriguez, Russell Sultzbach, and Burton Taylor as principals.

One of Schumann's great works for piano, the *Davidsbündlertänze*, is played throughout this ballet to inspire and accompany dances by vulnerable and susceptible young persons who listen and respond. They care deeply about what they hear and react with fervor to the intensity of concentration of the short, vivid dance pieces. Their dances express the joy and disappointments of love and youth.

AN EVENING'S WALTZES

Music by Serge Prokofiev. Choreography by Jerome Robbins. Costumes by Rouben Ter-Arutunian. First presented by the New York City Ballet at the New York State Theatre, Lincoln Center, May 24, 1973, with Patricia Mc-Bride and Jean-Pierre Bonnefous, Christine Redpath and John Clifford, Sara Leland and Bart Cook in leading roles.

The music for this dance ballet is five waltzes by Prokofiev from his *Symphonic Suite of Waltzes*. There is no story, only these persons dancing to these waltzes. Each of the waltzes is different, and a different atmosphere and mood are established for the dances. The three leading couples as well as the soloists and *corps de ballet* are formally dressed, as if they were attending a formal party.

Writing in the *Wall Street Journal* about the ballet, Peter J. Rosenwald said that "it has so much beautiful movement that it could almost bring back ballroom dancing as a national pastime. . . . From beginning to end it has that Robbins romantic style, warm and eloquent, full of effortless and thrilling lifts which are never showy for their own sake."

Deborah Jowitt in the *Village Voice* wrote: "Over the decorous unison waltzing of the *corps*, pairs of soloists enter one at a time to make violent small talk in dance. Small outbursts of movement, sudden changes of heart and direction interrupt the smooth surface of the waltzing. These couples are, perhaps, dancing out the thoughts and the verbal exchanges that occur at grand parties such as these, where a current of fashionable melodrama flows through the ballroom. The duet for Redpath and Clifford (replacing the injured Gelsey Kirkland and Helgi Tomasson at the last minute) is particularly effusive, with a hint of drastic coquetry."

EVERY NOW AND THEN

Music by Quincy Jones. Choreography by William Scott. Costumes designed by Hutaff Lennon and Jack Cunningham; costumes executed by Zelda Wynn. Lighting design by Gary Fails. First presented by the Dance Theatre of Harlem at the Uris Theatre, New York, April 26, 1975.

The ballet *Every Now and Then* was made by the ballet master of the Dance Theatre of Harlem, William Scott. His dances play with black folk dance, jazz, and ballet, mixing them together and merging the styles. Designed and laid out to be danced, the steps often appear spontaneous and improvised, like sudden expressions of a personal fantasy. The critic Arlene Croce of *The New Yorker* once noted in young amateur dancers on the "Soul Train" television program: "Every now and then, one of the boys will hurl himself into a *saut de basque*—playing at ballet."

FAÇADE

Ballet in one act. Music by William Walton. Choreography by Frederick Ashton. Scenery and costumes by John Armstrong. First presented by the Camargo Society at the Cambridge Theatre, London, April 26, 1931, with a cast that included Lydia Lopokova, Alicia Markova, and Frederick Ashton. First presented in the United States by the Sadler's Wells Ballet at the Metropolitan Opera House, New York, October 13, 1949, with Moira Shearer and Frederick Ashton in featured roles.

The music to *Façade* was originally written as a setting to certain poems by Edith Sitwell. The poet recited her verses accompanied by the music. The ballet has nothing to do with the poems and uses only the music, to which the choreographer has arranged a series of nine comic *divertissements* that poke fun at their subjects. The scene shows the façade of a large, light-colored house of the Victorian era.

First, two girls and a boy amble out on stage and dance a "Scottish Rhapsody" in appropriate native costume. This is followed by a number called "Yodeling." A milkmaid enters with a stool. Soon she is disturbed by three mountaineers, who turn her around as she stands posed on the stool and pay tribute to her fresh beauty. There is a yodeling contest, in which the girl enters with gusto. The music ripples and laughs with the happy young people. Next comes a "Polka," danced by a smart young lady.

Now two couples dance a "Fox Trot," which is followed by a "Waltz" executed by four girls. Two vaudeville dandies take up the "Popular Song" and perform it with quick, funny precision. The "Country Dance" features a silly country girl, a yokel, and an irate squire. A gigolo, overslickly dressed in evening clothes, and a debutante, who wears a long red dress and an absurd feather in her hair, now come forward and dance the "Tango." The gigolo bends the debutante backward, dips her low, runs a scale down her back with his fingers, and with a devilish air tries to overexploit her good nature. The debutante is amenable to any treatment, however, and finishes the dance considerably disheveled. All the dancers come forward now and join in a "Tarantella Finale."

FACSIMILE

Choreographic observation in one scene. Music by Leonard Bernstein. Choreography by Jerome Robbins. Scenery by Oliver Smith. Costumes by Irene Sharaff. First presented by Ballet Theatre at the Broadway Theatre, New York, October 24, 1946, with Nora Kaye, Jerome Robbins, and John Kriza.

A naturalistic ballet of ideas, *Facsimile* takes up a problem which is not only contemporary, but ageless. It is the problem of what modern man shall do with his time. Often apparently immune to authentic feeling, he takes refuge in the constant company of his fellow men, where he can conceal his lack of security. He arranges his life not only to conceal his real identity from his friends, but to hide it from himself. The ballet's program note reads: "Small inward treasure does he possess who, to feel alive, needs every hour the tumult of the street, the emotion of the theatre, and the small talk of society."

The scene of the ballet is a lonely stretch of beach. There is an improvised bathing tent at the left. On the right, disappearing in the distance, is an irregular line of pilings, marking the shore line. When the curtain rises, there is but one figure on stage: a woman in a bathing suit, who is idling away her time. The music is quiet and as lonely as the scene.

We see that the woman is bored. She seems to have nothing to wait for and walks about trying to find something to amuse her. She takes no pleasure in the scene and tosses away inanimate objects. Finally she goes over to her bathing tent, pulls the awning across it, and amuses herself slightly by watching her own shadow. Her own shadow is better than no society at all.

The woman turns and looks down the beach. Someone is coming! She is delighted and childishly runs behind the awning to surprise the stranger. A man strolls onto the scene. He does not see the woman and, just as she has done, tries to find something to amuse him. He plays with his beach towel, looks up and down the beach, thinks of nothing. He wonders why he is there. Now he sees the woman's shadow on the awning.

She steps out coyly. Both these vacuous personalities try to make something of themselves. Alone, they may be nothing, but together, they must pretend that this is not true. They introduce themselves, chatter, begin to flirt. They have nothing else to say to each other and grasp at flirtation like a straw. They therefore take their love very seriously.

But soon they tire even of this recourse. They come to life again as another man strolls toward them. Both imagine that the newcomer might be self-sufficient enough to amuse them. He turns out to be just as insecure as they are.

Now that they are a triangle, one woman and two men, the idlers try to make something out of nothing. The first man pretends to be annoyed at the intrusion of the second and claims the girl's whole attention. The girl plays along with him, and the intruder sees that this might be an interesting game after all. He flirts with the woman and tries to win her from his rival.

The woman now has a situation that amuses her immensely. She plays with the two men adroitly and watches closely to see their reactions. She knows that the important thing is to be so charming that the game will never end, for if either suspects that she is insincere, both will desert her. The men participate in the game for a short while, but the first man finally insists that she stop this nonsense and be his. The woman says, "No." Finally she has to take some way out and confesses that she likes the second man best. Her first lover storms at her and acts furiously jealous. He takes the woman and his rival and drags them across the beach. Soon all three are fighting together, their bodies tied in a writhing knot on the beach.

The woman is through. She cries out, "Stop!" The three figures untangle themselves, and when they see that the girl is really serious and actually prefers neither one of them, the two men leave the scene. The first man acts as if he had been hurt and misunderstood; the second tries to shrug off the incident: what difference could it possibly make to him? Now the woman is alone again. The incident has not made any difference to her, either. As she strolls away from the beach, there is a real question as to whether anything will ever make any difference to her.

FALL RIVER LEGEND

Ballet in eight scenes, with prologue. Music by Morton Gould. Choreography by Agnes de Mille. Scenery by Oliver Smith. Costumes by Miles White. First presented by Ballet Theatre at the Metropolitan Opera House, New York, April 22, 1948, with a cast headed by Alicia Alonso, Diana Adams, Peter Gladke, and John Kriza.

This modern melodrama is founded on fact. Fall River, Massachusetts, in the
summer of 1892 was the scene of a hideous crime that attracted the attention
of the nation. In that city, a respectable spinster by the name of Lizzie Borden
was said to have hacked to death with an ax her father and her stepmother.
Lizzie Borden was subsequently tried for this double murder. The jury, however, acquitted her, and she went back to her father's house and lived as a rec-
luse until she died. The murderer was never found.

In *Fall River Legend,* Lizzie Borden is hanged. Here she is called the Accused, and in the prologue of the ballet she faces the gallows.

PROLOGUE   Before the curtain rises, the music begins with loud shrieks of
sound that forebode terror. The orchestra quiets down, the curtain rises, and
we are about to be witnesses at an execution.

The gallows stands stark and bare, its rope dangling, against a dark, blue-
green sky. The Accused, in black, stands on the right with her pastor. Near
them is a black, leafless tree. On the left, the speaker for the jury mechanically
intones the jury's bill: that the jurors on oath present that on August 4, 1892,
the Accused with a certain weapon, to wit, an ax, did assault and kill her stepmother and father with twenty mortal wounds. The Accused stands in a spotlight on the right. She holds the pastor's hand and seems immune to feeling.
The speaker for the jury recalls aloud that the house where she committed
these murders was the house where she was born. As he remembers that she
lived there once with her father and mother in happiness, the drop curtain
rises, the gallows slides back to support a corner of the house, and the lights
rise on a typical Victorian home set back off the street. Except for the stoop and
the front door, the façade of the house is torn away to expose the interior. On
the left, we notice a tree stump set for chopping wood. We are to see the Accused in her childhood.

SCENE ONE: THE HOUSE OF THE ACCUSED—THE PAST   The sky that hangs over
the house is washed in hideous green. The Accused, dressed now in dark
green, stands before her room and watches time go back to the days of her
girlhood. Old neighbors and townspeople pass by. Her father and mother are
there. The Accused holds out her hands to them longingly, trying to claim
their attention, but they do not notice her. A young girl in white appears. We
know immediately that she is the Accused as a child. The Accused goes to her,
hovers over her as if to protect her, and follows her girlish dance steps to
hurdy-gurdy music.

The child runs to her mother. The mother caresses her daughter; the Accused pathetically fingers her mother's white shawl. A strange woman enters.
Her back is straight as a ramrod, her chin is held high; she is dressed in severe
black with a black boa about her shoulders. This woman marches, rather than
walks, and watches with the determined interest in everyone else's business
that only the spinster can have. The child is frightened of this woman; the Ac-

cused articulates this fright in a sudden tightening of her gestures: as the mature child, she is not only afraid, she knows why she fears. Instinctively the Accused goes to her father and kneels before him to guard him against this woman. But the adamant spinster comes forward; the father welcomes her and shakes her hand, not seeing his daughter as she kneels between them.

The spinster turns on the child and scolds her, apparently for no reason at all, but we see instantly that the spinster is acutely aware of the child's hatred that the Accused has expressed. Just as we note the woman's rudeness in scolding the girl in the presence of her mother, we see that the mother is indifferent. She is ill. She clutches at her heart and faints. A crowd gathers. The father and the child rush to her and hold her lovingly; they are helpless in their fear and shock. The spinster orders the child away from her mother and takes charge like a schoolteacher. The Accused, who has seen it all before, trembles; she holds her hands in front of her face to erase this memory. The child cries.

The mother recovers slowly from the attack, and the father leads her to the house. He turns at the door and bows to the spinster. The crowd disperses. The spinster walks proudly and primly down the street alone. The Accused turns her back on this woman.

The lights go down and a little time passes. When the stage is lit again, we see the child sitting on the steps by the door watching her mother and father dance. The Accused watches, too, as her parents move gracefully in a soft love duet. The child goes to her father, who holds her tenderly; then the mother lifts the girl into her arms. We are watching the ideally happy family. The Accused joins in the reliving of her childhood and with the girl dances gaily about her loving parents. She seems to lose all her hardness and bitterness; she forgets about the future as she and the child become one in their movements and one in their affection for the mother and father.

But the joyous dance is too much for the mother. She has another attack. Two passers-by run for help. The father lifts her carefully and carries her into the house. The Accused and the girl pray together for their mother. The spinster enters and goes immediately into the house. Two women come to the girl and dress her in black: her mother is dead. The Accused clutches the side of the house, hides her agony, and represses the hatred that must soon be asserted.

The father comes out into the street, looking for his daughter. The spinster stands beside him. The child runs to her father's arms and weeps. He attempts to console her, but the child breaks away from him and moves to enter the house. She cannot go in: the spinster, now in complete control, stands in the doorway.

The child returns to her father and kneels at his feet, begging him to allow her to see her mother. The woman in black marches up to the child and, taking her shoulders in her hands, shakes her viciously. The grieving father does not understand. He tries to separate them, then buries his face in his hands. He bows to the woman's authority and falls on his knees at her feet.

In the background, the Accused has turned to watch. Her grief and indignation are uncontrollable; her body writhes obscenely. The spinster sees the mother's white shawl lying on the ground. She goes to pick it up. As she does so, the Accused runs across the stage and leaps to her father's back, claiming him, denying him everything but grief. But he does not feel her presence. The spinster puts the white shawl over her shoulders. The father lifts her in his arms and takes her across the threshold. The door slams shut in the face of the Accused.

SCENE TWO: THE HOME OF THE ACCUSED—THE PRESENT   Many years have passed. The child has disappeared, and the Accused now lives her own part in the tragedy. She is a woman now, a young woman who ought to have been married years ago. As the lights come up, we see her father and her stepmother in the living room of the house. They sit opposite each other, rocking back and forth, reading books that they hold out stiffly in front of them. There is no music. In this oppressive silence, the Accused enters. She takes a chair between the two. All three rock in unison. The silence becomes taut and music begins quietly.

The house is moved forward to the front of the stage. The Accused rises from her chair and snaps her fingers desperately, demanding an end to this sitting and staring. Her father and stepmother do not pay any attention to this outburst. For a moment the Accused sits down again, then, nervously, almost without control, she runs up the stairs and down again, apparently for no reason at all. The stepmother glances up knowingly from her book and whispers to her husband. The Accused returns to sit and rock and stare. She gets up to look out of the window, but the woman in black follows her and snaps the window shade shut in her face. The Accused goes to her father and embraces him, but the woman pulls her away.

The Accused can bear it no longer; she goes out into the yard. The suspicious stepmother follows her for a moment, but sees she is alone and returns to the sitting room. Her husband places the white shawl about her shoulders and stands behind her chair.

In the yard the Accused meets her pastor. He is young and pleasant-looking, slightly deferential to her, and she is plainly attracted to him. They dance together, the girl participating in the dance with a kind of desperate and abandoned joy. She has no other companionship, no one knows the secret agonies and longings of her heart, and she does not know how to be happy in a normal way. The pastor is sufficiently acquainted with her family situation to be sympathetic and kind. The dance over, the two shake hands formally, both of them a little conscious of the absurdity of this convention.

The father opens the door and comes out to look for his daughter. He has acquired now the sternness and brusqueness of his wife. He disapproves of the rendezvous and tells the girl to come in. She does so reluctantly, and the pastor leaves the scene.

Back in the parlor, the family sit rocking again. The Accused moves from her chair and goes into the back hall. She re-enters the room with an ax in her hand. The orchestra sounds a sharp shriek on the strings. The stepmother cringes and seeks protection from her husband. The girl does not understand why she should be afraid and smiles to herself. She goes out into the yard, chops wood, and buries the blade of the ax in the chopping block. She goes back into the house with the wood, wipes her hands, and sits down again. Everything is still the same.

SCENE THREE: THE STREET BEFORE THE HOUSE   The house is moved back. We hear light and gay music, and young happy couples fill the street and dance together. The Accused opens the door and comes out to watch; her family remain seated in the parlor. Sitting on the doorstep, the girl observes wistfully the open happiness of youth. A soft and romantic *pas de deux* is danced by one couple who find themselves alone for a moment; then they are joined by other couples and leave the stage.

The Accused is alone and despondent. She thinks she must hate what she cannot have. The music snarls; she rises, leaps, and turns down the stage in a rapid diagonal. She almost runs into the ax, which still stands buried in the tree stump. She touches the handle. The music cries out in warning, and the girl creeps away from the ax in terror. She falls to the ground. As she rises, her eyes turn, fascinated, back to the ax. She moves toward it; her hand trembles. She is revolted by her thoughts and moves away.

Just as she does so, the young pastor enters with a bouquet of red roses. The music is low and tender. The girl takes the flowers and smoothes her hair. The pastor picks her up and holds her briefly as if she were a child. They begin to dance, and the girl forgets that romance seemed impossible for her five minutes before. The pastor asks her to come with him on a church picnic, and the girl responds eagerly.

Her happiness is short-lived. Her father and stepmother come out of the house and see her with the pastor. The parents creep up on the innocent lovers. The stepmother stares at the girl. The Accused falls to the ground and kicks her feet in an uncontrolled, childish tantrum. She rolls across the stage and finds herself looking straight at the ax. Meanwhile the stepmother is whispering to the pastor about the girl's abnormalities, telling him that she is perhaps insane. The pastor is respectful to the woman, but disbelieves her. The Accused rushes at her stepmother, scratching at the air in front of her. The woman accepts this as but another sign of the girl's insanity and threatens her. Then she and her husband beckon to the girl to come with them back to the house. The Accused gives them a quick look of appraisal, glances at the house, hesitates, and quickly, spasmodically, grabs at her mother's white shawl. Placidly she now goes to the pastor and takes his arm. They walk off together. For the first time in her life, the Accused has defied in action what she has always defied in her mind.

SCENE FOUR: A PRAYER MEETING The lights go down; the house turns. Over the house, the green sky darkens ominously. But when the lights come up, we find ourselves at a prayer meeting. The pastor stands in the midst of his congregation. The Accused looks on like an outsider: these happy people are like the lovers she saw dancing in front of her house, and she doubts that she can become one of them. The pastor perceives her thoughts, welcomes her, and the women of the church gather about the Accused and befriend her. One of the women kisses her and smiles. The Accused cannot believe her eyes. The congregation divides into two groups, dancing joyously to simulated organ music. The Accused hesitates to participate, but no longer watches as if she were an outsider.

Suddenly the congregation leaves the scene. The Accused and her pastor are alone. The music becomes dispassionately sentimental. The Accused falls to the floor and curls up like a child: never since childhood has she known such kindness as this. She rises; the pastor goes to her and takes her hand. Still the girl is afraid. The Accused looks into his eyes and sees there none of the deception, none of the duplicity she fears. Now she submits wholly to the young man's tender feeling for her and, all doubt gone, allows him to give her hope in a triumphant dance. The music mounts steadily in volume; the two figures move faster, circling and leaping. Then, with a quick cut in the music, the melody becomes soft and yielding. The girl kneels against her lover. He lifts her in his arms, and she curls up against him. He releases her for a moment, and they stand together, side by side, as the other couples in the congregation return.

To fresh, vibrant music, the Accused dances among the other lovers in an ensemble dance strongly reminiscent of a country revival meeting. She is carried high off the ground by two boys and shakes hands with the girls. Knowing happiness, she now has the right to participate. Her joy is open and she moves with quick spontaneity.

Her stepmother enters. When the Accused sees her, her body stiffens, her face contorts in pain, as if her heart were slashed with a knife. She falls to the ground, hysterical in her agony. The pastor reaches out to help her, but the woman in black draws him aside. The Accused sees them whispering together and, losing all control, seems to become as mad as her stepmother imagines her to be. The music whirls insanely. The congregation closes in on her in a semicircle of slow motion. The Accused writhes on the ground, rises, and walks in a trance.

The stepmother and the pastor come to her. The pastor puts her mother's white shawl about her shoulders and politely says good-by. The girl turns to stare after the pastor. She holds out her hand to him in one last plea. He does not see her. The stage darkens. The church turns, to become the house again. The stepmother leads her to the door. Her last hope is gone.

SCENE FIVE: INSIDE THE HOUSE   When the lights come up, the stepmother has gone into the house. The Accused remains on the doorstep. From this position she watches the happy young couples of the town move before her. Changed entirely, she observes them from the private distance of her mind. Her face is a mask. Her father and stepmother sit rocking in the parlor. She can no longer envy the lovers, because the possibility of being like them has been destroyed. Now she moves like an automaton, as if her every step were predetermined. She walks directly to the chopping block. Two cheerful girls walk down the street. The girl does not know they are there. She touches the ax, then picks it up and turns back toward the house. She has no doubt about what she must do. When she enters the parlor, her father and stepmother jump up in terror. The Accused merely looks at them. As the scene blacks out, her free hand moves up to cover her face.

SCENE SIX: THE PRESENT AND THE PAST   A drop curtain falls, to enlighten us on the goriness of the crime. We see depicted here the parlor suspended in mid-air, its chairs overturned; on the floor of the room streams of blood meet to form a red flood.

The Accused enters. She has removed her dress; her petticoat is spattered with blood. Her mother appears. The Accused begins to act out the wish she imagines to be fulfilled by her terrible crime. The mother must approve of the double murder; it is for her that the Accused has killed.

Her mother embraces her, and the girl rests content in her arms. But then the mother notices the red stains. The girl, now again the small child of the ballet's first scene, tries to hide the stains with the hem of her skirt. The mother slaps her hand. She examines the stains and sees that her daughter is covered with blood. She slaps the girl's cheek and pushes her forward. The child's arms hang limp, her fingers flutter. The mother rocks the naughty child against her breast. She smiles a little as she upbraids the Accused and vanishes in the night.

SCENE SEVEN: THE HOME OF THE ACCUSED   The drop curtain rises and the house is seen again. In time, this scene follows immediately after Scene Five. No longer dark, the sky in back of the frame dwelling is now hideously and grossly red. There is no sound, yet the atmosphere is tense, expectant. Neighbors are running up and down the street, frantically trying to locate the source of the ghastly outcries they have heard.

The Accused can be seen emerging from the back hall under the stairs. The orchestra is still quiet. She tries to straighten up the parlor hastily, but stops when she sees that people are looking in the window at her. Then quickly, in a desperate rush, she dashes for the front door. When she appears on the doorstep, the orchestra crashes and blares. The girl runs into the crowd and circles the street. The orchestra continues to play fortissimo as the girl cries out to the world the horror of her home.

Meanwhile townspeople have entered the house. Two men bring forward the bloody ax and the mother's white shawl, laced now with blood. They confront the girl. Her hands quiver before her face. Moving as in a dream, she takes her mother's shawl and holds it to her lips.

The pastor makes his way through the crowd to the Accused. He holds her, lifts her gently as if to protect her. The girl's feet kick at the air in a spasm of desperation. Then she collapses at the pastor's feet.

SCENE EIGHT: THE GALLOWS The house of the Accused disappears except for a piece of its framework, which forms the gallows we saw in the prologue. She stands with the pastor, awaiting her execution. The people of the town pass by and stare at her. She is not disturbed, for she is preoccupied with her own frantically rapid memories of her crime and what led up to it: the blissful childhood, the loving mother, the father destroyed in his weakness by the demon spinster, the love she has wanted to give all her life, and the love that must now die. She holds out her hand, grasping at her memories, kneels, and opens her arms. The pastor comforts her.

A mother and her small daughter, perhaps the Accused herself, come to see the condemned woman. Ironically, the child shakes her fists at the Accused. Contented couples pass and watch. The Accused lets her head rest briefly on the pastor's shoulder. There is not much time left. He kisses her and leaves her alone. The girl turns to the gallows and opens her arms, as if to welcome the hangman's noose. Her body twitches grotesquely; her neck breaks. The music finishes like thunder. The Accused has been hanged until she is dead.

FANCY FREE

Ballet in one act. Music by Leonard Bernstein. Choreography by Jerome Robbins. Scenery by Oliver Smith. Costumes by Kermit Love. First presented by Ballet Theatre at the Metropolitan Opera House, New York, April 18, 1944, with John Kriza, Harold Lang, and Jerome Robbins as the three Sailors; Muriel Bentley, Janet Reed, and Shirley Eckl as the three Passers-by.

This modern American ballet tells what happens to three sailors who go out on liberty in New York City. The time is "the present": any hot summer night. The scene is a side street in Manhattan.

The music is quiet when the curtain rises. Outlined against the dark city night is the interior of a bar. The entrance to the bar, on the right, leads out onto a street corner. There a bright street lamp shines down on the sidewalk. Inside the bar there are no customers; the lone bartender lazily dries and polishes beer glasses. He begins to read a newspaper. In the background the myriad lights of distant skyscrapers penetrate the sultry night like stars.

Through the side windows of the bar we can make out three sailors walking toward the corner. The music blares out. They rush toward the corner, pivot on the lamppost, and begin to dance in the street in front of the bar. Dressed in clean summer whites, the sailors are out to make the most of the night. They preen a little, adjust their hats to jazzy angles, and strut along the pavement in anticipation of the good time that must naturally come their way. Their dance is like an improvised vaudeville act; it's clear that the three are friends and that they can kid each other and laugh about it. If they have their way, this is going to be an evening to beat all the rest. They try to outdo each other with brief trick dance steps and laugh. Two of them push the third high up in the air between them. Inside the bar the bartender smokes and reads his paper.

The rowdy music that accompanies the sailors' dance slows down and softens. The three men know from experience that simple determination isn't going to get them a good time. They straighten their jackets, readjust their hats, and wonder what to do next: which do they want first—women, drink, or music? One of the sailors leans against the lamppost to consider the problem seriously. One of his pals joins him. Before these two have made up their minds completely, the third sailor enters the bar. His friends race in after him.

The three sailors strut up to the bar with a special salty air for the bartender's benefit. They order three beers, clink their glasses together, down the drinks in unison, and slam the glasses back down on the bar. The bartender eyes them suspiciously: who's going to pay? The sailors look at each other as if such a thought had never entered their heads. Finally one of them is tricked into paying by the other two. As he puts down the money, he tries to shrug off the fact that he always ends up with the short end of the stick.

Now that they've had one drink, the sailors remember that they don't want to drink alone. They look around the empty bar with amused disgust, hitch up their pants, and head for the door. The music is moody, waiting for something to happen. The sailors are getting slightly tired of each other; they wonder if the evening is going to turn out to be a bust, after all. One of them pulls out a stick of gum. He starts to unwrap it, then remembers his friends and splits it with them. The three chew thoughtfully and, one by one, flick the pieces of gum wrapper out into the street to see which one can flick it farthest. The winner wonders what difference it makes.

At this point, just as the three are about to relax into boredom, they straighten up as if lightning had struck. The music breaks out into loud, rhythmic boogie-woogie, and a terrific-looking girl walks by. She wears a tight-fitting blouse and skirt, high patent leather shoes, and carries a red handbag. The girl knows she is being watched; she smiles and by her walk suggests all the things the sailors are imagining. The sailors are struck numb; standing close together, they move as one body—bending so far forward to watch the girl that they almost fall on their faces.

The girl pretends that she hasn't seen them, which sends the boys into action. Suddenly they are three very different individuals, each trying to interest the girl in his own special way. They imitate her walk, laugh at her, grab her purse and toss it around, and all but lie at her feet to get the girl to recognize their existence. The girl wants to be angry and tries to act as if she is, but the boys sense that she's just kidding. When she laughs in warm, friendly recognition, the three sailors smile back and wonder—who saw her first? A small fight breaks out. Two of the boys lift the girl high. She kicks free and stomps off impatiently. The battle has left one sailor lying in the street. He watches as his two friends follow the girl, then lazily picks himself up.

He smoothes out his uniform and starts to go back into the bar. Then, as in a dream, he bumps into a small, cute girl, younger than the first. He apologizes for his clumsiness, smiles winningly, looks her up and down adroitly, and introduces himself. The girl smiles back. The sailor looks over her shoulder to be sure his friends have disappeared and asks her into the bar for a drink. The girl consents.

Inside, the bartender is still reading. The sailor and his girl climb up on two stools and order drinks. He is feeling his way with the redhead, but decides on the old routine. The music stops as he gives her a dazzling, rapid display of What-I've-Been-Through. His hands circle the air and zoom down to attack imaginary ships, and his body vibrates to machine-gun fire as he describes the terrors of life at sea. When the girl takes this in and doesn't laugh at him, just watches, the boy decides that she's not only cute, she's adorable. He asks her to dance.

The orchestra plays a low blues number as they move together slowly. The *pas de deux* they dance is instinctively intimate, and the intimacy—their mutual liking and attraction—is so natural and unforced that formality and doubt would be out of place. This is a made-for-each-other dance that makes sense in its alternate casualness and conviction. He dances with her as he would with any girl, then holds her closely, and she responds warmly to this way of showing how special she is. When the dance is over, he bends down and kisses her softly. The girl smiles and wipes her lipstick off his face. They move together back to the bar.

The sailor picks the girl up and sits her on a stool. He has started to pay for the drinks when a roaring rattle of sound breaks the romantic spell and ushers in his two friends. The two gobs barge into the bar with the first girl and stop dead in their tracks when they see him with a date. He grabs his girl and pulls her toward the door to avoid the intruders. But the girl stops him. The girls are old friends, apparently, and begin to carry on together as girls will.

The boy sees that the situation is hopeless and goes to join his pals at a table. More drinks are ordered. The girls sit down. There are only four chairs, and one of the sailors is left standing. He tries to sit on the first girl's lap—she seemed more experienced and tolerant—but she pushes him off. Two of the sailors dance with the girls, and the boy who found the redhead sits alone for a moment. Now he cuts in. The snare drum signals the quarrel that ensues:

who's going to dance with whom? The situation is hopeless. One of the boys has got to clear out or the night will be ruined.

The three sailors finally get together and agree that they'll have a contest to see which one of them can dance best. The girls will be the judges of the two winners, and the third man will scram. Two of the sailors join the girls at the table, and one of the boys begins a solo.

His dance is rowdy and energetic as he tries to outdo all the steps he thinks his friends might try. The girls are delighted at his fresh and arrogant skill and begin to applaud as he finishes his number by jumping up on the bar with one leap. There he poses for an instant, then jumps down, grabs up a beer, and flourishes his glass. The other two sailors razz him as the girls clap their hands.

The next variation is danced by the cute girl's first partner. His dance is subtler, relying more on sinuous, flowing rhythm than boisterousness, more on false modesty than overt bragging. The girls respond to his quiet dance with a sigh, and his friends hold their noses. He lies on the floor with his legs in the air as his number ends. The last sailor tries to combine the two styles of his friends and succeeds brilliantly in a snaky, Latin dance at the end of which he jumps down from a bar stool to kneel on the floor before the girls.

The girls don't know which ones to choose! They argue about it; then the boys argue with them and start to fight among themselves. The competition that began when the first girl passed by on the street turns into anger and rage, and they begin to tear each other apart. The girls cringe against the bar, thinking at first that this can't be serious, but as the battle goes on in earnest, they decide to get out of there fast. The sailors dive behind the bar in a tussle and don't notice that the girls have walked out on them. When they pause and wake up to this fact, they look at each other frantically and dive for the door. Out on the street they can't find the girls. They look at each other with amused disgust, straighten out their uniforms, nurse their aches and pains, and relax again.

What are they to do now? Maybe another drink will help. They re-enter the bar, down a drink apiece, and again the same sailor pays. The friends head back for the street. They stand there under the lamppost, as they did before they first entered the bar at the beginning of the evening. They split another piece of gum three ways; they tear off the paper and flip it into the street.

The music sounds noisily, and a beautiful babe promenades across the street —terrific, you understand? As before, the three bodies slant in unison as they follow her every step and wiggle. The girl struts off down the street on the left. The sailors seem to recover from her fascination and remember the bruises of the battle royal the last girls got them involved in. Each watches the others carefully, to be sure that this feeling is unanimous. This is just a stall. They begin to idle away from each other, laughing the blonde off, when one sailor strikes off like a streak of lightning after the girl. His friends follow. The cycle is endless.

NOTES Lincoln Kirstein, in his book *Movement and Metaphor* (1970), which analyzes fifty seminal ballets in the history of the art, reminds us that *Fancy Free* "remains the sturdiest characteristic national work" in the American repertory.

FANFARE

Classic ballet in one act. Music by Benjamin Britten. Choreography by Jerome Robbins. Lighting by Jean Rosenthal. First presented by the New York City Ballet at the City Center, New York, June 2, 1953, with a cast headed by Yvonne Mounsey, Todd Bolender, Frank Hobi, and Michael Maule.

Fanfare, which had its first performance on Coronation Night 1953, is a visualization of *The Young Person's Guide to the Orchestra*, a well-known work by the contemporary English composer Benjamin Britten. Britten's score consists of variations and a fugue on a theme by Henry Purcell, from *Abdelazor*. These variations and the final fugue illustrate, one by one, the different musical instruments, or group of instruments, that make up the modern symphony orchestra. The ballet is a set of dances arranged to these variations and fugue. A narrator stands at the side of the stage to introduce the ballet and the different instruments.

When the curtain rises, all the dancers who will later represent the different instruments of the orchestra are gathered together on stage under heraldic flags that depict ancient instruments. As Purcell's theme is played by the orchestra, the dancers imitate by noble gestures and attitudes the solemn dignity and nobility of the music. The dancers' costumes differentiate by color the four families of the symphony orchestra: the woodwinds are dressed in blue, the strings in orange, the brass in yellow, and the percussion in black. Each dancer's costume is embellished with a design that identifies the instrument portrayed. Each wears a crown.

After the opening theme has been stated, all the dancers exit. Now the narrator introduces the instruments. First, the woodwinds. The variation of piccolo and two flutes is characterized by a *pas de trois,* danced by three girls. Next, the clarinets, who are represented by a *pas de deux* for a boy and a girl. A lone girl dances to the music of the oboe. She moves in slow, beautiful adagio to its music. Next, two boys dance comically to the variation for two bassoons.

The strings now take the stage. The first and second violins are represented by groups of girls. They are followed by a girl and a boy who dance to the music of the violas. Two girls depict the cellos, while a boy mimes and dances the difficulties of the double bass. Finally the harp, represented by a ballerina all in white, fills the eye with precise and flowing grace to tingling arpeggios.

Next the brass—horns, trumpets, tuba, and trombones—are depicted. Finally, the percussion—drums, cymbals, gongs, etc. The variation which these instruments play is represented by three boys who characterize by horseplay and wit the sudden booms, rattles, crashes, and slaps of the percussion instruments.

Now that all the instruments of the orchestra have been demonstrated, the narrator tells us: "We have taken the orchestra to pieces. It remains to put it back together again. We shall do this in the form of a fugue."

The first voice of the fugue is taken by the woodwinds, one by one; next come the different strings; then the brass; and, at the end, the percussion. The four great families of the orchestra mingle on stage, depicting by a massive dance the cumulative power of all the instruments. The original theme by Purcell is again sounded by the entire orchestra, and all the dancers accompany the music with triumphant, noble flourishes.

Fanfare was revived by the New York City Ballet January 15, 1976, at the New York State Theatre, Lincoln Center, New York.

FANTASIES

Music by Ralph Vaughan Williams. Choreography by John Clifford. Costumes by Robert O'Hearn. Lighting by Ronald Bates. First presented by the New York City Ballet at the New York State Theatre, Lincoln Center, January 23, 1969, with Kay Mazzo, Sara Leland, Conrad Ludlow, and Anthony Blum.

A dramatic dance ballet for two couples, *Fantasies* is about reality and the ideal—the real persons we meet and the imagined ideal we sometimes make them into. The music is Vaughan Williams' *Fantasia on a Theme by Thomas Tallis.*

The Chicago critic Thomas Willis said: "The ballet is at once tender and passionate, joyful and wistful, *Romeo and Juliet* in a skewed mirror."

Writing after its première, Clive Barnes said in the New York *Times* that the twenty-one-year-old John Clifford, "the City Ballet's wunderkind, produced his second work for the company and it fascinated . . . It is a very good piece . . . and reveals a choreographer of more than usual interest . . . Here he is concerned with choreography that combines Soviet-style partnering with a very Tudoresque awareness of the psychological motivation of movement. It is a good work, arresting and moving . . . It was a privilege to be there in the theatre when Mr. Clifford's future first became apparent."

FEAST OF ASHES

Music by Carlos Surinach. Choreography by Alvin Ailey. Costumes by Jack Venza. First presented by the Robert Joffrey Ballet at the Fashion Institute of Technology, New York, September 30, 1962, with Françoise Martinet, Lisa Bradley, and Paul Sutherland in leading roles.

This dramatic ballet is based on García Lorca's famous play *The House of Bernarda Alba*. The story, narrated in modern dance techniques, tells the tragic plight of a young girl, Adella, who tries to escape the fatal decisions of her matriarchal family. Her love for her elder sister's fiancé causes a family disaster.

The music for the ballet is Surinach's *Doppio Concertino* and part of his *Ritmo Jondo*. The choreographer has said that he chose these scores "because of their texture, rhythm, color, and dynamics in relation to the theme of the dance drama. Also because, like the work itself, they are a stylization of real Spanish themes—both secular and religious. I have tried in the texture of the movement to re-create, with stylized modern movements, the quality of Lorca's drama—to start as the playwright and actor do with the natural gesture and meaning and to extend these into the intense and telling emotional language of modern dance. I have tried to suggest and comment upon Lorca's view of his Spanish milieu rather than imitate it. I have also tried through this movement to universalize this drama of matriarchal domination. And, last of all, I have tried to remain as faithful as one can in a transposition of this sort to the great play upon which it is based."

Reviewing *Feast of Ashes* in the Washington *Post*, the critic Jean Battey found it "a stunning work of theatre . . . It is magnificently conceived, moving from the daughter's relationship to her mother and family to the inner torment of her lover . . . The dance idiom is strongly that of modern dance (no one is on point), with strong use of Spanish dance to underline the brooding Spanish mood."

LA FÊTE ÉTRANGE

Ballet in two scenes. Music by Gabriel Fauré selected by Ronald Crichton. Book by Ronald Crichton. Choreography by Andrée Howard. Scenery and costumes by Sophie Fedorovitch. First presented by the London Ballet at the Arts Theatre, London, May 23, 1940, with Frank Staff, Maude Lloyd, and David Paltenghi in the principal roles. First presented in the United States by the Royal Ballet at the Metropolitan Opera House, New York, with Donald MacLeary, Anya Linden, and Ronald Hynd in the principal roles.

Based on an episode in a chapter in Alain Fournier's novel *Le Grand Meaulnes, La Fête Étrange* is a ballet about "the tragedy of sensitive adolescence, symbolized not only by the sequence of events, but by the gradual though pronounced change of mood; anticipation leading through happiness to ecstasy, which in its turn fades into sadness and disillusion." These words by Ronald Crichton, whose idea the ballet was, reflect the narrative action, which shows an adventure a country boy has one winter day with the inhabitants of a strange château.

There he wanders early one morning and is fascinated to find a lovely young girl, who mistakes him for a moment for her fiancé, a young nobleman she has come out of the house to meet. She returns to the house, her fiancé arrives, and the boy is about to leave when he meets with guests on their way to the wedding at the château. He joins them and in the second scene, on the terrace of the château, he again meets the lovely young girl. She and all the guests are kind to him, and excited by their warmth and elegance, the boy is happier than he has ever been. But this cannot last. The fiancé, jealous of the bride's kindness to the boy, denounces her and leaves her. The boy is heartbroken and tries in vain to console the girl, who goes into the house alone. The boy leaves and goes back into the country.

Reassessing this ballet after many years, the critic James Monahan wrote in *The Dancing Times* that it was still a beautiful work because "it carries just the sort of 'story-line'—and no more—which a ballet can well support. Ballet is the lyric poetry among the dramatic arts; it is at its weakest when it tries to be most dramatic and at its strongest either when it relies most on 'pure' dance or when, like lyric poetry, it is evoking mood and atmosphere rather than telling a story. There is very little story in *La Fête Étrange;* it is all, or almost all, mood and atmosphere—wonderfully evoked by Fedorovitch and Fauré, gracefully sustained by Andrée Howard."

FÊTE NOIRE

Music by Dimitri Shostakovich. Choreography by Arthur Mitchell. Scenery and costumes by Bernard Johnson. Lighting by Fred Barry. Pianist: Craig Sheppard. Conducted by Isaiah Jackson. First presented by the Dance Theatre of Harlem.

When the Dance Theatre of Harlem presented *Fête Noire* at the Spoleto Festival in July, 1971, the critic William Weaver called the ballet "a kind of black version of *Graduation Ball,* danced with precision and brio," and so indeed it is. The music is the *Concerto No. 2 for Piano and Orchestra* by Shostakovich. The setting is a huge ballroom where, responsive to the developing themes and moods of the music, the dancers celebrate an important occasion that demands of them their very best.

FIELD FIGURES

Music by Karlheinz Stockhausen. Choreography by Glen Tetley. Scenery and costumes by Nadine Baylis. First presented by the Royal Ballet, November 9, 1970, at the Theatre Royal, Nottingham, England. First presented in the United States by the same ensemble at the Metropolitan Opera House, Lincoln Center, New York, May 22, 1972, with Deanne Bergsma, Rudolf Nureyev, Vergie Derman, Michael Coleman, Sandra Conley, Wayne Eagling, and Peter O'Brien.

A dramatic dance ballet, *Field Figures* is performed to two pieces of music by Karlheinz Stockhausen: *Setz die Segel zur Sonne* ("Set Sails for the Sun") and *Verbindung* ("Connection"). They consist of instrumental improvisations that are variously processed by electronic techniques at the time they are played.

The setting is an abstract one of vertical rods and there is about the piece a sense of the magnetic field—what happens when certain bodies in certain situations attract and repel, satisfy and frustrate. The three girls and the four boys in the ballet are variously paired but there is one principal couple.

Writing in *The Times* of London, the critic John Percival said: "There is nothing pretty about *Field Figures,* but it is, to my mind, extraordinarily beautiful."

Richard Buckle in the *Sunday Times* of London said that *Field Figures* "is one of the most important creations of our time." Writing in the *Financial Times,* Andrew Porter called it "one of the most perfectly shaped, impressive and enthralling works in the repertory."

LA FILLE MAL GARDÉE (The Unchaperoned Daughter)

Ballet in three scenes. Music by Ferdinand Hérold. Choreography by Jean Dauberval. First presented at Bordeaux, France, 1789, and at the Grand Theatre, Paris, July 1, 1789. First presented in the United States in various versions beginning in 1794. Revived by Ballet Theatre, with music by Wilhelm Hertel and choreography restaged by Bronislava Nijinska and Dimitri Romanoff, at the Center Theatre, New York, January 19, 1940, scenery and costumes by Serge Soudeikine.

Many people who go to the ballet and chance to come across a work that was originally presented more than a hundred and fifty years ago imagine that such a ballet must be sad—perhaps an antique tragedy. But *La Fille Mal Gardée* is a comedy. The earliest of all the ballets in the current repertory, its universally comical situations are no doubt responsible for its survival.

Soon after the music begins, a painted drop curtain depicts the principal characters of the ballet. On the left are Lisette and Colin, the two lovers. A rotund Cupid painted at the top of the scene directs a pointed arrow at the heroine. Lisette's mother, Madame Simone, dominates the scene, trying to watch her daughter and be pleasant to the suitor she has chosen for her. The story contained in this picture gradually unfolds as the drop curtain rises. The ballet is set in a small provincial French town. The time is about two hundred years ago.

SCENE ONE: THE FARM OF MADAME SIMONE   Alongside the steep-roofed house of Madame Simone, a "rich farmerette," is the family barnyard. In back, a rushing stream cascades down a hill. Madame Simone sits on a bench at the left, whiling away the time of day. Two neighbors join her to gossip. She bustles off with them.

The music suggests the arrival of the heroine, and Lisette enters on the left. Dressed in a light-blue skirt with a red bodice, with blue ribbons in her hair, she is the picture of innocent, country prettiness. The day has just begun, and because she is supposed to be busy at one task or another, Lisette pretends to arrange several flowerpots on the bench. She bows to several of the village boys, bound for the fields with their scythes, as she waters the flowers. Colin, a good-looking farmer, enters on the left, carrying a rake. He sits down on the bench, and Lisette, anxious to be surprised by his arrival, absent-mindedly waters his head. Colin jumps up, and he and Lisette immediately begin to dance together. Their dance reveals that the two have been attracted to each other for some time, that this is not their first rendezvous. Colin lifts Lisette boldly, yet gently.

The love duet is interrupted by Lisette's mother. Directly she approaches, the two lovers rush to hide behind the bench. Madame Simone discovers them, however, and chases Colin around the stage. Hastily he embraces Lisette and rushes off. Madame Simone, in a high temper, proceeds to lecture her daughter on her duty to make a proper marriage. Lisette protests that she is absolutely innocent of any flirtation, but her mother persists in her rage. The two neighbors come in to watch the scene. Lisette finally secures her mother's forgiveness by offering her, with a sweet smile, one of her own flowers.

Trumpets announce the arrival of four of Lisette's friends. They are followed by a group of villagers. The young people want Lisette to join them. Dutifully she asks her mother's permission and she begins to dance. Colin sneaks in at the back and conceals himself in the crowd. He runs out and takes Lisette's hand when her mother stalks off. The two dance a lively duet, surrounded by their friends. The music is gay and sparkling. The conviviality is short-lived, however, for Madame Simone returns, sees Colin, and sends him packing. She makes a point of her daughter's idleness by presenting scythes to her four friends.

Lisette attempts to console herself by dancing with her friends as they celebrate the harvesttime. She tries to leave with them when they go, but her mother pulls her back. Lisette herself is now in a temper. She stomps, shakes her fists pathetically, cries, and hides her face in her hands. Her mother takes her hands away and tries to make amends. Colin has entered quietly and stands in back of Madame Simone. That is consolation enough for Lisette. She waves to him. Her mother notes the gesture, but cannot find a reason for it. Colin does not conceal himself for long, however. The impetuous girl rushes to him. They embrace briefly before Madame Simone leaps at them to drag Lisette back toward the house.

She sits her daughter down on the bench. Lisette rises and brings out a butter churn. Her mother fills the churn with cream and orders her daughter to work. Lisette churns away, and her mother leaves the scene. Colin leaps in behind Lisette. He places his hands on hers and easily persuades her to stop her work. He sits down on the bench beside her; Lisette, suddenly embarrassed at being alone with her lover, rises and dances. She turns softly and slowly, beguiling Colin with her sweet motion. When she finishes her dance with a series of rapid turns, Colin throws out to her a long blue ribbon. Lisette catches it and, holding the flowing ribbon above their heads, the two dance together romantically. Lisette tosses the ribbon back to Colin, who fixes it halter-fashion around her shoulders, after which the girl performs her steps as if by his command. Lisette pirouettes into his arms, Colin ties the ribbon about her, and the girl poses against her lover. The two then leave the stage.

Thomas, a vinegrower, enters with his son, Alain. Come to see Madame Simone by appointment, the obese Thomas is decked out in a bright-green suit; he is determined to be formal and correct. His son, determined to be playful and completely oblivious to his surroundings, leaps about the stage trying to catch butterflies in a net. Thomas reprimands him and pulls him to a bench.

Madame Simone, dressed in her best purple, arrives to greet the guests. With ceremonious gestures, she and Thomas discuss the suitability of a marriage between their children. Madame Simone is readily persuaded of Alain's eligibility when Thomas dangles a bag of gold in her face. The woman approaches to examine the young man, ascertains that he is sound of limb if not of mind, and gives her approval. She drags Lisette out to meet her fiancé. Dutifully the girl has changed her clothes for the occasion, but she has no idea of its real meaning. Both parents push their children toward each other. Both children step back in horror as they realize the meaning of their parents' interview. Each tries to escape, but the parents hold them secure. The curtain falls as they both kneel, their faces turned away from each other. Lisette's white dress and pink ribbons are for the wrong man. Madame Simone stands over them in an attitude of supreme happiness. During the scene change, Thomas and Madame Simone, accompanied by the neighbors, drag the engaged couple off to the village notary to make the marriage settlement final.

SCENE TWO: THE VILLAGE GREEN　On the painted backdrop, wheat fields are
seen in the distance. Sheaves of freshly cut wheat are propped up where the
workers have left them. A windmill stands over the fields on a hill at the back.
On the right is a great tree; two cows meditate nearby. The workers of the
village, colorfully dressed girls and their companions, pause for a general
dance. Lisette and Alain are pushed into the scene by their parents. Despite
all their complaining, the two are made to stand close together. They are able
to separate only when Thomas asks Madame Simone to dance. The aged couple cavort grotesquely about the green; it has suddenly occurred to Madame
Simone that she, too, might be quite a match, and she flirts with the vinegrower.

Meanwhile Colin has entered quietly on the right. He sees that his sweetheart has been promised to another and turns away. Madame Simone and
Thomas race off to pursue their flirtation elsewhere, and some of Lisette's
friends, noticing Colin's plight, encourage the girl to comfort the poor lad.
Lisette touches his arm. By her soft, endearing gestures the girl convinces him
that she herself has had nothing to do with the proposed match. Colin puts his
arms about her, and their foreheads touch. He kneels, and the two begin an
adagio to the melody of solo strings and an accompanying harp. The villagers
sit on the ground to watch the lovers. Lisette leaves the scene after the dance
is over, and Colin performs a bright, dazzling variation. Lisette returns for a
winsome, engaging dance in which she lifts her skirt softly, with innocent
coquetry. Her variation increases in momentum; at the end she turns brilliantly and cuts her movement off suddenly with a swift, pert pose.

Alain, who has been off chasing after butterflies, runs onto the scene, brandishing his net before him. He circles the stage in long, high leaps. Two of the
girls try to engage his attention. The youth ignores their flattery, but the girls
persist and dance on either side of him. Alain abandons them, jumping off into
the wings in pursuit of his hobby.

Thunder is heard and the scene darkens; lightning flashes illumine the hurried dashing back and forth of the villagers. Lisette and Colin follow as their
friends run for cover. Alain rushes in, trembling with fright at the lightning.
He hides his head under a girl's skirts and pushes her off toward safety. The
drop curtain falls.

SCENE THREE: MADAME SIMONE'S HOUSE　Lisette enters quickly to escape the
storm. Her mother follows and bustles about the room. Lisette pours coffee for
her, then sits at her feet as Madame Simone begins to work at her spinning
wheel. Lisette tries to sneak away, but her mother orders her to read a book
she gives her. Lisette looks at a page or two, then asks her mother the meaning
of one of the words. Madame Simone is horrified: she has given her daughter
the wrong book! A romantic novel, no less! The girl succeeds in crawling away
a few feet until Madame Simone seizes her from behind and draws her back to
her chair. She takes up her sewing again.

Colin opens the transom above the door and throws in a flower to Lisette.

Lisette turns around and sees him. Immediately her mother senses her agitation and commands her to be still. Colin, by passionate signs, beseeches her to dance for him. The girl persuades her mother to play the tambourine so that she can practice her dancing. Lisette dances flirtatiously for Colin's benefit. The old woman tires of the tambourine and falls off to sleep. Lisette approaches her on tiptoe. As the girl takes her key, her mother wakens and beats the tambourine. Lisette continues her dance, and at its conclusion Madame Simone kisses her in reward.

Boys and girls of the village enter, bringing with them sheaves of wheat, which they stack against a table. Lisette would like to follow them off, but her mother commands her to take her turn at the spinning wheel. Lisette stamps her foot and throws herself down in the chair to sulk. Her mother leaves the room.

The orchestra repeats the melody to which she and Colin danced so happily, and Lisette imagines what it would be like to be married to the man of her own choice. She puts her hands on her heart and blows a kiss toward the door. She sees herself surrounded by Colin's children, whom she scolds; she rocks her arms as if they held a child.

To Lisette's embarrassment, Colin is there in the room watching her. The sheaves of wheat are thrown aside, and her lover sits smiling at her. She sits beside him for a moment, then jumps up as he proposes to her seriously. Colin pleads with her—after all, she has just imagined herself as his wife—but the girl in her embarrassment and confusion denies her love and shoves the boy toward the door. Colin begins to lose his temper at her stubbornness and is delighted to find her even more flustered when she finds that the door is locked!

Lisette runs to the chair and sees that she can keep up the pretense no longer. Colin kneels at her feet and places his head in her lap. The two trade their scarves as a pledge of their love. Madame Simone can be heard approaching. Lisette tries to hide Colin—under the little table, in a small chest. In desperation, she pushes him into the hayloft and slams the door shut just as her mother enters.

Lisette thinks she is safe but she has forgotten Colin's scarf. Madame Simone spots it instantly and fetches a large switch to beat the girl. Lisette runs, but the old woman catches up with her, spanks her soundly, and, as an additional penalty, locks her in the hayloft!

Visitors are heard outside. Madame Simone admits Thomas and Alain, the village notary and his secretary following in their wake. Villagers accompany them to witness the marriage contract. The notary buries his face in his registry, the parents rejoice, and the preoccupied Alain toys with the spinning wheel. Madame Simone presents him with the key to the hayloft and tells the youth where to find his bride. Alain unlocks the door. Lisette and Colin step out sheepishly, their clothes and hair covered with hay.

Madame Simone is scandalized. Before all the village, her daughter has ruined the family's reputation. Lisette begs her to understand. Colin joins Lisette, and both lovers kneel before her. At first Madame Simone refuses to listen. Then she realizes that the notary can quite easily make another marriage contract and consents. Lisette kisses her joyfully. Colin kisses her. The two lovers kiss, and Madame Simone embraces them both.

Ballet in two acts. Music by Ferdinand Hérold, freely adapted and arranged by John Lanchbery. Choreography by Frederick Ashton. Scenery and costumes by Osbert Lancaster. First presented by the Royal Ballet at the Royal Opera House, Covent Garden, January 28, 1960, with Nadia Nerina, David Blair, Stanley Holden, and Alexander Grant in the principal roles. First presented in the United States by the Royal Ballet at the Metropolitan Opera House, New York, September 14, 1960, with the same principals.

Although other versions of the ballet are often danced, Frederick Ashton's re-creation of *La Fille Mal Gardée* is now permanent in the modern repertory. In 1960 Tamara Karsavina, the ballerina who danced in the ballet in Russia, recalled an earlier production in the Covent Garden program: "This production we now regard as the turning point in the history of ballet; a break-away from the formal, pseudoclassical tradition; a ballet of action instead of a succession of conventional dances which use the plot as a peg on which to hang a succession of *entrées, pas seuls, pas d'ensemble* . . . The story lends itself admirably to ballet treatment; there is not a dance in it that does not flow directly out of a natural situation. It is a charming period piece singularly compatible with the artistic trends of today . . ."

The music for the ballet, entirely restudied and arranged by John Lanchbery after consulting varied scores for the ballet by Hertel, Feldt, and others, is based on the 1828 score of Ferdinand Hérold, then chorus master of the Paris Opéra. After a pleasant overture, the curtain rises. An inner drop curtain depicts a charming rural landscape with a village in the distance. Arnold Haskell in the Covent Garden program describes the action when this inner curtain rises:

ACT ONE, SCENE ONE: THE FARMYARD "Lise, the only daughter of Simone, a widow and owner of a prosperous farm, is in love with Colas, a young farmer, but her mother has more ambitious plans.

"The dawn of a busy day on the farm is heralded by the cock and his attendant hens. Lise, disappointed at not seeing Colas, leaves a ribbon tied in a lover's knot, as a token of her devotion. He finds it and ties it to his staff. The lovers meet, but are interrupted by Simone, who sets her daughter a task of churning butter. Colas, in hiding in the loft, joins her. The work is shared and then forgotten as they declare their love.

"The farm girls summon Lise to play, but her mind is elsewhere. Her suspi-

cious and ever-watchful mother catches hold of her and chastises her. Just
then Thomas, the prosperous and wealthy proprietor of a vineyard, arrives
with his son Alain. Simone, aware of their mission, dismisses Lise. Thomas asks
her hand for his son, and when Lise returns, Alain, coy and clumsy, shows off
his paces. She is amused and a little shocked by his antics, but definitely not
interested. They set off for the harvest.

ACT ONE, SCENE TWO: THE CORNFIELD   "It is harvest time, and after working in the fields the harvesters, led by Colas, relax in a joyful dance. Lise and
Alain dance, but Colas intervenes, and the young girl makes it clear where her
preference lies. One of the harvesters plays the flute to the general merriment,
and Alain thinks he will have a turn, but the harvesters mock him and he is
rescued from their horseplay by his indignant father.

"The field is now left for the triumphant Colas, who dances with Lise.
Simone joins in the merriment. But suddenly they are interrupted by a storm
that drenches them, scattering them far and wide.

ACT TWO: INTERIOR OF THE FARM   "Mother and daughter, soaked by the
storm, return to the farmhouse. They sit down to spin: work, thinks the
mother, should keep Lise out of mischief. But she is overcome by sleep and
Lise, who has seen Colas through the gate, tries to take the key from her.
Simone awakes and, in order to remain watchful, plays the tambourine for
Lise to dance. But the tap grows feebler, she begins to nod, and now she is
fast asleep. Lise runs to the door and makes love to Colas through the
unfriendly bars. The knocking of the harvesters, coming for their pay, awakens
Simone. Colas enters with them and conceals himself in a pile of straw. Simone
tells her daughter to get on with her chores as she leaves to give the harvesters
a drink. Lise, thinking she is alone, dreams of the delights of married life.
Colas cannot resist, and comes out from hiding. She is bashful at first having
been taken by surprise, but once again they declare their love, exchanging
scarves as a token.

"As Simone reappears, Lise hustles Colas into her bedroom. The ever-
suspicious mother realizes that the lovers have been meeting, and in her turn
hustles Lise into the bedroom, locking the door.

"Alain and his father now arrive with a notary to complete the marriage
contract. When it is signed, Simone hands Alain the key to the bedroom. After
a moment of idiotic indecision, he opens the door, and to everyone's dismay,
Colas and Lise emerge. The lovers fall on their knees to ask Simone for forgiveness and a blessing. In spite of the fury of Thomas and Alain, urged on by
the notary and the villagers, she finally gives in amidst general rejoicing."

NOTES   Andrew Porter, music and dance critic of *The Financial Times*,
London, has said of this ballet: "The first act, in two parts, lasts just over an
hour; the second, thirty-six minutes. There is not an ounce of padding. Inven-

tion tumbles on invention, and the whole thing is fully realized in dance. The second act, in fact, is continuous, *durchkomponiert;* there is no possible break for applause except between the sections of the *grand pas de deux* just before the final gigue. The choreography is wonderfully fresh, and the shape of the scenes is beautifully balanced.

"There is comedy, sentiment, jollity, romance, flowing one into another. There is a clog dance for Widow Simone, brilliantly sustained; a 'parade' before the drop curtain which must be the most delightful of its kind ever done; a *valse des moissoneurs* in the first act which one would like to be twice as long; a stave dance; breathtaking 'Russian' lifts; passages which seem to be inspired by the virtuosity of the Georgians.

"Ribbons run like a motif through the first two scenes. They are used in a score of ingenious and beautiful ways, reaching their climax in a great maypole where the fleeting kaleidoscope of stage patterns is recorded by the plaited thread.

"To a far greater extent than any of the classics as we now know them, *La Fille Mal Gardée* seems to be all 'highlights,' without any of the stretches that we sit through for the sake of the best bits. And this cunningly varied and ceaseless flow of dance is constantly enlivened by the most brilliant inventions by the way, comic or touching, that give fullness to the ballet—far more of them than can be taken in at once."

Interviewed by the critic Don McDonagh in *Ballet Review* (Vol. 3, No. 4), Frederick Ashton observed that *La Fille Mal Gardée* is a really English work. "It has the Lancashire clog dance which is almost like a folk dance. *Fille* came about in a very odd way because of Karsavina. She was always after me to do it. I didn't particularly like the idea and I didn't like the music to the traditional version, by Hertel. I went back to Hérold, who did it originally . . . It was mostly a matter of selecting and curtailing. I always work out the structure of a ballet before I start—who's doing what and for how long. I don't do any steps until I'm with the dancers. The structure for *Fille* I worked out with John Lanchbery, marking the music. I have a great instinct for the right length of things. And I set that very tightly. It's a kind of minutage. And after I set that, in the case of *Fille* at least, it went very easily. Everything just flowed."

Readers are referred to David Vaughan's *Frederick Ashton and His Ballets* for more details on the genesis of *Fille Mal Gardée*. Vaughan has written in *Ballet Review* about Ashton and this ballet:

"He is a great comic choreographer. *La Fille Mal Gardée* is a perfect expression of his artistic benevolence. The dramatic complications are ingenious and of great concern to the characters involved. Yet the problems can be solved, the mistakes can be mended and the mistaken forgiven. As in Molière, all balance which can be attained is attained (the lovers marry) and any remaining sources of imbalance are neutralized (Molière's hypochondriac becomes a doctor himself, Ashton's Alain goes off with his umbrella).

"Each set of characters has its distinct style. The young lovers dance in a now playful, now softly melting classicism. The farmers' choreography combines classicism with folk dance borrowings to suggest the union of man with nature and a love of meaningful work. Simone, Thomas, and Alain derive from farce, pantomime, and music-hall. The dancing chickens, which some ballet-goers find annoyingly "unrealistic," may be there to be deliberately artificial, to emphasize right from the start that this ballet, however homely its subject, is not photographic naturalism, but instead uses the exaggerations of comedy to point to certain human truths."[*]

FILLING STATION

Ballet-document in one act. Music by Virgil Thomson. Choreography by Lew Christensen. Book by Lincoln Kirstein. Scenery and costumes by Paul Cadmus. First presented by Ballet Caravan at the Avery Memorial Theatre, Hartford, Connecticut, January 6, 1938, with Lew Christensen, Marie-Jeanne, Erick Hawkins, Michael Kidd, Todd Bolender, Eugene Loring, and Fred Danieli in the principal roles.

Filling Station is not only one of the first modern ballets on a familiar American subject, but one of the first ballets to employ American music, scenery, and costumes by an American, and American dancers. It was the first ballet on an American subject commissioned by Lincoln Kirstein for his Ballet Caravan, a small American company founded in 1936 which, with the Balanchine-Kirstein American Ballet, was to be the precursor of the present New York City Ballet.

Filling Station is an attempt to discover an American hero, a hero equivalent to the heroes of classical European ballets. The makers of the ballet have chosen a filling station attendant as their hero. The fact that the ballet succeeded in its aim was recently demonstrated by the marked success of its revival, which clearly indicated that the popular American myth of 1938 was still viable fifteen years later.

After a robust overture, the curtain rises on the interior of Mac's filling station. It is night. A neon sign advertising gas is seen in reverse against the large plate-glass window on the left. In the rear, there is a door leading to the station rest room.

Mac, the station attendant, is whiling away the lonely hours of the night reading a tabloid. He puts down the paper and begins to dance. He moves about the stage with vigorous leaps and turns. His dance is interrupted by a motorist who comes into the station to ask for directions. The motorist is dressed like a golfer in a comic strip: he wears violently colored checkered knickers, straw hat, and smokes a cigar.

Mac tries to direct him to his destination by pointing out the route on a

[*] Reprinted by permission of *Ballet Review,* Marcel Dekker, publisher.

map. When the motorist fails to understand, Mac produces a huge enlargement of the map to set him right. Behind this map, two truck drivers, friends
of Mac, sneak into the station while Mac gives the motorist final directions.

As soon as the motorist departs, the two truck drivers greet Mac and the
three men dance an athletic *pas de trois* that features cartwheels and somersaults. Their good fellowship is cut short by the arrival of a state trooper, who
accuses the truck drivers of speeding. The men deny this, and the state trooper
leaves after warning them severely.

The motorist in knickers returns, this time with his family and his golf gear.
His wife, a huge blonde in unbecoming slacks, towers over her husband and
constantly berates him. Their daughter, a constantly whining child, is clearly
in need of the rest room. While his wife and daughter disappear into the rear
of the station, the motorist entertains Mac and the truck drivers by practicing
golf. He is not happy for long, however. When wife and daughter return, they
combine to make life so miserable for him that he happily leads them back to
their car outside.

Now an intoxicated young couple drop by on their way home from a party
at the local country club. The girl stumbles in first, followed by her escort. She
is in no condition to dance, but insists on doing so. The boy supports her in
adagio poses, holding the girl's almost limp body upright when she collapses in
his arms.

As the couple finish this comic adagio, they are joined by Mac and the truck
drivers. By this time, the girl wants to dance with everybody. All the men join
her in a dance that is climaxed as she is tossed from one man to another and
thrown high into the air. When the unhappy motorist, who has momentarily
escaped from his wife and child, re-enters the station, the dance is at fever
pitch. Noting the newcomer, the girl jumps into his arms just as his wife comes
in after him.

The motorist tries to stay on the opposite side of the stage from his wife as
all join in the "Big Apple." But the celebration is soon broken up. A gangster
enters. He lines all the people up and instructs them to place all their jewelry
and cash in a bag he snatches from the motorist's wife. Everyone conforms to
his wish except Mac, who sneaks outside and turns out the lights.

Directly the lights go out, the stage is in confusion. Mac enters with a
flashlight, and soon the stage is filled with the beams of flashlights carried by
the others as they try to help Mac track down the gangster. Blinded by their
lights, the gangster shoots.

When the lights come up, it can be seen that the girl from the country club
is dead. All gather around her body. The state trooper enters and takes the
gangster off to prison. The girl's body is lifted high and carried off in solemn
procession. Just as the ballet seems about to end in a tragedy, the girl wakes
from the dead and waves at Mac as her cortege moves out of the station. Mac
saunters about for a moment, then returns to his newspaper.

NOTES *Filling Station* was revived by the New York City Ballet on May 12, 1953, at the City Center, New York. Jacques d'Amboise, Janet Reed, and Michael Maule danced the principal roles.

FIREBIRD

Dramatic ballet in three scenes. Music by Igor Stravinsky. Choreography by Michel Fokine. Scenery and costumes by Golovine and Bakst. First presented by Diaghilev's Ballets Russes at the Théâtre National de l'Opéra, Paris, June 25, 1910, with Tamara Karsavina as the Firebird, *Michel Fokine as* Prince Ivan, *and Enrico Cecchetti as* Kastchei.

Firebird marks Igor Stravinsky's entry into the field of ballet music. Perhaps his most famous score, the original ballet to the music remained dormant for many years. In 1954, to commemorate the twenty-fifth anniversary of the death of Diaghilev, under whose auspices the original had been created, the Royal Ballet produced in London a reconstruction of the original, with scenery and costumes by Natalie Gontcharova. This was made possible by Serge Grigoriev, Diaghilev's régisseur for many years, Lubov Tchernicheva, and Tamara Karsavina. The revival was first presented at the Empire Theatre, Edinburgh, August 23, 1954, with Margot Fonteyn as the *Firebird,* Michael Somes as *Prince Ivan,* Svetlana Beriosova as the *Tsarevna,* and Frederick Ashton as *Kastchei.* This production was first given in the United States at the Metropolitan Opera House, September 20, 1955, with the same principals.

Fokine has described in his book *Memoirs of a Ballet Master* how he envisaged the action of the ballet, and the background to the collaboration that produced the final work. In the Royal Ballet revival, the curtain rises on the enchanted garden of the sinister Kastchei. A high golden fence protects his golden fruit and the lovely princesses he has captured. The Firebird now appears, followed by Prince Ivan. The Firebird attempts to steal the golden apples from Kastchei's magic tree but Ivan captures her. He vows that he will not let her go unless she gives him one of her feathers. With her feather as talisman, he is assured of her magic intercession if he should ever need it. The Firebird yields to his entreaties and leaves.

Now in the growing darkness Ivan learns from the most beautiful of the captive maidens held prisoner by Kastchei how the evil magician entraps innocent travelers and turns them into stone. Ivan is attracted to the lovely creature who tells him this strange story and they dance. At dawn they kiss and part, the girl warning him not to follow her.

Ivan does not heed the warning. Following after his beloved, he opens the gate to Kastchei's magic garden and alarms sound, bells peal, and swarms of monsters rush out. Kastchei emerges, his enslaved creatures do him homage, and he approaches Ivan menacingly. The wicked magician tries to turn him to stone but just then Ivan remembers the Firebird's feather. He waves the feather in Kastchei's face and the Firebird instantly reappears. She compels Kastchei's monsters to dance until they collapse. Then, remembering the great egg that holds the soul of the magician, she orders Ivan to steal it. Finding it, Ivan throws the egg into the air. As it falls and breaks, Kastchei dies. Ivan then is free to marry his princess. All at the ceremony rejoice. The Firebird flies away forever.

Music by Igor Stravinsky. Choreography by George Balanchine. Setting by Marc Chagall. Lighting by Jean Rosenthal. First presented by the New York City Ballet at the City Center, New York, November 27, 1949, with Maria Tallchief as the Firebird and Francisco Moncion as Prince Ivan.

The composer of *Firebird*, Igor Stravinsky, once said that Russian legends have as their heroes men who are "simple, naïve, sometimes even stupid, devoid of all malice, and it is they who are always victorious over characters that are clever, artful, complex, cruel and powerful." Prince Ivan in this ballet is such a hero: he is a simple hunter who stumbles into the eerie garden of an evil monster, there falls in love with a beautiful princess held captive by the ogre, and rescues her with a supernatural power granted him by a magical bird of fire.

SCENE ONE: A FOREST As the music to the ballet begins, we have that first suggestion of the mystery and magic that will control Ivan's destiny. No sooner has the orchestra—with its low, throbbing strings and baleful trombones—given us a hint of darkness and foreboding, than the curtain rises to present us with an enormous painting of the ballet's heroine, the Firebird who will help the prince to free the world of one of its monstrous evils. The Firebird is depicted as bright, glorious, and triumphant—a fantastic creature, half bird, half woman. She has the face and arms of a charming young girl and a body of shimmering feathers that tapers off in orange-speckled flame. This colorful figure is painted against a background of amorphous, purple shapes. The music now suggests unimagined giants plodding across the earth and a fairyland peopled with primeval beings sadly singing an accompaniment.

Now the painted curtain rises. It is dark, and as the stage brightens slightly, we can see in the background trees so thickly crowded that the sun can scarcely penetrate. Here in the forest we are transported visually to the world of fantasy at which the music has hinted, and when the prince enters, his bow stretched tightly, ready to destroy any creature concealed in the thicket, we understand why he hunts with care. Ivan wears a costume more becoming to an untutored Russian peasant than to a royal prince, but this serves only to remind us that we are watching a story of a time before the primitive court of the Tsar was altered by European opulence.

Subdued, half-uttered cries come from behind the dark trees. Ivan looks about him, searching for the beasts that may lie waiting in the shadows, when a low, steady drum, followed by an answering horn, indicates that he is about to meet his prey. Suddenly the music whirs rapidly and brightly and from above a bright amber light races around and around the prince. Ivan, almost blinded, throws up his arms in astonishment and tries to avoid the shadow the light makes of his startled figure. He runs off, seeking the safe darkness. The music increases its speed, and on stage to its swift accompaniment dances the dazzling Firebird.

Her entrance is as strong and brilliant as the bright red she wears. As she crosses the stage in a series of swiftly executed leaps and poses, followed by that same amber light which announced her arrival, glints of light catch her figure in various attitudes to reveal the long red feather that rises high on her head. Her arms and shoulders are speckled with gold dust, and the shimmering red bodice reflects spangles of brilliance about her moving form. She dances frantically, in continuous movement, to music that mirrors her great joy in displaying vivid images of flight. Even here, in the secluded forest, the Firebird refuses to be earth-bound and seems to resist nature by performing dashing movements that whip the very air about her.

The prince emerges from the shadows to watch unseen. Wishing to capture this creature who moves so magnificently, he reacts with wonder as he discovers that this marvelous bird is also a ravishing woman. He follows her surreptitiously while the Firebird, unaware of the hunter who pursues her, darts about the stage climaxing her solo with rapid turns on point across the stage. This movement increases in momentum with the music, and just as her accelerating spin reaches its fullest force and the music its highest pitch, Ivan dashes forward and reaches out to catch the Firebird about the waist. Brought down to earth, she freezes at his touch, all movement ceasing. Slowly she backs away, in terror of the hunter, in modesty at sight of the man. She turns to escape, but Ivan, fascinated at her daring now that she is in his power, holds her secure. The Firebird, rigid with fear, her arms stiff across her body, falls back against him reluctantly, apparently resigned, but now her arms fly out and beat the air in a frantic effort to free herself.

Ivan will not release his prey, and the frightened Firebird, certain of death by his hand, pleads for mercy. The prince is moved to pity by this appeal for freedom and gently loosens his grasp. He holds out his arm, and the Firebird, in extended arabesque, falls across it, bending her head so that her headdress almost touches the floor at the prince's feet as she bows in tribute to his pity and courtesy.

Encouraged now by the prince's tenderness, the Firebird moves back to dance again. When she turns full circle, Ivan comes forward to support her. Moved by his compassionate strength, as Ivan is moved by her unclaimed love, the Firebird walks toward this man so strange to her. He holds her hand high, then she runs toward him, her body falling back full-length in mid-air. Ivan

catches her swooping body and supports her again, as she repeats this movement of ultimate sacrifice and trust. Assured of his sympathy, the Firebird now
dances with the prince.

Standing behind her, Ivan supports her arms with his own as the Firebird,
standing on point, bends her knees to the floor, then rises to his embrace. Legs
spread wide, she slides across the stage as Ivan holds her. The haunting melody of their *pas de deux* soars to its height as the Firebird is held motionless
on point, her right leg extended in stillness. Then she falls back, and Ivan
swings her around and around in great circles as her free arm flutters in flight.
Reminded by this of her greater freedom in the air, the Firebird moves as if to
leave the prince. He bows to her formally in homage, and in gratitude for his
generosity in releasing her, the Firebird takes from her breast a brilliant red
feather. She indicates to the prince that this feather is a magic charm: he need
only wave it in the air and she will come to his aid, should he ever require it.
Ivan, in respectful deference to the truly supernatural being he now understands the Firebird to be, thanks her and watches regretfully as she turns and
leaps gloriously into the wings. The prince follows, transfixed as the music
ends in enchanted serenity.

SCENE TWO: KASTCHEI'S GARDEN   While Ivan remains in the shadows, marveling at his encounter with the Firebird, we hear a gay melody from the orchestra. Ten young princesses run in, happily dancing to its tune. They wear
long peasant dresses with little caps, and their innocent, carefree gambols
make it impossible for us to believe that they are, in reality, captives of the
monster Kastchei who rules over the forest. Two of the young girls carry
scarves and, as the group dances with simple but elegant grace, these two
playfully direct the dancing of the others. They are all dancing together when
Prince Ivan startles them. Shocked at the intrusion of a stranger in their dangerous world, the princesses gather together and whisper excitedly. Ivan is
amused at their fear and approaches them. From a respectful distance, in
mock seriousness and formality, he beckons one of the maidens to come to
him. The princesses are agitated by this request and wonder at Ivan's audacity. Ivan insists, and one of the girls at last leaves the group. Ivan bows to her,
then whispers softly in her ear. The girl is shocked by what he says to her and
runs back to tell her friends. The maidens confer, and then the most beautiful
one of them all, in sweet and nervous modesty, steps forward to greet the
prince.

The two bow formally and, linking hands, lead the group in a *khorovod* or
Russian round dance, to the accompaniment of folklike themes. The chorus of
girls become so entwined about their two leaders that it is impossible for the
prince and the princess to remain long together. They close their arms about
one another, but their partners come amusingly to break their embrace. The
two lovers dance with their friends until the light begins to fade. A trumpet is
heard in the distance, and the girls gather together quickly in fear. The prin-

cess then hastily bids Ivan farewell and runs off with her companions. Ivan stands alone, bewildered at their behavior, as the music takes on mysterious darkness and hints of things unseen.

Ivan stares into the dark thicket about him and is suddenly afraid, but before he can leave the threatening darkness that seems to close in on him, a sharp crash of sound comes from the orchestra and dozens of weird monsters leap with a single bound into the stage and surround him. Green, brown, and multicolored creatures with hideous features and maimed limbs cavort about Ivan to fierce, militant beats from the orchestra. The monsters—some masked with the head of animals—divide into four groups and race backward and forward and sideways, each group trying to outdo the others in grotesque gestures of threat. One of the creatures is held upright, then thrown straight up into the air and caught by the others, only to be tossed up again. The music subsides, and all the creatures of this fantastic underworld fall on their faces as their master, Kastchei, enters menacingly. He is surrounded by the princess and her friends. Kastchei flourishes his dark cap at his creatures, and we glimpse his skeletonlike body. On his head he wears a spiked crown of burning gold. His fingernails, long as his hands, clutch at the air for victims to satisfy an insatiable appetite.

As Kastchei's slaves surround him in frantic attitudes of homage, Ivan moves to flee. But then he remembers the pledge of the Firebird, remembers that he need fear no danger, and brings out the magic feather. He runs, weaving in and out among the monsters, waving the charm in the air. The monsters try to close in on him. Kastchei stamps the earth in indignation and vows to kill the prince. To the theme to which they danced so playfully just a few moments before, the princesses encircle their evil lord and plead for mercy for Ivan. Kastchei dismisses them with curt disgust, but the prince, encouraged by the confusion he is causing among the monsters, races about with the brilliant red feather. The ogres step back, astounded at his fearlessness in the presence of the all-powerful Kastchei. Enormous snarls from the orchestra follow the prince as he provokes the demons to madness. Kastchei moves in to attack. Then a quick whir in the music proclaims the imminent arrival of the Firebird, come to Ivan's rescue.

The Firebird runs onto the scene with a magnificent leap, carrying over her head a naked golden sword. She hurriedly presents the sword to Ivan, then circles the stage in so rapid and fierce a spin that all the monsters are set to twirling with her. She exits quickly as Ivan falls upon Kastchei with the golden sword. The monster falls dead and Ivan, bathed now in the Firebird's brilliant light, holds the gleaming sword high in triumph as the music sounds his victory in a final crescendo.

The stage is dark. The prince stands alone among the fallen bodies of the monsters. The Firebird approaches. Harp strings are plucked gently. The prince finds the princess; he helps her rise. Both bow low before the beautiful

Firebird, thanking her for saving their lives. The princess' friends rise and do obeisance before the magical bird, and the Firebird bows to them in return.

Free now of mortals, the Firebird dances alone. The stage is completely dark save for the light that follows her. She rises on point, extends one leg straight out, and whips the air in daring turns. The Firebird now revives the fallen monsters. She gestures over them as the harp sounds swooping arpeggios and consigns them to an endless sleep. The orchestra plays softly a flowing lullaby. The mysterious eerie forest of Ivan's adventure becomes serene as she sets all at peace with graceful, birdlike movement. Her mission over, the Firebird moves across the stage in a flowing dance, now turning, now stepping softly. Her feet tremble to release her body back into the air. Compelled to leave the earth, she moves away, her body thrown back. The last we see of her is her golden hand fluttering against the dark curtain at the side of the stage. The scene blacks out.

SCENE THREE: THE COURT OF PRINCE IVAN   The music begins a quiet, subdued statement of an ancient Russian folk song. The melody that seems simple at first is changed gradually into a majestic song of thanksgiving. The music mounts in dignity and volume as light slowly comes up to show us a blue-green drop curtain. On this curtain are represented all those figures in fairyland who never will have any trouble in living happily ever after. Now that the music has asserted itself fully in praise and gratitude, we see two guards enter. They stand at attention in front of the curtain. The stage is fully lighted. Courtiers enter and bow to each other with each mighty chord from the orchestra, then join hands with the princesses who trip in to meet them. Now the drop curtain rises. Before another curtain of magical deep red, Ivan and his princess stand together. Pages enter with royal standards. A crimson carpet is pulled down the center of the stage, and onto it step Prince Ivan and his bride, in regal costume. All pay homage to the royal couple, and a page comes running out to present to the prince and princess a great wedding cake, aglow with hundreds of candles. The curtain falls as he kneels before them with his gift.

NOTES   The New York City Ballet production of Firebird has been revised over the years, like all ballets of any interest, and most importantly perhaps by Jerome Robbins and me at the New York State Theatre, May 28, 1970. Marc Chagall had wanted for some time to do new designs for the costumes and to make other changes. The new Firebird was an attempt, in fact, to present Chagall's paintings in action, with Stravinsky's accompaniment. This provided an opportunity to make changes, too, in the choreography. Jerome Robbins and I shared the work, he taking responsibility for the scenes involving large ensembles. Gelsey Kirkland, Jacques d'Amboise, and Gloria Govrin were the principal dancers in this revival. Barbara Karinska's costumes to Chagall's designs were acknowledged masterpieces of art and craft, like all her marvel-

York, April 30, 1969, with Birgit Keil and Richard Cragun in the principal roles.

A program note by Franz Willnauer reminds us that "genuine ballet art—like all genuine art—is ambiguous. It can be interpreted in many ways—from the stylized order of movements to the code of an incarnate calligraphy, to the symbolic dance drama of the human couple whose love and life are destroyed by the angel of death."

Set to Webern's *Passacaglia*, Op. 1, the ballet shows a life cycle in dance. A man is born. Curled up at first, he extends, is released, dances, finds a girl who comes down from above. They dance an impassioned *pas de deux* and then they are surrounded by a threatening group. Though they rejoin briefly, the girl is soon carried aloft. He reaches up for her but cannot reach her and, in despair, curls up on the ground, as at his beginning.

ORPHEUS

Ballet in three scenes. Music by Igor Stravinsky. Choreography by George Balanchine. Scenery and costumes by Isamu Noguchi. Lighting by Jean Rosenthal. First presented by Ballet Society at the New York City Center, New York, April 28, 1948, with Nicholas Magallanes as Orpheus, *Maria Tallchief as* Eurydice, *Francisco Moncion as the* Dark Angel, *Beatrice Tompkins as the* Leader of the Furies, *Tanaquil LeClercq as the* Leader of the Bacchantes, *and Herbert Bliss as* Apollo.

This ballet is a contemporary treatment of the ancient myth of Orpheus, the Greek musician who descended into Hades in search of his dead wife, Eurydice. With his music, Orpheus charms the God of the Dead into returning Eurydice to him. He promises not to look at her until they have reached the earth again. Eurydice, unknowing, persuades Orpheus to break this promise, thereby bringing about her irrevocable death. The ballet tells this story and its aftermath as simply as possible with its music, its dramatic action, and its dancing.

SCENE ONE: THE GRAVE OF EURYDICE   The first notes of the orchestra remind us that Orpheus's instrument was the lyre. A harp sounds descending scales in a slow, mournful rhythm accompanied by quiet strings. Eurydice is dead, and Orpheus cannot console himself with his own song. The curtain rises. Orpheus stands alone beside Eurydice's grave with his back turned. His arms hang limp, his lyre is discarded at his feet, and his head is bowed to the intensely blue sky that would pierce his sorrow with brightness. Three friends enter on the left, cross over to the grave, and place upon it relics of Eurydice. Orpheus does not notice them; he remains motionless when they place their hands on his shoulder to console him. He ignores their departure. The music ceases its slow lamentation, and Orpheus wakens from his grief. He takes up his lyre and begins a dance that expresses physical grief as well as mental anguish. He raises the lyre high above him in supplication, then holds the instrument in one hand as he dances. The song of the lyre is inadequate to his bereavement; yet the lyre is the only possession Orpheus has left, and in his dance he tries to make the instrument a partner to his woe. This effort fails, and Orpheus places the harp on Eurydice's grave, where he beseeches it to speak for her. Then he falls in despair at the grave and reaches out to pluck the lyre's strings. At this sound, a satyr and four wood sprites leap out from behind rocks in the background and attempt to distract Orpheus. Orpheus rises to meet these creatures who have been moved by his song and he darts in and out among them for a moment, but soon leaves them, to dance alone with his lyre. His misery is unabated and his pathetic figure seems to demand the sympathy of the gods he invokes to aid him. Again he stands beside Eurydice's grave with downcast eyes.

Now the prayers of Orpheus are answered. In the back, against the vivid blue sky, appears a strange, dark figure whose body is enveloped in black coils. The Angel of Death poses briefly, then moves forward toward the grieving poet. He approaches softly, so as not to disturb Orpheus in his reverie, and touches him. Orpheus stands immobile. The Angel of Death frees himself of the black coil that represents his power in Hades, raises Orpheus's arms high, and entwines the coil between his outstretched hands. As he wraps the coil about the silent musician, the Angel of Death by his intimate presence endows Orpheus with the power to accompany him on the long journey across the River Styx to Eurydice. The angel stands away from Orpheus and dances triumphantly for a moment, then prepares for the trip into Hades. He frees Orpheus of the bonds of death, then places over the minstrel's eyes a golden mask which must not be removed until the journey is over. Then he picks up the lyre, slips his arm through it, and beckons to Orpheus. Orpheus moves toward him hesitatingly; pliantly he stretches out his hand to grasp the angel's upturned palm. The open, widespread fingers of the angel close about his hand with the strength of steel. A trumpet sounds. The angel moves the lyre down his arm to rest on their clasped hands and begins to lead Orpheus on the downward journey. The music is slow and spacious as the two figures move toward the front of the stage. From above, a flowing white gauze falls in slow motion, and in front of this curtain the Angel of Death leads the blinded Orpheus on the tortuous journey. The progress in their descent into Hades is marked by bright objects that can be seen moving upward in back of the transparent curtain. The passage becomes difficult as the two figures cross the stage toward the left, and as they disappear, the angel, exhausted, pulls Orpheus over the ground. When they have gone, mysterious figures in back of the gauze push the curtain forward with a movement similar to the helpless beating of wings against a cage.

SCENE TWO: HADES   The gauze curtain rises swiftly, and crouched about the stage in fearful attitudes are the Furies, creatures of Hell who would destroy those who enter the Land of the Dead unlawfully. Bright cones of light from above illuminate their hideous and fantastic attire. The leader of the Furies proceeds to direct them harshly in a rapid, rhythmic dance. Orpheus and the angel enter on the left. The leader of the Furies turns and points at them menacingly, followed by her weird creatures. But the angel and Orpheus stand motionless. The Furies finish their dance, and their leader directs them to gather in a group. Tortured souls who have remained in the background now stir with great effort. They carry heavy burdens of rock on their shoulders and bend painfully under the strain. They set boulders down behind the group of Furies, as if to protect themselves, and all turn toward the two interlopers.

The Angel of Death moves away from Orpheus, slips the lyre from his arm, and, standing in back of the minstrel, places the lyre for Orpheus to play. But Orpheus does not understand—he cannot see—and the angel moves his hands so that they touch the strings of the harp. The angel plucks the strings, and now Orpheus comprehends and begins to play. His music is accompanied closely by two oboes and the orchestra. The lovely, soft melody of his lyre enchants the Furies, who are lulled to silence and rest. Yet Orpheus is still reluctant to play the harp as he once did, before Eurydice died, and the angel continues to exact the music from him. He knows that only by his great music will Orpheus persuade the ruler of Hades to release Eurydice. The two figures dance to the beautiful song, the angel constantly encouraging Orpheus to prolong the melody. The burdened, tortured souls move closer to hear more perfectly, and the music reflects their agony, which Orpheus's song has temporarily relieved.

But now the song is over. Orpheus bows stiffly in obeisance toward the back. In the dark recesses of the stage a strange shape begins to turn toward him. This is Pluto, God of the Underworld. Standing before him, her hands resting on his shoulders, is Eurydice. Orpheus does not move. Although he cannot see, he senses her presence and waits for Pluto's answer to his prayer. Eurydice moves forward, haltingly at first, with a slight limping motion, then more freely as her dance becomes syncopated. She turns to Pluto and beseeches him to come forward. Eurydice's arms move constantly to express her desire for freedom, and Pluto moves toward her. The Furies take Orpheus by the hand and bring him to Eurydice. Pluto joins their hands, and for a moment the two stand motionless before the god as Orpheus pledges not to look at his wife until they have ascended to earth. A blue stalactite descends from on high to symbolize the reunion, and the Dark Angel comes forward to lead Orpheus and Eurydice back to earth. He takes Orpheus by the hand, and all the inhabitants of the underworld circle the three figures, who move with hands joined to the front of the stage. The gauze curtain falls behind them, and the Dark Angel proceeds ahead, holding out Orpheus's lyre as a guide to the couple.

Orpheus and Eurydice dance together to a sumptuous melody as their journey begins. At first Eurydice merely follows Orpheus, imitating his steps as he leads the way. But the ascent is difficult, and their dance becomes for a short time a kind of portrayal of the hardships they undergo in passing unseen obstacles. Orpheus is blind, and when Eurydice is not holding him by the hand, she is lost to him. Eurydice puts herself in his way constantly: she longs increasingly for Orpheus to see her. Her longing is infinitely tender and appealing because of the warmth of the love in her own eyes; she therefore seems to tempt Orpheus to tear the mask from his face not so that he can see her, but so that she can see him as she remembers him. She wishes to help him as they proceed along the way, but the one way in which she cannot help him is by showing her love for him. Eurydice is tormented momentarily by the fact that, although they are really together once again, they are actually remote to each other: Orpheus, because he cannot see; Eurydice, because she cannot be seen by the man she loves.

The tempo and the theme of the dance change briefly as Eurydice moves away and dances before the blind Orpheus a gay and pleasant measure. She holds in her hands an invisible pipe, and plays upon it in celebration of their reunion. Orpheus catches the mood of her dance and joins her in it. Both are attempting to suppress the impassioned longings they feel so deeply. But Orpheus becomes even more intently aware of his lack of sight as Eurydice beguilingly dances out of his reach, and the principal theme of their *pas de deux* returns, this time prefaced with a short musical warning from the harp. On the extreme left, the arm of the Dark Angel still holds out the guiding lyre, and the two lovers turn to follow it. They start out as before, Orpheus leading and Eurydice duplicating his movements, but now Eurydice moves close to him in intimate contact. Orpheus tries to hold her, but she slides down to the floor, where his arms reach out desperately to find her. The melody mounts to a brief crescendo. Now that he cannot touch Eurydice, Orpheus abandons all patience and takes his head in his hands. Eurydice stands beside him, her face close to his, and he tears the mask from his eyes. There is absolute silence. Instantly she falls against him and dies. At first too stunned to move, Orpheus stretches out his arms, eager to touch her and to feel her touch. Invisible creatures of Hades push forward the gauze curtain to make good their promise and slip Eurydice away. Orpheus kneels alone, his open arms clasping the empty air.

Now that he has lost Eurydice until he himself shall die, Orpheus is afraid. Horns sound in terrifying judgment upon his fatal error. He remembers that the Angel of Death is still with him, just ahead, and he turns, half crawling, half running, to grasp his lyre. But just before his fingers reach the lyre, it disappears. Powerless now in the Land of the Dead, Orpheus knows that he is powerless, too, on earth; he crawls off in search of his lyre.

The gauze curtain rises rapidly when Orpheus has left the stage. Here again on earth the sky is still blue, but now it is bathed also in blood-colored lights.

There is a small hillock in the background. At the crash of a drum, there comes in from the left a tall Thracian woman with long red hair. This is the leader of the bacchantes, pleasure-seeking women who have not known love. She stalks the scene as if seeking desirable prey, moving with quick thrusts of legs and arms, looking to the right and left. She is soon followed by eight bacchantes, all with brilliant yellow hair. Orpheus enters carrying his mask. Immediately the bacchantes surround him. Their leader seems to demand his favor. Orpheus repulses her, indignant that she should try to sully his grief. The woman smiles her contempt and tries to take the mask from him. He runs, but the bacchantes are all around him. The leader embraces Orpheus savagely with her long arms, and the two fall to the ground. They roll over and over, and Orpheus frees himself, but the bacchante rises in triumph, holding his mask. Her face contorted with demoniac delight, she throws the mask out of sight. Orpheus cannot escape. The entire orchestra imitates his terror and the ferocity of the bacchantes with frenzied, rhythmic fortissimos. The bacchantes move in for the final attack. They push Orpheus back toward the hillock. He does not resist. They push him again. His head is bowed, his body listless. The bacchantes raise his arms, and for a brief moment they seem open in supplication. The leader stalks in on Orpheus and cuts off his right arm, then his left. He raises his head; she decapitates him. The body of Orpheus lies behind the hillock, torn to pieces. The bacchantes exit, strutting proudly, unregretfully.

SCENE THREE: APOTHEOSIS The stage is empty. Gradually the red disappears from the blue sky and the earth is bright once more. Again we hear the harp play the theme that opened the ballet, but now the accompaniment is different: this seems but a mere imitation of Orpheus's music. Apollo comes in slowly and approaches the grave of Orpheus. He kneels beside it and takes from behind the hillock a golden mask of the minstrel's face. Apollo holds the mask high, invoking the spirit of Orpheus as the God of Song, then holds it gently with his arm, as Orpheus held his lyre. The harp sounds as Apollo plucks the air before the mask, but the music—accompanied as it is by two horns—makes us all the more aware of the death of Orpheus and of Apollo's inability to call forth his music alone. Finally Apollo sets down the mask and stands poised over the grave of Orpheus. Slowly he moves his arm upward, and from the grave rises the lyre of Orpheus entwined in a long garland of flowers. The lyre rises higher and higher, carrying with it for the ages the tenderness and power of his song.

OTHER DANCES

Music by Frédéric Chopin. Choreography by Jerome Robbins. Costumes by Santa Loquasto. Lighting by Gilbert V. Hemsley, Jr. First presented at a Gala for the benefit for the Library of the Performing Arts at Lincoln Cen-

*ter at the Metropolitan Opera House, New York, May 9, 1976, with Natalia
Makarova and Mikhail Baryshnikov. Pianist: Jerry Zimmerman.*

Created for a special occasion, this dance for two has become a part of the
permanent repertory. Jerome Robbins, in *Dances at a Gathering* and *In the
Night,* had made enduring ballets based on Chopin's piano music. This work is
an extension of his interest in that music, as reflected in an admiration for the
two principal dancers. The music is four mazurkas and a waltz—the same
waltz used years ago by Michel Fokine for the first solo in *Les Sylphides.*

PAGANINI

*Ballet in seven scenes. Music by Sergei Rachmaninoff. Libretto and chore-
ography by Leonid Lavrovsky. Scenery by Vadim Rindin. First presented
by the Bolshoi Ballet at the Bolshoi Theatre, Moscow, April 7, 1960. First
presented in the United States by the Bolshoi Ballet at the Metropolitan
Opera House, New York, September 17, 1962, with Garosin Sekh in the
title role.*

The choreographer has written: "For many years I dreamed of making a ballet
about Paganini. Perhaps this wish derived from the impressions I formed in
my youth from reading the memoirs of Paganini's contemporaries and biographers, who described his uncanny expressiveness and the remarkable plastic
quality of his body, hands, and face. In the summer of 1959 I obtained a
recording of Rachmaninoff's *Rhapsody on a Theme of Paganini.* I was deeply
moved. The beautiful and convincing treatment of the musical work dedicated
to Paganini insistently called me, a choreographer, to respond in my own professional language."

The ballet depicts Paganini's recollections of his life, from which the violinist emerges as an inspired artist wrestling with evil forces. What are described
in the seven scenes are not actual facts of his life, but Paganini's meditations
on them. The scenes are marked: "First Improvisations," "Enemies," "A Meeting," "Loneliness and Despair," "Love and Consolation," "The Joy of Creative
Work and Death," "Finale—Stronger than Death."

In portraying Paganini, the choreographer was largely governed by Rachmaninoff's own wishes expressed in a letter written to Fokine. He wanted to
see Paganini with a violin, not a real one but a fantastic one that could be
impressed on the imagination. "Thus I felt that to bring Paganini to the stage,"
noted Lavrovsky, "the dancer performing his part must have his body and
movements tuned like a perfect instrument, thus symbolizing the beauty and
power of music itself. In this way the dancer's body, arms, fingers, his 'singing'
face, could help to create on the stage a vision of the fantastic violin Rachmaninoff so longed to see."

PAQUITA

Music by Léon Minkus, orchestrated by John Lanchbery. Choreography by Rudolf Nureyev "after the original by Marius Petipa." Staged by Marika Besobrasova. Costumes by Freddy Wittop. Lighting by Nananne Porcher. First presented at the Theatre Royal, Drury Lane, London, November 1965, with students of the Royal Ballet School. First presented in the United States by American Ballet Theatre at the New York State Theatre, Lincoln Center, July 6, 1971, with Cynthia Gregory and Michael Denard as the principals.

This entertaining dance ballet is all we now see of an original story ballet of two acts that enjoyed success for many years in France and Russia (*Paquita* is still in the Soviet repertory). First danced in Paris at the Opéra on April 1, 1846, by Carlotta Grisi, five years after her historic success in *Giselle*, the original choreography was by Mazilier and the music by Deldevez. The story tells of a Spanish gypsy Paquita who loves Lucien, a French nobleman. Their marriage appears to be impossible because of the difference in their social positions but all turns out well when Paquita discovers that she is, in fact, the daughter of a nobleman. The first Lucien was Lucien Petipa, brother of the great choreographer and ballet master Marius Petipa.

There have been a number of *divertissements* made from either the choreography or music of the Russian version of the French original, which had revised dances by Marius Petipa and music by Léon Minkus. Alexandra Danilova staged a one-act *Paquita* for the Ballet Russe de Monte Carlo, September 20, 1949, at the Metropolitan Opera House, New York, with Danilova and Oleg Tupine in the principal roles. The Grand Ballet of the Marquis de Cuevas from 1948 and, from 1951, the New York City Ballet for some years danced a *pas de trois* arranged to some of Minkus' music to *Paquita*. The latter, with Maria Tallchief, Nora Kaye, and André Eglevsky, was first presented at the City Center, New York, February 18, 1951, with costumes by Barbara Karinska.

The *divertissement* as arranged by Nureyev, exuberantly Spanish in character, has as its principal feature six variations for soloists, ballerina, and *premier danseur*. Enclosing these solos are group ensembles. The first introduces all the girls, who herald the arrival of the ballerina. Next, as the lights go down and the girls arrange themselves in a long diagonal across the stage, her partner enters to lead her in a dance. An interesting aspect of this *pas de deux* is that the girls who accompany the leading dancers reflect in their movements the steps and gestures of the ballerina. Eight girls and the soloists dance now to the playful rhythms of castanets. The harp now introduces the first of the six variations and it is always very interesting to see these Petipa dances. Like the variations in another of his masterworks, *The Sleeping Beauty*, they remind us of his great achievement in the classic ballet. We do not make dances like this now, perhaps, but we could make nothing if we had not had dances like these by Petipa to teach us.

After variations by two of the soloists, the *danseur* and the ballerina perform their individual dances. The circle is closed by brilliant dances for two more girls. The ballet ends in a joyous finale, the ballerina performing a dazzling variation.

NOTES Reviewing *Paquita* in the Washington *Post*, the critic Jean Battey Lewis wrote that Cynthia Gregory, in the ballerina's role, "used her extraordinary technique to dance with a wonderful freedom. Balances were held with elegant aplomb, phrases were finished with a triumphant flourish, and she tossed off 32 fouettés, punctuated by double fouettés, with breezy precision." (October 30, 1972)

Writing of the first *Paquita* and its great ballerina Carlotta Grisi, Théophile Gautier wrote in *La Presse*, Paris, on April 6, 1846: "This ballet, where the action is perhaps a little too melodramatic, is a complete success. The richness and strangeness of the Empire costumes, the beauty of the decor, above all the perfection of Carlotta's dancing, are responsible for this success. Her final steps in the piece are of unimaginable daring and difficulty: these are a kind of hopping on the very tip of the toe with a sudden turn made with a dazzling quickness which inspires a mixture of pleasure and fear, for its execution appears impossible, although she repeats it some eight to ten times. Thunderous applause greeted the ballerina, who was called on to perform the dance twice again after the fall of the curtain."

Readers who wish to know more about Carlotta Grisi, the first Giselle, and other great ballerinas, should read *The Ballerinas* by Parmenia Miguel.

PARADE

Music by Erik Satie. Book by Jean Cocteau. Choreography by Leonide Massine. Scenery and costumes by Pablo Picasso. First presented by Diaghilev's Ballets Russes at the Théâtre du Châtelet, Paris, May 18, 1917, with Leonide Massine, Lydia Lopokova, Nicholas Zverev, Maria Chabelska, and Leon Woizikowski in leading roles. First presented in the United States by the City Center Joffrey Ballet at the City Center, New York, March 22, 1973, with Gary Chryst, Eileen Brady, Gregory Huffman, Donna Cowen, and Robert Talmage in leading roles.

Renowned collaboration of the Diaghilev era, unique combination of the gifts of Satie, Cocteau, Massine, and Picasso, *Parade* proves yet again in the 1970s the genius of the Diaghilev Ballets Russes in generating artistic collaboration of the highest order. When relatively few of the ballets created under Diaghilev's direction can be seen in our theaters (only *Petrouchka, Firebird*—in another version, *Spectre de la Rose, Apollo,* and *Prodigal Son*), in a recent season, it is refreshing to have the impresario's incomparable gifts demonstrated again for a new generation. Until its American revival, *Parade* had not been seen for forty-seven years.

Parade has long been considered a landmark for its introduction of cubism into the theater. The idea of the ballet was Jean Cocteau's. It was he who persuaded Satie and Picasso, who had never worked with the Ballets Russes, to collaborate on this undertaking in the midst of World War I. Subtitled a "Realistic Ballet," the work was intended to heighten realism; Guillaume Apollinaire, writing in the program, put the word *surrealism* onto the printed page for the first time to describe *Parade*. This would seem to point to a contrast the ballet makes visible on the stage—a contrast between performers in a traveling circus, the real people, and their managers or impresarios—public relations men who attempt to persuade the public to enjoy their arts.

Street circuses used to be common in Paris, and it is one of these that is the subject of the ballet, where the huckstering managers parade their talent to passers-by before the start of the show, with the hope that they will pay to come inside.

Massine, *Parade*'s choreographer, has said, in describing his method of making ballets, that it is sometimes the music, sometimes the theme, or the period and atmosphere of the action. With *Parade*, "the music was supreme, although the theme, too, interested me." Satie's score, like Picasso's settings and costumes visually, radically reflected new directions in sound and sense, mixing everyday noises, the real, with the imaginative expectation.

The action of the ballet is direct and straightforward, with none of the mystery associated so often with the avant-garde. After a series of almost solemn, quasi-religious chords in a brief musical prelude, there is a brief quiet that reveals a drop curtain of "early Picasso" portraying a rustic backstage scene of players relaxing before a performance. This inner curtain rises to show a scene by the same artist that is clearly different: a curtained booth, askew but making sense at once as a stage for the public to view a performance. Here parades an odd creature, the like of which has never been seen walking—a huge, pipe-smoking man made up of angles and planes and no softness. This is the French Manager, who introduces the Chinese Conjuror, who emerges from the curtained booth to amuse us with tricks—sword swallowing, etc.—to simulated oriental music. In a splendid multicolored costume he fairly dazzles us with his entertainment and then disappears behind the curtain.

There is a flourish and another huckster comes out, this the Manager from New York, his costume an amalgam of skyscrapers and curious angles. He carries a megaphone and a sign reading PARADE. He consults and commiserates with his French colleague, then introduces his specialty, a Little American Girl, a perpetual child in white middy blouse with a bow in her hair. To the menacing sound of multiple typewriters and gun shots, she dances a machine-age number, all winsomeness and cute charm. But her dance is more than that—it epitomizes, in small compass, the European image of America as heard by an acute ear and reflected by an acute eye in 1917. The imagery is almost totally derived from popular songs and movies. As the music imitates American dance rhythms, the little girl runs the gamut of stock U.S. melodrama—cops and robbers, rescue from a storm at sea, etc., at the end of which she bounces off as cheerily as she entered. At the end, her Manager is just as disappointed as his predecessor: no audience responds enough to come into their theater. He and the French Manager cannot understand this indifference.

Now in silence comes a brown-and-white Horse, grinning from ear to ear. Somewhat bashfully he entertains us, too, and prances out. The curtains close behind him. When they part again, we see two Acrobats, a girl and a boy, who dance a circuslike *pas de deux*, simulating tricks of the ring and high wire.

After the Acrobats finish, to the sound of a screaming siren the two Managers and the American Girl return. Next, the Horse and the Conjuror, finally the Acrobats, all in a reprise of their acts. In unison, they urge us, the audience, to come into their theater to see more. When we do not, they form a kind of cortege and the Horse lies down. The curtain falls as the music of the beginning is heard again.

NOTES   There are many accounts of the origins of *Parade* but none more complete than those in *Cocteau*, Francis Steegmuller's biography of the librettist, in Leonide Massine's autobiography, and in Douglas Cooper's book, *Picasso Theatre*. Cooper, Picasso's collaborator, assisted the revival by the City Center Joffrey Ballet, and also wrote about it at length in *Dance and Dancers* magazine. He said of the presentation, which had been re-created by Leonide Massine himself:

"The famous drop curtain, revealed during the opening section of the music, showed one of the most romantically evocative and tender of all Picasso's circus compositions. But behind it lay a surprising and colorful contemporary reality. A proscenium opening, decorated with scrolls and a lyre, was painted red and yellow, and set among whitish buildings, with dark windows, and some dark-green foliage. The Chinese Conjuror had a scarlet tunic, strikingly patterned in yellow and grey, over black trousers with a yellow pattern. The two Acrobats had sky-blue tights with bold ornamental motifs in white, while the Little American Girl had a dark-blue middy jacket over a white skirt.

"Each of these turns was presented successively by one of the two so-called Managers, dancers raised to eleven-foot-high figures by an elaborately carpentered, descriptively symbolic superstructure rising from their shoulders. Both wore a sort of formal evening dress and a top hat, but were equipped with buildings and other attributes to establish their national character: thus the American had the Woolworth building, a megaphone and some flags, while the French Manager had houses, trees, a staff and a long-stemmed pipe.

"Massine cleverly characterized each role in his choreography, which made much use of mime. The subtly emphasized rhythms beaten out by the four legs of the Horse, in an enchantingly comic, acrobatic dance without music, was a triumph of his invention. While the Managers were made to convey the force of their huckstering and despair by ungainly movements, by demonstrative and angry steps and by towering over all around them.

"Massine had the good fortune to find in the Joffrey Ballet a marvelous group of young dancers who worked with him brilliantly in this recreation of *Parade*. For it is a ballet which requires the performers to show style, precision of movement, perfect timing, athletic prowess, great powers of mime and especially a sense of enjoying what they are doing. Gary Chryst, assuming Massine's original role (the Chinese Conjuror), displayed that nervous intensity, speed, suavity, and air of mystery which is required for the character. His flickering hands, his shuffle, his leaps and especially his elevation were superbly timed and amazing to watch, as were the mimed passages of his dance where he finds an egg in his pigtail, digests it and recovers it from the toe of his shoe, or swallows a sword or eats fire.

"Donna Cowen, the first native-born American ever to dance the role of the Little American Girl, showed a marvelous sense of ragtime and was by turns pert, droll and captivating as she danced and mimed her way through the episodes of the ungainly typewriter, of the encounter with Indians, of the wreck of the *Titanic* or of the rosy dawning. The graceful and wistful *pas de deux* for the two Acrobats, who tumble, climb ropes, perform trapeze and walk a tightrope, was danced with great feeling and dexterity by Brady and Huffman. The Managers and the Horse gave their numbers with great distinction and all the fun and noise of the fair. The music was rendered in strict accordance with Satie's published score so that the incidental sound effects were confined to a typewriter, a ship's siren and some revolver shots at the appropriate times."

Cooper recalls that in staging the ballet, Massine was able to consult with dancers living in New York who had once appeared in various roles, notably Maria Chabelska, Vera Nemtchinova, Lydia Sokolova, and Michel Pavloff, while Boris Kochno also made a contribution from Paris. Lydia Sokolova in her memoirs had written prophetically: "*Parade* was so delightful that I am sure it would be a favorite if it could be done today."

PARADISE LOST

Music by Marius Constant. Choreography by Roland Petit. Libretto by Jean Cau. Scenery by Martial Raysse. First presented by the Royal Ballet at the Royal Opera House, Covent Garden, London, February 23, 1967, with Margot Fonteyn and Rudolf Nureyev. First presented in the United States by the Royal Ballet at the New Metropolitan Opera House, New York, May 10, 1967, with the same cast.

This ballet is based not on John Milton but on a poem by Jean Cau: "Every paradise is found in order to be lost." What happens is that we first see a huge egg, outlined in neon, then in lights a countdown that flashes 5 . . . 4 . . . 3 . . . 2 . . . 1 . . . and then the birth of Man who turns out to be Adam. He walks down a ramp and the dancing begins.

In the words of Alexander Bland of *The Observer,* the action "is traced in a long series of solos and duets which make the first half of the ballet one of the most stimulating dance experiences in a long time—Adam exploring his nature and powers; his first intimation of pain and the birth of Eve; their mutual suspicion thawing into complete harmony; the change wrought by the Serpent, Eve twisting into seduction and Adam into aggressive sexuality, ending in a denouement as theatrically breath-taking as Nijinsky's leap in *Spectre de la Rose.*" The hero runs and jumps headfirst into a huge mouth of Eve.

Innocence is further destroyed by an attacking crowd and God's wrath finally descends. Peter Williams wrote in the *Sunday Times* of London: "The fall is frozen in yet another sublime 'fallen-angel' composition—Man crashed to earth with his body curved across the neck of the sorrowing Woman."

PAS DES DÉESSES

Music by John Field. Choreography by Robert Joffrey. First presented by the Robert Joffrey Ballet Concert at the Kaufmann Auditorium, Y.M.H.A., New York, May 29, 1954, with Lillian Wellein (Taglioni), Barbara Gray (Grahn), Jacquetta Kieth (Cerrito), and Michael Lland (Saint-Léon).

Inspired by a romantic lithograph of 1846 by Bouvier, *Pas des Déesses* re-creates the ballet style of that day. At the start, four dancers are seen in the pose of this famous print. Each represents a famous dancer of the romantic era in ballet and each of the dances that follow displays the qualities made famous by the quartet—the languorous Danish ballerina Lucile Grahn, the darting Italian, Fanny Cerrito, and the floating Marie Taglioni, all strongly supported by the gallant Arthur Saint-Léon. The air of competition among the three ballerinas echoes the delicate rivalry which existed among these celebrated dancers.

The music for the ballet is by the Irish piano virtuoso John Field (1782–1837), who originated the name and style of the Nocturne. The ballet uses selected nocturnes, rondos, and waltzes.

The first *Pas des Déesses* was performed at His Majesty's Theatre, London, during the 1846 season by Taglioni, Cerrito, Grahn, and Saint-Léon. Choreography was by Jules Perrot.

PAS DE DIX

Classic ballet. Music by Alexander Glazunov. Choreography by George Balanchine. Costumes by Esteban Francés. Lighting by Jean Rosenthal. First presented by the New York City Ballet at the City Center, New York, November 9, 1955, with Maria Tallchief and André Eglevsky; Barbara Fallis, Constance Garfield, Jane Mason, Barbara Walczak, Shaun O'Brien, Roy Tobias, Roland Vasquez, and Jonathan Watts.

The music for this dance for ten (two principals plus four girls and four boys) is taken from a ballet score I have always liked since my student days in Russia, Glazunov's *Raymonda*. I danced in Petipa's original production of this ballet at the Maryinsky Theatre when I was studying at the Imperial Ballet School. Some years ago, for the Ballet Russe de Monte Carlo, Alexandra Danilova and I put together our version of Petipa's last act—the nuptial festivities of the Hungarian lady Raymonda and the Count Jean de Brienna—a dance ballet that follows the narrative.

Except for one brief variation, all the music for the *Pas de Dix* is taken from this same act, but there is no attempt here to approximate Petipa's original, which no one remembers accurately, anyway. What I have done instead is to try to make an entertaining spectacle with no story, simply a series of dances for a ballerina, her partner, and a small ensemble. The music will be familiar, I think, to those who know the Russian repertory.

PAS DE DUKE

Music by Duke Ellington. Choreography by Alvin Ailey. Scenery and costumes by Rouben Ter-Arutunian. First presented by the Alvin Ailey City Center Dance Theatre at the City Center, New York, May 11, 1976, with Judith Jamison and Mikhail Baryshnikov.

Created for a special gala occasion and to honor the late Duke Ellington, this ballet was a *pas de deux* for two performers with radically different preparations—one a star of a modern dance company, the other a star of classic ballet. The choreographer brought the two together for a jazz ballet and made for the classic dancer a modern role he had not thought possible. The result was a memorable duet.

Clive Barnes recalled afterward in the New York *Times* that "it was remarkable how well Mr. Baryshnikov had absorbed the Ailey technique, and how well the two of them went together. It was sheer fun and Mr. Ailey was at his most persuasively inventive. It is always a delight to see Mr. Baryshnikov doing jazz movements—he performs a little naughtily, like a bright child talking faultlessly in a foreign language with a charming and slightly accentuated accent."

PAS DE QUATRE

Divertissement. *Music by Cesare Pugni. Choreography by Jules Perrot. First presented at His Majesty's Theatre, London, July 12, 1845, with Marie Taglioni, Carlotta Grisi, Fanny Cerrito, and Lucile Grahn.*

This short ballet is probably the most famous *divertissement* in the history of dance. It displayed in one work four of the greatest ballerinas of its time, bringing these talents together for several memorable performances that have excited the curiosity of dance lovers for more than a hundred years. At this distance, it is impossible for us to tell exactly what *Pas de Quatre* looked like as a ballet, but information about what it resembled, and the unprecedented occasion it undoubtedly was, has come down to us in lithographs and reviews. If the greatest ballerinas of the United States, France, England, and the U.S.S.R. were to appear together in a ballet today, we should have some approximation of the excitement caused by the original *Pas de Quatre*. If such a *Pas de Quatre* seems impossible today, we must remember that it also seemed impossible in 1845.

Among all artists there is bound to be competition, and in the 1840s it seemed unlikely that any four of the great ballerinas would consent to dance on the same stage. Marie Taglioni had been acknowledged the finest dancer in the world when she created the title role in *La Sylphide* in 1832, and even thirteen years after her first famous role, she was still considered supreme in the realm of the romantic ballet that she had helped to create. But with the coming of the romantic era, there were also other ballerinas who danced in similar ballets: exceptional among these dancers were Fanny Cerrito, who was acclaimed in the early 1840s, Carlotta Grisi, who danced in 1841 the first performance of *Giselle*, and the Danish ballerina Lucile Grahn, who had successfully danced Taglioni's role in *La Sylphide*. The fact that each ballerina had danced *Giselle* (Taglioni, Cerrito, and Grahn undertook Grisi's original role in 1843) gives us an indication of their rivalry. There was, in short, so much natural jealousy between these four—and each faction of the public showed so great an amount of enthusiasm for its chosen goddess among them—that it appeared unlikely that the ballerinas would expose themselves to any common venture.

The man who thought otherwise and acted with persistence until he achieved his goal was the enterprising manager of His Majesty's Theatre in London, Benjamin Lumley. "The government of a great state was but a trifle compared to the government of such subjects as those whom I was *supposed* to be able to command," he recollected almost twenty years after the event. "These were subjects who considered themselves far above mortal control, or, more properly speaking, each was a queen in her own right—alone, absolute, supreme."

Lumley was encouraged to assemble the four ballerinas by a success he had brought off in 1843, when Fanny Cerrito danced at his theatre in a *pas de deux* with Fanny Elssler, the fifth great ballerina of this period. Why Elssler was not invited to participate in Lumley's assembly of ballerinas in 1845 is perhaps partially explained by this earlier triumph, but not altogether so. For Elssler's fame equaled, if it did not actually exceed, Taglioni's. No doubt that is exactly the point. Taglioni's superiority was unquestioned throughout Europe until Elssler made her début at the Paris Opéra in 1834. From this point on, the rivalry between the two was bitter. Elssler taunted Taglioni and her admirers by threatening to dance *La Sylphide*, which no other dancer yet dared to do. When Elssler essayed Taglioni's famous role in this ballet in 1838, open war broke out, and seven years later it must have been clear even to Benjamin Lumley that between these rivals there could never be peace. Théophile Gautier, who was to become the originator of *Giselle*, the friend and critical sponsor of Carlotta Grisi, wrote in 1837 that Fanny Elssler's dancing had a special quality that distinguished her from all other dancers and proceeded to make his point clear in a fashion that must have made the rivalry between the newcomer and the "Sylphide" intense: ". . . it is not the aerial and virginal grace of Taglioni, it is something more human, more appealing to the senses. Mademoiselle Taglioni is a Christian dancer, if one may make use of such an expression in regard to an art proscribed by the Catholic faith; she flies like a spirit in the midst of transparent clouds of white muslin with which she loves to surround herself, she resembles a happy angel who scarcely bends the petals of celestial flowers with the tips of her pink toes. Fanny is a quite pagan dancer; she reminds one of the muse Terpsichore, tambourine in hand, her tunic, exposing her thigh, caught up with a golden clasp; when she bends freely from the hips, throwing back her swooning, voluptuous arms, we seem to see one of those beautiful figures from Herculaneum or Pompeii which stand out in white relief against a black background . . ."

And Elssler was not praised only in Europe. She came to the United States in 1840 for a three-month tour and did not return to Europe for two years— two years during which she became the toast of the nation. She was welcomed by President Martin Van Buren, escorted by his son, entertained by Congress, carried on the shoulders of adoring crowds, and so universally acclaimed that she could declare, with accuracy, that "never was an artiste more completely seated in public sympathy." In nineteenth-century America she anticipated the exclusive success enjoyed by Anna Pavlova seventy years later.

But Benjamin Lumley also had grounds for being discouraged. His predecessor at His Majesty's Theatre had announced, but had been unable to present, Taglioni, Cerrito, and Elssler in a special performance. Circumstances,

too, contrived against him. He had chosen Jules Perrot, the former partner of
Taglioni and the choreographer who had collaborated on *Giselle*, to arrange
the dances for the *Pas de Quatre*, and everyone was ready to begin—except
one of the ballerinas. Carlotta Grisi, Perrot's wife, seemed unable to fulfill her
engagement on time. She was dancing in Paris; how was she to get to London
for rehearsals? Lumley tells us how: "A vessel was chartered . . . to waft the
sylph at a moment's notice across the Channel; a special train was engaged
and ready at Dover; relays of horses were in waiting to aid the flight of the
danseuse, all the way from Paris to Calais."

When Grisi arrived, Perrot began to work on the most difficult assignment a
ballet master ever had. He had not only to invent an ensemble that the four
ballerinas would perform together, he had also to devise individual dances that
would display ideally the particular artistry of each performer without distracting from the excellence of her sisters. In Lumley's words, "no one was to
outshine the others—unless in their own individual belief." Perrot had worked
closely on other projects with each of the four dancers previously and knew
their temperaments; as the finest *danseur* of his time and a choreographer of
equal fame, he also knew his job.

He seemed to succeed. The ballerinas were content with what they were to
dance together and pleased with their variations; the costumes were ready, the
theater sold out. And then came the problem of who was to dance first—or,
rather, last, for the final variation in every ballet, as in regal processions, according to Lumley, is performed by the superior artist. Cerrito, Grisi, and
Grahn agreed that Taglioni, because of her unprecedented fame, should occupy this place of honor. But as to the penultimate variation, the ladies
disagreed: who was to be closest to Taglioni? Cerrito and Grisi vied for the position and quarreled on stage. Finally Grisi lost her temper, called Cerrito "a little chit," and the two ballerinas vowed they would never appear together.

Perrot, in despair, told the bad news to the manager. Lumley recalled what
the choreographer said: "*Mon Dieu!* Cerrito won't begin before Carlotta, nor
Carlotta before Cerrito, and there isn't anything that will make them change
their minds: we're finished!" And Lumley also recalled what he replied: "The
solution is easy . . . In this dilemma there is one point on which I am sure the
ladies will be frank. Let the oldest take her unquestionable right to the envied
position."

Perrot returned to the stage to try this ruse. When he told the two ballerinas
the manager's decision, everything suddenly changed: they "tittered, laughed,
drew back, and were now as much disinclined to accept the right of position
as they had been eager to claim it." The trick worked! Taglioni was at this
time forty-one, Cerrito was twenty-eight, and Grisi twenty-six: the reverse
order was thus established, with Grahn, who was twenty-four, leading with the
first variation. Lumley says that "the *grand pas de quatre* was finally performed on the same night before a delighted audience, who little knew how
nearly they had been deprived of their expected treat."

What this audience saw was recorded by several critics, and approximations of the performance have been given us in modern representations of this *divertissement*. When the curtain went up, the four ballerinas appeared before a romantic background. They entered in a line, holding hands; each was dressed in billowing muslin and each wore in her hair a crown of white flowers, except Cerrito, who wore flowers in the knot at the back of her head. The ballerinas smiled, walked to the footlights, and bowed. The audience could not believe it. One member of the audience did not want to believe it and threw down from the gallery a shower of placards that declared Cerrito the peer of all dancers in the world. The audience was embarrassed and frightened of the possible consequences, but then someone laughed, the dancers smiled, and the music began.

The *Pas de Quatre* commenced in soft stillness as the four ballerinas moved toward the backdrop and arranged themselves in charming tableau about Taglioni, who looked down upon her sisters with an expression of sincere sweetness. Even the slightest display of jealousy was impossible now, for each artist was thoroughly aware that the ballet would surely fail if any of them failed to be as perfect as Perrot imagined they were and that they would be responsible. And so they knelt about Taglioni, opened their arms to her in a gesture of affection and respect, and smiled as innocently as she did. They changed their position, and the graceful Taglioni seemed to fall back in their welcoming arms.

The actual dancing began with a short variation by Grahn to quick, lively music. This was followed by a *pas de deux* by Cerrito and Grisi, which came to an end as Taglioni crossed the stage in high, light leaps that seemed to make her a part of the air. This introduction was merely a hint as to what was to follow in the four virtuoso variations. Grahn came first, dancing quickly, lightly, turning and hopping on point, moving about the stage with the controlled vigor of shining youth. Next, as the music changed, Carlotta Grisi stepped forward and danced with a sharp but airy vibrancy, a solo that summed up in a few short minutes her great fame.

Taglioni and Grahn, the oldest and the youngest, now danced together to a brief romantic measure. Cerrito was posed gracefully on stage with them, apparently waiting for them to finish their duet. Suddenly she cut this dainty and quiet sequence short, darting forward like an arrow released from the taut bow and describing a long, swift diagonal of accelerated turns. She finished her variation in a display of still, balanced poses contrasted with unparalleled verve and speed.

Taglioni, as the last of these great dancers, had the most difficult variation of all: she had to show the audience that what they had rejoiced in so far could be climaxed. And this she did, not by dancing in any fashion novel to her, but in a manner that epitomized her reputation: she moved with supreme lightness and she moved effortlessly, dazzling the audience with controlled poses even in midflight. And she moved with unquestioned authority, with the highest knowledge of her great gift and of her own faithful obedience to it, pausing in perfect balance with the grace and refinement of the mature artist.

Now, at the end, the three other ballerinas joined her. They all danced together, each trying to outdo the others in a final display of virtuosity. Then, as if they all understood that competition was in vain, they arranged themselves again in the tender tableau with which they had begun. Taglioni raised her arms over her head and looked down upon the other three, who gathered about her quietly and looked toward the audience with pensive, beguiling smiles, as if they had never moved.

NOTES And what was the critical opinion of this *Pas de Quatre?* The *Times* of London called it "the greatest Terpsichorean exhibition that ever was known in Europe . . . Never was such a *pas* before. The excitement which a competition so extraordinary produced in the artists roused them to a pitch of energy which would have been impossible under other circumstances, and hence everyone did her utmost, the whole performance being a complete inspiration . . . The whole long *pas* was danced to a running sound of applause, which, after each variation, swelled to a perfect hurricane . . . Bouquets flew from every point, an immense profusion, as each *danseuse* came forward, so that they had to curtsy literally in the midst of a shower of floral gifts. Cerrito's wreaths and nosegays were more than she could hold in both her arms . . . The front of the stage was almost covered with flower leaves."

The critic of the *Illustrated London News* reported: "No description can render the exquisite, the almost ethereal, grace of movement and attitude of these great dancers, and those who have witnessed the scene may boast of having once, at least, seen the perfection of the art of dancing. . . ."

The best accounts of three of the four ballerinas are given by their contemporary Théophile Gautier. Gautier did not review the *Pas de Quatre,* but he speaks here of Taglioni the year before the London *divertissement:* "Mademoiselle Taglioni is not a dancer, she is the embodiment of dancing . . . Fortunate woman. Always the same elegant and slender form, the same calm, intelligent and modest features; not a single feather has fallen from her wing; not a hair has silvered beneath her chaplet of flowers! As the curtain rose, she was greeted with thunders of applause. What airiness! What rhythmic movements! What noble gestures! What poetic attitudes and, above all, what a sweet melancholy! What lack of restraint, yet how chaste!"

Gautier speaks of Cerrito two years after the *Pas de Quatre:* "Fanny Cerrito's principal qualities are grace of pose, unusual attitudes, quickness of movement, and the rapidity with which she covers ground; she bounds and rebounds with an admirable ease and elasticity; there is a charming grace about her whole body. . . . She radiates a sense of happiness, brilliance, and smiling ease which know neither labor nor weariness. . . ."

Of Carlotta Grisi, Gautier had this to say at the time of her début at the Paris Opéra (1841): "She is possessed of a strength, lightness, suppleness and originality which at once place her between Elssler and Taglioni." Two years later he was to write that "Grisi's dancing has a quite special style; it does not resemble the dancing of either Taglioni or Elssler; each one of her poses, each one of her movements, is stamped with the seal of originality."

Pas de Quatre with its original cast was performed only four times (July 12, 15, 17, and 19, 1845). Queen Victoria and the Prince Consort attended the third performance. Three of the original cast—Taglioni, Cerrito, and Grisi—danced in a revival of the *divertissement* that was performed twice in Lumley's theater: on July 17 and 19, 1847. Carolina Rosati replaced Lucile Grahn in these performances. Rosati at this time was only twenty years old; fifteen years later, in Russia, she was to dance the leading role in *The Daughter of Pharaoh* (Pugni), the first great success of the ballet master Marius Petipa.

A year after the first performance of the original *Pas de Quatre*, Taglioni, Grahn, and Cerrito danced together at Lumley's theater in a ballet called *The Judgment of Paris* (Pugni-Perrot). The ballerinas danced the parts of three goddesses in this *divertissement*, which was hailed almost as loudly as *Pas de Quartre*. *The Judgment of Paris* was Marie Taglioni's last new ballet.

Marie Taglioni retired soon after she danced the revival of *Pas de Quatre* and died impoverished in Marseille, France, in 1884, at the age of eighty. Fanny Cerrito, at the time of her appearance in London, had yet to achieve her fullest fame and in the 1840s and 1850s secured for herself additional triumphs. She died in 1909 at the age of ninety-two. Carlotta Grisi had new successes after the famous *divertissement*, creating the title role in *Paquita* (Mazilier-Deldevez) in 1846 and dancing at the Imperial Theatre in St. Petersburg. She was seventy-eight when she died in 1899. Lucile Grahn, the youngest of the *Pas de Quatre* ballerinas, had danced in Russia before she came to London for Lumley's *divertissement*. Trained in her native Denmark by the great Danish ballet master Auguste Bournonville, Grahn made her début at the Royal Theatre, Copenhagen, in 1835. In this theater Grahn danced a version of *La Sylphide* created for her by Bournonville (1836). This production of the famous ballet has been in the repertory of the Royal Danish Ballet ever since it was first performed. Grahn died in 1907 at the age of eighty-six.

Another historic presentation of *Pas de Quatre* took place January 24, 1972, at the City Center, New York, at the Gala Performance for the Dance Collection of the New York Public Library. Anton Dolin, who had reconstructed the ballet for American Ballet Theatre in 1941, did so again, this time bringing together Carla Fracci as Taglioni, Violette Verdy as Grisi, Patricia McBride as Cerrito, and Eleanor D'Antuono as Grahn.

LES PATINEURS (The Skaters)

Ballet in one act. Music by Giacomo Meyerbeer. Choreography by Frederick Ashton. Scenery and costumes by William Chappell. First presented by the Vic-Wells Ballet at the Sadler's Wells Theatre, London, February 16,

1937, with a cast headed by Margot Fonteyn, Robert Helpmann, and Harold Turner. First presented in the United States by Ballet Theatre at the Broadway Theatre, New York, October 2, 1946. Scenery and costumes by Cecil Beaton. Nora Kaye, Hugh Laing, and John Kriza danced the leading roles.

Some people watch ice skating and say how like dancing it is. *Les Patineurs* shows us how dancing, among other things, can imitate ice skating. The ballet has no story; it simply organizes what any of us might see at a skating rink into a series of nine *divertissements*. The music, arranged by Constant Lambert, is based on selections from Meyerbeer's operas *L'Étoile du Nord* and *Le Prophète*. The Ballet Theatre production is described here.

The music is whistling, thumping holiday fare. The scene is any secluded skating pond, the time, night. Snowy branches of barren trees hang over the pond; brightly colored paper lanterns light up the forest. Four couples skate across the scene. Two pretty girls follow them, slipping and turning on the ice. One of the boys in the skating party falls; his girl brushes him off, and they exit. A boy in bright green rushes in and treats us to a quick, dazzling display of virtuosity and skates off as though he'd done nothing at all.

The harp signals a romantic melody, and two lovers enter. The boy carries the girl high on his shoulder, sets her down, and she turns close to the ground. The couple are dressed in white and seem at home in the snow-laden scene. They circle the stage, the boy lifting the girl softly to the right and left. For a moment they separate; then they rejoin, and the boy spins the girl around and around. They skate away, hand in hand.

Eight couples—the girls in bright red and the boys in yellow and blue—fill the skating area. Two girls take over the pond and dance brightly to a tinkling tune. The lovers join the eight couples and dance with them a gay ensemble. The boy in green circles the stage, then leaves. Now the ensemble moves with a slower grace. The boy in green now shows off among them, and all watch him. When he is finished, they turn to watch four girls who are skating apart from the crowd; then all skate off in a circling line.

The boy in green and the two girls who danced the first *divertissement* perform a *pas de trois*. Soon they are followed by two other girls, who do an incredible number of fast, accelerated *fouettés*. The boy in green hails the others in the party to come back, and everyone promenades. Snow begins to fall. The girls resume their *fouettés*, whirling away faster than ever as the exhilarating music comes to a climax. The boy in green is challenged by their skill to turn faster than ever and he is spinning like a top when the curtain falls.

PAVANE

Music by Maurice Ravel. Choreography by George Balanchine. Lighting by Ronald Bates. First presented by the New York City Ballet at the Hom-

mage à Ravel at the New York State Theatre, Lincoln Center, May 29, 1975, with Patricia McBride. Conducted by Robert Irving.

This work of Ravel's, the *Pavane pour une Infante Défunte,* or *Pavane for a Dead Child,* is perhaps the best-known of his compositions after the ever popular *Boléro.* This popularity is perhaps due to the name of the piece; everyone feels sentimental about the mere idea of it. Yet Ravel himself felt that the work owed its success to its "remarkable interpretations." He wrote: "Do not attach to the title any more importance than it has. It is not a pavane for a dead child but, rather, an evocation of the pavanes that could have been danced by such a little princess as painted by Velásquez at the Spanish court."

The dance to this music is arranged for a girl who responds to a ghostly idea among the living. The dictionary defines a pavane as a slow, stately dance. So does this girl perform it, in a flowing white gown, gossamer and a preparation for the shroud.

As the curtain rises, the girl, veiled, stands at the back of the stage. She shields her eyes in grief, then begins to dance. Cradling her hands as if to hold a child, the girl moves like the wind, yet royally, in a processional manner. In control of her long train, she lets it swirl about her, then covers her face with it and stands alone, grieving.

NOTES   The critic Byron Belt wrote after the premiere, in the *Long Island Press:* "*Pavane* is an undulating treatment of mourning, at once poignant and sensuous. Patricia McBride, swathed in white, uses a long scarf in the manner of an Art Nouveau Isadora Duncan, but it is carried off with such fragile beauty that the work seems astonishingly fresh and strong . . . *Pavane* . . . was created for a dancer magnificently able to dominate the stage completely with her virtuosity."

PELLÉAS AND MÉLISANDE

Music by Arnold Schoenberg. Choreography by Roland Petit. Scenery and costumes by Jacques Dupont. First presented by the Royal Ballet, March 26, 1969, at the Royal Opera House, Covent Garden, London, with Margot Fonteyn, Rudolf Nureyev, and Keith Rosson in the principal roles. First presented in the United States by the same ensemble at the Metropolitan Opera House, Lincoln Center, New York, May 5, 1969. Conducted by John Lanchbery.

The choreographer of this ballet, Roland Petit, has written his own synopsis of the action and a comment:

"Mélisande is lost in the forest. Golaud finds her and falls in love. She senses that another destiny awaits her and when Pelléas, Golaud's brother, arrives, he and Mélisande instantly recognize that it has come.

"Golaud leads her away, but she returns to Pelléas with her long hair streaming round her. Golaud becomes tormented by jealousy and, seeing the lovers together, he stabs Pelléas. Mélisande dies of a broken heart. Reunited in death, the lovers are resurrected for Eternity from their forest grave.

"Pelléas and Mélisande like Romeo and Juliet are part of a legend which has through the centuries taught subsequent generations about love. The forces that unite or divide, that kill or revive them still constitute the very substance of love.

"Today love does not have to come under the same judgment as of old, nor to surmount the same obstacles, but love itself is the same, with fewer frills and furbelows, even, perhaps, stripped naked. This is why I have chosen to play down the circumstances that we connect with Pelléas and Mélisande. Instead, I have attempted to portray them as they appear in us. Hounded by an identical destiny, we see in them what we feel happening in ourselves."

The ballet is arranged to the tone poem of the same name by Arnold Schoenberg, who wrote that "inspired entirely by Maeterlinck's wonderful drama, I have tried to mirror every detail of it."

Reviewing *Pelléas and Mélisande* after its first performance, in *The Observer* of London, the critic Alexander Bland noted that the ballet was featured at a gala to celebrate Margot Fonteyn's thirty-fifth year with the Royal Ballet: "It has been an incredible career which has seen her steadily progress to that peak of artistry where, like a mature draughtsman, she can express everything with almost nothing. She packs richness into simplicity, conceals technique under nonchalance and melts emotion into classical economy and integrity . . . There is one effective moment when Mélisande dominates the stage with a tent of gauzy tresses . . . in which Pelléas becomes voluptuously entangled."

LA PÉRI

Music by Norbert Burgmüller. Choreography by Jean Coralli. Book by Théophile Gautier and Jean Coralli. First presented at the Théâtre de l'Académie Royal de Musique, Paris, July 17, 1843, with Carlotta Grisi and Lucien Petipa. Presented in a new version by Frederick Ashton, by the Royal Ballet at the Royal Opera House, Covent Garden, February 15, 1956, with Margot Fonteyn and Michael Somes. Music by Paul Dukas. Scenery by Ivor Hitchens. Costumes by André Levasseur. First presented in the United States by the Royal Ballet, September 26, 1957, at the Metropolitan Opera House. Presented in a new version by George Skibine to the Dukas score at the Opéra, Paris, December 1966, with Calire Motte and Jean-Pierre Bonnefous. Setting by Robert D. Mitchell. Costumes and lighting

by Nicholas Cernovich. First presented in the United States by the National
Ballet of Washington, with Andrea Vodehnal and Steven Grebel, at the
Lisner Auditorium, Washington, February 26, 1967.

According to Persian mythology, *péris* are fallen angels who assume the form
of elfin sprites. There have been many ballets created around the story of
Iskender and his search for the lotus, the flower of immortality, and his encounter with a *péri*. Iskender wanders far and wide searching for the flower,
which he finds at last in the hand of a lovely sleeping *péri*. He steals the flower
but cannot leave, for he adores the girl he sees lying before him. When she
wakens, the *péri* senses his want, and dances to play upon his desire so that
she may regain the flower. Iskender is bewitched and in exchange for a kiss
would give her the world. He returns the flower. "Then the lotus seemed like
snow and gold like the summit of Elbourz in the evening sun. The form of the
péri appeared to melt into the light emanating from the calyx. Iskender saw
her disappear. And realizing that this signified his approaching end, he felt the
shadow encircling him."

This story and its heroine have fascinated choreographers and dancers for
more than a hundred years. There have been many dances based on the original two-act ballet with Théophile Gautier's scenario. Grisi, Pavlova (in a version by Clustine, 1921), Spessivtzeva (in the ballet by Leo Staats, 1921),
Markova (in Frederick Ashton's first version, 1931, for the Ballet Club, London), Yvette Chauvire (in the version by Serge Lifar, 1948), and others. The
Dukas score was commissioned by the Russian ballerina Natalia Trouhanova
and first performed by her in Paris, April 22, 1912.

PERSEPHONE

Melodrama in three scenes. Music by Igor Stravinsky. French text by André
Gide. Choreography by Kurt Jooss. Scenery and costumes by André Barsacq.
First presented by Ballets Ida Rubinstein at the Opéra, Paris, April 30,
1934, with Ida Rubinstein in the title role. Revived in a new version by the
Royal Ballet, with choreography by Frederick Ashton at the Royal Opera
House, Covent Garden, London, December 12, 1961. Scenery and costumes
by Nico Ghika. Svetlana Beriosova appeared in the title role.

The ballet tells the story of Persephone, daughter of Zeus and Demeter, goddess of fertility, who was taken away to the Underworld by Pluto, its king. In
the first scene, "The Abduction of Persephone," Persephone on "the world's
first morning" is warned not to pick the narcissus, for whoever breathes its fragrance must come to see a vision of Hades. But Persephone admires the flower
and as she smells it she glimpses the sorrowful Shades of the Underworld, who
must endlessly wander until the end of time. She has pity on them. Eumolpus,

the high priest, tells Persephone that if she will go to the Underworld the lot of the Shades will be happier. Pluto claims Persephone, who descends to the Underworld.

In the second scene, "Persephone in the Underworld," she has become Queen of the Shades. With her descent, Pluto has banished spring from the earth. Biting a pomegranate presented to her by Mercury, she recalls the earth above, her mother, and her earthly husband, Demaphoon. Eumolpus relates that the earthly winter will not last forever and that it is Demeter's plan to cause Demaphoon to teach men to till the soil, thereby bringing them salvation. Through his intercession, Persephone is reborn and goes to rejoin her earthly husband.

"Persephone Reborn," the final scene, shows the goddess reunited with her mother and husband; spring returns to the earth. Having restored the seasons, Persephone realizes that her destiny lies with the Shades and that she must again return to rule over them at Pluto's side. Taking a torch offered her by Mercury to light her way back into the darkness, Persephone makes her farewell.

PETROUCHKA

Ballet burlesque in one act, four scenes. Music by Igor Stravinsky. Choreography by Michel Fokine. Book by Stravinsky and Alexandre Benois. Scenery and costumes by Benois. First presented by Diaghilev's Ballets Russes at the Théâtre du Châtelet, Paris, June 13, 1911, with Vaslav Nijinsky as Petrouchka, *Tamara Karsavina as the* Ballerina, *Alexandre Orlov as the* Moor, *and Enrico Cecchetti as the* Charlatan. *First presented in the United States by Diaghilev's Ballets Russes at the Century Theatre, New York, January 25, 1916, with Leonide Massine, Lydia Lopokova, and Adolph Bolm in the principal roles.*

Petrouchka tells the story of a puppet with a human heart, a creature of straw who comes to life only to be disbelieved. Characters similar to Petrouchka, half comic, half tragic, have been common to popular theatrical tradition in Europe for hundreds of years—characters such as Pierrot and Puck, clowns no one will ever take seriously, funny men who are always unlucky but who somehow manage to have in the end more wisdom than anybody else; funny men such as Charlie Chaplin's tramp. *Petrouchka* is ballet's representation of this universal character, of what the creators of the ballet knew in their youth as the "Russian Punch and Judy Show." At first the puppet is happy to be a mere automaton. Then he falls in love with a beautiful dancer and tries to win her, though all the world seems against him. He loses her, dies, and everyone laughs. He wins by returning for the last laugh himself.

Maria Tallchief in *Firebird*. Photo by George Platt Lynes.

Edward Villella in *Brahms-Schoenberg Quartet*. Photo by Martha Swope.

Violette Verdy in *Liebeslieder Walzer*. Photo by Martha Swope.

Suzanne Farrell and Jacques d'Amboise in *Apollo*. Photo by Martha Swope.

Suzanne Farrell and Arthur Mitchell in *Agon*. Photo by Martha Swope.

Rudolf Nureyev in *Petrouchka*. Photo by Rosemary Winckley.

Natalia Makarova in *Don Quixote*. Photo by Rosemary Winckley.

Mikhail Baryshnikov in *Don Quixote*. Photo by Kenn Duncan.

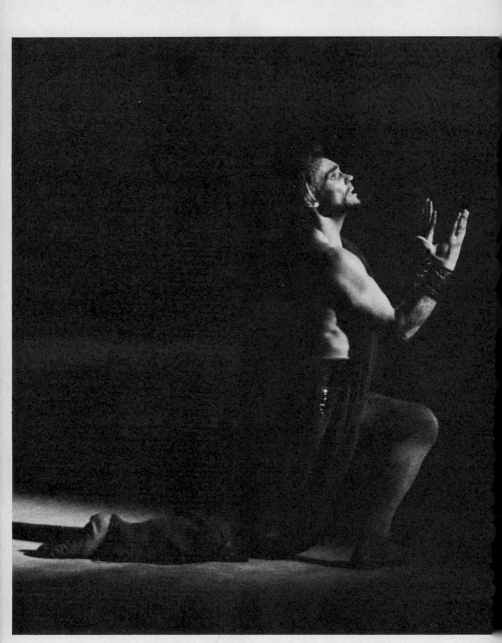

Vladimir Vasiliev in *Spartacus*. Photo by Rosemary Winckley.

Suzanne Farrell and Peter Martins in *Jewels* ("Diamonds").
Photo by Costas.

Violette Verdy, Carla Fracci, Eleanor D'Antuono, and Patricia McBride in *Pas de Quatre* at the Gala to Save the Dance Collection of the New York Public Library, 1972.
Photo by Martha Swope.

Karin von Aroldingen in *A Midsummer Night's Dream*. Photo by Costas.

Sara Leland and Bart Cook in *Tchaikovsky Suite No. 3*. Photo by Costas.

Suzanne Farrell and Peter Martins in *Concerto in G*. Photo by Martha Swope.

Suzanne Farrell and Peter Martins in *Concerto in G*. Photo by Beverley Gallegos.

SCENE ONE: THE SHROVETIDE FAIR   The first scene of the ballet is set in a great public square in old St. Petersburg. The year is 1830; the season, winter —the last week before Lent, when all the populace gather together for final feasting and celebration. Even before the curtain rises, the orchestra tells us it is carnival time, as the cheerful blatancy of the music swells and varies to bring up images of a surging festival, where everyone is determined to have a good time in his own way. Peasants, gypsies, soldiers, and well-dressed folk, all in holiday attire, mingle in the snow-covered square. Fair booths decorated with bright bunting and flags surround an open area, and in the back stands the largest booth of all. It has blue curtains drawn across it like a stage. Above the booth, in Russian, are the words "Living Theater." Behind it are the spires of government buildings topped with flags. The crowd tries to keep warm by moving constantly; its members stamp and throw their arms around their chests as they talk to each other; some buy hot tea at a booth with a large, steaming samovar. But the cold weather serves only to intensify their good spirits. Everyone seems to be happy and carefree in the pursuit of a traditional pleasure all can share. The open, undisguised merriment of the music whirls with the circling crowd and its quick-changing rhythms accentuate the variety of noises that refuse to blend into one tune—the loud, comradely greetings, the laughter, the shrieking of persistent barkers, the vigorous dancing of three enthusiastic peasants.

The crowd hears a barrel organ grinding away in the distance, but its small sound is almost immediately drowned out by the hubbub in the square. The organ-grinder enters, playing a street song, and the people stand aside to watch his approach. With him comes a girl who carries a little rug under her arm and a triangle. She spreads the rug over the snow, strikes the triangle in a steady beat to secure everyone's attention, and begins to dance to a gay tune. Her dance is clearly designed to show the crowd how rapidly she can turn on one point without stopping; and as people begin to be impressed by her virtuosity, the organist shows off too, by grinding out the song with one hand and duplicating it on a cornet he holds with the other. When he finishes, he begins to play again his rather mournful street song, while on the other side of the stage a rival team of entertainers has appeared to attract the crowd away. There another dancer begins to turn to the tune of a hurdy-gurdy, and a new group forms about the girl and her accompanist. The organist and his partner glance over at the newcomers and speed up the tempo of their act. The two dancers and the two instruments compete openly: each of the girls imitates the other's movements, and the crowd watches first one and then the other as if they were looking at a tennis match. Finally the girls have spent all their energy and the contest is over. Both end their dances in identical positions; the spectators applaud, reward both couples, and everyone is delighted.

The square is now packed with people, who mill about greeting one another and conversing as the orchestra renews the raucous overture. Rowdy peasants come in and dance an animated Russian folk dance to the amusement of some of the crowd. The scene is now feverish with liveliness and hearty good spirits, and the music reaches a high volume to duplicate this enthusiasm. Two drummers step out from behind the blue-curtained stage at the rear and walk forward. The crowd stands back. The drums roll commandingly; everyone looks toward the stage; a loud chord from the orchestra is cut off sharply. A man with a high-peaked hat pokes his head through the curtains. This is the Charlatan, the showman in charge of the "Living Theater." Everyone is silent as they watch him. He is a showman who entertains by magic, and when he steps out from behind the curtains, no one is quite certain what he will do. His long black robe decorated with mysterious signs, his white face, and his menacing gestures attract the crowd strangely. He takes out a flute. The orchestra sounds a few weird bars suggestive of incipient evil. Then the Charlatan surprises us by playing on his instrument not an Oriental incantation, but a pleasant melody, beseeching in its repetitions. This is his magic song, the music that will bring to life the unseen show behind the closed curtains. The crowd waits, fascinated. The Charlatan gives a sudden imperious signal. The curtains fly back. We see a stage separated into three small compartments. In each compartment rests a motionless puppet, staring out at the audience with blank expression. The three figures are supported by high armrests. In the center is the prima Ballerina, with perfect, Dresden-china features and pink cheeks. She poses rigidly, waiting to be wound up. On the left is the Moor, with white eyes and a white mouth set in a coal-black face. He wears a turban, a bright blouse with a sash about his waist, and trousers of gold brocade. On the right, completely relaxed, is Petrouchka. His face is a white mask, his body is limp, like that of a rag doll. His costume has no conventional design: the loose-fitting trousers that hang down over black boots, the blouse ruffled at the neck, the haphazard cap—all make his figure absurd. While the ballerina and the Moor hold themselves erect, Petrouchka's head lolls to the side. Of the three, he is the least eager to move or to be moved. Lifeless as he is, Petrouchka therefore seems to be more natural. The ballerina and the Moor are posed tensely, ready to spring into activity, but Petrouchka's attitude suggests that perhaps he is tired of being a puppet.

The three puppets remain still as the Charlatan finishes his invocation to his magical gods. The ensuing music is low and mysterious. The Charlatan cuts it short by sounding his flute three times, whereupon Petrouchka, the ballerina, and the Moor instantly wake up and move their feet to the sharp and lively rhythms of a Russian dance. The puppets still stand, and their feet move so fast on and off the floor that their bodies seem suspended. They have come to life so spontaneously, and their feet mark each accent of the dance with such energetic unison, that it is difficult to believe they were inert but a moment before. The music becomes more demanding in its tempo, but the puppets follow the dance perfectly, as if they were toy soldiers obeying the beat of a snare drum. Now they abandon their armrests and step down. The crowd gives them room, and, to the great pleasure of the spectators, the puppets act out a dumb

show almost as mechanically as they danced. Both the Moor and Petrouchka
are enamored of the ballerina. The Moor flirts with her, and the ballerina
seems to favor him, upon which Petrouchka, in a jealous rage, attacks his rival.
The Charlatan signals for the drama to stop, and the three puppets involun-
tarily return to their dance routine. The stage grows darker, and the crowd begins to wander off. The Charlatan makes another signal, and the puppets immediately cease all movement and become rigid and still. The curtain falls.

SCENE TWO: PETROUCHKA'S ROOM   Now we are taken behind the scenes, into
the private lives of the puppets. Petrouchka's room is a barren cell. The peaks
of icy high mountains are painted all along the walls, near to the floor, while
up above, near the ceiling, is a border of puffy white clouds. The room has
been decorated, the set implies, for a character not altogether of this world.
On the right wall hangs a large portrait of the Charlatan. A door on the left is
embellished with satanic figures carrying pitchforks. Petrouchka is suddenly
tossed into the room through this door by the Charlatan. The door slams shut.
Petrouchka makes a feeble effort to pick himself up, but wonders whether it is
worth it. His wooden gestures indicate that everything is hopeless. Here he is
in prison again, with nothing to look at but a picture of his master. A piano
takes up a despondent theme that embodies Petrouchka's despair, while the
rest of the orchestra tries to drown it out. He moves about the room helplessly,
he tries to open the door, he pounds on the walls, hoping that someone will
release him. Then, all alone, he rages against the world that ignores him. As
trumpets blare a loud fanfare, Petrouchka turns to the portrait of the Charlatan and shakes his fists in challenge to the evil magician who limits his life to
public performances.

As if to prove that he is worthy of a better fate, Petrouchka then does a little dance in which he imitates human expression of feeling. The piano accompanies him. His arms are stiff, but when he holds them close to his heart and
then opens them in a gesture of hope, we see that the puppet understands
more than the dumb-show version of love. He is a marionette who might become human, but cannot because of the Charlatan who made him. His hatred
of the Charlatan is his hatred of his inarticulate self, that part of his dual nature that can but pathetically copy the human gestures for the human emotion
his other nature feels so intensely. He arouses our pity because we see that his
rage against the world is also his rage at himself. His clumsy wooden limbs try
in vain to express their freedom, and his white face is a mask of sorrow.

But Petrouchka's whole attitude changes when he turns to see that the
ballerina has entered his prison. Now the music is gay and lighthearted and
Petrouchka jumps about joyfully. The ballerina, who stands motionless on
point, registers shock at this inelegant expression of pleasure. She makes the appropriate formal gestures of delicate disapproval and turns to go. Petrouchka is
beside himself with anxiety and proceeds to increase the ballerina's distaste by

leaping higher to attract her attention. Clearly, the ballerina has had enough of the uncontrollable puppet. She turns and leaves.

Once again Petrouchka is in despair and again, to the accompaniment of the piano and the overpowering orchestra that represents the world he fights against, he gives himself up to his grief. The Charlatan will always think him a mere puppet; the ballerina will never regard him as anything but an idiotic buffoon. He flings his exhausted body about the room, bangs against the walls, finally succeeds in tearing open a large hole in the right wall, and collapses when he sees that it leads nowhere.

SCENE THREE: THE MOOR'S ROOM   The Moor, too, has been imprisoned by the showman, but his abode is ornately decorated and sumptuously furnished. Everything is splashed with color. A large couch, covered with the skin of a tiger and backed with cushions, is on the left. Tall, bushy palm trees are painted on the walls. Serpents and ferocious beasts depicted in bright colors peer out into the room through thick jungle foliage. On the right is a door ornamented with a snake rampant. On the couch lies the Moor. He is playing idly with a coconut. The music is slow, almost lazy, as the Moor amuses his indolence by tossing the coconut and catching it. Unlike Petrouchka, the Moor is satisfied with his abode and appears happy whiling away the time of day like the caged beast contentedly resigned to an imitation jungle. He is also unlike the clown in his inhumanity: he is all puppet. He is soon bored with his simple pastime and tries to vary it with complications: by grasping his toy with his feet and letting it fall, by catching it in many ways. But this is not sufficient for the Moor's entertainment. He grows angry with the coconut. He shakes it, as an animal would shake the head of a helpless victim. He hears something inside, but he cannot break the coconut. He pulls out his scimitar, places the coconut on the floor at his feet. The music crashes with his effort to break the coconut in two, but it is hard as a rock. The Moor is astonished. He stares at the mysterious object that can withstand his mighty blow and decides that it must be magical. He kneels then, bows and worships his plaything as he would worship a god.

The door moves aside, and a roll on a drum signals the entrance of the ballerina. She dances in, horn held to her lips, and steps gaily about the room, the beat of the drum accompanying the tune she plays. The Moor forgets his fetish and watches her with great pleasure, a pleasure which the music expresses with brief cries. The ballerina is charmed by this simple response, so different from the open approval of Petrouchka, and obliges the Moor by dancing a waltz. He is delighted beyond mere approval by this performance and insists upon dancing too. His motions are primitive alongside her elegant steps, but he nevertheless tries to make his crude dance fit the rhythm of the ballerina's waltz. He fails miserably and persists in his own private rhythm as the orchestra imitates the chaos of their duet by opposing different melodies. The Moor is now infatuated with the dainty ballerina and demonstrates his affection by pulling her toward the couch. The ballerina pretends to be aghast at this behavior, but secretly she is charmed also and scarcely resists when the Moor holds her on his lap. Their amorous dalliance is interrupted, however, by strange noises from outside. One of Petrouchka's melodies is proclaimed on the trumpet, and the clown thrusts his arm in at the door in an effort to wedge himself into the room. He has imagined the plight of the ballerina and has come to her aid! The couple jump guiltily as he forces his way in; they spring apart. The jealous Petrouchka berates the Moor for his behavior and approaches him menacingly as the music resounds his rage. The Moor recovers from the surprise of Petrouchka's sudden appearance and replies with animal grunts. Then he draws his scimitar and begins to chase the clown around the room. The ballerina faints on the couch, the Moor closes in on Petrouchka, whose end seems certain until he makes a quick dash for the door and escapes. The Moor is about to pursue the interloper, when he remembers the ballerina. He drops his sword, goes back over to the couch, and pulls the ballerina back onto his lap. The curtain falls as his head bobs up and down in savage satisfaction. The private lives of the three puppets have turned out to be almost identical to the dumb show they acted before the public: Petrouchka always loses.

SCENE FOUR: GRAND CARNIVAL   The Shrovetide Fair, the outside world, has gone on while we watched the inner drama backstage, and the music now takes us back to the festivities. Very little time has elapsed, for the stage is not yet dark and the celebrating crowd is by no means ready to go home. The puppet theater in the back is dark and silent. Stimulated by their continuous refreshment, the peasants are all laughing and whipping themselves up to a final high pitch of excitement. A group of nursemaids emerge from the multitude, line up, and start a traditional dance to a Russian folk song that is exhilarating in its open melody; the crowd sways to the rhythm of the dance. The nursemaids' round is interrupted by deep, plodding notes from the orchestra, which herald the arrival of a trained bear. The bear swaggers clumsily onto the scene, led by his trainer, who laughs at the fears of the spectators and directs the bear in a few simple tricks. Then follows the dance of the coachmen, whose performance outrivals all the others in color and vigor. The theme to which the nursemaids danced is heard again, and the nurses join the coachmen. The couples seem to exhaust themselves in joyous abandon, but gain fresh strength with each step. Garishly dressed masqueraders—a demon, various animals—scurry about in the square trying to frighten people, but almost everyone is involved in the dance, in watching it at first, then imitating it while standing still, then participating fully, so that the stage gradually becomes a mass of whirling color. The frenzied beat of the music, and its increasingly raucous volume, intoxicates the dancers, and—as night descends on the scene and snow begins to fall—their movements in this picture frame of old Russia surge with a final expression of carnival fervor.

The enthusiasm of the revelers has not allowed them to notice that in the back, within the puppet theater, there are signs of activity behind the drawn curtains. They all turn, as they hear strange noises inside the theater, and wait expectantly. Petrouchka comes running out, the music sounds his fanfare, and we see that he is trying to escape from the Moor, who dashes out after him. The crowd is struck dumb by this apparently spontaneous life in the puppets and looks on, fascinated, as the clown tries to avoid the blows of the Moor's scimitar. The Moor's animal strength overpowers Petrouchka. The clown is cornered. He covers his head with his arms, shaking with fright. The Moor, with one blow of his sword, strikes him down. Petrouchka doubles up in pain. The music reflects his agony and his great effort to remain alive, but his legs stretch out, his whole body quivers spasmodically, and he is dead.

His death has been so realistic that the people who surround his body cannot believe that he is a mere puppet; a crime seems to have been committed. Someone calls a policeman, who observes the dead clown and hauls out the Charlatan to give an account of the strange goings on. The Charlatan is much amused at his suspicions and picks up the body to show everyone they are mistaken. Petrouchka is now a limp rag doll, a creature who could never have been anything but lifeless. The policeman is satisfied, people shake their heads, the crowd begins to leave slowly. The Charlatan remains alone, holding the puppet, and the stage is almost completely dark. He turns to re-enter the theater—perhaps to put the errant clown back in his cell—when Petrouchka's fanfare blares out loudly to stop him in his tracks. He looks up: on the top of the theater the ghost of Petrouchka shakes his fist at the Charlatan—and at everyone else who will not believe he is real.

NOTES The idea of *Petrouchka* was first of all a musical idea. Stravinsky had finished *Firebird* and was about to begin work on his next project for Diaghilev—*The Rite of Spring*—when he interrupted his plans to compose a purely nonballetic piece. He wanted to write a piece for piano and orchestra in which the piano would seem to be attacked by the mass of instruments. It would fight back, flourish a bit, but then the large orchestra would win out.

Stravinsky began to think of this composition as a contest between a puppet, represented by the piano, and the orchestra. After he had finished it, he tried to find an idea that would express the image that had been in his mind as he composed. He found it in a word, *Petrouchka*, "the immortal and unhappy hero of every fair."

He conveyed his idea to Diaghilev, who, upon hearing the music, decided to produce a ballet on this theme as soon as possible. The painter and designer Alexandre Benois collaborated with the musician and the impresario on the story, which Michel Fokine choreographed for Nijinsky, Karsavina, Orlov, and Cecchetti.

Although it is perhaps the most famous ballet in the modern repertory, *Petrouchka* has but recently been revived with sufficient competence to remind us that its first production was a very great one indeed. Stravinsky has written in his *Autobiography* (1936): "I should like . . . to pay heartfelt homage to Vaslav Nijinsky's unsurpassed rendering of the role of Petrouchka. The perfection with which he became the very incarnation of this character was all the more remarkable because the purely saltatory work in which he excelled was in this case dominated by dramatic action, music and gesture. The beauty of the ballet was greatly enhanced by the richness of the artistic setting which Benois had created for it. My faithful interpreter Karsavina swore to me that she would never relinquish her part as the dancer, which she adored. But it was a pity that the movements of the crowd had been neglected. I mean that they were left to the arbitrary improvisation of the performers instead of being choreographically regulated in accordance with the clearly defined exigencies of the music. I regret it all the more because the *danses d'ensemble* of the coachmen, nurses and mummers, and the solo dances, must be regarded as Fokine's finest creations.

Carl Van Vechten describes Nijinsky's Petrouchka in this way: "He is a puppet and—remarkable touch—a puppet with a soul. His performance in this ballet is, perhaps, his most wonderful achievement. He suggests only the puppet in action; his facial expression never changes; yet the pathos is greater, more keenly carried over the footlights, than one would imagine possible under any conditions. I have seen Fokine in the same role, and although he gives you all the gestures the result is not the same. It is genius that Nijinsky puts into his interpretation of the part. Who can ever forget Nijinsky as Petrouchka when thrown by his master into his queer black box, mad with love for the dancer, who, in turn, prefers the Moor puppet, rushing about waving his pathetically stiff arms in the air, and finally beating his way with his clenched fists through the paper window to curse the stars? It is a more poignant expression of grief than most Romeos can give us."

Many famous dancers have since appeared in the role—Massine, Woizikowski, Jerome Robbins, Michael Kidd, Børge Ralov. Fokine revived the ballet for the Royal Danish Ballet in 1925, and for Ballet Theatre, October 8, 1942.

Petrouchka was revived by the Royal Ballet on March 26, 1957, with Alexander Grant, Margot Fonteyn, and Peter Clegg in the principal roles. Rudolf Nureyev danced the role for the first time with this company on October 24, 1963. Nadia Nerina was the doll and Keith Rosson the blackamoor. Mary Clarke wrote in the *Dancing Times:* "Let it be said at once that Nureyev captures to perfection the sawdust quality of the part. His first fall in the opening scene is just a crumble of a puppet body and all the way through one feels that the gloves contain no hands, just useless stuffing. This, of course, heightens the pathos of the character, the little pigmy soul that aspires to human loves and fears without a human body to support them. The scene in Petrouchka's cell is, as yet, only sketched; it will develop with more performances . . . but the final moment on the top of the booth, when the immortal soul asserts itself for the last time, is marvelously done. Everybody's heart must have trembled just a little bit when watching this."

Petrouchka is a ballet for which I have some sentimental recollection. In the Diaghilev production, whenever anyone was sick or unable to dance I took his part in the ballet. At one time I thought I had danced almost every male part in the ballet!

Petrouchka was revived in New York, March 13, 1970, by the City Center Joffrey Ballet under the supervision of Leonide Massine, assisted by Yurek Lazowski and Tania Massine. The principal roles were taken by Edward Verso, Erika Goodman, Christian Holder, Yurek Lazowski, and Zelma Bustilio. Noting that the ballet had not been seen in New York for twelve years, the critic Anna Kisselgoff wrote in the New York *Times* that "the spell of the decor, based on the original designs of Alexandre Benois, the magic of Igor Stravinsky's miraculous score and the radically expressive choreography of Michel Fokine are as strong as ever."

American Ballet Theatre revived *Petrouchka* June 19, 1970, at the New York State Theatre, with Ted Kivitt, Eleanor D'Antuono, and Bruce Marks in the principal roles. Clive Barnes in the New York *Times* called this production, staged by Dimitri Romanoff and Yurek Lazowski, "A sumptuous and authentic new staging that is part homage to the past and part reaffirmation of Ballet Theatre's historically classic role in American dance's future."

PICNIC AT TINTAGEL

> *Dramatic ballet in three scenes. Music by Arnold Bax. Choreography by Frederick Ashton. Scenery and costumes by Cecil Beaton. Costumes executed by Helene Pons. Lighting by Jean Rosenthal. First presented by the New York City Ballet at the City Center, New York, February 28, 1952, with Francisco Moncion as the Husband (King Mark), Diana Adams as the Wife (Iseult), Jacques d'Amboise as her Lover (Tristram), and Robert Barnett as the Caretaker (Merlin).*

Today, on the west coast of England, stands "wild Tintagel by the Cornish seas," a rocky promontory reaching out into the water. Here we find the ruins of an ancient castle celebrated by poets and chroniclers for centuries as the stronghold of King Arthur and his Knights of the Round Table. One of King Arthur's trusted knights was Tristram, who brought the beautiful Irish maid Iseult to Cornwall to be the wife of his uncle, King Mark. The love story of Tristram and Iseult has inspired writers from the time of Geoffrey of Monmouth to the times of Tennyson, Swinburne, Wagner, Hardy, Edwin Arlington Robinson, and Jean Cocteau.

This modern ballet recalls the story of Tristram and Iseult in a setting that is centuries later. The time is 1916, the year Sir Arnold Bax composed *The Garden of Fand,* the ballet's score. The place is Tintagel.

SCENE ONE   The curtain rises as the music begins. The melody is soft and magical, weaving in sound a mysterious spell. The scene is dominated by arches of gray, slatelike stone, the ruins of the castle where the romance of Tristram and Iseult took place almost a thousand years ago. A man is on stage. He is the caretaker. Dressed in green tweeds with a cap, he moves about the scene as if only he understood it, as if he shared some secret with the ancient castle that tourists could not understand.

Tourists enter on the right. They are a motoring party, dressed in the long dusters of the time. We see a man, his wife, and another man. Two other men follow behind. The husband looks about and goes over to the caretaker. As soon as he turns his back, the second man goes to the wife and takes her hand in his. She glances nervously at the other two men in their party, who are watching them, and cautions him to be discreet. The husband comes to take his wife on a tour of the castle, and they exit. As they leave, the wife waves to the second man, who walks off in the opposite direction.

The woman's maid enters, followed by her master's chauffeur and footman, who carry picnic baskets. A cloth is laid on the ground, the baskets are opened, goblets and a bottle of wine are set out, and the servants leave. The second man enters and asks the caretaker if he has seen the woman. He leaves. Now the woman inquires after the man and goes off in search of him.

The caretaker, alone, looks about quickly and takes up the bottle of wine. He opens the bottle, reaches into his pocket, gestures magically over the bottle, and then replaces it on the picnic cloth. All the picnickers return. The maid pours wine for her mistress and the second man, who stand together as the others sit on the ground. The two lovers look in each other's eyes, make a toast, and drink. As the glasses touch their lips, a trumpet is heard and the music bursts into thunderous sound. The party is alarmed, and all leave the stage.

SCENE TWO   The chauffeur and footman, magically transformed into two heralds, rush in bearing the flag of King Mark. The caretaker turns around and around in the center of the stage as the scene, almost at his command, is magically transformed. The ruins disappear, and in their place, rising from the ground, stands a colonnade that graced a room in King Mark's castle. The caretaker's wish has come true: the man and the woman have drunk the magic potion, to become Tristram and Iseult, and again he is Merlin, the magician, who can stand aside and watch the workings of his mysterious art.

Merlin leaves the scene, and King Mark enters with Iseult and Tristram. Except for their costumes, they are the same as before: two men in love with the same woman. King Mark knights Tristram with his sword, and Tristram kisses the hand of his king. Then, for a brief moment, Tristram is alone with Iseult.

The lovers snatch at the opportunity to be together. They are unaware that one of King Mark's knights watches them from the colonnade in the rear. Tristram lifts Iseult lovingly in his arms. Brangaene, Iseult's maid, rushes in and separates the lovers. She warns them to be careful, that the king approaches.

King Mark enters, and Brangaene dances with Tristram so that the king will suspect nothing. Two knights propose a hunt to the king. Mark assents and asks Tristram if he will join them. Tristram, anxious to be alone with Iseult, pleads some excuse. The two knights watch this and whisper together. Iseult observes their suspicions and separates the two talkers. Now Iseult herself whispers to Brangaene how delighted she is that she and Tristram can be alone at last.

King Mark thinks it strange that Tristram will not accompany them, but leaves the scene for the hunt. His knights and heralds follow. Iseult, alone, seeks Tristram, running in and out among the arches of the colonnade. She is unaware that one of the king's knights has entered surreptitiously and concealed himself behind one of the columns to watch her. The music is quiet, expectant.

Tristram enters, and the two lovers run together from opposite sides of the stage. The orchestra commences a restrained, almost suppressed, romantic melody that gains gradually in intensity. Tristram kneels, and Iseult falls back over his shoulder. They kneel together. The spying knight moves to watch them more closely. As the melody gathers to a soaring crescendo, Tristram lifts Iseult straight into the air.

The lights dim and the music quietens. The lovers are almost motionless, content merely to be alone together, but their passion returns. To the call of a flute, Iseult entwines her body about Tristram, and the two fall to the ground in a close embrace.

The quiet of the music is broken by a sudden, shocking fortissimo. The false knight rushes out. Tristram attacks him. Brangaene, much alarmed, goes to her mistress. A herald enters with two crossed swords, and the flags of King Mark return. Mark, who has been forewarned, enters and points accusingly to Tristram. Iseult goes to her husband to plead with him, but he brushes her aside. The two knights suggest to the king that he engage Tristram in a duel. Tristram accepts the challenge, and the two men take swords from the herald and begin to fight. As she tries frantically to separate the duelers, Iseult is stabbed. The heralds holding the flags of the king let them fall to the ground. King Mark renews his attack upon Tristram and wounds him fatally. As he falls, Tristram grasps the arm of the king and sinks slowly down. King Mark moves over to stand over Iseult's body.

SCENE THREE   The lights dim. Merlin returns, and the principals in the ancient tragedy disappear. Darkness envelops the scene briefly. When light returns, the castle has vanished and in its place we see again the ruins—dark fingers of stone against the sky. The wife and her lover stand together in their motoring coats, as we left them, about to drink the magic wine. They still look into each other's eyes, and for an instant we feel that they will never cease being Tristram and Iseult. But the husband steps in. He pushes his friend away. His wife's lover stands there, not understanding, holding out his glass: what has he done, he wonders?

The caretaker comes forward, and the stage darkens about him. Alone now in the castle, he holds up the crossed, gleaming swords of Tristram's mortal combat for Iseult. The curtain falls as the music that began the ballet returns us to the twentieth century, suggesting also that, at Merlin's command, the cycle might begin all over again.

NOTES Frederick Ashton's first ballet for the New York City Ballet, *Illuminations*, had been such a success in 1950 that the American company immediately asked the distinguished English choreographer to return to the United States and mount a second work. Ashton's obligations as principal choreographer of the Sadler's Wells Ballet made it impossible for him to do this until two years later. In the meantime, however, he had agreed with the directors of the New York City Ballet on a subject: a modern treatment of the legend of Tristram and Iseult. Ashton and Cecil Beaton, who was to design the work, traveled to Tintagel, in Cornwall, England, where they observed the ruins of the ancient castle associated for centuries with the love story of Tristram and Iseult.

Ashton wished to use as a score for his new ballet *Iseult at Tintagel* (1915), by Sir Arnold Bax, Master of the Queen's Musick. The score, however, was found to be too short for his needs, and consultation with the composer suggested alternative music—Bax's *The Garden of Fand* (1916), which had had its first performance in the United States, by the Chicago Symphony Orchestra under Frederick Stock. Ashton adopted this score, cast the ballet, and in a very short space of time staged his new work.

Walter Terry reported in the New York *Herald Tribune* that *"Picnic at Tintagel*—musically, pictorially, choreographically, dramatically," was a "theatre piece of which the New York City Ballet may be justly proud . . . Not only has Mr. Ashton used well the dramatic urgency of time but he has also choreographed with craftsmanlike shrewdness and considerable artistry . . . The love duet itself is a work of great beauty . . ." On the occasion of the New York City Ballet's first presentation of *Picnic at Tintagel* in Europe, at the Edinburgh Festival in August 1952, the New York *Times* reported that the ballet "was swift, exciting and dramatic, and is likely to occupy a permanent place in British ballet."

THE PIED PIPER

Ballet in two parts. Music by Aaron Copland. Choreography by Jerome Robbins. Lighting by Jean Rosenthal. First presented by the New York City Ballet at the City Center, New York, December 4, 1951, with a cast headed by Diana Adams and Nicholas Magallanes, Jillana, Roy Tobias, Janet Reed and Todd Bolender, Melissa Hayden and Herbert Bliss, and Tanaquil LeClercq and Jerome Robbins.

The Pied Piper is a dance ballet set to Copland's *Concerto for Clarinet and String Orchestra;* its title has nothing to do with the famous Pied Piper of Hamlin and refers instead to the clarinet soloist. Copland's score (1948) was not written with a ballet in mind, but *The Pied Piper* derives its inspiration directly from the music, so that we are always being reminded visually of what we are listening to.

Many people imagine that ballets without stories, ballets that are based simply on music—and music which was not composed for ballet in the first place—are a dull prospect. Of course, it is natural for all of us to like stories; but with a little careful listening and watching, it is just as natural for us to be entertained by a visual spectacle based on a musical narrative. After all, we begin to like stories first because we hear them, listen to them, before we learn how to read. If we listen to music in the same way, we find ourselves just as entertained: we don't have to know how to read it. *The Pied Piper* is another ballet that proves how much fun we can have if we recognize this.

Before the music begins, the curtain rises. The stage is dark, and as our eyes try to see what is there, we can barely discern a man walking out from the side toward the center. He is wearing a plain business suit and carrying a clarinet. He looks around him at the bare stage, where there is no scenery—only ladders left propped up against the back wall by stagehands, and a few idle, unpainted flats standing at the left. He looks up, where a little light filters down to illuminate the plain back wall and the radiators that cling to it. He plays a few testing scales on the clarinet and ambles across the stage to the right-hand corner. There he finds a music stand, a lamp, and a high stool. He turns the music stand so that it faces the stage, adjusts the lamp, opens the music, and sits down. Harp strings are plucked softly. Low strings reflect their chords, and the piper begins to play.

The clarinet melody is slow, quiet, sounding lonely and lyrical on the empty stage. Slowly two great doors in the back wall begin to open, and a bright slash of light widens and fans out from the doorway, making an aisle of light across the stage. Two dancers, a girl and a boy, stand silhouetted in the doorway. They are listening to the mysterious music, which seems to come from nowhere. Attracted by its sweet melancholy, they walk forward, holding hands. Both of them wear rehearsal clothes. The door closes behind them.

They bow their heads as they stand facing the soloist, then their bodies fall back into a dance that responds irresistibly to the plaintive romance of the music.

The boy supports the girl in low turns and high, soft lifts. The *pas de deux* is tender and yearning, the pace slow, the steps wide, open, and reaching. The dancers pause as a spotlight at the front of the stage throws their shadows against the back wall, then move over to the right, seeking refuge at the source of the music. Another girl enters on the left with a boy. They watch their shadows on the wall. The first couple cross the stage and the boy lifts the girl high over his head as the strings piercingly sound the climax of the melody. Now they join the other two for a moment. All bow low to their shadows on the back wall. A group of dancers wander in and, with the intruding couple, watch as the lovers finish their dance. In the slow rhythm of the dance and the music, lights come up and fade one by one to make the whole stage picture balance in the romantic mood. Lights at the back, against the wall, and on the sides shine directly onto the stage, making a carpet of yellow light. The scene grows dark again, and the boy lifts the girl off into the wings toward the disappearing yellow light.

The dancers who have been standing quietly, watching the love duet, look at the soloist. The stage is now lighted, and we see that all the dancers wear rehearsal clothes—shirts and sweaters and tights of varied colors. The piper begins a cadenza as the romantic music fades behind, and gradually the dancers gather together to listen. Others straggle on, see the group, and listen too. This is music that seems to be asking a question, in quick, lively, darting phrases. The atmosphere is expectant. Instinctively the boys and girls are attracted by the piper's song, and their bodies, almost uncontrollably, begin to answer its phrases. A blond girl's hand shakes to the music, and she holds it out at the end of her arm as if it didn't belong to her. The hand creeps around to the back of her neck, and soon her whole body is miming the music.

The solo ends after a swift climbing scale; the music is curtly and demandingly rhythmic. A redhead seems to go crazy with the insistence of the piper's call. Mysteriously she finds herself climbing on a boy's shoulders. Another boy begins to chase her. Other boys crowd in, there is a scuffle—the boys fighting, but not touching, pointing their fingers like guns.

Drawn to the scene by the light, driving melody, another couple enter. They join the redhead and her partner. The boys and girls separate into two groups and follow their leaders. When a final lead couple is seen to emerge, the boy chases the girl in mock seriousness, turns, and she chases him. Now the whole group is dancing, responding to the music with spontaneous and spasmodic jerkings and jivings as it becomes brisker and hysterically carefree. In different groups, they run back and forth, crisscrossing the stage. Then, suddenly, all the dancers are flat on the floor. Their bodies remain quiet for a minute, but then the music drives at them again with sharp, shrieking calls and they bounce on the floor. Their arms reach up into the air, then their legs. The redhead tries to control her dancing legs by pressing down on the top of her head, as if to put a lid on the vitality created by the music, but her whole body begins to vibrate. The others rise automatically to the music's call, and the stage is a mass of hurried, comic twitchings to the loud beat of the music.

Now the song of the clarinet above the music attracts the dancers like a magnet, and they gather round the piper. But his music drives them back across the stage. Grouped closely together on the side, they reach up their hands to the clarinet's high, piercing song and bow down low when the piper sounds a low note. This low note begins a fast ascending scale and propels them again into motion, and in one movement all the dancers dash across the stage toward the piper. They fall at his feet in a wave, and the music explodes on a final high note.

PIÈGE DE LUMIÈRE (Trap of Light)

Ballet by Philippe Hériat. Music by Jean-Michel Damase. Choreography by John Taras. Scenery by Félix Labisse. Costumes by André Levasseur. First presented by the Grand Ballet du Marquis de Cuevas at the Théâtre de l'Empire, Paris, December 23, 1952, with Rosella Hightower, Vladimir Skouratoff, and Serge Golovine in leading roles. First presented in the United States by the New York City Ballet at the City Center, New York, October 1, 1964, with Maria Tallchief, André Prokovsky, and Arthur Mitchell in leading roles. Supervision and lighting by David Hays.

The creator of the idea for this ballet, Philippe Hériat of the Academy Goncourt, has described the background and action:

"From time to time, escaping convicts reach the heart of the virgin forest. Forever lost to a civilization whose stern laws alone await them, they form their own communities, living on the spoils of the hunt—the skins of wild beasts, serpents, exotic birds, and giant butterflies. This existence, cut off from the world, furnishes the ballet's theme: the scene is set in such an encampment.

"A young convict joins the band of runaways. They welcome him to their midst and, as night falls, they build a fire to lure from hiding those butterflies who appear at twilight. Species of every kind swarm through the forest. The most agile, the Iphias, and the most beautiful, the Morphide, linger a while together; but even love cannot distract them from the fatal flames. Before this trap of light the massacre begins. The young convict snares the Morphide, and the Iphias sacrifices himself to save her. She escapes, leaving with her captor the glittering traces of their encounter—gold pollen from her wings. Now, like his insect prey, he, too, becomes a hunted creature."

PILLAR OF FIRE

Ballet in one act. Music by Arnold Schoenberg. Choreography and book by Antony Tudor. Scenery and costumes by Jo Mielziner. First presented by Ballet Theatre at the Metropolitan Opera House, New York, April 8, 1942, with Nora Kaye as Hagar, *Hugh Laing as the* Young Man from the House Opposite, *Lucia Chase as the* Eldest Sister, *Annabelle Lyon as the* Youngest Sister, *and Antony Tudor as the* Friend.

This ballet tells a story to a piece of music that was inspired by a story. Schoenberg's *Verklärte Nacht* (*Transfigured Night*) is based on a nineteenth-century German poem called *Weib und die Welt* (*Woman and the World*), which had a theme daring for its time. In the poem there are two characters, a man and a woman who walk together in a cold, moonlit wood. They are lovers. First the woman addresses the man. She tells him that she has sinned, that she is going to have a child that is not his. All this happened, she tells her lover, before she was sure of his affection, at a time when she was desperate for any kind of security. She has learned since that sensuality is no security at all and that her new love for him is the blessing she really sought. The man replies that she must not feel guilty, that their mutual love is so great that even her child will be unblemished, that it will be in reality his child. He says that, as the light of the moon embraces the dark night, her love for him will transfigure the child, just as his love for her has transformed him. There is no need for forgiveness: they have love.

Such is the story of *Pillar of Fire;* but because it is a ballet, it takes this story and presents it dramatically, introducing additional characters, giving us a picture of the community in which such an event can take place, motivating the principal characters and their actions as completely as possible. The time is about 1900. The place is any town. The curtain rises to a low throbbing of strings. We see a wide street, lined with houses, under a darkening sky. The street narrows and vanishes in the distance. In the foreground, on the right, stands a high, narrow house, its woodwork embellished with Victorian scrolls. On the front steps a girl sits, brooding. She is plainly, almost severely, dressed; her long dark hair is braided about her head. She sits absolutely erect, her whole body seeming to delight in an intense placidity that is belied only by the clenched fists in her lap. This is Hagar, who lives in this house with two sisters.

The music is dark, heavy, oppressive; yet within this gloom, the principal melody cries out yearningly. Hagar watches the townspeople pass by in the twilight. Young people walk in the street, young people in love, and we sense immediately that Hagar has never been like them. Spinsters walk down the street with exaggerated daintiness, and Hagar turns away in disgust. She herself is not a young girl, but already she is frightened: she cannot be like the beautiful young girls in love, and the spinsters suggest the only alternative. She smooths back her hair, and we see that she is not unattractive.

Her two sisters emerge from the house. One is older, prim, and straitlaced; the other is young, a blond girl with long curls, soon to become a woman. The contrast between these two is apparently the same as the difference Hagar has noted in the passers-by. The younger sister is obviously spoiled, and when the older sister seems to reprimand Hagar for sitting apart from them, the young girl pokes fun at her. A young man comes across the street to their door. Hagar is delighted to see him. He is her only friend, and she is in love with him. Now she is no longer moody, but she hesitates to display her true feelings before her family. She knows them too well. The friend observes this and, being a very polite, conventional young man, is pleasant to her sisters.

The sisters, in turn, are more than civil to him. They are thoroughly aware that he has come to the house mainly to see Hagar, but the one—older, strong, possessive—and the other—young, demanding, accustomed to having anything she wants—soon draw his attention to themselves while Hagar watches. The young sister sidles up to him, flirting with cunning innocence. The friend observes her manner, is charmed by her blind youth, and ignores Hagar. The spinster is delighted at this sudden success of her favorite and asks the friend into the house. He goes in, and Hagar again is alone. It occurs to no one that she would enjoy going with them.

Hagar's despair turns to anger and hatred. It is not enough that her sister has dominated her family; she must also dominate all those who come in contact with it. The girl sees her last hope of freedom gone: her friend is hopelessly ensnared. And so she tries to forget her hope that he will respond to her love. The house across the street aids her forgetfulness. Lights come up inside the house, and Hagar sees through the walls all she has imagined must take place within it. For this is a place where love is celebrated all night long, where bold, unpolite men come to meet their women.

Shadows of lovers embracing are thrown against the walls of the house, and Hagar reaches out in open longing. She is taken aback when a man comes out of the house and glares at her. He walks jauntily, confidently, putting himself on display a little. She pretends to be embarrassed when he looks at her boldly and openly. Under any other circumstances this man would seem absurd to her, but now he embodies all the longings that Hagar cannot satisfy in a normal way, and she is attracted to him and the mysterious life in the house across the street. The man gives her a final look and goes back inside.

Now Hagar's young sister returns with the friend. The friend observes Hagar and has no understanding of her dilemma. Instead of questioning her, instead of helping her, it is much easier for him to succumb to the designs of the younger girl. Now more a woman than a child, the girl curls herself around his affections with the sinuousness of a cat. Hagar sees that her older sister has succeeded in making of the younger a frightening, pretty projection of her own willful selfishness and turns away in horror at the contrast between the girl's innocent beauty and inner evil. Should she warn the friend? How can she? He would laugh and not believe her. And so she watches as the girl takes her friend's arm and goes off with him for a stroll in the moonlight.

As they disappear, Hagar is frantic. She despises not only her sisters, but the man who will be duped by them. She contorts her body obscenely to express the depth of her disgust. Feeling now completely severed from all she might hold dear, she turns instinctively toward the mysterious house. The man who watched her in the street sees that she is still alone and leaves the house to join her.

Hagar welcomes him, and the two dance together. The girl loses all sense of modesty and decorum and for the first time in her life gives open expression of her feelings. The man encourages her passion. When Hagar leaps across the stage, he seizes her in mid-air, cutting short her flight of freedom, directing her warmth only to himself. He takes her by the hand and leads her to the house. Now eager to learn its secrets, Hagar enters ecstatically.

When she leaves the house a little later, she is alone. The conventions she renounced to discover love renew their hold on her to expose her act as sin, and she is filled with remorse. Now she has nothing, for she has rapidly learned the inadequacy of the kind of life led by the bold young man.

Her older sister enters and sees the guilt on Hagar's face. Neighbors passing by seem to know of her guilt, and Hagar, bitterly ashamed, seeks some friendly response from the crowd. She is shunned by everyone, even by the sordid people who frequent the house she has just left. These lovers-in-experience look at her in contempt while the youthful lovers-in-innocence scarcely see her.

The younger sister and the friend return from their walk. While the older sister mingles with a group of spinsters, confirming the shame Hagar has brought on the family, the young girl cavorts with new playmates from the house across the street. She is delighted to discover how nice they are.

The tormented Hagar can turn to no one. Obediently, like a child, she goes with her sisters toward the house. The two women say good night to her friend, as if to apologize for her behavior. The scene blacks out.

The street and the houses have vanished when the scene is lit again. The three sisters find themselves outcasts from society because of Hagar's indiscretion. Secretly her two sisters are delighted at her defection; but they are angry at what it has cost them and they repudiate her. The friend comes to her with his sympathy and help, but Hagar cannot bear to confront him with her evil. She seeks recognition instead from the townspeople, from the loose women, from men like her seducer. All are aghast at her downfall and will not help. Finally, in desperation, she reaches out pathetically to the seducer himself. He looks at her as if he'd never seen her.

Seeing her final despair, the friend returns. Hagar twists away to flee, but now the young man will not let her go. He holds her strongly, yet tenderly, tells her that she has forgotten his love and that he is there to stand by her and welcome her as his own. The girl is overwhelmed with his loving kindness and dances with him a *pas de deux* that is not only passionate, but tender. Hagar now possesses the permanent love that she despaired of finding. The lovers disappear for a moment, then we see them again, walking away in the distance, their hands clasped, their shoulders touching. They move slowly away out of sight in a deep green forest to the singing romantic music.

NOTES   In 1973 American Ballet Theatre filmed for television the full-length *Pillar of Fire* under the supervision of Antony Tudor. Sallie Wilson, Gayle Young, Marcos Paredes, Bonnie Mathis, and Ellen Everett were the principal dancers.

The ballerina Sallie Wilson, who has excelled in the title role of this ballet, had a number of interesting things to say about working with the choreographer Antony Tudor in an interview with the writer John Gruen, first published in *Dance Magazine*, March 1975. Excerpt: "Tudor makes you aware of the fact that when you are stepping on the stage, you're not coming in from the wings, but from where you are . . ."

PINEAPPLE POLL

Comic ballet in three scenes. Music by Sir Arthur Sullivan, arranged by Charles Mackerras. Choreography by John Cranko. Scenery and costumes by Osbert Lancaster. First presented by the Sadler's Wells Theatre Ballet at the Sadler's Wells Theatre, London, March 13, 1951, with Elaine Fifield as Pineapple Poll, David Blair as Captain Belaye, and David Poole as Jasper. First presented in the United States by the Sadler's Wells Theatre Ballet at the Buffalo Theatre, Buffalo, New York, October 23, 1951, with Maryon Lane as Pineapple Poll and David Blair and David Poole in their original roles.

Pineapple Poll is a Gilbert and Sullivan ballet, based on one of the *Bab Ballads* of Gilbert and on a selection of Sullivan's music from the famous operettas that he wrote with Gilbert's collaboration. Like *H.M.S. Pinafore* and *The Pirates of Penzance, Pineapple Poll* is typically and charmingly British. It is the first ballet to exploit the universal fame of the Royal Navy and, like our own native ballets *Rodeo* and *Fancy Free,* gives us a story that is both happy and sentimental.

The story of the ballet takes its cue from Gilbert's ballad the *Bumboat Woman's Story.* (A bumboat is a boat carrying provisions, vegetables, trinkets, and so forth, to ships at anchor.) This ballad tells the history of the bumboat woman, Pineapple Poll, who joyfully recalls her past by saying:

My cheeks were mellow and soft, and my eyes were large and sweet,
Poll Pineapple's eyes were the standing toast of the Royal fleet!

A bumboat woman was I, and I faithfully served the ships
With apples and cakes, and fowls and beer, and half-penny dips,
And beef for the general mess, where the officers dine at nights,
And fine fresh peppermint drops for the rollicking midshipmites.

SCENE ONE: PORTSMOUTH; A PUBLIC SQUARE   Poll's history in the ballet begins one day in spring in a public square at Portsmouth, the great port in South England. Painted statues of the god and goddess of the sea stand on either side of the stage, framing the scene. The buildings—shops and naval supply stores—are clean and brightly painted. In the distance, over the shoulder of the statue of an admiral that stands in the background, we see the pointed roofs of warehouses and masts of anchored ships. On the right stands a pub, the Steam Packet. Jasper, potboy at the pub, is busy polishing the window that advertises wines and spirits.

Jasper turns and watches longingly as two pretty girls come into the square, dancing with a sailor. The sailor is dressed in a typical British seaman's uniform of the late nineteenth century; the girls wear colorful summer dresses. Two other tars enter the Steam Packet; a crowd of girls come in with a group of sailors, take partners, and dance. Two girls who are left without partners go to the door of the pub and knock. Two sailors come out to join them, and the waltzing couples pause for refreshment. The sailors call Jasper to bring them pots of beer, and the potboy runs frantically back and forth from the pub to the street with tankard after tankard. Finally he, too, is in need of refreshment and downs two mugs of beer before he reaches the sailors. The hearty tars toss him about, and he retreats to the door of the Steam Packet to watch them renew their dance. The vigorous dance ends with all the girls sitting on their partners' knees.

The music is bright and merry, a triangle tinkles, and Pineapple Poll dances into the square. She is dressed in a candy-striped dress and wears green ribbons in her red hair. She carries on her head a basket filled with flowers and trinkets, and soon all the sailors are surrounding her. Poll sells most of her wares and begins to dance. From the door of the pub, Jasper waves to her. She does not acknowledge his greeting, and he places his hand over his heart, signifying his love for her. He, too, would like to buy a trinket from Pineapple Poll and goes through all his pockets, one by one, searching for the one coin he knows he possesses. He finds a piece of silver and approaches Poll hopefully, but she treats him like any other customer and when he gives her the flower he has purchased, she throws it on the ground. Poll, however, consents to dance with him briefly, and Jasper holds her in his arms until he sees that his love is not requited; he returns to the pub.

The girls and the sailors promenade about the square, and Poll, without a partner, picks up the flower Jasper gave her and for a moment reconsiders. Then she tosses it away again and circles the stage. She and all the girls stop their dancing at this point and watch breathlessly the entrance of Captain Belaye:

Of all the kind commanders who anchor in Portsmouth Bay,
By far the sweetest of all was kind Lieutenant Belaye.
Lieutenant Belaye commanded the gunboat, *Hot Cross Bun,*
She was seven and seventy feet in length, and she carried a gun.

The tars salute their captain while the girls begin to swoon. Captain Belaye, dark and handsome, wears a blue jacket, white duck trousers, and an officer's cap at a natty angle. Belaye jauntily inspects his crew, who automatically line up before him. He straightens one of the sailor's neckerchiefs and tries to act as if he were oblivious to the admiring glances of the girls. Casually he touches Poll's cheek, and she steps back in a romantic daze.

The orchestra sounds a drum roll, and Belaye begins to dance. His merry, rapid dance depicts the routine of life at sea: he peers through an imaginary long glass, climbs imaginary ropes, and orders his crew about. The crew, who stand in back of him during this solo, throw their hats in the air at a final dazzling display of virtuosity by their commander. The girls rush to surround him. The tars take their swooning partners out of the square, lest they begin to devote all of their time to the side-whiskered captain. Poll is the last reluctant girl to leave the scene and whirls out of sight, dizzy with love for the captain.

Belaye is alone for a moment, but soon he is joined by a pretty overdressed young lady and her chaperone. This is Blanche, the girl he wants to marry, accompanied by her aunt, Mrs. Dimple. Blanche is all decked out in red, white, and blue and clearly is in love with her fiancé's navy. Mrs. Dimple, in black, wears a high feathered hat and brandishes an umbrella, which gets in the way every time the captain tries to speak to her or to Blanche. He and Blanche snatch a few moments together; he embraces her, and the music is romantic. But Mrs. Dimple is on the job again; the music mimics her busybody authority as she scolds the two lovers. They begin to dance together, but Mrs. Dimple good-humoredly interferes again and in the process drops her umbrella and shawl over and over again. When she turns away to look about the square, Belaye kisses Blanche; upon the return of the crowd, he escorts her and Mrs. Dimple to another part of the town.

Poll observes his departure disconsolately, and all the girls follow her example in a slow ensemble dance that is listless and despondent. The sailors try to cheer the girls up, but the girls will have none of them. The tars are a little angry now and play tug of war with their sometime sweethearts. When they end up flat on their backs, they vow vengeance on their handsome captain.

Good Captain Belaye dances back in at this point, and again the girls are in a daze. The sailors rage as the girls reach out to touch him and blow him kisses frantically. Belaye reprimands them as if they, too, were members of his crew, but the sailors are still jealous and threaten him. He dances in their midst and is tossed about by the men, as the girls continue flirting. Belaye dances gaily down through a line of adoring girls, who kneel and try to touch him as he passes, and the curtain falls.

SCENE TWO: THE QUAYSIDE   Night has fallen. A drop curtain places us on a dock that stretches out into Portsmouth Harbor. *H.M.S. Hot Cross Bun* is seen at the right. Above the ship's anchor chain a nude figurehead winks amusingly. Across the water a lighthouse stands at the end of a long seaside quay, where the Lord Nelson Tavern and the customhouse face us. Captain Belaye strides across the scene and mounts the gangway, shaking his head at the impertinent lasses of Portsmouth town.

Pineapple Poll follows him. She knows that the *Hot Cross Bun* has been ordered back to sea and is sad that she will not see Belaye for some time. Then, on the right, at the foot of the gangway, she discovers a discarded sailor's uniform. Suddenly her face brightens and she rushes off into the wings.

Liberty has expired for the crew of the *Hot Cross Bun,* and in slow single file the sailors make their way across the dock to their ship. When they have disappeared up the gangway, Poll returns. She now wears white sailor's pants and her mood has changed completely:

> And I went to Lieutenant Belaye (and he never suspected me!)
> And I entered myself as a chap as wanted to go to sea.

Poll is delighted at the ruse, whirls happily, puts on the blue jacket, takes the ribbons out of her hair, and adjusts the sailor hat at a jaunty angle. Now she is ready for sea. She steps up the gangway with salty determination.

The music now sounds a pathetic strain, and Jasper arrives on the scene. He is looking for Poll and has come to the dock as a last resort. He cannot find her and, as he looks down at the water, he fears the worst. Suppose she has thrown herself into the sea, all for the love of Captain Belaye! Jasper doesn't quite believe it, but soon he finds it impossible to believe anything else: there on the dock is Poll's hair ribbon and there are her discarded clothes. Jasper shakes his fist at the *Hot Cross Bun* and weeps for his lost love. He knows she is dead. He holds Poll's dress against his shoulder, as if she were still dancing with him, and caresses the dress. Slowly he walks away.

SCENE THREE: ON BOARD H.M.S. HOT CROSS BUN   The curtain rises, the music brightens, and we find ourselves on the afterdeck of Captain Belaye's ship. In the back, under the poop deck, is the captain's cabin. The white ensign of the Royal Navy flies free in the wind. Belaye is at the helm. The crew lines up at quarters on deck, and Captain Belaye leaves the helm to put them through their paces. He dances before them, long glass in hand. The crew watch respectfully, all that is except the sailor Pineapple Poll, who adores her captain so much that she can barely keep in line. At Belaye's command, Poll spreads her arms wide and the rest of the crew, in a close line, turn around her, like an anchor chain winding around a capstan.

Although the crew seem to be exhausted and Poll is plainly seasick, Belaye has other tasks for them to do and orders them to aim one of the ship's guns at a target he spies in the distance. The crew haul out a cannon, set it in place, load it, and stand ready. Belaye walks over to fire the gun and is astonished to see his crew hold their hands to their ears and run to the starboard side. The cannon is delayed in firing, and when it finally explodes, Pineapple Poll falls back in a dead faint. The other sailors don't know what to do, and Belaye tries to revive this supersensitive member of his crew. He is holding Poll in his arms when she recovers, and this is sufficient to send her into another swoon.

At this point Belaye sees that the *Hot Cross Bun* has reached its destination: Portsmouth again! He takes a ring out of his pocket and smiles. He all but drops Poll, runs across the deck, and leaps over the side to the dock. Poll is left alone for a moment and assumes that all the crew will go ashore. But then she observes that the men are behaving in a curious fashion, very unlike the seafaring type, and a number of curious incidents come back to her:

We sailed that afternoon at the mystic hour of one,—
Remarkably nice young men were the crew of the *Hot Cross Bun.*
I'm sorry to say that I've heard that sailors sometimes swear,
But I never yet heard a Bun say anything wrong, I declare.

When Jack Tars meet, they meet with a "Messmate, ho! What Cheer?"
But here, on the *Hot Cross Bun,* it was "How do you do, my dear?"
When Jack Tars growl, I believe they growl with a big big D—
But the strongest oath on the *Hot Cross Bun* was a mild "Dear me!"

One sailor, striding across the deck with affected saltiness, stops to primp girlishly at the porthole of the captain's cabin. No wonder, Poll says to herself, that:

Belaye would admit that his men were no great use to him,
"But then," we would say, "there is little to do on a gunboat trim.
I can hand, and reef, and steer, and fire my big gun too—
And it is such a treat to sail with a gentle well-bred crew."

Poll begins to wonder where Captain Belaye has gone and picks up his long glass to train it on the town. One of the crew points out that she's looking through the wrong end and grabs the instrument to have a look himself. Captain Belaye leaps back aboard, and they are delighted at his return until they see that he is not alone. He lifts over the side his new bride, Blanche, and Mrs. Dimple.

When the sailors see Blanche in her wedding dress, they fall over in a mass faint. All but Poll, that is, who is so angry that she goes to the captain and claims him for her own. Blanche will not believe her, and Poll takes off her hat and jacket to prove that she has been intimate with Belaye on the ship. Belaye cannot believe his eyes. No one can believe their eyes when all the sailors tear off their false beards and turn out to be girls too!

Blanche now hates her new husband and will not listen when he tries to explain that he is surprised by all this. She is threatening to leave him when the real "Jack Tars," the real crew of the *Hot Cross Bun*, climb over the bulwarks to berate their captain for sailing away with their girls. Attacked from all sides, Belaye can do nothing. Some of the girls swoon and fall over the helm. But the sailors will have no more nonsense. They grab the girls, throw them on the deck, and stand over them triumphantly. Belaye leaves with his Blanche and her aunt.

The girls seem delighted at this reconciliation and rock contentedly back and forth in their sailors' arms. Now Jasper enters with Poll and they dance together happily. Poll is joyful that at least one man can be constant in his affections! Captain Belaye and his new wife have now settled their argument and they enter with Mrs. Dimple. Belaye is in full-dress uniform—gold epaulets and cocked hat. Mrs. Dimple carries his regular jacket and cap; she goes and presents them to Jasper. The potboy puts both of them on. Poll kisses him, admires his appearance, and they leave the scene to the sailors.

The crew of the *Hot Cross Bun* dance a vigorous, rowdy number and then hail the return of Jasper. Poll joins Jasper; he lifts her high in his arms, then releases her, and Poll dazzles the assembled crowd with rapid, whipping turns on point. Belaye and Blanche return; Poll circles the stage swiftly and then rejoins Jasper. The crew and their girls stand aside as Jasper and Belaye, arm in arm, lead the procession of principals. When these two come to the front of the stage, they separate and stretch between them a large Union Jack, which they drape about Mrs. Dimple's shoulders. She kneels between the two happy couples, umbrella in one hand, trident in the other. Some of the sailors move forward and lift her high over the deck. They begin to turn her as the other sailors and their girls circle them, and the curtain falls as Mrs. Dimple, ruling Britannia with all her might, smiles down upon all the happy lovers.

A POEM FORGOTTEN

Music by Wallingford Riegger. Choreography by Eliot Feld. Scenery and costumes by José-Luis Cuevas. Lighting by Jules Fisher. First presented by the American Ballet Company at the Brooklyn Academy of Music, New York, October 22, 1970, with Daniel Levans, Edward Henkel, Christine Kono, Cristina Stirling, Elizabeth Lee, Larry Grenier, James Lewis, and Richard Munro. Conductor: Isaiah Jackson.

A recollection of childhood, boyhood, and youth, *A Poem Forgotten* is a narrative work to the *Concerto for Piano and Wind Quintet* of Wallingford Riegger.

The curtain rises, and we see on stage, his back to us at first, a boy, naked to the waist, going through the ritual of being born. He falls back, sucking his thumb, his father helps him, and gradually he learns to crawl, jump, and walk. No sooner does he do so, however, than his mother emerges with a little sister for him. The two children play as the parents make love. Against a backdrop of boyhood images, the father carries the mother away and the children are alone.

A red beanie on the back of his head, the boy now jumps down from a bench and tests his adolescent strength. His sister, fascinated also by her growing attractions, sits on the bench while the boy enjoys seduction by a girl in purple. When she goes, however, the boy hides his face in shame and wants to cry out. He joins his sister on the bench and wiggles his thumb.

After an interval, he and the sister sit rocking as three rowdy boys play roughly. He joins them: there is some trouble, but the girl in purple breaks it up. This scene is caught in a frozen tableau, with the boy stretched out on the floor. The three hoodlums now attack the girl in purple as the sister, watching, lifts her dress above her waist, wishing it were her. The boy goes to lie at his sister's feet as his father re-enters, carrying the boy's mother.

NOTES   Anna Kisselgoff in the New York *Times* called *A Poem Forgotten* "a brilliant, personally phrased essay on a young man's memories of his adolescence. Its idiom . . . is really expressive, not expressionist, and this is not a minor ballet . . . Daniel Levans, so obviously slated to become an exceptional dancer, was outstanding."

POÈME DE L'EXTASE (Poem of Ecstasy)

Music by Alexander Scriabin. Choreography by John Cranko. Designed by Jürgen Rose. First presented by the Stuttgart Ballet at the Württemberg State Theatre, Stuttgart, March 24, 1970, with Margot Fonteyn, Jan Stripling, Bernd Berg, Heinz Clauss, Richard Cragun, and Egon Madsen in principal roles. First presented in the United States by the same ensemble at the Metropolitan Opera House, New York, July 21, 1971.

The choreographer John Cranko expressed the essence of his ballet, derived from a story by Colette, in his own words: "At a party given by a great diva, there appears among the guests a young man who falls in love with her. At first she is flattered, then she remembers, more and more vividly, her former lovers, realizes that her life is already fulfilled and finally sends him away."

The ballet is set to the *Poème de l'Extase* of Scriabin and also to that composer's *Sonata No. 9*, orchestrated by Wolfgang Fortner.

The American critic Hubert Saal wrote in *Newsweek* (August 2, 1971): "Fonteyn is wonderful. In that frenetic atmosphere, she stands out as the one distinct figure, delicate but strong, nobly resigned to age. 'What I like about the ballet,' she says, 'is that it's all one piece—the decor, the music, the choreography. It all goes together in a special period style and requires its own posing and line and fresh possibilities for *arabesques*. It's remarkable the number of different things you can do with *arabesques*. I suppose it's really the most important movement in ballet . . . Few ballerinas are lucky enough to get a new ballet, much less a role tailor-made for my personality. I can act my age. It's about someone looking back on her memories rather than forward to them. It's something I can put myself into easily, like a nice coat.'"

The British critic John Percival wrote at great length about *Poème de l'Extase* in *Dance and Dancers* magazine:

"Cranko's intention was to get away from the little-girl image to which ballerinas are mostly confined. They spend most of their lives playing sixteen-year-old princesses, adolescent peasant girls, neglected younger daughters, and other similar characters, with a whole host of our feathered friends (swans, firebirds, bluebirds) for light relief. As Cranko remarked, an actress as she grows up graduates to new and often more interesting roles, a dancer is stuck with much the same kind of role all her life. His first idea was to make a ballet based on *Medea* but he decided the story could not be made clear enough in dancing. So after various possibilities had been discussed, he announced that he had settled on a plot based on Colette's novel *Break of Day*. At the premiere, one disgruntled colleague complained of having read the book in preparation and found it completely irrelevant. I could not agree: the novel to my mind provides both the situation and the motivation—but the story has undergone a complete change of setting and therefore of emphasis and development in Cranko's treatment.

"The idea is, briefly, that a mature woman (not old, but past her youth) has a young man fall in love with her. After some hesitation, she rejects him because she has built a contented life for herself and carries with her the memory of her former lovers; she prefers to keep all that as something already achieved, and concentrate on her life now rather than risk a new adventure that might be disappointing. Don't run off to read the novel for an idea of what the ballet looks like—Colette's heroine lives in a cottage near the sea and works in her garden; Cranko's heroine is a fine lady with a salon, clearly in a fashionable town where there is lots of society. In a brief program note he describes her as a great stage star, but I don't think there is any real indication of this in the ballet—only that she is clearly much admired and respected by the guests who throng the room where the first scene takes place.

"I don't know whether the ballet's chosen style dictated the choice of music or vice versa, but they go marvelously together. A program note acknowledges that choreography and production draw their inspiration from the work of the painter Gustav Klimt (1862–1918), who was one of the practitioners of the style known variously as *Jugendstil* (so called after the Munich magazine which served as a rallying point for the movement) or Art Nouveau. Richly ornamented, sensuous, full of natural-looking forms organized in a very artificial way, it is a style well suited both to ballet and to today's taste, besides providing an apt parallel to the swirling, swooning, orgiastic music of Scriabin's *Poem of Ecstasy*.

"Cranko's designer, as on several earlier occasions, is Jürgen Rose, who has made the ballet as stunning visually as in every other respect. The settings have a remarkable amount of detail in them and much rich coloring, so that you might expect the dancers to be lost in the confusion, but in practice it is all so meticulously worked out that every detail remains clear. And the work evokes its chosen model without in any way losing its own individuality.

"The first scene—perhaps prologue would be more accurate—is set in an elaborately furnished period drawing room. The walls are champagne colored, with decorations in red and blue. Above a large round seat rises an ornate wire structure supporting a huge pale orange bowl from which curls a faint whiff of smoke suggesting incense; above this is a multi-colored hanging bowl lamp that mirrors its shape. At the side and in a recess at the back are smart black and white upright chairs.

"The people who enter are dressed in smart frocks with big hats, or in formal jackets with ties; the atmosphere is one of studied ease, very formal informality. Their movements are very artificial too, with particularly elaborate ways of holding or moving their hands. They move about like people at a party waiting for the real point of the party to arrive. A young man enters at the back, at first unnoticed by the others: more eager, more earnest and less affected than the rest, he seems slightly out of place, and clearly he feels a certain coolness on their part towards him, for he goes to sit alone in an alcove.

"Suddenly a woman enters quietly from the opposite corner. She has her back to us but at once we know that she is the one who has been awaited. Graciously and with studied charm she acknowledges the greetings of the assembled company. But now the youngster, too, comes to her, a little too warmly for a stranger, and she turns away from him, but he persists in paying attention to her. For a moment she seems rather annoyed, but her carefully held poise continues, and when he returns after everyone else has gone, she dismisses him with a single gesture of one arm. Alone, she lies on her couch . . .

"The lights dim; when they come up once more the walls of the room and all furniture except the couch have disappeared (and the couch vanishes, too, once she has got up from it). At the back of the stage, a vast curtain tumbles billowing from above, followed by another: they are painted with multi-colored swirling patterns of great beauty. The boy has returned; like the woman he is now dressed in a simpler, more stylized version of the realistic clothes they wore before. We have left reality for the world of her imagination, and now the visions of her past lovers come to her, wrapped in great cloaks of red, blue, black and white or white and gold. First all of them together; then they go and return one by one, this time appearing in turn from behind those great curtains. Without their cloaks they look almost naked, but their flesh-colored tights are embroidered each with a different jewel-like pattern. Each dances with her in turn, and each time the boy tries to intervene and take the place of this rival from the past, so that this part of the ballet (the greater part, in fact) becomes a tumultuous series of solos, duets and trios.

"Jan Stripling is the first to appear: tall, slim but strong, mature and quietly forceful in appearance and manner. Next Bernd Berg: smaller, more impetuous, in some respects a little like Egon Madsen, who plays the youngster; and this similarity is emphasized by giving them a kind of danced duel in which they echo each other's leaps and turns. Now Heinz Clauss, a little older than the others in appearance, and very gentle but with the air of a hard core of strength in reserve. Finally Richard Cragun, almost Bacchic in appearance and overwhelming in the youthful virility with which he hurtles round the stage.

"Now the boy is again alone with the woman and for a moment his hopes rise as she caresses his head while he kneels before her. But even while she pulls his head against her body, she is gazing across to where the four lovers have again returned, this time all together. They seize her and run with her held between them in a great circle round the stage; they lift her high above them, wrapped in their cloaks like a statue of winged victory. Then, two by two, they take the corners of those great curtains at the back and, as the music reaches its last orgasmic climax, run with them diagonally right across the stage. The curtains fall from where they hung, billowing behind the running men, right across the stage and out of sight. The light begins to dim. Realizing his fate, the boy backs away out of sight and out of the woman's life. She stands alone, looking after her visions and again raising one arm, this time to reach after them. But it is not a sad longing she feels, rather a sense of fulfillment. She raises both arms and curls them round her head, smoothing her face with a caressing movement, then her hands drop, first to her breasts and then to hang by her side. And as she stands there, a smile, a look of ineffable joy comes over her face.

"It is a marvelous role for Fonteyn. She has caught exactly the visual style of the ballet—that first entrance, her hands held at a slight angle, her arms curving gently down, her hip thrust a little to one side so that her dress also flows curvingly, her head alertly poised: you know at once that she is going to be exactly right. The personality too: even though she comes on with her back to you, there is not for a moment any doubt (and would not be, even if you did not recognize her) that here is the star—both in real life and in the character she is playing. But more than this: there is depth and warmth too, there is a living person there, not just a dancer, but a woman, not a conventional ballerina but a great dance-actress. And the best thing about this performance is that the humanity of it is achieved through the deliberately artificial style. It is not a question of two different aspects, a mannered exterior and a natural interior, nor a question of achieving humanity in spite of the artificiality, but actually through the elaborate artifice. The poses and movements, any one of which could have come from a painting of this period, are necessarily contrived, stylized, yet at the same time they express the emotions in a natural way. See how she stands with the back of one hand against her lips, her body and arms a carefully contrived pattern of curves and angles—it could look simperingly shallow, but it does not, it conveys the feelings of a woman who has accepted a certain way of life but can look within herself with truth and understanding.

"Fonteyn's dancing in *Poème* (and I must stress that it is a real dancing role, not just an acting part) is mainly in duets, trios or larger ensembles with her five partners. And what partners they are. All four of the visions are so strong, they look so handsome and manly, they dance with such fire and strength, they support her with such tenderness and firmness too; and each emerges also as a real individual. Cragun has the role needing most virtuosity (some of the leaps in which he swirls in the air are fantastically unexpected and yet done with such apparent ease)—but all of them have to dance hard, and they all do it well. You would be hard put to it to find another company which could cast these four roles successfully—and that is without mentioning Madsen in the lead, who has to keep up with all four of them right through the ballet, dancing like a dream—yet what you notice more than his dancing is the way he brings the boy to life, the eagerness of his admiration for the woman at the beginning, contrasted with the artificiality of the rest of the assembled company; his engaging mixture of diffidence and assertiveness; the way he responds to the challenge of each remembered rival; and the look of absolute brokenheartedness on his face at the end when he realizes he is defeated."

PRESENCE

Music by Bernd Alois Zimmermann. Choreography by John Cranko. Scenery and costumes by Jürgen Schmidt-Oehm. First presented by the Stuttgart Ballet at the Württemberg State Theatre, Stuttgart, May 16, 1968. First presented in the United States by the same ensemble at the Metropolitan Opera House, New York, June 20, 1969, with Marcia Haydée, Richard Cragun, and Heinz Clauss in the principal roles.

A ballet for the well-read, *Presence* has as its main characters Don Quixote, Ubu Roi, and Molly Bloom. The choreographer has said that the characters are in no way intended as literal copies after Cervantes, Jarry, and Joyce, but are rather the omnipresent reflections of certain of their aspects common to us all.

Presence, said Cranko, "is a series of portrait-dialogues revealing the protagonists: Don Quixote, the Dreamer, who hardly knows whether he is a part of a dream or reality, whether he himself is the dream or is conceived by the dream of another; Roi (King) Ubu, the Mighty, a remorseful and naïve Cain who seeks to destroy everything that stands in his way; and with them, Molly, the Woman—Goddess, Prostitute, Virgin in one—the Mother of us all, and the Creation of us all." The ballet is in five episodes, each in the form of a pantomime.

In an interview in *Opera News* (October 11, 1969), in which he discussed much of his work in detail, John Cranko recalled that originally *Presence* "was an idea that came from the composer . . . It has no rhythm at all, just structures and textures; this bit's spiky and that bit's oily, this bit's flat and that bit's high. Zimmermann chose the three characters—Ubu, Molly Bloom and Don Quixote—and I used them in alternating sequences of pantomime and dance."

PRINCE IGOR

Ballet in one act. Music by Alexander Borodin. Choreography by Michel Fokine. Scenery and costumes by Nicholas Roerich. First presented by Diaghilev's Ballets Russes at the Théâtre du Châtelet, Paris, May 18, 1909, with Adolph Bolm, Sophie Fedorova, and Helen Smirnova in the principal parts. First presented in the United States by Diaghilev at the Century Theatre, New York, January 18, 1916, with Bolm, Lubov Tchernicheva, and Sophie Pfanz.

Set to the music of the "Polovtsian Dances" from the second act of Borodin's opera *Prince Igor*, this is purely a dance ballet, without any connection with the plot of the opera. When it was first performed with full chorus and orchestra, the ballet served to introduce to Western Europe the unimagined color of Russian music and dancing combined in a striking single work.

The scene, when the curtain rises, is suffused in the violet light of the approaching dawn. The light of two campfires is thrown against two great tents made of animal skins. Gathered about the fires, the men and women of the Polovtsy tribe sleep soundly. In the distance, around other campfires, other members of the tribe are curled in sleep. A lone warrior stands on watch.

One of the sleeping girls begins to stir. She raises her arm, rises, and stretches. As soon as she is fully awake, she goes from group to group, gradually waking the whole tribe. The somnolent music becomes expectant in its rhythm, as the drowsy villagers prepare for their daily tasks. The sun rises, and the people's dark garments take on their vivid natural colors.

The girl moves forward, turns rapidly, and begins to dance to the music. Other girls join her dance; in the back a group of youths accompany them. The young warlike villagers are unable to contain the vigor which sleep has stored up within them; they seek to release their energy. The girls sit on the ground as one of the boys comes forward and dances with keen strength, spinning swiftly to the pulsating rhythm of the music. The girls surround him, gyrating with brilliant turns. As the youth concludes his dance, the girls fall at his feet.

A great warrior, the leader of the tribe, moves forward, brandishing a brilliant sword. A dozen girls appear, as if at his silent command, and dance softly. Their primitive costumes are embellished with flowing gauze, which follows their movements in dancing waves. A girl in white, with long braided hair, is among them. The music mounts in intensity; the girls sit on the ground and a brave warrior leaps over their heads. He dances fiercely, called by some distant battle call. The girls dance in a group, as a formation of warriors circle their leader. The warrior slides forward, brandishing his weapon, and the entire ensemble forms a warlike tableau to the insistent demand of the music.

The men gather in the center of the stage and dance around and around to the demanding tempo. The girls enclose them in a wide circle of whirling movement. Suddenly the music hesitates. The two groups cross the scene quietly, then the men move up behind the girls and lift them high. The youths slap their thighs in their enthusiasm for battle and they race back and forth across the stage.

Six of the Polovtsy girls come to the front and dance with an energy that emulates the warriors' strength. They are joined by the girls dressed in gauze, who reassert the femininity of their sex. But the warlike dancers take over again, stomping the ground with their feet and clapping their hands to the beat of the music. The finest warrior of them all comes forward and, as the entire tribe beats out the rhythm of his dance, the brave Polovtsian dances a whirling climax to the ballet. He comes forward to the footlights and continues his dance, turning like a persistent top. The whole tribe gathers behind him and turns with him. The scene is alive with whirling movement as the curtain falls.

PRINTEMPS

Music by Claude Debussy. Choreography by Lorca Massine. Costumes designed by Irene Sharaff. First presented by the New York City Ballet at the New York State Theatre, January 13, 1972, with Violette Verdy in the principal role.

Describing *Printemps* in her review of the premiere in the New York *Post*, Frances Herridge said the ballet "was a picture of Spring, come gently to life— all innocence and sweet frolic, full of freshness and grace, and utterly feminine in the romantic spirit of time past. It was as though Isadora Duncan, inspired by Botticelli's *Primavera*, had gamboled with her girls to the lyrical music of Claude Debussy."

The dance indicates the years' remaking and shows how a new spring spirit can take over from the old.

THE PRIVATE LESSON

Music by Georges Delerue. Choreography by Flemming Flindt. Decor and costumes by Bernard Daydé. First presented at the Opéra Comique, Paris, April 6, 1964. First presented in the United States by the Royal Danish Ballet at the New York State Theatre, New York, December 17, 1965, with Mette Hønningen, Henning Kronstam, and Mona Kiil.

Based on a play by Eugène Ionesco, *The Private Lesson* tells of a lesson given by a psychopathic ballet master.

The scene is the ballet master's classroom. His pianist is preparing for the day's lesson when the bell rings and a young girl arrives. She is shown to the dressing room. When she returns ready for her practice the ballet master enters. The lesson at first goes well, but with complicated exercises on *pointe*, the pupil has difficulties and complains. The pianist is sent away. The ballet master insists that the girl continue, becoming more and more incensed. The dancer is almost hypnotized by him. In the end, the ballet master loses his temper and strangles her.

The pianist returns and the ballet master behaves like a little boy who is sorry and asks for help. She reproaches him indulgently and together they carry the girl's body away. Again the pianist prepares for a lesson. She picks up some overturned chairs when suddenly the bell rings . . .

PRODIGAL SON

Ballet in three scenes. Music by Sergi Prokofiev. Choreography by George Balanchine. Scenery and costumes by Georges Rouault. First presented by Diaghilev's Ballets Russes at the Théâtre Sarah Bernhardt, Paris, May 21, 1929, with Serge Lifar in the title role, Felia Dubrovska as the Siren, Michael Fedorov as the Father, and Leon Woizikowski and Anton Dolin as Servants to the Prodigal Son. Revived by the New York City Ballet at the City Center, New York, February 23, 1950, with Jerome Robbins as the Prodigal Son, Maria Tallchief as the Siren, Michael Arshansky as the Father, and Herbert Bliss and Frank Hobi as Servants to the Prodigal Son. Lighting by Jean Rosenthal.

The story of the prodigal son is told first in the Bible: ". . . A certain man had two sons. And the younger of them said to his father, Father give me the portion of goods that falleth to me. And he divided unto them his living. And not many days after the younger son gathered all together, and took his journey into a far country, and there wasted his substance with riotous living. And when he had spent all, there arose a mighty famine in that land; and he began to be in want . . . And he would fain have filled his belly with the husks that the swine did eat: and no man gave unto him. And when he came to himself he said, How many hired servants of my father's have bread enough to spare, and I perish with hunger! I will arise and go to my father, and will say unto him, Father, I have sinned against heaven and before thee, and am no more worthy to be called thy son: make me as one of thy servants. And he arose and came unto his father. But when he was yet a great way off, his father saw him, and had compassion, and ran, and fell on his neck, and kissed him. And the son said unto him, Father I have sinned against heaven, and in thy sight, and am no more worthy to be called thy son. But the father said to his servants, Bring forth the best robe, and put it on him; and put a ring on his hand, and shoes on his feet: And bring hither the fatted calf, and kill it; and let us eat, and be merry: For this my son was dead, and is alive again; he was lost, and is found . . ." (St. Luke, 15:11–24)

This ballet tells the parable dramatically, with certain necessary omissions from and additions to the original story, but with the central theme preserved.

SCENE ONE: HOME   The curtain rises almost immediately after the orchestra has played the first few bars of a strong, high-spirited theme. The scene is opulently colored. A painted backdrop depicts the distant view and imaginative sky line of the ancient Near East. A bright yellow sun hangs in a rich blue sky over a port with a lighthouse watching over the sea. At the right, in the back, is the opening to a tent; on the left, toward the front, stands a low picket fence with a small gate. Two boys, friends to the prodigal son, are busy about the scene, hurriedly arranging a store of large wine jugs as if they are preparing for a long journey. The prodigal son emerges from the tent, followed by two sisters. He is dressed in a short blue tunic and an open vest. His sisters, dressed in long, flowing garments, try to engage his attention, but the carefree youth ignores them to greet his friends. He picks up one of the wine jugs and throws it to one of them playfully. The music becomes terse in tempo, and the prodigal son dances vigorously in response to its pounding rhythm. With robust gaiety he seems to act out for his friends the adventures in store for them away from home and to reveal, at the same time, an innocent, headstrong spirit that urges him to seek those adventures. His sisters are frightened at his strong determination to leave home so selfishly and watch apprehensively. The prodigal son leaps about the stage with boundless energy, oblivious to their care. His dance stops in an open gesture when he looks up, to find himself face to face with his father, who has come out of the tent. He is embarrassed for an instant and steps back.

As a new, poignant melody begins, the father beckons to his children. They come and sit before him, the son unwillingly, but obediently. The son's attention wanders, and the father patiently turns his head back to the family circle. He holds up his arms over his children and looks upward in humble prayer.

He touches their heads softly. The son turns away in protest at the ritual, but his father persists gently. When the son twists his body away, the father takes the boy's hand and places it on his sisters' hands.

The tension between the son and the father increases; the son turns away in disgust, leaps up, and flaunts his indifference in his father's face. The father rises and stands motionless and unprotesting in his grief, as his son dances in defiance before him. The son's temper is so-high and his eagerness to leave home so intense that his sisters watch in terror and sadness. His dance is closely similar to his first dance, but here he is emboldened by anger. He ignores his family, beckons to his two friends, and points toward the open highway. They gather together their gear and run off through the gate, closing it hastily behind them. In a final gesture of rebellion, the son turns rapidly in the air before his father, dashes across the stage, and jumps high over the fence after his companions. The sisters stand close to their father in sympathy, but the old man walks forward slowly, raises his hand in unacknowledged farewell, and stands for a moment watching. Then he motions his daughters to the tent and follows them into their home. The scene blacks out.

SCENE TWO: IN A FAR COUNTRY   The backdrop has been changed when the lights come up again. Still heavily colored, it now depicts an open tent furnished with a festive table. The small, symbolic fence that figured in the first scene stands as it was, on the left. A loud, crashing march heralds the arrival of a group of revelers, who enter on the left in a close line. They wear short tunics and white tights. All of them are bald. The manner in which they cross the stage to the raucous music is grotesque. As they separate, the beautiful, jubilant melody that will dominate the scene receives its first statement from the orchestra. They go over to the fence, turn it upside down, and we see that the prop is also a long black table. The table is moved back. The revelers form in short lines before it and hop across invisible lines toward each other, playing some fantastic game. Four of them lie down on the stage and spread their legs to form a star. One of the revelers lies across the middle of the star as the others move forward and rotate the pattern their companions have made. Their frolic is renewed until the prodigal son enters on the right with his two friends.

The revelers cease their play and gather in a close group on the other side of the stage; they are just as frightened as the intruders. The prodigal son doesn't see them at first. Then he approaches carefully, urging his friends to follow. They refuse, and he abandons his fears, to greet the strangers with open cordiality. He tries to shake hands with one of them, then with another, but all the revelers pull their hands back. He doesn't understand. They touch his rich clothes covetously and come closer. He hesitates and moves away apprehensively, but his friends force him back and he remembers the wine they have brought with them. He tells his companions to give the revelers drink, and immediately the situation changes. The revelers form a parade behind him, and the prodigal son is carried on the shoulders of his two friends. Everyone is now his friend. He is lifted up and, from above, shakes hands with all of his new companions. They throw him side to side in jovial welcome. Then he dances between his two fellows as everyone watches admiringly. He grasps their hands elatedly, and all the revelers rush to shake his hand. The whole group dances boldly and vigorously with the prodigal son. He jumps over the table as the dance ends, and all gather about him.

The siren comes in, dancing on point slowly and seductively to a tune of Oriental character. She wears a tight red tunic about her slim body, a high headdress, and from her shoulders there trails a crimson cape of velvet. The men watch her intently; the prodigal son is dazzled by her strange beauty and the confidence with which she fascinates. She turns slowly, wrapping the cape around the upper part of her body, then unwinds the garment. She handles the cape as if it were a part of her own body—an animate object obedient to her will. When the cape is fully extended behind her, the siren steps back over it, pulls it up between her legs, and winds it around them. Holding the cape with one arm, she dances proudly. She seems oblivious to the fact that she is being watched; this dance seems to please her more than it could please anyone else. She drops the cape and falls to her knees in an attitude of conventional despair. Then she rises, proud and assertive, to turn intricately on point. She throws the cape behind her, falls back on her arms, and, moving slowly on her hands and points, drags it across the floor. Then she kneels low and pulls the cape up over her head, covering her body completely.

The prodigal son, now helplessly attracted, moves from behind the table and pulls the cape away. The siren rises on point, unsurprised. He tosses the garment aside as she turns to look at him. The prodigal son becomes now as obedient to her desire as the castoff raiment. He stands transfixed as the siren dances before him. She turns with strong, sinuous grace and holds out her arms in a gesture of approval and welcome. She approaches him closely; the prodigal son places his hands on her waist; they move backward in response to her lead. The siren pushes him back against the table. The revelers gather about them, and the siren is thrown back high above the table, into the waiting arms of her accomplices. She sits in triumph over the suppliant prodigal son, who lies on the table beneath her.

The siren is lifted down and sits facing the prodigal son. His eyes look down. His two friends begin a dance to amuse the group. Relieved by this distraction, the prodigal son watches with the others, but glances at the siren when her eyes leave his face. The siren touches his hand and moves her fingers up his arm to caress the golden medallion that hangs about his throat. He looks her full in the face.

His friends finish their dance, kneel before the table, and everyone applauds. The siren and the prodigal son come forward, watching each other intimately. They stand apart. It is as if he were imitating her movements. The siren falls back in his arms. She repulses his caress and entwines her arms back around his neck, and the two dance forward. They pause, and he puts his head between her legs, rises, and the siren sits proudly on his shoulders. Then she slides down his back. She stands on point before him and coils her leg about him, holding him fast, as he turns her. She releases him, and he pulls her over his back; the siren's hands reach out for her feet so that her body forms a hoop about him. Her body snakes about him completely, and slowly she slides to the floor. He steps out of the coil, rolls the siren upright, and holds her under her arms. Her knees rest on his feet as he moves across the stage. Now the prodigal son becomes bold and caresses the siren openly. He sits at her feet, his knees drawn up. She approaches him and sits on his head while resting her feet firmly on his knees. Now she rises straight up, arrogant in her voluptuousness and power. She steps away, and the prodigal son lies supine. She lies back across his body; their legs tangle. Now powerless, the prodigal son lies entwined in the siren's grasp. She gestures in insidious exultation.

The music pounds and shrieks fiercely. The prodigal's two friends pull the couple apart. Their companions are now reveling in drunkenness and force the prodigal son to join them. They drag his exhausted body about the stage while the siren watches from the table. He seeks her help, but the profligates carry her above the table and she pours wine down his throat as he slides down the table beneath her. They lift him high and carry the siren under him. Both are held by the waist as their bodies fall back hideously. They embrace frantically, are finally released, and two drunkards crawl under their legs. The prodigal staggers from group to group in his intoxication and falls against the table, where he cannot distinguish one of his companions from another. The siren watches him expectantly. He rushes up on the table, but the revelers tilt it up high under him and he slides down it, all his strength spent. The siren places her pointed toe on his chest in triumph.

The table now stands up on end. The revelers conceal themselves behind it. The prodigal is shoved back against the table, where he rests helpless. Hands reach out from either side and move down his body. The friends rush out from behind, turn him upside down, shake him, and collect his gold greedily. They stand aside as the siren is carried out. She stands upright on a man's shoulders, her arms akimbo. She gets down and gathers up all the remaining gold. Now the thieves rob the prodigal of all his outer garments, even his shoes. He is still unaware of what they have done to him, and the debauchers celebrate by crawling over and under each other, like eels. The siren yanks off the prodigal's gold medallion, kisses it, and exits. Her companions leave the scene, running across the stage, back to back, like many-legged insects.

The prodigal son wakens slowly from his stupor. He slides down the table to the ground and falls on his face. He pulls himself back up, gripping the table with agonized effort. He looks down at his hands, then at his body. He remembers and holds his head in disbelief. Stretching his hand up plaintively in despair, he acknowledges the betrayal of his friends and his own self-betrayal. He falls to the ground, sees water, crawls to it, drinks, and curls up like a child. He rises, looks behind him at the scene of his debauchery, and struggles off on his knees.

The profligates return, bringing their loot with them. The siren follows. The table is now turned upside down to form the gate and fence. The siren's companions run to the fence, arrange themselves within it, and the siren joins them. One of the men lifts high the end of her crimson cape, others begin a rowing motion, and the table becomes a ship, the siren's cape its sail, and her arched body its figurehead. Her companions blow their trumpets, and the scene blacks out.

SCENE THREE: HOME   The stage is set as it was for the first scene. The prodigal son, covered now with a thin and tattered black cloak, crawls across the stage, supporting his exhausted body with a staff. The music is dark, almost funeral-like in its persistent beat. The traveler's progress is slow and, to him, endless, for he has no idea where he is. He looks about hopelessly. Suddenly he sees the gate to his home. He staggers toward it, reaches out his hand, touches it, and collapses with the effort.

His sisters emerge from the tent. One of them sees him and calls to the other. Together they go to him and open the gate to lead him in lovingly. The piercing melody of the music reflects their great joy. They stand on either side of their kneeling brother as their father comes out. They are so happy that they do not move. The father remains near the door of his home. The son slowly and hesitatingly raises his head and looks up at his father. He beseeches him with outstretched arms. The father does not move. The son twists away toward the fence, but he has no sooner moved than his father raises his hand to keep him. He turns back toward his home, bows his head to the ground, and stretches his arms out behind in self-denial. With head still bowed, he crawls toward his father slowly, wretchedly. He falls full length just as he nears him, reaches out to drag himself forward by grasping his father's feet. He pulls himself up, clinging to his father's arms. The father reaches out to gather him close in forgiveness, love, and protection and, holding him like a child, he covers his son with his cloak.

THE PROSPECT BEFORE US

Dramatic ballet in seven scenes. Music by William Boyce. Choreography by Ninette de Valois. Scenery and costumes by Roger Furse. First presented by the Sadler's Wells Ballet at the Sadler's Wells Theatre, London, July 4, 1940, with Pamela May, Mary Honer, Margaret Dale, Frederick Ashton, Robert Helpmann, and John Hart among the principals. First presented in the United States by the Sadler's Wells Theatre Ballet at the Pabst Theatre, Milwaukee, Wisconsin, November 3, 1951, with Svetlana Beriosova, Pirmin

Trecu, Stanley Holden, Pauline Harrop, and Michael Hogan among the principals.

The Prospect Before Us, or *Pity the Poor Dancers,* is a comedy based on eighteenth-century English art, music, and theatrical history. The art is that of the colorful caricaturist Thomas Rowlandson (1756–1827), one of whose drawings, entitled *The Prospect Before Us,* gives the ballet its name; the music is an arrangement by Constant Lambert of selections from the works of the English composer William Boyce (1710–79); and the history is taken from an incident related in John Eber's *History of the King's Theatre.*

The King's Theatre and its rival, the Pantheon, were popular London theatres of the time. Rowlandson's engraving shows us the stage of the Pantheon, where the celebrated French dancers Mademoiselle Théodore and Monsieur Didelot are dancing a ballet before an enthusiastic audience. But there were also enthusiastic audiences at the King's Theatre. The ballet *The Prospect Before Us* tells us the story of these two theatres—the intense rivalry of their managers, the resorting to any means to achieve success, the fierce competition for guest artists, and the pitiable condition of dancers who did not know from one day to the next on which stage they would appear.

SCENE ONE: THE STAGE OF THE KING'S THEATRE, 1789 After the orchestra has played a brief, charming overture, the curtain rises on a ballet rehearsal backstage at the King's Theatre. Five ladies of the ballet await the direction of Monsieur Noverre, the great ballet master, who stands on the right studying a choreographic chart. Madame Noverre sits in the background, knitting. Monsieur Didelot, the *premier danseur,* paces up and down, wondering when the devil Noverre will get on with the show. Mademoiselle Théodore, the *première danseuse,* wanders in. She sits down on the stage and blithely tries on one pair of dancing slippers after another while her fellow performers fret. Finally she finds a pair that suits her, and the rehearsal resumes. Monsieur Noverre pulls Monsieur Didelot into the rehearsal, and this *premier danseur* automatically supports Mademoiselle Théodore in a series of poses. He is not the least bit interested in dancing with her, and when he lifts her indifferently, the girl begins to complain. Didelot rages back at her.

Mr. Taylor, the manager of the King's Theatre, enters with a party of guests. The manager of the Pantheon Theatre, Mr. O'Reilly, wanders in to see what his chief competitor is up to. He trips over some of the dancers and watches the rehearsal with broken, humble envy. When the great Vestris is given a chance to rehearse his variation, he is so disdainful of these spectators that he merely indicates with his fingers the difficult steps he will dazzle them with in actual performance.

The visitors parade off the stage, and the rehearsal ends. When Mr. Taylor returns, Monsieur Noverre and his wife attack him with a demand for more money. As the three squabble over a contract, Mr. O'Reilly tries vainly to find

out how much money Taylor is giving them. Finally Taylor accedes to Noverre's demands and he and his rival are alone.

Mr. Taylor and Mr. O'Reilly sit down on chairs at the back of the stage.
Poor O'Reilly sits wrapped in thought as Taylor regales him with stories of the
dancers, the unprecedented success they will have, and the money he will rake
in. He brings out a bottle and offers his friend a drink. O'Reilly hardly notices
his glass and drinks almost automatically as he sits sulking, thinking that all
this might be his. But suddenly O'Reilly leaps up from his chair, claps his
friend on the back, and is all expansive good humor. Taylor is bewildered by
this change of mood, but listens patiently as O'Reilly gabbles about the beauty
of the dancers and congratulates him on his good fortune. Soon O'Reilly staggers off and Mr. Taylor sits alone, wondering what on earth could have happened to change his rival's mood so quickly.

SCENE TWO: THE BURNING OF THE KING'S THEATRE   Mr. Taylor finds out the
answer to his rival's strange behavior soon enough. It is June 17, 1789. A drop
curtain depicting the burning of his theatre falls on the previous scene. Mr.
Taylor ambles by, not noticing that anything is wrong. O'Reilly enters and
calls his attention to a blazing wreckage. Taylor despairs. The dancers come
into the street to watch the fire, and O'Reilly instantly directs them toward his
theatre, the Pantheon, where new, profitable jobs await them. Mr. Taylor tries
to get between his rival and his dancers, but O'Reilly steps over his back to
welcome Monsieur Noverre and his wife and take them on to his theatre.

SCENE THREE: A LONDON STREET   Four kids in ragged clothes run into a
street in the poor section of the city. A half-dressed harridan looks down from
the window of a nearby house as they play aimlessly, tumbling and dancing
and clapping hands. They hear a parade approaching and sit down, their
backs to the footlights, as a strange procession enters. A horn player and
drummer announce the arrival of a party of poor, impoverished dancers, who
enter carrying a model of the Pantheon Theatre. Mr. O'Reilly is evidently not
paying them very well, for written across the model of his theatre is the legend
"Pray Remember the Poor Dancers."

SCENE FOUR: THE STAGE OF THE PANTHEON THEATRE   Mr. O'Reilly's opening night has come, and he sits watching the first performance of the ballet in
a stage box on the left. Mr. Taylor observes his rival's success from the opposite box on the right. Dancers enter and, before a conventional pastoral
backdrop, enact a *divertissement* with some semblance of plot. Mr. Taylor is
anxiously looking for empty seats in the house and does not give his full attention to the ballet. Mr. O'Reilly is delighted with the dancing and when Monsieur Didelot wanders about the stage, anxiously looking for his love, does not
in the least hesitate to direct him toward the right girl.

A girl in the *corps de ballet* stands in front of poor Mr. Taylor, obstructing his view of the stage. When another girl prevents Mr. O'Reilly from watching the stage, he flirts with her openly and outrageously, and all but pulls her into the box with him. Soon Mr. O'Reilly gets so carried away by the wonder and beauty of this performance in his own theatre that he, too, must become a part of the *divertissement*. He steps out of his box onto the stage and stumbles about awkwardly among the dancers. He is gradually enveloped by the *corps de ballet* and becomes, at the end of the ballet, a grotesque and embarrassed figure of the final tableau. The curtain falls as O'Reilly poses thus in triumph and Taylor, in his box, despairs at his rival's success.

SCENE FIVE: THE STAGE OF THE NEW KING'S THEATRE Some time has passed: it is now 1790. Mr. Taylor has secured funds and has rebuilt the King's Theatre. The curtain rises on the stage of the new theatre, its equipment refurbished to duplicate the first scene of the ballet. The stage is dark. Four men stand near the footlights, disputing. Their shadows are thrown up against the back wall of the stage, making a comic enlargement of their obviously petty argument. One of the men is Mr. Taylor; the others are his lawyers, who prance about daintily examining a contract as they pursue their legal dialectic. The problem is: can Mr. Taylor, with his New King's Theatre, oblige Monsieur Noverre and his dancers to return, or has Mr. O'Reilly of the Pantheon a legal right to their continued services? O'Reilly observes the dispute.

The lawyers decide in favor of O'Reilly, who oddly enough is impatient with his advantage. He has grown tired of the whims, tempers, and persistent demands of the great choreographer and wishes to be rid of dancers forever.

SCENE SIX: THE BURNING OF THE PANTHEON Hardly has Mr. O'Reilly had a chance to return to his theatre with his problem than the Pantheon catches on fire, and, as in Scene Two, we are treated to the pyrotechnical drop curtain. Mr. O'Reilly dances a jig of delight before his flaming theatre and sees himself happily released from the uncertainties of the world of ballet. He is so delighted with the fire that he turns around and warms his pants near its flames.

His dancers, the girls first, flee the burning wreckage. They flee with obvious pleasure: perhaps they, abetted by the dauntless Mr. O'Reilly, have had a hand in the holocaust! Mr. Taylor welcomes them with open arms. Monsieur Noverre and his wife are the last to accept their former manager's greetings and to accompany him back to the New King's Theatre. Mr. O'Reilly, his troubles now but a heap of ashes, looks upon the smoking scene with the uncontrolled relish a stepfather might feel in seeing off to school a thankless child. He will pay for it, in the end, but now he is happy.

SCENE SEVEN: THE STAGE OF THE NEW KING'S THEATRE Back at Mr. Taylor's new theatre, Monsieur Noverre is again rehearsing his dancers on their home stage. Monsieur Vestris uses the back of one of the chairs for a bar and warms up for his solo, while the ballet master and his wife hover busily over the *corps de ballet*.

Mr. Taylor enters, followed by the inevitable parade of lawyers. Now that the Pantheon has burned down, there is no problem: the French artistes can return to the King's Theatre without fear of suit from Mr. O'Reilly. Mr. Taylor shakes hands with the lawyers one by one, and they dance about him joyfully.

In the midst of this celebration, Mr. O'Reilly stumbles in. He has lost his wig and his coat, and his stockings flap about his ankles: he is very drunk. Whether he is drunk because he is happy or drunk because he is sad, we cannot at first determine, but it soon appears that he has had second thoughts: again he is jealous of Mr. Taylor, who always seems to have all the luck, what with his faithful dancers, his friends to lend him money, and his brand-new theatre.

As soon as he sees the dancers, he begins to imitate them, ruthlessly and absurdly, burlesquing both the ladies and the gentlemen in their artificial poses. When they reprimand him, he apes their movements even more outrageously. Finally O'Reilly collapses on the floor, where he sits with affected dignity. Monsieur Noverre cannot quite believe that he can be so intoxicated. The rank odor of spirits that the besotted manager breathes upon him causes the dancing master almost to swoon. The dancers are aghast at this scandalous interruption to their rehearsal and exit in a huff, followed by Monsieur Noverre and his wife. O'Reilly hoots at them, and as Madame Noverre passes, he grabs hold of her skirt and almost pulls her to the floor.

Mr. Taylor sees nothing for it but to give his unfortunate friend more to drink: it would be useless to *stop* him from drinking. The two sit side by side, as they did at the end of Scene One, Mr. Taylor happy and triumphant, bragging of his good fortune, whispering stories about the dancers, and clapping poor Mr. O'Reilly on the back again and again to display his bumptious good nature. After all, business is business, he seems to say, one must not cast out one's rivals. And business is business, also, to Mr. O'Reilly, who all of a sudden, drunk as he is, comes to. He slaps Taylor on the back and staggers about the stage, almost falling into the orchestra, wholly possessed with a new and brilliant idea. He clutches his rival's bottle of whisky in his arms and, zigzagging, nearly tripping, he stumbles off into the wings. Mr. Taylor, left alone, recalls that O'Reilly was similarly jubilant some while back, when, just as now, he had no right to be. Drunk as O'Reilly is, could he be plotting another ruse? Could he? After all, there is a limit to the number of new King's Theatres. The curtain falls.

PULCINELLA

Dramatic ballet in one act. Music by Igor Stravinsky, based on scores by Giambattista Pergolesi. Choreography by Leonide Massine. Scenery and costumes by Pablo Picasso. First presented by Diaghilev's Ballets Russes at the Théâtre National de l'Opéra, Paris, May 15, 1920, with Leonide Massine as Pulcinella, Tamara Karsavina as Pimpinella, Vera Nemtchinova as Rosetta, Lubov Tchernicheva as Prudenza, Stanislas Idzikowski as Caviello, Nicholas Zverev as Florindo, Enrico Cecchetti as Il Dottore. First presented in the United States by the New York Music Guild in Chicago, 1933, with choreography by Laurent Novikoff.

Stravinsky's score for *Pulcinella* is based on music by the great Neapolitan, Giambattista Pergolesi. The story of the ballet is based on an early eighteenth-century Italian manuscript found in Naples, and its principal characters are taken from the *commedia dell'arte*, the popular Italian masked comedy, which, beginning in the sixteenth century, captured the imagination of all of Europe with its universal types: the pathetic Pierrot, the heartless and flirtatious Columbine, the deathless Pulcinella (Punch, to the English-speaking world), and others. The ballet tells a new variation of Pulcinella's immortality.

A narrow street in Naples is the scene. A volcano can be seen in the distance, over the bay at the end of the street. The end house to the left is that of Tartaglia, whose daughter, Rosetta, is beloved by the youth Caviello. The end house to the right is that of *Il Dottore* (the doctor), whose daughter, Prudenza, is beloved by Florindo.

At the beginning of the ballet Caviello and Florindo enter to watch the houses of their sweethearts. Soon Prudenza and Rosetta look out of their windows. They smile at their suitors, seemingly encouraging them, then pour water out over their heads. The doctor, meanwhile, has discovered the presence of the boys and drives them away.

Pulcinella enters—the familiar figure with a long, pendulous red nose. He dances in the street to the tune of a small violin he plays. His dance and his music attract the girls. Prudenza, who clearly adores him, tries to embrace him. Pulcinella chases her back into her house. Rosetta appears, properly chaperoned by her father, Tartaglia. She tells him that she is in love with Pulcinella and must marry him. Tartaglia upbraids her for loving the ugly little man, but Rosetta ignores him. She tries to interest Pulcinella, who is as indifferent to her as he was to Prudenza. She dances before him. Enchanted, Pulcinella kisses her and takes her for a partner in a dance.

Pimpinella, Pulcinella's wife, discovers the two dancing together. The husband protests that he is innocent, that he still loves only her; Pimpinella is at length convinced of it, and the couple dance.

Meanwhile the two suitors, Caviello and Florindo, have been watching the street. They have seen that Pulcinella is the favorite of both Rosetta and Prudenza, and they are furious with jealousy. Their rage is still more inflamed when it becomes obvious that Pulcinella dares to reject the advances of the girls.

They attack Pulcinella, both jumping on him at once. Pimpinella screams for help, and both Rosetta and Prudenza rush out to help. The boys flee, and poor Pulcinella, left in the hands of three women, all eager to assist him, is almost torn in two by their fierce sympathy.

Summoned by their fathers, the two girls return to their homes. Pulcinella dances with his wife.

Florindo and Caviello have been waiting for this moment. They re-enter the street, disguised in black cloaks, carrying swords. Just as they run for him, Pulcinella sees them. He crosses himself hurriedly and pushes his wife into their house. Before he can enter too, he is caught by the two boys. Florindo strikes him dead with his sword. The murderers leave. Pulcinella gets up as if nothing had happened to him. He turns down the street and disappears.

The stage is empty for a moment. Then an astonishing thing happens. Four little Pulcinellas enter, carrying on their shoulders a fifth Pulcinella, apparently dead. They lay the corpse down in the street and dance.

Tartaglia and the doctor come out with their daughters, to see what has happened. The two girls, horrified to see their Pulcinella lying thus in the street, helplessly hover over his body. The doctor examines Pulcinella and declares him dead.

A magician joins them and assures the girls that he can bring Pulcinella back to life. The four little Pulcinellas and the two girls anxiously await the result of his mysterious incantations. The two fathers stand aside, disbelieving. After pommeling Pulcinella's body thoroughly, the magician commands him to live again. Pulcinella gets up, and the onlookers rejoice. The two girls swear to him that he is their only love.

Their fathers, however, remain unconvinced, even by appearances. To prove these skeptics wrong, the magician takes off his long cloak and wig: *he* is the real Pulcinella! His friend, Fourbo, has been the body.

Fourbo and Pulcinella trick the two fathers into retreating into their homes. Pimpinella comes into the street and, seeing two Pulcinellas, runs away in horror. Fourbo, still alias Pulcinella, brings her back.

Now everyone tries to get into the act. Caviello and Florindo enter, wearing Pulcinella disguises, to renew their romances with Rosetta and Prudenza. The girls accept them. Pimpinella, Rosetta, and Prudenza are dancing with three fake Pulcinellas. The real Pulcinella intervenes and kicks each of his imitators. While his friend Fourbo seeks safety in the magician's costume, Pulcinella unmasks the other two impostors before their girls.

The doctor and Tartaglia, still astonished by the goings on, are persuaded by Fourbo, the magician, to permit their daughters to marry Florindo and Caviello. The fathers agree. Pulcinella dances joyfully with Pimpinella, and the magician declares that they and the other two couples are man and wife.

NOTES Massine's *Pulcinella* was first presented in the United States by the City Center Joffrey Ballet, in 1974. The New York première was at the City Center, October 9, 1974.

Music by Igor Stravinsky. Choreography by Jerome Robbins and George Balanchine. Scenery and costumes by Eugene Berman. Lighting by Ronald Bates. First presented by the New York City Ballet at the Stravinsky Festival, 1972, at the New York State Theatre, Lincoln Center, June 23, 1972, with a cast headed by Edward Villella and Violette Verdy. Conducted by Robert Irving.

I am proud that the painter Eugene Berman, who died December 14, 1972, soon after *Pulcinella* was completed, designed this ballet for us. His help, friendship, and collaboration were essential. I had long felt that the original idea of the ballet from the Diaghilev days was just not interesting enough for the stage any more. But Jerome Robbins and I loved the music. So did Stravinsky's friend Berman, who was of course almost an Italian, so immersed was he in Italy, living there, painting there, knowing that beautiful country, its art and its traditions and theater, too, in all its variations. Berman was a kind of specialist in the *commedia dell'arte*, the improvisational theater identified with the great natural mimicry of the clowns of Naples, what Lincoln Kirstein has called the "underground manual idiom of scurrilous tricks and gesture." It was just those tricks that inspired us to do this new ballet with Berman to Stravinsky's music and I am glad that we did it. Robbins and I enjoyed putting the piece on; we even enjoyed dancing in the first performances, and if the ballet doesn't last as we made it, both of us know that Berman's part in it ought to. Good painters go on forever.

You just have to read the story of the first *Pulcinella*, described above in the first version, to see how complicated it all was for the audience to understand. Our idea was to simplify so that everything would be clear, and we hit on a variation of not only the Pulcinella myths, but the Faust myth, too. We decided that Pulcinella, a Neapolitan scamp, would make a pact with the devil to save his skin. He would then, as would be expected, renege on his promise, but his girl would rescue him, in spite of his having given her a hard time all along. Jerome Robbins and I had worked together before on a compressed story ballet, *Tyl Ulenspiegel*, where he, as the hero, made the whole of a personal as well as political and religious plot idea wonderfully clear in a matter of minutes. (One of the reasons Robbins is such a great choreographer is his great gift as a dancer; we can't remember that too often.)

To see the ballet and enjoy it, I hope words are not really necessary. It might be good to hear the recording that Stravinsky conducted of his lovely music (Col. ML-4830) and to read Robert Craft's notes on that album. As for the action:

Berman's superb drop curtain of Pulcinella and Stravinsky's signature rises on a graveyard scene. Eight Pulcinellas as pallbearers bring to his tomb a white skeleton recumbent on a catafalque. The Pulcinellas are beside themselves with grief. They put the skeleton in the tomb, nevertheless, weeping and wailing all the time.

The Devil arrives. At the tomb, he obliges the skeleton to look over the list of sins the deceased Pulcinella has committed, etc. He then tempts the deceased to sign a pact by which he will rise from the dead if he obeys the Devil in the future. The skeleton signs and then, miraculously, comes out of the grave a full-fledged Pulcinella. His girl, who had despaired at his death, rejoices. She cannot believe that her love has been restored to her. Pulcinella, however, intent on a reunion with his fellow comics, repulses her cruelly. The Devil drags him away to meet several fascinating ladies. In a brief scene in a brothel, the ladies, at the Devil's command, respond to his desires.

Pulcinella leads on a group of his fellow clowns as the baby Pulcinellas watch. He dresses then in a woman's dress and in this disguise, suddenly becoming a beggar, is seen asking for alms at a street fair of acrobats. This is simply a disguise for thievery, of course. The police spot him. He eludes them, then just as the police think they have cornered him, all his identical Pulcinella friends turn up and they don't know *whom* they are chasing. Victorious over the law, Pulcinella passes out the loot among his friends. He gives too fast, however, and there is nothing left for himself! Alone, he laments. A skeleton appears, brought onto the scene by the Devil; Pulcinella shivers in terror at this reminder of the pickle the Devil got him out of. Now when his girl comes onto the scene, he does not dismiss her rudely. The chorus sings as the Devil gives him a scroll; this is the pact he has signed.

A funeral procession of another Pulcinella passes. The Devil reminds Pulcinella of the flames of hell that await him. Then a young boy appears, blond and attractive, especially to the Devil, who can't keep his eyes off the boy. Suddenly blind to all else, the Devil follows the boy. Pulcinella has again escaped.

He and his girl are reunited. Pulcinella indicates that for some reason he is terribly, terribly hungry; ravenous, in fact. So a long table and a huge pot are brought in. Quickly, a potful of pasta is produced out of the pot. Pulcinella and his friends eat so much they collapse. The Devil arrives with his scroll again. Before he knows what has happened to him, Pulcinella's pals put him in the pot and give the scroll to their friend.

The scene shifts now to a solo by the girl, followed by one for Pulcinella, dressed now all in a white costume festooned with black balls. The brass in the orchestra begins a richly melodic section and the *pas de deux* for the two lovers begins. A dance of celebration for all the villagers follows, after which Pulcinella and his girl come forward to the front of the stage, with all their friends, to blow kisses to the audience.

PULCINELLA VARIATIONS

Music by Igor Stravinsky. Choreography by Michael Smuin. Scenery by Jack Brown. Costumes by Stanley Simmons. First presented by American Ballet Theatre at the Metropolitan Opera House, New York, July 11, 1968.

The program note reads: "Stravinsky, feeling sympathetic affinities with the music of Pergolesi, produced in this composition what is, in effect, a portrait of Pergolesi and his time." Similarly, the ballet presents, without a plot or story, a dance impression of the world of *commedia dell'arte,* the world of Punch and Harlequin and Columbine.

NOTES Writing of this production, Walter Terry in the *Saturday Review* said that *"Pulcinella Variations* turned out to be a delight, the best work of choreography yet by Michael Smuin, a highly virtuosic dancer in the company . . . What he has done is to retain the antic nature of the *commedia dell'arte,* for he has choreographically distilled its very essence from all its many flavors."

PUSH COMES TO SHOVE

Music by Franz Joseph Haydn and Joseph Lamb, arranged by David E. Bourne. Choreography by Twyla Tharp. Costumes by Santo Loquasto. Lighting by Jennifer Tipton. First presented by American Ballet Theatre at the Uris Theatre, New York, January 9, 1976, with Mikhail Baryshnikov, Marianna Tcherkassky, Martine van Hamel, Clark Tippet, and Christopher Aponte as principals. Conductor: Akira Endo.

A mix of old and new music, time past and present, new and old dance, *Push Comes to Shove* displays the genius of the contemporary dancer in rare and droll combinations. Doris Hering wrote in *Dance Magazine:* "It's like a giant Euclidean doodle with a firm undercurrent of pure ballet logic."

Push Comes to Shove introduces ballet's first modern folk hero, in a modified Chaplin style. He appears, in practice clothes and derby hat, in front of the curtain as the piece begins and starts to react to Joseph Lamb's *Bohemian Rag 1919.* Two girls join him and under the palsy-walsy horseplay there is a wry suggestion of feeling. Which doesn't last long. For before we know it the stage picture has changed to a formal area, the music is Haydn's *Symphony No. 82 in C,* and the vaudeville hero is now *premier danseur* and acting and dancing like one for real. Except maybe he is a pugilist, ready to knock 'em all out. The fancy girl dancers who take over the stage scare him off and then another group of girls seizes the stage, dancing to Joseph Lamb again. The hero comes and goes, there are dance situations that make jokes. Both sides, as epitomized in the hero, part hoofer/beatnik/street crazy, part *danseur noble,* are played off against each other. The hero dances this schizophrenia for all he is worth. His derby hat, which is like an ever present talisman throughout the ballet, being played with and tossed about, reminds us of the dual nature of what is happening: a modern audience watching a new ballet danced by remarkable classical performers trained in an old technique. *Push Comes to Shove* holds the mirror up to the audience and to the dancers and the company they keep.

Time said that *Push Comes to Shove* "just might be the most important dance event of the year." Frances Herridge wrote soon after the premiere in the New York *Post:* "Baryshnikov is so irresistible with his Peck's Bad Boy insouciance and his spoofing of bombast that you don't notice at first how amusing the rest of the group is . . . There are speeded-up sequences reminiscent of Mack Sennett. There are manipulated duets that made puppets of the ladies. And there are loose nuts everywhere. In short, there's not a dull moment."

Writing about the ballet in the *Times* of London, the critic John Percival said: "At the heart of *Push Comes to Shove* is a hilarious performance by Mikhail Baryshnikov. In effect, he is playing the Twyla Tharp role: the little bundle of nerves and muscles, glaring out from a moplike fringe. Sheer energy is his *métier* here, manifested in sudden bursts of wild spinning or fantastic jumps. But it is put over with an absolutely cool manner and a vaudeville comic's timing.

"In fact, Baryshnikov by no means carries the work alone. Martine van Hamel, just coming into bloom as a ballerina (I saw her charming Sylphide, and heard everyone raving about her Swan Queen and her Raymonda), has an aloof allure that is irresistible. Making up a trio of contrasted personalities, appearances and manners is Marianna Tcherkassky, small and pertly pretty.

"Those three principals dance a wickedly funny *pas de quatre* with a black bowler hat in the prelude, which is set to Joseph Lamb's *Bohemian Rag,* and each of them leads one movement of the main ballet, which is danced to Haydn's 'Bear' Symphony. Yes, the two musical styles do go together, thanks to the unfailing ingenuity of Tharp's invention. The mixture of tradition and irreverence even passes into Santo Loquasto's costume designs, which make the men wear woollen leg-warmers beneath their calf-length velvet pants."

THE RAKE'S PROGRESS

Dramatic ballet in six scenes. Music by Gavin Gordon. Choreography by Ninette de Valois. Book by Gavin Gordon. Scenery and costumes by Rex Whistler. First presented by the Sadler's Wells Ballet at the Sadler's Wells Theatre, London, May 20, 1935, with Walter Gore as the Rake and Alicia Markova as the Betrayed Girl. First presented in the United States by the

Sadler's Wells Ballet at the Metropolitan Opera House, New York, October 12, 1949, with Harold Turner as the Rake *and Margot Fonteyn as the* Betrayed Girl.

This ballet is based on the series of paintings of the same name by the great English satirist William Hogarth. Hogarth showed in this famous work the gradual corruption of an adventurous youth who suddenly found himself endowed with unlimited money. The scenery and costumes, the characters—their situation and their dancing—are a vivid reproduction of eighteenth-century London, its people, and their habits as Hogarth saw them. The music is an appropriate eighteenth-century style.

SCENE ONE   The curtain rises on a drop curtain that depicts a street in eighteenth-century London. Georgian houses, public buildings, and a church line both sides of a cobblestone street that extends into the distance. When this curtain rises, we find ourselves in the elegant apartment of the rake. There are doors left and right, and across the back there is a large window. The rake is a youth who has recently come into a fortune, and this morning all the merchants, hangers-on, and toughs who hope to profit by his good luck are paying their daily call. He is still in his night clothes, but this doesn't prevent a tailor from measuring a new coat for him. The rake seems to enjoy this attention, however, and is hardly disturbed when his jockey informs him that his horse won an important race the day before. Now a fencing master takes over and beseeches the rake to practice at his art. The rake obliges him briefly, then practices the horn under the direction of a musician.

The rake begins to dress, and all come to his assistance when needed. When he is fully dressed, he turns to his dancing master. The dancing master takes out a violin and, as he plays on the instrument, shows the rake fancy steps. The rake is not very agile, despite his youth; the truth is that he is not accustomed yet to the gestures of the youthful rich.

The dancing lesson is interrupted by an altercation at the door. There a determined old woman is arguing familiarly with the maid. She forces the maid, her daughter, into the room and follows after. The old harridan upbraids the rake for seducing her daughter and threatens blackmail. The pretty girl obviously does not approve of this procedure and is embarrassed when the rake gives her mother money. They leave the scene, and the dancing lesson continues. The drop curtain falls as the rake succeeds in affecting the manner, if not the skill, of the dance his teacher has set him.

SCENE TWO   Three ladies of the town, apparently on their way to a party, parade the street in front of the drop curtain. The rake's maid and her mother pass them. When the curtain rises, we find ourselves in a bedchamber. The room is hardly private, however, for the two women sitting at a table on the right are clearly of loose character. They are drinking and gossiping together. Three other winsome bawds are exchanging jokes in the center of the room;

they guffaw lustily at the slightest innuendo. In the back, on the left, in a curtained alcove, is an unmade bed. A lush painting of Venus and Mars in a gilt frame hangs on the back wall, giving the room an air of hopeful respectability.

Soon a friend of the rake's swaggers into the room, followed by the rake himself. Rake he is determined to be: he is drunk and delighted with himself. The girls take immediate advantage of him and his friend, treating them as if they were the only attractive men in the world.

The guests are treated to *divertissements* by a professional dancer, who does an eighteenth-century version of the striptease by removing her stockings, and a female ballad singer, who creaks out a song. This song delights the drunken rake, who throws his arm about the ballad singer and insists upon joining her. The music goes to his head, unfortunately, and he begins to pass out.

He is revived, however, as the girls begin to dance. Soon everyone in the room is dancing, whirling and whirling about in a manner that reflects the rake's intoxication. The rake expresses his admiration for this display by throwing coins about the room. One of the rowdy girls scurries about trying to pick up all the money, while the others devote themselves to affected gaiety to amuse the rake. The curtain falls, leaving the rest of the bawdy scene to our imagination.

SCENE THREE   Before the drop curtain, three creditors lie in wait to accost the rake. He strolls in haughtily. They present their bills, which are long overdue, and demand payment. Evidently the rake has run through his inheritance rather rapidly, for he is not in the least condescending: he is afraid. The pretty maid whom we met in the first scene comes into the street. As we might have expected, from her annoyance with her demanding mother, she does not despise her seducer. On the contrary, she observes him with some sympathy and intercedes in his quarrel with the creditors. The poor serving maid tells the men that she will pay the bills! The rake appears to be unimpressed by this expression of love, but the creditors are pleased with her promise; they exit. The rake goes on down the street, immediately forgetting the trouble he has had. The girl does a dance that expresses her love for the rake and the impossibility of its fulfillment.

SCENE FOUR   The rake has seriously come down in the world, for this time the curtain rises on a low gambling dive. The rake, no longer dressed in finery, enters and joins three burly-looking characters in a game of cards. Cleaned out in the higher-class gaming rooms and brothels, he imagines that he can easily regain his losses among such ignorant folk. His fellow players are cleverer than he thinks, however, and luck seems to be against him. He begins to lose steadily. He clings to his few coins as if they were the last moments of a happy life. It is not difficult for us to imagine that the betrayed girl, the lovely chambermaid he has spurned, would have a great deal of pity for him. The poor devil cannot bear to lose: he loses not only his money, but his connection with reality, as he hopes that this last bet will bring back all the opulence of his former life—the tailors and jewelers and race-track touts indebted to *him* again, much wine, many women, and endless song. Simultaneously he sees that if he loses, he will enjoy none of these things: that leaves, for him, poor fellow, nothing. The last wager is made, the last card is turned up, the tables are turned; he is wiped out! Less rake than pauper, the unfortunate fellow collapses.

SCENE FIVE   Before the curtain, the betrayed girl dances alone, hoping that the rake, who has now been put in the debtor's prison, will be released and come back to her.

SCENE SIX   When the curtain comes up again the scene, like the rake's progress, has gone from bad to worse: we are in a madhouse, a dark place and damp, where therapy consists of filthy isolation. The more dangerous lunatics can be seen behind iron grilles, posing as kings and cardinals. Creatures less preoccupied sit in an open area. One of these men entertains himself and his fellow madmen by a grotesque dance with a rope, which outlines in the air the images that haunt him.

The outside door clangs open, and the rake is thrown into the cell. The men watch the new inmate while he tries, as they did, to escape. When he falls to the floor exhausted, they display their individual manias for his benefit. While the rake looks at them, we think for a moment that he is not really mad, that there has been some mistake: an eighteenth-century solution to a down-and-outer's problem, some gross misjudgment. But we are wrong. The rake rises and dances like a demon.

The girl he has betrayed comes to visit him and tries pathetically to make him remember her, but now this man's only thought is to escape from her, to escape from everyone, to get out. He attacks the door again, and again he falls to the floor. The lovely girl attempts to mend his agony by sweet and loving gestures that might give him some hope. Her thoughtfulness and devotion are contrasted vividly with the fashionable world that her lover has left, when some well-dressed ladies enter the asylum and observe the inmates for entertainment and diversion.

The rake becomes hysterical, catatonic, and thrashes about the floor uncontrollably. He dies in the midst of his paroxysms. The betrayed girl holds him close in her arms, weeping that her love might have saved him, weeping that he did not understand the path of self-destruction.

RAPSODIE ESPAGNOLE

Music by Maurice Ravel. Choreography by George Balanchine. First presented at the New York City Ballet's Hommage à Ravel at the New York State Theatre, Lincoln Center, May 29, 1975, with Karin von Aroldingen and Peter Schaufuss in leading roles.

Ravel knew Spain well. The Spanish composer Manuel de Falla has recalled that "Ravel's Spain was a Spain ideally presented by his mother, whose refined conversation, always in excellent Spanish, delighted me, particularly when she would recall her youthful years spent in Madrid."

I found the music exciting for its vigor, clarity, and wonderful flamenco from the first and tried to arrange some expressive yet simple dances for passionate young persons.

RAYMONDA

Ballet in three acts. Music by Alexander Glazunov. Choreography by Marius Petipa. First presented at the Maryinsky Theatre, St. Petersburg, January 19, 1898. First presented in the United States in abbreviated form by the Ballet Russe de Monte Carlo at the City Center, New York, March 12, 1946, with choreography by Alexandra Danilova and George Balanchine. First presented complete by the Kirov Ballet at the Metropolitan Opera House, New York, September 16, 1964, with Irina Kolpakova as Raymonda, Vladilen Semenov as Jean de Brienne, and Gennady Selutsky as Abderachman.

Glazunov's music for *Raymonda* contains some of the finest ballet music we have. And Petipa's original choreography, which I remember from student appearances at the Maryinsky Theatre, was superb. But his story was nonsense, difficult to follow, and, in the words of an old Russian balletomane Prince Lieven, "it has everything but meaning," as you will see. It takes place in medieval Hungary.

ACT ONE, SCENE ONE   Raymonda, betrothed to Jean de Brienne, who is away at war, celebrates her birthday at the home of her aunt, a countess. Jean sends his fiancée gifts, among them a tapestry portrait of himself, and announces that he will arrive the next day. But Abderachman, a Saracen chief, pays an unexpected visit to the castle. He admires Raymonda, attempts to lure her with rich gifts.

ACT ONE, SCENE TWO   Raymonda dreams that her lover descends from his portrait and leads her into the garden to dance a *pas de deux*. But this vision is dispelled and in Jean's place Raymonda finds the sinister Saracen, who renews his advances. Raymonda swoons.

ACT TWO   At a reception the countess gives in honor of the Saracen, Raymonda anxiously awaits Jean's arrival. But Abderachman approaches her passionately and insists that she dance with him. She accepts and the Saracen then commands his retinue to entertain Raymonda with jugglers and dancing. Moors and Spaniards join in a dance that becomes fierce with intensity; at its height the Saracen attempts to abduct Raymonda. At that point, who should arrive but Jean de Brienne, accompanied by his old father, King Andrew II of Hungary. Raymonda rushes to Jean's arms. He and his followers threaten Abderachman and his retinue, but the king intervenes and proposes single combat for the rivals. The ensuing duel is furious and Abderachman falls.

ACT THREE   A festival is being held at Jean de Brienne's castle to celebrate his marriage to Raymonda. The festival begins with a *grand pas hongrois* in which Raymonda dances a variation and Jean a final solo before the lovers are united forever.

NOTES   Rudolf Nureyev staged his version of the complete *Raymonda* with the Royal Ballet's touring company at the Festival of Two Worlds in Spoleto in 1964. Doreen Wells and Nureyev appeared in the principal roles. Act III of this production, with scenery and costumes by Barry Kay, was presented by the Royal Ballet at the Royal Opera House, Covent Garden, July 16, 1966, with Doreen Wells and David Wall. Alexander Bland, reviewing this and other ballets on the same program in *The Observer,* wrote that David Wall "finally and triumphantly established himself as the most promising British dancer since the war, heading for the international class. In *Les Sylphides* he gave . . . an almost faultless performance, very much in the Nureyev style; his young boy in *The Invitation* . . . was rather more than adequate: and finally he came up at the end of the evening to give his *Raymonda* solo a mixture of dash, control, musicality, and style of which any Kirov dancer could have been proud."

Nureyev staged *Raymonda* for the Australian Ballet in 1965. In 1972 he mounted it for the Zurich Ballet in a production designed by Nicholas Georgiadis, in 1975 for American Ballet Theatre. In Zurich, Nureyev and Marcia Haydée danced the first performance. Reviewing it in *Dance and Dancers* magazine, the British critic John Percival wrote:

"The Zurich Ballet is more used to appearing alone in some quite ambitious productions, but I doubt whether its dancers have tackled anything as taxing as Nureyev's *Raymonda.* This has been completely rethought and drastically changed since the two previous productions Nureyev has mounted. The good features of those productions remain: the marvelous Glazunov score, full of dreamy waltzes and exciting rhythms; some brilliant solos preserving Petipa's choreography; and the biggest of all classical roles for a ballerina (now even augmented beyond what we saw before). These virtues have been increased, too; the score is now played complete, and almost in the composer's original order, except for one change in Act Three to give the hero an extra solo; and the new choreography which Nureyev has added is well devised to show off the dancers and to make the best of the preserved Petipa.

"The trouble with *Raymonda* has always been the story . . . Nureyev has found a surprisingly simple way to make sense of the whole. He takes his cue from the fact that there was always a dream sequence, designed to allow

Raymonda a duet with her admirer Jean de Brienne in the early part of the ballet, although the plot did not actually introduce him until near the end. Nureyev considerably enlarged this dream to cover not just one scene but a substantial part of Act One and almost the whole of Act Two.

"What happens now is that Raymonda is first seen playing with her friends (two girls and two troubadours) while preparations are going on all around for her marriage as soon as Jean gets back from the wars. Pretty soon he arrives with the King of Hungary (in whose forces he has been serving) and offers her a present: a tapestry banner he has brought back from the Crusades. Left alone, Raymonda imagines the dark Saracen warrior from whom Jean won this. She falls asleep, and in her dream the banner grows until it becomes the Saracen's tent. The traditional love duet with Jean remains, but in addition there are scenes alone with the Saracen, Abderachman; others in which he and Jean phantasmagorically exchange places; and others again in which both appear dancing with her and her friends. For a while Abderachman persuades Raymonda (and her girl friends) to remain with him, enjoying the divertissement of Spanish and oriental dances he provides; but at last the nobly retiring Jean is provoked into challenging his rival. They compete at archery, fight with lances on horseback, and finally engage in a duel with swords, in which Jean, with one mighty blow, shatters his enemy's helmet and wounds him, presumably fatally. Now Raymonda can unreservedly give Jean her heart and her hand—and at this point she wakes up to find him and her friends come to look for her. Thus Act Two ends happily, and Act Three is, as usual, the wedding celebration.

"This makes a more interesting story, for its own sake and also as a portrait of Raymonda's inner struggle. The presence of the troubadours, poetic exponents of the artificial conventions of courtly love, among her friends is evidence that she is not really ready, when the ballet starts, for the wedding which is imminent. Together the friends play at being in love, but Raymonda's games are still childish. Jean's devotion is at first too reticent to awaken her; only when her dreams conjure up the dark figure of her animus, and Jean proves able to defeat this imagined rival, does she come to terms with her hidden longings.

"The role of Raymonda thus becomes dramatically interesting, and Marcia Haydée (who danced the first four performances of the production) makes the most of this. But it is still, above all, an immensely demanding virtuoso role, with so many solos that I lost count, each showing off a different aspect of technique—leaps, turns, balances and so on. There is a beautiful lyric solo with a scarf; a solo in which she jumps repeatedly to land with a stabbing thrust on full point; and of course that haunting last-act solo with its hints of melancholy beneath a surface of surpassing grandeur."

Nureyev staged his production of *Raymonda* for American Ballet Theatre in New York in 1975. Cynthia Gregory and Nureyev danced the first performance. John T. Elson wrote in *Time* magazine:

"*Raymonda* is a two-hour experience in pure dance. And what dancing there is! . . . The incandescent Miss Gregory danced the role as if it had been created for her alone, carrying out variation after variation—six in all—with radiant confidence. The breathtaking pauses at the peak of her balances last only a second or so; yet they seem to embody T. S. Eliot's haunting lines in *Burnt Norton:* 'At the still point of the turning world . . . There the dance is, but neither arrest or movement.'"

Marius Petipa's original scenario for *Raymonda,* including his instructions to the composer, Glazunov, has been translated by Debra Goldman for *Ballet Review* (Vol. 5, No. 2).

RAYMONDA VARIATIONS

Music by Alexander Glazunov. Choreography by George Balanchine. Scenery by Horace Armistead. Costumes by Karinska. First presented by the New York City Ballet at the City Center, New York, December 7, 1961, with Patricia Wilde and Jacques d'Amboise in the leading roles.

I have already mentioned in speaking of *Pas de Dix* how I have always liked the music Glazunov wrote for the ballet *Raymonda.* This ballet also has music taken from Glazunov's score for *Raymonda,* but it is music of an entirely different character from *Pas de Dix.* Originally called *Valse and Variations,* the ballet consists of dances for two principals, soloists, and a *corps de ballet.* There is no story, only the music to dance to.

When the curtain goes up, twelve girls stand posing in an elegant garden. They dance for us and then the principals, another girl and then a boy, join them. Next, the girl and the boy are alone for an adagio. This is followed by a series of nine variations, or solos, by five of the girls and the two principals. The ballet concludes with a coda and a finale by all the dancers.

To try to talk about these dances in any useful way outside the music is not possible; they do not have any literary content at all and of course have nothing to do with the story of the original ballet *Raymonda.* The music itself, its grand and generous manner, its joy and playfulness, was for me more than enough to carry the plot of the dances.

THE REAL McCOY

Music by George Gershwin. Choreography by Eliot Feld. Setting and costumes by Rouben Ter-Arutunian. Lighting by Thomas Skelton. First presented by the Eliot Feld Ballet at the New York Shakespeare Festival Public Theatre, December 7, 1974, with Eliot Feld in the leading role. Pianist: Gladys Celeste Mercader.

The Real McCoy recaptures the past and projects it into the present. With the authenticity of George Gershwin's music as a floor to walk on, the action has other points to make, too, about the American Dream. The hero of the piece, a bright, brash young man, a mix of James Cagney and Fred Astaire, indicates at the start that any kid can be a star, like Astaire maybe. Perhaps he is, in fact, George Gershwin? The painted backdrop of rainbows reminds us that much is being sought after, in the '30s fashion.

A guy in a top hat, with cane, and a blonde on a chaise longue turn the sofa into a canoe and go paddling. They meet curious adventures. At the end, the hero dances frantically. Seeking a cocktail feeling of joy or experiencing the Real McCoy?

REFLECTIONS

Music by Peter Ilyich Tchaikovsky. Choreography by Gerald Arpino. Lighting by Jennifer Tipton. First presented by the City Center Joffrey Ballet at the City Center, New York, February 24, 1971, with Erika Goodman, Dana Sapiro, Denise Jackson, Glenn White, and Henry Berg as the principals. Cellist: Warren Lash. Conducted by Walter Hagen.

Arranged to Tchaikovsky's *Variations on a Rococo Theme for Violoncello and Orchestra*, *Reflections* is a dance ballet with no plot beyond the beauties of the score. This music, not often enough heard, is of interest to those who know only Tchaikovsky's familiar works. There is, first of all, the statement of the theme, danced by a group of seven girls. Seven variations then follow, the first two danced by girls, the third a *pas de deux*, the fourth a *pas de trois* for three girls, the fifth another *pas de deux*, the sixth yet another, and the seventh an ensemble for all the dancers. There is no setting, only the dancers providing absorbing displays of reflected virtuosity to the music.

THE RELATIVITY OF ICARUS

Music by Gerhard Samuel. Text by Jack Larson. Choreography by Gerald Arpino. Set and costumes by Rouben Ter-Arutunian. Lighting by Thomas Skelton. First presented in New York City by the City Center Joffrey Ballet at the City Center, October 17, 1974, with Ann Marie DeAngelo as the Sun, Russell Sultzbach as Icarus, and Ted Nelson as Daedalus. Soprano: Joan Bell. Conducted by Seymour Lipkin.

The story of two men, father and son, who escaped from the labyrinth on self-made wings, has been told many times. This ballet is a variation on that story, based on the poem by Jack Larson and the music by Gerhard Samuel.

Daedalus was the builder of the Labyrinth on the island of Crete. He and his son Icarus were later imprisoned in the Labyrinth. To escape from it and the Minotaur, the monstrous man-bull who dwelt there, they fashioned wings of feathers and wax, which enabled them to fly. Icarus, however, flew too near the sun, the wax on his wings melted, and he fell into the sea, thenceforth called Icarian.

The text by Jack Larson for the music that accompanies the action follows:

As it was with Icarus,
Imprisoned in the labyrinth of his father's creation
Punished by the echoes of a monster's satisfaction
He wished to escape in wings from the confusion of earth.
As it was with Icarus,
Wanting to fly from memories of a Minotaur's birth
Away from mutilated bodies of handsome young men
From the echoes of rape and massacre of young women:
As it was with Icarus,
Out of the labyrinth in wings of things of feathers and wax
Straining free of gravity into air currents that relax
He took flight into the transforming softness of the clouds.
As it was with Icarus,
Even the clouds mushroom in echoes of thunderous shrouds
And though he flies straight as light, like light he'll curve near the moon
And return to the labyrinth a trillion light years too soon.
As it was with Icarus,
Soar to the sun, it's only a mass of multiplied light
Transmuting its brilliance into the curvature of night
Like his too warm wings, the escape expands as it contracts.
And disappears from space as impermanent as wax.
As it was with Icarus,
So it is with all of us.*

The action of the ballet takes place in a remarkable luminous and reflecting setting that catches light and movement, expanding and focusing, deflecting and returning, in much the same way as interpretations of myth invariably return to the primal story.

First the Sun, a lovely girl, dances around a raised area on which Daedalus lies. The Sun reveals him to us and from Daedalus springs full-armed his son Icarus. Bound to his father by cords about his wrists, Icarus is taught to fly. The cords, however, make it impossible for him to fly free of Daedalus.

Daedalus is enamored now of the Sun, and would follow her, sensing even the danger he sees in loosening the cords and abandoning his son. But the boy is more deeply tempted than the father. To free himself, he strangles Daedalus. The liberated Icarus then plunges into an endless fall. The Sun turns again about the earth.

In a long, discursive essay, "Arpino's *Icarus:* Confrontations with the Fall," in *Dance Magazine* (January 1975), Richard Philp writes: "Nobody was unmoved by *Icarus* . . . I believe that we all seem to have seen something in the ballet which is familiar; it holds a mirror up before us and reflects experience which is difficult to reject, or accept . . .

"For one of the simplest interpretations, with which the ballet's strongest supporters are content to settle, I borrow a quote from Nietzsche's *Zarathustra:* 'Many a one hath cast away final worth when he hath cast away his servitude.'

"Wherever *Icarus* is danced, the ballet will continue to evoke comment and interpretation which will have to deal to some extent with the meaning of myth and the nature of human freedom. Visually, I think of *Icarus* and remember the struggling movements outwards, away from, beyond; conversely, there is also a sense of restriction, withdrawal, retreat. To rephrase Nietzsche: When Icarus casts off his servitude [to Daedalus], he is in effect casting away himself; Icarus, like many of us, cannot function without the flexing pressures of obligation."

REMEMBRANCES

Music by Richard Wagner. Choreography by Robert Joffrey. Set by Rouben Ter-Arutunian. Costumes by Willa Kim. Lighting by Jennifer Tipton. First presented by the City Center Joffrey Ballet at the City Center, New York, October 12, 1973, with Francesca Corkle and Jonathan Watts as principals. Conducted by Seymour Lipkin. Pianist: Stanley Babin. She, Who Sings: *Donna Roll.* She, Who Remembers: *Jan Hanniford.*

Remembrances is a ballet about looking back. As a woman sings her recollections of past love, a woman who remembers remains at her side to watch and reach out toward a danced re-enactment of the past.

The program recalls that Richard Wagner, in 1849, having taken an active role in the revolutionary movement in Germany, was forced to flee with his wife, Minna, and to settle in Switzerland. There, in Zurich, he met a wealthy silk merchant, Otto Wesendonck, who, at his wife Mathilde's urging, became Wagner's patron. It was not long before "something dangerously like a love affair" developed between Mathilde and Wagner.

Some of Wagner's work is inextricably linked with his relationship to Mathilde. In 1853 he wrote for her personal album a sonata that is described by one of his biographers, Paul Bekker, as "a summary of the past and a promise for the future, a delicate act of homage to the woman who had inspired the music

which was now to flow from him in an almost unbroken stream." Written on
the manuscript of the sonata, as a motto, is the inscription: "Do you know
what will follow?"

Mathilde Wesendonck and Wagner became artistic collaborators a few years
later, when in 1857–58 he set to music five of her poems. The poems are enti-
tled *Der Engel* (*The Angel*), *Stehe Still* (*Stand Still*), *Im Treibhaus* (*In the
Greenhouse*), *Schmerzen* (*Tears*), and *Träume* (*Dreams*). Wagner said that
Im Treibhaus and *Träume* could be described as "studies" for *Tristan und
Isolde*.

In 1935 Arturo Toscanini discovered a lost, unpublished piece of Wagner's
known as the *Porazzi Theme*, which the composer had played on the afternoon
of his death. Dating from 1859, this theme had been jotted down on the back
of a sketch for *Tristan*, relating to the lovers' invocation to the night.

These musical works of Wagner's are the score for the ballet and set the
scene for its backward look.

The ballet carries as its motto this quotation from Shelley:

Music, when soft voices die
Vibrates in the memory.

The pianist begins the music in the dimly lit auditorium. The house slowly
darkens with the quiet music. Soon a girl in a long dress walks slowly across
the stage. She reaches out in a gesture of longing and sits down. Following her
now comes another girl, her double, who is to sing what the first girl feels and
acts as she watches the scene that flows before her.

A girl dances with a boy, it is apparently long ago and almost lost to the
memory but soon other images come back, the lovers are among friends, four
other couples. The scene appears to be a clearing high above a cavernous bay,
the sea shimmering in the distance; the setting resembles an oculus that is
focused on a far-off place, the sea, mountains, enclosed in a curved landscape
of the memory.

Two couples dance to the music of the first song. Then later, the lead girl,
alone, dances and seems to suffer, but her lover rejoins her.

There is a recognition between the woman who watches her past and the
girl who dances it. Others now dance to the low threnody of strings. Finally,
the girl is left by herself, kneeling. She rises; her partner returns. Later among
the happy couples, the lovers seem to expire. She, Who Remembers reaches
out to them and gestures to She, Who Sings. But her young image only looks
back at her.

NOTES Writing in *Dance and Dancers* about *Remembrances*, Patricia
Barnes referred to the ballet as "perhaps the best thing Robert Joffrey has yet
achieved. . . . It is a lushly romantic work, matching the music's soul and
passion. . . . Corkle has always been a brilliant young technician. In *Remembrances* Joffrey has seen another side of her. One is tempted to say that this

ballet has made her a great dancer. She performed it as if her heart was on fire, with a sincerity and depth that were remarkable. In her movement there was a dramatic tension and in her musicality a wealth of understanding of what can transform a simple movement into art.

"Jonathan Watts . . . was here making his first stage appearance in nine years. . . . He is now dancing better than ever, even after such a long lay-off period. Always an immaculate stylist, in *Remembrances* he was superb, partnering with tenderness, possessing elegant *ports de bras* and unforced dignity."

LES RENDEZVOUS

Ballet divertissement *in one act. Music by François Auber, arranged by Constant Lambert. Choreography by Frederick Ashton. Scenery and costumes by William Chappell. First performed by the Sadler's Wells Ballet at the Sadler's Wells Theatre, London, December 5, 1933, with a cast headed by Alicia Markova, Stanislas Idzikowski, Pearl Argyle, Ninette de Valois, and Robert Helpmann. Revived with new decor by William Chappell, November 16, 1937. First presented in the United States by the Sadler's Wells Theatre Ballet at the Northrop Auditorium, Minneapolis, Minnesota, November 7, 1951, with Elaine Fifield and Pirmin Trecu in the principal roles. First performed by the Royal Ballet at Covent Garden, London, May 7, 1959.*

Les Rendezvous is a dance entertainment set to music from Auber's *L'Enfant Prodigue*. In a private park, young couples promenade and dance to give appropriate expression to youthful sentiments that take hold of their ebullient spirits. There is no plot.

The curtain rises on a bright, sunny scene. A high white fence of wrought iron stands out against a light-green back cloth. The gate to the park, in the center, is open. The orchestra plays music that is light and charming, music suggestive of the good nature we always feel when we watch boys and girls show their happiness by dancing together. Trumpets sound a fanfare and the ballet begins.

Young couples out for a stroll dance into the park one by one from the corners of the stage. They are all dressed in white; the girls wear pink ribbons in their hair and pink sashes, and the boys wear belts of light blue. The young people move back and forth across the park. Finally there are six couples. They stand on either side of the gate, and a seventh couple enters. They pass down the line formed by their friends, greet them effusively, and then, more formally, shake hands.

Now the couples divide into different groups and fill the stage with shifting, quick movement. The boys dance alone briefly, then leave the stage to a couple who dance a short *pas de deux*. The boy lifts the girl off into the wings;

the music is rapid and joyful, the lift is long and slow, and there is an effect of joyfulness mixed with romance. Other boys enter and lift their partners more rapidly, more in direct imitation of the music. Six girls surround the romantic couple when they return, and the introduction to the ballet finishes as the boy again lifts the girl into the wings.

Four girls dance a bright *pas de quatre*. They are joined by their partners and leave the stage as the boy of the lead couple enters and dances a bold leaping-and-turning variation to brilliant, flourishing music. The boy gestures toward the gate, his girl rejoins him there, and they leave the stage together. The other couples have returned and form three tableaux about the stage. The boy, reaching out to his partner who kneels below, comes back, leading his girl forward, and the two of them dance a slow, romantic duet. Four of the boys lift the girl to their shoulders as the adagio ends. There she poses gracefully, as the girls gather about her raised figure, hold hands, and enclose her with a circle of arabesques.

The music becomes saucy and bouncing. A girl bounds on stage with two partners, turning from the arms of one boy into the arms of the other. The two boys lift her high into the air, release her, and their steps quicken to the hastening music. The *pas de trois* finishes as all three kneel.

Next the lead girl dances alone. She leaps onto the scene, turns dizzily, delighting us with her deft, swift movement. She is very pretty, apparently in love, and enjoys showing off a little. Boys emerge from the wings one by one and bow to the girl, in tribute to her beauty and her masterful dance. She bows gratefully in return and leaves the stage on the left.

Rhythmic handclaps are heard off-stage. Six boys run into the park to dance in unison a strong, buoyant ensemble, dazzling with its long, high leaps, multiple turns, and the quick, steady certainty with which they finish their brilliant sequence of movement. A trumpet fanfare announces the arrival of six girls, who join their partners for a brief dance before the reappearance of the ballerina, who whirls about the stage. The *corps de ballet* returns and forms a background for another virtuoso variation by the ballerina's partner, who places his hands on his shoulders and spins like a top.

Four girls approach the boy and blindfold him. He plays their game for a moment, then turns in their midst and rushes off as the ballerina enters on the right to hop backward on point in a long diagonal. All the couples are now on stage. They bow to each other and bid their partners a fond farewell. One by one, they leave the park through the gate. When the ballerina disappears into the wings, her partner leaps after her in a high trajectory. Four girls, who remain in the park, pose amusingly, as if the fun has just begun.

REQUIEM CANTICLES

Music by Igor Stravinsky. Choreography by Jerome Robbins. Lighting by Ronald Bates. First presented by the New York City Ballet at the Stravinsky Festival, June 25, 1972, at the New York State Theatre, Lincoln Center, New York, with Merrill Ashley, Susan Hendl, Bruce Wells, and Robert Maiorano as principals. Soprano: Elaine Bonazzi. Bass: William Metcalf. Conducted by Robert Craft.

Stravinsky's *Requiem Canticles,* for contralto, soloists, and orchestra, first performed in 1966 at Princeton, New Jersey, was selected by Jerome Robbins as one of his ballets for our Stravinsky Festival in 1972. That event, which marked the composer's ninetieth birthday, also mourned his death as we hope he would have wished us to do, with celebration. *Requiem Canticles* was the final ballet of the Festival.

Stravinsky had earlier informed the New York City Ballet that he planned the *Requiem Canticles* "as an instrumental work originally, and I composed the threnody for wind instruments and muffled drums, now at the center of the work, first. Later I decided to use sentences from six texts of the traditional Requiem service, and that time I conceived the triangulate instrumental frame of the string *Prelude,* wind-instrument *Interlude,* and percussion *Postlude.* The *Requiem Canticles* are concert music, but the celebration of death is to be played in memory of a man of God, a man of the poor, a man of peace."

Robbins's *Requiem Canticles* was an appropriate finale in dance to what was, for many of us on both sides of the footlights, a memorable week.

A *Village Voice* critic said of the ballet: "Mr. Robbins's piece, conducted by Robert Craft, accentuated the energy heard in the music. Here were granite blocks of black-clothed dancers staring out at the audience in the *Prelude* and shaking in tight spasms. The choral sections followed, with the *Exaudi* bringing in slow gestures and walkings, the *Dies irae* frenzied with lifts and aimless striding, the *Tuba mirum* showing Bruce Wells as a sort of Angel Gabriel ready to call everyone to judgment, the non-vocal *Interlude* leaving the stage to four dancers full of expectation, *Rex tremendae* bringing back the corps in their block phalanxes, Merrill Ashley bursting out of a semicircle of corps in *Lacrymosa,* the *Libera me* letting the corps members converge on one another on their knees and making room for short solos by Miss Ashley and Susan Hendl before the group goes into asymmetric attitudes; and finally the drums and bells of the *Postlude* setting off a mechanism of ticking bodies, limbs, and finally just heads in open-mouthed, silent cries of fear and marvel."

REVENGE

Dramatic ballet in four scenes with prologue. Music by Giuseppe Verdi. Choreography by Ruth Page. Book by Ruth Page with the collaboration of Nicolas Remisov. Scenery and costumes by Antoine Clavé. First presented by Les Ballets des Champs-Élysées at the Théâtre de l'Empire, Paris, October 17, 1951, with Sonia Arova as Azucena, Vladimir Skouratoff as Manrico, Jacqueline Moreau as Leonora, and Gérard Ohm as the Count di Luna. First presented in the United States by Ruth Page Ballets at the Civic Opera House, Chicago, November 26, 1955, with Sonia Arova, Oleg Briansky, Alicia Markova, and Bentley Stone in the principal roles.

Like the ballet *Carmen, Revenge* is also based on a great popular opera— Verdi's *Il Trovatore.* The ballet is faithful to the opera's theme of passionate revenge and condenses into a comparatively short space of time the principal elements of the musical drama. The time is the sixteenth century. The place is Spain.

PROLOGUE: THE COURTYARD OF THE CASTLE OF THE COUNT DI LUNA   The elderly Count di Luna has two infant sons, of whom he is very proud. One day an old gypsy woman is discovered hovering over the cradle of one of these boys. The child's nurse, suspecting sorcery, sounds the alarm, and the old count's servants capture the gypsy. The hag pleads that she meant no harm, that she was only interested in reading the child's fortune. She is driven out of the castle, but when the child becomes ill, she is brought back. At the count's order, she is burned at the stake for sorcery. His child recovers.

The old gypsy's young daughter, Azucena, dances in despair as the flames of her mother's burning light the distant sky. Gentlemen of the count's household stand on the steps of the courtyard watching the fire with indifference. Azucena vows to avenge her mother's horrible death. She steals the count's other son and flees into the night.

SCENE ONE: THE CASTLE   Twenty years have passed. The old Count di Luna is dead. On his deathbed he urged his remaining son never to abandon search for his brother. Unknown to the new count, his brother still survives as Manrico, whom Azucena has brought up as her own son.

Both the Count di Luna and Manrico are in love with the beautiful Leonora, lady in waiting to the queen. Leonora favors Manrico, and the count, enraged that the girl should prefer a ragged gypsy to a nobleman, is determined to separate them. Leonora escapes with Manrico to a gypsy camp.

SCENE TWO: THE GYPSY MOVEMENT   The Count di Luna traces the two lovers and comes in person to the gypsy camp. There he challenges Manrico to a duel. The young gypsy, warned by a premonition, reluctantly consents to this contest, and the two brothers, completely ignorant of their relationship, begin to fight. Manrico gains the upper hand and might easily slay the count. The premonition returns, and he stays his hand. Azucena regrets that her ward has not killed the count; after twenty years, she can still think only of revenge.

The count, enraged by jealousy and Manrico's contempt, is determined to force his love on Leonora. He sends her to prison with Manrico.

SCENE THREE: IN FRONT OF THE PRISON   The two lovers endure torture in prison by the count's order. Leonora, in desperation, promises that she will marry the count if he will set Manrico free.

SCENE FOUR: THE BETROTHAL   The marriage ceremony has been arranged. Manrico, who does not know that she has arranged for his release, accuses Leonora of faithlessness. But Leonora, unwilling to marry the count, has taken poison and urges Manrico to seek his freedom. Manrico discovers what she has done and weeps as she dies in his arms.

The Count di Luna orders Manrico's execution. The youth bids farewell to his foster mother, who despairs that her revenge means such a sacrifice. But when Manrico is dead, she weeps no more. She turns to the Count di Luna in fierce triumph. Glorying in her revenge, she holds out to him the locket that hung about the neck of his brother twenty years before. To the count's horror at this secret, Azucena responds with demoniac exultation: she has had her revenge at last.

REVERIES

Music by Peter Ilyich Tchaikovsky. Choreography by John Clifford. Costumes by Joe Eula. Lighting by Ronald Bates. First presented by the New York City Ballet at the New York State Theatre, December 4, 1969, with Conrad Ludlow, Anthony Blum, Johnna Kirkland, Gelsey Kirkland, and ensemble.

The fourth ballet by John Clifford, *Reveries* uses music from Tchaikovsky's *Suite No. 1* (the first, third, fourth, and sixth movements). The plot of the ballet is the plot of the music.

The curtain rises after a brief orchestral introduction. The first movement, marked *Introduction and Fugue,* is staged for a boy and twelve girls who, dressed in flowing pink, surround their romantic hero. He is seen in a spotlight, center. Detached at first, he kneels and watches the girls dance, then joins them under the dark, starry sky. His dance is like magic, and they all seem to respond like flowers in the wind. He leaves the girls then to commence to dance to the fugue. The boy returns to dance and fall at the feet of his Muses. They soon leave, the scene darkens and he, too, departs.

To the third movement of Tchaikovsky's Suite, *Intermezzo*, the dance begins in a diagonal of light on a dark stage. Four boys and four girls face each other. The stage brightens, a boy lifts on a girl in white, and the orchestra plays a romantic theme. The couple dances, he catching her under the arms as she leaps. As the music ends, he kneels before her, then holds her as she falls into his arms. A brilliant soloist in blue dances in dynamic contrast to the lyricism of the lovers.

The *Marche Militaire* is led by a girl who matches the brilliance of Tchaikovsky's melody with the help of a small group of four girls. The finale, *Gavotte*, brings the four principals together in a climactic ensemble of complication and exuberance.

NOTES Clive Barnes wrote in the New York *Times:* "*Reveries* is John Clifford's best piece to date, and is a lovely piece of choreography. . . . He really illuminates the music. There is a sumptuous and love-rapt *pas de deux* for Johnna Kirkland and Conrad Ludlow, and beautiful solos for Anthony Blum and Johnna's brilliant kid sister, Gelsey Kirkland. . . . The entire piece is elegant yet fun."

Arlene Croce, editor of *Ballet Review*, wrote of John Clifford in *Playbill* in 1969: "The youngest of the New York City Ballet's dancer-choreographers is twenty-one-year-old John Clifford. Clifford came to New York from Los Angeles and was awarded a scholarship to the School of American Ballet, where he entered the choreography workshop in 1966. He made his choreographic debut with *Stravinsky Symphony* in the spring of 1968 and has revised it steadily ever since. His second ballet, to Vaughan Williams' *Fantasia on a Theme of Thomas Tallis*, is a lyrical work about two real people and a dream couple whom the real people prefer to one another. Premièred early this year, *Fantasies* was a hit with both critics and audiences, and Clifford has been invited to stage his next ballet for the company's Sixth Annual Spring Benefit on May 8, on the same program with new works by George Balanchine and Jerome Robbins. Robbins, who returns this spring to choreograph for the company after more than a decade's absence, provided Clifford with his earliest inspiration. Shortly before spring rehearsals began, Clifford was to be found at the State Theatre, where Robbins was taking class.

" 'I've been watching Jerry work on his new piece,' he told an interviewer. 'I'm rehearsing it but I don't know if I'm going to be in it yet. The way he squeezes everything he can get out of you! I can't do that yet. He's a rhythm choreographer of course—he uses every last bit of rhythm. And he's so thorough. I think he thought about *The Cage* for years before he did it, thought it all out and knew exactly what he wanted to do. When I first joined the company I would watch every performance of *The Cage* and people would say, "Well, John, what did you like this time?" The first large-scale choreography I ever saw was the film of *West Side Story*. I've seen it more than twenty times. When it came out again recently, I went back. I think it affected my spatial concepts when I began to choreograph. I used to try and set bits of movement in the background that only ended up confusing the stage picture. I was choreographing selectively as if for a camera. I didn't realize that in the theater the spectator has to have a central focus because he's stationary; he can't move around like a camera picking up this and that. You know those funny, insectlike things the girls do in *The Cage?* Well, they do a lot with their arms and hands you really can't see, but only because the stage is so dark. I wish it could be brighter. I'd like to do a horror ballet like that some day. Actually, whether you do story ballets or not depends on the music. I consciously try to do something different in each piece. The Stravinsky—a neo-classical abstract work. Mr. B. thought it would be good for me to work with that score. Next, a long romantic piece with a bit of a story. Now I'm using Bernstein's *Prelude, Fugue and Riffs*. It's a jazz score from the same period as Stravinsky's *Ebony Concerto*, but it's not going to be set as a "jazz ballet" in that sense because it would look dated. I don't read music or have a record-player. I go to the library and listen to records. When I hear something I like, I file it away in the back of my mind. I hadn't heard the *Tallis* until about a year ago, on the Coast, when somebody played it for me. I didn't care for it too much then. But it came back to me for *Fantasies*. When I'm making a piece, I don't try to get the dancers to consciously project a meaning. I don't tell them what they're supposed to do except over coffee. Ideally, you just want the dancer to be. You try and get the ones you know will look right for the part in the first place, then things happen. . . . I have projects going all the time. This company is so full of terrific dancers but we have such an enormous rep they don't often have the energy to show off. Right now, in addition to the Bernstein, I'm choreographing a Bartók ballet over at the school, and a rock ballet—rock music. It's only a 7½-minute piece but it's the hardest thing I've ever done. I tried doing classical *pas de deux* movements but it didn't work, it looked too contrasty. Then I did regulation discothèque and hated it. Now, last night, I had them all just walk. It was better. I want to do all kinds of things—multimedia . . . using singers and speech . . . opera. I have this terrific idea but I won't talk about it. I think Lincoln Kirstein thinks I'm mad.' "

RITE OF SPRING (*see* LE SACRE DU PRINTEMPS)

RITUALS

Music by Béla Bartók. Choreography by Kenneth MacMillan. Designer: Yolanda Sonnasend. First presented by the Royal Ballet at the Royal Opera House, Covent Garden, London, December 11, 1975, and introduced to

*the United States by the same ensemble April 27, 1976, at the Metropolitan
Opera House, New York.*

Set to the *Sonata for Two Pianos and Percussion* of Bartók, *Rituals* is a dance
ballet about Japanese formalized sport and theatre. The first scene shows the
preparation for combat and self-defense for which movements have been
derived from Japanese boxing, sumo wrestling, and a Japanese form of Tai-
Chi. The second scene is inspired by the Bunraku Puppet Theatre and the
third shows a "very emotional situation"—the birth of a child—in the impressive style of some forms of Japanese theatre.

The Royal Ballet visited Japan in 1975, which gave the choreographer Kenneth MacMillan an opportunity to watch the Kabuki theatre and Nō plays.
The studied lack of emotion in the Japanese theatre inspired him to make a
work of that character in ballet.

THE RIVER

*Original score by Duke Ellington. Choreography by Alvin Ailey. Costumes
by Frank Thompson. Lighting by Gilbert V. Hemsley, Jr. Special lighting
by Nicholas Cernovitch. First presented by American Ballet Theatre at the
New York State Theatre, Lincoln Center, New York, June 25, 1970, with a
cast headed by John Prinz, Alexandra Radius, Hans Ebbelaar, Marcos
Paredes, Eleanor D'Antuono, Cynthia Gregory, Ivan Nagy, Dennis Nahat,
Sallie Wilson, and Keith Lee. Conducted by Jaime Leon.*

A quotation from the musician Duke Ellington prefaces the ballet: ". . . of
birth . . . of the well-spring of life . . . of reaffirmation . . . of the heavenly
anticipation of rebirth. . . ." The work itself is the result of collaboration between Duke Ellington and Alvin Ailey. In its musical entirety, the work consists of a *Prologue*, an *Epilogue*, and eleven sections. These are entitled:
*Spring, Spring Run, Meander, Giggling Rapids, Falls, Vortex, Lake, Main-
stream (Riba), Two Cities, The Sea (Mother),* and *Spring.*

First presented by American Ballet Theatre in an unfinished state that was
later completed, on June 29, 1971, *The River* was appraised by critic Jean Battey Lewis of the Washington *Post* as a work with "an alive and joyous quality,
a life force that carries along its series of solos, duets and group dances in a
headlong sweep. . . . *The River* is not only a well-spring of free, unforced,
imaginative movement. It is also a tribute to Ailey's gifts as a director and
developer of talent that he has created passages which capture so sensitively
the strengths of some of Ballet Theatre's finest dancers."

Writing of *The River* soon after its première, in *The Saturday Review,* the
critic Walter Terry said: "The Ailey ballet *The River,* with an original score
by Duke Ellington, was not completed by première time, so for the season it

was given in part as 'six dances from a work in progress.' A full appraisal, of
course, must wait, but the Ailey dance brilliance—wonderful freshets of movement designs to delight the eye—are already there. There are patterns of mass
motion that are utterly beautiful, but there are also such choreographic con-
centrates as Eleanor D'Antuono's incredibly fast solo *Vortex;* Cynthia Gregory
(with either Ivan Nagy or Gayle Young) in a cool and graceful *pas de deux,*
surrounded by ensemble movements, called *Lake;* Dennis Nahat's jaunty
Mainstream; and the curiously haunting *Two Cities,* danced by Sallie Wilson
and Keith Lee, each in separate pools of light, each lonely, each reaching out
across the unseen barrier of river, of distance, of divisiveness, of solitary spirit,
however you care to interpret it, and, finally, bridging the abyss."

A year later, Deborah Jowitt wrote in the *Village Voice:* "Alvin Ailey has
added three more sections to *The River.* One, called *Sea,* certainly rounds the
whole piece out, since the sea people, Erik Bruhn and Natalia Makarova, can
now open the ballet by pulling away from the 'spring' (Keith Lee) in a receding wave and return at the end in a slow, coiling floor duet that seems to
spawn that wellspring again. *Meander,* for Mimi Paul, Ted Kivitt, and Ian
Horvath, is a playful, jazzy, carelessly sensuous *divertissement*—very nicely
danced, but not terribly compelling in its movement concept. *Giggling Rapids*
features Bruhn and Makarova in a fast, almost kittenish exchange. She has a
beautifully innocent body to go with her strength, and both are exuberant performers. As for the whole idea, well, the crowd loved seeing these two jazz it
up (so good-sporty of them), but watching Bruhn reminded me of Cathy Ber-
berian singing Beatles songs. Technique and persona not completely compatible with the material.

"There were other good things in *The River.* Dennis Nahat did marvelous
things with the rhythmic shape and impetus of his little solo in *Falls,* and
Eleanor D'Antuono has mastered *Vortex* completely, so that now her turns and
swirls unleash little spurts of power without obvious effort or preparation."

RODEO

*Ballet in two scenes. Music by Aaron Copland. Choreography and book by
Agnes de Mille. Scenery by Oliver Smith. Costumes by Kermit Love. First
presented by the Ballet Russe de Monte Carlo at the Metropolitan Opera
House, New York, October 16, 1942, with a cast headed by Agnes de Mille
as the* Cowgirl, *Frederic Franklin as the* Champion Roper, *and Casimir
Kokitch as the* Head Wrangler. *Revived by Ballet Theatre at Rhine-am-Main
Air Force, Frankfurt, Germany, August 14, 1950.*

Rodeo, subtitled "The Courting at Burnt Ranch," is a love story of the American Southwest. The problem it deals with is perennial: how an American girl,
with the odds seemingly all against her, sets out to get herself a man. The girl

in this case is a cowgirl, a tomboy whose desperate efforts to become one of the ranch's cowhands create a problem for the cowboys and make her the laughingstock of womankind.

SCENE ONE   The corral of Burnt Ranch. The ballet's brief overture begins with a crash of cymbals and continues with a rowdy, rhythmic melody reminiscent of the wild west. The music becomes quiet, and the curtain rises on the corral of Burnt Ranch. The time is Saturday afternoon, the time of the weekly rodeo, about the turn of the century. Against an orange-red sky whose intense heat seems to bear down on the scene, a high wooden fence encloses the parched, dusty ground of the corral. Half a dozen lazy cowhands stand about, idling away the time. Among them stands the cowgirl, self-assertive in a bright red shirt, brown hat tilted back over her head, and brown pants and boots. Long pigtails hang down her back. One of the cowhands holds his hand up to shield his eyes from the glaring sun and looks out into the distance. Another cowboy rides in, twirling his arm over his head in a lassoing motion. The cowgirl hitches up her pants, as if to prepare for the rodeo that is about to begin. The cowboys tell her that she can't come along and ride off rapidly. Not to be outdone so easily, the cowgirl decides to follow them and rushes off to the right, roping the air with a fast-turning arm.

Three cowhands ride on vigorously. Six of their fellows join them, and all dance wildly, imitating in their movements the jolts and tricks of the rodeo. The music is fierce and a challenge to the dancers. The cowgirl re-enters and tries to join one of the groups. The cowgirl secretly hankers after the head wrangler, and watches him anxiously. He and the others motion to her to go away—she isn't wanted. The girl is used to this kind of treatment, however, and stays put, trying to compete in the rodeo. She disgraces herself, and the head wrangler is about to lose all patience with her.

But suddenly the corral is transfigured by the arrival of girls in city clothes—Eastern friends of the rancher's daughter, who have come out with her to get a taste of ranch life. The cowboys slap their thighs in enthusiastic welcome; the girls wave to them with their handkerchiefs and giggle among themselves in feigned bashfulness. The cowgirl is both contemptuous and envious of their finery; she is visibly disgusted by their silly flirting.

The champion roper steps out to show off his skill before the girls. When the head wrangler steps over to them politely and takes off his hat to the rancher's daughter, the cowgirl can bear it no longer and rides off in a jealous fit of petulance. Four women from the ranch come out to watch the rodeo. They are entertained until the cowgirl rides in on what appears to be a bucking bronco. All the women raise their hands in despair at this foolish show-off. The cowgirl falls. The Eastern girls rush over to her and can't control their laughter: never in *their* born days has a *girl* done anything like that. The cowgirl is furious. She gets up and thumbs her nose at the women. Soon, alone with the cowboys, the girl sees that she's made a fool of herself all around; the

women may laugh at her, but the men are worse: their silence makes her despair. She tries to regain her old familiarity with them. They ignore her and
stare into the distance. The head wrangler jerks his thumb toward the house,
telling her to leave the corral. He is the one man in the world the girl respects:
smothering her tears, she obeys him.

The rodeo is over. The girls wave at the champion roper as he leaps away.
The scene darkens, the music softens, the womenfolk cross the stage, moving
slowly, bravely, yet wistfully, and there is created an impression of what home
is like after a tiring, busy day. The cowboys cross the stage behind the women,
and when the girls step backward, hesitating in their homeward march, the
men move forward to them, place their arms about their waists, and move forward again with them.

The couples disappear. The cowgirl re-enters and tries to attract the head
wrangler's attention. But it's as if she weren't even there: he goes to the
rancher's daughter, who stands demure in her long blue dress with ribbons in
her hair, lifts her softly, and takes her off into the night.

The cowgirl dances for a moment alone, trying to shake off what she knows
has happened to her. She isn't any good as a woman and she's a miserable failure as a cowhand. The head wrangler returns. He doesn't understand what's
wrong with this strange girl. A cowboy calls to him, and he leaves before the
girl can tell him. The womenfolk try to call the girl home; she ignores them.
The champion roper crosses the back of the corral, snapping his fingers in private anticipation of the Saturday night dance at the ranch house. He disappears. The cowgirl falls to the ground, all alone now with her problem. The
stage blacks out around her.

A bright blue drop curtain, decorated with galloping wild horses, falls in
front of the scene. Four couples rush out and begin a square dance. A caller
shouts out directions to the dancers, and the couples respond by moving
quickly into more intricate patterns as he commands. Soon they are out of
breath, but turning still more rapidly and now shouting as they run around
and around in a circle, faster and faster. They run off into the wings.

SCENE TWO   The ranch house. The curtain rises on the ranch house. The
cowgirl is sitting alone on a bench at the left, watching three cowboys dance a
jig to a jazzy piano accompaniment. One of the cowboys is the champion
roper, dressed now in his Saturday-night best—violet shirt, a loud vest of
cowhide, and striped yellow pants. He jumps high into the air and clicks his
heels together repeatedly. The cowgirl, still dressed in the dusty clothes of the
corral, feels out of place, though she is making an obvious effort to enjoy herself. The boys finish their jig. Three couples come in and dance about the
room, oblivious to whether anyone is watching them. Two of the couples waltz
into the parlor as the remaining pair quarrel: the boy kisses the girl, and she
rushes out.

The boy despairs of women and sits down beside the cowgirl. She tries to comfort him, man to man. But another girl has come in looking for a partner. She sees the boy alone, lifts her dress flirtatiously, and runs out. He chases after her. The cowgirl can see no hope for such an idiot. The champion roper strides back in and notices the lonely girl. He doesn't know what the matter is; but since this is Saturday night and dancing time, he can see only one cure. He tells her to get up and dance. The cowgirl says she doesn't know how to dance. Well, first, he tells her, you'd better look a little cleaner. He tries to fix her face up and smacks the dust off her bottom.

Just as the girl is beginning to forget about the head wrangler, he comes in and goes over to the rancher's daughter. The cowgirl forgets all about the champion roper. He loses patience with her; after all, he's just as interested in other girls as she is in the head wrangler: He was only trying to make her have a good time. When the champion roper walks out on her, the girl begins to cry. She looks at the romantic dancing couple and falls to the floor in tears.

Gradually the room fills with people. The bench is moved back, and everybody gets ready for a community dance. The girls line up on one side, the boys on the other. Bravely, the girl decides to try again and hopefully stands in line with the girls. The boys approach and take their partners; the cowgirl is left standing alone! The music becomes sweet and lyrical; the couples form a circle; the boys lift the girls tenderly high above them; the girl turns away.

The champion roper dances in, jumping high in the air, clicking his heels together, breaking the romantic spell. When he finishes this bit of exhibitionism, he comes over and leans on the girl's shoulder. She stifles a sob. The other couples leave the scene. The roper puts his hand under her chin and tells her to cheer up, to try to dance with him again. He opens his arms wide, the girl smiles, hitches up her belt, comes close to him, and everything is all right for a few seconds while they dance.

Everything is spoiled, however, by the head wrangler and the rancher's daughter, who come back and remind the cowgirl of her real love. The roper catches her watching them; before he can do anything about it, she has run away. The roper sees a girl walking alone and pursues her into the wings.

All the cowboys and their girls dance now, filling the scene with violent color and vigorous movement. The couples clap their hands joyously in rhythm to the music. They stop dancing all at once and stare, as the cowgirl comes in, dressed from head to foot in bright red. The girls are shocked by this lack of taste; the boys are eager to find out what it means.

The champion roper goes to her, hitches up his pants, and asks her to dance. Even in her new dress the girl hitches up her clothes, too. They dance. The violins saw away at a square-dance theme, and the moving couples form a circle around them.

The cowgirl finds herself standing between the head wrangler and the roper. Both want to dance with her. The wrangler has forgotten the rancher's daughter long enough to notice the cowgirl. The roper and the wrangler throw the girl back and forth between them. She tries to escape, but the wrangler grabs her and tries to kiss her. The roper steps in and says, "No! She's my girl!" He takes her face in his hands and kisses her hard. He kisses her again, harder. Both of them wake up: they've both been wrong all along and didn't know what was happening. The head wrangler rejoins the rancher's daughter, and the whole group dances happily. As the curtain falls, the girls step into stirrups formed by the boys' hands and stand poised high over their heads. The cowgirl and the roper look into each other's eyes.

NOTES *Rodeo* has been a steady favorite in the United States and on American Ballet Theatre's many tours abroad. That was proved especially true when the company revived the ballet in 1972, in New York, at their engagement at the City Center. Writing of that performance in *Dance Magazine,* the critic Nancy Mason said: "America was ripe for *Rodeo* when performed by Ballet Russe in 1942. We were at war; national feeling was running high. Although Women's Lib may now quibble about the theme—'How to get a man'— *Rodeo* isn't dated because it deals with basic emotions.

"The action's set on a ranch in the Southwest and concerns a tomboy (Christine Sarry) who prefers riding a horse to wearing a dress. She's the tagalong of the cowboys, desperately and unreciprocally in love with the Head Wrangler (Marcos Paredes). Aaron Copland's music offers rowdy and rhythmic accompaniment.

"There couldn't be better casting for the tomboy. Christine Sarry even looks the part with her cropped brown hair and stubborn expression. What's more, she's a superb actress and comedienne; a powerpacked little dynamo who can stir laughter or tears. One really feels for her plight and wishes her well. Projecting incredible energy, she'd meet any challenge by pushing back her hat, hitching up her trousers, then diving right in. Shyness underlies this gumption. Here's a girl more at home on the back of a horse than in any social situation.

"The turning point arrives at the Saturday night dance, where Chris is finally persuaded by the Champion Roper (Terry Orr, alternating with William Carter) to put on a dress and join the party. A few minutes later she dashes in and everything halts abruptly. Gone are the baggy trousers; in their place, a sensible red jumper and ankle-length boots; on her face, a triumphant, excited grin. The Head Wrangler does a double-take. Then there's a competition between him and the Champion Roper for her heart.

"In *Rodeo* virtuoso tap dancing was used for the first time in a ballet. It also focused international attention on utilizing American folk themes in ballets. It changed the course for the musical theater; the next year Agnes de Mille choreographed *Oklahoma.*

"What a happy thought that *Rodeo* is back in the active repertoire. The company performs it with infectious zeal and good feelings. It's a perfect vehicle for Christine Sarry; Terry Orr delights with his easygoing and confident

Roper interpretation. And it's good to see William Carter. . . . He created an honest and charming 'big brother' feeling."

In his book *Inside American Ballet Theatre,* Clive Barnes records a long interview with Agnes de Mille on the origins of *Rodeo.*

RODIN, MIS EN VIE

Music by Michael Kamen. Choreography by Margo Sappington. Costumes by Willa Kim. First presented by the Harkness Ballet at the Harkness Theatre, April 17, 1974, with Jeanette Vondersaar, Chris Jensen, and Zane Wilson in principal roles.

Rodin's sculpture come to life is the interesting idea behind this unusual ballet, which uses a specially commissioned score by Michael Kamen. Many familiar works by the great French artist (who once sculpted Nijinsky) are seen here in varied characterizations. The ebb and flow of the movement of sculptural bodies is seen to have a different quality from usual dance action and gesture. We are reminded of what must have attracted Rodin to dance and what must have generated some of his idealized figures as well as the power of his memorable studies and groupings. The work concludes in a dramatic tableaux with all of the figures "draped like some Dantesque vision," in Patricia Barnes's phrase, "over a vast scaffolding . . . It was particularly impressive."

ROMANCE

Music by Johannes Brahms. Choreography by Eliot Feld. Costumes by Stanley Simmons. Lighting by Jennifer Tipton. First presented by the American Ballet Company at the Brooklyn Academy of Music, New York, April 20, 1971, with Anna Laerkesen, Christine Sarry, Elizabeth Lee, Cristina Stirling, John Sowinski, Richard Munro, Daniel Levans, and Kenneth Hughes. Pianist: Harry Fuchs.

A dance ballet for four girls and four boys to some of Brahms's later piano music, *Romance* has no narrative action. The drama of the piece and the atmosphere of each of the dances derive from the choreographer's response to the music and the response of his dancers to that impulse. The dances are accompanied by a pianist who sits at his instrument on the left side of the stage. There are benches on stage and the costumes and deportment of the dancers suggest a formal occasion. The four couples appear in various combinations and ensembles; at one point two boys perform a display piece. The music is drawn from nine piano works, mostly intermezzos (Opus 116, Opus 118, Opus 119, and a final *Capriccio,* Op. 76). These pieces are in many ways ideal for dances; they are brief, about three or four minutes each, and can be easily heard, and seen, as continuous, though there is no thematic connection.

A thematic connection, of course, can be given in dance form, and while romance is indeed the theme of the ballet and several couples are wrapt in it to the exclusion of everything but speed in conquest and fulfillment, the ballet plays its variations on the main subject: frustration, wrong matches, ill-fated meetings. The evocation here of different situations in love—tenderness, regret, jealousy—is what *Romance* is all about. If you do not know these piano pieces by Brahms, I commend them to you.

ROMEO AND JULIET

Shakespeare's tragedy of *Romeo and Juliet* has been turned into dance by many choreographers. The six ballets described below are the most familiar:

Ballet in three acts, based on the play by Shakespeare. Music by Sergei Prokofiev. Libretto by Leonid Lavrovsky, Sergei Prokofiev, and Sergei Radlov. Choreography by Leonid Lavrovsky. Décor by Pyotr Williams. First presented at the Kirov State Theatre of Opera and Ballet, Leningrad, January 11, 1940, with Konstantin Sergeyev and Galina Ulanova in the title roles, A. V. Lopukhov as Mercutio, and S. G. Karen as Tybalt. Revised and presented at the Bolshoi Theatre, Moscow, December 28, 1946. First presented in the United States by the Bolshoi Ballet at the Metropolitan Opera House, New York, April 16, 1959, with Galina Ulanova and Yuri Zhdanov in the title roles.

The Soviet production relates Shakespeare's story in thirteen scenes, with a prologue and epilogue.

PROLOGUE   Friar Laurence, sage and philosopher, blesses the marriage of Romeo and Juliet. The three figures stand motionless in tableau in front of three arches.

ACT ONE, SCENE ONE: THE MAIN SQUARE OF VERONA   As dawn breaks, Romeo, son of Montague, is seen wandering alone about the deserted streets of Verona. Three servants leave the house of Capulet and walk across the square to join some girls in the inn. They are soon embroiled in a quarrel with two servants of Montague, the sworn enemy of their house. Swords are drawn and a fight starts. More and more people, including Benvolio, nephew of Montague, and Tybalt, nephew of Lady Capulet, join in the fray. Paris, who has come to Verona to seek the hand of Capulet's daughter, Juliet, reaches the square when the fighting is at its fiercest. Montague and his hated rival,

Capulet, unsheathe their swords and attack each other. The tocsin rings; its sound, reverberating through the city, brings crowds to the square. The prince of Verona then appears. He stops the fighting and an edict, forbidding disturbances in the city streets, is proclaimed. Tybalt leaves, cursing the Montagues.

Before the curtain, in a transitional *Front Scene*, the Capulet household is preparing for a ball. Juliet's nurse, carrying a beautiful dress, stops to reprimand some servants who have stolen food from the kitchen.

ACT ONE, SCENE TWO: JULIET'S ROOM   In her room, the walls covered with tapestries, Juliet plays hide-and-seek with her nurse instead of dressing for the ball. Lady Capulet comes into the room and tells Juliet that Paris has asked for her hand in marriage. Juliet protests that she is too young, but leading her to the mirror, her mother shows her that this is not so.

Front Scene: The preparations for the ball are almost finished. The servants carry in food and wine.

ACT ONE, SCENE THREE   The guests, including Verona's most illustrious citizens, troubadours, and many friends of Juliet's, arrive for the ball; among the last to come are Paris and his page.

Front Scene: Hearing music, Romeo's friends Mercutio and Benvolio decide to disguise themselves and go to Capulet's ball. They persuade Romeo to join them. He puts on a domino mask.

ACT ONE, SCENE FOUR: THE BALLROOM OF THE CAPULETS' PALACE   Juliet with all their guests awaits the arrival of her parents, who now enter. Paris presents Juliet with a bouquet. The ball now begins with a formal dance during which the men lay cushions at the feet of the ladies, kneel and kiss the hems of their skirts. The ladies and gentlemen then dance separately, followed by a slow and stately ensemble. Now Juliet, who has been arranging flowers and watching, dances herself. The dance of the guests is resumed briefly and then Juliet dances again. Romeo and his friends enter. He is enchanted by Juliet and approaches her. Paris, however, intercedes. Mercutio dances to distract the guests. As they dance together, Romeo tells Juliet how beautiful she is. His mask falls from his face and Juliet sees him for the first time. Juliet is captivated. This man she could really love. But then Tybalt appears and thinks he recognizes Romeo, a sworn enemy of the family. He tells old Capulet. Romeo quickly puts his mask back on. Although Tybalt there and then wishes to attack Romeo, Mercutio comes between them.

Front Scene: After the guests have left, Juliet learns from her nurse that it is none other than Romeo, son of her father's enemy Montague, with whom she has fallen in love.

ACT ONE, SCENE FIVE: THE GARDEN   Juliet cannot sleep and comes out on her moonlit balcony. She can only think of Romeo, whom she suddenly sees in the garden. They confess their love for each other and dance.

ACT TWO, SCENE ONE: THE MAIN SQUARE OF VERONA Revelers throng the square. There are dances for the crowd and waitresses at the inn. A procession enters carrying an image of the Madonna. Benvolio and Mercutio flirt with ladies at the cafe and dance with the waitresses and there is another ensemble for the revelers. The nurse pushes her way through the crowds, looking for Romeo to give him a message from Juliet. He enters the square and the nurse whispers to him.

Front Scene: Romeo reads that Juliet has consented to be his wife and rapturously presses the letter to his heart.

ACT TWO, SCENE TWO: FRIAR LAURENCE'S CELL On a simple table stand some flowers and a skull, which the friar is contemplating when Romeo enters. Romeo kneels before the friar and asks him to marry them secretly. Nervously waiting for Juliet to come, his hands play with the skull and the flowers. Juliet, wearing a black cape, rushes in. Friar Laurence marries them and hopes that their union will end the strife between the Montagues and Capulets.

Front Scene: The Montagues and Capulets are in the main square as the procession of the Madonna moves across. Mercutio buys fruit and gives it to his friends. Tybalt bursts into rage when a peddler's tray accidentally knocks into one of his companions. Both families are cruelly sensitive now to any possible offense.

ACT TWO, SCENE THREE: THE MAIN SQUARE OF VERONA Revels continue in the square with a tambourine dance. Mercutio dances with waitresses at the inn. Tybalt enters and challenges Mercutio to a duel. Romeo tries to call it off and make peace but Tybalt mocks him and goads Mercutio into fighting. Mercutio is hit, struggles bravely against death but dies. Tybalt leaves, laughing. Romeo tries to hear Mercutio's heart and mourns. The body is borne out. Just as Romeo follows after, Tybalt comes back, insolent, swaggering. Romeo draws his sword, dashes up the stairs, and kills him. Romeo flees. The Capulets rush from their palace with the nurse. Lady Capulet so laments her kinsman's death that she is carried out gesturing wildly on his bier. The prince of Verona declares Romeo an exile for life.

ACT THREE, SCENE ONE: JULIET'S ROOM At dawn the next morning, Romeo opens the curtain onto the balcony and watches the sun. Juliet pulls the curtain back and the two lovers dance an impassioned *pas de deux.* But the household is stirring and Romeo must go. He embraces Juliet for the last time. As he leaves by the balcony, Juliet's parents and Paris enter with the nurse. Paris tries to woo Juliet but is scorned. Hurt by Juliet's rebuff, Paris leaves. Juliet tells her parents that she will not marry him. They are angry and threaten to disown her. The mother and the nurse leave and the father tries to force Juliet to submit to his will. She dances in despair when he has finally left her alone. Then quickly she finds her cape and runs out.

Front Scene: Juliet rushes to Friar Laurence.

ACT THREE, SCENE TWO: FRIAR LAURENCE'S CELL Juliet prays and relates her plight. She sees a dagger on the table and seizes it. Gently taking the dagger from her, Friar Laurence gives her instead a phial of sleeping potion which she must drink. She will then fall asleep, he tells her, and her parents, thinking her dead, will bury her in the family tomb. Meanwhile, Romeo, warned by Friar Laurence, will return under cover of darkness and take her away from Verona.

ACT THREE, SCENE THREE: JULIET'S BEDCHAMBER It is evening and Juliet is with her family and Paris. She consents to marry Paris, they dance together, and her parents are jubilant. The nurse brings the wedding gown. Juliet is alone. She knows she must drink the potion but delays in a dance of indecision. She then quickly swallows the potion and falls back on the bed. Soon it is morning. Her friends come with troubadours to celebrate her engagement. Paris enters, eager to see his bride. But the wedding dress lies on a chair and Juliet still sleeps. Her mother comes and orders the nurse to waken her. She goes to the bed but starts back with a cry of terror. Juliet lies lifeless on the bed. All weep.

ACT THREE, SCENE FOUR: A STREET IN MANTUA Romeo, alone, expresses his sorrow at his separation from Juliet. Outpacing Friar Laurence's messenger, Romeo's servant Balthasar arrives from Verona with the news that Juliet is dead. Stunned by grief, Romeo does not know what to do, then decides that he must go to his beloved.

ACT THREE, SCENE FIVE: THE CAPULET TOMB Many attend Juliet's funeral and her body is placed in the family vault at the top of a flight of steps. Paris prays there and leaves. It grows dark. Romeo comes in, mounts the steps, removes her shroud and holds Juliet in his arms. He kisses her, then picks her up to carry her briefly down the steps. He ascends again, holding her high over his head, and places her on her tomb. He then drinks a phial of poison and dies, falling back down the steps. Juliet now awakes from her sleeping potion. She sees Romeo and at first thinks him perhaps asleep, as she has been, but he is dead. She takes his dagger at once and stabs herself. She falls back over his body.

EPILOGUE Over the bodies of their children, the Montagues and the Capulets, followed by the populace, take each other's hands and swear to end their feud. All kneel.

NOTES Prokofiev's score to *Romeo and Juliet* was completed September 8, 1935, soon after his return to Russia from Paris. It was first performed at a concert in Moscow in October of that year. Prokofiev's plan at that time was that the ballet should end happily, with Juliet resurrected in her tomb and a final joyous *pas de deux* for the two lovers. This idea received some criticism and the composer abandoned it. He said at the time: "I have taken special pains to achieve a simplicity that will, I hope, reach the hearts of all listeners. If people find no melody and no emotion in this work of mine, I shall be very sorry; but I feel that they will, sooner or later."

Some time elapsed before the score was first used for ballet, and this was in Brno, Czechoslovakia in 1938. Meanwhile, two suites arranged by Prokofiev were played in the U.S.S.R. and the United States.

The Soviet choreographer Leonid Lavrovsky published notes about his conception of the ballet, which was first produced in 1940: "The depths of passion and ideas, the intensity of feeling conveyed by the protagonists of Shakespeare's tragedy, demand the fusion of dance with mime. In ballet, words are absent and the effect of every phrase of mime must correspond with the spoken language of the stage characters. Mime should never descend to trivial, commonplace, imitative gestures, but become a genuine theatrical performance, in which characters, emotion, and passion are expressed by the movements of the body, instead of by the varied intonations of the voice. Ballet is a choreographic play in which the dancing must arise naturally from the mimed action, or the mimed action be the logical sequence of the dancing."

A film of Lavrovsky's *Romeo and Juliet* was produced in the U.S.S.R. in 1954, with Galina Ulanova.

When the Bolshoi's *Romeo and Juliet* was first presented in New York, Edwin Denby, writing about it for *The Hudson Review* (now included in his book *Dancers, Buildings and People in the Streets*), spoke of Ulanova's vividness:

"Bending her neck toward her partner in a lift of the Bedroom Scene, the gesture had the tragic quiet Pasternak speaks of. Or take the opposite kind of moment. Faced with marriage to County Paris, Juliet, her mantle flung round her, desperately rushes along the apron to Friar Laurence; armed by him with the sleeping potion, she flings the mantle round her again, and rushes desperately along the apron back home. The fling, the rush, the exact repeat are pure 'Perils of Pauline.' But Ulanova's art at that moment is so brilliant the audience breaks into delighted applause.

"You can find out something about Bolshoi style by trying the gymnastics of Ulanova's fling and rush yourself. Standing in the middle of the room, fling an arm across your chest, and at the same time raise the breastbone as high as it will go, bending it over at the top so it pushes the neck back. Don't let go, keep forcing the breastbone further, but in addition push the neck forward as hard as you can, and lift your head until you feel 'desperately resolved.' (It may make you cough.) And now, keeping the stance you are in unchanged, rush about the room with an incredible lightness and rapidity. If your family is watching, they will pick you off the floor, and urge you to try harder.

"The special stance of fling and rush you just tried (it involves a backbend between the shoulder-blades) is not classical. It has been called the pouter-pigeon silhouette by Walter Terry, and that is just how it looks. But when Ulanova does it, you feel it means, 'Here is my heart.'

"But if you notice that, you also notice her feet. In light runs on toe (bourrée steps) they seem to touch the floor sensitively. You see how keen the pointed foot looks in the air, during attitudes, arabesques, and passés, how clearly the leg defines and differentiates the different classic shapes. Below the waist Ulanova is a strict classicist; above the waist she alters the shape of classic motions now slightly, now quite a lot, to specify a nuance of drama (for example, the pouter-pigeon silhouette). Neither element—the lightness below or the weight above—is weakened for the sake of the other; the combined motion keeps fluid. And often while one movement is ebbing to its end, another seems already welling up in the midriff."

Narrative ballet in one act, based on the play by Shakespeare. Music by Frederick Delius. Choreography by Antony Tudor. Scenery and costumes by Eugene Berman. First presented by Ballet Theatre at the Metropolitan Opera House, New York, April 6, 1943, with Alicia Markova as Juliet, Hugh Laing as Romeo, Nicolas Orloff as Mercutio, Antony Tudor as Tybalt, and Jerome Robbins as Benvolio.

This dramatic ballet compresses into one vivid act the tragic love story of Romeo and Juliet. Within a single-unit setting representing the ordered golden beauty of the Italy of the Renaissance, the narrative proceeds without scenic interruption; and what might be spoken of as "scenes," in an ordinary dramatic spectacle, move together and coalesce with a flow that suggests the inevitability of the tragedy itself.

The score for the ballet is an arrangement by Antal Dorati of selected works by Delius: *Over the Hills and Far Away, The Walk to the Paradise Garden, Eventyr,* and *Brigg Fair.*

PROLOGUE The curtain rises immediately on a drop curtain depicting the entrance to a palace in Verona. There are two great arches to the left and right, and in the center, cut out of the curtain, is a draped entry. A spotlight centers on this doorway, and Romeo steps out cautiously. He looks behind him, and Rosaline, a beautiful girl, follows him. Romeo takes her hand and attempts to embrace her. Rosaline warns him that he is too hasty, and Romeo follows her impatiently within.

Now members of the opposing families of Montague and Capulet dance onto the scene and challenge each other. The two leaders of the factions, Mercutio and Tybalt, are eager for a contest, and the two groups commence dueling. But the heads of the two houses at variance with each other enter with their wives and order their kinsmen to desist. The men reluctantly abandon their fighting and bow to the peers. It is apparent that their battle will be renewed at the first opportunity. Romeo and his friend Mercutio remain behind when the others have left. Only the entrance of the fair Rosaline persuades them that they have better business elsewhere.

BALL AT THE HOUSE OF THE CAPULETS The drop curtain rises on a wide, open area of red marble enclosed by a decorative colonnade. Couples in richly embroidered costumes are dancing in elegant, courtly fashion. The music softens, and Juliet enters on the right. She lingers slightly, hesitating to step into the ballroom, for she knows what awaits her. She greets her parents warmly, yet formally. Capulet turns to introduce her to a young nobleman, Paris, but Juliet seeks instead the company of her cousin Tybalt. The understanding Tybalt consoles her, but also reminds her of her duty and leads her to Paris. The assembled company begin to dance again, and Juliet accepts Paris as her partner.

Romeo enters on the right. He looks directly at Juliet. Juliet, her back to Paris for a moment, glances back at him. As Paris bends down to kiss her hand, Juliet looks across the room toward Romeo. The dance continues, and Romeo chooses a partner to join the ball. The two couples dance on opposite sides of the room. The set pattern of the dance separates them, and Juliet and Romeo despair of meeting. Soon the entire company circles the hall and the dance ends. The guests proceed to move toward the rear for refreshment, and Romeo and Juliet are alone.

Romeo falls at her feet and declares the overpowering love he has felt since he saw her. He rises, their faces touch, and they kiss. Then, formal again, the two bow to each other and begin to dance together a delicate, flowing measure. When the dance is over, they realize that they must separate and both say their farewells. But as they turn to go, they move together again and kneel.

Mercutio and Tybalt emerge from the banquet hall. Juliet's nurse urges her away, lest there be trouble. Tybalt warns Romeo and turns to Juliet questioningly, and all depart.

ROMEO WOOS JULIET IN THE CAPULET ORCHARD The lights dim. White drapes are drawn across the back colonnade. Four torchbearers enter on the right, followed by Romeo and Mercutio. Romeo is preoccupied and will not listen to his friend's appreciation of the beauty of the evening. Mercutio grows impatient and tells his friend that the romance he contemplates is out of the question. The music builds in intensity, and Romeo refuses to heed Mercutio's advice. Mercutio leaps to the back of one of the torchbearers and urges Romeo to follow them to a tavern. Romeo pretends to go, then conceals himself. The others return to look for him, but soon follow after Mercutio.

Two couples enter. Romeo holds his arm across his face, lest he be recognized. The couples disappear, and Romeo dances alone. Above the colonnade at the rear, Juliet looks down into the orchard and sees her lover. She is enchanted and rests her head sweetly on the balcony railing, wondering when he will look up and see her. Romeo glances up and blows kisses to her. She returns the kisses, but warns him away. Just as he hides behind a pillar on the right, Juliet's nurse comes into the garden. No sooner has she departed than Tybalt and Paris stroll by. When they are alone again, Romeo holds out his hands to Juliet and from above she gestures to him yearningly. Romeo gestures defiance of their families and proposes marriage. Juliet consents.

BETROTHAL OF ROMEO AND JULIET BY THE FRIAR Drapes are drawn across the colonnade, and Friar Laurence stands in his cell. Romeo enters. He is impatient and afraid and paces the floor. There is a sound at the door, and Romeo rushes to see who it is. Friar Laurence pulls him back warningly. Romeo's back is turned as Juliet runs into the room. He turns to her, and the two kneel before the friar, who blesses them. Juliet rises, turns rapidly, and falls low in Romeo's arms. Then she rushes off into the night, promising him that her nurse will bring him a message.

STREET SCENE The curtains are drawn back, the friar disappears, and the open area becomes the street. It is still night. A cripple and a blind man enter, followed by the gay Mercutio and a friend. Romeo enters, followed by Juliet and her nurse. The nurse beckons Juliet away. The concern of the lovers is contrasted with the friction between their families, for Tybalt has entered and threatened Mercutio in earnest. The two fight, their kinsmen join the battle, and the music is ominous, like the sound of an approaching storm. Mercutio is stabbed by Tybalt and dies in Romeo's arms.

Romeo recovers from his grief and attacks Tybalt. He leaps to his back, forces him down, and stabs him to death. Now there is no hope of reconciling the two families. Romeo does not know what to do. Friar Laurence enters and takes the dagger from him. Finally the youth is persuaded that he must flee for his life.

Juliet and her nurse enter the square and see what has happened. Juliet weeps for Tybalt, but then, suddenly desperate, instructs the nurse to run to Romeo and reassure him.

ROMEO'S FAREWELL TO JULIET The scene is Juliet's bedroom. Day is breaking. Juliet rises first and dances joyfully, with a sweet, youthful happiness, as Romeo watches her from the bed. She returns to him, he lifts her, and they embrace. Romeo prepares to leave. He must escape from Verona. They will meet elsewhere. Juliet weeps because of her happiness and its quick ending. They kiss. Romeo departs, and Juliet falls back on the bed, still weeping.

PREPARATIONS FOR THE WEDDING OF JULIET TO PARIS Some time passes, and handmaidens to Juliet enter with her nurse to prepare her for the marriage her parents have insisted upon. They waken Juliet. Instantly she sits up and looks off into the direction that Romeo took when he left her. She cannot believe that this day she must marry another man. The nurse holds her in her arms and tries to comfort her. Juliet rises and protests to her father that she cannot marry Paris. Capulet refuses to listen to her or to his wife, who tries to intercede for Juliet.

Then, to the accompaniment of a melody almost unbearable in its sweetness and pathos, Juliet's four handmaidens form a tableau beside her. They hold before her a wedding dress of gold, and Juliet slips her arms into it as if the cloth were on fire.

When she is dressed, she weeps softly in her father's arms. Her father blesses her and places on her head a shining crown. She is presented with a bouquet of white flowers. Friar Laurence enters, and Juliet falls into his arms. When they are unobserved, the friar gives her a vial containing a secret drug and instructs her to drink it without delay: all may yet be well.

Juliet walks away, drinks the contents of the vial, whirls frantically, and swoons. Her family gathers about her. Six women bear slowly across the stage a great cloth trimmed in somber black.

PROCESSION TO THE TOMB Two of Juliet's attendants head her funeral procession. Juliet lies on a bier carried high by her black-cloaked kinsmen. Her father and mother follow behind. When the procession has passed, the women holding up the cloth of mourning disappear to reveal another scene.

SCENE IN THE VAULT OF THE CAPULETS We are in Juliet's tomb. She lies immobile on her bier, her hands pressed together at her breast. Romeo enters. He imagines that his beloved is dead and drinks a vial of poison. He falls at the foot of the bier.

Juliet gradually revives from the drug she has taken. She rises. Romeo sees her, pulls himself up with difficulty, reaches out for her, and—when Juliet comes to him—lifts her with his remaining strength. He falls. Juliet understands what has happened. She spins around and around frantically. Romeo rises again and lifts her in his arms. He holds her for a moment, then collapses across her bier. He dies. Juliet looks down upon him. She takes out his dagger, waits for a moment, and—rising suddenly on point, as if to meet the happiness only death can bring her—stabs herself in the heart. She falls across her lover's body and, with her last gesture, touches his face.

NOTES Tudor's Romeo and Juliet was revived by American Ballet Theatre, July 22, 1971, at the New York State Theatre, Lincoln Center. The critic Deborah Jowitt wrote in the Village Voice: "What Antony Tudor did in his 1943 Romeo and Juliet, now revived by Ballet Theatre, makes it one of the

most brilliant and interesting of recent ballets. In particular, he has worked
with the structure of the play so as to situate it in the kind of Renaissance time
and space with which Shakespeare's work has so many affinities.

"As Wylie Sypher pointed out in his *Four Stages of Renaissance Style,* the
plot of *Romeo and Juliet* is an essay in symmetry and proportion. Capulet is
weighed against Montague, Romeo's passion against Paris's suitability, love
against hate, night against day, rashness against prudence, etc. Time is compressed into forty-two hours; space is defined and confined by the walls of
Verona's chambers, gardens, piazzas. There is none of the depth, irregularity,
or ripeness of the later *Hamlet* or *Macbeth.*

"Tudor has set his version of this sad and lyrical equation in what might be
compared to a continuous Botticelli frieze. There is an emphasis on elegant,
agitated, fastidiously sensual flow rather than on volume. It is as if Tudor had
speeded up the heartbeat of the play, so tremulous is one's reaction to it. His
space, like Botticelli's, is almost more medieval than Renaissance: depth is
created by temporary hierarchies, events separated in time can coexist in
space. When Romeo and Juliet wind through the pillars of the piazza in an ecstatic return from their wedding, they are small upstage figures, seen through
the minor bustle of the square. When Juliet, enveloped by the nurse, weeps
over Tybalt down left, their figures are balanced by those of Romeo and Friar
Laurence consulting hastily down right. And the two tableaux are separated
by a temporary 'wall' formed by two watching women. Tudor's use of these
women is another odd detail. They witness the action from different positions,
like those little faces in the corners of certain medieval paintings.

"The effect of all this compression on the spectator is fascinating. There is
no blood, thunder, bombast; the action is drawn lightly over you like a veil
while you sit in a state of almost febrile tension. Events, briefly sketched, flow
out of each other; even what Tudor has chosen to show or not show is
revealing. Nothing seems to have any preliminaries. The Montague boys' decision to attend the Capulet ball is conveyed to Mercutio's brusquely beckoning
finger, while the powerful effect of the lovers' first meeting on Romeo and his
friends is shown more fully. Letters are not delivered, potions are drunk, marriages are arranged at high speed and with pictorial clarity.

"Eugene Berman's marvelous pillars, archways and porticos hold and shape
the action, add to the morbid delicacy of atmosphere. When a curtain is drawn
to reveal the ball in progress, the dancers first appear cramped, too large for
the space they inhabit—another painterly touch. Tudor's choice of excerpts
from Delius is extremely unusual. The music meanders along its own path—
painting a lush, summer atmosphere that is neither dramatically nor rhythmi-
cally assertive, but full of feeling. Often it creates a curious tension between
its dreamy flow and the action of the play. For instance, the insistent little tap-
pings and steppings of the court dances begin to be almost ominous against
the inconclusive music.

"Since nothing in this ballet ever really stops, pauses for large scale 'dance numbers' would have been unthinkable. Tudor has built the dancing out of gesture so subtly and naturally that you are not aware of anything but the continuous unfolding of this lyrical disquisition on action. There is a ball scene, of course, quietly and slowly built up. There is no *grand pas de deux* for the balcony scene: alone on the stage floor, Romeo bursts into an exulting stammer of leaps and postures and wide-flung gestures, while Juliet on the balcony above returns his passion with slow and happy stretchings and curvings of her body and arms. Even the morning-after-the-wedding scene turns into a dance imperceptibly through a series of muted rushings, claspings, near-swoons.

"Because nothing seems calculated, no particular moments of dance can be easily isolated. Pointe work has a special expressive function. Juliet steps up onto pointe as if some delicate emotional balance were at stake, or as if she were on unfamiliar ground. In some of her steps, she might be swooning upward."

The critic Marcia Siegel wrote in the Boston *Globe:* "Antony Tudor's *Romeo and Juliet* is a beautiful ballet. An extraordinary ballet. I think it's the best new ballet I've seen this year, even though it's really a revival, originally choreographed in 1943 for the infant Ballet Theatre. Restaged July 22 by that company, with Carla Fracci and Ivan Nagy in the opening-night title roles, it's a deeply moving and interesting work. I don't know when I've seen a ballet with such clarity and distinction of detail.

"Tudor saw the perennial story in quite intimate terms, encompassed in one act with several scenes. This makes for a tighter production—the story moves quickly, building to its powerful tragic end, without the long interpolations of sword-play and ceremony that pad out more grandiose Romeo and Juliet ballets. There's considerably less display dancing, smaller crowds, and less exposition, but I think this makes sense. Tudor's ballet is about the star-crossed lovers. The John Cranko and Kenneth MacMillan versions we've seen here in recent years are about the spectacular possibilities of a full-length ballet based on Shakespeare's play—quite a different thing.

"Fracci and Nagy are splendid as the doomed couple. Fracci is one of our best actress-dancers, and Nagy, released by Tudor's unstereotyped movement from the conventional suffering nobility of his other roles, was more convincing, more alive to the dramatic situation than I've ever seen him. All their scenes together breathed wonder and changeableness, joy touched with disbelief, a sort of shining despair.

"Tudor set the ballet in the Italian Renaissance, and much of the movement looks like the paintings and court dances of the period—the men with one leg turned out and pointing a fashionable toe, the women tilting back with their weight thrust mincingly forward. At times the company looked awkward with these stylizations, but Bruce Marks as Tybalt, Rosanna Seravalli as Lady Capulet, and Bonnie Mathis as Rosaline showed me immediately what the shape of the movement is, how it works. What intelligent character dancers these three are!

"There's more in this ballet, both in its dancing and production, than I can discuss in one day, but Tudor's choice of Delius' music is indicative of his unusual concept. The elegaic, rich-textured, but not especially dancy score seems at first too impressionistic to support the tragedy. But in fact it reinforces the ballet's delicate romanticism and isn't overpowering as the more familiar Prokofiev *Romeo and Juliet* usually is.

"Eugene Berman's multilevel set suggests both the scaffolded flexibility of a Shakespearean stage and the columns and perspective of an Italian painting. . . .

"I went back to see Antony Tudor's *Romeo and Juliet,* given by American Ballet Theatre, and found it as fascinating as I had the first time. It's a ballet of ideas—not philosophical or moral preachings, but ideas about how to present a classic story.

"Ballets are produced in such quantity here, and with so little attention to durability, that they often seem to be a matter of choosing new spices to liven up the same old hamburger. Tudor's *Romeo* constitutes a rethinking of every aspect of the narrative ballet. He uses all theatrical elements to suggest the depth and universality of the theme, instead of just letting us recognize what we already know about it.

"Eugene Berman's opening drop shows a small Romanesque building, possibly a tomb, suspended against a blue sea or sky, just hanging there, a door to something insubstantial and timeless. Classical allusions keep recurring quietly. You notice during the principals' first duet that the other guests at the Capulets' ball have seated themselves beyond some pillars, at a dinner table in another room. Their backs are to the audience; they are too close to the stage for realism. They look flat, like the background of a Renaissance painting. Juliet's friends, dressed like Botticelli nymphs, lift a shroud across the stage where Juliet's drugged body lies, and stand there throughout the funeral procession, echoing the statues perched atop the colonnaded set.

"The changes of scene—there are about ten of them—are accomplished in a variety of ingenious ways, many involving characters in the ballet. In fact, two 'attendants' watch the whole ballet from a bench downstage, moving around to draw curtains and even, at one point, simulating a wall. They are spectators of the tragedy who also help present it to us, and at the same time they belong to the House of Capulet as servants. This is an Elizabethan device as well as a classical reference. Realistic theater didn't come along till the late nineteenth century, and Tudor isn't offering us a modern romance. Other critics have objected to the extremely stylized quality of this *Romeo,* as if that were a drawback, and as if *all* ballet weren't a stylization to begin with. I suggest that Tudor's concept of production has the same elevating effect on the story that Shakespeare's poetry has."*

* Reprinted from Marcia B. Siegel's book, *At the Vanishing Point,* 1972.

Ballet in eleven scenes with prologue, based on Shakespeare's play. Music by Sergei Prokofiev. Choreography by Frederick Ashton. Scenery and costumes by Peter Rice. First presented by the Royal Danish Ballet at the Royal Theatre, Copenhagen, May 19, 1955, with Mona Vangsaae and Henning Kronstam in the title roles. First presented in the United States by the Royal Danish Ballet at the Metropolitan Opera House, New York, September 26, 1956.

Frederick Ashton's ballet follows this scenario:

At Verona there is constant feuding between the families of Montague and Capulet. A party of young men from Montague's household are present at an entertainment at Capulet's house. Among them is Romeo, who falls in love at first sight with Juliet, Capulet's only child. Romeo and Juliet declare their love for each other. They are secretly married by Friar Laurence. The brawls are continued. Romeo's friend Mercutio is killed by Tybalt, of the House of Capulet. Romeo kills Tybalt and is forced to flee. He takes refuge with Friar Laurence.

Meanwhile, old Capulet decides that Juliet shall marry Count Paris. The friar, hoping to bring about a reconciliation, advises Romeo to say farewell to Juliet and to hide in Mantua. When he learns of old Capulet's decision, he gives Juliet a sleeping draught which will produce a deathlike sleep. Juliet is believed dead, and is buried in the vault of her ancestors. The friar's message to Romeo miscarries. Supposing that his wife is indeed dead, Romeo hurries to the tomb, and commits suicide over her body. Juliet wakes too late, finds Romeo dead, and kills herself with his dagger.

Ballet in three acts after William Shakespeare. Music by Sergei Prokofiev. Choreography and staging by John Cranko. Décor and costumes by Jürgen Rose. In the repertory of the National Ballet of Canada. First staged by John Cranko for the ballet of La Scala, Milan, at the Teatro Verde, in Venice, July 26, 1958; this production was extensively revised and first presented by the Stuttgart Ballet at the Württemberg State Theatre, Stuttgart, December 2, 1962. The Stuttgart Ballet production was first presented in the United States at the Metropolitan Opera House, New York, June 18, 1969, with Marcia Haydée as Juliet, *Richard Cragun as* Romeo, *Jan Stripling as* Tybalt, *and Egon Madsen as* Mercutio.

The scene is Verona.

ACT ONE, SCENE ONE: THE MARKET PLACE As day breaks, Romeo, son of

Montague, is found declaring his love to the fair Rosaline. With the sunrise, the market place fills with townspeople, among whom are members of the two rival families, the Capulets and the Montagues. Tempers flare and a quarrel develops. The Duke of Verona appears and warns the two factions that death will be the ultimate punishment if the feud does not stop. Romeo and his friends Benvolio and Mercutio make reluctant peace with Tybalt, a kinsman of the Capulets.

ACT ONE, SCENE TWO: JULIET'S GARDEN IN THE CAPULETS' HOUSE   Juliet receives her first ball dress from her mother, Lady Capulet, and learns that she is to meet the noble Paris to whom she will be betrothed on the following day. Now she must bid farewell to her childhood.

ACT ONE, SCENE THREE: OUTSIDE THE CAPULETS' HOUSE   Guests appear for the Capulets' ball, among them Rosaline. Romeo and his friends, masked, follow her to the ball.

ACT ONE, SCENE FOUR: THE BALLROOM   Juliet dances with Paris but suddenly she and Romeo behold each other, and it is love at first sight. Tybalt, suspecting Romeo's identity, tries to start an argument but is prevented by Juliet's father who abides by the laws of hospitality.

ACT ONE, SCENE FIVE: JULIET'S BEDROOM   On the balcony outside her bedroom Juliet dreams of Romeo. He appears below in the garden. They declare their eternal love.

ACT TWO, SCENE ONE: THE MARKET PLACE   A carnival is in progress in the main square. Romeo, indifferent to the gaiety around him, is discovered by Juliet's nurse, who brings him a letter from her. She asks Romeo to meet her at the chapel of Friar Laurence.

ACT TWO, SCENE TWO: FRIAR LAURENCE'S CELL IN THE FOREST   In his cell, Friar Laurence joins the young lovers in marriage.

ACT TWO, SCENE THREE: THE MARKET PLACE   At the height of the carnival, Romeo returns to the square. Tybalt accosts him but Romeo declines to fight. Mercutio, angered, engages in a duel with Tybalt, and dies at his hands. Romeo, distraught, turns on Tybalt and kills him.

ACT THREE, SCENE ONE: THE BEDROOM   In Juliet's bedroom the lovers are awakened by the sunrise, and Romeo, under sentence of exile, must leave Juliet and Verona. Lord and Lady Capulet enter with Paris, but Juliet rejects him.

ACT THREE, SCENE TWO: FRIAR LAURENCE'S CELL IN THE FOREST   Juliet, appealing for help to Friar Laurence, receives a potion from him that will place her in a deathlike sleep. He explains that Romeo will find her in the family tomb and both can escape together.

ACT THREE, SCENE THREE: THE BEDROOM   Juliet agrees to her marriage with Paris. After he leaves with her parents, she takes the sleeping draught and is thought to be dead when her family and friends discover her.

ACT THREE, SCENE FOUR: THE CAPULET FAMILY CRYPT   Romeo, who has never received Friar Laurence's message revealing the plan, believes Juliet to be dead and rushes to her tomb. There he finds the mourning Paris and kills him. Embracing Juliet for the last time, he plunges his dagger into his heart. Juliet awakens to find Romeo dead. Grief-stricken, she kills herself.

Reviewing a performance of Cranko's ballet by the Stuttgart Ballet at the Metropolitan Opera House in the spring of 1973, the critic Andrew Porter wrote in *The New Yorker:* "There can be little dispute that Prokofiev's *Romeo and Juliet* is the most successful full-length ballet score written since Tchaikovsky's. I have seen it set to movement in six different versions, and only one of them—Serge Lifar's, for the Paris Opéra—was without marked merit. John Cranko's, created for the Stuttgart Ballet in 1962, and chosen for the opening night, last week, of the company's current Metropolitan season, is a very successful dance drama that has worn well. It continues to display the special virtues and strongly individual character of the troupe for whom it was made, and provides extended, uncommonly telling roles for the major stars—Marcia Haydée, Egon Madsen, and Richard Cragun—that shine in the splendid ensemble. The Royal Ballet, they say, dances best in New York; perhaps the Stuttgarters do so, too. I was bowled over on the first night by the power and eloquence of their presentation, and certainly Jürgen Rose's *Romeo* scenery and costumes never look as handsome and striking as they do on the Metropolitan stage. Dramatic force, potent projection, is a mark of German dancing; in Stuttgart, with his international team of dancers, Mr. Cranko has combined this force with Royal Ballet 'school,' developed his artists by composing new works for and 'on' them, and created one of the world's leading companies.

"Approaches to a Shakespeare ballet are almost as diverse as those to a Shakespeare opera. Prokofiev in his *Romeo* score devised appropriate melodies and motifs for the characters and their attributes (Juliet as a girl, Juliet as a woman, Romeo's ardor, Mercutio's wit, etc.), wrote movements that mount to passionate climaxes in the right places, supplied the necessary (and some unnecessary) ensemble dances, and achieved all this with his wonted flair for theatre music. Leonid Lavrovsky did the original choreography; his version was first performed, in Leningrad, in 1940. He worked on the piece with Prokofiev (and once told me how tiresome and silly the composer had been—

wanting, for a while, a happy ending, not wanting to lose a Dance of Carpet Sellers that he had somehow managed to bring in). While Prokofiev's 'libretto' was, so to speak, the plot, the characters, and their emotions, the choreographer added a more detailed attention to Shakespeare; in his version specific lines from the play seem often to ring out from the motion of the dancers: Romeo's 'O! she doth teach the torches to burn bright' when first he sees Juliet, his 'I do protest I never injur'd thee' to Tybalt, and then, after Mercutio's death, 'Fire-ey'd fury be my conduct now,' Juliet's 'My only love sprung from my only hate,' her 'Is there no pity sitting in the clouds?,' and many others. By comparison, Ashton's version for the Royal Danish Ballet, in 1955, to the same score, was a Lamb's Tale that became lyric poetry in the duets for the lovers. Kenneth MacMillan's *Romeo* for Covent Garden, ten years later, borrowed Cranko's solutions to the structural problems set by Prokofiev's ensembles, and acquired its special character from the detailed concentration on Juliet's development. In the monologues and duologues of MacMillan's version there is the same sense found in Lavrovsky's of words just below the surface of the dance. The successive quatrains and couplets of the antiphonal sonnet spoken by Romeo and Juliet when first they meet ('If I profane with my unworthiest hand') are transmuted into plastic imagery. Cranko's *Romeo* is more generalized, less intense in its close-ups. We do not follow the balcony and bedroom scenes 'line by line'; his approach, like Prokofiev's, is less literary. But the dances do not lack emotion, and they flow effectively. Cranko's presentation of the world around the tragedy—the street scenes, the assembly of Capulet's guests, the ball—is the most successful of all; a theatre flair kin to Prokofiev's is apparent in his handling. I miss Juliet's pas de deux with Paris on the wedding morning, a poignant moment in both the Lavrovsky and the MacMillan versions; the Friar Laurence scenes are rather skimpy, and Act III passes too swiftly. (Lavrovsky did well to insert a solo for Romeo in Mantua, corresponding to 'Is it even so? then I defy you, stars!') Comparisons are helpful in description; in its own right, Cranko's *Romeo* is an excellently vigorous, youthful, unrhetorical yet affecting work, couched in a fluent, eclectic choreography that I suppose could be called free-Fokine with modern ingredients, and very skillful in its theatrical shaping.

"The first night presented the nonpareil cast of Miss Haydée and Mr. Cragun in the title roles and Mr. Madsen as Mercutio. The second brought a new Juliet, the young Joyce Cuoco, touching and vulnerable, a promising actress and fleet technician—prone, in fact, to phrase some of the lyrical choreography too crisply. The Romeo and Mercutio swapped roles: Mr. Madsen now made a courteous, romantic Romeo, rather less boldly ardent than Mr. Cragun had been, while as Mercutio Mr. Cragun lacked only the twinkling beats with which Mr. Madsen had tripped through the Queen Mab solo. Jan Stripling's cold, strong Tybalt, the contrasted interpretations of Paris from Reid Anderson (a formal wooer) and Vladimir Klos (more tender), and Andrew Oxenham's bright Benvolio deserve mention; so do the unforced buoyancy, verve, and warmth with which the whole company took the stage."*

Ballet in three acts. Music by Sergei Prokofiev. Choreography by Kenneth MacMillan. Scenery and costumes by Nicholas Georgiadis. Lighting by William Bundy. First presented by the Royal Ballet at the Royal Opera House, Covent Garden, February 9, 1965, with Rudolf Nureyev and Margot Fonteyn as Romeo and Juliet. First presented in the United States by the Royal Ballet at the Metropolitan Opera House, New York, April 21, 1965.

The English critic and editor Peter Williams has said, "The game of love and death is the theater's trump card, and Shakespeare was no fool about what made good theater, the rules of which have varied little in any language from the threshing floors of Greece until the present day." Kenneth MacMillan's version of *Romeo and Juliet,* while based on the Prokofiev score used by a number of choreographers, varies substantially in treatment and detail.

ACT ONE, SCENE ONE: THE MARKET PLACE   The curtain rises on a dark stage. Then, to pizzicato strings, the stage is gradually lighted, revealing the market place. It is early morning, and the market is not yet busy. Romeo enters and tries to declare his love for the lovely Rosaline, who rejects him. Romeo joins his friends Mercutio and Benvolio, and, as day breaks and the market begins to fill up with butchers and farmers, Romeo takes off his cape and watches idly. A girl tries to entice him away. With two other harlots, she becomes involved with Romeo and his friends. A quarrel now develops between Tybalt, a nephew of Capulet, and Romeo. The Capulets and Montagues are of course sworn enemies and a fight begins. The heads of the two families join the dispute and do not assist a solution. The Prince of Verona appears and is obliged to order them to cease their feuding. All place their swords on the ground at his command, in front of the slain, but the two families stand opposite each other, obstinate in their rage.

ACT ONE, SCENE TWO: JULIET'S ANTEROOM IN THE CAPULETS' HOUSE   After a brief musical interlude, the curtain rises on a bright and cheerful room. There are large bird cages to the right and left, and Juliet's nurse sits waiting. Juliet runs in and we are reminded at once that this girl who will become a tragic figure is at heart a child of fourteen. She plays with a doll. She reacts like a spoiled child, too, when her mother and father come in with Paris, whom she does not like. But Juliet is nevertheless interested somewhat in anyone who

* From *A Musical Season* by Andrew Porter (Viking Press); © 1973 Andrew Porter. Originally in *The New Yorker.*

would express interest in marrying her; she yields to her father's insistence and is nice to him. When the Capulets and Paris leave, Juliet wants to resume her play with the doll, but the nurse points out that her childhood is over, that she is a young woman now, about to be beloved. Juliet clutches her heart. The curtain falls.

ACT ONE, SCENE THREE: OUTSIDE THE CAPULETS' HOUSE Two huge iron gates guard the entrance to the Capulet palace, where guests are arriving for a masked ball. Romeo, Mercutio, and Benvolio, disguised in masks, enter. Romeo flirts with a lady who drops a rose for him to pick up—the fair Rosaline. Then he and his friends dance a vigorous, high-spirited *pas de trois*. They decide then to follow the lady into the ball. They are aware that they do so in some danger.

ACT ONE, SCENE FOUR: THE BALLROOM Romeo and his friends arrive at the height of the festivities. Still infatuated with Rosaline, Romeo follows her. He comes face to face with Juliet for a moment. As Juliet dances with Paris, Romeo watches, bewitched. As Paris kneels to kiss her hand, Juliet turns, sees Romeo, and is visibly disturbed. She is given a mandolin and strums it as six of her friends dance. But their dance is interrupted by one for Romeo, as if Juliet could not get him out of her mind. He dances marvelously for her alone, and kneels at her feet, taking her mandolin. But Paris quickly intercedes and Juliet dances. Romeo, irresistibly drawn to her, comes to join Juliet, catching her about the waist. Mercutio, seeing that Romeo is entranced with Juliet, dances to distract attention from him. Later, Tybalt recognizes Romeo and orders him to leave, but Capulet intervenes and welcomes him as a guest in his house.

ACT ONE, SCENE FIVE: OUTSIDE THE CAPULETS' HOUSE As the ball breaks up and the guests depart, Tybalt follows Romeo out. Lord Capulet intervenes and Tybalt is restrained from pursuing Romeo.

ACT ONE, SCENE SIX: JULIET'S BALCONY Unable to sleep, Juliet comes out on her balcony, throws off her scarf and leans against a column. She thinks of Romeo. Suddenly he is there, below in the garden. She runs swiftly down the long flight of steps to him. He drops his cloak and goes to her. He puts his hand to her heart and then dances for her. Now they dance together, confess their love, and the die is cast.

ACT TWO, SCENE ONE: THE MARKET PLACE The market bustles with activity; buyers and sellers jostle together, hooded monks mingle with the crowd. Romeo, who can think only of Juliet, watches as a wedding procession passes and dreams of the day he will marry her. Her nurse enters on the right, seeking Romeo. She gives him a letter in which he rejoices: Juliet has consented to marry him, but with their families so opposed, they must do this secretly.

Thinking only of his bride, Romeo dances joyfully, then embraces the nurse and rushes out.

ACT TWO, SCENE TWO: THE CHAPEL   The music is somber as the curtain rises on Friar Laurence's cell. The monk enters and prays. First Romeo and then Juliet and the nurse come. All kneel before the monk. Friar Laurence joins the hands of the two lovers, hoping that their union will end the strife between the Montagues and the Capulets. The nurse weeps.

ACT TWO, SCENE THREE: THE MARKET PLACE   Meanwhile, the crowd in the market place is still celebrating. Interrupting the revelry, Tybalt tries to pick a fight with Romeo. At such a time, Romeo will not duel his wife's kinsman. But Tybalt will be fought with and before anyone can intercede, Mercutio has accepted the challenge and the two enemies fight with swords. Romeo begs Mercutio to stop. Tybalt stabs Mercutio in the back. Mercutio staggers. He still tries to fight, but dies with gaiety, his sword becoming for a moment his guitar as he plays his own lament. As Mercutio dies, Romeo in revenge attacks Tybalt and kills him. Romeo is exiled. Lady Capulet holds the body of her nephew, swaying back and forth in her grief as her husband watches helplessly.

ACT THREE, SCENE ONE: JULIET'S BEDROOM   Romeo and Juliet lie together on a canopied bed. He kisses her as the sun comes through the window. She sleeps on for a bit but soon they rise to dance ecstatically of their mutual joy. At the end they are sick with sadness that they must part. After a long kiss Romeo rushes to the balcony and away, while Juliet hurries back to bed just as the nurse enters. Her parents soon follow with Paris. Juliet, to her father's rage, repulses Paris. The nurse begs her to bahave, but she cannot. She prays to her father to forget this marriage. When he will not she throws herself on the bed and cries like a child. But the family closes in on her, bearing down and insisting. Juliet seems to reconsider but instead of going to Paris and being nice to him she circles him on point. Capulet will tolerate this no longer; he and his wife take Paris away. They leave Juliet lying in despair. She sits up then at the foot of the bed, vulnerable yet sure, tormented but determined to find a way out for herself and her lover. She takes up her cloak, gestures toward the balcony as if that would bring Romeo back, prays frantically, and then rushes off to see Friar Laurence.

ACT THREE, SCENE TWO: THE CHAPEL   Juliet falls at the friar's feet and begs for help. He gives her a phial of sleeping potion which will make her fall into a deathlike sleep. The monk further undertakes to warn Romeo that Juliet has taken the potion and is not really dead but that she must be rescued from the family tomb.

ACT THREE, SCENE THREE: JULIET'S BEDROOM   Juliet, back in her room, hides the phial under the pillow. When her parents come, she begs her mother's pardon. Her father is pleased that she seems to have come to her senses. Juliet dances for Paris but resists any real contact with him. He kisses the hem of her dress. Her parents decide not to force matters and then Juliet is alone. She goes to the bed for the phial, but is frightened at the possible consequences of taking it. Suppose she will really die? What if the potion does not work at all and she is compelled to marry Paris anyway? She sits at the foot of the bed and again she is a child, younger than we saw even at the beginning, caught up in a fate beyond her. But she takes the phial, drinks the sleeping potion, and expires on the bed.

The next morning Juliet seems to be asleep when six friends of the bride enter with flowers. They remark how quiet she is and try to waken her. The nurse comes in with Juliet's wedding dress and then her parents arrive. The nurse falls full length beside the bed when Capulet declares that his daughter is dead. All lament.

ACT THREE, SCENE FOUR: THE CAPULET FAMILY CRYPT   The curtain rises on the grim interior of an underground cavern. Juliet lies on a bier in the center. Her family mourns and monks with candles lament her passing. Paris remains behind to bid farewell to Juliet, but Romeo, disguised as a monk, throws off his cloak and attacks him. Paris is killed. Believing Juliet to be dead (the message from Friar Laurence has miscarried), but not believing it possible, Romeo lifts her from the bier and holds her. He dances with the dead body of his beloved, trying to revive her, but she falls back always in his arms. He places her on the tomb, then drinks a phial of poison that he has brought with him. Juliet wakes, but as she moves off the tomb she sees Romeo's body. She takes his dagger, which he has dropped near Paris's body, plunges it into her breast, and embraces Romeo.

Ballet in three acts. Music by Sergei Prokofiev. Choreography by John Neumeier. Scenery and costumes by Jürgen Rose. Lighting by Jorgen Mydtskov. Produced by John Neumeier assisted by Ray Barra and Henning Kronstam for the Royal Danish Ballet at the Royal Theatre, Copenhagen, December 20, 1974. First presented in the United States by the Royal Danish Ballet at the Metropolitan Opera House, New York, May 20, 1976.

A compression of four crucial days in April of a Verona long ago, this *Romeo and Juliet*, after defining the strife between the two enemy families, shows the rise and fall of the love of the daughter of one for the son of the other. The frame of the ballet, while showing the background of the city and the carnage engendered by hatred, focuses on intimacy. The *pas de deux* govern the action.

ACT ONE: THE FIRST DAY   Crowds throng the market place of Verona in front of the house of the Capulets on the day before the Feast of San Zeno, the city's patron saint. Infatuated with Rosaline, Juliet's cousin, Romeo pays court to her. Servants of the rival houses of Capulet and Montague clash until the Prince of Verona insists upon a cessation of hostilities.

The Capulets, entertaining at a huge ball, introduce their daughter Juliet to the Count Paris, whom they have selected as her husband. Crashing the party, Romeo finds himself face to face with a creature unimaginable to him. Juliet responds in similar fashion and, after the ball, under her balcony, the two meet to declare their love under the moon.

ACT TWO: THE SECOND DAY   In the midst of celebrations in the city, Romeo proposes marriage to Juliet and they are wed in secret by Friar Laurence. Back in the center of the town, unaware of what has taken place elsewhere, cousins of the newly wed pair, Mercutio and Tybalt, fight a duel, in which Mercutio, of Romeo's family, is killed. Coming upon the action, Romeo, in horror, and unable to prevent this outcome, challenges Juliet's cousin Tybalt and kills him.

ACT THREE: THE THIRD DAY   Tybalt's funeral calls out all the Capulets. Romeo, after his wedding night with Juliet, is obliged to flee because of his part in the duel. Endeavoring to escape her marriage to Count Paris, Juliet consults Friar Laurence, who arms her with a potion that will cause her to appear dead for a day. Pretending to assent to her parents' will, Juliet takes the potion.

ACT FOUR: THE FOURTH DAY   Believing her dead, Juliet's parents mourn deeply. Her funeral is prepared. Romeo, on his way to Mantua, learns of her death and races back to Verona, seeking Friar Laurence, who might have explained the liberation he and Juliet had arranged. He fails to find him and goes to Juliet, who is laid out in her tomb. Believing her dead, he stabs himself. Awakening from her day's sleep, Juliet finds her beloved at her side. Finding him dead, she kills herself with his dagger.

The critic George Dorris has written an important essay, "Prokofiev and the Ballet," which examines in detail the scores of *Romeo and Juliet* and other ballets by that composer (*Ballet Review*, Vol. 4, No. 6).

ROOMS

Music by Kenneth Hopkins. Choreography by Anna Sokolow. First presented at the YM-YWHA, New York, February 24, 1955, with Beatrice

Seckler, Eve Beck, Donald McKayle, Jeff Duncan, Jack Moore, Sandra Pine, Judith Coy, and Paul Sanasardo.

Anna Sokolow has written of this work: "I wanted to do something about people in a big city. The theme of loneliness and non-communication evolved as I worked. I like to look into windows, to catch glimpses of unfinished lives. Then I ask: 'What is there, and why?' Then I thought of using chairs as if they were rooms, each dancer on his own chair, isolated from all the others though physically so close to them."*

Rooms has been danced by the Alvin Ailey Company, by the Netherlands Dance Theatre, and by the City Center Joffrey Ballet (September 7, 1967). Reviewing the latter production, Clive Barnes wrote in the New York *Times:* "The pattern of *Rooms* is the pattern of a run-down rooming house. Eight straight-backed people are found sitting on eight straight-backed kitchen chairs. The chairs are their rooms, their patch of frightening privacy in an alien world. The people in the rooms, remote, removed, separate in the way of separateness of cities, are trying vainly to connect with life. They fail.

"Miss Sokolow shows us, with a series of dance images accurate enough to be painful, the shabbiness of their aspirations. A man dreams of escape, a girl dreams of love, a boy sees a false world as a flurry of jazz. Miss Sokolow forces us to peek into the windows of an apartment house we have all, however fleetingly, visited, but would prefer to forget."

THE ROPES OF TIME

Music by Jan Boerman. Choreography by Rudi van Dantzig. Scenery and costumes by Toer van Schayk. First presented by the Royal Ballet at the Royal Opera House, Covent Garden, London, March 2, 1970, with Rudolf Nureyev, Diana Vere, and Monica Mason in the principal roles. First presented in the United States by the same ensemble at the Metropolitan Opera House, New York, May 13, 1970, with the same principals.

The ballet is prefixed by a quotation from the British writer and critic Richard Buckle: "Every journey we make is an adventure into the unknown; each arrival a birth and each departure a death." The characters in the ballet are a Traveller, Life, and Death.

The curtain rises on a dark stage. A man stands to the left, on top of a hemisphere, or egg, where he balances for a moment, then falls, to the sound of crashing glass. The pinnacle rises and out from under the Traveller is born.

* From *The Modern Dance, Seven Statements of Belief,* edited by Selma Jeanne Cohen, Wesleyan University Press, 1966.

Dancing amidst ten boys young like himself, the Traveller becomes an individual and begins his life journey. Death enters and watches. So, too, does Life. The Traveller dances with her but Death cuts in and the Traveller is caught between. So begins the journey in which the two dominant figures accompany the venturing Traveller to the end. No sooner does he succeed in showing self-mastery than he is brought back, as it were, to earth. He returns at last to his birthplace to die.

In an interview about his ballet, Rudi van Dantzig said that the inspiration for it was a performing artist he much admires who has sustained a career well beyond the usual span, triumphing over age and adversity. The Traveller as performing artist, on trial before the public, is thus an important aspect of the ballet.

A ROSE FOR MISS EMILY

Music by Alan Hovhaness. Choreography by Agnes de Mille. Costumes and scenery by A. Christinia Giannini. Lighting by Gene Lowery. First presented at the North Carolina School of the Arts, Winston-Salem, October 24, 1970, with Gemze de Lappe and David Evans in leading roles. First presented by American Ballet Theatre at the City Center, New York, December 30, 1970, with Sallie Wilson and Bruce Marks in leading roles. Lighting by Tom Skelton.

The choreographer Agnes de Mille has said of her ballet: "It is a story of narcissism . . . self-love, possessiveness and destruction. It is a story about a woman who eats up all the things she loves and then destroys herself."

Miss de Mille's program note reads: "Preoccupation with the morbid is a marked characteristic of the American psyche. It has passed into great literature with Edgar Allen Poe, William Faulkner, Ambrose Bierce and Shirley Jackson.

"This little melodrama, suggested by the masterpiece 'A Rose for Emily' by William Faulkner, seems, because of its stark terror, to lie outside normal experience; it is, however, universal.

"In every life there is an aspect of the personality sealed off and entombed, protected from the abrasive and healing effects of reality, cherished because it is safe, and because it is comforting. This buried person, this self-haunted mourner dotes on experiences and events that are ended, living on a febrile and false world of reflections. We call this sealing off memory; it can be and often is, a form of death."

The curtain rises to the ominous sound of low drum rolls and piano chords. A group of children stand in front of a house in the Old South. There is a jalousied porch, overgrown with creeping vines. The young persons act as if something mysterious has happened within; they seem to giggle in their dread of the unknown. A girl does an imitation of the la-de-da lady of the house, who can be seen dimly behind a scrim. The scrim rises and Miss Emily is seen, in a long gray dress. She dances but hobbles in her attempt to be glamorous. She suffers as a girl comes to give her a rose. The girl drops the flower before Miss Emily can take it and, giggling, leaves. Miss Emily places the rose on a couch, where a cover seems to hide a laid-out figure.

Now, looking in a mirror, the distraught woman recalls her past. A back curtain rises and we are in a scene recollecting her youth. Five girls in red are seen dancing. As Miss Emily looks back, the girls enclose her in a semi-circle, she embraces them and becomes, too, a girl in red—one of them. She is suddenly alone. A man comes to her. They dance together passionately, suppressed feeling rising to the surface. She crawls to his feet, asking for something he seems unable to give. She is embarrassed then and gets up. The man gives her a rose, which she secures at her shoulder, and the dance is resumed. It finishes as she claims the man, holding him fiercely in her arms.

There is silence as four masked couples enter. They appear to be a bit scandalized by what they see, but the man joins them. Miss Emily watches in horror as a young girl in pink blows him a kiss. Two other girls are attracted to him, too. Miss Emily tries to take him away, clinging to his back. She begs him; he rejects her; in suppressed fury she wraps her scarf around his neck and strangles him. He falls back on the couch, and dies. Her body trembles at his death, but she covers him and poses there, fascinated by a vision of her own glamour.

In a dance of triumph and self-justification, she relives the earlier scene, seeing herself and her lover as one of six happy couples. Putting back on now her old lady's dress of gray, she writhes on the floor in despair, reaching out for her lover.

The young people of the first scene return. They observe that Miss Emily has died. Placid at that discovery, they take up the body of Miss Emily and place it on the couch, on the blanket of rotten flowers that has covered the body of her lover all these years. One of them then lifts up a corner of the cover to look underneath.

LA ROSE MALADE

Music by Gustav Mahler. Choreography by Roland Petit. First presented by Les Ballets de Marseille at Le Palais des Sports, Paris, January 10, 1973, with Maya Plisetskaya. First presented in the United States by the Bolshoi Ballet at the Metropolitan Opera House, New York, September 18, 1974.

Set to music from Mahler's *Symphonies No. 2* and *5*, this ballet is based on the poem by William Blake:

O Rose, thou art sick!
The Invisible worm,
That flies in the night,
In the howling storm,
Has found out thy bed
Of crimson joy;
And his dark secret love
Does thy life destroy.

The complete ballet, in three long parts, expands these eight lines into a dance work that has no plot but attempts to capture certain moods, feelings, and passions reflective of the poem. Only one of these parts was danced at the American premiere, by Plisetskaya and Alexander Godunov.

Choreographed especially for the Soviet ballerina by Roland Petit, *La Rose Malade* was created during Plisetskaya's residency in Paris with Petit's company in 1972.

LE SACRE DU PRINTEMPS (The Rite of Spring)

Ballet in two parts. Music by Igor Stravinsky. Choreography by Vaslav Nijinsky. Book by Igor Stravinsky and Nicholas Roerich. Scenery and costumes by Nicholas Roerich. First presented by Diaghilev's Ballets Russes at the Théâtre des Champs-Élysées, Paris, May 29, 1913, with Marie Piltz as the Chosen One. *Rechoreographed by Leonide Massine and presented by Diaghilev's Ballets Russes at the Théâtre des Champs-Élysées, 1920, with Lydia Sokolova as the* Chosen One. *First presented in the United States, with new choreography by Massine, at the Academy of Music, Philadelphia, April 11, 1930, under the auspices of the League of Composers. Martha Graham danced the leading role in the first American presentation.*

Stravinsky has said that the "violent Russian spring" that seemed to begin in an hour was like the whole earth cracking. . . . It was "the most wonderful event of every year of my childhood." In 1910, when he was finishing *Firebird*, the composer had an unexpected vision: "I saw in imagination a solemn pagan rite: wise elders, seated in a circle, watching a young girl dance herself to death. They were sacrificing her to propitiate the god of spring." The ballet that resulted from this vision made musical and theatrical history. The score, long a masterpiece of the modern repertoire, has become more popular in the concert hall than in the theater, although there continue to be a number of ballet versions (one by Kenneth MacMillan for the Royal Ballet, with scenery and costumes by Sydney Noland, May 3, 1962, was introduced in North America the following year, May 8, 1963).

Subtitled "Scenes of Pagan Russia in Two Parts," the ballet returns us to a time when primitive rites dominated the lives of the Russian tribes. Every year spring was consecrated by a human sacrifice.

FIRST TABLEAU: ADORATION OF THE EARTH   A musical prelude recalls man's first relations with the world about him. The curtain rises. In a wasteland scene dominated by great masses of stone, young girls and boys sit in separate groups. They do not move, they wait and watch, as if expecting some sign from the stone shafts they revere. The girls rise, as if drawn by the abundance of Nature to which the music calls their attention. A wise man stands among the dancers; the girls rush around and around him. Now he moves toward the sacred mound of the enclosure. The girls follow and bow before him. The opening phrase of the ballet—the quiet, plaintive cry of man against all-powerful Nature—is repeated.

The strings sound strong, persistent chords that rouse the young men. To the virile beat of the music, they begin to dance, their movements accelerating at its demand, their feet stamping, stamping the earth. The girls join in the dance, the music becomes joyous, and the adolescents abandon themselves to the swift, exuberant rhythms of the orchestra.

This music changes sharply. A new, penetrating melody shrieks warningly and disturbs the young people. The happiness of the boys and girls shifts abruptly to fierce savagery. They split into different groups; the boys face the girls and move toward them. The boys seem bent on attack, but at the last minute they hesitate; they move back and forth in an almost helpless effort, ignorant of their own true intent. The rhythmic crescendos give place to the soft trilling of flutes. Now the boys break their formation, and each carries a girl away.

Four boys remain on the scene. They choose four girls, lift them up on their backs, and dance slowly, bending low under the weight of their burdens in imitation of the plodding chords of the music. This "Round Dance of Spring" gradually increases in volume, and all the adolescents participate. All the dancers step back as the trilling flutes repeat their love call.

Drums herald the beginning of a contest between two rival tribes. Groups of men from each tribe engage in vigorous games. In the midst of their activity, the wise man, represented in the orchestra by a portentous melody on the tuba, tries to interrupt the games. The stronger theme of the games at first drowns out the wise man's theme, then recedes. The men turn to the wise man. There is a brief, taut silence, then all the men fall to the ground and worship the earth.

The drum rolls loudly, and all rise to dance, as if they had felt the pulse of the earth and been renewed by its power. The dance grows frenzied in its intensity. The curtain falls.

SECOND TABLEAU: THE SACRIFICE   Night is about to fall as this second scene begins; the setting sun has turned the sky scarlet. The girls sit near the wise man at a fire. One of these girls must be chosen by the others to make the sacrifice to the earth: this girl must dance herself to death. The music is calm; the figures on stage are quiet and they are unafraid. The girls regret what they have to do, but they are resigned to it with a kind of physical tiredness that the music reflects. They do not feel that they are victimized by Nature, but rather that they must obey what they believe to be its rules.

Soon the girls rise and move in the patterns of the "Dance of the Mysterious Circles." Their movements are trancelike, as if they themselves were not to make their dreadful decision. Their inspiration arrives, and they rush to the periphery of the scene; the chosen one stands alone in the center of the stage.

Now begins the dance that glorifies the victim. The chosen one remains motionless as the girls and men of the tribe whirl around her. All are transfixed at her power. They invoke the spirit of their ancestors, terrified anew by the force of Nature. Marking the relentless, sharp rhythms of the music with their feet, their dance reaches an ultimate expression of uncontrolled glory in sacrifice.

All the tribe members retire to watch the chosen one. The orchestra sounds strong, militant chords, trumpets blare harshly, cutting the air. The dance of the chosen one begins. The brutal savagery of the demanding music compels her to imitate it. Brief moments of comparative quiet, which seem at first to be periods of rest and release, are in reality more deadly because of the thrashing force that follows them. The girl is now wholly a part of the music, part of the earth. Hypnotized by her movements, the tribe joins in the violent dance. The chosen one begins to lose her strength, but—forced on by the convulsive violence of the music—is endowed with a new, superhuman compulsion. When it seems that Nature can demand no more, the girl is pushed into a fresh frenzy. Then she falls. She is dead.

The men of the tribe catch her up in their arms and hold her high over their heads before the sacred mound. The people of the tribe rush around her, holding up their arms. At the last slapping crescendo of the music, they fall to the earth.

NOTES   The first assistant to Nijinsky in the creation of the first version of *Le Sacre du Printemps*, Dame Marie Rambert, who later founded ballet in Britain and developed the gifts of Tudor, Ashton, de Mille and many others, has written in a way no one else can match of the background of this ballet in her autobiography, *Quicksilver* (1972):

"It was the painter Roerich who first suggested the subject of *Sacre du Printemps*. He then worked on the theme with Diaghilev, Stravinsky and Nijinsky. It was to be prehistoric Russia and represent the rites of spring. Stravinsky had finished his magnificent score by 1912, and we started the rehearsals with the company that same year.

"Nijinsky again first of all established the basic position: feet very turned in, knees slightly bent, arms held in reverse of the classical position, a primitive, prehistoric posture. The steps were very simple: walking smoothly or stamping, jumps mostly off both feet, landing heavily. There was only one a little more complicated, the dance for the maidens in the first scene. It was mostly done in groups, and each group has its own precise rhythm to follow. In the dance (if one can call it that) of the Wisest Elder, he walked two steps against every three steps of the ensemble. In the second scene the dance of the sacrifice of the Chosen Virgin was powerful and deeply moving. I watched Nijinsky again and again teaching it to Maria Piltz. Her reproduction was very pale by comparison with his ecstatic performance, which was the greatest tragic dance I have ever seen.

"The first night of that ballet was the most astonishing event . . . at the first sounds of the music, shouts and hissing started in the audience, and it was very difficult for us on the stage to hear the music, the more so as part of the audience began to applaud in an attempt to drown the hissing. We all desperately tried to keep time without being able to hear the rhythm clearly. In the wings Nijinsky counted the bars to guide us. Pierre Monteux conducted undeterred, Diaghilev having told him to continue to play at all costs.

"But after the interlude things became even worse, and during the sacrificial dance real pandemonium broke out. That scene began with Maria Piltz, the Chosen Virgin, standing on the spot trembling for many bars, her folded hands under her right cheek, her feet turned in, a truly prehistoric and beautiful pose. But to the audience of the time it appeared ugly and comical.

"A shout went up in the gallery:

"'Un docteur!'

"Somebody else shouted louder:

"'Un dentiste!'

"Then someone else screamed:

"'Deux dentistes!'

"And so it went on. One elegant lady leaned out of her box and slapped a man who was clapping. But the performance went on to the end.

"And yet now there is no doubt that, musically and choreographically, a masterpiece had been created that night. The only ballet that could compare with it in power was Bronislava Nijinska's *Los Noces*, created in 1923. She, like her brother, produced a truly epic ballet—so far unexcelled anywhere."

Music by Igor Stravinsky. Choreography by Maurice Béjart. First presented by the Ballet of the Twentieth Century at the Théâtre Royale de La Monnaic, in December 1959. First presented in the United States by the same ensemble at the Brooklyn Academy of Music, New York, January 26, 1971, with Tania Bari and Jorge Donn in principal roles.

The choreographer of this version of *Le Sacre*, Maurice Béjart, has written:

"What is Spring but an immense primordial force, which after long sleeping under the mantle of winter, suddenly bursts forth, kindling new life in all things. . . . Human love, in its physical aspects, symbolizes the act by which the divinity creates the Cosmos and the joy the divinity thereby derives. At a time when the borders that divide the human spirit are gradually crumbling, we must begin to speak in terms of the culture of all mankind. Let us avoid folklore that is not universal and only retain the essential forces of mankind which are the same the world over and throughout all periods of history.

"Let this ballet then be stripped of all the artifices of the picturesque in a Hymn to this union of Man and Woman in the innermost depths of the flesh, a union of heaven and earth, a dance of life and death, as eternal as Spring."

Rejecting, therefore, the original scenario of Stravinsky and Roerich, this *Sacre* celebrates instead the mating of a young man and woman. Writing in the New York *Times,* Anna Kisselgoff has said that Béjart's "use of group patterns and rhythmic pulse gives this *Sacre* an underivative look. . . . The chosen maiden is not sacrificed literally but thrown into a physical union with an equally virginal male. . . . The Puritans did not ban Maypole-dancing in England for nothing and Béjart has given his strikingly designed fertility ritual the primitive physical force it needs. It works."

The English critic Peter Williams has written in *Dance and Dancers* magazine: "The mass ritualistic movements leading up to the final orgasmic moment make pretty powerful theatre, in which the music plays a vital part."

Rudolf Nureyev danced Béjart's ballet on March 12, 1971, at the Palais des Sports, Brussels.

John Taras choreographed a new version of *Le Sacre* for La Scala, Milan, December 9, 1972. Natalia Makarova danced the principal role. Scenery and costumes were designed by Marino Marini.

June 21, 1976, Glen Tetley's version of *Le Sacre,* created in 1975 for the Munich Opera Ballet, was first presented in the United States by American Ballet Theatre at the Metropolitan Opera House, New York. Scenery and costumes were by Nadine Baylis, lighting by John B. Read. The cast was led by Mikhail Baryshnikov, Martine van Hamel, and Clark Tippet.

The action depicts a vernal sacrifice and renewal of the human spirit.

Bill Zakariasen wrote in the *Daily News* after the first performance in New York: "Those expecting pagan rites of ancient Russia were no doubt disappointed, yet for the first time in my experience, the choreography matched the elemental power of Stravinsky's music."

SACRED GROVE ON MOUNT TAMALPAIS

Music and lyrics by Alan Raph. Choreography by Gerald Arpino. Set designed by Robert Yodice from a concept by Ming Cho Lee. Costumes by David James. First presented by the City Center Joffrey Ballet at the City

Center, New York, November 2, 1972, with Starr Danias, Russell Chambers, and Russell Sultzbach in leading roles. Conducted by Sung Kwak.

From antique times, men and women have gone to sacred groves to celebrate the earth's renewal every spring. Mount Tamalpais, in Marin County, California, overlooking San Francisco Bay and the Pacific beyond, is the scene of this extensive dance ballet that explores the drive, innocence, and sophistication of contemporary youth. There is a pastoral marriage and evidence of other commitments ". . . to build from a moment onward/to build a beginning./ Come to the wall around you/Come through the wall around you./ Come and see/look and see/follow me." The score, with lyrics, which includes the *Canon in D* by Johann Pachelbel, was commissioned by the Foundation for American Dance, Inc.

The action depicts a wedding ceremony and the attendant celebration, followed by the birth of a son who represents a kind of prophet to the young persons on Mount Tamalpais.

NOTES Writing about the ballet in the New York *Times*, Clive Barnes said that "Mr. Arpino has conceived his ballet as an exaltation of the human spirit. Californians (perhaps) in a Greek mood are dancing out fancies of renewal. Two lovers—Starr Danias and Russell Chambers—produce, quite suddenly, a full-grown son, Russell Sultzbach. . . . Miss Danias dances like a still thought in a quick world—there is a special quietness to her lyricism, a youthful melancholy, that Mr. Arpino so instinctively picks up. He creates beautifully for her, and Mr. Chambers, ardent and provocative, makes her a nicely matched partner. The assertive radiance of Mr. Sultzbach was also used to strong effect."

In a special portfolio by Olga Maynard on Gerald Arpino's "Berkeley ballets" for *Dance Magazine* (September 1973), the choreographer is quoted as saying that *Sacred Grove on Mount Tamalpais* polarizes its audiences: "'For some (for whom the distance is too far from the real Mount Tamalpais, and the Berkeley life-style), the ballet is incomprehensible. It is not a work that should be approached intellectually, but as an experience. But people come to me, in every city that The Joffrey dances *Sacred Grove on Mount Tamalpais*, to say that it has made them feel beautiful again. I am very grateful for that. . . .

"'The choreographer cannot deliberately make a ballet to appeal to an audience; he has to start from personal inspirations. He has to trust the ballet, to let it stand on its own strengths—or fall on its weaknesses. If it reaches the audience, then he is lucky that round!

"'In *Trinity* and *Sacred Grove on Mount Tamalpais* I have been able to look at the world through the eyes of the young—to touch the heart of the matter of what it is to be young in this place and time. I could not have done this unless I had gone to Berkeley.

"'The choreographer (especially in the United States) needs Berkeley. Ma-

terialistic things, from which art cannot be separated, force us into certain perspectives, they sometimes narrow those perspectives, as tall buildings confine
the sight of the sky. At Berkeley, The Joffrey had a true freedom, and our
company was able to refresh and to replenish its spirit. Joffrey and I are very
conscious of the free spirit that identifies this company; the dancers are very
important to the company. They *are* The Joffrey.

"'As artists, they are very sensitive to an atmosphere and at Berkeley we all
felt, very intensely, the free, open spirit that is the stamp of The Joffrey.'"

SALTARELLI

*Music by Antonio Vivaldi. Choreography by Jacques d'Amboise. Scenery
and costumes by John Braden. Lighting by Ronald Bates. Dedicated to the
Drs. B. and L. Krynski. First presented by the New York City Ballet at the
New York State Theatre, Lincoln Center, May 30, 1974, with Christine
Redpath, Merrill Ashley, and Francis Sackett as principal dancers.*

The *saltarello,* an old Italian court dance, derived from the word for "jump,"
also had its popular manifestation among the people. Clive Barnes has said
that it might be regarded as the Roman counterpart of the southern *tarantella.*
This ballet by Jacques d'Amboise, a dance occasion without narrative, is performed on a *saltarello* base to music by Vivaldi (the *Concerto in D Minor*
F.XI No. 19 and the *Concerto Grosso in D Minor,* Op. 3, No. 11). *Saltarelli* is
a reworking of an earlier work mounted in 1973 for the Ballet de San Juan in
Puerto Rico.

Writing in *The Record,* Barbara Archer said that the ballet "reflects the ease
and breeziness Jacques d'Amboise usually brings to his own dancing. As its
name suggests, the ballet transmits a constant energy."

Using seven dancers, the ballet varies lively presentation with quiet *pas de
deux.* "There is a certain poetic touch," wrote Clive Barnes in the New York
Times, "that through a chain of associations, can recall the tenderness and
melancholy of Picasso's blue and rose periods."

SARABANDE AND DANSE

*Music by Maurice Ravel. Choreography by Jacques d'Amboise. Costumes
by John Braden. Lighting by Ronald Bates. First presented at the New
York City Ballet's Hommage à Ravel at the New York State Theatre, Lincoln Center, May 29, 1975, with Colleen Neary in the principal role. Conductor: Robert Irving.*

Ravel wrote orchestrations of Debussy's *Sarabande* and *Danse* as a tribute to the great French composer who had died in 1918. Since the compositions are in effect dance works it was only natural that Jacques d'Amboise should have used them for our Ravel Festival in 1975. He did so for dance works expressive of the music without any specific narrative idea.

SCÈNES DE BALLET

Classic ballet in one act. Music by Igor Stravinsky. Choreography by Anton Dolin. First presented by Billy Rose at the Ziegfeld Theatre, New York, December 7, 1944, as part of the revue The Seven Lively Arts. *Alicia Markova and Anton Dolin danced the leading roles. Presented by the Sadler's Wells Ballet at the Royal Opera House, Covent Garden, London, February 11, 1948, in a new version with choreography by Frederick Ashton and scenery and costumes by André Beaurepaire. Margot Fonteyn and Michael Somes were the principal dancers.*

Stravinsky wrote the music to this ballet after the forms of the classical dance, and the work consequently has no literary meaning or plot. In the composer's words, "The parts follow each other as in a sonata or in a symphony in contrasts or similarities."

The pattern of the ballet follows the divisions of the score. *Scènes de Ballet* is danced by two soloists and a *corps de ballet* of four boys and twelve girls. Stravinsky specified different dances for the eleven parts of his score.

The brief opening fanfare heralds an introduction by the *corps de ballet,* "Moderato." Now the ballerina dances a variation to bright, quick rhythms. After a brief pantomime section, "Lento," the *pas de deux* begins. In the Sadler's Wells production, the ballerina in the adagio is supported by five men. As they support her in pirouettes at one point, she keeps turning and another partner steps in to support her. A variation for the *danseur* "Risoluto," is followed by a variation for the ballerina. During her dance, her partner kneels before her and holds his hand to his heart; the four boys recline about him. There is another brief pantomime "Andantino," a final dance by the *corps de ballet,* "Con moto," and an apotheosis. Here the music gradually mounts in grandeur; the ballerina and her partner stand together in the center of the stage, and about them the *corps de ballet* are arranged in their original tableau.

Music by Igor Stravinsky. Choreography by John Taras. First presented at the New York City Ballet's Stravinsky Festival, June 22, 1972, at the New York State Theatre, Lincoln Center, with Patricia McBride and Jean-Pierre Bonnefous in the leading roles.

Well-known in Britain in Frederick Ashton's version, *Scènes de Ballet* is not familiar enough in America and my colleague John Taras at the New York City Ballet made a new ballet to this music for our Stravinsky Festival. The dancing celebrates the beauty of the score, which was arranged originally as a showpiece for an eminent dancer and her partner.

Writing in the *Daily News* after the premiere, the critic Sam Norkin said: "Taras has devised sweeping, lyrical movement for his two soloists, Patricia McBride and Jean-Pierre Bonnefous, who danced in the lavender mood of the decor. The trumpet solo for their pas de deux was sensitively played by Theodore Weis."

SCHEHERAZADE

> *Dramatic ballet in one act. Music by Nikolai Rimsky-Korsakov. Choreography by Michel Fokine. Book by Alexandre Benois. Scenery and costumes by Léon Bakst. First presented by Diaghilev's Ballets Russes at the Théâtre National de l'Opéra, Paris, June 4, 1910, with Ida Rubinstein as Zobeide, Vaslav Nijinsky as the Favorite Slave, and Enrico Cecchetti as the Chief Eunuch. First presented in the United States by Gertrude Hoffman's Saison Russe at the Winter Garden, New York, June 14, 1911.*

Color is the dominant element in this lavish ballet, color as brilliant and resplendent as the Eastern sun—color in music and dancing, in lush decor, and in the burning passions that consume the principal characters in the story. Those who are familiar with Rimsky-Korsakov's music, which the ballet uses, know that it is an orchestral suite—program music appropriate to a series of stories told by the beautiful Scheherazade to fascinate her husband. The makers of the ballet chose to abandon the composer's musical scheme and to fashion a dance drama out of the first story in the *Arabian Nights*, a drama that would embody all the mystery, passion, and violence that all these tales contained.

The first movement of the suite, the section known as "The Sea and Sinbad's Ship," is played by the orchestra before the curtain rises. Its music insinuates an Oriental atmosphere, prognosticating the voluptuous adventure the ballet relates and intimating the excitement and deadly risks attendant upon it. The second movement begins; the curtain rises.

The scene is the great hall of an Oriental palace. Rich hangings of purple and green and orange are looped from the ceiling, creating an impression of abundant wealth that spends itself on every conceivable extravagance. On the left a purple stairway carpeted with golden cloth leads to the upper reaches of the palace. In the back there are three small blue doors decorated with silver stars. The king, Shahriar, sits upon his royal cushion. He ignores the members of his court as he turns constantly to caress Zobeide, his favorite concubine and leader of his harem.

The scene is relaxed and luxurious, the music languid. Eight girls of the harem recline lazily on multicolored cushions. Shahriar evidently wishes not to be distracted from his dalliance as he rests in the cool, open room. But his brother, Shah Zeman, who sits beside him, endeavors to engage his attention. Shahriar's chief eunuch, an obese, conniving caricature of a man, waddles before him, unctuously suggesting entertainment. Shahriar grants him permission by his silence, and the chief eunuch claps his hands. Three girls dressed in gold run out, bow to their master, and sit down together to perform a preface to their specialty. Shahriar holds Zobeide in his arms and does not notice them. The girls rise and dance sinuously. No one is amused.

The chief eunuch and several attendants assist Shahriar to rise. He is a tall man, whose costume is covered with jewels; a high gold collar surrounds his proud bearded face. His brother looks with hatred upon Zobeide, who stands beside her lord and master, her supple, yielding body scarcely disguised in transparent gauze and myriad ropes of pearls. She pleads with Shahriar for a favor. He refuses and points off into the distance. He commands a hunt in the forest. Zobeide is enraged: she has been embarrassed before the entire harem. She stalks away and flops down on a cushion, to look on with sulking defiance.

Shah Zeman, suspicious of Zobeide's fidelity to his brother, seizes upon the sudden tension between the two lovers and whispers his fears to the king. Shahriar listens. Although he is annoyed by her behavior, he disbelieves the gossip about his favorite. Shah Zeman persists, and briefly the king is a willing listener. Zobeide turns away contemptuously. The king calls over several of his attendants and gives them secret instructions. They bow and retreat.

All the girls save Zobeide rise from their cushions to bid their lord farewell and to wish him luck on the hunt. Four of the girls circle him. He protests lightly, but when four others surround him, he bends down to kiss two of the concubines. The girls dress him for the hunt. Shahriar looks over at Zobeide, enraged by her rage and by her power over him.

The chief eunuch brings in silver halberds. The trumpeting music heralds the start of the expedition. Shahriar attempts to persuade Zobeide that she has no cause for her anger. The sullen concubine resists his explanation at first, then fondly bids him farewell. All the girls kneel and hold up their hands beseechingly as Shahriar walks past them with his entourage toward the waiting expedition. Several girls wave to him. The chief eunuch exits with his master.

Now free from care and eager to enjoy their own pleasure, the harem women gather together and whisper excitedly, like schoolgirls. The light dims. They run to the back of the room and peer through the keyholes of the locked doors. They consult again and exit, bringing with them chests of jewels. One of the girls pulls in the chief eunuch, who protests helplessly. The girls surround him and, by the movement of their bodies, try to secure a favor. The eunuch refuses. All the girls circle about him, but the adamant eunuch shoos them off. One of the girls steals the big ring of keys he carries at his waist. He chases her and takes them back. The girls kneel about him, and the eunuch's resistance begins to disappear. Shall he, or shall he not? The girls see that he requires a bribe and dangle dazzling necklaces before him. The eunuch consents.

He walks to the doors at the back and unlocks one of them. Three Negro slaves dash out, like quick stallions, to their waiting lovers and throw them down upon the cushions. The second door is unlocked; three other couples are reunited in heated, reclining embraces. It is as if the girls, each momentarily out of favor with the king, are rejoicing openly in their contempt for his fickle affection as they welcome the eager advances of their secret lovers. The slaves, who so seldom gain admittance to the harem, cover their bodies with frantic kisses.

Zobeide pleads with the chief eunuch to open the third door. He turns away. Zobeide stamps and insists. The eunuch demands payment. She takes up a necklace, throws it at his feet, and now, consumed by her desire, drags him impatiently toward the door. She stands beside it in a voluptuous pose, slithering like a cat. The door opens. The favorite slave sneaks out with wary delight. He sees Zobeide; she stands breathless, her head thrown back, as he touches her body intimately. The chief eunuch exits.

The girls of the harem and their lovers abandon themselves to riotous dancing. Servant boys enter. Zobeide and the favorite writhe together on the cushions. The favorite slave springs up, and everyone watches as he throws himself into a vigorous dance. Now the entire group moves about the stage in whirling circles. The music whips their natural excitement into a frenzy of pleasure. The favorite slave holds the group fascinated with his bold leaps and assertive passion. The room becomes a whirling mass of climactic, flashing color. Zobeide and her lover are lost to each other on the king's divan. At its height, Shahriar rushes in, his scimitar raised threateningly. The hunt was but a ruse designed by his brother to expose the unfaithfulness of Zobeide.

The group rushes away from him like a receding wave. The king's men stand poised, with their swords ready to strike them down. Zobeide and the slave are so involved in their ecstasy that at first they do not notice. The slave springs up as he sees the king; Zobeide gropes back toward the corner of the stairs and tries to press her body into the wall. The slave dashes across the stage. Shah Zeman cuts him down in mid-flight, and the slave falls. His legs rear up into the air, his body refusing to die. The shah strikes again, and the slave expires. The king's soldiers chase the slaves and the concubines, killing them mercilessly at his command. The eunuch is stabbed to death.

Zobeide pleads with the king for her life as his men close in on her with their scimitars. He orders them aside and the repentant woman kisses his hand. The king pulls his hand away. Zobeide reminds him of his devotion to her and her faithfulness to him. For a moment Shahriar believes her and is fascinated again by her loveliness. He embraces her and kisses her. As he raises his eyes, his brother kicks viciously at the body of Zobeide's secret lover and reminds him of her betrayal. He pushes her away. He hesitates. He does not wish to kill the woman he loves, despite her infidelity, for her repentance ap-

pears so genuine, but his kingly honor demands that a price be paid for his
abused pride. He stands irresolute. His cohorts move toward Zobeide. Before
they reach her, she pulls out a dagger and stabs herself in the belly. Her body
doubles up over her arm. She is dead. The men drop their swords. Shahriar
raises his arms in despair and weeps over her. His pride seems as nothing compared to his lost love.

NOTES *Scheherazade,* the work that popularly identified the "new Russian
Ballet" in the early days of Diaghilev's Ballets Russes, has managed to be in the
active repertory of one company or another ever since. Its initial fame is understandable when we recall that its subject matter was new to its first audiences and when we remember its principal dancers. Tamara Karsavina soon
took over the role of Zobeide, while Nijinsky continued in the part of the favorite slave. Carl Van Vechten wrote that "Karsavina's *Zobeide* is a suggestive
picture of languorous lust, and Nijinsky, as the principal slave, alternates between surprising leaps into the air and the most lascivious gestures; like some
animal, he paws the reclining Sultana." The librettist of the ballet, Alexandre
Benois, wrote that Ida Rubinstein was "absolutely inimitable . . . in her
proud, cunning and unrestrained passion" and that Nijinsky as the favorite
slave was "half-cat, half-snake, fiendishly agile, feminine and yet wholly terrifying."

What has happened to *Scheherazade* since, is best reflected in a review by
Edwin Denby in the New York *Herald Tribune:* "Seen on a ballet program
today, *Scheherazade* . . . is an illustrious warhorse foundering in dishonor.
Not that there isn't some kind of life left in the old girl. The bundling and the
clinches are still fine for laughs and whistles and cries of 'Take it off' . . . A
great many people register sex all over the stage with an earnestness that is
disarming rather than embarrassing. But one wonders what *Scheherazade*
looked like when it scandalized our parents or when Parisians swooned at the
lushness of it in 1910. In the 1910 photographs the slave girls look soft and
abandoned. Nijinsky bounded about them like a panther in thrilling spasms
that grew to a paroxysm of death at the climax. Bakst the great decorator—the
Berman of his day—dazzled the public by the sensual shock of the brilliant
decor. And the 'slavic harmonies' of Rimsky's score dunked the orgy on the
stage in a bath of gold.

"Nowadays the small orchestra, the clumsily executed decor, the earnest but
overworked dancers can't create any sense of abandon. The trouble is that
there is no dance form, nothing for them to do as dancers. There is only miming and hubbub, and that doesn't keep for thirty years. A dance ballet can
keep fresh because of its form, because arms and legs stay arms and legs; but
when the dancers have to pretend to be something they aren't, a ballet disintegrates into a charade."

The first production of *Scheherazade* in the United States was not rehearsed
by Fokine and not authorized by him. It remained for Diaghilev's Ballets

Russes to present the first authentic version in this country, January 17, 1916, at the Century Theatre, New York. Nijinsky danced *Scheherazade* with Diaghilev's company for the first time in the United States on April 15, 1916, at the Metropolitan Opera House.

SCHERZO À LA RUSSE

Music by Igor Stravinsky. Choreography by George Balanchine. Costumes by Karinska. First presented by the New York City Ballet at the Stravinsky Festival, June 21, 1972, at the New York State Theatre, Lincoln Center, New York, with Karin von Aroldingen and Kay Mazzo in leading roles.

This is a lovely piece of music by Stravinsky that he originally composed for a movie in Hollywood but was never used. It lasts about five minutes but it is a charming, accurate evocation of an old Russian dance, and I liked very much arranging it for two girls and their girl friends in our Stravinsky Festival. It is certainly a Russian dance, as I recall such things from my childhood and my training in ballet there, but I do not mean the piece as any kind of sentimental gesture to the past. All of my dances to Stravinsky music are reflections of what he and I, together, might have done. My luck was that our working together lasted so long.

SCHERZO FANTASTIQUE

Music by Igor Stravinsky. Choreography by Jerome Robbins. First presented at the New York City Ballet's Stravinsky Festival, at the New York State Theatre, Lincoln Center, June 18, 1972, with Gelsey Kirkland, Bart Cook, Victor Castelli, Bryan Pitts, and Stephen Caras. Conducted by Robert Irving.

At the beginning of our Stravinsky Festival at the New York State Theatre—the festival that celebrated the ninetieth birthday of the composer, who had died the previous year—I said that without music there can be no dance and that Stravinsky, more than any other composer, created music for dancers. The *Scherzo Fantastique*, an early work, first performed in 1909, gives us an idea not only of what the young composer most admired in those days but an idea of what he was to become. It is a piece for large orchestra lasting about sixteen minutes. The impresario Diaghilev heard the first performance, and it was this piece, and *Fireworks*, that interested him in the possibility of Stravinsky's composing music for ballet.

Jerome Robbins arranged to *Scherzo Fantastique* a dance for a girl and four boys, an exuberant work with no narrative that reflected the youth and brio of the score.

Writing about it in the *Daily News*, Sam Norkin said that "the ballet is appropriately swift and buoyant. The dancers spend most of their time spinning aloft, conceding to gravity only grudgingly. Gelsey Kirkland in filmy yellow was a delightful sprite in counterpoint to the men in the cast.

SCHERZO FOR MASSAH JACK

> *Music by Charles Ives. Choreography by Lar Lubovitch. Costume consultant, John Dayger. Lighting consultant, Beverly Emmons. First presented by American Ballet Theatre at the City Center, New York, January 17, 1973, with Daniel Levans, Ruth Mayer, Keith Lee, Bonnie Mathis, William Carter, Christine Sarry, and Ian Horvath in the leading roles. Assistant to Mr. Lubovitch: Ernest Pagano. Violin: Alexander Horvath. Piano: Howard Baer.*

An impressionistic dramatic dance about the Old South, *Scherzo for Massah Jack* presents and comments on aspects of antebellum plantation mythology and reality. The choreographer, Lar Lubovitch, describes his ballet as "a pure dance piece to illuminate the music of Charles Ives." The ballet develops its themes much as Ives developed the music for his *Trio*—by exploiting the variations possible on old American tunes and hymns. What Ives does with the song "My Old Kentucky Home" is similar to the choreographer's idea to probe and reveal new aspects of the familiar—here the pathos, absurdity, and tragedy of a familiar racist drama.

SCHUBERTIADE

> *Music by Franz Schubert. Choreography by Michael Smuin. First presented by American Ballet Theatre at the City Center, New York, January 1, 1971, with Paula Tracy and Vane Vest, Cynthia Gregory and Gayle Young, Sallie Wilson and Marcos Paredes, Diana Weber and John Prinz, and Eleanor D'Antuono as principal dancers.*

A pianist plays Schubert waltzes and *Ländler* on stage for this dance ballet, named for what the Viennese call a Schubertiade—a civilized time at home for friends and family with fine music to play and dance to. And there is an intimate family atmosphere to the ballet, where children are present, too. Relationships between persons at the party become apparent as we go along; there is a sense of competitiveness among the boys, the girls are eager to outdress their peers, and it is clear how a number of the young couples feel about each other.

Writing in *Dance and Dancers* magazine, Patricia Barnes said that in
Schubertiade "a mood is created and there is enough variety in the dancing to
keep one's attention happily engaged. Diana Weber and John Prinz, in particular, have been given some of the most attractive choreography in the ballet.
The brief, playful *pas de deux* was a delight and Prinz's virtuoso solo later on
demonstrated his buoyance and excellent beats to fine effect. Weber, a meticulously precise young dancer, improves all the time . . . and it was nice to see
Terry Orr, dashing and elegant, in another well-constructed male solo. Smuin,
himself a brilliant dancer, really knows how to choreograph for men. Among
the rest, Cynthia Gregory, Eleanor D'Antuono, Paula Tracy, Sallie Wilson and
Gayle Young stood out, and at a later performance I was also impressed with
the charm and delicacy of Karena Brock replacing D'Antuono."

SCHUMANN CONCERTO

*Ballet in three movements. Choreographic concerto by Bronislava Nijinska.
Music by Robert Schumann* (Piano Concerto in A minor). *Scenery and
costumes by Stewart Chaney. First presented by Ballet Theatre at the Metropolitan Opera House, New York, September 27, 1951, with a cast headed
by Alicia Alonso and Igor Youskevitch.*

The romantic mood of Schumann's music is the inspiration for this abstract
ballet. Two central figures represent the romantic center of the ballet, and
above this couple a *corps de ballet* of boys and girls dance as a background.
The setting is romantic, too. Three gray stone arches draped with red cloth
frame a backdrop that depicts a high, desolate cliff.

FIRST MOVEMENT: ALLEGRO AFFETTUOSO   When the curtain rises, after a
long musical introduction, we see on stage the ballerina, who stands in an attitude of wistfulness. She is dressed all in white, in full romantic costume. To
the right is her lover, who holds out his arms to her longingly. The couple and
the small group of girls who stand to either side of them begin to dance. What
they dance has no plot in any usual sense; they exit and re-enter, not continuing a pattern they have started, but simply dancing along with the dynamics
of the music. The piano in the concerto represents no one in particular. When
the music becomes vigorous, groups of boys cross the stage in high leaps. The
premier danseur dances with one of these groups and exits. The ballerina now
performs a variation. Her partner returns to watch as she circles the stage with
rapid turns. They leave the stage to the *corps de ballet* briefly. The music becomes quiet; six of the girls form a tableau. The ballerina rejoins them, still
turning, to the accompaniment of soft trills of the piano. Three of the boys lift
her high, carry her around the stage and off into the wings. She and her part-

ner return, as the last chords of the first movement begin, and join the *corps de ballet* to dance its final measures.

SECOND MOVEMENT: INTERMEZZO The light dims. Eight girls in rust-color skirts covered with black net join other girls dressed in softly tinted dresses to form a backdrop for a *pas de deux* between the ballerina and her partner. Alternately, with the rhythm of the music, the *premier danseur* supports the ballerina in swift pirouettes that stop sharply with the music's hesitation and high lifts that end, again, with pirouettes. As the dance progresses, the ballerina turns more and more rapidly; her white dress seems to be in a perpetual whirl about her moving figure.

THIRD MOVEMENT: ALLEGRO VIVACE The scene brightens, and a new backdrop reveals in the distance ancient ruins, overrun with moss and weeds and grass. A luminous yellow sun in a cloudless sky shines down on the nostalgic vista. The ballerina and her partner return. Three boys go to the front of the stage and recline to watch the ballerina dance. Soon they rise and, with a second group of men, stand at either side of the stage as the ballerina moves across it. She leaves the scene now to her partner, who dances brilliantly down a diagonal formed by the male *corps de ballet*. All the girls come back and reform a tableau, as the two principals dominate the scene. The ballerina encircles her lover with accelerated terms; he spins in the air, as the music reaches a crescendo of joyousness, and carries her off into the wings. The different units of the *corps de ballet* fill the stage with movement until the principals join in for the finale. The curtain falls as the ballerina is lifted high above the group. Her lover stands facing us with outstretched arms.

SCOTCH SYMPHONY

Classic ballet in three parts. Music by Felix Mendelssohn. Choreography by George Balanchine. Scenery by Horace Armistead. Costumes by Karinska and David Ffolkes. Lighting by Jean Rosenthal. First presented by the New York City Ballet at the City Center, New York, November 11, 1952, with Maria Tallchief, André Eglevsky, Patricia Wilde, Frank Hobi, and Michael Maule in the principal roles.

When the New York City Ballet appeared at the Edinburgh Festival in August 1952, I had my first opportunity to see the great massed demonstration of parade units from the Scottish regiments in the famous nocturnal Military Tattoo. I greatly enjoyed this spectacle, as I also enjoyed seeing Scotland as a whole. It occurred to me that when my company returned to New York, we might do a Scottish ballet. Scotland, after all, was the scene of the first great romantic ballet, *La Sylphide,* and a new ballet might well recollect this fact as it also remounted dances in the Scottish manner. Mendelssohn, too, had written his *Scotch Symphony,* and this music seemed to me appropriate for the idea I had in mind.

Back in New York, we decided to do the ballet *Scotch Symphony* almost immediately, omitting the first movement of Mendelssohn's score, which is not appropriate for dance.

In the first movement of the ballet there are general dances by the ensemble, all in appropriate Scottish costume: there is a *pas de trois* by a girl and two boys, and there are solo passages for the girl.

The second movement is an adagio for a ballerina and her partner that represents, without a story, the general mood and atmosphere of the romantic ballet as epitomized in such ballets as *La Sylphide.*

The third movement is again an ensemble, in which the ballerina and her partner participate with *pas de deux* and variation, joining the soloists and *corps de ballet* in a finale.

SEA CHANGE

Music by Benjamin Britten. Choreography by Alvin Ailey. First presented by American Ballet Theatre at the Opera House, Kennedy Center for the Performing Arts, Washington, D.C., October 26, 1972, with Sallie Wilson and Royes Fernandez as principals.

A dramatic dance for a girl and her drowned lover, *Sea Change* is introduced with two notes in the program: "Love transcends all bounds—including death," and a lyric from *The Tempest:*

Full fathom five thy father lies;
Of his bones are coral made;
Those are pearls that were his eyes;
Nothing of him that doth fade,
But doth suffer a sea-change
Into something rich and strange . . .

The action is divided into four parts, corresponding to the music of Benjamin Britten's *Four Sea Interludes* from *Peter Grimes,* the ballet's score.

In the first part, *Dawn,* the death of a fisherman at sea is mourned by his friends. In *Sunday Morning,* a girl, the dead man's wife, remote and detached, dances midst a vigorous dance by the young men of the village. In *Moonlight,* her love for the lost mariner is recapitulated as we see them dance together. In the final *Storm,* love appears to transcend death and the lovers are reunited.

The late John Cranko also made a ballet called *Sea Change.* Set to music by Sibelius, with scenery and costumes by John Piper and presented first by the

Sadler's Wells Theatre Ballet at the Gaiety Theatre, Dublin, Ireland, January 18, 1949, the ballet told the story of another village situation. A ship goes to sea, there is a storm and all but one of the men return. While the villagers rejoice in their deliverance, the wife of the lost seaman, a young bride, interrupts the scene in a wild outpouring of grief. At the end, she scans the horizon in quiet despair. The critic Clive Barnes has called *Sea Change* "John Cranko's first major ballet."

SEA SHADOW

Music by Michael Colgrass. Choreography by Gerald Arpino. Setting by Ming Cho Lee. First presented by the Robert Joffrey Ballet at the Delacorte Theatre, Central Park, New York, September 5, 1963, with Lisa Bradley and Paul Sutherland. Music for the first performance was a movement of Ravel's Concerto in G for Piano and Orchestra.

Called "a poem-in-dance," *Sea Shadow* is a dramatic *pas de deux* in which a sprite from the sea visits a dreaming boy on a beach. The ballet might be called a modern treatment of the Ondine theme, for attracted as the boy is by the sea sprite, it becomes clear that she will lead him not only to happiness but also to his death. In a mesmeric, underwater rhythm, the dance is performed to a score by the contemporary composer Michael Colgrass. The critic Walter Terry has called *Sea Shadow* "one of the most beautiful duets in all ballet."

THE SEASONS

Music by Alexander Glazunov. Choreography by Marius Petipa. First presented at the Hermitage Theatre, St. Petersburg, February 7, 1900. First presented by the Stuttgart Ballet, in a production by John Cranko, at the Württemberg State Theatre, Stuttgart, June 15, 1962. Completely revised by Mr. Cranko in a new version which was first presented in the United States at the Metropolitan Opera House, New York, April 30, 1971.

While the first ballet to Glazunov's great score (one that is more familiar, from excerpts we know, than we suspect) included four danced tableaux of the seasons and an apotheosis, John Cranko's production also makes of the work a major opportunity for a reigning ballerina. He provides her with no less than three of the seasons—Winter, Summer, and Autumn. (Spring is led by two girls.) Each of these parts of the ballet is supported by soloists and *corps de ballet*, but the emphasis is on personal virtuosity and dance display. Summer and Autumn are both *pas de deux*, the latter rivaling the former in exuberance.

When *The Seasons* was first presented in America, Clive Barnes wrote in the New York *Times* that "Cranko has never choreographed with more authority. . . . The dancing has a range, scope and sheer bigness that have to be associated with the Bolshoi Ballet and nothing else. . . . Cranko's pure dance choreography has more vigor than it ever had. . . . The dancing is the best the Stuttgart has ever given us."

SEBASTIAN

Ballet in one act and three scenes. Music and libretto by Gian-Carlo Menotti. Choreography by Edward Caton. Scenery by Oliver Smith. Costumes by Milena. First presented by Ballet International at the International Theatre, New York, October 31, 1944, with Francisco Moncion in the title role. Restaged with new choreography by Agnes de Mille for American Ballet Theatre, May 27, 1957, with Lupe Serrano and John Kriza in principal roles. Restaged with new choreography by John Butler for the Netherlands Dance Theatre, Amsterdam, Autumn 1963, and introduced to the United States in 1966 by the Harkness Ballet, with Brunilda Ruiz, Lawrence Rhodes, Roderick Drew, Hester Fitzgerald, and Sarah Thomas in principal roles. Scenery and costumes by Jacques Noel, lighting by Nicholas Cernovich.

This dramatic ballet is set in Venice at the end of the seventeenth century. The prince, in love with a notorious courtesan, has two possessive sisters who wish to break up the affair. They steal her veil, knowing that its possession will enable them to exercise black magic over her. Constructing a wax image of the courtesan, they cover it with her veil and plan to kill her by piercing the image with arrows. But the Moorish slave Sebastian, who has loved the courtesan, substitutes himself for the wax figure and takes the deadly arrows. By his self-sacrifice, he breaks the evil power, reuniting the prince with his beloved.

SECRET PLACES

Music by Wolfgang Amadeus Mozart. Choreography by Gerald Arpino. Setting by Ming Cho Lee. Lighting by Thomas Skelton. Pianist: Stanley Babin. Dedicated in living memory of Lorraine Squadron. First presented by the City Center Joffrey Ballet at the City Center, New York, February 20, 1968, with Lisa Bradley and Dermot Burke.

A dance for two young lovers, *Secret Places* is performed to the second movement of Mozart's *Piano Concerto No. 21 in C Major* (K. 467). The dance begins in silence. The curtain rises on a dark woodland scene where the rays of the sun barely penetrate. On the left stand three golden trees. A girl enters.

She walks through the glade, touches gently one of the trees, then goes. A boy comes from the opposite direction, looks about, leaves. The girl returns but this time as she starts to go her walk speeds up and becomes almost a dance step. Similarly with the boy; and as the two go and return yet again, just missing an encounter, their steps accelerate in speed and intensity so that there is an urgency in the air. Finally, as she leaps backward into the air, the boy is there to catch her, she is safe, they are together and the dance, with the music, begins.

Thoughtful and introspective with the score, the dance mirrors quiet joy, cautious discovery, exultation, and celebration of first love. At the end, the boy holds the girl high, she descends in a graceful pose, and they walk off into the forest.

SEPHARDIC SONG

Traditional music arranged by Manuel Valls. Choreography by Eliot Feld. Setting and costumes by Santo Loquasto. Lighting by Jennifer Tipton. First presented by the Eliot Feld Ballet at the New York Shakespeare Public Theatre, May 30, 1974, with Naomi Sorkin, George Montalbana, Suzanne Erlon, Valerie Felt, and Elizabeth Lee. Flute, Paul Dunkel; guitar, Fred Hand; soprano, Meria Sargon.

This is a dance ballet performed to Iberian Jewish songs that are sung at the side of the stage. There is an atmosphere and feeling of the nearby sea in ropes or nets that are set against a sunset in the background. The persons who inhabit the ballet seem to be fisherfolk. There are different combinations. Four girls begin the piece, weaving in and out in a kind of chain to the songs that are being sung. Wives of fishermen at sea, they await their return. Later, one comes—or is he a lover?—to dance with one of the girls. The idea appears to be that everyone here is beloved—a friend, perhaps a lover—at any event all united and unafraid.

Reviewing the ballet for *Dance News*, the critic Nancy Goldner wrote: "This is one of those deceptively simple ballets, in which dancers 'just dance' . . . Feld has really caught the essence of lament because he discovers its neutrality—neither sad nor happy, but a mixture; in short, lyrical. As such it is a profound embodiment of the music, traditional Spanish songs, with their tantalizing off-key Flamenco mode."

In 1975 a new setting by Ming Cho Lee and costumes by Stanley Simmons replaced the first designs.

SERENADE

Classic ballet in four parts. Music by Peter Ilyich Tchaikovsky. Choreography by George Balanchine. Costumes by Jean Lurçat. First presented by

*students of the School of American Ballet at the estate of Felix M. Warburg,
White Plains, New York, June 9, 1934. Presented by the producing company of the School of American Ballet at the Avery Memorial Theatre, Hartford, Connecticut, December 6, 1934, with Kathryn Mullowney, Heidi
Vossler, and Charles Laskey in the principal roles.*

Named after its music—Tchaikovsky's *Serenade in C major for String Orchestra*—*Serenade* tells its story musically and choreographically, without any extraneous narrative. Because Tchaikovsky's score, though it was not composed
for the ballet, has in its danceable four movements different qualities suggestive of different emotions and human situations, parts of the ballet seem to
have a story: the apparently "pure" dance takes on a kind of plot. But this
plot, inherent in the score, contains many stories—it is many things to many listeners to the music, and many things to many people who see the ballet.

Most people would agree that a nonprogrammatic piece of music doesn't
have to have a story to be a pleasure: we enjoy symphonies by Tchaikovsky
and Mozart just as much as we enjoy a symphony with a story, such as Beethoven's *Pastorale*. *Serenade* is programmatic only insofar as its music is
programmatic.

To tell a story about something is simply a very human way of saying that
we understand it. Making a ballet is a choreographer's way of showing how he
understands a piece of music, not in words, not in narrative form (unless he
has in mind a particular story), but in dancing.

The four movements of Tchaikovsky's score are danced in the following
order, without interruption: (1) Piece in the Form of a Sonatina: *Andante non
troppo, Allegro;* (2) Waltz; (3) Tema Russo: *Andante, Allegro con spirito;* (4)
Elegy. Twenty-eight dancers in blue costumes dance the ballet before a blue
background.

FIRST MOVEMENT   The orchestra plays the strong and spacious opening
chords of the brief Andante section and repeats them deeply before the curtain
rises. When we see the stage, a group of girls stand in a tableau of crossing
lines. It is night. The shadowed light that shines upon them is soft. They are
motionless at first, then respond to the music as the light brightens and the
new melodious Allegro is heard.

The girls dance in small groups, forming patterns on the stage. One girl
dances alone, turning, posing, leaping among the others. Others seem to imitate her originality, but then all are whirling faster and faster in a wide circle
together. Suddenly, quickly, each girl stands motionless in the same tableau
that opened the ballet, and the familiar chords of the introductory Andante are
repeated.

One girl comes in late. She finds her place in the group and stands with the
other girls. A boy enters at the back of the stage. As he walks forward toward the girl, her friends leave the stage.

SECOND MOVEMENT   A waltz begins as the boy reaches the girl. They begin to dance together, the girl moving away from him, then rejoining him. When her friends re-enter, the girl dances joyously among them; then she and her partner lead them in a dance, the boy lifting the ballerina high in front of the group. The waltz slowly and softly ends, and the group walks off to the tempo of its concluding rhythms.

THIRD MOVEMENT (the fourth movement in the original suite)   Five girls remain on stage. They sit together on the stage as the music is quiet, turning toward each other in gentle movements. They rise and, at the first sound of the brilliant Russian melody, respond immediately and dance with open gaiety. A boy rushes on and meets a girl; they dance together; and when the ensemble runs off, as the music finishes, we see that the girl has fallen to the floor, her head buried in her arms. She is alone.

FOURTH MOVEMENT   Another girl brings a boy to her. This girl walks behind the boy, guiding him forward: it is as if she moved him, as if he saw only what she wished. When they reach the fallen girl, the boy helps her to rise and now dances with the two of them. He remains with them, dancing with one of them alone, then both together, until there comes a time when he must choose. The girl who possessed him first, the girl who brought him to the other, claims him irrevocably and he leaves with her. The forsaken heroine collapses, revives briefly, and then is lost. Three boys lift her straight up above their shoulders. Her body arches back slowly as they carry her forward in a quiet procession; her arms open wide.

NOTES   *Serenade* was my first ballet in the United States. Soon after my arrival in America, Lincoln Kirstein, Edward M. M. Warburg, and I opened the School of American Ballet in New York. As part of the school curriculum, I started an evening ballet class in stage technique, to give students some idea of how dancing on stage differs from classwork. *Serenade* evolved from the lessons I gave.

It seemed to me that the best way to make students aware of stage technique was to give them something new to dance, something they had never seen before. I chose Tchaikovsky's *Serenade* to work with. The class contained, the first night, seventeen girls and no boys. The problem was, how to arrange this odd number of girls so that they would look interesting. I placed them on diagonal lines and decided that the hands should move first to give the girls practice.

That was how *Serenade* began. The next class contained only nine girls; the third, six. I choreographed to the music with the pupils I happened to have at a particular time. Boys began to attend the class and they were worked into the pattern. One day, when all the girls rushed off the floor area we were using as a stage, one of the girls fell and began to cry. I told the pianist to keep on playing and kept this bit in the dance. Another day, one of the girls was late for class, so I left that in too.

Later, when we staged *Serenade*, everything was revised. The girls who couldn't dance well were left out of the more difficult parts; I elaborated on the small accidental bits I had included in class and made the whole more dramatic, more theatrical, synchronizing it to the music with additional movement, but always using the little things that ordinarily might be overlooked.

I've gone into a little detail here about *Serenade* because many people think there is a concealed story in the ballet. There is not. There are, simply, dancers in motion to a beautiful piece of music. The only story is the music's story, a serenade, a dance, if you like, in the light of the moon.

Serenade has seen a number of different productions. It was produced by the American Ballet, the company made up of our dancers at the School of American Ballet, in its first season, at the Adelphi Theatre, New York, March 1–15, 1935. It was staged for the Ballet Russe de Monte Carlo, October 17, 1940, at the Metropolitan Opera House, with costumes by Lurçat and a cast headed by Marie-Jeanne, Igor Youskevitch, and Frederic Franklin. In 1941 *Serenade* was mounted for the South American tour of the American Ballet Caravan in a new production with costumes by Alvin Colt. In 1947 it was staged for the ballet of the Paris Opéra. On October 18, 1948, *Serenade* became part of the permanent repertory of the New York City Ballet. This production has costumes by Karinska.

The leading role in *Serenade* was first danced by a group of soloists, rather than by one principal dancer. In a number of productions, however, I arranged it for one dancer. But when the New York City Ballet was to make its first appearance in London, at the Royal Opera House, Covent Garden, in the summer of 1950, it seemed appropriate to introduce the company by introducing its principal dancers and the leading role was again divided and danced by our leading soloists.

Serenade is now danced by many ballet companies in the United States and abroad. A few years ago I finally succeeded in expanding the ballet so that it now uses all of the score of the Tchaikovsky "Serenade for Strings," something I had wanted to do for a long time. The interesting thing is that while some knowing members of the audience noticed this change and spoke to me about it, the critics didn't seem to notice at all! Perhaps they had seen the ballet too often!

Serenade was danced by students of the School of American Ballet at their annual program in 1974, at the Juilliard Theater, Lincoln Center, New York.

Don Daniels has written a long essay, "Academy: the New World of *Serenade*," in *Ballet Review* (Vol. 5, No. 1, 1975–76).

SERENADE IN A

Music by Igor Stravinsky. Choreography by Todd Bolender. Costumes by Stanley Simmons. Pianist: Madeleine Malraux. First presented at the New York City Ballet's Stravinsky Festival, June 21, 1972, at the New York State Theatre, Lincoln Center, with Susan Hendl, Robert Maiorano, Robert Weiss, and ensemble.

Stravinsky's *Sonata in A for Piano* is dated 1925 and lasts twelve minutes—just long enough for each of the four movements to fill one side of a ten-inch recording in those days. Stravinsky never resented specifics about time. When we were working on new ballets together he always wanted to know precisely how long a particular dance or *pas d'action* would last, so that his music would be a perfect fit.

Todd Bolender arranged a dance ballet to the *Sonata* for our Stravinsky Festival. There are four movements—*Hymne, Romanza, Rondoletto,* and *Cadenza Finale.*

Writing after the premiere in the New York *Post,* the critic Frances Herridge said that "the solos and duets are lovely. The movement is softly romantic and stunningly danced by the long-legged Susan Hendl in one of her most important roles to date."

The New York City Ballet was fortunate to have the French pianist Madeleine Malraux play the music on this occasion.

THE SEVEN DEADLY SINS

Music by Kurt Weill. Choreography by George Balanchine. Libretto by Bertolt Brecht. First presented by Les Ballets 1933 at the Théâtre de Champs-Élysées, Paris, June 7, 1933, with Lotte Lenya and Tilly Losch in the leading roles. First presented in the United States by the New York City Ballet at the City Center, New York, December 4, 1958, with Lotte Lenya and Allegra Kent in the leading roles. Translation by W. H. Auden and Chester Kallman. Scenery and costumes by Rouben Ter-Arutunian.

This is a ballet in song and dance about the seven deadly sins—sloth, pride, anger, gluttony, lust, avarice, and envy. The words and music were commissioned by Les Ballets 1933, for which I did the choreography. Twenty-five years later, when the New York City Ballet was about to celebrate its tenth anniversary at the City Center, Lincoln Kirstein, who had seen the original production, suggested that it might be revived.

Kurt Weill's Three-Penny Opera had been playing to full houses in New York for some years and the time seemed to be ripe for presentation of another important Weill-Brecht collaboration. When Lotte Lenya consented to participate and to sing the leading role again, I knew we would indeed have to do it.

I did not remember many details of the original production, which had been performed for only a few weeks in 1933, but working with Weill's score and the libretto, a great deal came back to me. Rouben Ter-Arutunian's setting and costumes were immensely helpful in making the work unified.

The ballet is the story of two Annies, a singing Annie who narrates the progress of a silent dancing Annie in her search for enough money to build a home for her family back in Louisiana. Annie travels to seven American cities, in each of which she encounters a sin. Annie I is the experienced alter ego of the innocent Annie II. Sings Annie I

"She's the one with the looks, I'm realistic;
She's just a little mad, my head is on straight.
You may think you can see two people,
But in fact you see only one
And both of us are Annie."

At the beginning, we see Annie's family gathered under a fringed lampshade, lamenting Annie's indolence. They call her "Lazy Bones," ask her to "think of us" and to send money for the "little home down by the Mississippi." In Scene 1, "Sloth," Annie I photographs Annie II compromising innocent passers-by for blackmail.

In Scene 2, "Pride," Annie works as a cabaret dancer in Memphis and talks about art, which Annie I deprecates. Speaking for Annie's family, she explains that

"When a man has paid for his evening,
He expects a good show in return . . .
Leave your pride to those who can well afford it . . ."

In Scene 3, "Anger," Annie is in Los Angeles working as a movie extra. While she is sickened at the cruelty she sees there, Annie I sings that "open disapproval of injustice is widely disapproved," and that "Unforgiving anger is from the Devil."

Scene 4, "Gluttony," takes place in Philadelphia, where Annie II does well as an acrobatic dancer. Because of her career, however, she must diet heavily. "Gluttons," sing the family, "never go to heaven."

Scene 5 is in Boston, where Annie is loved by a wealthy man but loves another. The singing Annie persuades her that love for love's sake is nothing but "Lust."

In Scene 6, "Envy," in San Francisco, Annie II envies others while Annie I sings:

"Don't let the flesh and its longings get you,
Remember the price a lover must pay,
And say to yourself when temptation besets you—

What is the use?
What is the use?
Beauty will perish and youth pass away."

Scene 7, "Avarice," sung by the family, shows Annie set up in Baltimore:

"She must be doing all right
And raking it in
To get in the news like that . . ."

After the seven years and the seven cities and the seven sins, the two Annies return to the little house in Louisiana. The family sings:

"Who fights the Good Fight and all Self subdues
Wins the Palm, gains the Crown."

SHADOW OF THE WIND

Ballet in six parts. Music by Gustav Mahler. Choreography by Antony Tudor. Scenery and costumes by Jo Mielziner. First presented by Ballet Theatre at the Metropolitan Opera House, New York, April 14, 1948, with Igor Youskevitch, Hugh Laing, Dimitri Romanoff, Alicia Alonso, John Kriza, Mary Burr, Ruth Ann Koesun, Crandall Diehl, Diana Adams, Nana Gollner, Muriel Bentley, and Barbara Fallis in principal roles.

Shadow of the Wind is based on Mahler's *Song of the Earth*, a symphony for alto and tenor with orchestra. The critic Alfred Meyer has observed of this song cycle which is based on ancient Chinese texts: "It is not the earth that sings, and the poems deal less with the aspects of nature than with the philosophy of human existence."* The choreographer has said that his ballet symbolizes the impermanence of existence, the Chinese philosophy of accepting the mutations of life and bowing before them. Like the seasons, human experience is cyclical and has no sudden beginning or end.

In keeping with his interpretation of the score, the setting for Tudor's ballet is also Chinese. To the first song for solo tenor, "The Drinking Song of Earthly Woe," five men, one an old poet, another an old warrior, dance to the words: "O man, what is the span of thy life?/Not a hundred years art thou permitted to enjoy/The vanities of this earth!" The second song, for alto, about loneliness in autumn and the passing of life, is transposed in dance terms to be a presentation of an abandoned wife: "Autumn in my heart too long is lasting. O sun

* See THE SONG OF THE EARTH, page 560.

of love, never again wilt thou shine to dry my bitter tears?" The tenor's song of
youth describes a pretty Chinese landscape with a green and white porcelain
pavilion in a little pool that is reached by a bridge of jade. "My Lord Summons Me" is the name of the dance for a girl, a boy, and the ensemble. "The
Lotus Gatherers" is the title of the next section, which is performed by a girl
and the ensemble to a contralto solo about beauty, where youthful maidens
pluck lotus flowers at the shore, where lovers play at longing. The fifth part,
"Conversation with Winepot and Bird," is accompanied by the tenor lament
that all life is woeful and wine the only reality. The final dance, "Poem of the
Guitar," is performed to Mahler's "Farewell" for contralto: the poet waits for
his friend for a last farewell but looks to the coming spring to waken the world
anew.

SHADOWPLAY

*Music by Charles Koechlin. Choreography by Antony Tudor. Scenery and
costumes by Michael Annals. First presented by the Royal Ballet at the
Royal Opera House, Covent Garden, January 25, 1967, with Anthony Dowell, Merle Park, and Derek Rencher in the principal roles. First presented
in the United States by the Royal Ballet at the new Metropolitan Opera
House, May 2, 1967, with the same principals.*

Shadowplay is an allegory about growing up. The scene is the jungle, where a
Boy with Matted Hair sits alone. Creatures from the jungle world surround
him and although he would prefer to be alone, he sees that he cannot remain
passive to relationships. "Arboreals and Aerials"—monkeys and bright birds—
come and then a dominating male figure called "Terrestrial" confronts the boy.
He will not, however, submit to his will. The boy is then drawn to a "Celestial" figure, a beautiful goddess whose remoteness enchants him, but again
masters his feelings after two close encounters. He is now a different person
and his air of authority as he sits alone in the jungle affects the animals, too,
who ape his civilized gestures and would copy his example. Then instinctively
he copies theirs and scratches himself; the end is something like the beginning.
   Shadowplay is set to music by the French composer Charles Koechlin
(1867–1950), who wrote seven orchestral works on themes drawn from *The
Jungle Book* by Rudyard Kipling. The score of the ballet consists of the last of
these, *Les Bandar-Log*, and selections from *La Course de Printemps*. The
ballet uses *The Jungle Book* situation as a point of departure for larger
allegory. The critic Clive Barnes wrote after its New York *première* that the
ballet "has as many meanings as an onion has layers, but basically it seems to
be about the realms of experience and the attainment of grace . . . Tudor has
produced a strange and engrossing work, a ballet that even at first glance has
the look and feel of a major work."

Shadowplay was presented by American Ballet Theatre in 1975 for Mikhail Baryshnikov.

SHÉHÉRAZADE

Music by Maurice Ravel. Choreography by George Balanchine. Lighting by Ronald Bates. First presented by the New York City Ballet at the Hommage à Ravel at the New York State Theatre, Lincoln Center, May 22, 1975, with Kay Mazzo and Edward Villella as principals. Conducted by Robert Irving.

Our plans for the Ravel Festival at the New York City Ballet were well advanced when I decided that I wished to add yet another work. *Shéhérazade* was Ravel's first piece composed for orchestra and one of his first works to be performed in public. His friend Tristan Klingsor, the painter and poet, had told Ravel tales of his travels in the East and the composer, attracted since his childhood to the exotic, the mysterious and fantastic, began work on an elaborate conception of an opera based on Galland's *A Thousand and One Nights*. He actually only finished the *Overture*, which is used for this ballet. Later, Ravel set three of Klingsor's poems as a song cycle, for yet another version of *Shéhérazade*.

The ballet's action is simple to describe—it is a dance for a girl and boy accompanied by two couples and eight girls. If it all seems to take place in another world remote from the present time, well, that is a way of thinking of Shéhérazade and the tales she told.

SINFONIETTA

Music by Malcolm Williamson. Choreography by Frederick Ashton. Costumes by Peter Rice. First presented by the Royal Ballet at the Royal Shakespeare Theater, Stratford-on-Avon, February 10, 1967, with Doreen Wells and David Wall in principal roles.

Sinfonietta is a modern ballet with new music by one of England's leading young composers and a new design idea conceived by one of Britain's art colleges. Against the backdrop on stage moving shapes and light patterns are projected to accompany the dances. There is no story.

The ballet, like the music, is in three parts: toccata, elegy, and tarantella. The first is arranged for two couples, the second for a girl and five boys. This part, the elegy, has been called by the English critic Andrew Porter a "new Rose Adagio in a marvelous modern idiom." Here the girl is held and carried so that she seems never to touch the ground. The final movement is a brisk and gay tarantella for the ensemble from which one of the boys darts in and out to perform brilliant and challenging variations.

Music by Paul Hindemith. Choreography by Jacques d'Amboise. Lighting by Ronald Bates. Dedicated to Bunny and Arthur Horowitz. First presented by the New York City Ballet at the New York State Theatre, Lincoln Center, January 9, 1975.

The late Paul Hindemith, one of the half-dozen leading composers of the present century, came from Germany to teach at Yale University in 1940; he remained there the rest of his life. Lincoln Kirstein has noted that Hindemith, an extremely prolific composer, "was particularly interested in dancing." Among his earliest compositions were the famous *Triadic Ballet; Nobilissima Visione* (St. Francis): Massine/Tchelitchew (1938); and *Herodiade* for Martha Graham (1944). I myself greatly enjoyed working with Hindemith's music on several occasions. So, too, did Jacques d'Amboise in this ballet, arranged to the *Sinfonietta in E.* The work is a dance occasion, based on the music itself, without story.

SITUATION

Choreography by Hans van Manen. Decor and costumes by Jean-Paul Vroom. Lighting by Oliver Wood. First presented by the Netherlands Dance Theatre at the Circustheater, Scheveningen, Holland, April 20, 1970. First presented in the United States by the same ensemble at the Brooklyn Academy of Music, New York, April 1, 1972.

Situation is a series of dances to a series of sounds, all set in a specific place, a room lined with graph paper, measuring 27 × 20 × 14 feet and with a digital clock on the wall, telling the precise time. This room contains its own story as the dancers come and go through one door to varied sounds: hunting, shooting, machine gun fire, a water tap, a bath filling, a jet engine, walking in gravel, rain on the street, and mosquitoes. The dancers are anonymous, stretching like gymnasts, coupling, responding to the sounds in different ways, responding too to brief periods of silence. Certain sounds appear to turn certain dancers on, others turn them off. There is rejection, satisfaction, unfulfillment, amusement, as the dance reflects the sounds in ways that appear individual to the performers.

SLAUGHTER ON TENTH AVENUE

Dramatic ballet within a musical revue. Music by Richard Rodgers. Chore-ography by George Balanchine. Scenery by Jo Mielziner. Costumes by Irene Sharaff. First presented by Dwight Deere Wiman in the musical revue On Your Toes *(Richard Rodgers-George Abbott-Lorenz Hart) at the Imperial Theatre, New York, April 11, 1936, with Ray Bolger, Tamara Geva, and George Church as the principal dancers.*

The ballet *Slaughter on Tenth Avenue* was not a separate dance number in the great musical comedy *On Your Toes*, but a ballet that was part of the story. This story, a take-off on Russian ballet, had for its central theme a question very appropriate for its time: how could an American upstart hope to make good in a famous Russian ballet company?

Junior (Ray Bolger) was the American. Almost overnight he found himself a member of this famous Russian company when he successfully substituted for a dancer who had fallen ill. But young Junior didn't like the ballets the company danced. Sergei Alexandrovitch (Monty Woolley), the company's impre-sario, preferred ballets in the lush, pseudo-Russian, romantic style.

Junior thought he knew how to remedy this situation. He himself came from a vaudeville family, he knew a lot about music, and he tried to induce the company to accept an idea for a new kind of ballet. The ballerina (Tamara Geva) was all in favor of the idea, but the pompous Russian *premier danseur* (Demetrios Vilan) was jealous of Junior's talent and immediately began to plot against him. Only the enthusiasm of the company's rich patroness permitted Junior to proceed with his plan.

Rehearsals for the new ballet began. It was called *Slaughter on Tenth Avenue* and told a modern story of love and death. Junior himself was to dance the hero, a hoofer who one night visits a low dive on New York's West Side. Here he meets the strip-teaser (Tamara Geva), dances with her, and the two fall in love. But the girl is married to the big boss (George Church), who has been watching his wife dance so warmly with one of the customers. He breaks up the dance, fights with the hoofer, and pulls a knife on him. Accidentally he stabs the girl. She dies. The hoofer attacks the big boss and kills him. He dances around the body.

We learn that the ballet will end with the hoofer's suicide. He has killed the murderer, but is himself a murderer. The girl is dead; he has nothing to live for.

The day of the *première* of the new ballet approaches. Already *Slaughter* is popular with the company. But the *premier danseur* is determined that it shall fail and that Junior shall leave the company. To ensure his ends, he hires a group of gangsters, men very similar to the tough guys standing around the bar in the Tenth Avenue joint depicted in the ballet. The *danseur* gives these men tickets for a box near the stage for the opening night of the ballet, instructs them to eliminate Junior, and tells them how they can do it without being caught. At the end of *Slaughter on Tenth Avenue*, Junior is supposed to shoot himself. If they shoot him from the box, the ballet will end as planned, the curtain will fall, and no one will have any idea who committed the crime.

The gangsters agree. On the night of the *première*, they sit in a box in the theatre overlooking the stage. *Slaughter on Tenth Avenue* begins. We watch the action, are moved by the lyrical *pas de deux* danced by the hoofer and the girl, then see her murdered. As she dies in her lover's arms, the ballerina who is playing the girl speaks to Junior. She warns him of the plot against his life, which she overheard just before the rise of the curtain. She tells him that the gangsters will not dare to kill him if at the end of the ballet he keeps on dancing: he must change the ending and not shoot himself! The ballerina has called the police; they are sure to arrive in a matter of minutes.

When the big boss has been dispatched, Junior begins his dance of despair around the dead man's body. Then he improvises, dancing so artfully a frantic dance of death that the audience is unaware of any change. He moves faster and faster, incredibly spinning with ever greater energy, when his last strength seems to be spent. As he almost collapses on the stage from exhaustion, the police arrive. They arrest the frightened gangsters and the *premier danseur* amid tremendous applause for the new ballet. *Slaughter on Tenth Avenue* is a hit. Junior is the dancer of the hour. His success assured, the upstart hoofer marries the American girl he has loved all along and lives happily ever after.

NOTES   *On Your Toes* was the first musical I choreographed in the United States. Working with Lorenz Hart, Richard Rodgers, and George Abbott on this show made my job a pleasure from the start. The team of Rodgers and Hart represented for me, as it did for so many Americans, superb entertainment in the musical theatre. These men devised over the years a seemingly endless series of revues that were melodically and lyrically filled with great wit, touching humor, and eminent theatricality. After *On Your Toes*, it was my privilege to work with them on three other revues. *On Your Toes* was also my first association with the fine artist and comedian Ray Bolger, whose dancing throughout the show, and in *Slaughter*, will scarcely be forgotten by those who saw it.

THE SLEEPING BEAUTY

Classic ballet in three acts, with prologue. Music by Peter Ilyich Tchaikovsky. Choreography by Marius Petipa. Book by Marius Petipa and Ivan Vsevolojsky, after tales by Charles Perrault. Scenery and costumes by Ivan Vsevolojsky. First presented at the Maryinsky Theatre, St. Petersburg, Rus-

sia, January 15, 1890, with Carlotta Brianza as the Princess Aurora, *Paul Gerdt as the* Prince, *Marie Petipa as the* Lilac Fairy, *Enrico Cecchetti as* Carabosse, *Varvara Nikitina as the* Enchanted Princess, *and Enrico Cecchetti as the* Bluebird. *First presented in Western Europe by Diaghilev's Ballets Russes at the Alhambra Theatre, London, November 2, 1921. Staged by Nicholas Sergeyev after the choreography of Marius Petipa. Additional choreography by Bronislava Nijinska. Orchestration of Prelude to Act Three and the Princess Aurora's variation in Act Three by Igor Stravinsky. Scenery and costumes by Léon Bakst. The cast included Olga Spessivtzeva as the* Princess Aurora, *Pierre Vladimiroff as the* Prince, *Lydia Lopokova as the* Lilac Fairy, *Carlotta Brianza as* Carabosse, *Felia Dubrovska, Lydia Sokolova, Bronislava Nijinska, Lubov Egorova, and Vera Nemtchinova as the* Fairies, *Ludmilla Shollar as the* White Cat, *Lydia Lopokova as the* Enchanted Princess, *and Stanislas Idzikowski as the* Bluebird. *Revived by the Sadler's Wells Ballet at the Sadler's Wells Theatre, London, February 2, 1939, in a new production staged by Nicholas Sergeyev after choreography by Marius Petipa. Scenery and costumes by Nadia Benois. The cast included Margot Fonteyn as the* Princess Aurora, *Robert Helpmann as the* Prince, *June Brae as the* Lilac Fairy, *and Mary Honer and Harold Turner as the* Bluebirds. *Revived by the Sadler's Wells Ballet in a new production under the supervision of Nicholas Sergeyev at the Royal Opera House, Covent Garden, February 20, 1946. Additional choreography by Frederick Ashton and Ninette de Valois. Scenery and costumes by Oliver Messel. Margot Fonteyn as the* Princess Aurora, *Robert Helpmann as the* Prince, *Beryl Grey as the* Lilac Fairy, *and Pamela May and Alexis Rassine as the* Bluebirds *headed the cast. First presented in the United States by the Sadler's Wells Ballet at the Metropolitan Opera House, New York, October 9, 1949, with Margot Fonteyn and Robert Helpmann, Beryl Grey, Moira Shearer, and Alexis Rassine. Catherine Littlefield, Director of the Philadelphia Ballet, produced a complete version of* The Sleeping Beauty *with her own choreography at the Academy of Music, Philadelphia, February 12, 1937. This version was later produced at the Lewisohn Stadium, New York, July 29 and 30, 1937.*

The crashing, commanding chords of the brief overture to *The Sleeping Beauty* herald the special magic of the fairy tale the ballet relates, a fairy tale that is rich and formal in presentation, but warm and intimate in effect. Tchaikovsky and Petipa have so fashioned Perrault's story of the sleeping princess (*"La Belle au Bois Dormant,"* from *Mother Goose*) for the theater that notions of reality are suspended in favor of belief in characters who can live forever, in a curse of black magic that can put a forest to sleep for a hundred years, and in a beneficent fairy whose magic can rescue all goodness from evil. The time is unimportant, as is the place. The nameless mythical kingdom of the mythical King Florestan XXIV becomes the scene of our imagination.

The intensity of the music demands the attention, focusing it, as it were, on the splendor of the opening scene. The overture to *The Sleeping Beauty* also contains in miniature the story it introduces. Concealed within the opening regal chords is a theme that represents the fairy Carabosse, the evil fairy who will cast a spell upon the ballet's heroine and her family. This music is quickly interrupted by the melodious harp, which introduces a soft, slow, magical, compassionate theme—the melody of the Lilac Fairy, whose beauty and goodness will triumph over the evil fairy's challenge.

Now the music changes to a march tempo, quietly at first, then more assertively. The melody swells. The curtain rises.

PROLOGUE: THE CHRISTENING   The hall of King Florestan's palace is high-ceilinged. Great arches of stone cross the back of the stage; through them can be discerned the foliage of the garden. Drapery of resplendent color and ornament warms the spaciousness of the scene. On the right, on a small platform, stands the canopied cradle of the Princess Aurora, guarded by two nurses on each side. Two heralds stand at the back. Almost immediately the king's master of ceremonies, Cattalabutte, enters in elaborate full dress. With great flourish, he busies himself seeing that all is ready for the ceremony. Satisfied, he comes forward, gives a page his stick of office, and scans the list of guests who have been invited to attend the christening of the princess.

Twelve ladies in waiting enter the chamber. They circle the stage and ceremoniously ask Cattalabutte if they may see the child. He consents and leads them over to the cradle, where they hover over the princess. Cattalabutte directs a page to notify the king that all the preparations have been made and nervously unrolls the guest list again to check his memory. The ladies retire from the cradle and stand to one side. A fanfare sounds in the distance; it grows louder; three pages enter. To the blaring of trumpets, the king and queen approach. They pause for a moment under the silk canopy that is held high above them by Negroes dressed in gold and survey the scene. Then their attendants drop their trains. The queen goes to the cradle. She kisses the princess and greets the ladies in waiting, who bow to her. She joins the king, who stands in conference with Cattalabutte. After a brief consultation with their servant, the two monarchs mount the steps to their thrones.

An arpeggio on the harp announces the arrival of the fairy godmothers of the princess. The royal fairies are preceded by their pages, who enter two by two and bow to their sovereigns. Five of the fairies enter in a group: the Fairy of the Crystal Fountain, the Fairy of the Enchanted Garden, the Fairy of the Woodland Glades, the Fairy of the Songbirds, and the Fairy of the Golden Vine. Eight maids of honor attend them. Last of all comes the Fairy of the Lilac, accompanied by six cavaliers, one for each of the fairies. The cavaliers carry, on plush cushions, the gifts the fairies have chosen for their godchild. The Lilac Fairy leads the group forward. The fairies bow low to the king and queen, who welcome them cordially, and arrange themselves about the royal cradle to bless the princess. They bow again to the king and queen and leave the scene.

The maids of honor come forward in two lines and, to the syncopated rhythm of a new melody, they dance in linear patterns. They are joined by the cavaliers, who leap boldly in the air. The fairies return, and all dance together briefly. The queen thanks the Lilac Fairy for the dance and asks the group to continue. The Lilac Fairy bows.

A new tender theme is heard, accompanied by runs on the harp. The fairies and their partners arrange themselves in five moving circles, the Lilac Fairy in the center. Two of the girls in the back are lifted to their partners' shoulders and turned around and around so that they appear to be swimming high in the air. The fairies come forward to the footlights. One by one, the fairies pirouette rapidly and pose in attitude supported by their cavaliers. The maids of honor lie at their feet in respectful obeisance.

The tableau is broken; the music subsides, then regains in volume; in a hushed pause, the royal nurses bring the small princess to the center of the stage. There is a magical rushing run on the harp, and the Lilac Fairy is lifted high above the princess. She blesses the babe with her wand. The *pas de six* is over. The harp plays for a moment, the tempo changes, and the fairies leave the stage while the maids of honor dance a new sprightly measure in unison.

Now each of the fairies returns to perform a variation before the assembled court. These variations are very short; they have no literal significance, and the attributes of the different fairies cannot be read into them; but the different music and different dances that Tchaikovsky and Petipa devised for the six fairies gives each of the variations an individual, distinctive character. First is the Fairy of the Crystal Fountain. She enters and waits for her music to begin. Its movement is slow and leisurely; its melody, calm. The fairy dances forward and moves back and forth across the stage on her points, her body in graceful repose. As her feet mark the retarded rhythm of her music, her head and arms depict the quiet sweetness of the melody. She kneels to the king and queen as her variation ends and leaves the stage.

The Fairy of the Enchanted Garden emerges to dance with quick steps to a brighter tempo—music which carries her into swift pirouettes that accelerate as she moves across the stage. For the Fairy of the Woodland Glades, the music is characterized by a soft, tempered pizzicato. This fairy's skill in quiet, slow movement is revealed in the daring figure that highlights her dance: she dances forward on one foot, her other foot extended before her. With subdued brilliance her extended foot moves back, and the girl stands poised for a breathless moment in arabesque. This figure is repeated as she continues to move forward. Then her dance becomes luminous and light, with rapid dancing on point. She ends her variation standing on point, with open arms, one leg raised pertly before her.

In a flashing yellow costume, the Fairy of the Songbirds dances now to a hurried, tinkling melody, her arms moving ecstatically in simulated flight, her bright head turning to the shimmering elevation of the rhythm. She is followed by the Fairy of the Golden Vine, whose dance is characterized by the curt, staccato movement of her head and the quick pointing of the index fingers of both her hands—the so-called "Finger Variation." The tempo of the music increases sharply, and the brilliant fairy whirls to a quick, sudden stop.

The Lilac Fairy comes forward. She stands toward the back of the stage. The orchestra begins a sumptuously melodic waltz, and the Lilac Fairy accompanies its flowing line with extended, open movements in which her raised point traces small circles in the air. Then she turns in arabesque; she pauses briefly each time her body is seen in profile. In the rapid complexity of its movement and in the fullness of the magnificent waltz, the variation of the Lilac Fairy sums up in splendid grandeur the dances of all the other fairies.

Now the cavaliers dance. The maids of honor join them with light, precise movements. The fairies reassemble at the front of the stage. Their cavaliers hold them in attitude. The fairies' gifts are presented to the king and queen. The queen leaves the throne and delightedly examines the presents. There is a deep, rumbling sound, like an earthquake, off stage. Some of the courtiers imagine it to be only thunder, but the king is apprehensive. The queen trembles for the safety of her child, and the master of ceremonies cowers. A page rushes in and gestures helplessly to the king, pointing off to the left. The king understands suddenly and rushes over to Cattalabutte and demands to see the invitation list. He scans it rapidly, then dashes the scroll to the floor in a gigantic rage. Cattalabutte's fate is averted momentarily by the frightening appearance of two great rats, who emerge from the left and dance a few insidious steps. They run back out. Before the court has recovered, they return with other rats, pulling along behind them an enormous black coach. Standing majestically in the coach is the fairy Carabosse, the hunchbacked godmother of the Princess Aurora, whom the forgetful Cattalabutte has neglected to invite to the christening. She grasps at the air in her fury; her black chariot circles the stage, sweeping all the courtiers aside.

Assisted by her four rodent attendants, Carabosse steps down. The music gives a low warning. Her face is a hideous blue-white mask covered with moles and magical, shining spangles. Her long black dress is tattered and dusty, yet she wears it as if it were ermine. Carabosse hobbles forward on her stick and inquires fiercely of the king, by gesture, "Why was I forgotten? Do you realize what this will mean to the fate of your child?" Already, the king is afraid. He points to Cattalabutte as the real culprit. Carabosse approaches the cowardly master of ceremonies, who kneels at her feet. He throws up his hands, begging for mercy and to protect himself, but Carabosse reaches out her talonlike fingers and tears off his wig, which she throws at the hungry rats. Now, deprived of all his dignity, the courtier attempts to escape.

Carabosse raises her stick and, with a quick thrust in the small of his back, sends him flying. She caresses the rats, who form a small square about her as she dances blithely. She gestures to the royal couple, pointing to the cradle:

"Your daughter will grow up . . . She will grow up to be a beautiful princess . . . the most beautiful princess of them all; and then"—Carabosse brings down her stick loudly; the music thunders—"and then . . . she will die! . . . She will prick her finger, no one will prevent it, and she will be a beautiful dead princess." The wicked fairy cackles with glee as the king tries to comfort the distraught queen. He motions Carabosse imperiously away, but the evil fairy persists in laughing at his discomfort. She whips her great black cape through the air to the sound of the harp.

The Lilac Fairy steps out. Carabosse tries to approach the cradle to repeat her curse. The Lilac Fairy holds up her wand in quiet defiance; Carabosse stumbles back. All the other fairies gather around her to guard the cradle. She threatens them with her stick, but the good fairies stand placidly impervious. The hideous, servile rats surround the grotesque Carabosse, and she dances a final, frantic jig, at the end of which she holds up her hand in triumph. She climbs back into her carriage; as she stands under its high roof of black plumes, shaking her fists at the whole court, the obedient rats draw the black chariot off. The thunder subsides.

The queen weeps in the king's arms. He cannot comfort her. The Lilac Fairy comes to them. The lovely melody that identifies this good fairy fills the hall. She gestures toward the cradle and gives them this message in pantomime: "Your daughter, the princess, will grow up to be beautiful, and it is true that she will prick her finger and seem to die . . . but in reality she will only go to sleep . . . she will sleep for a hundred years, and all the court with her . . . but one day a prince, as handsome as she is beautiful, will come to the princess . . . she will wake at his kiss, and all will live happily ever after."

The king and queen bow to the Lilac Fairy and thank her. The release from the evil curse of Carabosse causes the court to be joyful. All the fairies bow to the king and queen, and then the entire assembly turns toward the cradle of the Princess Aurora. The queen stands over her daughter; the ladies in waiting and the maids of honor kneel in homage, and the fairies stand in attitudes of infinite protectiveness. The curtain falls.

ACT ONE: THE SPELL   The scene is the garden of the palace. A colonnade of huge columns, topped by ancient statues, sweeps in a curve about a high fountain toward the right to support a great arch of stone over the back of the garden. Thrones for the king and queen are arranged at the right. On the left, a flight of wide stone steps leads up toward the palace. Peasants idle in the distance. Ladies in waiting and their cavaliers walk about the garden, marveling at its beauty and anticipating the day's festival. For today is the Princess Aurora's sixteenth birthday, and the king has decreed a celebration in her honor. The king has also invited the court and kingdom to entertain four foreign visitors: princes from England, India, Italy, and Spain, who have come long distances to meet the young princess and pay court to her.

Three old hags in black, their dark hoods concealing their faces, stoop to-

gether over spindles. As they sew, they keep looking about cautiously. Cattalabutte enters. He has aged somewhat in the sixteen years that have passed, but
still flourishes his cape and stick at every opportunity. The old women dance
away from him. Cattalabutte regards them suspiciously. They try to escape,
but the master of ceremonies catches them. He takes the spindles from them
forcibly and stands over them threateningly. The women cower at his feet as
Cattalabutte reminds them that for sixteen years, ever since the curse of the
wicked fairy Carabosse, the king has ordered that no spindles be brought
within a mile of the Princess Aurora. He is interrupted by the arrival of the
king and queen, who are followed by the four princes. The old women scurry
into a corner.

The king greets Cattalabutte and wonders what his courtier holds concealed
in the hand behind his back. Reluctantly Cattalabutte holds out the dread
spindles. The king is shocked and furious. Cattalabutte points to the weird
women; the king commands them to come forward. He tells them that they
must hang for this offense; how otherwise can he protect his daughter from the
spell of Carabosse? The women kneel at his feet and plead for forgiveness. The
king is adamant. To a sudden crescendo of surging, pulsating music, the queen
steps forward and asks the king to relent. After all, this is Aurora's birthday
and the women are truly sorry. The king smiles and consents.

The king and queen mount their thrones, carrying fresh garlands. A group
of peasant girls enters. They bow deeply to their lord. The courtiers gather on
the steps, and the four princes stand to one side as the girls commence to
dance to a flowing waltz. The girls weave in and out under the garlands and
arrange themselves in circles that travel around the stage in opposite directions. Cattalabutte thanks them when the waltz is over, and they bow to the
monarchs.

Four musicians enter, carrying golden instruments, followed by eight girls—
friends of the princess. The four foreign princes stand ready to greet the guest
of honor. The music is expectant. The four princes look toward the back of the
garden and peer down the colonnade, hoping for a glimpse of the princess.
Softly the music hesitates. In the distance, under the arch, we see a beautiful
girl in a pink dress embellished with silver. She poses for an instant and disappears like an apparition. Then, brilliantly, to a burst of music, she is on stage,
dancing joyfully with the sweet, innocent exuberance of youth. The four
princes approach her. The princess goes to her mother, who embraces her
warmly, then to the king, who kisses her on the forehead. The king then introduces her to the foreign princes, who bow low to her. She responds gently. The
harp plays a rushing cadenza; all the other instruments are silent, waiting; there
is a brief hush, a momentary interval of preparation like the soprano's measured
intake of breath before a great aria commences. The "Rose Adagio" begins.

The four princes move to the front of the stage in a line. One by one, the
princes support the Princess Aurora as she dances softly and openly her preparatory steps. Then she steps back; standing on point in attitude, she greets

the first prince. Holding her right hand, he turns her in attitude, as she maintains the graceful pose. When she has come full circle, the prince releases her hand; both hands are raised to form a crown above her head for a moment of balance; then the second cavalier steps forward to hold her right hand. This design is repeated. Finally, as the last prince releases her, the princess extends her body in arabesque and holds this position with breath-taking equilibrium.

One of her suitors now supports Aurora, who modestly displays her dancing skill without conveying the least impression that she is unlike any other young girl who is beautiful and happens to be dancing. Sweetly holding her hands to her cheek, the princess leans forward. She is lifted high in the air. When she is released, she dances alone in a small circle, her arms invoking the melody of the music, her strong points tracing its rhythms.

Each of the enamored princes now presents Aurora with a freshly picked rose. The theme is played softly by the oboe. One prince supports her as the others come forward, one by one, with their gifts. The princess pirouettes swiftly as she accepts each of the flowers. Then, charmingly, she leaves her suitors and presents their flowers to the queen. She moves to the back of the stage and dances forward. Armed with fresh roses, the princes kneel at her feet. As she pirouettes past them, the princes hold out their flowers; the princess pauses in her turning to receive each rose. She holds the flower to her breast for a moment, then tosses them in the air as her dance continues.

The music approaches its fullest, final expression. One of the princes holds her hand as the princess stands again on point in attitude. He releases her, and she sustains her pose as if it were effortless. Then, moving only her arm, she takes the hand of the second prince, to prepare briefly for a second, longer balance. Her modest confidence in balance increases as the adagio comes to a conclusion. When the fourth prince releases her, she stands in what seems perpetually perfect balance until the final chord breaks the enchantment. She runs off into the garden.

The eight friends of the Princess Aurora dance to a tinkling, blithe melody. Soon the princess returns. The four princes beseech her to dance again. She turns to her mother, who encourages her with a smile, and the princess begins a *pas seul*. After posing in attitude and arabesque, she goes to the corner of the garden. She dances forward on point in a diagonal line with slow precision. Step by step, she bends her right knee and brings her right leg up so that it touches gently the back of her supporting leg. The diagonal completed, she dances backward toward the corner in a series of pirouettes, each of which ends in secure, perfect position. The princess circles the garden, with brilliant, accelerating spins, and leaves the stage.

When friends commence to dance, the princess comes back. She dances toward the front with high, broad leaps in which she kicks her front foot forward—a movement that gives her dance a new urgency. She circles the stage again, this time with open, free turns rapidly executed. The tempo of the music builds with her speed, with her joy in dancing.

On the right, in the corner, half concealed by the crowd, an old woman in black emerges. She watches the happy princess, and when Aurora circles near her, holds out a present to the princess. Aurora, barely stopping, takes it and dances on, delighted with the strange, new object. The gift is a spindle! The king rises in terror and warns the court. Everyone attempts to stop Aurora's dance and take the spindle from her. But the innocent, impetuous girl is so charmed by the spindle that she cannot cease to play with it. Suddenly, she pricks her finger. Instantly, she falls to the ground.

The king and queen rush to her. The angry monarch orders the court to find the criminal who presented the princess with the fatal spindle. The princess herself has no idea of what has happened. She stirs, looks into her father's disturbed face, and shakes her head slowly, as if to say, "Don't worry, nothing is wrong." Similarly she comforts her distraught mother. To prove that everything is all right, the anxious girl rises and begins to dance again. She moves rapidly, the music accelerates ominously, and there is a clap of thunder. The princess falls into her father's arms. The cymbals clash in evil triumph, and the old woman in black steps out. She throws aside her cape: she is the fairy Carabosse, come back to court to fulfill her prophecy. She cackles with delight. The princess seems to die. Armed courtiers chase the evil fairy as she runs into the garden.

A trumpet sounds, then the harp, and the melody of the Lilac Fairy is heard. She enters with her wand and comforts the king and queen, telling them that the princess, as she foretold, is not really dead, she is merely asleep, and this is the beginning of the spell that will last a hundred years. The king and queen thank the Lilac Fairy and bow humbly. Courtiers take up the princess and carry her slowly up the steps to the palace. The Lilac Fairy ascends the stairs; the last members of the court disappear. She holds out her wand, casting a spell over the kingdom.

The stage grows dark; the garden fades in the distance. From the ground, enormous shrubs, great branches of foliage rise magically and seem to entwine the garden and the palace, smothering them in sleep. In a small point of light, the Lilac Fairy can be seen dancing softly, waving her magic wand, as the palace and its people, obedient to her command, go to sleep for a hundred years.

ACT TWO: THE VISION   A brief orchestral introduction features the sound of hunting horns, and when the curtain rises on a wooded glen, we are prepared for the entry of the royal hunting party. The scene is the forest of King Florestan XXIV, a part of the forest remote from the sleeping palace; the time, one hundred years later. The setting sun glows in the distance over rocky hills that enclose a still stream. As the hunting party comes upon the scene, it is apparent that the style of dress has changed considerably. Duchesses and dukes, marchionesses and marquesse stride about the wood in their colorful riding habits. Gallison, tutor to Prince Florimund, the leader of the hunt, totters onto the stage exhausted. Prince Florimund follows. Dressed in red riding habit, with high red boots and a feathered hat, the prince bows to his guests. A countess approaches him and makes a suggestion. The prince responds lazily and motions her away gently. The persistent countess does not acknowledge the rebuff, however. She has in mind a game of blindman's buff and persuades the tutor to bind his eyes. The old man obliges her and chases after the royal couples, who egg him on by whipping their riding crops at his feet. He stumbles around, becomes dizzy, and takes the hand of what he imagines to be a beautiful lady. He is somewhat staggered as he takes the handkerchief from his eyes and finds himself embracing a peer.

The game has not amused the guests sufficiently and they turn to other entertainment. Reluctantly the prince yields to the countess' persuasion and takes her as his partner in a stately mazurka. Peasants enter the wood at the conclusion of the dance and perform a farandole, a round dance in which the boys and girls join hands and curve about the stage in a continuous serpentine line. Every member of the hunting party is diverted by the farandole except the prince, who is moody and preoccupied. The hunting horns sound again. Attendants bring in spears for the hunt, and the lords and ladies prepare to leave. But the prince has suddenly changed his mind and urges his guests to leave without him. He will remain in the forest for a little while and rejoin them later. The countess is visibly upset at her inability to attract the prince away; she attempts to change his mind; the prince dismisses her.

Now alone in the glen, the prince walks about. Night falls; the setting sun becomes the new moon. He stares out over the lake, hoping that the beautiful scene will settle his gloom. He turns away dejectedly and walks forward. Just as he turns his back, the theme of the Lilac Fairy is heard and a magical boat floats onto the lake from the right. Its gossamer sail hangs from a silver mast; motioning the boat forward is the Lilac Fairy, who stands with upraised wand in the great sea shell that forms the boat's hull. The boat stops at her command, and the fairy steps down to earth. Still preoccupied with his own thoughts, the prince does not see her. As he moves back toward the lake, he is astonished by her presence. He bows deeply.

The Lilac Fairy then begins to instruct the prince in the cause of his woe. In a palace not far from this forest, she tells him, sleeps a beautiful princess, a princess so lovely that his mind must have envisaged her all his life. This princess has been asleep for a hundred years, yet she is only sixteen. She will sleep forever unless she is kissed by a prince who loves her.

The prince is enchanted, but somewhat skeptical, and impatiently asks the Lilac Fairy to let him see the princess. The fairy consents to show him a vision of the Princess Aurora. She points her wand to the left, and concealed within a dark tree trunk we see a misty vision of the princess. The specter disappears as quickly as it came. The prince demands to see more of her; already he is enamored of Aurora. The Lilac Fairy now allows the vision of the princess to enter in person.

The princess comes in on the right. Still the beautiful young girl of the first act, her movements are now soft and romantic. A haunting melody begins, dominated by the cellos, lending the scene a dark, mysterious atmosphere. The prince lifts Aurora high off the ground and, when he lets her down, attempts to embrace her. Fairies who have followed the princess pull him away from her, and he watches as she dances alone. The fairies form a circular tableau in the center of the scene. The princess moves about this circle, momentarily disappearing from the prince's sight. He pursues her softly, patiently, yet never catches up to her. Finally he holds her for a brief moment in his arms. The vision relaxes against him for an instant and then leaves him, like a phantom. He beseeches the Lilac Fairy to call her back again.

The sixteen nymphs dance for a short interval, and suddenly the princess returns to their midst. The flowing music becomes strongly rhythmical. Standing in the center of the stage, she dances quickly, with staccatolike urgency, a brilliant variation that excites the prince's love for her. He holds out his arms and she vanishes.

The nymphs fill the scene again with their dancing, and the princess makes a final, spinning, illusory appearance. The prince asks the Lilac Fairy, "Where has she gone? Where can I find her again?" The Lilac Fairy calms his curiosity and tells him that to find the princess, they must sail across the lake to her father's palace, where the princess lies asleep. She motions for him to follow, and the curtain falls as the Lilac Fairy's magical boat disappears in the midst of the lake.

ACT THREE, SCENE ONE: THE AWAKENING   The orchestra plays a long overture, the composition that was designed originally to accompany the journey of the Lilac Fairy and the prince toward the palace, a slowly paced interlude during which the fairy's magic barge passed slowly across the lake, surrounded by a panorama of dense forest and splendid vistas of the enchanted palace.

When the curtain rises, the Lilac Fairy and the prince have already disembarked. The fairy leads the prince across the stage from the right. He follows several paces behind her, looking about him cautiously, both amazed and delighted at the sleeping forest. Only shadows can be distinguished in the background. The two walk off at the left and reappear almost immediately behind a gauze curtain. Light emerges from behind; the palace can be seen, rising high on the summit in the distance. On the ground, two guards, frozen in an attitude of perpetual slumber, sleep away their watch. The prince stares at them, unbelieving. The Lilac Fairy leads him off; the light is extinguished, only to come up again in a moment in a high-vaulted chamber—the boudoir of the Princess Aurora. The Lilac Fairy enters first, holding her wand before her. She enters through a maze of great columns entangled with cobwebs, beckoning to the prince to follow. In the half-darkness, on the left, a silken bed canopied with royal drapes dominates the apartment. Guards stand in a line, motionless, sleeping against their upright spears.

The prince enters, marveling at the oppression of the sleeping rooms and the splendor they still contain. He glances incredulously at the sleeping guards. The Lilac Fairy motions him forward to the bed. In the dim light, he sees the sleeping princess. He hesitates, not wishing to disturb her sleeping beauty. The Lilac Fairy waves her wand, and he steps forward toward the bed. Curled in an attitude of peaceful contentment, the princess lies in deep slumber, her head on an ancient, dusty pillow. The prince bends down toward her face; the Lilac Fairy gestures with her wand; he kisses her softly. The music mounts to a vivid crescendo. The princess stirs, wakens, and rises slowly as the prince gathers her in his arms.

The light flashes out, and miraculously the giant spiders who hover over the chamber rise and vanish; the cobwebs are disentangled from the great pillars and gradually fall away. The light comes up slowly, royal pages stand against the high columns, and we see before us the great hall of King Florestan's palace.

ACT THREE, SCENE TWO: THE WEDDING   The lofty columns of stone support high-vaulting arches. In the distance, great, sweeping staircases climb up to the farther reaches of the castle. The thrones of the king and queen stand at the right.

With pomp and ceremony, as if he had not been disturbed by more than a night's sleep, the courtier Cattalabutte enters with all his old-time flourish. He struts about the hall as if he himself were responsible for the festivities that are about to follow.

The king and his queen enter regally. Cattalabutte bows to them and escorts them to the dais. Courtiers and ladies in waiting with their escorts dance in and promenade about the hall to the virile rhythms of a polonaise. Six other ladies enter. As the dance theme is repeated quietly, the special guests who have been invited to attend the wedding of Princess Aurora and Prince Florimund dance in to pay their respects to the parents of the bride.

These royal guests are perennial fairy tale characters. First comes the White Cat, held high on a pillow which her escorts carry on their shoulders. She paws the air plaintively and washes her face. Behind her comes Puss in Boots, who watches her possessively while waving his hat in greeting. Bluebeard and his wife, Goldilocks and her prince, Beauty and the Beast, and Florestan, the crown prince of the kingdom, and his two sisters follow behind. Last of all come the enchanted princess and the bluebird. Now, led by the Lilac Fairy, all six of the Princess Aurora's fairy godmothers enter in all their glory.

All the courtiers and guests arrange themselves in a great circle about the hall. Prince Florestan, Aurora's brother, and their two sisters step out and stand at the back of the stage toward the right. A lovely, lilting waltz begins; to its enchanting melody, the three dance a *pas de trois*. When the waltz ends, each of the two girls dances a short variation to music that is light and sparkling in its tinkling sound. Prince Florestan rejoins them, and all three leap off into the wings.

The next *divertissement* features the White Cat and Puss in Boots. This oboe mimes their mewing as Puss in Boots tries to ensnare the winsome cat in a love trap. The White Cat pretends to resist Puss's caresses, but actually she is delighted. Finally Puss can contain himself no longer and puts an end to the flirtation by carrying his ladylove off.

The Enchanted Princess enters with the Bluebird. Both flutter their arms in light, airy motions of flight and commence a *pas de deux*, perhaps the most dazzling dance duet of the entire ballet. The Bluebird, in his variation, seems to be suspended in soaring flight.

Another *divertissement* enacts the tale of Little Red Ridinghood. Four pages bring small trees onto the stage. Red Ridinghood walks lightly through the wood, treading as softly as possible, glancing behind her at every turn. The wolf enters with a bold leap and conceals himself behind one of the trees. The girl passes; he steps out in front of her. Red Ridinghood tries to pretend that he is just another passer-by, like herself, and, holding her basket close, proceeds on her way. The wolf is fooled only for a moment: quickly he throws her over his shoulder and runs off.

Now the moment for which all the court has been waiting finally arrives. Princess Aurora and Prince Florimund enter. A spotlight brightens the brilliant white the bride wears for her wedding day, and all the lords and ladies bow. The royal couple come forward and begin to dance. Their *pas de deux* is gracious and formal. The Princess Aurora reveals, in her mastery of movement and balance, a maturity and perfection for which the "Rose Adagio" was but a youthful rehearsal. Still charming, the youthful princess is now about to be married, and her radiant poise reflects the lesson her love has taught. Prince Florimund supports his bride gallantly, lifting her effortlessly, holding her confidently—by each of his gestures and motions drawing the court's attention to her loveliness. As the *pas de deux* concludes, its tender music ascends to a pitch of everlasting joy. The princess turns with incredible speed on point and dives toward the floor. The prince catches her falling figure and holds her in the daring pose.

A final *divertissement* is offered by the Three Ivans, who perform a virile, stomping Russian dance for the bride and groom. The court is now at the height of good humor, and when the Princess Aurora returns to dance briefly alone, everyone is suddenly saddened by the fact that soon she will go away with her prince. But everyone watches closely this last dance of their princess; the entire assembly is infected by her happiness. Now the whole court—all the fairies, all the nobles, all the fairy tale figures—joins the bride and groom in a spirited mazurka, at the end of which the guests form a circle about the prince and princess who, standing in close embrace, become, in reality, a part of that fairy tale world that brought them together. Everyone kneels to them.

NOTES The success of *The Sleeping Beauty* described here—as presented by the Royal Ballet (then the Sadler's Wells Ballet) in 1946, in London, and three years later in the United States—has led to many other productions. All of these, including new productions by the Royal Ballet itself, retain the main outlines of the story and the principal dances, while adding variations of character, new dances and ensembles to accompany changes in scenery and costume. Notable productions are those of the Leningrad Kirov Ballet (filmed in 1965, with Alla Sizova and Yuri Soloviev), the National Ballet of Washington (staged by Ben Stevenson), and the National Ballet of Canada (staged by Rudolf Nureyev). The latter, with Veronica Tennant as the Princess Aurora and, as guest artist, Rudolf Nureyev as Prince Florimund, was presented on film by Public Broadcasting Service television in the United States at Christmastime 1972 in color. Rudolf Nureyev first staged the ballet independently for La Scala, Milan, September 17, 1970, with scenery and costumes by Nicholas Georgiadis. Margot Fonteyn and Nureyev danced the première.

Nureyev has said of *The Sleeping Beauty* (in an interview in *Dance and Dancers*, January 1972): "It is really a kind of *Parsifal* of ballet and very important to the whole ballet world. It's very long and very lush, and there is nothing you can really cut. Since I had been brought up on the Kirov version, my production was naturally inspired by that."

In writing of Nureyev's *Sleeping Beauty* soon after its New York première in 1973, Andrew Porter in *The New Yorker* reviewed much of the ballet's history: "In ballet history, the usual order is reversed; the Romantic works come first, then the Classical. And the Petipa-Tchaikovsky *Sleeping Beauty*, first performed, in St. Petersburg, in 1890, is the grandest, fullest, and finest achievement of Classical ballet—its 'definitive statement' and an enduring inspiration to later choreographers. Balanchine, Ashton, and Kenneth MacMillan all proclaim their debt to the inventions of Petipa. Brought from Leningrad to London by Nicholas Sergeyev, *The Sleeping Beauty* became, in 1939, the foundation of the Royal Ballet's work, and the dancers, directors, ballet masters, and teachers who have gone out from Covent Garden to play leading roles in ballet across six continents have all been brought up on *Sleeping Beauty* as ballet's Bible. Meanwhile, in Leningrad itself, *The Sleeping Beauty* remains the work that shows Maryinsky-Kirov dancing at its purest and most poetic. The Kirov company brought its *Sleeping Beauty* to London twelve years ago, and left a new mark on all subsequent Western productions. The influence was continued, in a highly personalized variant, by the participation of the ex-Kirov dancer Rudolf Nureyev in the Royal Ballet performances and then by his own stagings of the work—at La Scala, in 1969, and now for the National Ballet of Canada. With a *Sleeping Beauty* 'produced, staged, and with additional choreography by Rudolf Nureyev after Marius Petipa,' the Canadian company made its Metropolitan début last week. It offered an exceedingly grand presentation of the piece—from a scenic point of view the grandest, in fact, that I have ever seen.

"When Auguste Bournonville, that great Romantic choreographer (whose

La Sylphide is another work in the Canadian repertory), visited Petersburg in 1874, he was distressed by what he saw: 'Much as I wanted to, I could not discover action, dramatic interest, logical continuity, something that would even remotely remind one of common sense. And if, on occasion, I did succeed in finding a trace of something like it (as, for example, in Petipa's *Don Quixote*), the impression was immediately obscured by an endless number of monotonous bravura appearances.' Ivan Alexandrovich Vsevolozhsky, appointed Director of the Imperial Theatres in 1881, changed all that. He instituted production councils in which scenarist, choreographer, composer, and designer got together to plan a new work. Of *The Sleeping Beauty* he was both scenarist and costume designer; Tchaikovsky, 'in large letters,' dedicated the published score to him. Composer and choreographer worked closely together. Petipa told Tchaikovsky exactly how many measures he wanted for each episode, and specified the tempo, the style, even the scoring. Princess Aurora's first variation should be accompanied by violins and cellos pizzicato, and harps; at Carabosse's unmasking, at the end of Act I, 'a chromatic scale must sound in the whole orchestra'; the Sapphire of Act III, being of pentahedral cut, required an accompaniment in 5/4 time. When, during rehearsals, the Panorama music of Act II came to an end before the great panorama of painted canvas had rolled its full course, Tchaikovsky composed extra music, whose length was determined, literally, by the yard. The three collaborators played each his different role in giving unity to the elaborate *féerie*. Vsevolozhsky had his conception of a glittering dance pageant mounting to its climax in an apotheosis—paean to imperial splendor (a paean in the precise sense, since the ending would show Apollo costumed as Louis XIV). Petipa had his sharp-cut scheme for a balanced and well-varied sequence of dances. And Tchaikovsky? He always delighted in the evocation of past centuries. Petipa's blueprint checked his tendency to sprawly form. And he poured out his heart. It is Tchaikovsky's music that gives character to the heroine and expresses the 'inner theme' which raises *The Sleeping Beauty* above the level of a pretty divertissement.

"Most of the fairy tales that adults go to the theater to see again and again— *Swan Lake, Cinderella, Hansel and Gretel*, the *Ring*—symbolically enshrine truths about human experience and human behavior to make their pleasures more than incidental. *Swan Lake*, for example, is a drama involving conflict and character; it gives scope for dramatic expression, for acting, and for diverse striking interpretations. By comparison with Prince Siegfried in *Swan Lake*, Prince Florimund of *The Sleeping Beauty* is a cipher. What does he do to deserve his princess? The briar thicket surrounding his bride is no dangerous Magic Fire through which only the dauntless can pass. And similarly, by comparison with the brave, pathetic Odette and the formidable temptress Odile, Princess Aurora is a passive heroine played upon by circumstance. Can we find a moral in *The Sleeping Beauty* beyond that guest lists should be kept up-to-date lest awkwardness result? Perrault, who wrote the fairy tale on which the ballet is based, suggested, 'What girl would not forgo her marriage vows, at least for a while, to gain a husband who is handsome, rich, courteous, and kind?' Not enough! In a preface to the Penguin edition of Perrault, Geoffrey Brereton remarks that it is 'tempting to adopt the nature-myth interpretation and see the tale as an allegory of the long winter sleep of the earth'— but adds that 'the allegory, if it is one, is obscure.' Tchaikovsky's interpretation was simpler. His *Sleeping Beauty* is a struggle between good and evil, between forces of light and forces of darkness, represented by the benevolent Lilac Fairy and the wicked fairy Carabosse. The prelude, a straightforward exposition of the music associated with the two characters, suggests it; the consistent employment of melodies related to or derived from these themes—the Lilac Fairy's transformation of the Carabosse music at the close of Act I, the Carabosse figuration that propels Aurora's dance with the spindle, the opposition of the two themes in the symphonic entr'acte that precedes the Awakening—makes it clear. These two forces shape Aurora's destiny, and although she initiates nothing, with just a little stretching of the imagination we can accept the declaration of the Russian composer and critic Boris Asafiev that the heroine's three adagios (the Rose Adagio, in E flat; the Vision Scene appearance, in F; the Grand Pas de Deux, in C) tell 'the story of a whole life—the growth and development of a playful and carefree child into a young woman who learns, through tribulations, to know great love.' It is in this sense that Margot Fonteyn, since 1939 our leading Aurora, dances the role.

"That question 'Can we find a moral?' prompts others. Is it right to look for one? Does the 'meaning' of *The Sleeping Beauty* not lie simply in its patterns of movement, as does that of, say, *Ballet Imperial*, Balanchine's homage to Petipa and Tchaikovsky? While spectacle, pure dance, expressive dance, narrative, and symbolism must mix in any presentation of the work, what importance should be given to any single ingredient? Different productions have provided different answers. The Kirov's has modest décor; the dances shine as rich, perfectly cut jewels in a quiet, rather dowdy setting; this Leningrad *Beauty* is not a drama but a long, lyrical poem in varied metres, spun on a thread of radiant narrative. Kenneth MacMillan's presentation, at the German Opera, in Berlin, in 1967, was very grand indeed to look at (the epochs were moved forward, so that Aurora fell asleep in the reign of Catherine the Great and woke a century later, under Alexander II) and also rather dramatic—yet the main emphasis was again not on the story but on the dances, both Petipa's and those that MacMillan added, in brilliant emulation. The famous old Covent Garden version, which did more than twenty years' hard service (and in 1949 introduced the company to New York), balanced all the ingredients listed above, but toward the end it fell apart; though the central Petipa episodes were lovingly preserved, around them was a ragged patchwork. The 1968 replacement was softly romantic, lavishly sentimental in appearance, and did not last long; I have not seen its successor, which opened at Covent Garden in March.

"Nureyev's production for the National Ballet of Canada is different again. The décor, by Nicholas Georgiadis, is even more sumptuous than Barry Kay's in Berlin, though it does not sparkle so brightly. Mr. Kay produced a jewelled effect, of diamonds, rubies, sapphires, with the softer gleam of pearl and opal in the Vision Scene; Mr. Georgiadis prefers an impression of old gold, with touches of rich colors that are muted as if by a layer of fine dust; in the final scene the dominant tone becomes rust red. David Hersey's subtly elaborate lighting subdues the colors still further and blurs distinctions between them; a prevailing amber glow neutralizes all shades in the Vision Scene except when follow spots fall on the principals, or the attendant fairies enter pools of white light stage-front. Blackness at the back strikes an unsuitably sombre note at the christening party of the Prologue; Aurora's wedding, I think, also calls for a more splendid general blaze. All the same, the lighting is carefully and imaginatively wrought. There are some excellent stage effects: a streamer of red ribbon flies across the stage, to shape itself as Carabosse and her retinue; a boat for Florimund and the Lilac Fairy glides magically through the obstacles on the way to the palace. The tableau of sleeping courtiers through which the prince, marvelling, picks his way is a triumph for designer, producer, and lighter at once. Mr. Georgiadis's architecture, substantial and imposing, leaves plenty of space for the dance. His multitudinous costumes are beautiful both in detail and in massed effect. Only the cut of the tutus, which are large, floppy, and thus line-obscuring, is unhappy.

"Nureyev's handling of the piece is extremely elaborate, from the first moment of the fairies' entrée; they come on four at a time, *bourrée*ing hand-in-hand, each group with an attendant cavalier, who then lifts the leader while she draws her companions through the mazes of a most un-Petipalike procession. The second fairy variation is danced in duplicate, which is unusual, but in the score the variation does bear the names of two characters (Coulante, Farine). Nureyev's main innovation in the Prologue is to divide the role of the Lilac Fairy into two: a 'Principal Fairy,' who does the dancing, and a Lilac Fairy 'proper,' who turns up at the party, last guest to arrive, only after Carabosse has spoken her curse. Crinolined and heavily draped, an ambulant tea cozy, this fairy can do little more than glide about and wave her wand. Carabosse is played by a woman, as she was by Natalia Dudinskaya in Leningrad a decade or so ago, and she is played by Celia Franca in terms of offended dignity rather than evil malice. Her retinue roughs up the good fairies in a rather infelicitous sequence. Amid all this complication, and with the roles of good and evil genies reduced, the point of the Prologue is not clearly made. The fact that the fairies are endowing young Aurora with the gifts characterized in their variations is unstated, and a newcomer might watch the scene without even becoming aware that a royal infant is the focus of the festivities. The knitting bee, at the start of Act I, becomes another production number, involving slatterns, cat's-paws, halberdiers, hangmen, and a good deal of fussy activity. At the close of the act, the four minor princes, lunging at

Carabosse, run one another through. But Petipa's lovely inventions for Aurora are respected, even if eight minstrel girls figure too prominently in parts of the Rose Adagio. Veronica Tennant, Aurora at both performances I saw, places the choreography precisely, apart from a tendency to push forcefully into arabesque. She does not convey much sense of a developing character, and her dancing lacks, above all, legato—that feeling for a flowing line which links one image to the next. It is stop and start again—sequences chopped into short phrases. And this is a general company fault, observable in most of the solo dancing. The musical director, George Crum, has it, too; Tchaikovsky's long melodies do not flow smoothly enough. The anonymous orchestra is proficient but a bit short on strings. Some of Mr. Crum's rhythms are sludgy and undramatic.

"When, in Act II, Prince Florimund arrives, in the person of Rudolf Nureyev (who dances fourteen of the sixteen New York performances), he gives a splendid demonstration of that phrasing command which, so to speak, keeps the line going through the rests. In Petipa's original the Prince was not a large dancing role (the brilliant male technician of the Petersburg company, Enrico Cecchetti, created not the Prince but the Bluebird—and also Carabosse); Nureyev has enlarged it. He has given himself three variations in Act II, the second of them done to Panorama music shifted to an earlier point in the act. Aurora's second solo has been rewritten, without the alternating *relevés*, and not improved. The voyage to the palace and the Prince's entry are, as I said, strikingly achieved. After the Awakening, the climax of the story, there is a letdown. It is mainly Petipa's fault; here, surely, there should be a *pas de deux* for the Princess 'whose radiant beauty' (in Perrault's words) 'seemed to glow with a kind of heavenly light' and the Prince 'who hardly knew how to express his joy and gratitude'—but, instead, the curtain drops after a few bars. In the old Covent Garden version the difficulty was solved by moving straight into the wedding celebrations, and for the 1968 production Ashton composed a tender new *pas de deux* to the music of the entr'acte. In the Canadian version, on the opening night, Miss Tennant and Nureyev made things worse by expressing no great interest in one another. Reactions in this production were often inadequate. Earlier in Act II, the Prince showed little surprise when the Lilac Fairy joined him but behaved as if fairy apparitions were an everyday occurrence. Act III in the Canadian *Beauty* opens not brilliantly but quietly, with the Sarabande, originally the penultimate dance, brought forward. Then things follow much their usual course. The *pas de quatre* of Jewels becomes a *pas de cinq*, with the Diamonds a twin set. (The male Diamond is allotted Sapphire's 5/4 solo variation.) Bluebirds are placed before Cats; Red Ridinghood, Hop-o'-My-Thumb, and Cinderella are omitted; so, unfortunately, is the apotheosis. Again, the plot point—that all the characters of fairyland have assembled to pay homage to the royal couple—is not potently made, but again there is a display of dense dance patterns around the solos, with much rich 'doubling at the octave' in Nureyev's favored manner.

"The National Ballet of Canada was conceived when the Sadler's Wells/Royal Ballet, after its New York triumphs in 1949, went on to appear in Toronto. The official début was late in 1951; the company comes of age with a *Sleeping Beauty* that shows it need yield nothing in scale of presentation to the London company."*

March 15, 1973, the Royal Ballet produced a new version of *The Sleeping Beauty*. Designed by Peter Farmer, with lighting by William Bundy, the ballet used the choreography of Marius Petipa with new and additional dances by Kenneth MacMillan. Antoinette Sibley was the *Princess Aurora*, Anthony Dowell the *Prince*. The fairy variations were danced by Jennifer Penney, Laura Connor, Alfreda Thorogood, Anita Young, Lesley Collier, and Deanne Bergsma (the *Lilac Fairy*). Lesley Collier and Michael Coleman were the *Bluebirds*. Clement Crisp reviewed it in *The Financial Times*: " 'A magical fantasy'—thus I. A. Vsevolozhsky, director of the Imperial Theatres and guiding spirit in the creation of *The Sleeping Beauty* as librettist and designer of the costumes, wrote to Tchaikovsky when he commissioned the score. *Beauty* is, of course, several things: the supreme achievement of Petipa's genius; the pinnacle of nineteenth-century ballet; a *ballet féerie* designed to delight a court audience and pay discreetly flattering homage to the Tsar, whose servants the artists of the Imperial Ballet were. For us it is the signature work of the Royal Ballet—symbol of the company's maturity in the 1946 staging, testimony to the international standing of the troupe at the triumphant New York opening in 1949.

"The 1946 staging was decorated by Oliver Messel, and after the austerities of the war it looked supremely opulent. Five years ago a new production, with designs by Henry Bardon and Lila de Nobili—*à la manière de Doré*—was a brave attempt at rethinking the piece; but it lacked airiness, space in which Petipa's inventions could breathe; and hence the new production by Kenneth MacMillan with designs by Peter Farmer, given at a gala in the presence of Her Majesty the Queen last night to pay tribute to the American Friends of Covent Garden whose generosity has paid for this much-needed revision.

"The result is entirely worthwhile. This new staging is Vsevolozhsky's 'magical fantasy,' with steps restored, some choreography renewed, other sections embellished. The *Beauty* has been reawakened, and the whole staging is a reassertion of MacMillan's love and understanding of the classic tradition of which he is a product. To detail the various innovations must wait until later viewings of the production; suffice it to say that the spirit of this great ballet is honored throughout. MacMillan has done his homework—*Beauty* is a well-documented ballet—and both the spirit of the piece and its choreographic structure have been honorably displayed.

"It is the special merit of Peter Farmer's settings that they give ample room

* From *A Musical Season* (Viking Press); © 1973 Andrew Porter. Originally in *The New Yorker*.

for the dances. Each act of the ballet is conceived in one color: the Prologue is almost entirely blue—the most difficult shade to bring off on stage—and in amid the soaring arches of King Florestan's palace, which suggest a properly magical setting for a fairy tale, the arrival of the fairy godmothers had been staged with extraordinary skill as they enter down mysterious flights of stairs hidden from our eyes.

"For Act One we are in a garden setting which, at first viewing, seems too ingratiatingly pretty, but here—as throughout the evening—I was conscious of the care taken that nothing should obscure the impact of the dances. In the Prologue, the Fairy variations glittered diamond-sharp against the indigo darkness of the palace; with Aurora's appearance we could see the majesty of Petipa's inventions plain, and Antoinette Sibley was in superb form as the young princess, and later as the vision, and ultimately and most brilliantly as the bride.

"Carabosse—Alexander Grant, tremendous here as throughout the evening—is placed on stage under the guise of a courtier, and the spell is cast, and the Lilac Fairy intervenes, with a real feeling for the magical element that sustains the whole action of the piece. In this scene, as at every point during the action, there is a concern for dramatic credibility; MacMillan has reworked small incidents that have become dully traditional, and the action is carried forward with a nice appreciation for period style.

"The first two acts are set in a suitably fantastic and improbable realm of fairy enchantment; but with the hunting scene we enter a world which, as Vsevolozhsky intended, has some historical reality. The whole development of the staging moves from the imaginary, dream-like setting of Aurora's youth into the clarity and formal elegance of the age of Louis XIV in which she must awake from Carabosse's enchantment.

"The Prince Florimund is Anthony Dowell, princely in style and technique; his journey to Aurora's palace—with its use of panorama as demanded by Tchaikovsky's music—is true theatrical magic and the celebrations of the final act are grand and beautiful. Further comment must wait until the *Beauty* enters the repertory next week: until then a welcome for the production, and for the excellence of the company's performance."

For a contemporary Soviet Russian appraisal of Marius Petipa's achievement in *The Sleeping Beauty*, an essay by Vera Krasovskaya in *Dance Perspectives*, No. 49, is of interest. Yuri Slonimsky's monograph, *Marius Petipa*, translated by Anatole Chujoy in *Dance Index* VI, Nos. 5 and 6 (1947), remains the classic account of that master's work, by the renowned Soviet critic and historian. Also of interest is *Russian Ballet Master: the Memoirs of Marius Petipa*, edited by Lillian Moore and translated by Helen Whittaker (New York, Macmillan, 1958).

Now the wheel has come full circle. The Sadler's Wells Ballet production of *The Sleeping Beauty*, designed by Oliver Messel, which introduced the ballet to the modern audience, has been mounted anew by American Ballet Theatre, which staged it at the Metropolitan Opera House, New York, June 15, 1976, with Natalia Makarova and Mikhail Baryshnikov. The production was staged by Mary Skeaping, after Petipa; the lighting was by Nananne Porcher.

Margot Fonteyn's performance in the original Messel production by the Sadler's Wells Ballet in New York in 1949 has been recalled by the critic Dale Harris in *Ballet Review* (Vol. 4, No. 6): "The ultimate proof of Fonteyn's skill was to make her last-act variation into the climax of the entire evening, to transform into the apex of Aurora's good fortune a simple dance designed to provide a lyrical contrast with the *grand adage* that precedes it and the strong male solo and boisterous coda that succeed it. In 1949 there was no male solo and the coda was used for the Three Ivans. Fonteyn's triumph was compounded of all her virtues: the slow opening section showed off her nobly proportioned body, its perfect placement, the pliancy of her back, the clarity and continuity of her line from fingertips to feet, the ballerina head and face which gave focus to the body's expressiveness by directing the audience's attention where she wanted it to be. In the sequence to the perky violin solo, as she flicked her wrists while raising her arms she would draw the rhythm taut by raising her eyes a fraction later than her arms. The same kind of rubato informed her phrasing of the *petits battements frappés* to the pizzicati, so that she seemed to be toying with the music, teasing it out, flirting with it. Yet in the final section her fast, sure *piqué* turns were thrilling precisely because they accorded so exactly with the music's strong, driving rhythm. Fonteyn's musicality was awesome."*

Clive Barnes in a long appraisal of American Ballet Theatre's revival of the ballet entitled "A Promise Fulfilled" (the New York *Times*, June 27, 1976) discussed the virtues of the Oliver Messel production and its meaning for the company's dancers and the contemporary audience.

The critic Tobi Tobias wrote an interesting historical overview of *The Sleeping Beauty* entitled "Inheritance" for the first issue of American Ballet Theatre's magazine *On Point*, Summer 1976.

SMALL PARADES

Music by Edgard Varèse. Choreography by Glen Tetley. Decor and costumes by Nadine Baylis. Lighting by John B. Read. First presented by the Netherlands Dance Theatre in March 1972. First presented in the United States by the same ensemble at the Brooklyn Academy of Music, New York, March 30, 1972.

A dance ballet to contemporary music in a chaste, modern setting, *Small Parades* is performed to five famous pieces by Varèse: *Intégrales, Density 21.5,*

* Reprinted by permission of *Ballet Review*, Marcel Dekker, publisher.

Octandre, Hyperprism, and *Ionisation.* Arranged for ten dancers, the ballet is divided into five parts, like the music, and performed without interruption.

Writing after its U.S. premiere, Clive Barnes said in the New York *Times* that *Small Parades* "is a ballet of space and emotion. Its vocabulary is a perfect amalgam of classic ballet and modern dance, and its structure has a natural strength . . . Tetley uses classic dance here almost as a commentary on his modern-dance experience. These Dutch dancers are the perfect expression of this revealing choreographic ambiguity."

SOLITAIRE

Music by Malcolm Arnold. Choreography by Kenneth MacMillan. Scenery and costumes by Lawrence Shafer. First presented by the Sadler's Wells Theatre Ballet, June 7, 1956, with Margaret Hill, Sara Neil, and Donald Britton. First presented in the United States by the Royal Ballet at the Metropolitan Opera House, New York, September 17, 1957, with scenery and costumes by Desmond Healy.

Solitaire is a playful *divertissement* arranged to the *English Dances* of Malcolm Arnold. Its choreographer calls the ballet "a kind of game for one" and the ballet follows the efforts of an attractive girl to be included in a group of other young people. Time and again she tries to join in their games but is always rebuffed. In the end, she is as alone as she was at the beginning. While this sounds somewhat sad, it is not, because both the music and the dances have a gaiety and warmth that suggest inner as well as conscious security. The girl is lovely, she dances superbly. It is perhaps the people she wants to be with who are missing something!

SOME TIMES

Music by Claus Ogerman. Choreography by Dennis Nahat. Scenery and costumes by Rouben Ter-Arutunian. Lighting by Nananne Porcher. First presented by American Ballet Theatre at the New York State Theatre, Lincoln Center, New York, July 14, 1972, with Mimi Paul, Martine van Hamel, Naomi Sorkin, Ian Horvath, and Dennis Nahat and ensemble.

A ballet about young people in these times, this ballet, without a narrative, plots the interaction of the sexes in a series of dances. A lone girl moves through a social scene as if she were alone. Two boys and a girl fantasize together. The scene, an abstract one, might be any contemporary place in which young persons might be alone, and be themselves.

SONATINE

Music by Maurice Ravel. Choreography by George Balanchine. Lighting by Ronald Bates. First presented by the New York City Ballet at the Hommage à Ravel at the New York State Theatre, Lincoln Center, May 14, 1975, with Violette Verdy and Jean-Pierre Bonnefous. Pianist: Madeleine Malraux.

This little dance ballet opened our Ravel Festival at the New York City Ballet in 1975. The year 1975 was the one hundredth anniversary of Ravel's birth. I have always loved his music, from the time I made a bit of a waltz from his *Valses Nobles et Sentimentales* in Russia, and so we thought it would be a good idea to celebrate this wonderful composer's life and work by arranging new dances to as many scores as we could. We did seventeen ballets, sixteen of them new. Some were very long, like *L'Enfant et les Sortilèges*, with lots of costumes and a big production. Others, like *Sonatine*, were only a few minutes long, simply using Ravel's music and making what we could of it.

The pianist and the dancers are on stage together when the curtain goes up on the ballet. The pianist begins to play; the girl and the boy stand and listen. They like what they hear, apparently, for they begin to move to it, following its line, and gradually becoming imbued with its spirit.

THE SONG OF THE EARTH

Music by Gustav Mahler. Choreography by Kenneth MacMillan. First presented by the Stuttgart Ballet Company, November 7, 1965. First presented in the United States by the Royal Ballet at the new Metropolitan Opera House, April 25, 1967, with Anthony Dowell, Donald MacLeary, Georgina Parkinson, Jennifer Penney, and Ann Jenner in leading roles.

Mahler regarded his *Das Lied von der Erde* as a "symphony in songs." The work is set for tenor, alto, and orchestra. Mahler found the text for his songs in a volume of translations of the Chinese poet Li-Tai-Po (702–763) and others. The poems speak of earthly woe, loneliness, youth, beauty, drunkenness and the spring, and farewell, not, in other words, celebrating nature so much as expressing a philosophy of a lifetime. To the last poem, the composer added these lines:

> The lovely earth, all, everywhere,
> Revives in spring and blooms anew,
> All, everywhere and ever, ever,

* See also SHADOW OF THE WIND.

Shines the blue horizon,
Ever . . . ever . . .

The choreographer has said that his ballet is about Death. "This theme comes out very strongly. But I can't say that the man who moves among the dancers like Death actually is Death. That would be too specific. The Germans call him *der Ewige*, the one who is always there, and it is difficult to find an English equivalent. The direct translation would be The Eternal, but probably the best description is in the last line of the last poem, 'Forever . . . forever . . .'

"The Death figure is not at all evil. In fact, he is . . . just there, always hanging about. He wears a colorless mask without any marks on it, and it makes him look like the others, only just that much different. Basically the theme of the ballet is quite simple: a man and a woman; Death takes the man; they both return to her and at the end of the ballet—in the last poem—we find that in Death there is the promise of renewal."

While Kenneth MacMillan has said that people expecting a line by line translation in stage action of the text of the songs are bound to be disappointed, he has tried, as with *Images of Love*, to distill what is spoken, "and to find imagery for the ideas behind the words. My interest was to create movements to describe the essence of the poems."

Since the songs are sung in the theatre in German, a translation of them by Alfred H. Meyer is given here:

THE DRINKING SONG OF EARTHLY WOE

Wine in the golden goblet is beckoning,
But drink not yet, first I will sing you a song!
The Song of Sorrow, let its mockery laugh itself into your soul.

When sorrow approaches, the soul's gardens lie desolate,
Joy and song wither and die.
Dark is life, is death.

Lord of this house!
Thy cellar holds the fullness of golden wine!
Here, this lute I call mine own!

To play upon the lute, to empty glasses,
These are things that fit each other.
At the proper time a goblet full of wine
Is worth more than all the kingdoms of this earth!
Dark is life, is death!

The firmament in its eternal blue, and the earth,
These will long endure, will blossom in springtime.
But thou, O man, what is the span of thy life?
Not a hundred years art thou permitted to enjoy
The idle vanities of this earth!

Look there below! In the moonlight upon the graves
There crouches a wild, ghostly figure—
An ape it is! Hark how his howling
Shrills out into the sweet airs of this our life!

Bring on the wine! The time has come, my comrades!
Drain your golden goblets to the dregs!
Dark is life, is death!

THE LONELY ONE IN AUTUMN

The mists of autumn build their blue wall over the sea;
With hoarfrost covered, stands the grass;
It seems as if an artist had strewn the dust of jade over delicate blossoms.
The flowers' fragrance has spent itself;

A cold wind bows them to earth.
Soon the withered, golden leaves
Of lotus flowers will be scattered upon the waters.
My heart is weary. My little lamp
Has gone out, a-crackling, minding me of need for sleep,
I come to you, blest resting-place!
Yea, give me rest; for I need quickening!

I weep and weep in all my solitude.
Autumn in my heart too long is lasting.
O Sun of Love, never again wilt thou shine,
Gently to dry my bitter tears?

OF YOUTH

Midway in the little pool
Stands a pavilion of green
And of white porcelain.
Like the back of a tiger
The bridge of jade arches
Across to the pavilion.

In the little house friends are seated,
Beautifully gowned, drinking, gossiping;
Some are writing verses.

Their silken sleeves glide
Backwards, their silken caps
Hang from the back of their necks.

On the smooth surface of the quiet pool
All is mirrored
Wondrously.

All stands upon its head
In the pavilion of green
And of white porcelain.

Like a half-moon stands the bridge,
Reversed in its bow. Friends,
Beautifully gowned, are drinking, gossiping.

Of Beauty

Youthful maidens are plucking flowers,
Plucking lotus flowers at the edge of the shore.
Between bushes and leaves are they sitting.
Gathering blossoms in their laps and calling
To each other in jest.
The golden sun plays about their forms,
Reflected in the quiet water.
The sun mirrors their slender limbs,
Their sweet eyes,
And a zephyr with gentlest caress raises the fabric
Of their sleeves, wafts the magic
Of their perfume through the air,
O see, beautiful youths at play
On fiery horses, over there at the edge of the shore,
Glistening from afar like rays of the sun;
Between the green branches of the willows
Fresh youth is making its way!
The steed of one whinnies for joy
And shies and rushes past.
Over flowers, grasses, gallop his hoofs,
Whose stormy stamping crushes the fallen blossoms.

Heigh! How his mane flies in the breeze,
How his nostrils dilate!

The golden sun plays about the forms,
Reflecting them in the quiet water.
And the loveliest of the maidens
Sends him long glances of yearning.
Her haughty bearing is no more than feigned.
In the sparkle of her wide eyes,
In the darkening of the eager glance,
Ascends the plaint of the passion of her heart.

THE DRUNKEN ONE IN SPRINGTIME

If life is no more than a dream,
Why bother?
I'll drink, till drink no more I can,
The whole, live-long day!

And when no longer I can drink,
When throat and soul are full,
I'll stagger on till to my door,—
And sleep, and sleep, and sleep.

What hear I, awakening? List!
A bird sings in a tree.
I ask him whether Spring has come,
I feel as in a dream.

The birdling twitters, Yes! the Spring
Overnight has come!
In contemplation deep I brood,
While birdling sings and laughs!

Anew I fill my goblet
And drain it to the dregs
And sing until the moon shines bright
In the dark'ning firmament!

And when no longer I can sing
Again to sleep I'll go.
For what matters Spring to me?
Drunk only let me be!

FAREWELL

The sun is sinking 'neath the hills.
Evening descends into the vales
With its cool, quiet shadows.
Behold! As a bark of silver
The moon rises into the blue heaven.
I feel the motion of a gentle wind
Behind the dark pines.

The brook sings its music through the dark.
The flowers grow pale in the twilight.
The earth breathes the quiet of rest and sleep.
All longing goes a-dreaming.
Weary humanity is homeward bound,
To seek anew in sleep
Forgotten fortune, youth.
Birds are perched upon their branches.
The world falls into sleep.
The cool wind is in the shadow of my pines.

I stand here and await my friend, for a last farewell.
I long, O friend, at thy side
To drink in the beauty of this evening.
Where are you? You leave me long in solitude!
I wander to and fro with my lute
On paths thick with soft grass.
O Beauty! O World, drunk with love eternal—life!

He climbed from his horse and gave his friend a farewell cup; asked him
Whither he was going, and why it needs must be.
He spoke, his voice choking: O, my friend, Fate in this world has not
been kind to me!
Whither am I bound? I go, I wander into the mountains.
I seek rest for my lonely heart.
I am wand'ring toward my native place, my home.

I shall no longer seek the far horizon.
My heart is still and waits for its deliverance.
The lovely earth, all, everywhere,
Revives in spring and blooms anew,
All, everywhere and ever, ever,
Shines the blue horizon,
Ever . . . ever . . .

The English music and dance critic Andrew Porter has written:
"MacMillan has shaped his response to the score in pure movement. No
decor. No costumes. No picturesque lighting. And no 'acting.'

"The music of *The Drinking Song of Earthly Woe* leaps up and the boys
leap on in a bounding, unforced surge of invention, patterning the energy and
the soaring, plunging emotional contours of the movement. The slow movement, *The Lonely One in Autumn,* is quietly and simply danced by four girls,
sometimes partnered, sometimes not ('O Sun of Love, will you never shine
again, gently to dry my bitter tears?'). There follow three scherzos. *Of Youth*
tells verbally of a cultivated social scene, a pavilion of green and white porcelain where friends sit, chatter, write verses. MacMillan finds playful, exqui-
sitely articulated invention—and when the tenor sings of the reflections in the little pool ('everything standing on its head') the soloist is momentarily inverted!

"In *Of Beauty* the choreographer keeps more specifically to the poet's narrative: the girls plucking flowers by the stream, the boys crashing in on their
prancing horses; the love-glance that unites one couple. In *The Drunkard in
Spring,* set for four boys, MacMillan has treated drunkenness with great delicacy. It could so easily be vulgar, but his handling is as poetic, as lyrical, as
Li-Tai-Po's and Mahler's. There is a wonderful moment when a question is
asked: no conventional mime-signal, but a new unforced image that seems to
sing.

"Throughout, MacMillan works with extraordinary economy. Only twenty
dancers are involved, and the second half of the finale, the *Farewell,* the
longest movement, is set only for three: the ballerina, her human partner, and
der Ewige, the eternal one. A half-mask sets him apart from the others, even
while he joins in their dances.

> "Whither am I bound? I go, I wander into the mountains.
> I seek rest for my lonely heart.
> I am wandering toward my native place, my home.
>
> I shall never roam in foreign lands.
> My heart is at rest and waits its hour!

"And then Mahler adds the words already quoted. Solos, *pas de deux, pas
de trois* succeed one another. Human parting, eternal beauty. It is all so simple, so clear, so poetic."

SONG OF THE NIGHTINGALE

*Dramatic ballet in two scenes. Music by Igor Stravinsky. Choreography by
Leonide Massine. Scenery and costumes by Henri Matisse. First presented
by Diaghilev's Ballets Russes, February 2, 1920, Paris. Revived by Dia-*

ghilev's Ballets Russes, 1925, with choreography by George Balanchine and with Alicia Markova in the principal role.

This work, based on the story of "The Nightingale" by Hans Christian Andersen, is both an opera and a ballet; it has also been arranged by the composer as a symphonic poem. First performed as an opera, the score was revised to exclude voices for ballet performance. The opera consisted of three acts. In the ballet the first act was omitted, but it is necessary to mention its contents here.

The scene of Act One is the home of the nightingale, a wood in China, near the palace of the emperor. A fisherman glides his boat across a lake. He sings to himself. As his boat goes into the distance, we hear the magical song of the nightingale. At the emperor's order, the imperial chamberlain and his followers come to the wood to hear the nightingale. As they seek its voice, they mistake other sounds for the song of the bird. They are led to the nightingale by a humble scullery maid. The courtiers are disappointed in the bird's ordinary appearance, but delighted at its song. The nightingale accepts their invitation to sing at court.

SCENE ONE: THE IMPERIAL PALACE When preparations have been made for his arrival, the Emperor of China enters his court. The nightingale is brought before him. The bird waits until the emperor signals her to begin her song, then commences.

The emperor is so enchanted with the song that he tells the bird she may have anything she wants. The bird replies that she has moved the emperor to tears and that is all the favor she requires.

Now the noble ladies, noting the high favor in which the lowly nightingale is held by their emperor, try to imitate her song. They fail miserably.

A gift arrives from the Emperor of Japan: a mechanical nightingale, beautifully wrought in gold and set with gems. The song of the toy bird delights the emperor and his court, and they forget the presence of the real nightingale. When the emperor tires of the toy and turns to ask the bird to sing again, she has disappeared. The angry monarch thereupon banishes the bird from his kingdom and makes the toy bird principal songster at his court.

SCENE TWO: THE EMPEROR'S BEDCHAMBER The mechanical nightingale stands by the emperor's bedside. The emperor is dying. Death stands ready to welcome the monarch, and courtiers prematurely prepare the way for his successor. Spirits taunt the emperor with a list of his good deeds and wrongdoings. He cannot bear their chatter and calls for music. He begins to expire.

The song of the nightingale is heard. The return of this beautiful music delights the emperor, and Death is so struck by the wonderful song of the nightingale that he asks the bird to continue to sing.

The bird consents if Death will permit the emperor to live. Death makes this bargain and vanishes as the nightingale again takes up her song.

The emperor recovers completely and again offers to do any favor the bird wishes. The nightingale replies that his tears are her best reward and that she will sing to him every night until the rise of the sun.

Officials of the court, come to continue the deathwatch, enter the bedchamber. They are astonished to find the emperor standing in all his majesty, ready to receive them.

NOTES *Le Rossignol* (*The Nightingale*) was originally composed as an opera in three acts, which Serge Diaghilev presented for the first time at the Paris Opéra, May 26, 1914, under the direction of Pierre Monteux. Alexandre Benois designed the scenery and costumes. This work was first presented in the United States at the Metropolitan Opera House, New York, on March 6, 1926, with Marion Talley in the principal role.

Stravinsky revised his score for symphonic performances, eliminating the first act of the original. He was persuaded by Diaghilev that this new arrangement of his music might be suitable for ballet, and, now called *Le Chant du Rossignol,* the work was presented, with the choreography by Leonide Massine.

A new ballet to this music was my first assignment for Diaghilev's Ballets Russes, soon after I joined the company. I chose for the leading role in the ballet the young artist Alicia Markova, who had just joined Diaghilev's company, when she was only fourteen years old. We saw Markova dance in London, in 1924, at the studio of Serafima Asafieva, where she was a brilliant student. Diaghilev engaged her—the youngest dancer ever to belong to his company—immediately after seeing her dance.

Music by Igor Stravinsky. Choreography by John Taras. Scenery and costumes by Rouben Ter-Arutunian. First presented at the New York City Ballet's Stravinsky Festival, June 22, 1972, at the New York State Theatre, Lincoln Center, with Gelsey Kirkland as the Nightingale, *Elise Flagg as the* Mechanical Nightingale, *Francisco Moncion as the* Emperor, *Penny Dudleston as* Death, *and Peter Naumann as the* Fisherman.

When we were planning our celebration of Stravinsky's ninetieth birthday at the New York City Ballet, one of the composer's works that came immediately to mind was the *Song of the Nightingale,* which had been missing for too long a time from the ballet theatre. The ballet master John Taras undertook the choreography, which retells the lovely story in a most effective way. Writing after the premiere in the *Daily News,* the critic Sam Norkin said:

"John Taras' version of this fairy tale ballet with lavish, colorful decor by Rouben Ter-Arutunian was seen for the first time last night. This is the tale of the Chinese emperor who banishes his live nightingale in favor of a mechanical one, to his regret. Compassionately, the real bird returns in time to save the emperor from the throes of death. The intriguing character solos were beautifully designed and executed. The corps flourished long ribbons and there was a courtiers' pageant. This elegant new ballet belongs in the repertory."

SONGS OF A WAYFARER

Music by Gustav Mahler. Choreography by Maurice Béjart. First presented by the Ballet of the Twentieth Century at the Forest National Arena, Brussels, March 11, 1971, with Rudolf Nureyev and Paolo Bortoluzzi. First presented in the United States by Rudolf Nureyev and Friends at the Uris Theatre, New York, March 1, 1977, with Nureyev and Johnny Eliasen.

It has been said that Mahler's songs are the way to his symphonic works. The *Lieder eines fahrenden Gesellen* (*Songs of a Wayfarer*) indeed leads thematically to sections of the First and Fourth Symphonies, but it is in the beautiful simplicity of the songs, the words here by Mahler himself, written after an unhappy love affair, that we begin to catch the complexities the composer was later to develop. The songs in this case, sung by a man accompanied by orchestra, tell the story of a young man who cannot forget the loss of a girl who marries another. This theme is another variation on Schubert's *Die Schöne Müllerin*. At first, the man is sick with grief and despair. Later, turning to nature, he is partially revived but in a wild impetuous third song the dagger that stabs his breast returns and he cannot escape the girl's dominion over him. The final song begins with the poet saying that eyes of blue are sweet but fill me with fear and I must say goodbye to all I hold dear. He continues to wander, lonely at night, finding rest under a linden tree, finally, where pain is forgotten.

It is important to know what the words are about, for although this ballet does not reproduce the suggested action of the poem, its subject is the hero's state of mind. The other dancer who moves with him is his alter ego, representing his states and shifts of mind. They are the only two performers, and the emotions the hero lives through in his loss constitute the choreographic fabric.

After the premiere of *Songs of a Wayfarer* in Brussels, the critic John Percival wrote to *Dance and Dancers* magazine that the character Nureyev portrays "exists pure and undiluted by any element of story telling, diversion or contrast—just fifteen minutes of sheer theatrical impact which holds the huge audience spellbound."

LA SONNAMBULA (*see* NIGHT SHADOW)

LA SOURCE

Music by Leo Delibes. Choreography by George Balanchine. Costumes by
Karinska. Lighting by Ronald Bates. First presented by the New York City
Ballet at the New York State Theatre, Lincoln Center, November 23,
1968, with Violette Verdy and John Prinz in principal roles.

My admiration for Delibes as a composer of music for ballet is no secret, I believe; with Tchaikovsky, who knew his music well, of course, and Stravinsky,
he is for me one of the three great musicians of the dance. Some years ago, in
1950, to music from his superb ballet score *Sylvia,* I arranged a *pas de deux*
that was danced by Maria Tallchief and André Eglevsky, and is still danced
by others, with some success. This was later expanded into a *divertissement*
for the New York City Ballet. That, however, was not enough and I kept wanting to use more of Delibes's music. The result is *La Source,* which uses music
from that work and from *Naila,* too. *La Source* puts together an earlier *pas de*
deux of that title with elements from the *Sylvia Pas de Deux and Divertisse-*
ment.
    The ballet is in effect an extended *pas de deux,* with a soloist and a *corps de*
ballet of eight girls. The curtain rises on an empty stage—only a blue background—soon after the music starts. A boy carries on a girl and their dance begins. After an adagio, each does a variation. The soloist and girls dance now to
wonderfully familiar music by Delibes. In the midst of the ensemble, the couple return and the stage is left to them. The boy dances a second variation, as
does the girl. The ensemble takes the stage again briefly, before the girl and
boy return for a final flourish of dancing.

NOTES Writing in *Dance and Dancers,* Patricia Barnes wrote of an early
performance: "The two dancers, Violette Verdy and John Prinz, dance the
work wonderfully well . . . The choreography and music for Prinz's second
solo are strongly rhythmic, and the dancing given to him is pure virtuosity—as
an example, a passage of whirling turns in *arabesque* which Prinz manages
with admirable dexterity. This gives way to a precise pizzicato solo for Verdy
ending in a *manège* of turns . . . Verdy gives the ballet just the right radiance,
and Prinz in his first created leading role confirmed that he is one of the most
interesting young dancers in America, or indeed, anywhere."

SOUVENIRS

Music by Samuel Barber. Choreography by Todd Bolender. Scenery and
costumes by Rouben Ter-Arutunian. Lighting by Jean Rosenthal. First pre-

sented by the New York City Ballet at the City Center, New York, November 15, 1955, with Edith Brozak, Ann Crowell, Carolyn George (Three Young Girls), Arthur Mitchell (Attendant), Roberta Meier and Richard Thomas (Husband and Wife), Todd Bolender (A Man About Town), Roy Tobias (Another Man About Town), Jillana and Jonathan Watts (A Lady and Her Escort), Wilma Curley and Robert Barnett (Bride and Groom), Irene Larsson (The Woman), John Mandia (The Man), Jane Mason (A Maid), Herbert Bliss (Man in Grey), Patricia Savoia, Dido Sayers, Ronald Colton, Gene Gavin, Walter Georgov (Hotel Guests), and Eugene Tanner (An Attendant).

The designer of *Souvenirs,* Rouben Ter-Arutunian, accurately sets the stage in a recollection published in *Dance Perspectives:* "The costumes were taken from the era of silent films and based on a set of fashion plates Todd Bolender had found . . . The ballet was a spoof of a certain aura of pre-World War I, and the set was more a series of prop pieces than a decor as such. There was the prop of the elevator; a few palms, suggesting the court of a European-type spa; a round banquette, found often in the vestibules of these hotels. Later there was a set of doors; a couch with a tiger, and a beaded curtain; then, at the end, a pole with banners and a virile lifeguard. There was a minimum of decor. The emphasis was on the costumes, which brought out the satire."

The time is 1914, the scene the Palm Springs Hotel. In six swift episodes the ballet shows us some of the guests and what they are up to: how they make their entrance to the hotel and try to get acquainted; how a bride and groom can get mixed up in a corridor with a Man About Town and his Lady; how girls at dances pine for partners and how one who is pretty can dance with four men at the same time; how a wife can make a new conquest over an argument with her husband; how a siren entices a Man About Town into her boudoir and feigns to protect herself with a gun; how, on the beach the next afternoon, a lifeguard is the center of attention.

The music for *Souvenirs,* originally composed as a suite for two pianos, uses old dance forms that were popular in the days before World War I. The work was orchestrated by the composer for the New York City Ballet.

SPARTACUS

Ballet in four acts. Music by Aram Khachaturian. Choreography by Yuri Grigorovich. Scenery and costumes by Simon Virsaladze. First presented in this version by the Bolshoi Ballet at the Bolshoi Theatre, Moscow, April 9, 1968, with Vladimir Vasiliev, Yekaterina Maximova, Maris Liepa, and Nina Timofeyeva in principal roles.

Not the first Soviet ballet to this story, this one by Grigorovich appears to have attracted the most acclaim. A synopsis of the action, based on classical sources such as Plutarch, relating the fate of the Roman slave Spartacus, follows:

ACT ONE, SCENE ONE: SUBJUGATION   The Roman legions terrify their captive empire. The army leader is Crassus, cruel, ruthless, and coldly flamboyant. After campaigns in Thrace, where the land has been pillaged and burnt, he brings back Thracian captives to Rome to sell as slaves. Among them are Spartacus and his wife, Phrygia. Spartacus expresses his love of freedom and his refusal to be reconciled to his new state of slavery.

ACT ONE, SCENE TWO: THE SLAVE MARKET   The captives are left at the wall of the capital. Men and women are separated so that each will get a better price for the slave dealer from the Roman patricians. Phrygia is parted from Spartacus. Phrygia is desperate in her grief. Her beloved Spartacus has been reduced to slavery, and she herself is subject not only to Rome but the Roman master who has purchased her, and taken her from her husband forever.

ACT ONE, SCENE THREE: ORGY   Phrygia has been bought by Crassus, and taken to Crassus's villa in Rome. Aegina, Crassus's concubine, mocks Phrygia's unhappiness and fears. For her, wine, gold, lust, power, and murder are the only facts of pleasure. Crassus is holding an orgiastic party for his friends. As the climax to this, two masked gladiators are brought in. They are to fight blindfolded until one of them is killed. They fight with blind and deathly intensity until one is slain. The victor takes off his mask. It is Spartacus.

Spartacus looks down at his unwitting victim with a terrified compassion. He has been forced to murder a fellow man, a slave like himself. What has he done? What more will he be forced to do?

ACT ONE, SCENE FOUR: THE GLADIATORS' BARRACKS   Spartacus, returned to the Gladiators' Barracks, is full of remorse. He calls upon the gladiators to break their chains and escape from their shameful captivity. With superhuman efforts they do this, and overcoming their guards flee to freedom.

ACT TWO, SCENE ONE: THE APPIAN WAY   It is night. The gladiators, escaping in glory, meet shepherds resting by the wayside. Inflamed with the spirit of revolt they call the shepherds to join them, and Spartacus's band is joined by many brave men. It is now an army, dedicated to remove the yoke of Rome. Spartacus is proclaimed its leader.

Alone, Spartacus muses on his forced acceptance of power. He is determined to lead his slave army to victory and to free thousands of Rome's victims. But he realizes that he first must find Phrygia and release her from Crassus.

ACT TWO, SCENE TWO: CRASSUS'S VILLA   Spartacus discovers Phrygia in

Crassus's villa to the south of Rome, and they are joyfully reunited. Meanwhile Crassus is giving a feast for the Roman patricians at which Aegina is also present.

Aegina contemplates Crassus and herself. She not only wants power over Crassus, but wishes to dominate the entire world. He tries to achieve it with power and cruelty, and she with cunning and duplicity. But they share the same ambitions—power, glory, and riches. Both need to acquire all and relinquish nothing.

ACT TWO, SCENE THREE: CRASSUS'S DEFEAT The patricians pander to Crassus and praise his power and victories. But the praise is cut short by the terrifying news that the villa is all but encircled by the advancing army of Spartacus. Crassus, Aegina, and the patricians depart in defeat, leaving Spartacus in possession of the villa.

Spartacus ponders on his victory. The Roman legions' success rests solely on the weapons of the legionnaires and the submission of the conquered. The Roman leaders themselves are cowards.

ACT TWO, SCENE FOUR: THE CONTEMPTUOUS GENEROSITY OF SPARTACUS Crassus has been captured and is brought before Spartacus, whom he recognizes as his former gladiator. The rebel soldiers want to execute the Roman general out of hand, but Spartacus asserts his authority and permits Crassus to save his life with the same kind of trial the tyrant imposed upon gladiators. But this time the singlehanded combat will not be blindfolded. The rebels are warriors, not murderers. Crassus fights Spartacus but is no match for him. At point of death Crassus pleads for mercy. With a gesture of contempt the rebel leader lets him go.

ACT THREE, SCENE ONE: CONSPIRACY The dishonored Crassus swears revenge, and Aegina fans his hatred. He calls his soldiers once more into the field, and Aegina sees them off to battle. Left alone, Aegina is full of hatred for Spartacus, fearing she might lose Crassus. She vows vengeance.

ACT THREE, SCENE TWO: THE ENCAMPMENT OF SPARTACUS Aegina steals into Spartacus's camp by night. Phrygia's fears are not helped by Spartacus's attempts to console her. Spartacus is told by a messenger that the Roman legions are advancing on him. He now puts forward his plan of battle, and the weaker among his captains are frightened by the daring of his tactics. Spartacus now calls upon all of them to take an oath of loyalty.

Spartacus, left to his thoughts, notes that the rebel forces will be defeated if there is dissension among their leaders. For all this death in battle is preferable.

ACT THREE, SCENE THREE: TREASON The faithful captains of Spartacus await his signal to start the combat and follow him at once. Those of weaker

mettle might have followed their example, but Aegina appears out of the darkness bringing wine and whores. They succumb to temptation and fall easily to
the advancing vanguard of Crassus's army. Crassus himself rewards Aegina for
her help.

Crassus now knows that his revenge will not be complete until Spartacus
has been killed, for he cannot forgive the humiliating stain to his honor he
suffered as the captive of a slave. He will overtake the remainder of Spartacus's army and annihilate it.

ACT THREE, SCENE FOUR: THE FINAL BATTLE   Spartacus's troops are encircled and his army is fast dwindling in the face of vastly superior forces.
Spartacus is still fearless and begins to counterattack the legionnaires. Cunningly the Romans ambush him, triumphantly raising him on their spears as he
dies a hero's death. Phrygia comes on to the battlefield to find his dead body.
She is heartbroken.

NOTES   The first Soviet ballet Spartacus had choreography by Leonid Ya-
cobson, music by Khachaturian, book by Nikolai Volkov, décor by Valentina
Khodasevich, and was first presented at the Kirov State Theatre in Leningrad,
December 27, 1956, with Makarov and Zubkovskaya in the principal roles of
Spartacus and Phrygia. Another treatment of the same story was made by Igor
Moiseyev, with designs by Alexander Konstinovsky, and given at the Bolshoi
Theatre, Moscow, March 11, 1958. This version, presented in the United
States at the Metropolitan Opera House, New York, September 12, 1962, by
the Bolshoi Ballet, featured Dmitri Begak and Maya Plisetskaya in the main
roles.

Writing in the British magazine Dance and Dancers about her impressions
of the Grigorovich Spartacus, Patricia Barnes said: "Grigorovich's choreography and conception are brilliant. This is an immensely moving work, filled
with imaginative theatrical strokes and performed with blazing intensity by
Mikhail Lavrovsky, who at this performance dominated the ballet. The dances
are fairly clearly divided between the coldly neo-classic steps given to Crassus
and his armies and the more plastique work, expressive and eloquent, for Spartacus and his followers.

"Particularly successful has been the way Grigorovich has used his male
dancers. Never have I seen an ensemble used with such sweep and grandeur,
and rarely has a dance work on such an ambitious scale succeeded so well in
putting across its ideas and dramatic theme with such a minimum of mimetic
fuss.

"The opening is startlingly effective. Crassus is seen standing in the center
of the stage, arm raised, the lower half of his body surrounded by a wall of
shields. Seconds later it is seen as the soldiers of his army spill forward filling
the vast stage in a profusion of silver uniforms, shields and swords.

"The tragic ending is in its way as admirable as the ballet's opening. The black-clad grieving figure of Phrygia is lifted high by the followers of Spartacus and the body of her husband is handed up to her, together with his battle shield. She lays the shield on his chest and, eyes cast down, sorrowfully contemplates the dead Spartacus. It is a beautifully conceived scene and brings the curtain down on a work of truly heroic dimensions.

"Mikhail Lavrovsky's Spartacus is a wonder to behold. It is a superbly thought-out role and Lavrovsky has explored every dramatic nuance of it. From our first view of him as a slave in bondage, through his moments of resolution as he vows to free the slaves in captivity, until his final battle, he never departs from a characterization that is deeply felt and powerfully projected.

"A particularly superb episode is a gladiator fight. Two men, blindfolded, are brought in for the entertainment of Crassus's court, and fight for their lives. One kills the other—he takes off his helmet, and it is Spartacus, grieving over the fellow slave he has been forced to kill. As he stands there his face reflects the bitter anguish of his heart and with it we see the beginnings of his revolt, the first stirrings of his determination to free himself and his fellow-slaves from his ruthless captors.

"Almost as impressive was the sweetly passionate portrayal of Phrygia by Natalia Bessmertnova. Her dancing, so extraordinarily individual, had the elegiac beauty of a poem and her dark eyes and pale face caught at the heart.

"In a role that was created by Maris Liepa (and one could see how brilliant he must have been), young Mikhail Gabovich was extraordinarily good. If he looked on the young side, he could hardly be blamed, being under twenty, and he nevertheless gave a portrayal of genuine power. He presented Crassus as a warrior both arrogant and heartless, and his dancing was lithely elegant.

"The last of the four principal roles, Aegina, is the least interesting, being rather more of a stereotype. It was performed on this occasion by Svetlana Adyrkhaeva, who danced with a sveltely voluptuous allure.

"Finally, the dancing of the company, for which no praise could be too high. The men in particular outdid themselves in convincing one that the stage was filled with hundreds. Their attack and technical mastery was constantly outstanding."

Clive Barnes in the magazine of the Friends of Covent Garden, *About the House,* said that the Grigorovich *Spartacus* was "undoubtedly the most successful Soviet ballet since *Romeo and Juliet.*" The Grigorovich *Spartacus* was performed by the Bolshoi Ballet in London for the first time July 17, 1969.

LE SPECTRE DE LA ROSE

Ballet in one act. Music by Carl Maria von Weber. Choreography by Michel Fokine. Book by J. L. Vaudoyer. Scenery and costumes by Léon Bakst. First presented by Diaghilev's Ballets Russes at the Théâtre de Monte Carlo, Monte Carlo, April 19, 1911, with Vaslav Nijinsky and Tamara Karsavina.

First presented in the United States by Diaghilev's Ballets Russes at the Metropolitan Opera House, New York, April 3, 1916, with Alexander Gavrilov and Lydia Lopokova.

This is a ballet danced by two people, a romantic *pas de deux*. The ballet has a simple story, but the story is so slight that we must refer to the actual dancing for an impression of the ballet. Its first performances convinced audiences that it was possible for two dancers, alone on a stage, to create a story and at the same time to create a mood in which that story could become real, like a lyric poem.

Le Spectre de la Rose is based on a poem, a poem by the nineteenth-century French poet and novelist and great critic of the ballet Théophile Gautier. Just as Gautier adapted the work of another poet, Heinrich Heine, to produce the romantic classic *Giselle,* so his own creative work gave to another age the inspiration for another romantic ballet. In Gautier's poem a rose addresses the girl who wore it to a ball. The rose is grateful for having danced with her all evening, grateful even for death on her breast, and tells the maiden that his ghost will continue to dance, at her bedside, all night long, to express his love.

The ballet *Le Spectre de la Rose* has a real setting but, as in *Giselle,* it is a dream that comes to life within this setting that creates its romanticism. The music is Carl Maria von Weber's *Invitation to the Dance,* as orchestrated by Hector Berlioz.

The curtain rises on a young girl's boudoir. The room is formal, high, and cool, with immense windows that look on to a garden. There is a bed on the right and on the left a small dressing table. The colors are blue and white, and as we look at the walls and the furniture and see the moon through the French windows, we imagine that the girl who lives here is demure and innocent. The room is uncluttered, plain in spite of its elegance; it makes you interested in the life it contains. The young girl enters. She is dressed formally, in a long white gown. She takes off the cape she wears about her shoulders, unties her bonnet, and we notice that she holds in her hand a red rose. She refuses to relinquish it as she moves about the room, turning slowly, dancing with an invisible partner, remembering the excitement of her first ball. She has come back from the dance to her familiar surroundings and finds the room a little old-fashioned; it has not changed as she imagines she has changed. She is in love. She presses her lover's rose against her cheek and sits down in a white chair near one of the windows. Half-asleep from fatigue, she still wishes to relive her first encounter with romance. But sleep soon overtakes her. Her hand falls from her face, and the red rose slips from her fingers to the floor.

There is almost no sound for a moment, and then suddenly, buoyantly, the orchestra plays at full volume a quick, intoxicating waltz. As this rush of sound fills the room, through the open window the spirit of the rose leaps in a high, smooth trajectory to stand poised behind the girl's chair. He dances alone as

the girl sleeps, moving about the room effortlessly, seeming to touch the floor
almost against his will, dancing with the lightness of the rose petals that adorn
his body.

He touches the girl, and now—awake in her dream—she dances with him.
When the two dance together to the soaring waltz, the young girl moves with
the grace of the spirit she has invoked; as they glide and leap about the room,
their dance is absolutely continuous, never-ending, unbroken in its flow of
movement into movement; the only thing that can stop it is the music. The girl
is inspired by her partner as naturally as she held the rose to her cheek and—
with his strong, but tender, aid—she becomes not simply a beautiful young girl
in love with love, but a part of the romantic night.

The dream cannot last. The waltz melody fades. The girl goes to her chair
and sits as before, her arm limp at her side, pointing to the rose on the floor.
The spirit of the rose hovers gently over her head in farewell and in a continuous movement rushes toward the window. He disappears into the oncom-
ing dawn at the high point of a leap that seems never-ending.

The light of the sun disturbs the girl. She moves in her sleep, then wakens
lazily, rubbing her eyes, not yet aware of where she is. She is still thinking of
the spirit of the rose and looks for her mysterious partner. He is not there! She
sees she is alone in her own room and that she must have been dreaming.
Then she sees the rose on the floor at her feet. She picks it up gently and holds
it against her breast, content that the dream is still with her.

Mikhail Baryshnikov first danced Le Spectre de la Rose at a performance
during the first Hamburg Ballet Festival, dedicated to the memory of Nijinsky,
June 22, 1975. Lynn Seymour was the girl. She had been advised on her role
by Margot Fonteyn, who had known the recollections of Tamara Karsavina.
Baryshnikov learned his role from André Eglevsky, the great premier danseur
who had learned it from Fokine himself. John Percival reported to Dance and
Dancers that he had never seen Baryshnikov "dance better in anything, and I
have never seen this role so well done. It was a very demanding version of the
choreography that he performed, but he danced at full strength throughout
. . . His immensely powerful leaps were done with such soft strength, and he
evoked perfectly the mixture of sensuousness and romance which is the ballet's
essence." In 1976, Baryshnikov danced the role for the first time in the United
States with American Ballet Theatre in a production with costumes by Stanley
Simmons. Marianna Tcherkassky was the girl.

Nancy Goldner wrote in Dance News after the 1976 revival by American
Ballet Theatre: "For once a legendary ballet made immediate sense. In a flash
the story became important and full of implication. One could really see and
feel the specter as an essence of nature and the sleeping beauty's shy, cautious,
and finally rapturous acknowledgment of the rose as a story about maturation.
As the dreamer, Tcherkassky was perfect . . . the perfect straight lady to
Baryshnikov's more exotic role. He was a marvel of strength and clarity, but
the fantastic aspect of his specter was that he reincarnates a historical style

without looking mannered . . . The gentle but insistent way he insinuated himself into the girl's mind was a masterful fusion of contradictory impulses. Similarly, his approach to the steps was robust while his body was curling, introspective. Even in the big soaring jumps were his eyes and head lowered, somehow hidden. He was utterly manly, yet utterly a personification of spirit. One could recognize in this *Spectre* the Fokine who made the male solo in *Les Sylphides.*"

On December 6, 1976, the American Ballet Theatre production was seen on WNET television in the program "In Performance at Wolf Trap."

In an account of his training for *Le Spectre de la Rose,* the dancer Mikhail Baryshnikov has recalled (in the book *Baryshnikov at Work*) that the ballet requires a very special style. He characterizes it as "a kind of broken, soft harmony. It calls for the dancer to dance in a less stretched-out way, almost a little 'off.'"

SQUARE DANCE

Music by Arcangelo Corelli and Antonio Vivaldi. Choreography by George Balanchine. Lighting by Nananne Porcher. Square Dance Caller: Elisha C. Keeler. First presented by the New York City Ballet at the City Center, New York, November 21, 1957, with Patricia Wilde and Nicholas Magallanes in the leading roles.

Ballet and other forms of dance of course can be traced back to folk dance. I have always liked watching American folk dances, especially in my trips to the West, and it occurred to me that it would be possible to combine these two different types of dance, the folk and the classic, in one work. To show how close the two really are, we chose old music also based on ancient dances and a new setting, put the musicians on the stage on a platform like a bandstand, and invited the famous square dance caller Elisha C. Keeler to call out the dances. The dances he called out seem to be folk dances, but of course all the steps were purely classic. The spirit and nerve required for superb square dancing are close to what we always want in ballet performances, which is one way perhaps of explaining why so many American dancers are so gifted. The American style of classic dancing, its supple sharpness and richness of metrical invention, its superb preparation for risks, and its high spirits were some of the things I was trying to show in this ballet.

The music, all for strings, consists of Corelli's *Saraband, Gigg,* and *Badiniere* from the *Suite for Strings,* and Vivaldi's *Concerti Grossi,* Op. 3 and Op. 10, and the *Violin Concertos,* Op. 3 and Op. 12, *Concerto for Violin and Strings in E major,* Op. 3, No. 12 (first movement), and *Concerto in B minor,* Op. 3, No. 10. Much of this eighteenth-century music was of course derived from old folk dance forms and rhythms that were later refined for the courts of Europe.

In 1976 we decided to revive *Square Dance* at the New York City Ballet, but with some changes, doing it without the caller and with the orchestra in the pit. I also put in a new dance for the boy. Kay Mazzo and Bart Cook danced the first performance of this revival, May 20, 1976, at the New York State Theatre. The following day, Anna Kisselgoff in the New York *Times* noted that while in the first version, you would have heard a call by Mr. Keeler and the music would repeat with the dancers performing the step, now the lead dancer calls the tune by dancing to it and the others follow him. "He is the caller, but uses movement instead of words."

SQUARES

Music by Zoltan Szilassy. Choreography by Hans van Manen. Decor and costumes by Bonies. First presented by the Netherlands Dance Theatre at the Théâtre de la Ville, Paris, June 24, 1969. First presented in the United States by the same ensemble at the Brooklyn Academy of Music, New York, March 30, 1972.

Squares is a way of looking at dance in a setting that frames the action. The setting, on a raised platform, invariably a variation on the square, varies: it is an enclosure, an upright outline, or a frame of light, fluorescent or ultraviolet. It hems the ten dancers in, liberates them, or sets them off.

STARS AND STRIPES

Ballet in five campaigns. Music by John Philip Sousa, adapted and orchestrated by Hershy Kay. Choreography by George Balanchine. Scenery and lighting by David Hays. Costumes by Karinska. First presented by the New York City Ballet at the City Center, New York, January 17, 1958, with Allegra Kent, Robert Barnett, Diana Adams, and Melissa Hayden and Jacques d'Amboise in the leading roles.

Ever since I came to the United States I have liked watching parades and listening to Sousa's marches. For many years in the back of my mind was the hope that one day I might find an opportunity to do a ballet using his music. The problem was always the arrangement of the music for dancing and it was not until I had heard Hershy Kay's arrangement of Gottschalk's music for *Cakewalk* that I thought I had found a solution. I talked about the possibility with the composer, who was just as enthusiastic as I was about Sousa. We went over all the pieces we might use and planned their arrangement together. Kay's score was just what I wanted.

We dedicated the ballet to the memory of Fiorello H. La Guardia, the late mayor of New York City who had epitomized America to so many of us for so many years.

The ballet is a kind of balletic parade, led by four "regiments." The five campaigns or movements feature each regiment in turn and at the end they all combine. In the first movement, to Sousa's *Corcoran Cadets* a majorette leads twelve girls. Another girl leads the second campaign in the *Rifle Regiment* march. *Thunder and Gladiator* march is danced by a regiment of boys, and the fourth, to the *Liberty Bell* and *El Capitan* marches, is a *pas de deux*. All regiments participate in the fifth campaign, the *Stars and Stripes* finale.

Karinska created brilliant costumes for this ballet and it seemed to me that David Hays's setting, and the final display of the American flag he arranged, were ideal.

THE STEADFAST TIN SOLDIER

Music by Georges Bizet. Choreography by George Balanchine. Setting and lighting by David Mitchell. Lighting by Ronald Bates. First presented by the New York City Ballet at the Saratoga Performing Arts Center, Saratoga, New York, in July 1975, with Patricia McBride and Peter Schaufuss. Conducted by Robert Irving.

Hans Christian Andersen's stories are endlessly interesting. I am always coming back to them—sometimes for ballets. This particular story, which I first arranged in *Jeux d'Enfants* in 1955, tells of a toy soldier who goes through an endless series of trials and difficulties for the sake of a doll who does not pay any attention to him. At the end, both toys fall into a fire. What happens in the ballet is a little different, but I hope clear. The doll is an automaton ballerina, a bit like the toy made by Dr. Coppélius but with more soul. She is so enchanted with herself that she just keeps on rejoicing in her steps and gestures. She adores herself and ignores entirely the soldier, who presents her with his heart. Still, she ignores him. Her dancing so overheats her that she opens the window for relief. A draft rushes into the room and sends her up the chimney. The tin soldier mourns her and rejoins his platoon. All he has left is his paper heart.

THE STILL POINT

Music by Claude Debussy. Choreography by Todd Bolender. First presented by the Dance Drama Company, 1954, with Emily Frankel and Mark Ryder. First presented in New York, April 10, 1955, at the YMHA. Presented by the New York City Ballet, March 14, 1956, with Melissa Hayden

Suzanne Farrell in *Union Jack*. Photo by Beverley Gallegos.

Gelsey Kirkland and Edward Villella in *Tarantella*. Photo by Martha Swope.

Patricia McBride and Jean-Pierre Bonnefous in *Who Cares?* Photo by Rosemary Winckley.

Merrill Ashley, Renee Estopinal, and Susan Pilarre in *Concerto Barocco*. Photo by Costas.

Violette Verdy and Jean-Pierre Bonnefous in *Sonatine*. Photo by Martha Swope.

Patricia McBride and Edward Villella in *Dances at a Gathering*. Photo by Martha Swope.

Kay Mazzo and John Prinz in *Dances at a Gathering*. Photo by Martha Swope.

Peter Martins in *Tchaikovsky Pas de Deux*. Photo by Costas.

Peter Martins in *Coppélia*. Photo by Costas.

Kay Mazzo and Peter Martins in *Duo Concertante*. Photo by Martha Swope.

Suzanne Farrell and Peter Martins *Chaconne*. Photo by Martha Swope.

Helgi Tomasson in *A Midsummer Night's Dream* Photo by Costas.

Allegra Kent and Jacques d'Amboise *Afternoon of a Faun*. Photo by Mart Swope.

and Jacques d'Amboise in leading roles. Presented by the City Center Joffrey Ballet, September 24, 1970, with Pamela Johnson and Dennis Wayne. Lighting by Jennifer Tipton. Assistant to Mr. Bolender: John Mandia.

The Still Point, which takes its title from T. S. Eliot's poem *Four Quartets*, is a dance drama arranged to music by Debussy—the first three movements of the *String Quartet*, Opus 10, transcribed for orchestra by Frank Black. The drama is about a young girl who, lonely at first and rejected, finds love. She endures jealousy, embarrassment, and torment as her girl friends rejoice in young love. Rejected by them, she rejects herself and suffers. She so wants a young man of her own that she dreams, too, and simply waits, fearing a little a real encounter. Finally, a boy comes, watches her as she dreams, then touches her shoulder. She reacts at first as if she had been stung and appears to resist him. Realizing that he has found an extraordinarily sensitive girl, the boy is gentle with her. She watches him dance, then they dance together, becoming closer, too, in thought, as they touch. They find in each other, at the end, the dreams they have had.

NOTES　Writing in *Dance Magazine* of *The Still Point*, the critic Doris Hering said that "Mr. Bolender has uncanny insight into the feelings of young women. His girl in *Mother Goose Suite*, his debutante in *Souvenirs*, and the tortured protagonist of *The Still Point* are all sisters under the skin—poignant sisters seeking fulfillment in romantic love. Of them all, the girl in *The Still Point* is the most touching because she is delineated with the most depth and at the same time with the most simplicity. In fact, simplicity is the prime virtue of this little ballet. Mr. Bolender has had the courage and the care to let the dancing speak out honestly without any mimetic overlay. And in Melissa Hayden and Jacques d'Amboise in the leading roles; and Irene Larsson, Roy Tobias, Jillana and John Mandia in secondary roles, he found responsive instruments. As the lonely girl, Melissa Hayden wove endless nuance and pathos into her portrayal, and yet the danced outlines were contained and beautifully clear. As her friend, Jacques d'Amboise communicated the steady masculinity that we have associated heretofore only with Igor Youskevitch."

STIMMUNG

Music by Karlheinz Stockhausen. Choreography by Maurice Béjart. First presented by the Ballet of the Twentieth Century at Brussels University, Brussels, Belgium, 1972. First presented in the United States at Carnegie Hall, New York, by the same ensemble, February 14, 1974.

This ballet is a full-evening concert occasion based on the ambience of sound, a ballet that requires the attention of an evening's entertainment, without intermission. It was inspired by a piece of music, the title of which, *Stimmung*, carries a number of interesting meanings. Perhaps the best of these meanings, and the clearest for the dance involved here, is what might be called voiced atmosphere, or ambience. It is important to realize what the composer meant in thinking of the piece that accompanies the ballet and what the choreographer contemplated in the course of his composition to this music. Béjart describes his intention, plus the action:

"The ballet *Stimmung* is born from music and through music, and has no other purpose than to prolong in space, by tangible forms, the vibration which comes from the voice, the inner self, the absolute center of man—and which strives to touch this absolute vibration (which some call divinity).

"The ballet is ritual—'magic names'—and magic gestures. Doesn't every gesture which completely absorbs our being, and which is performed with complete concentration, have some impact on the total life of the cosmos? 'I raise my little finger,' said a Zen master, 'and the course of the stars is disturbed.'

"In *Stimmung* the gestures of life become gestures of dance as the dancers interpret and join daily life, inspired by the different intonations of the accompanying voices creating the diverse 'ambience' which succeed each other in the course of the day.

"As in life, from time to time man passes from sadness to joy; eroticism becomes prayer; joy transfigures the ritual; abstraction becomes lyricism; dance—mathematical equation; humor appears under each attitude and (visible or invisible) directs this ceremony which pretends to be serious without taking itself seriously.

"Ten dancers create the subject matter and its multiple combinations, such as the image of the 'Tekraktys' of Pythagoras, the triangle that contains the first ten numbers which are the basis of all mathematical combinations. The eleventh dancer in turn will incarnate himself in this interrogation until, when the cycle is completed, only the breath (which is the beginning and the end of everything) continues to exist.

"No improvisation is permitted, but each dancer finds himself or herself confronted by a series of possibilities which can be resolved differently each performance. The steps, which are 'regulated,' can be combined and repeated by each performer in a different way a number of times, which depends only on the imagination, the schemes, and the mutations which the act itself undergoes each performance according to the singers' inspiration."

The inspiration of the singers is, of course, largely dependent on what the composer has written. He has said that the work was built upon a series of "magic names" assembled for him by an American anthropologist, the names of some thirty deities from varied religions and cultures: Vishnu, Uranus, Uwoluwo, Rhea, Venus, et al. These names are invoked in the sung text. Stockhausen has recalled that the title of the piece, *Stimmung*, originally meant "harmony of pure intervals . . . In addition, and far from the least important, the German word 'Stimmung' corresponds to the notion of fluidity, of frame of mind (for example, one speaks of 'gute Stimmung'—good ambience— or of 'schlechte Stimmung'—bad ambience). It evokes the harmonious resonance of man and his environment. Finally the word 'Stimmung' includes 'Stimme,' meaning voice!"

The work is sung by six singers, who enter simultaneously with the dancers at the start of the piece. Seated about a lamp on a raised platform at the back of the stage, they sing meditatively, their voices amplified so that the softest nuances are heard. Each singer has a command of nine models and eleven magic names that he can, after a "scheme of form" and according to the context, introduce freely. "The others," writes the composer, "can react to these models and magic names with some 'transformations,' 'digressions variées,' 'oscillations,' 'unisson.' Nothing is directed.

"Surely Stimmung is meditative music. Time is abolished. One listens to the inside of the sound, to the inside of the harmonic spectrum, to the inside of a vocal INSIDE, with the most subtle undulations. It is scarcely explosive. All the senses are awakened and calm. In the sensuous beauty shines the beauty of the eternal."

THE STONE FLOWER

> Ballet in three acts. Music by Sergei Prokofiev. Libretto by Mira Prokovieva, based on a story by Pavel Bashov. Choreography by Yuri Grigorovitch. Scenery and costumes by Simon Virsaladze. First presented by the Bolshoi Ballet at the Bolshoi Theatre, Moscow, February 12, 1954. Revised and presented by the Bolshoi Ballet at the Kirov State Theatre of Opera and Ballet, Leningrad, July 6, 1958. First presented in the United States by the Bolshoi Ballet at the Metropolitan Opera House, New York, May 4, 1959, with Vladimir Vasiliev, Marina Kondratieva, Maya Plisetskaya, and Vladimir Levashev in the principal roles.

The Stone Flower, Prokofiev's last ballet, writes the choreographer Yuri Grigorovitch, "tells of the fate of the stone carver Danila who wishes to see the full power of stone and to show its beauty to the people. The creative urge which possesses Danila and the desire to create more perfect art is the leitmotif of the ballet."

ACT ONE Danila, a young craftsman, desires to create a malachite vase that will be as simple and beautiful as a flower. He is not satisfied with one vase he has made; the secrets of the malachite seem to elude him. His mind is full of these problems as he meets his beloved Katerina and goes with her to their betrothal party. There Severyan, a bailiff, attempts to purchase the vase Danila has made, but the artist refuses to sell. In the course of the ensuing argument, Severyan becomes fascinated by Katerina and tries to embrace her. Danila and their friends defend the girl and force the bailiff to leave. There is a lyrical scene between the lovers and Katerina departs.

Danila smashes the vase and begins work on a new piece of malachite. The spirit of the malachite appears and with a touch of her hand shapes the stone, but as she disappears the stone resumes its original form. Danila pursues the spirit, who sometimes appears as a fairy, sometimes as a lizard, finally revealing herself to be the Mistress of the Copper Mountain. There she leads Danila to her underground realm where she is surrounded by maidens who are the spirits of the various precious stones. Danila is dazzled as he watches the blossoming of these fairy stone flowers.

ACT TWO   Katerina, missing Danila, dances pensively alone. Severyan attempts to seduce her, but she defends herself with a sickle and he is forced to leave. Danila, meanwhile, is learning the secret of the malachite as he works away in the palace of the Mistress of the Copper Mountain, who is enthralled by him. Katerina searches for Danila at the village fair. There again she is compelled to defend herself against Severyan, who tries to carry her off. The Mistress of the Copper Mountain now enters, transfixes Severyan, places him under a spell, and leads him to his death.

ACT THREE   Still searching for her beloved, Katerina comes into the forest. As she rests there beside a fire, a fair maiden emerges from the flames and leads her to the Copper Mountain. In the palace, Danila has realized his dream. He has created a stone flower. As the spirits of the stones dance in crystalline patterns, the mistress of the palace again tries to tempt him. But Danila's thoughts are only of Katerina. He realizes that he must leave the palace. Angered at his rebuff, the Mistress of the Copper Mountain decides that Danila will be turned into a statue and kept at the palace.

When the fire maiden brings Katerina, there is an emotional *pas de trois* between the boy and the two girls who love him. Danila in the end chooses Katerina and the fearlessness of their love obliges the Mistress of the Copper Mountain to release Danila from her spell. The young lovers return to their village, to share with them the joy of their love and the secret of creating beauty from stone. The Mistress of the Copper Mountain appears to bid them goodby, and vanishes.

NOTES   Describing the ballet, the choreographer has written:

"The foundation for the musical and choreographic structure of the ballet is the combination of the real-life scenes and fantastic dreams. The dance language is fundamentally based on folk choreography. The scene of the party, with the ceremonial features, is constructed in the form of a Ural dance rhapsody.

"Fantastic scenes utilize the classical dance. The movements of the classical dance characterizing the world of the Mistress of the Copper Mountain have a sharp, clean-cut style, emphasizing the nature of formation of stones and crystals. In the dances of the stones there should be reflected the sparkling, shining play of reflected beams. Dances of the main characters Katerina and Danila are also classic, the courage of the human heart showing broadly in the ballet. These dances are quite different from the dances of the stones, since we are dealing with a human quality. The dances of Katerina and Danila have elements of folk dancing and features of Russian painting technique.

"The classic dance also serves as a foundation for the character of the Mistress of the Copper Mountain. This fantastic creature personifies the splendor and beauty of nature. She has two faces; the face of powerful and strong secret force and the face of human justice, full of feminine charm. The author, Bazhov, makes her appear both as a lizard and as the spirit of malachite. This contradictive character determines the means for creating the character for the ballet. Her dances tend to be classic in style for the stone dances and must have very flexible elements for the sliding lizard so vividly created by Bazhov.

"A special role in the ballet is played by Severyan, the bailiff. He is a ruthless, soulless person—the only negative person in the story. Naturally the style varies from the style which outlines the other characters. Severyan, as with other characters of the ballet, must be expressed with full dance and plastic language which the choreographer must create."

SUMMERSPACE

Music by Morton Feldman. Choreography by Merce Cunningham. Scenery and costumes by Robert Rauschenberg. Lighting by Nicholas Cernovich. First presented by Merce Cunningham and his Dance Company at the American Dance Festival, Connecticut College, New London, Connecticut, August 17, 1958, with Merce Cunningham, Carolyn Brown, Viola Farber, Cynthia Stone, Marilyn Wood, and Remy Charlip. First presented by the New York City Ballet at the New York State Theatre, April 19, 1966, with Anthony Blum, Kay Mazzo, Patricia Neary, Sara Leland, Deni Lamont, and Carol Sumner. Lighting by Ronald Bates.

Summerspace, which Merce Cunningham has subtitled "a lyric dance," is the second work by this distinguished modern dancer for the New York City Ballet (the first being *The Seasons*, created for Ballet Society in 1947). The music, a commissioned score, is composed in Morton Feldman's graph system. The background by Robert Rauschenberg is a pointillist skyscape and this idea is continued in the costumes. The choreographer revised his original work for the ballet idiom. There are six dancers—four girls and two boys.

Writing about his original production in *Dance Magazine*, Merce Cunningham recalled that the principal momentum behind the piece "was a concern for steps that carry one through space, and not only into it. Like the passage of birds, stopping for moments on the ground and then going on, or automobiles more relentlessly throbbing along turnpikes and under and over cloverleafs. This led to the idea of using kinds of movement that would be continuous, and could carry the dancer into the playing area, and out of it."

The resultant space-play is a continuum of movement that appears to swim in an intense haze of summer heat. The stage space here is a field, in fact, rather than the usual proscenium-enclosed space with a center of interest, and as the choreographer explains, since all points are of equal usage, "one does not lead to any particular other. The eye is not guided but allowed to jump throughout the space. The corners, in a conventional theatre stage, are nuggets that can sparkle. The momentum, too, is different. In a general way, the Balanchine dancers proceed in a vertical accent. 'He usually likes the accent down.' The force of *Summerspace* is horizontal. The stillnesses are dealt with as that, and not as positions in preparation." (From an interview with Merce Cunningham in *Ballet Review,* Vol. 1, No. 4.)

SWAN LAKE

Dramatic ballet in four acts. Music by Peter Ilyich Tchaikovsky. Book by V. P. Begitchev and Vasily Geltzer. First presented, with choreography by Julius Reisinger, at the Bolshoi Theatre, Moscow, March 4, 1877, with Pauline Karpakova in the leading role. This incomplete and unsuccessful production was superseded by a new choreographic version by Lev Ivanov and Marius Petipa, which was presented for the first time in a complete, four-act production at the Maryinsky Theatre, St. Petersburg, February 8, 1895, with Pierina Legnani in the double role of Odette-Odile. *Act Two of this version was presented for the first time at the Maryinsky Theatre, St. Petersburg, February 29, 1894, with Legnani as* Odette. *Scenery by Botcharov and Levogt. First presented in western Europe in complete form in Prague, Czechoslovakia, June 27, 1907, with choreography by Achille Viscusi. First presented in the United States at the Metropolitan Opera House, New York, December 20, 1911, with Catherine Geltzer as* Odette-Odile, *Mikhail Mordkin as* Prince Siegfried, *and Alexandre Volinine as* Benno. *This production was staged by Mordkin after the Petipa-Ivanov choreography. Scenery by James Fox. First presented in England in complete form by the Sadler's Wells Ballet at the Sadler's Wells Theatre, London, November 29, 1934, with the Petipa-Ivanov choreography reproduced by Nicholas Sergeyev; Alicia Markova as* Odette-Odile, *Robert Helpmann as* Prince Siegfried. *Scenery and costumes by Hugh Stevenson. Presented complete by the San Francisco Ballet, in a version staged by William Christensen, 1940. The revised Sadler's Wells production, with scenery and cos-*

*tumes by Leslie Hurry, was first presented in the United States October 20,
1949, with Margot Fonteyn and Robert Helpmann. Presented complete with
the original choreography of Lev Ivanov staged by David Blair, by the Atlanta Civic Ballet, August 24, 1965. Presented complete with Ivanov's choreography staged by David Blair by American Ballet Theatre at the Civic
Opera House, Chicago, February 16, 1967. Scenery by Oliver Smith. Costumes by Freddy Wittop. Lighting by Jean Rosenthal. Presented in varied
versions by many companies.*

Musically, and as a dance drama, *Swan Lake* is undoubtedly the most popular
of all classical ballets. It is possible to see at least a major portion of the complete *Swan Lake*—the famous second act—danced by almost every ballet company in the world. And the ballet is a favorite of ballerinas as well as audiences. All leading dancers want to dance *Swan Lake* at least once in their
careers, and all audiences want to see them dance it. To succeed in *Swan Lake*
is to become overnight a ballerina. Petipa and Ivanov are to the dancer what
Shakespeare is to the actor: if you can succeed in their choreography parts,
there is a suggestion that you can succeed at anything.

Why is it that *Swan Lake* has been so consistently popular with both audiences and dancers for so long a time? What about its chief rivals in the classical repertory—*Giselle, The Sleeping Beauty,* and *Coppélia*—why are they not
as popular? If we set aside practical considerations (unlike *Swan Lake,* these
other ballets cannot successfully be shortened into one-act versions; the part
does not provide the spirit of the whole), we find the answer in *Swan Lake*'s
romantic and tragic story and the music that accompanies its unfolding.

The heroines of these other classics all have some relation to the real world—
they are peasant girls or princesses. Strange things may happen to them, but
they live within determined conventions. The heroine of *Swan Lake* has another story. She is a princess of the night; she is all magic, a creature of the
imagination.

On one level, her story is a girl-meets-boy story: girl meets boy, girl loses
boy, girl gets boy, and then both are lost. What prevents this from being silly
is the character of the girl. She is Queen of the Swans, a beautiful bird, except
for the brief time—between midnight and dawn—when the mysterious sorcerer,
Von Rotbart, allows her to become a beautiful woman. In the world of sky and
water she is at home, but in the real world, where romance is possible, she
seems to be irretrievably lost. The great love she comes to have for a worldly
prince is doomed at its start; she has no control over her destiny.

The Swan Queen is the opposite of the Firebird, the bird triumphant; she is
immediately pathetic, a creature whose initial fear and consuming love interest
us immediately. The dignity and courage and authority she possesses as Queen
of the Swans become, in the ballet, the dignity of the woman in love. Humanly
speaking, even in this magical world she inhabits, she is never unreal or absurd

to us, because we see that love does not shatter her dignity; rather, it ennobles her beauty and explains her universal appeal.

ACT ONE: THE GARDEN OF PRINCE SIEGFRIED'S CASTLE   Before the curtain rises, an overture warns us of the impending tragedy of the story. After the woodwinds have introduced the principal romantic theme, and the strings have taken it up, there is a faltering: a soft, gradually building questioning by the strings. And the answer comes in boldly asserted warnings by the crashing of cymbals and resounding trumpet calls. But soon, over these crescendos, the romantic theme returns at full, conquering volume. It quietens, and the curtain rises.

This is Prince Siegfried's twenty-first birthday, and the young prince is celebrating the occasion in the garden of his ancestral palace. Young people from the surrounding estates have come to pay tribute to him. Benno, friend to the prince, is talking to a group of twelve young men. Wolfgang, the prince's old tutor, comes in merrily and is almost immediately attracted to the bottles of wine that stand on a table at the right. The atmosphere is one of anticipation, and as the trumpets blare the climax of a spirited march, the host enters. The handsome prince is not haughty; neither is he familiar. He is delighted to see his friends, thanks them as they congratulate him, claps his old tutor on the back affectionately, and prepares to enjoy the festivities that have been arranged in his honor.

First there is a *pas de trois,* danced by two girls and a boy. (Since the Diaghilev company's second-act version of 1911, this *pas de trois* has often been performed as a *divertissement* in Act Two. Sometimes it is danced by Benno and two cygnets, sometimes by a first huntsman and two swan princesses, as in the production by the Sadler's Wells Theatre Ballet. Where the *pas de trois* is not interpolated in Act Two, the music for the variation of the *danseur* is almost invariably used for a variation by Benno.) For the dance of the two girls and a boy, the music is lightly melodic and flowing. Now each dances alone: the first girl performs to blithe, tripping music that increases in speed; the boy, to strongly accented rhythms that mark the precision of his *entrechats* and turns in the air; and the second girl, to a light, almost joking theme. Climactic music accompanies the final display of virtuosity that all three perform.

While most of the assembled guests have been watching the dance, the old tutor has been privately celebrating the prince's coming of age by drinking as much wine as possible. Just as everyone begins to enjoy the party, the conviviality is disturbed by the entrance of the princess mother and her four ladies in waiting. Siegfried goes to his mother and escorts her into the garden. She observes his friends with considerable disdain; there is an effort to hide the wine bottles, and poor old Wolfgang finds himself in obvious disfavor. The princess mother indicates to her son that his coming of age is hardly the occasion for levity. He responds to this opinion dutifully, but with apparent resistance.

Siegfried is further disturbed when his mother points out to him that he must soon choose a wife. Her suggestion is in the nature of a command, and Siegfried turns stubbornly away. Tomorrow night, his mother reminds him, his birthday will be celebrated formally at a court ball, and there, from among the loveliest ladies of the land, he must select his future wife. Siegfried sees that argument is impossible; as he kisses his mother's hand and leads her out of the garden, he seems to bend to her will.

Wolfgang gestures his pleasure at the departure of the dominating princess mother. He attempts to restore the spirit of the happy occasion by claiming that, old as he is, he can dance better than any of the younger men. Everyone laughs at him, but Wolfgang is not to be outdone. He approaches one of the village maidens, who giggles as he takes her by the hand and begins to dance. The melody to which he partners her is subdued and charmingly sentimental, sweetly echoing the joys of youth. Soon Wolfgang is having such a good time that he tries to surpass himself by whirling his partner around and around. In the process he becomes dizzy and falls to the ground, taking his partner with him.

Now Prince Siegfried is convinced that the only thing to do is to enjoy himself to the utmost: tomorrow, after all, is another day. The prince signals that the celebration should continue. Wine is poured for all the guests, and village couples dance a vigorous polka that completely restores to the gathering its natural spirit of gaiety. Still Siegfried broods; the celebration has failed to dispel his apprehension in regard to the morrow.

Night begins to fall. Benno knows that Siegfried must be distracted for the remainder of the evening. He hears the sound of fluttering wings overhead, looks up, and sees in the sky beautiful wild swans in full flight. Against the sound of harp and strings, the oboe sounds softly the theme of these enchanted birds. Benno suggests that the prince form a hunting party and go in search of the swans. Siegfried consents; crossbows are brought, and flaming torches are provided to light the way through the woods. The village girls circle the stage and exit. Wolfgang alone is unwilling to accompany the hunting party. As the full orchestra takes up the mysterious and doomful theme that heralded the swans, Wolfgang tells Siegfried that he is too old, that he will remain in the garden. The young men bid him good-by and rush off into the night. The curtain falls as the old tutor stands alone in the center of the empty garden, his bottle his only friend.

ACT TWO: A LAKESIDE   While the curtain is lowered, the music continues to develop the theme of strange foreboding. Then all is quiet for a moment. As the music resumes, the curtain rises on a forest scene; a great lake, its shining surface undisturbed by the wind, shimmers in the moonlight. The music begins again. The hunting party enters, led by Benno. All carry crossbows. The men look above them through the trees, searching for the swans; they are astonished to see that the swans have settled on the lake and, within a few feet of them, are placidly gliding by. Leading the group of swans is a beautiful white bird, apparently their queen. The diamonds in her crown reflect spangles of light over the dark water.

A flourish from the orchestra heralds the arrival of the prince. The hunting party bows to him. Benno hastens to point out to Siegfried that the swans can be seen close by. The prince directs the men to hasten along the lakeside ahead of the swans; he is about to follow them off, when he sees something in the distance that gives him pause. He stops, close by the lakeside, then retreats hurriedly across the glade to conceal himself. . He has seen something so strange and extraordinary that he must observe it closely in secret.

No sooner has Siegfried hidden himself than the most beautiful woman he has ever seen enters the quiet glade. He cannot believe his eyes, for the girl appears to be both swan and woman. Her lovely face is enclosed by swan feathers, which cling closely against her hair. Her pure white dress is embellished with soft, downy swan feathers, and on her head rests the crown of the Queen of the Swans. The young woman thinks she is alone. She poses in arabesque, then remains almost motionless, softly bending her cheek down against her shoulder in a gesture reminiscent of a swan smoothing its feathers. The music informs us of the pathos of this gesture, and Siegfried is so enchanted by the magical creature that he enters the glade. He moves quietly, lest he disturb her.

The girl is terrified, her whole body trembles, her arms press against her breast in an attitude of almost helpless self-protection; she backs away from the prince, moving frantically on points that drive desperately against the ground. Her arms seek the air for freedom, for escape. The prince, already in love, begs her not to fly away. The girl looks at him and gestures that she is afraid. Siegfried wonders why. She points to his crossbow and draws her arm back as if to let fly an arrow, then holds her arm over her face, cowering with fear. The prince indicates that he will never shoot her; he will protect her. The girl bows to him in gratitude.

The prince now asks her who she is, why she is here? The girl's hands enclose the crown on her head: she is Odette, Queen of the Swans. The prince salutes her and says that he will honor her, but how is it that she is the Swan Queen? The Swan Queen asks for his patience and points to the lake. The lake, she indicates, was made by her mother's tears. Her mother wept because an evil sorcerer, Von Rotbart, made her daughter into the Swan Queen. And swan she must always be, except between midnight and dawn, unless a man should love her, marry her, and never love another. Then she will be saved and be a swan no longer.

Siegfried holds his hands to his heart and says that he loves her, that he will marry her and never love another. He swears his faithfulness. Now angry at the fate of his love, he demands to know where this Von Rotbart hides himself. Just at this point, the magician appears at the lakeside. His owl-like face is a hideous mask; he reaches out his claws, beckoning Odette to return to him. [In one-act versions of *Swan Lake*, this lengthy mime passage is often shortened and the music is used to accompany a dance in which the prince, his bow set aside, follows the dancing Swan Queen, lifts her as they circle the stage, embraces her, and supports her gently in poses until she breaks away from him at the entrance of Von Rotbart.] Von Rotbart points menacingly at Siegfried. Odette moves between them, begging Von Rotbart for mercy. Trumpets sound in blaring, warning crescendo. The prince seizes his bow, kneels, and aims it at the magician. Odette beseeches him to stop and runs diagonally across the stage toward Siegfried. She touches his stretched bow and stands over it and her lover in extended arabesque. Von Rotbart disappears. Siegfried rises and embraces Odette. The music quietens. The prince puts his arm about the girl, and they go toward the forest.

The prince tells the girl that she must come the next evening to the court ball. He has just come of age and must marry and at the ball he will choose her as his bride. Odette replies that she cannot come to the ball until she is married—until Von Rotbart no longer has power over her—otherwise the magician will expose her and their romance will perish. She knows, she tells Siegfried, that Von Rotbart will stop at nothing to keep her in his power, that he will contrive artfully to make Siegfried break his promise to her, and that should he do so, should be be faithless, Von Rotbart will cause her own death. Siegfried again swears his faithfulness.

When the lovers have left the glade, Odette's charges, all the swans who, like herself, assume human form only between the hours of midnight and dawn, dance in from the lakeside. They form a single serpentine line that moves toward the front, then face the audience in a triangular grouping.

Soon Benno, the prince's friend, comes upon the dancing swans. They encircle him, rushing past him with their fluttering arms. Benno, unaware of the mystery of these creatures, thinks only of the hunt. The swans cower in fear and rush together in a close group by the lakeside. Benno hails the rest of the hunting party. The huntsmen marvel at his discovery and aim their crossbows at the swans. Suddenly the music crashes warningly; Siegfried runs in and behind him comes Odette. The Swan Queen stands before the group of trembling swans and stretches out her arms to protect them; the huntsmen must kill her first. As Odette begs the men for mercy, Siegfried orders them to lower their bows and to respect the magical birds. When the huntsmen have learned that, like Odette, the swans are really unfortunate girls in the hands of an evil magician, they remove their caps and bow in apology to the maidens.

Siegfried and Odette again vanish into the forest, the huntsmen leave the scene, and the swan maidens come forward in three columns to dance. They dance to a charming waltz; their ensemble is dominated by two swan maidens who emerge from the group to dance in unison between lines formed by their friends. When the dance is over, the swans gather together in picturesque groupings to form a final tableau.

Now the swan maidens gather at either side of the stage. Siegfried enters with Benno. The harp sounds a series of arpeggios. The prince searches for Odette among the swans. He does not find her. The huntsmen return and stand among the swan maidens. Siegfried stands with his friend in the center of the glade. At the back, behind them, Odette enters softly. She touches Benno's shoulder, poses for a brief second in arabesque, then comes forward. It is as if she had not seen the prince. The harp is plucked gently. Odette rises on point, then sinks slowly to the ground. She rests on her left knee, her right leg stretched before her. She bends down low, her arms reach forward like enclosing wings, and to the quiet rhythm of the music her body stirs expectantly. Siegfried comes forward, reaches down to her hands, and raises her. The solo violin begins quietly the wistfully romantic theme of the adagio. Odette pirouettes with slow, romantic adroitness in his arms. Now her love supports her as she bends low in a deep arabesque. Each of the huntsmen, observing the beauty of this love duet, now stands between two swan maidens, his arms about their waists.

Odette moves to Benno, and the prince admires her loveliness as his friend holds her in arabesque. The beautiful Swan Queen returns to her lover, moves in supported attitude, then rests for a moment against his breast. She moves now slightly away, rises on point, takes Siegfried's hand, and then—raising her right leg straight before her—removes her hand from his; for a fraction of a second, as she lifts both arms up, the idyllic nature of this dance is luminously clear: the relation of Odette and Siegfried is one of complete sweetness and absolute trust. Odette falls back, and Benno catches her gently in his arms as her right leg closes against her left. Benno lifts her up, she returns to the prince, nestles against his shoulder as he embraces her softly, and the movement is repeated a second time. Siegfried puts his arms about Odette at its conclusion and leads her toward the lakeside. The swan maidens turn in arabesque, to the gently hopping rhythm of the woodwinds, and cross the stage before the lovers. As the solo violin resumes, Odette and the prince run forward quietly between the swan maidens. Siegfried lifts Odette high in his arms to the violin's music; he lifts her again, and then she pirouettes in his arms. He continues to lift her effortlessly to the demand of the theme; she turns to his encircling arms, then moves away on point with a gesture of obeisance and love.

Now a number of the swan maidens are arranged in a diagonal line across the stage. The huntsmen, standing in back, lift some of the girls to their shoulders. The prince moves back. Odette goes to him, and Siegfried opens his arms to her. She turns away then and, hopping softly, moves in arabesque down the line formed by her charges. Siegfried follows her adoringly and, taking her about the waist, lifts her at arm's length high above his head. He lifts her again, releases her, and, as she reaches the end of the diagonal, lifts her to carry her to the right side of the stage. The violin repeats the theme of the first lifts of the adagio, and this time, to the melody, Odette executes supported arabesques followed swiftly by pirouettes that she terminates with an open pointing of her leg to the left. These movements are repeated with the music.

The swan maidens are now grouped on the left. After the final pirouette, Siegfried stands close behind Odette. She leans back softly against him and balances. The prince opens his arms as Odette opens hers and gently he moves her arms close to her body, as if he were quieting her frightened wings. Siegfried moves slightly from side to side, gently rocking his love. Odette rushes away, seemingly compelled to resist the embrace, and balances in arabesque, both arms encircling her head. From behind, the prince takes her arms, moves them back close to her body, and Odette leans back against him, now confessing the power of her love for him.

The adagio nears its end. Siegfried turns the Swan Queen slowly as she stands on point, her right foot trembling in *petits battements*. She turns a final series of slow pirouettes in his arms and then is held by the prince; both arms over her head, her left leg extended to the side. Siegfried holds her thus, then releases her; she balances for an instant and then, holding her pose, falls to the side; at the last breathless moment she is caught in the arms of her lover's friend. The adagio is over. The two lovers and Benno leave the stage.

Four cygnets appear and dance with bright, youthful precision a *pas de quatre* that is accompanied by lightly bouncing music of great charm. This is followed by a dance for two swan princesses. Here the music is openly joyous, uninhibited in its bounding, youthful expression of happiness in newfound love.

Just as this dance ends, we notice that dawn is approaching. Odette returns and dances a variation that is at first modestly lyrical; her arms stretch back and her neck arches backward as she balances in arabesques, and we feel that to this beautiful woman such a pose is the most beautiful and natural thing in the world. The music increases in momentum, and the variation finishes with a dazzling diagonal of rapid pirouettes across the stage.

The swan maidens are alerted by the coming light and prepare to return to the lake. Odette, in their midst, comes forward and—from the front of the stage toward the back—executes to the driving rhythm of the rapid music a series of quick, desperate movements that reflect her fear at her departure from her lover. Siegfried beseeches her to stay, but she cannot. Benno kneels before her. Now impelled to become again the Swan Queen, she rushes toward Benno and stands in full flight on his extended knee. Siegfried reaches out for her, lifts her down gently. The swan maidens have responded already to the return of the mysterious music that presaged the first appearance of the magical creatures: Odette and Siegfried are alone. Von Rotbart appears by the lakeside, beckoning Odette to come to him. She is helpless and must obey. She holds out her arms yearningly toward Siegfried, but her feet carry her back toward the lake. Her body trembles with helplessness, and she glides farther and farther away from him, to disappear in the new dawn. Siegfried reaches out toward her, unable to console himself by her promise to return.

The huntsmen enter the glade. Benno comforts the prince, and then, at the sound of wings overhead, all look up to see the swans in full flight, led by their queen. The curtain falls.

ACT THREE: THE GREAT HALL OF PRINCE SIEGFRIED'S CASTLE   The time is the following evening. The ball that the princess mother has arranged in honor of her son is about to take place. After a long and regal musical introduction, the curtain rises on the hall of the palace. There is a roll of drums, and a march begins. Here in the great hall, the royal thrones are placed on a dais to the right; on the left, with a short flight of steps leading down to the ballroom, is the formal entrance. Across the back, stretching into the distance, is a long, curved colonnade.

A flourish of music marks the entrance of two royal pages. The prince and his mother enter the room. The assembled guests bow to them as they proceed to the dais. The princess mother turns to speak to her son. Siegfried looks out over the ballroom with a blank stare; he is thinking of his meeting with Odette and his vow to be faithful to her. His mother, jealous of his preoccupation, addresses him somewhat in the manner of Gertrude upbraiding Hamlet: "Are you ill? You must pay attention to our guests; they are beginning to remark your strange behavior." The prince throws off his thoughts and assures his mother that he will not fail in his obligations.

Ambassadors from foreign lands, attired in colorful native costume, have come to pay tribute to the prince on his coming of age. A trumpet sounds a flourish, and a herald announces the arrival of six beautiful girls invited by the princess mother as prospective brides for her son. The girls are attired identically in stunning evening dresses and each carries a large feathered fan. The princess mother nods to them, and they begin to dance before the prince to the strains of a courtly waltz.

Siegfried pretends to watch them, but actually he thinks only of the lakeside glade and his meeting with Odette. His mother taps him on the arm and warns him that he must dance with his guests. The prince descends from the dais and dances briefly with each of the would-be brides. He dances automatically, with no interest, holding the girls casually about the waist and scarcely looking at his partners. The girls are dismayed at his indifference, but cannot display their displeasure too markedly lest their hostess be disappointed in them. Siegfried returns to the dais and again sinks into melancholy.

The princess mother rises and approaches the prospective brides. She thanks them for the lovely waltz and congratulates them on their beauty. Now she turns to the prince, asking him to confirm her opinion. Siegfried gestures that the girls are very pretty, indeed, but he does not wish to marry any of them. He loves another. He bows coldly to the girls. As his mother upbraids him, the music is interrupted suddenly.

Again the trumpet sounds a flourish. All the guests turn to watch the door. A herald hastens to inform the princess mother that a strange couple has arrived. He does not know who they are, but avows that the woman is a creature of rare beauty. Siegfried looks expectantly toward the door. His mother orders that the guests be admitted. There is a crash of cymbals, the room darkens mysteriously, and the music hurries warningly into a repetition of the theme that marked the fate of the Swan Queen.

The light returns, and a tall bearded knight enters with his daughter. As the knight introduces himself and his daughter, Odile, to the princess mother, Siegfried—excited almost beyond control—stares at the beautiful girl. Although dressed in somber black, she is the image of his beloved Odette. [Although not originally designed for the same dancer, Odile for many years has been danced by the same ballerina who performs the role of Odette; Odette-Odile has become the most famous dual role in ballet.] Odile returns his stare with a steady glance of cold, but passionate, interest. In the distance, framed by an arch of the colonnade, Odette is seen holding out her hands to Siegfried. The prince is so enchanted by the girl he supposes to be the Swan Queen that he does not notice Odette's warning. The vision of the Swan Queen fades. Siegfried takes Odile by the hand. Now he foresees that the ball will be a happy occasion after all! He escorts Odile into the palace garden. Odile's father watches their departure with interest. Unknown to the prince, he is in reality not a knight at all, but Von Rotbart, the evil magician, who has transformed himself and his conniving daughter in order that Siegfried will be deceived and break his promise to Odette never to love another. Convinced that his trickery will doom Odette and Siegfried, Von Rotbart turns to the princess mother with a gracious smile. She is charmed by his flattery and—hopeful that her son will marry a lady of rank, as Odile appears to be—invites Von Rotbart to sit beside her on the dais.

Now the guests from foreign lands, who have come to honor the prince on his birthday, come forward to dance. First, two Spanish couples dance a quick and supple *divertissement* to the sound of music reminiscent of the melodies and rhythm of Spain. Next five Hungarian couples line up and, to the slow, anticipating measures of the music, commence a *czardas* that gathers in speed to end in a whirling finish. A vigorous Polish mazurka danced by eight couples concludes this series of *divertissements*. Von Rotbart indicates his appreciation of this entertainment to the princess mother and then suggests that his daughter, Odile, is the most beautiful dancer at the ball. Just as the princess mother is about to wonder where her son has taken Odile, Prince Siegfried appears with the stunning girl. Von Rotbart leaves the dais and tells Odile that the time has come for her to dance before the princess mother and Prince Siegfried. The orchestra sounds a rhythmic flourish, and the *pas de deux* between Odile and the prince begins. [When it is performed as a separate *divertissement*, this dance is known as the "Black Swan," or "Magic Swan," *pas de deux*. As a *divertissement*, the *pas de deux* necessarily lacks the dramatic impact it possesses as a part of the complete *Swan Lake*.]

This dance dramatically displays the cunning of Odile and the infatuation of the prince. In opposition to the adagio of Act Two, it has another kind of grace: it is full of pride and arrogance, rather than tenderness; it has the cold, dazzling light of a bright diamond. As Odile goes to Siegfried, Von Rotbart stands on the right, watching with guile and satisfaction. The prince welcomes his new love with joy: now his mother and the whole court will see how wonderful she is. Odile pirouettes across the ballroom floor, then turns rapidly in Siegfried's arms. Von Rotbart calls to her, and she goes obediently to her father, standing in arabesque with her hand on his shoulder. Von Rotbart whispers in her ear. Odile looks back at the prince and nods. She has grown confident with the success of her disguise and, when she returns to the prince, is determined to display her power over him with even more breath-taking skill. Siegfried supports her adoringly as she bends low in arabesque, but then Odile lets go his hand to stand alone, poised, balanced, splendidly self-sufficient. She goes back to Von Rotbart, and this time the impetuous prince follows her. After receiving more instructions from her father, she rejoins her lover, who supports her with glowing pride in bold and confident movements. For a moment the two are separated. They promenade across the ballroom floor, Odile walking with masterful authority and steely confidence, and meet in the center of the stage to resume the dance. Suddenly Odette again appears in the distant colonnade. Von Rotbart immediately notes her presence and signals to Odile, who steps between Siegfried and the vision. Odette extends her clasped hands to Siegfried, despairing of her fate if he abandons her. The enchanted Siegfried has no idea that she is there; the cunning Odile smiles at him—a cold, even smile in which he can discern nothing but warmth for his passion. The vision of Odette persists, and Odile becomes angry at this interference. She runs to Siegfried and places her hands over his eyes. Siegfried is so infatuated that he regards this gesture as flirtatious and fails to see that Odette, all hopes gone, has vanished, weeping, in the distance.

The *pas de deux* continues. Odile, now the winning seductress, carries her conceit still farther, and the innocent prince is utterly in her hands. The dance ends as the prince kneels before Odile and the proud, evil girl stands over him in high, conquering arabesque. With the final note of the music, she gives a curt, triumphant toss of her head.

The prince now dances a variation expressive of his great joy in rediscovering the girl he supposes to be Odette. Odile follows with a quick final dance designed to whip Siegfried's passion still further, and she succeeds in this brilliantly. Her variation contains a dazzling circling of the stage with small, swift turns, a series of quick, close movements performed in a straight line from the front of the stage to the back, and finally a series of thirty-two *fouettés*. These relentless, whipping turns sum up her power over the prince and, with disdainful joy, seem to lash at his passion. Helplessly bewitched, he rejoins his enchantress for a brief final dance.

Siegfried then approaches Von Rotbart and asks for Odile's hand in marriage. Von Rotbart immediately consents. Siegfried announces his decision to his mother, and Odile bows before the princess mother. Von Rotbart, still unsatisfied, addresses the prince further: he asks Siegfried to swear an oath of fidelity of Odile, asks him to promise that he will never love another. Siegfried's love for Odile is so great that he is offended by this request, and then, too, he knows that he has heard those words before. Why should they be asked again, he wonders. He looks at Odile, and his fate hangs in the balance. The music hesitates. He takes the oath. At that moment there is a crash of thunder. The ballroom darkens. The theme of the abandoned Odette screams above the orchestra. Quick flashes of light show the frightened courtiers fleeing the ballroom, the distraught princess mother, and Von Rotbart and Odile standing before the prince in a final triumph of self-revelation. Their hideous, cruel laughter Siegfried cannot bear, and he turns to see in the distance the pathetic figure of Odette, reaching out to him helplessly, her body racked with sobs. He falls to the floor in an agony of guilt.

ACT FOUR: THE LAKESIDE   The swan maidens have gathered by the side of the lake. They are sad and wistful at the fate of their queen. Their grief is reflected in the still tableaux they form with a group of small black swans who have joined them and in the dance the little swans do with their elders to soft, tender music. They yearn for the return of Odette. When she appears, weeping, they try to comfort her, but she tells them they do wrong to give her false hope. "I have been betrayed and I must die: the magician has won."

The music cries out with her grief, and she runs toward the lake. Two swan princesses intercept her and urge her to wait. They remind her that Siegfried is only human, that he could not have known the power of sorcery and thus could have had no suspicion of Von Rotbart's design. "You must wait," they advise her, "and hear the prince." "No," she gestures, "I have lost him and could not bear it."

Some of the swans hear Siegfried in the distance, calling for Odette, and tell her that he approaches. The Swan Queen orders a group of little swans to stand before her so that the prince will not discover her. Siegfried rushes into the clearing and frantically searches for Odette among the swans. Desperate, he asks the swans if they have seen her; he is about to abandon hope when the swans that surround Odette bend down and he sees her standing among them. He runs to her and takes her in his arms, asking for her forgiveness, swearing his infinite love. They go into the forest, and the swan maidens continue their dancing. When the lovers return, Odette has forgiven her lover, but she tells him—with tears streaming down her smiling face—it is no use, for what is her forgiveness alongside her death, which now must surely follow. "Von Rotbart is relentless. My life was forfeit if I should be betrayed. Only in death am I released from his power."

Now Odette dances to music that is tenderly beautiful. She moves softly in a long diagonal enclosed by the swans and, at the moment of her imminent death, expresses her undying love for the prince. Von Rotbart, enraged at Odette's delay, hovers over the scene disguised as a monstrous owl. He vows vengeance on her and all the swans. The swan maidens tremble as Siegfried defies Von Rotbart, who is momentarily overpowered by the strength of the prince's love for Odette.

The lovers embrace as Von Rotbart disappears. Odette then reminds the prince that only in death will she be released from Von Rotbart, only in death will she be free to love him forever. Her gestures are dramatic and sure as she tells him this, and suddenly she rushes across the stage in a swift diagonal to the shore's edge and throws herself into the lake as the music reaches a surging climax. Siegfried is motionless for a moment and stands helpless among the grieving swan maidens. Then, knowing that life without Odette will be nothing, he declares that he will follow her. He runs down the same diagonal that Odette took to the lakeside and drowns himself.

Siegfried's sacrifice of his love that Odette might not be destroyed by the evil magician has caused Von Rotbart's downfall. Again the malevolent owl-like creature appears, but only briefly. He lingers among the distraught swan maidens only long enough to see that love has triumphed in the end. He dies.

The stage darkens. The music softens. The swan maidens form two diagonal lines at the right, and as the light of day gradually rises in a soft glow, we see their figures bent low to the ground in grief at the loss of their queen and in gratitude for their own liberation from the evil sorcerer. Then, on the waters of the lake, a gleaming jeweled bark glides into view, its ornaments brilliant in the morning sun. Odette and Siegfried, clasped in each other's arms, move in the magical bark to a new and perpetually happy life. The swan maidens raise their heads, and their arms move softly, like ripples on the water, in quiet farewell to their queen.

NOTES   March 4, 1952, was the seventy-fifth anniversary of the first performance of *Swan Lake*. In observance of this occasion, Anatole Chujoy wrote the following authoritative article in the April 1952 issue of the informative and popular publication, *Dance News:* "Troubled less than it is in our days, a civilized world would have rested from its labors on March 4 to celebrate an important occasion in the history of ballet and music, the diamond jubilee of *Swan Lake*, the greatest romantic-classic ballet of all times.

"*Swan Lake*, as it were, stands at the highest point of the curve which represents the history of the source of all ballet as we know it today—the romantic-classic era which began with *Giselle* in 1841 and ended with *Les Sylphides* in 1909—the greatest period the classic dance has ever known. *Swan Lake* is often accepted as a strictly classic ballet; actually it is much more a romantic ballet. In conception, content, structure and emotion it is much closer to *Giselle*, for example, than to *The Sleeping Beauty*. In fact, it owes some of its choreographic invention to *Giselle*.

"*Swan Lake*, which has been variously called the greatest ballet of all times and an old war horse, was first presented on March 4, 1877, at the Moscow Imperial Bolshoi Theatre.

"Two years earlier, in the spring of 1875, the Director of the Bolshoi Theatre, V. P. Begitchev, commissioned Tchaikovsky to compose a score for a ballet then called *The Lake of the Swan*, based on a libretto written by the director himself, who was also a playwright of sorts, in collaboration with Vasily Geltzer (the future father of Catherine Geltzer, subsequently the famous prima ballerina of the Moscow Theatre [and the first to dance the complete *Swan Lake* in the United States]).

"Tchaikovsky hoped to create in *Swan Lake* a score that the Bolshoi Theatre would accept with the same regard as orchestras accepted his symphonic works. This hope was not realized. The choreographer assigned to the ballet was Julius Reisinger, a hack ballet master who possessed neither the talent nor the taste to choreograph a work to the music of a major composer.

"The ballerina, Pauline Karpakova, was a run-of-the-mill dancer past her bloom, who insisted upon interpolating sure-fire 'numbers' from other ballets in her repertoire to replace some of Tchaikovsky's music which she could not appreciate, understand or even count. The première of the ballet was to be a testimonial gala in her honor and she was not going to take any chances.

"When the première of *Swan Lake* took place it was a disappointment to everybody, especially to its composer. Herman Laroche, a well-known music critic, composer and friend of Tchaikovsky, wrote about the première as follows:

"'If during the creation of the ballet he [Tchaikovsky] had pictured fairy-tale splendor and brilliance he must have felt a bitter disappointment when he saw the work of the ballet master on the stage. I must say that I had never seen a poorer presentation on the stage of the Bolshoi Theatre.

"'The costumes, decor, and machines did not hide in the least the emptiness of the dances. Not a single balletomane got out of it even five minutes of pleasure. The greater, however, was the joy of the melomane. From the very first measures of the introduction one felt the hand of a true master; a few pages later we knew already that the master was in excellent humor, that he was fully at the height of his genius.'

"It cannot be said that *Swan Lake* was a total failure. It had a moderate success with the spectators and it remained on the stage until 1883 during which time it was given thirty-three performances.

"According to another contemporary of Tchaikovsky, N. Kashkin:

"'It [*Swan Lake*] was kept in the repertoire until the scenery was worn to shreds. The music also suffered a great deal. The substitution of the original numbers with others was practiced to an even greater extent, and toward the end almost a third of the music of *Swan Lake* had been substituted with that from other ballets, usually from the most mediocre ones.'

"When the scenery finally gave out the directorate of the Bolshoi Theatre took *Swan Lake* off the repertoire, and the ballet was not revived until January 1901, when Alexander Gorsky, a talented choreographer not sufficiently appreciated by his contemporaries and almost entirely neglected by historians, staged a new version of it.

"The version of *Swan Lake* which came down to our generation dates back to the St. Petersburg production choreographed by Lev Ivanov and Marius Petipa and first presented at the Maryinsky Theatre on January 17, 1895, more than a year after the death of Tchaikovsky.

"The production of *Swan Lake* at the Maryinsky came about in a rather unorthodox manner. The initiative for it stemmed from Ivanov, not from Petipa, as is generally supposed.

"After Tchaikovsky died of cholera on November 6, 1893, there was a general upsurge of interest in his work. His operas were being revived by Imperial and private opera houses, his orchestral compositions, even those which earlier had not been successful, were being played by symphonic organizations all over Russia.

"On March 1, 1894, an evening honoring the memory of Tchaikovsky was given at the Maryinsky Theatre. The program included several excerpts from the composer's operas and what is now called Act II of *Swan Lake*, independently staged for the occasion by Lev Ivanov, Marius Petipa's assistant who carried the unpretentious title of second ballet master and *regisseur*, the same Ivanov who had staged in 1892 Tchaikovsky's *The Nutcracker*.

"The role of Odette, the Swan Queen, was taken by Pierina Legnani, the great Italian ballerina, who had made her debut at the Maryinsky the year before in the ballet *Cinderella*, in which she introduced to St. Petersburg balletomanes her famous thirty-two *fouettés*. The short ballet caught the imagination of the audience.

"Petipa saw the performance and decided to profit by its success. He ordered a repetition of the performance at a gala evening and on that occasion placed his name alongside Ivanov's (and ahead of it) as choreographer. The second performance had an even greater success and Petipa decided to revive the whole ballet.

"Richard Drigo, the composer of the ballets *Talisman, The Magic Flute* and others, who was then conductor of the Maryinsky, was commissioned by Petipa to clean up the Moscow score. Drigo, on the whole, did a conscientious job, but found it necessary for some reason to eliminate several numbers from the ballet and substitute for them a few of Tchaikovsky's short 'salon pieces,' among them *Op. 72 Nos. 11, 12*, and *15*, as well as one number in Act III by an anonymous composer (Drigo himself, perhaps).

"Outside Russia there has often been speculation about what choreographer staged which part of the ballet. Indeed on several occasions the entire ballet, through sheer negligence, has been credited to Petipa, which is not only historically incorrect but also a great injustice to Ivanov. It has been established beyond any doubt that Petipa staged Act I (called Act I, Scene 1 in the original St. Petersburg version) and most of Act III (called Act II in the original version). Ivanov staged Act II, which constitutes the familiar one-act version (called Act I, Scene 2 in the original version), and Act IV (called Act III in the original version).

"Unlike the Moscow opening, eighteen years before, the St. Petersburg première on January 17, 1895, was a huge success. The occasion was also a testimonial gala for Pierina Legnani, who danced the double role of *Odette-Odile* and could not restrain herself from injecting her thirty-two *fouettés* from *Cinderella*, this time as the coda of her *pas de deux* in the ballroom scene (Act III).

"The two acts of *Swan Lake* which Lev Ivanov was permitted to stage were a great achievement for the choreographer and the culmination of his long but frustrated career at the Maryinsky, too little of which is known to the outside world.

"In staging the two acts Ivanov went contrary to the basic artistic direction in ballet during the second half of the nineteenth century, which aimed to demonstrate the technical proficiency of the dancer and the spectacular solution of complicated technological choreographic problems. Ivanov built Acts II and IV on musical principles, thus breaking a strong and generally accepted tradition. An excellent example of this is the adagio in Act II.

"In Petipa's ballets the adagio usually unfolds against the background of a picturesque backdrop or an immobile group of dancers who do not take part in the action. Ivanov's composition of the adagio in Act II is a duet with an active ensemble which accentuates and participates in the dance of the two principals. It is motivated entirely by the construction of the music, which was inspired, according to memoirs of Tchaikovsky's friends, by the vocal duet in his opera *Ondine*, the score for which he had destroyed before the opera was ever produced.

"This may sound less than revolutionary now, but in 1894 it was quite a step forward, so much so, in fact, that no choreographer dared to take a similar step until Michel Fokine, at the very height of his avant-garde Fronde'ism, utilized Ivanov's idea in *Les Sylphides* in 1909. Fokine also made use of some of Ivanov's choreography in *The Dying Swan* which he staged for Anna Pavlova in 1905.

"But Ivanov did more than just violate the canonical principles of the construction of the adagio by subordinating it to the problems of the musical themes. His two acts of *Swan Lake* very effectively dethroned the ballerina as the alpha and omega and, one might say, the *raison d'être* of the ballet. For some forty years Petipa constructed his ballets *ad majoram ballerinae gloriam*. The ballerina was all that mattered and everyone and everything else was on the third plane. Not so in *Swan Lake*. Here Ivanov treated the ballerina only as one of the protagonists. Here she either participates in the dances together with other dancers or alternates with them, or, if she performs a solo passage, the other dancers echo or accompany her. But no one leaves the stage for her variation, no one freezes into the painted backdrop.

"The adagio in Act II is a remarkable example of Ivanov's choreography, a testimonial to his choreographic and musical genius, but it is not the only example. One has but to think of the witty and compositionally perfect *pas de quatre* of the cygnets, the man's variation, and especially the entire last act to realize the great talent of Ivanov that was never allowed to achieve full bloom because of Petipa's dictatorial position in the Imperial Theatre.

"An appreciation of Lev Ivanov in English and an analysis of his work on *Swan Lake* and *The Nutcracker* is still to be done, and this writer hopes to do it before very long. It can be said here, however, that Ivanov's two acts of *Swan Lake* have been an inspiration to many contemporary choreographers whose origin was in prerevolutionary Russia. If one man can be considered the precursor of modern ballet, especially in the musical approach to choreography, that man was Lev Ivanov.

"Since its St. Petersburg première *Swan Lake* has never left the stage. The greatest ballerinas of prerevolutionary Russia, among them Mathilde Khessinska, Olga Preobrajenska, Anna Pavlova, Tamara Karsavina, and Olga Spessivtzeva, have vied for the privilege of dancing it.

"The current production of *Swan Lake* in Russia is based on the Ivanov-Petipa version, revived by Agrippina Vaganova in 1935. It is being given both in Moscow and Leningrad and is unquestionably the most popular ballet of the repertoire of both state theatres. It is also the ballet always presented on gala occasions and it is safe to say that every American and Western European diplomat and dignitary visiting Moscow has seen it.

"In Western Europe the full-length *Swan Lake* is only being given by the two British companies, the Sadler's Wells Ballet and the International Ballet. Both productions are based on the St. Petersburg version and both were staged by Nicholas Sergeyev, a former *regisseur* of the Maryinsky Theatre.

"The familiar one-act version of *Swan Lake* dates back to the Diaghilev Ballets Russes, which presented the ballet first in two acts [November 30, 1911, at the Royal Opera House, Covent Garden, London, with Mathilde Kchessinska, *prima ballerina assoluta* of the Imperial Theatre and Vaslav Nijinsky. Mischa Elman played the solo violin passages for these performances] and later in one act (ca. 1925). With the exception of the small French groups, nearly all professional contemporary ballet companies in America and Western Europe have a one-act version in their repertoire, based more or less on the Ivanov choreography."

Swan Lake is always changing. That is as it should be. Tradition in performance is, unlike teaching, discontinuous, as my friend Lincoln Kirstein has said. It is always interrupted, depends on shifts of directorships, changes of parts, whims of choreographers, dancers, designers, musicians, and the public. Only recently has a way been found to make permanent a record of a performance and I imagine that in the future it will be possible to know about a number of "definitive" *Swan Lakes*. But I also suspect that artists will want always to change it, to remake it for themselves. That is what many of us have done, and I hope will keep on doing.

My own version of Act Two, for example, first presented by the New York City Ballet November 20, 1951, retained then only the central *adagio* and the *pas de quatre*. But I have made many changes in the ballet since and we have new scenery and costumes, too, by Rouben Ter-Arutunian.

In England, the Royal Ballet, which has revised its production a number of times, has arrived at a useful compromise by retaining its older, Sergeyev version of the original in the repertory of its national touring company and presenting newer versions at Covent Garden and on international tours. This keeps the old well intact and at the same time makes possible innovation. One of the major revisions in the Royal Ballet's production was December 12, 1963, when Robert Helpmann staged a production with scenery and costumes by Carl Toms that had new dances by Frederick Ashton and restagings of other dances by Rudolf Nureyev and Maria Fay. Margot Fonteyn and David Blair danced the principal roles.

The Bolshoi Ballet and the Kirov Ballet productions of the complete *Swan Lake* have become familiar. Other productions of interest include a version by Vladimir Bourmeister for the Moscow Stanislavsky Ballet (1953), Rudolf Nureyev's staging for the Vienna State Opera (1964), with Margot Fonteyn and himself, and Erik Bruhn's production for the National Ballet of Canada (1967).

Bruhn's production was fortunately filmed for television in Canada. Produced and directed by Norman Campbell, with scenery and costumes by Desmond Healy, this National Ballet of Canada presentation featured Lois Smith, Erik Bruhn, and Celia Franca. In an hour and a quarter, Bruhn compressed for the television audience the entire ballet, employing new choreography and new arrangements, too, of the score. This version was presented in the United States by the Public Broadcasting Service, July 17, 1972, over Channel 13, New York.

On June 27, 1972, Natalia Makarova of American Ballet Theatre danced *Swan Lake* with the Royal Ballet in London. Clement Crisp wrote in London's *Financial Times:* "Odette and Odile are both magical beings, the one enchanted, the other an enchantress; the particular distinction of Natalia Makarova's interpretation was marvelously to convey this quality of magic.

"Her entrance as Odette is quite extraordinary; the Swan Queen is terrified, a fraught creature at Siegfried's appearance, trembling in his arms. Like Melisande when Golaud finds her, she is lost, a prey to unfathomable terrors, and throughout this first encounter we are made aware how heavily Von Rotbart's spell lies upon her. Infinitely pathetic, she seems not of this world and the menace of the enchanter's presence never seems to desert her during the whole of the act. The result is a profoundly moving characterization, expressed through dancing of exquisite perfection.

"With the Kirov, Makarova's Odette was a marvel; now it seems even more amazing. The great sound-act duet pours out in an unbroken cantilena, long-breathed, phrased with the inevitability of genius. The pure, classic schooling, the lightness that imbues her every movement, make the dancing float on the music—albeit Makarova demands slow tempi and is not, I would hazard, the most musical of dancers. But an *assoluta* is to be allowed her own way with the score, and the means amply justify the end when it results in an interpretation at once classically controlled, in the Kirov manner, and totally communicative of the Swan Queen's tragedy.

"In her Kirov performances, Makarova's Odile was something below the standard of her Odette; this is now no longer true. She plays the third act with prodigious brilliance; the choreographic variants she offers are acceptable since the enchantress in the ballroom shines with a hectic glitter that is totally compelling. No prince could resist this malign beauty, and Donald MacLeary's fine Siegfried is no exception. He is obsessed with her, and very properly so; Makarova's shining presence is hypnotically attractive—witness the fact that after prolonged stage calls following her variation, the truth of her impersonation seemed to carry right through them: we were not cheering a ballerina but Von Rotbart's creation.

"If the fourth act seemed slightly flat, I would blame the production rather than the interpreter; it is unfamiliar to Makarova, and not particularly effective anyway. What shone through the relative dullness of the staging here was the beauty of her style, with its delicacy and impeccable placing, the expressive force of her poses, and such small but thrilling things as a *pas de bourrée* which seems to meet the ground with a feathery lightness. I imagine that some viewers will consider Makarova 'cold' as Odette; her performance is still absolutely true to the canons of the Kirov style in which the very statement of the choreography must contain the essence of the role without any external 'acting' —and I find it entirely satisfying. My only hope is that her interpretation be preserved on film—it is essential for future generations to be able to study it, and to marvel at its magnificence."

There have been a number of films made of *Swan Lake,* or parts thereof (the Royal Ballet's Act Two, with Margot Fonteyn, for example). David Vaughan in *Ballet Review,* Vol. 4, No. 1, wrote at length of the Kirov Ballet's film.

When the first edition of this book of ballet stories first appeared, in 1954, there was only one complete four-act version of *Swan Lake* before the public in the West—the Royal Ballet's, described above. Since then, many other four-act productions have materialized, and in the United States it has been possible to see different versions by the National Ballet, American Ballet Theatre, in a notable staging by David Blair, the Bolshoi Ballet, the Kirov Ballet, the National Ballet of Canada, and the Stuttgart Ballet, among others. The one by John Cranko for the Stuttgart Ballet prompted these remarks by the choreographer: "I am always surprised by productions of *Swan Lake* that claim to have used all the music. Such a production would last about as long as *Die*

Meistersinger. While opera lovers can take this length, balletomanes tend to enjoy shorter fare. Something must go and I have, therefore, cut the well-known waltzes and *pas de trois* from Act One and put in their place the equally beautiful but seldom performed *pas de six*. This gives Siegfried the opportunity to dance and also to develop the character. The Black Swan *Pas de Deux* remains in the place Tchaikovsky intended, and in the fourth act the Drigo *pas de deux,* which always seemed too slight for the situation, has been replaced by the beautiful *Elegy for Strings.* I have tried to base my own work on the classic/romantic style of Petipa, working freely and in my own manner, but not losing sight of the great man's direction. Consequently most of the second act has been retained in its usual form. For the opening of the fourth act and the famous elegiac entry of the swans I have 'borrowed' from various Soviet productions. However, all the musical repetitions have been cut and the drama has been strengthened accordingly so that the prince emerges as a living person who experiences a tragic ordeal, rather than being a human crane who simply lifts the ballerina. The national dances have been woven into an overall dramatic arrangement instead of being pointless *divertissements.* What of the ending? There have been many 'happy endings,' where the lovers are reunited after death in 'fairyland,' but I believe that Tchaikovsky intended to write a tragic ballet. Consider the situation: Siegfried proves unworthy, he breaks his vow and unconsciously confuses outward appearances with inner reality, . . . he is a tragic hero and must be vanquished. The tone of the music, especially in the fourth act, is tragic. In the imperial theatre the Tsar (surrounded by so many tragedies) made it an unwritten rule that everything must close happily. But Odette and Siegfried are not the sort of lovers who can 'live happily ever after.'"

Reviewing Margot Fonteyn's *Autobiography* in the New York *Times* (May 15, 1976), the critic Anna Kisselgoff recalled that the ballerina, on May 3, 1972, offered "at the age of 53 an unforgettable *Swan Lake* with Rudolf in New York that surpassed the effort of any younger ballerina that season. The idea of a technique drenched in emotionalism (for this was the secret of that night's success) is not usually associated with the most regal of the Royal Ballet's ballerinas.

"Yet that is a notion about herself that she accepts fully. Writing of the early years of the Nureyev-Fonteyn partnership, she describes the contrast between the two dancers this way: 'It was paradoxical that the young boy everyone thought so wild and spontaneous in his dancing cared desperately about technique, whereas I, the cool English ballerina, was so much more interested in the emotional aspects of the performance.'"

LA SYLPHIDE

Ballet in two acts. Music by Jean Schneitzhoeffer. Choreography by Philippe
Taglioni. Book by Adolphe Nourrit. Scenery by Pierre Ciceri. Costumes by
Eugène Lami. First presented at the Théâtre de l'Académie Royale de
Musique, Paris, March 12, 1832, with Marie Taglioni as La Sylphide *and*
Mazilier as James. *Marie Taglioni danced the title role when the ballet was*
introduced to London (1832), St. Petersburg (1837), and Milan (1841).
A version of La Sylphide *was presented in the United States for the first*
time on April 15, 1835, with Mademoiselle Céleste in the leading role. It
was subsequently danced in the United States by the same ballerina; by
Augusta Maywood (1838); Amélie Galster (1839), sister-in-law of Marie
Taglioni; and by Fanny Elssler (1840). In 1836 Sylphiden *was presented*
by the Royal Danish Ballet in a version by Auguste Bournonville with mu-
sic by Herman Løvenskjold. Lucile Grahn danced the Sylphide *in the first*
performance of this version, which has been in the active repertory of the
Royal Danish Ballet ever since. Taglioni's La Sylphide *was revived in 1946*
by the Ballets des Champs-Élysées, Paris, with choreography by Victor
Gsovsky, scenery by Serebriakov, and costumes by Christian Bérard. Nina
Vyroubova and Roland Petit danced the principal roles. The Royal Danish
Ballet danced the ballet in the United States for the first time at the Met-
ropolitan Opera House, New York, September 16, 1956. Harald Lander
staged La Sylphide *for American Ballet Theatre in San Antonio, Texas, No-*
vember 11, 1964, with Toni Lander and Royes Fernandez. Music arranged
and composed by Edgar Cosma after Løvenskjold. On May 20, 1967, Carla
Fracci and Erik Bruhn danced in this production at the New York State
Theatre. Erik Bruhn staged it for the National Ballet of Canada in Toronto,
December 31, 1964, with Lois Smith and himself in the leading roles. These
were later taken by Lynn Seymour and Rudolf Nureyev.

Once a curiosity but now popular in repertories in the United States, Canada,
England, and the continent, *La Sylphide* deserves continuing attention. Ballet
history was changed completely by the work. Marie Taglioni who danced it
and the men who created the role for her made a revolution in the art of dancing that we still witness whenever we go to the ballet and see a world of story
—of sylphs, ondine, swan queens, and firebirds—that is both real and fantasy,
settings that are both ethereal and natural, costumes of flowing white, satin toe
shoes, and dancers who rise on *pointe* and are lifted magically into the air by
their partners. The era of the romantic ballet begun by this ballet is still much
with us.

ACT ONE   The story of *La Sylphide* is a romance of old Scotland. The scene is the living room of a Scottish farmhouse. The time is 1830. The room is large and high. On the left a fire blazes in a great fireplace; a huge stone mantel rises from it to the rafters. The mantel is hung with trophies of the hunt—colorful stuffed birds, powder horns, and flintlocks. A staircase runs up the back of the room to the upper story, and a bright plaid decorates the banister. Near the first landing of the stairs is a high, peaked window through whose diamond-shaped translucent glass we can discern the break of day.

This is the wedding day of James Reuben, the young Scots peasant who lives in this house with his mother. The bridegroom sleeps restlessly in a high wing chair drawn close to the fire. He is dressed for his wedding: kilts, cap with high feather. His dark head stirs against the back of the chair; he is dreaming. His dream is with us in the room, and we understand his restlessness. For kneeling on the floor at his feet, her long white dress against the bridegroom's bright tartan, is the diaphanous, winged sylphide, who glances with quiet happiness about the room and seems with her penetrating gaze to look into the eyes of her dreaming lover.

Gurn, another young peasant, rests in a corner against the fireplace. In his deep sleep, Gurn is not disturbed by the realization of his friend's dream; he himself dreams of Effie, James's bride-to-be, and the love he will lose this day.

The sylphide rises effortlessly and circles about the chair. She looks down upon the sleeping James with wistful longing, moving around the room with a lightness and grace that make her wings more than a part of her costume. James turns his head as she dances about him; he is still asleep, but in his dream he watches every gesture she makes. Creature that she is from another world, the sylphide now seems a part of this room. Her smile is the considered smile of possession; she is both beautiful and serious, and her face tells us that her love is great enough to endure beyond James's dream. Should James respond to her love, we feel that this dream might become permanent.

James stirs in his sleep. He wakens suddenly and beholds the sylphide before him. He reaches out for her desperately. Frightened now by reality, the sylphide eludes his grasp. She rushes toward the fireplace. She disappears like the smoke from the dying embers. James moves his hand to his forehead in disbelief at the apparition: was she really there, after all? He becomes frantic and unable to understand the mystery and decides to question Gurn. He shakes his friend awake rudely. Did he see the beautiful vision? How long have we slept? Gurn is a little embarrassed at his own dream and is about to tell James yes, he saw the beautiful girl, but he sees that his friend is not talking about Effie, the bride, but about someone quite different. He wonders at his friend.

James is angry at Gurn for allowing himself to sleep so soundly. He is still trying to piece together the fragments of his dream when he hears his mother approach. She comes in from another room with Effie. Reminded by his bride's presence that he has scarcely thought of her, James is embarrassed. Gurn greets the bride first. The beautiful young lass smiles at him. Gurn can hardly control himself, he is so moved by her loveliness; meekly he presents her with a rare bird he killed yesterday while hunting. Effie accepts the gift, but turns to her fiancé. Why, she wonders, is he preoccupied? Has he no greeting for her? James shakes off his dream and kisses her fondly. They embrace. Effie cannot see James's face as he stares over her shoulder into the fireplace. His mother and Gurn watch him curiously.

Again James kisses his bride. Amused by his own formality, he kisses her hand and tells her that this is the day he has long awaited. Effie sees that he is sincere and his old self again. She is therefore a little annoyed when Gurn steps in, takes her hand and tries to kiss it too. She shakes her finger at him, and James, seeing that he has a rival in his friend, jokes with him about it. Gurn, however, is in no mood for jokes and walks away to nurture his private dream.

James's mother embraces her son and Effie. The lovers kneel before her; she blesses them and hopes for their eternal happiness. Effie and James look into each other's eyes; in her sight, he has forgotten his dream.

Now the music brightens and becomes festive with the arrival of Effie's bridesmaids. The young peasant girls, dressed in brilliant plaids, surround the lovers and wish them well. Gurn approaches. The girls giggle at his discomfiture: after all, he might choose one of them instead of Effie, who is already spoken for. The unhappy Gurn pleads with them to intercede for him; can't anything be done, he wonders, before it is too late? The girls put him off and bring out the wedding gifts they have for Effie: bunches of freshly picked flowers, decorative cloths, and simple jewelry. The bride is delighted with the presents, tries on the jewelry, and drapes the new material over her shoulder.

She and her friends do not notice James as he walks away from them and stares into the fire. Gurn watches him suspiciously. What can be wrong with his friend? James turns his head to look at the precise spot where he last saw the sylphide. He catches his breath and jumps back, startled. Someone is there! He reaches out his arms hopefully, and out of the dark corner steps not his sylphide, but a frightening figure: Old Madge, the village sorceress. The girls are pleased and run over to her. Old Madge stumbles forward, bent low over her crude walking stick. Her ragged clothes are filthy; her stringy gray hair hangs loose about her white, ghostly face. She cackles hideously and walks straight over to James and looks up into his face. His fear turns to anger. He orders her away. Madge cowers pathetically, and the girls are shocked at James's behavior.

The bridegroom stalks away. The girls persuade Madge to tell their fortunes. Effie is the first to hold out her hand. She asks the sorceress if her marriage will be a happy one? Effie does not really have any doubts; it is, after all, the conventional question. Old Madge nods her head and grins, "Yes, you will be happy in marriage." Emboldened by this answer, Effie asks another question: does James love her? James looks over at the group. The witch says, "No," smiling the same toothless smile as she shakes her head. James will tolerate this no longer. Old Madge cackles ominously. He picks up a broom and drives the hag from the room.

Effie, reassured by James's indignation, tells him that she never doubted his love and that Old Madge is a proverbial liar. James believes her and is comforted. As long as Effie is with him and he can look into her eyes, he, too, has no doubt.

His mother comes to take Effie away. It is time for her to dress for the wedding. Mother Reuben laughs at her son when he doesn't want to let Effie go. She takes the girl by the hand and leads her and her bridesmaids up the stairs. Effie glances back at James, who smiles at her reassuringly.

But now, alone in the room, James has his doubts. He cannot get his dream out of his mind, though rationally he knows it is nonsense. Effie is his real love and so she will remain. But will the dream recur? What would he do if it did? Could such a vision really exist? As he asks himself these tormenting questions, he feels a draft. He turns around, and there—standing in the window—is the sylphide! She is leaning against the window frame; her hands are clasped before her; her expression is one of sweet sadness; and her eyes look down, refusing to meet James's glance. James goes to the window and asks her why she is so sad. Before she vanished so mysteriously, the sylphide was blithe and happy; what can be troubling so beautiful a girl? The sylphide replies that she loves someone who does not love her. James turns as if to move away, but the sylphide continues. He must know, she says, that she loves him. She is the one who brought him the beautiful dream; she is the one who will always watch over him and keep him from harm. Gurn, who has been sulking in a dark corner near the fireplace, emerges from the shadows to watch closely.

James reminds the sylphide that he is to be married this very day. The sylphide knows. Tears fall upon her cheeks. She murmurs that there can be no more beauty in her life: she must die. She starts to leave. James can suppress his secret no longer. He kneels before her and tells her that since she disappeared from his sight he has not been able to forget her for a single moment; he has tried, for he owed it to his love for his fiancée, but he could not: he has loved her as she loves him.

The sylphide dances about the room. James is enraptured to see his dream become real and to find the creature even more graceful in life. She moves toward the window, beckoning James to follow her. He does not move. She whispers softly into his ear. The unhappy bridegroom looks toward the stairs and hangs back. The sylphide watches him and sees the source of his anxiety. Lightly, without seeming to have the least idea of what it is, she takes up the plaid Effie has left behind on the chair, puts it around her shoulders, and poses demurely with downcast eyes as the bride. James can resist her no longer. When the sylphide kneels at his feet, he draws her to him and kisses her.

Gurn is now convinced of his friend's faithlessness and dashes up the stairs to Effie. James and the sylphide are frightened. Excited voices approach. Quickly the sylphide cuddles up in a corner of the huge chair. James throws the plaid over her just as Gurn and Effie, in her bridal gown, rush down the stairs. Her friends follow. Gurn accuses James of having kissed another woman in this room. But where is she? James asks him; he laughs and swears he has been quite alone. Effie and Gurn see no one, but Gurn notes the plaid that covers the chair. James trembles. Gurn pulls the plaid away, and underneath is . . . nothing! The sylphide was vanished! James is as surprised as his friend, but immediately reassures Effie, who now berates Gurn for allowing his jealousy to govern his sense of truth. The girls ridicule Gurn mercilessly, and he slinks out of the room.

James's mother enters with the wedding guests—her friends as well as the friends of the happy couple. Refreshments are served, toasts are made, the bagpipes tune up, and soon everyone is either dancing or talking volubly. Everyone, that is, except James. As all the other young men of the village surround the bride, James stands apart, reminded anew of the sylphide. Effie breaks away from her admirers and reminds the bridegroom that he has not asked her to dance. James is shocked at his forgetfulness, and the two begin to dance. The other guests stand back and watch them. The couple dance together happily until the formal pattern of the peasant dance forces them to separate for a moment. At this point the sylphide returns. She is seen only by James, and the other guests are astonished—when James rejoins Effie—to see him turn his head away from his bride. The *pas de deux* becomes a *pas de trois*: every movement of Effie's is imitated and elevated by the sprightly sylphide. The guests join Effie and James in a general dance, while the sylphide runs hither and yon, now visible, now concealed by the turning couples.

James tries not to lose sight of her and whirls Effie around and around as he frantically pursues the sylphide. Effie is so happy she doesn't notice his anxiety. The sylphide continually eludes him, and James can no longer see her. The dance stops, and some of the guests surround James and inquire about his strange behavior.

They are put off, however, by the beginning of the wedding ceremony. The guests stand in formal groups about the fireplace, where James and Effie stand with his mother. The ritual begins. The couple start to exchange wedding rings. James take off his own ring and holds it at Effie's finger tip. He moves to slip it on her finger, when the sylphide darts out from nowhere and takes the ring from his hand. The guests gasp at the sudden disappearance of the ring. James turns away from his bride. The sylphide whispers to him that she will die if he marries anyone else. James is so appalled at this possibility that he now sees his course: he must prevent such a tragedy. The sylphide beckons to him and stands there in the room by the window before his wedding guests; the bridegroom vanishes.

Effie dissolves in tears. No one can understand how or why James has abandoned her thus. Gurn rushes in and announces that he has just seen the bridegroom running across the moor with another woman. Effie will not believe it. Gurn tries to comfort her, assuring her that she can be certain of his love. Mother Reuben and all the guests gather about the troubled bride. Effie sits down in the chair by the fire. The plaid is placed around her shoulders, her wedding veil is removed. Gurn kneels beside her.

ACT TWO Eerie music suggestive of an unnatural world marks the beginning of this second scene, which will unravel the mystery of the magical sylphide and confront the romantic James with his destiny. When the curtain rises, it is still night. On the left, a small fire throws grotesque shadows against the walls of a small, dark cave. The surrounding forest is impenetrably black. The witch, Old Madge, emerges from the cave and stands over the fire. Hovering over the flames, she invokes her demons, beseeching them to obey her commands. With her crooked walking stick, she draws a magic circle about the fire, then hurries into the shadows of the cavern. She returns with her sisters in witchcraft: hunchbacked, cackling hags who gather about the circle. The hideous women hang a huge black caldron over the fire and dance around and around it. Suddenly Old Madge orders silence and, walking up to stand over the caldron, she points her finger downward in unquestioning command. The other witches are silenced by this gesture and wait expectantly for some result. Old Madge orders them to dance again; as they circle the fire, smoke and steam and blue flame arise from the caldron, illuminating the forest for a few flashing moments. The conflagration in the caldron simmers down, and the old women crowd around to see what remains inside. With an imperious sweep of her arm, Old Madge tells them to stand back. The sun is about to rise, and they must hasten their work. Madge takes her stick and pokes it into the caldron; when she pulls it out, we see on the end of the stick, like a banner, a lovely shimmering scarf. The old women grab at it, but Madge holds it to her breast; only she is aware of the power of this beautiful scarf. She orders her sisters away, and all the witches disappear into the cave.

In the distance, the sun rises brightly over the fields of heather and we see a clearing in a thickly wooded glade. The green trees hang down over the scene, almost obscuring the witches' cave. Dew covers the ground as the morning mist settles on the earth.

On the right, James enters the forest. No longer dressed like a typical Scots peasant, James wears a costume befitting the bridegroom of his sylphide: white tights and a plaid vest. He carries a bird nest in his hand. Carefully he examines the colorful eggs and replaces them. He looks about the forest for his love, but she is not to be found. As he begins to approach the cave, he discovers the sylphide standing by his side. He is astonished at the suddenness of her appearance and asks her where she has been hiding. The lovely girl smiles back at him so beautifully that James leaves off his questioning. As if to show him how she appeared so swiftly and silently, she dances about the forest like a magical sprite; the tips of her toes seem to require only the air to support

them in flight. James is bewitched anew by her charm and becomes apprehensive when the sylph darts in and out behind the trees. He holds out the
bird's nest and tells her he has brought her a gift. The sylph shrinks back; and
we see suddenly that she is not frightened because James has probably harmed
the eggs in the nest, but because the living birds who fly about the forest are
moved by a power quite different from the mysterious force that makes her a
sylphide as well as a woman. The sylphide is afraid of the nest. Scrupulously
she takes it between her hands and runs to place it high on an overhanging
branch. James smiles warmly at what he believes to be her tenderness; lightly
the sylphide moves her finger tips over her diaphanous white gown.

James draws her to his side. The sylphide places her head on his shoulder
for a moment, and James moves to take her face in his hands. Before he can
do so, the sylphide has danced away toward the back. James observes her as
she calls forth a band of sylphs, who pay homage to her and to him. The
sylphs surround the happy lovers, and James would dance with his bride; but
every time he turns to take her in his arms, she is mysteriously gone and before him stands another sylphide. This happens repeatedly, and James becomes frantic in his search. Then, just as if nothing had happened, the sylphide
is at his side again, looking up into his eyes. James is satisfied, but again the
vision disappears: all the sylphs seem to fly away in the blazing light of the
sun.

Alone, James considers that he has made a mistake. Yesterday, in his mother's
house, the sylphide was always appearing and vanishing mysteriously, but that
he could understand—for there he alone shared her secret; but here in the forest with her, with no one to see, why should she wish to escape *him?* She had
sworn that she loved him and would love him eternally, and yet she would be
loved only from afar. Was his love an illusion, he wondered?

On the left, close to where he last saw his beloved, the branches rustle.
James is startled to see Old Madge come out of her cave. In his present state
of mind, he greets her like an old friend. He remembers his rudeness of yesterday and hastens to apologize. Old Madge tells him not to mind, she understands the momentary follies of youth—but why is he here in the forest? What
has happened?

James tells her briefly that he has run away with his true love, the most
beautiful girl in the world. Why then does he look so dejected, Madge
inquires? "Because," James tells her, "the sylphide is never with me: I search
for her, and she is not to be found; I reach out to touch her beside me, and she
eludes my embrace."

Madge offers to help him with her occult powers. James, willing to try any
device to still the sylphide's flight, beseeches the witch to ease his state of
mind and secure his permanent happiness. Old Madge holds out the bright
magic scarf and offers it to James. She instructs him to place this scarf about
the sylphide's shoulders, and then the sylphide will never fly again: her light,

transparent wings will fall to the ground and flutter no more; she will be his, on earth.

James is delighted with this magic and kneels before the witch in gratitude. Old Madge's eyes gleam with triumph as she looks down upon him. Then she hurries away into the dark cavern as she sees the sylphide approaching. James runs to his bride and embraces her. She responds warmly to his affection and seems to be charmed by the gift he offers her. James places the scarf about her shoulders. As the cloth touches her flesh, the sylphide clutches at her heart in a spasm of agonizing pain. Her wings fall to the ground. She stumbles forward. James, struck dumb by this outcome, tries to hold her in his arms and comfort her. The dying sylphide looks at him in horror and pushes him away. Slowly her body relaxes, and she lies dead before him, like a leaf fallen from a tree.

As James kneels beside her, weeping, the mirthful cackle of Old Madge ricochets against the dark walls of her hidden cavern. The sylphide's winged sisters emerge from the trees above. They do not comfort the despairing hero, but take the sylphide tenderly in their arms. As they lift her from the ground, they themselves are lifted up; the branches of the trees overhead move back, and high into the clear sky the winged creatures carry their dead queen.

James is inconsolable in his grief. The softness of the music that has carried his ideal love away forever is interrupted by the shrill, open sound of joyous bagpipes, reminding him of his home and the happiness he might have found there. Across the forest, in the distance, we see a wedding procession moving over the moor. Gurn and Effie, arm in arm, lead the happy party, and the curtain falls as the faraway church bells sound their welcome.

NOTES The National Ballet of Washington presented *La Sylphide* in the version by Elsa Marianne von Rosen in 1969. When Margot Fonteyn, dancing this ballet for the first time, appeared in this production October 3, 1969, the critic Clive Barnes wrote: "After seeing Dame Margot it seemed only remarkable that she had never danced the role before. It suited her perfectly, for she brings to these Romantic ballets a most exquisite sense of period style.

"The ballet is a kind of Victorian nosegay—sweet, sentimental and yet completely acceptable upon its own period terms. . . . Dame Margot fitted into its ardors with effortless grace. . . . she conveys the mystic character of the sylph with a seductive mixture of femininity and charm. It recalls her beguiling performance in Ashton's *Ondine*, all thoughtless wiles and innocent raptures."

When American Ballet Theatre staged a new production of *La Sylphide* in New York, July 8, 1971, the staging was by the Danish dancer, choreographer, and producer Erik Bruhn. Clive Barnes commented in the New York *Times* the next day: "By far the best aspect of the production is Mr. Bruhn's staging. This is far more authentic than the first production of *La Sylphide* he created for the National Ballet of Canada some years ago. Indeed, it follows the original fairly carefully and with considerable sensibility.

"The only major addition is a brief new solo for Effie, which is reasonable enough. As is common nowadays, the hero, James, dances the second male solo in this act, and his rival, Gurn, dances the first. Mr. Bruhn takes further than any other production the current trend to romanticize Gurn and to remove him from the original comic tradition, and I can see no harm in this, even though it eliminates some of the traditional pantomime.

"There were other details of the production I was less happy about. I would like to have seen more stage machinery used—this is part of that particular period. I regret the omission of some of the smaller touches that are usually introduced—such as the Sylphide, on persuading James to run away from home, bringing him his cap. There were even details of choreography missing— including James's quite celebrated turn-and-a-half, where he ends a sequence with his back to the audience facing his ballerina.

"These are quibbles, but perhaps the kind of details that give authenticity to the authentic. But at last Ballet Theatre has found a good and valid version of this very important classic, and it will fit well into the company's repertory.

"At this first performance, the Sylphide was danced by Carla Fracci, with Ted Kivitt as her swain, James. Miss Fracci, with her fugitive smile wreathing the corners of her mouth, her tarlatan skirt frothing, and her shy yet captivating manner, is the epitome of the Romantic ideal, when, poetically, women often meant to be more myth than reality. And her dancing had the right febrile grace.

"The Sylphide herself is all spirit—an image rather than a character, an unattainable sex symbol for an age that in polite literary terms had no explicit sex but merely its lost promise. James, the Highland lad, who, rather foolishly, throws away everything to follow her into the heather, has more of the dimensions of reality, and Mr. Kivitt acted with a simple forcefulness.

"Probably the most rewarding character in *La Sylphide* is that of Madge the Witch, who ruins James and insures all ends unhappily. This is now played by Dennis Nahat, who is wearing one of the two or three most interestingly twisted noses I have ever encountered, and glowers with genuine power. It is a good idea to have this role played by a man—it often is in Denmark—and Mr. Nahat, with his unfailing sense of style, is already good and will soon be even better."

Erik Bruhn performed the role of Madge in New York, in August 1974, in the production of *La Sylphide* he had staged for the National Ballet of Canada. Writing in *Dance Perspectives* about his famous roles in the essay "Beyond Technique," Erik Bruhn recalled the first time he appeared as James in *La Sylphide*: "It was a pretty difficult assignment—to do James at the age of 23. I would consider any age between 18 and 24 as the right age for James on the stage. Of course we are all that age at one time or another. But to play him that way is possible only if you can achieve and sustain an idea about how you see him. To play yourself or to play your own age is not enough; to play young when you are young is very hard. When you are mature you can look on youth from a certain distance and this makes you objective. But when you are terribly involved with what is happening to you at this age it is difficult to re-create this. Some people would say that when you look back it isn't the truth you are seeing anymore, it is what you think the truth is. Yes, the role is also what you think it is. It is what you bring to it—your thoughts, your mind. You give life to the role by bringing to it what is true for you at that moment.

"For me, James is the youngest in the gallery of Romantic ballet heroes. He is an idealist, a poet. In the end when he tries to grasp his ideal and tries to make her a real woman, he dies. Without this dream, this illusion, he can no longer exist. All he wants to catch is a dream which exists only in his head and which nobody else can see. He is a true escapist. Nobody can actually get hold of James. His mother, his fiancée—none of the real people understand him. But when he is alone with his dream he is quite himself; he is a total being. When the dream is gone, he must die with it. He believes only in this dream and it is sad that he could never grasp reality. James dies without knowing that he is licked, which becomes a very beautiful thing.

"Unlike James, Albrecht in *Giselle* is on the point of entering maturity. He realizes that he has done something terrible and that he must suffer. If he can survive his night of remorse he will come out the better for it. He pays the price as James never did. Therefore he can live."

For an interesting analysis of the difference between the Bournonville style and the classic style taught in Russia, as well as for a penetrating account of *La Sylphide,* readers are referred to the book *Baryshnikov at Work,* where the dancer describes with Charles Engell France characteristics of performances he has known.

LES SYLPHIDES

Classic ballet in one act. Music by Frédéric Chopin. Choreography by Michel Fokine. Scenery and costumes by Alexandre Benois. First presented by Diaghilev's Ballets Russes at the Théâtre de Châtelet, Paris, June 2, 1909, with Anna Pavlova, Tamara Karsavina, Maria Baldina, and Vaslav Nijinsky as the principal dancers. Fokine's first arrangement of this ballet was presented on March 21, 1908, in St. Petersburg, under the title Chopiniana. The dancers were members of the Imperial Ballet; Pavlova and Oboukoff danced a classical pas de deux to the "Waltz," which was the only part of the original production without a realistic setting or suggestion of plot. The second production, given by Fokine's students, April 6, 1908, was wholly classical; like the first "Waltz," it had no plot, and the musical structure was altered. Preobrajenska, Pavlova, Karsavina, Nijinsky, and Bekeffy were the principal dancers. This second version was costumed in the long white ballet dress made popular by Marie Taglioni in La Sylphide. The title of this famous ballet of Taglioni's was Diaghilev's inspiration for the new name he applied to Chopiniana when it was first presented in Western Europe in

*substantially the same form as its second production. First presented in
the United States in its authorized version by Diaghilev's Ballets Russes at
the Century Theatre, New York, January 20, 1916, with a cast that included
Lydia Lopokova, Lubov Tchernicheva, Xenia Maclezova, and Adolph Bolm.
An unauthorized version, not credited to the choreographer and not supervised by him, was presented in the United States by Gertrude Hoffman's
Saison des Ballets Russes on June 14, 1911, at the Winter Garden, New
York, with Maria Baldina, Lydia Lopokova, and Alexandre Volinine as the
principal dancers.*

No one knows exactly when the first *ballet blanc,* or white ballet, was first performed. It is probable that this kind of ballet, which involved a new conception of dance based on ethereal atmosphere, soft music, and diaphanous white
costumes, was first performed before *La Sylphide;* but it was *La Sylphide,* and
the dancing of its ballerina, Marie Taglioni, that made the *ballet blanc* famous. *Les Sylphides,* its twentieth-century namesake, has carried this fame
into our time more than any other ballet.

For the *ballet blanc* did not remain popular. Théophile Gautier, who first
used the phrase, was complaining in 1844 that since *La Sylphide* the Paris
stage was so dominated by white gauze, by tulle and tarlatan, that the "shades
became mists of snow in transparent skirts" and "white almost the only color
in use."

And so the misty white ballets gradually passed out of fashion. The ballets
that replaced them for half a century were more concerned with dancing than
with mood—more devoted to elaborate, regal stage spectacle, and the development within this frame of the classic dance, than to simple stories of fantasy
and ethereal romance.

Les Sylphides restored the *ballet blanc,* now embellished with the developed classic dance; but it did so without a story. Here, instead of characters
with definite personalities and a narrative, we have simply dancers in long
white dresses and a *danseur* in white-and-black velvet, whose movements to
music invoke the romantic imagination to a story of its own. It is the music,
and the care with which the classic dance embodies it, that tells us the story of
these magical creatures who dance in the light of the moon.

The overture, *Prelude, Opus 28, No. 7,* to the ballet is quiet and contemplative. The curtain rises on a secluded wood near an ancient ruin, where
lovely girls in white are grouped about the scene in a still, charming tableau.
The light is bluish white, soft, and misty. As the *Nocturne, Opus 32, No. 2,*
commences, some of the girls begin to dance to the light, airy melody. They
are joined by the principal dancers, who stand in a cluster at the rear.

Now a girl dances a variation to a gentle but joyous waltz, music suggestive
of beautiful and controlled happiness.

The next dance, like the *Mazurka, Opus 33, No. 3,* that accompanies it, is
not as soft; it is bolder, more open and free, but still restrained in its ex-

uberance as the ballerina bounds diagonally across the stage in *grand jetés,* over and over again.

A variation to another mazurka, *Opus 67, No. 3,* is danced by the *danseur* after the girls have formed a decorative tableau about the stage.

When the overture is repeated, the sylphs form picturesque groups, the girls kneeling about central figures. The *danseuse* who now enters comes softly, pauses, and seems to listen to a distant call. She moves among the groups adroitly and sweetly, but completely removed from them in her rapt attention to what she might hear.

The *Waltz, Opus 64, No. 2,* commences, and the *danseur* lifts the ballerina across the stage from the wings. She appears to be so light that it must require no effort to hold her. She is released, and the *pas de deux* begins. Throughout this dance, as the music increases in momentum, the girl responds with unhesitating swiftness and flight to the inspiration of the music and the night: she abandons herself to the air.

The stage is empty for a moment, there is no music; then, to the final buoyant *Waltz, Opus 18, No. 1,* the dancers return, move diagonally across the stage, mingle, brush past each other, and fill the stage with movement like the swift fluttering of butterfly wings. The principal dancers join them for short solos; and at the final chords, there is a swift, silent rush and all are standing still, in the same tableau in which we first saw them.

NOTES *Les Sylphides* is associated with many famous dancers. Fokine staged his work for the Royal Danish Ballet on October 21, 1925 (in a revised version), for René Blum's Ballet Russe de Monte Carlo in 1936, and for Ballet Theatre in 1940.

In the first Diaghilev production in Paris, the first solo, Waltz, was danced by Karsavina; the second, Mazurka, by Anna Pavlova; the third, Mazurka, by Nijinsky; the Prelude, by Maria Baldina; the *pas de deux,* Waltz, by Pavlova and Nijinsky; and the final Waltz, by all the soloists and the *corps de ballet.* Vaslav Nijinsky danced *Les Sylphides* in the United States on April 14, 1916, at the Metropolitan Opera House.

The music for Fokine's first arrangement of the ballet that was later to become *Les Sylphides* was orchestrated by Glazunov. Music for the second version was orchestrated by Keller and Glazunov. Music for the Diaghilev production was orchestrated by Stravinsky (his first Diaghilev commission), Tcherepnine, Glazunov, and Liadov. Later orchestrations include those of Vittorio Rieti and Lucien Caillet.

On January 13, 1972, *Chopiniana,* the work on which *Les Sylphides* was based, was presented for the first time outside Russia:

Music by Frédéric Chopin. Staged by Alexandra Danilova after Michel Fokine. Pianist: Gordon Boelzner. First presented by the New York City

Ballet at the New York State Theatre, Lincoln Center, with Kay Mazzo,
Peter Martins, Karin von Aroldingen, and Susan Hendl in the principal roles.

The title *Chopiniana* derives from a suite of four piano pieces by Chopin, orchestrated by Alexander Glazunov (*Opus 46*, 1894). Fokine, planning these
for a charity performance ballet, asked the composer to add the *C Sharp
Minor Waltz* (for Anna Pavlova and Mikhail Oboukoff, Nijinsky's teacher).
This first *Chopiniana* was danced March 21, 1908, comprising five scenes: a
Polonaise in Polish court dress; an evocation of Chopin and his Muse who
repels nightmares of dead monks in his Mayorquin monastery; a Mazurka for a
peasant wedding; the Waltz; and, as finale, a Tarantella based on Fokine's
memory of a Capri festival.

A second (this current) *Chopiniana* introduced April 16, 1908, used
different piano pieces orchestrated by Maurice Keller, retaining Glazunov's
Waltz but eliminating all character dancing and mime for a visualized abstraction. Set in three days, Fokine described: "Some of the *corps de ballet* groups
accompanying the dancing of the soloists were staged by me, just before curtain time." Diaghilev produced it in his initial Paris ballet season, June 2,
1909, under his own title as *Les Sylphides*, with Pavlova, Karsavina, and
Nijinsky, in a long blond wig which the designer Alexandre Benois said
"seemed a trifle comic when I saw it on stage . . . his slightly caricatured appearance made the artist look like a figure from some old beaded reticule or
painted lampshade." Some critics frowned on piano music in arrangements
made then (and later) by Keller, Liadov, Rieti, Malcolm Sargent, Sokolov,
Stravinsky, Taneef, Tcherepnine, etc. Scenery was by Benois; later by A.
Socrate, Leon Zak, etc. In 1932, for René Blum's Ballets du Théâtre de Monte
Carlo under Balanchine's artistic direction, a Corot landscape was used. Fokine
restaged his work for the Royal Danes in 1925 as *Chopiniana*, by which it was
familiar in Russia before and since. In 1936, for Les Ballet Russes de Monte
Carlo, he altered music and steps for the male solo. Other changes have crept
in over sixty years, some due to individual dancers of which Fokine complained; others to the memories of rehearsalists after his death in 1942.

Costumes and scenery suggested the "romantic" (classic) lyricism of the
1830s. However much long skirts evoked Taglioni, Fokine's choreography
surpassed any *tableaux vivants* inspired by static popular lithographs of the
period. This was the first ballet as a whole (with precedents from Ivanov and
Gorsky) in which movement itself projected from important music was a prime
factor rather than a propulsive accompaniment. Fokine's fluent pattern held no
pretext for virtuosity or pageantry. Layers of sentiment or sentimentality have
tended to dull the force, logic, and ingenuity of this academic masterpiece. The
original was planned for large opera house stages; later, scenic frames shrunk
spatial possibilities due to the need for touring smaller theaters, while musical
tempi increasingly decelerated. The present recension is not offered as a pious

museum restoration but as a testimony of approximate efficiency in a context of its contemporary choreographic vitality.

Reviewing *Chopiniana* in *Dance News*, the critic Nancy Goldner wrote: "The decision to strip *Les Sylphides* of its scenery, costumes, orchestration, and by implication its sense of period, even genre—as the City Ballet has done with *Chopiniana*—will strike some as cantankerous and perverse; to others, like myself, a stroke of genius. While watching American Ballet Theatre's production during the last few seasons, I have been continually discovering that there is sturdy, tightly constructed, and subtle but unmistakable climax-building choreography underneath all the aspects that bring historicity to the ballet but have little to do with choreographic fact. One went to see *Les Sylphides* for great performances.

"Now we can more clearly see *Chopiniana* for great choreography as well. On the most obvious level, we can see what choreography is in the legs, since the girls wear short white tunics. It is easier to see that Fokine has been brilliantly economical. Alexandra Danilova's staging has also brought out the choreography's precision and deliberateness. The ensemble looks more vivid, more important. The placement of dancers now looks more linear, lending to the pretty formations a welcome touch of austerity. With this production, one also becomes more aware of lovely repetitions and the fact that *Chopiniana* is, in one aspect, a study on entrances and exits. The ballet is as beautiful as ever, but it is not of a genre. The City Ballet production, in other words, does not preclude style, just stylization. In its de-interpretation, it restores and preserves. This is useful."

NOTES *Ballet Review* (Vol. 4, No. 5) published in 1973 an interview with the ballerina and teacher Alexandra Danilova that is of special interest in view of her part in the staging of the New York City Ballet revival of *Chopiniana:*

BALLET REVIEW "How did you think the New York City Ballet's *Chopiniana* turned out?

ALEXANDRA DANILOVA "Well, I think the first performance was beautiful, and I think the angle that we took is very interesting, and it was very clever of Mr. B. to suggest all these things, because *Chopiniana* is usually done with long skirts, blue flowers—

BR "But this was really radical.

AD "But it is not, if you think that from the beginning it was done with the piano. Chopin never orchestrated. And in Paris people said it was illogical to orchestrate Chopin when he wrote strictly for piano.

BR "Was it the Glazunov orchestration?

AD "Yes, it was Glazunov, then it was Stravinsky, then it was Dorati. So Mr. Balanchine wanted to go right back as like it was done, and now we have the ballet done with the piano, so this time they say why is it not with orchestra?

BR "The principal criticism has been that the ballet was done for a particular reason with the costumes that it had, that when Fokine made the ballet the whole mood and the whole aura of the piece had a lot to do with the production and that these elements were very important to it.

AD "I think a little bit different. I don't know what they wore originally because it was done for annual school performance, and they probably, like we have, just had that white wardrobe tutu past the knee. But then when Diaghilev bought *Sylphides* from Fokine he asked I think Benois to do the costumes, and Benois did the costumes which we wear for forty or fifty years, let's say. And then the time come when the costumes are not necessary, like the scenery is not necessary. So it is a good angle to put just in tunic to see all the beauty of the movement.

BR "I, personally, thought it was very beautiful.

AD "But it is always—you can't please everybody. Don't forget that all our geniuses go twenty-five years ahead of the audience. The beginning, people spit when Stravinsky *Petrouchka* and *Firebird* was played. And now it's the classic. It took twenty-five years for public to catch up, and they love *Petrouchka*. They have such a habit of having *Sylphides* done the way Diaghilev did, but why not to show another angle? I know some people wrote me a letter that they just can't go and see old *Sylphides;* they think it's too heavy.

BR "I thought it was both interesting and beautiful, but many people thought a part of what the ballet meant to them was gone.

AD "Well it's too bad if they take so personally, but a lot of times you come to the rehearsal and admire the ballet before it's done with the costumes, and sometimes costumes ruin the ballet. But this was absolutely pure like crystal. There was pure art of Chopin and pure choreography of Fokine."

SYLVIA

Ballet in three acts and four scenes. Music by Léo Delibes. Choreography by Louis Mérante. Book by Jules Barbier and the Baron de Reinach. Scenery by Chéret, Rubé, and Chaperon. Costumes by Lacoste. First presented at the Théâtre de l'Opéra, Paris, June 14, 1876, with Rita Sangalli as Sylvia and Louis Mérante as Amyntas. Revived at the Paris Opéra, by Léo Staats, December 19, 1919, with Carlotta Zambelli; by Serge Lifar, February 12, 1941, with Lycette Darsonval; by Albert Aveline, 1946. First presented in Russia at the Maryinsky Theatre, St. Petersburg, December 15, 1901, with Olga Preobrajenska in the title role. First presented in England in a one-act version, produced by C. Wilhelm, at the Empire Theatre, London, May 18, 1911, with Lydia Kyasht as Sylvia.

Until recently, *Sylvia,* or *The Nymph of Diana,* was more familiar to the English-speaking world for its music than for its dancing. Its original choreography survives only at the Paris Opéra, where the production has long been one

of the glories of France. To the rest of the world, selections from the ballet's
score, selections such as the often-played *Valse Lente* and *Pizzicato Polka*,
have been the principal reminders of the ballet's existence. These selections, as
a matter of fact, are so familiar to us that we sometimes forget that they are
part of a score for a three-act ballet and that this particular score was extraordinary for its time, as it remains for ours. The American critic Carl Van Vechten reminded us some years ago that before Delibes composed his ballets,
"music for dancing, for the most part, consisted of tinkle-tinkle melodies
with marked rhythm." Before *Sylvia* and *Coppélia*, Delibes' first great ballets,
ballet music was universally subservient to the dancer: it had no drama to it
and merely accompanied the steps of a dance with embellishing sound.
Delibes changed all that, fusing drama with lyric melody, to become the father
of modern ballet music, the inspiration of Tchaikovsky in his own ballet scores,
and the precursor of Igor Stravinsky.

The story of Delibes' ballet *Sylvia* is a return to mythology. Sylvia, nymph
of Diana, chaste goddess of the hunt, is loved by a mortal, Amyntas, the shepherd. The gods contrive against the romance until, with godlike privilege, they
change their minds and the nymph and the mortal are united forever.

ACT ONE: A SACRED GROVE   The orchestra plays an Olympian prelude before
the curtain rises. In this regal-sounding music—with its majestic trumpet calls
suggestive of a royal hunt and its alternate light, open, joyous melody—we
have a brief musical picture of the ballet's story.

The curtain rises on a grove sacred to the goddess Diana. Dominating the
scene is a statue of Eros, the child god of love, armed with his bow and
arrows. It is night. Magical creatures of the wood, fauns and dryads, cavort
about by the light of the moon. The fauns flirt playfully with the dryads and
finally succeed in ensnaring the creatures with garlands of flowers. But the sylvan lovers soon pause in their flirtations. A stranger is approaching! They conceal themselves to watch in secret.

Amyntas, the shepherd, enters the grove. He thought he had heard singing
and dancing and looks about suspiciously. He sees nothing and cannot understand. Some nights ago he looked into this place and saw dancing a lovely
nymph, the most beautiful girl he had ever beheld. Perhaps he was dreaming,
but no—there is a soft horn call and soft, rustling, tripping music, as if a mysterious, unfelt wind had disturbed all the leaves of the forest.

Amyntas hides and observes the scene as his beautiful nymph, Sylvia, comes
into the wood with her followers. They dance in honor of the chase, the pursuit of their patron goddess. Their innocent joy in the hunt seems to be
curiously out of place as they dance before the statue of Eros, who would
surely think them unnatural creatures to be so satisfied. Soon the girls tire and
rest.

Now it happens they are observed by another. Orion, giant hunter of the
forest, loves Sylvia in secret and wishes to abduct her. He is disturbed when

some of the nymphs find the shepherd's crook and cloak lying on the ground and is immediately jealous. Sylvia orders her nymphs to seek out the intruder in the sacred grove, and Amyntas is brought before her. Enraged that a man has cast his eyes upon her and intent above all on preserving her purity, Sylvia determines that he must die. She draws her bow, though the young man is obviously in love with her. The love that he feels, Sylvia decides, he himself is not responsible for: it is some mischief of Eros. She therefore aims her bow at the statue.

Amyntas, shocked at this offense to the god who has inspired his love for her, runs across the wood and stands before the statue of Eros to protect it. But Sylvia has drawn her bow: her arrow sinks into the shepherd's breast, and he falls to the ground. Now the statue comes to life and Eros retaliates by aiming his arrow at Sylvia's heart. The girl collapses, clutching at her heart. Her nymphs gather about her, fearing that she is dead, but Sylvia holds out the arrow of Eros and says that she has not been hurt, it is nothing. She departs from the forest as day begins to dawn.

Villagers enter the forest and pay tribute to Eros. They do not notice the body of Amyntas. As soon as they depart, Orion enters in search of Sylvia. When he discovers the dead shepherd, he rejoices that he now has no rival and makes a new plan: he will capture Sylvia with a golden chain. Orion is observed by a straggling peasant, who remains on the scene in hiding to see what will happen.

Sylvia returns to the forest. Orion hides. The girl, remorseful at the death of the shepherd, hovers over his body. We wonder at her change of heart and then recall that she brushed off Eros' arrow too lightly. Orion takes advantage of her lack of vigilance, throws the chain of gold about her, lifts the struggling nymph into his arms, and runs toward the inner darkness of the forest.

A peasant who has seen all this is unable to help Sylvia. He runs to tell the other peasants that Amyntas is dead. His friends try to revive Amyntas, but the shepherd does not stir. An old magician comes forward and presses a rose to the shepherd's lips, and he returns to life. When he discovers, however, that Sylvia has disappeared, he wishes himself dead again. The sorcerer comforts him and tells him that perhaps Sylvia loves him; perhaps the arrow of Eros really touched her heart. Amyntas is then told of Sylvia's capture by the hunter Orion. He instantly prepares to save her; before departing, he bows to the statue of Eros. The statue again comes to life: Eros points the way to Orion's hiding place, and Amyntas sets out to rescue his beloved.

ACT TWO: THE CAVE OF ORION   Orion watches as his captive wakens. As soon as she opens her eyes and sees her abductor, Sylvia attempts to escape from him. But the weapons of the hunt have been taken from her, and she has no defense. She is impervious to his declarations of love, and the repulsed Orion grows angry. Sylvia placates him with wine, which the hunter has never tasted before. His servants willingly prepare it at their master's suggestion.

At first the wine merely increases Orion's passion, and the nymph dances before him to encourage him to drink more. He does so, but—tiring of the dance—seizes Sylvia in his arms. She easily eludes him, and the intoxicated giant falls to the ground.

Still she cannot escape. Orion has blocked the entrance to the cave with a huge boulder. The girl prays to Eros. The god appears to her, takes her by the hand, and leads her into the forest. There he turns around and, with an impatient godlike gesture, causes Orion, his grotto, and his servants to vanish into the earth.

The sound of a hunting horn causes her to rush to the nymphs she has abandoned, but Eros reminds her of Amyntas, who more than anyone grieves over her disappearance.

ACT THREE, SCENE ONE: A WOODED LANDSCAPE ON THE SEACOAST   Amyntas is still unaware of Sylvia's rescue; he enters lonely and dejected soon after the curtain rises on a celebration in honor of the god Bacchus. The sea stretches into the distance behind the trees; at the left is the sacred temple of Diana. Bacchantes dance and present grapes to the god of wine.

A ship is seen approaching the shore. A pirate captains this ship and as it reaches shore, he interrupts the festival and attempts to interest the natives in the purchase of slave girls. In reality, this pirate is Eros, who wishes to return Sylvia to Amyntas. Eros urges the veiled slave girls to surround the shepherd, but the moody Amyntas takes interest in only one of the girls, who seems to him strangely familiar. The girl dances before the youth to a pizzicato melody. He is completely delighted with her and when she removes her veil, he is overcome with happiness. He clasps Sylvia in his arms.

Orion bursts in on the scene. Eros has not been able to suppress the hunter, and Sylvia, knowing the giant's power, rushes into the temple of her patron goddess. Amyntas prepares to engage Orion in combat, but Orion runs past him to force the doors of the temple.

ACT THREE, SCENE TWO: THE TEMPLE OF DIANA   A distant roar that grows louder and louder reminds us of the anger of the gods. Lightning flashes. Within her temple, Diana, her bow drawn tight, stands over Sylvia, who kneels before her protectress. Orion dashes toward Sylvia. Diana releases her bow, and the evil hunter is pierced through the heart.

The angry goddess, who divines the real reason for Sylvia's fears, asks her how it has happened that she is in love. Sylvia confesses that Eros wounded her with one of his darts. Upon this declaration, Eros removes his disguise. Diana threatens him, but the god of love reminds her that once upon a time even she was grateful for his gift of love: the one time Diana was moved by his power and kissed the sleeping Endymion by the light of the moon.

The embarrassed goddess, confronted by her one fault, forgives Sylvia for breaking her vow never to love. She rises to her high seat in her temple with

Eros. All her handmaidens bow low to the god and goddess, and the village peasants stand amazed as Amyntas and Sylvia—having received the blessing of Olympus—are transfigured by their love.

NOTES   Frederick Ashton revived *Sylvia* in London, September 3, 1952, with scenery and costumes by Robin and Christopher Ironside. Margot Fonteyn, Michael Somes, John Hart, and Alexander Grant danced the principal roles as they also did September 29, 1953, when the Sadler's Wells Ballet brought it to New York.

SYMPHONIC VARIATIONS

Classic ballet in one act. Music by César Franck. Choreography by Frederick Ashton. Scenery and costumes by Sophie Fedorovitch. First presented by the Sadler's Wells Ballet at the Royal Opera House, Covent Garden, London, April 24, 1946, with Margot Fenteyn and Michael Somes, Pamela May and Brian Shaw, and Moira Shearer and Henry Danton. First presented in the United States by the Sadler's Wells Ballet at the Metropolitan Opera House, New York, October 12, 1949, with the same cast but with John Hart replacing Henry Danton.

This classic dance ballet is arranged to Franck's *Symphonic Variations* for piano and orchestra. There is no story, only a mood created by the setting and costumes, the music, and the dancers' response to it.

When the curtain rises, six dancers are on stage. Three girls stand forward in a line parallel to the front of the stage. In the back, turned away from us, are three boys. The backdrop is of abstract design: curved and slanting black lines on a light green cloth.

The orchestra begins. The dancers do not move: they stand quietly in youthful meditation on the music. Directly the piano begins, the girls commence to dance. As if activated only by the instrument, they pause as the orchestra takes up the theme. A variation on the theme is stated, and one of the boys comes forward. He takes turns dancing with the three girls, then remains still as they dance about him. Now he holds the girls, one by one, as they whirl in his arms.

The girls rest as the two other boys join the leading male soloist in a line similar to that which was formed at the beginning by the three girls. The three dance—the two boys on the outside miming in motion the part of the orchestra, while the soloist, in the center, takes the part of the piano. The boys dance now to the girls, who respond to their statement of a theme. Two of the girls dance alone, then with one of the boys. They retire; another boy takes the center of the stage and dances a variation.

The principal ballerina now comes forward and, while the boys in the background dance quietly, she moves with sweet splendor to the music of the piano. The male soloist joins her, and they dance a *pas de deux*.

After this romantic sequence, all six dancers move together. Now they are not so much separate individuals responding to the music, as one group animated by the same theme. The boys and girls divide, come together in couples, and make swift, open patterns about the stage while the music rushes toward its conclusion. Their swift ebullience is broken at the end, as the dancers resume the meditative poses with which the ballet began.

NOTES Ashton has said of his ballet and the time it was composed, just after World War II, in *Frederick Ashton and His Ballets:* "My mother died in 1939, just before the war. So I was independent at last, although it didn't do me any good. Almost as soon as the war started I had to go into the R.A.F. Everyone was being called up—all the dancers and everyone I knew in the theatre—and I wanted, I suppose, to share their agony. I must say, I thought it was the end of everything. It was a period of enormous frustration to me because I felt I hadn't said nearly enough to be ready to die on it.

"The importance of the war was that it gave me a period to think and read a good deal and also, because I was rather unhappy, I went in for mysticism. I read St. Theresa of Avila and St. John of the Cross and lots of books about mystics and mysticism. After all, one was told that it was the end of the world.

"During the war, the tendency in all the ballets seemed to become much too literary and dramatic. During the last part of the war, I was stationed at the Air Ministry as an Intelligence officer and I saw everything that was going on, although at this stage I couldn't do any work myself. It was very frustrating, and originally I think that *Symphonic Variations* was very much over-choreographed. I remember doing a tremendous amount of eliminating, especially in the finale; I pared and pared and pared until I got the kind of purity I wanted. You see, when I started I was going to do something very complicated, with lots of people and a sort of seasonal theme. But then I thought one day that six dancers would be enough. When one begins to do things one is apt to overcharge everything, and if things get too intense, one blurs the vision of the audience. By simplifying, you make it easier for an audience to take in your intentions.

"With *Symphonic Variations* I had to do a lot of experimenting to find the sort of movement that I wanted. That was what took the time, but once I had achieved it the rest went fairly well. I was able to ride on the music quite a bit because I knew it very well and I'd listened to it during the war. I'd always hoped I would get round to using it one day."

Margot Fonteyn has also written of the time of the creation of this ballet: "When *Symphonic Variations* was almost finished, Michael Somes had to have an operation on the cartilage in his knee. The first night of *Symphonic* was postponed for something like two months while Michael had his operation and got back into training.

"When we started to rehearse it all again Fred took out a lot of things and simplified and purified the choreography. Instead of having his usual deadline for the dress rehearsal and the first performance, he had time to reassess the choreography. I think that's one reason why it turned out to be one of his masterpieces. I remember a lot of discussion and all sorts of different ideas and versions and several different endings, and Sophie Fedorovitch at the rehearsals and coming in each day to say what she thought. A lot went into revising *Symphonic*. It's probably the only ballet he's ever had the opportunity to revise before the first night."

The critic and dancer David Vaughan, writing in *Ballet Review*, has said of this ballet: "The postponed première of Ashton's *Symphonic Variations* was for him a kind of manifesto similar to *Apollo*—a clearing away of literary and scenic paraphernalia, just six dancers on an open stage, given an illusion of even greater spaciousness by Fedorovitch's airy decor. If Ashton had shown at various times in his earlier career the influence of Nijinski and Massine, to say nothing of Pavlova and Duncan, there were moments in *Symphonic Variations* that inevitably, maybe coincidentally, suggested Balanchine's masterpiece, especially in the passages of supported adagio involving three women and one man. But more important was the final distillation of Ashton's own classicism: it marked the beginning of his exploration of various motifs that became trademarks of his *pas de deux* at that time—the skimming lifts with *batterie* or *pas de bourrée* just off the floor, the scissor-like movements, the *arabesques élancées*. Notable also was the courage to be simple, to leave out anything extraneous to the piece's lyric utterance: there is never any sense of strain after the ingeniously original lift or step, indeed, some of the most eloquent passages are the transitions when the dancers join hands in a simple run.

"*Symphonic Variations* was, then, a kind of summation, and a consummation, of Ashton's career up to that point, made possible, no doubt, by the kind of fallow period he had been obliged to go through during his war service, however frustrating that must have been at the time. From there he could move on to the inevitable next step in the development of British ballet—or at any rate of the Wells, as it acquired official recognition as the national ballet in the form of the royal charter—the creation of full-length ballets that could stand alongside the classics of the repertory, *Giselle, Swan Lake, Sleeping Beauty*, and the rest."

David Vaughan's biography *Frederick Ashton and His Ballets* examines in detail the making of this ballet and its subsequent history in performance.

The British writer James Monahan, whose admiration for this ballet is well known, has again described it in his book *The Nature of Ballet* (London, 1976).

SYMPHONIE CONCERTANTE

Classic ballet in three movements. Music by Wolfgang Amadeus Mozart.
Choreography by George Balanchine. Scenery and costumes by James Stew-
art Morcom. Lighting by Jean Rosenthal. First presented by Ballet Society
at the City Center, New York, November 12, 1947, with Maria Tallchief,
Tanaquil LeClercq, and Todd Bolender in the principal roles.

Set to Mozart's *Sinfonia Concertante in E flat major for Violin and Viola* (K.
364), this ballet follows closely the design of the music. It has no story. Its
gold backdrop represents the formal classical frame into which both music and
dancing fit. The three parts correspond to the three movements of the score.
There are two ballerinas, corresponding to the solo instruments, a *danseur,* a
group of six secondary soloists, and a *corps de ballet* of sixteen dancers.

FIRST MOVEMENT: ALLEGRO MAESTOSO   The curtain rises and the stage is
empty. The music begins, allegro maestoso. After the opening chords, eight
dancers emerge from either side of the stage, dancing to the light, quick
rhythm of the music. They arrange themselves in a pattern that encloses the
front part of the stage. The six soloists enter and dance in a close line. Now
they move to the back and dance forward in rapid, crossing diagonals.

The introductory passage is over. Quietly the solo instruments are heard. All
the dancers move to the sides of the stage, and slowly the ballerinas enter at
the back. They meet in the center of the stage and dance together. Then, as
the violin alone is heard against the orchestra, one of the ballerinas dances
briefly alone. The other ballerina succeeds her as the viola returns with the
same melody. The two dancers follow the turns of the solo instruments
throughout the ballet, dancing together and alternately. They do not represent
the instruments in any literal sense; their dances are simply accompanied by
the instruments. The ballerinas leave the stage when the violin and viola are
silent, returning when the instruments are heard again. Three girls enter with
each of the ballerinas in turn and support them in brief, extended poses, after
which the two dance together.

The opening section of the first movement is now repeated. The *corps de*
ballet kneels, and the two ballerinas enter as they did at the beginning. The violin, which took priority over the viola, now takes a secondary position. The
ballerinas dance closely together, almost touching, as the two instruments in-
tertwine the melody. One of the ballerinas supports the other as the violin
plays in the background against the dominant viola. Then both pirouette off
while the *corps de ballet* accompanies the final orchestral bars. All kneel on
the last chord.

SECOND MOVEMENT: ANDANTE   The six soloists remain on stage as the *corps* exits. The second movement begins, and the girls dance forward slowly. They separate and retire as the two ballerinas enter with the *danseur,* who supports each of the girls in turn to the music. When the principal theme of the movement is stated by the orchestra, the six soloists cross the stage with measured pace. The *danseur* leads the ballerinas to the back, the soloists dance, then the ballerinas move forward again to dance to the intricate alternation of violin and viola. The movement ends as softly as it began. As the three principals exit, the six soloists enclose them in a moving semicircle.

THIRD MOVEMENT: PRESTO   To the high-spirited, joyous finale, the two ballerinas and their partner take turns in dancing alone and in the brief duets and trios. The *corps de ballet* forms a moving background to their movements. Each of the principals circles the stage brilliantly. The dancing becomes brisk with the clipped, delightful cheerfulness of the music. The girls flick their wrists elegantly as the movement draws to its conclusion, then dance together with the principals, who kneel before the group as the ballet ends.

NOTES   This ballet is a good example of how dancing might aid appreciation of the music. Mozart's *Sinfonia Concertante* is long and difficult; to the inexperienced listener it might be boring; perhaps only the musician likes it immediately. The ballet, on the other hand, fills the time measured by the music with movement and seems to shorten the length of the music. What seemed dull at a first *hearing,* is not so dull when the ballet is first *seen.*

It is interesting that although Mozart wrote no music for ballet, of all composers his music is most adaptable for ballet, of all composers his music is the most danceable. Children who hear Mozart's music without knowing what it is, instinctively wish to dance to it. They appreciate its true quality better than their elders, who are often too impressed by Mozart's greatness to listen to his work with unaffected ears.

SYMPHONIE POUR UN HOMME SEUL (Symphony for a Man Alone)

Score by Pierre Schaeffer and Pierre Henry. Choreography by Maurice Béjart. First presented by the Ballets de l'Étoile in 1955 with Michèle Seigneuret and Maurice Béjart in the principal roles. First presented in the United States by the Ballet of the Twentieth Century at the City Center, New York, November 30, 1971, with Suzanne Farrell and Jorge Donn in principal roles.

One of the ballets that established the international fame of European choreographer Maurice Béjart and his subsequent ballet company, the Ballet of the

Twentieth Century, *Symphony for a Man Alone* was the first dance work to use an electronic score, a popular complement to dance from that time forward. The signature of the ballet has been given by the choreographer himself. Béjart writes:

"How reply to the clamor of the crowd? . . . with violins? With oboes? And what orchestra can boast of rendering that other cry which man in his solitude is powerless to utter? Let us leave the sound of the violoncello, too easy for present-day man, his daily epic and collective anguish. Footsteps, voices and familiar sounds will suffice. Footsteps press upon him, voices go through him, who make love and war, the whistle of bombs or the tune of song . . . May the modern dancer, without costume or decor, be without drum or trumpet. To the rhythm of his own heart, if he is sincere, dance will be the more true."

The choreographer's response to the demands of his audience produces in this case the situation of a man, alone, entrapped, as in a prison, among strands of rope hanging from above. The man is haunted throughout the ballet by a girl, an illusive figure with whom he cannot establish any kind of permanent relationship. He tries, but the girl always at the crucial moment vanishes or escapes his grasp. At the end, he seems to despair. Man, alone, no matter what the quality of the music to accompany his solitude, seeks another.

SYMPHONY IN C

Classic ballet in four movements. Music by Georges Bizet. Choreography by George Balanchine. First presented under the title Le Palais de Cristal by the Paris Opéra Ballet at the Opéra, July 28, 1947, with Lycette Darsonval, Tamara Toumanova, Micheline Bardin, Madeleine Lafon, Alexandre Kaliujny, Roger Ritz, Michel Renault, and Max Bozzoni as principals. Scenery and costumes by Léonor Fini. First presented in the United States by Ballet Society at the City Center, New York, March 22, 1948, with Maria Tallchief, Tanaquil LeClercq, Beatrice Tompkins, Elise Reiman, Nicholas Magallanes, Francisco Moncion, Herbert Bliss, and Lew Christensen in the principal roles.

Symphony in C is not based on a story, but on the music to which it is danced. Bizet's symphony is in four movements; each of these movements develops different themes, different melodies. Correspondingly, in the ballet, there is a different dance scheme and development for each of these four movements. Each movement has its own characteristic ballerina, *premier danseur*, and *corps de ballet*. Toward the end of the ballet, when the different groups have danced their special parts of the symphony, all the groups combine with their ballerinas for a kind of dance summing up of all that has gone before. There is no scenery, only a blue background; the dancers are dressed in classical ballet costumes.

FIRST MOVEMENT: ALLEGRO VIVO   The curtain rises before the music begins.
Two small groups of girls begin to dance with the opening chord. As the orchestra plays the first theme and repeats it, the two groups dance in opposition, first dancing all together, then alternately following the movements of
two leaders.

The ballerina appears as the second theme is announced by the oboe and
strings. She dances forward in crisp, open movements to the rhythm of the
melody, turning gracefully as she poses and balancing for a moment as she
waits for the theme to begin anew. Her dance now becomes brisk and
flourishing. She pirouettes swiftly as the two soloists join her, balances again
briefly, and leaves the stage.

After the orchestra has given an intimation of the first theme and horns have
played a short transition, two boys enter to support the soloists. The ballerina
returns with her partner. She dances around the stage, retires to the rear, and,
as the first theme of the movement returns, leads the ensemble. On the last
clipped chord she stands supported in a quick, graceful pose.

SECOND MOVEMENT: ADAGIO   The *corps de ballet* moves slowly to the introductory passage. A second ballerina enters with her partner as the soft central
theme of the movement is sounded by the oboe. She is lifted low off the floor
and moves as if in slow motion, then is lifted high, her legs describing sweeping arcs in the air. Her partner supports her in long, slow lifts and held poses
while the *corps de ballet* gathers about her. As the movement ends, the
ballerina falls back in her partner's arms.

THIRD MOVEMENT: ALLEGRO VIVACE   Here the music is spirited and lively.
Six girls, in a third *corps de ballet,* dance forward; two couples join them to
leap across the stage; and, finally, a third ballerina and her partner enter to
circle the stage in broad leaps. They dance together briefly, turning rapidly in
the air together, and rush off into the wings. Soon they return, repeat their
dance, and lead the *corps de ballet* to the bright, ebullient music. At one point
the boy lifts the ballerina off the floor and drops her, pushing her forward, so
that she seems to bounce to the music. The entire group joins in the final
measures, the *corps de ballet* kneeling as the ballerina is held in a graceful
pose at the last chord.

FOURTH MOVEMENT: ALLEGRO VIVACE   In the final movement, the principals
of the first three movements join with a fourth ballerina and her partner in an
exhilarating display of virtuosity that becomes at times a contest. The fourth
ballerina and her accompanying group dance first. They are followed by the
ballerina of the first movement and her *corps de ballet*. The ballerina of the
Adagio movement appears next, then the ballerina of the third movement.

The thirty-two girls who have made up the four *corps de ballet* now line the
stage at the sides and across the back. All four ballerinas dance in their midst,

each executing the same brilliant steps. Their partners enter for their turn, while secondary soloists dance behind them. At the close, all forty-eight dancers—soloists and *corps de ballet*—join the principals in a brilliant finale. As the last chord of the music sounds, the ballerinas turn quickly and fall back over their partners' arms as the secondary soloists are lifted high behind them in a climactic tableau.

NOTES *Symphony in C* was originally mounted for the Paris Opéra during my visit there as guest choreographer in 1947. For the Opéra, I staged revivals of three ballets: *Apollo, Le Baiser de la Fée,* and *Serenade,* and although the two latter ballets had never been seen in Paris before, at the end of my engagement I wished to stage a new work especially for the principal dancers of the Opéra.

It seemed fitting to select for this new work music by a French composer. I accordingly chose the little-known *Symphony in C Major* written by the French master Bizet when he was only seventeen years old. Composition of the ballet was completed in about two weeks.

The ballet was staged for Ballet Society in New York the following spring. When this company became the New York City Ballet seven months later, *Symphony in C* was the concluding ballet on the first program. The ballet has been a part of the permanent repertory of the New York City Ballet ever since.

In 1973, the New York City Ballet made a series of films for television in Berlin. Writing about the film of *Symphony in C* the critic Robert Greskovic said in *The Soho Weekly News:* "Though this and the 15-or-so other films of Balanchine's ballets were made for TV, this projected print made a dazzling image. Unlike the Tharp tape, the filming here plays no camera tricks. With the exception of some close-ups for the *adagio pas de deux* of the second movement, the camera maintains its eye as a transfixed spectator from an imaginary vantage point about the twentieth row center of a visionary theater. The familiar white tutus of the female dancers and (alas, equally familiar) black sequined leotards, tights and white sweat socks of the male dancers are neutrally and delicately set off by a consistently cool, pale olive background. The cast is Karin von Aroldingen, Jean-Pierre Bonnefous—first movement; Allegra Kent, Conrad Ludlow—second movement; Sara Leland, John Clifford—third movement; and Marnee Morris, Victor Castelli—fourth movement. The full-stage picture is always clear and yields the full force of this work by the company at its very best. With the brisk flow that Robert Irving's magic-wand baton makes of this symphony, Bizet via Balanchine strikes a focus/blend of perfection throughout. The careful camera make-up gives everyone in the cast a theatrical patina that glows and radiates a screen persona to the performance. (Especially glamorous here is von Aroldingen . . .) The angle of vision hovers slightly above the floor space, defining a steady rake to the dancing plane that opens at you like the palm of a hand extended in formal presentation. The depth of field grows physical as the choreographic/symphonic lines occupy more and more space with diagonal and flanking formations. The paths that the solo dances describe become lines of force that draw their length in after-images of energy. As the fourth movement shifts into the repeats of the finale, the space further deepens as it fills with the *corps de ballet* and soloists from the preceding three movements. That horse-shoe formation of ballerinas has never looked so precise and pure as legs and arms rapidly angle and arc in unison and frame the principals' and soloists' coda sections like a rainbow of warm white light."

SYMPHONY IN E FLAT

> *Music by Igor Stravinsky. Choreography by John Clifford. First presented at the New York City Ballet's Stravinsky Festival, June 20, 1972, at the New York State Theatre, Lincoln Center, with Gelsey Kirkland, Peter Martins, and ensemble.*

Stravinsky's first symphony, dedicated to "my dear teacher N. A. Rimsky-Korsakov," was first performed in 1907. The young dancer and choreographer John Clifford, who had done his first ballet to Stravinsky's *Symphony in C* for us, and other fine ballets since, was a natural to undertake the choreography for this work's presentation at the New York City Ballet's Stravinsky Festival. There are four movements—*Allegro moderato, Scherzo allegretto, Largo,* and *Finale, Allegro molto.* The dancing is the choreographer's story of the music; what he sees happening in it.

Reviewing the ballet the next day in the *Daily News,* Sam Norkin wrote of *Symphony in E Flat:* "Intricate maneuvers and groupings are complemented by the expert pas de deux and solo sections for Gelsey Kirkland and Peter Martins. Tiny Gelsey is a fine lyric dancer who can turn into a pocket dynamo or fly away without warning. She is an exciting thing to observe."

SYMPHONY IN THREE MOVEMENTS

> *Music by Igor Stravinsky. Choreography by George Balanchine. First presented by the New York City Ballet at the Stravinsky Festival, 1972, at the New York State Theatre, Lincoln Center, June 18, 1972, with Helgi Tomasson, Sara Leland, and Edward Villella in principal roles. Lighting by Ronald Bates. Conducted by Robert Craft.*

I remember Stravinsky's talking to me about this music during World War II, when I visited him in Hollywood. It is a magnificent, major work, and I had wanted for many years to make a ballet to the music. The appropriate opportunity came in 1972, when we were preparing the Stravinsky Festival at the New York City Ballet.

The score is a short one for a symphony—about twenty-one minutes—and is in three movements. Stravinsky has written that "the formal substance of the symphony exploits contrasts of several kinds, one of them being the contrast between the principal instrumental protagonists, harp and piano. Each instrument has a large obbligato role in a movement to itself, and only at the turning-point fugue . . . do the two play together and unaccompanied."

"Composers combine notes," Stravinsky said. Choreographers combine movements and the ones I arranged for this music follow no story line or narrative. They try to catch the music and do not, I hope, lean on it, using it instead for support and time frame. If I were to try to relate that a boy and sixteen girls begin the ballet, that would not be very interesting, or that a girl in purple dances with eight others to music for clarinet, piano, and strings soon follows. What is really interesting is the complexity and variety of the music, from the propulsive drive and thrust of the vigorous opening (which also closes the ballet) to the developed use, almost like a concerto, of the piano in the first movement, the harp in the second and the two together in the finale.

The central movement, Andante, is a *pas de deux*. One writer has called this a "strangely quiet, sensuous, meditative interlude with a pronounced Eastern tinge." I had not thought of that but paraphrasing Stravinsky, how and in what form the things of this world are impressed upon my dance is not for me to say.

After the ballet was in our repertory, I heard that the first movement of the symphony was actually composed as a possible accompaniment for a film about China and that the second movement was also composed (but not used) for a film project—the apparition-of-the-Virgin scene for the film of Werfel's *Song of Bernadette*.

TALES OF HOFFMANN

Ballet in prologue, three acts, and an epilogue. Music by Jacques Offenbach, arranged and orchestrated by John Lanchbery. Choreography by Peter Darrell. Design by Alistair Livingstone. Lighting by John B. Read. Scenario by Peter Darrell from stories by E. T. A. Hoffmann. First presented by Scottish Theatre Ballet at the Kings Theatre, Edinburgh, Scotland, April 6, 1972, with Peter Cazalet as Hoffmann. First presented in the United States by American Ballet Theatre at the New York State Theatre, Lincoln Center, New York, July 12, 1973, with sets and costumes by Peter Docherty and with Cynthia Gregory and Jonas Kage in the principal roles.

Those who are familiar with Offenbach's opera of this title, or with the popular

film, will know all about E. T. A. Hoffmann, the German teller of tales whose
stories have already made ballet history in *Coppélia* and *The Nutcracker*.

PROLOGUE: A TAVERN OUTSIDE AN OPERA HOUSE   Hoffmann is drinking with
friends while awaiting the arrival of La Stella, his latest love, who is appearing
at the opera. He is asked to explain the meaning of three souvenirs on his table
but at first refuses. La Stella arrives and gives her maid a note for Hoffmann
which, unseen by him, is intercepted by Counsellor Lindorf. Hoffmann, now a
little drunk, agrees to tell the stories behind the three souvenirs and the tales
proper begin:

ACT ONE (THE FIRST TALE): THE CONSERVATORY IN SPALANZANI'S HOUSE
Spalanzani, an inventor, has invited some friends to see his latest invention,
the lifelike mechanical doll, Olympia. Hoffmann as a very young man observes Olympia from afar and tries to meet her. Spalanzani announces that
Olympia will dance for his guests, but first insists that Hoffmann put on a pair
of magic spectacles. Hoffmann immediately falls in love with Olympia and
asks her to marry him. Spalanzani, delighted with the success of his deception,
agrees at once. Hoffmann, whirling Olympia about in a dance, loses the magic
pair of glasses. The doll thereupon falls apart and poor Hoffmann realizes he
has been tricked.

ACT TWO (THE SECOND TALE): THE MUSIC ROOM OF ANTONIA'S HOME   Ten
years have passed. Hoffmann, in love with Antonia, is taking music lessons
from her father. Behind her father's back, Antonia flirts with Hoffmann while
dancing to his playing. When they are discovered, the father warns Antonia
that too much exertion will be fatal to her. Doctor Miracle suddenly appears.
He promises to cure Antonia and hypnotizes her into believing that she is a
great ballerina. Hoffmann returns and Antonia, enthralled by her vision, im-
plores him to play so that she may dance again. Urged on by Doctor Miracle,
Hoffmann reluctantly does so until, overcome, Antonia dies in his arms.

ACT THREE (THE THIRD TALE): DAPERTUTTO'S SALON   Now an older and
more serious man, Hoffmann has turned to religion for comfort from his earlier
disappointments. He finds himself in the salon of Dapertutto, who tries to lure
him again to the enjoyment of sensual pleasures but without success until the
arrival of Giulietta, a lovely courtesan. Encouraged by Dapertutto, Giulietta so
seduces Hoffmann that he even renounces his faith. Then he realizes, when his
reflection disappears in a mirror, that he has lost his immortal soul. In his anguish he prays that he may be forgiven and, as his reflection reappears,
Giulietta and Dapertutto are drawn into the mirror and vanish.

EPILOGUE: THE TAVERN   Hoffmann, his stories told, is offered more drink by
the sinister Counsellor Lindorf. La Stella emerges from the opera house look-

ing for Hoffmann and finds him in a drunken sleep, her note crushed on the ground. Sad and disappointed, she is led away by Lindorf. Hoffmann, roused from his stupor, realizes that yet again he has been duped by the evil presence that has pursued him throughout his life.

THE TAMING OF THE SHREW

Ballet in two acts after Shakespeare. Music by Kurt-Heinz Stolze after Domenico Scarlatti. Choreography and production by John Cranko. Scenery and costumes by Elizabeth Dalton. Lighting by Gilbert V. Hemsley, Jr. First presented by the Stuttgart Ballet at the Wurttembergische Staatstheater, Stuttgart, Germany, March 16, 1969, with Marcia Haydée and Richard Cragun in the principal roles. First presented in the United States by the same ensemble at the Metropolitan Opera House, New York, June 12, 1969.

The Taming of the Shrew turns out to be just as amusing to see in dance form as it is in the spoken theater. The action of the ballet follows closely that of the play:

ACT ONE, SCENE ONE: OUTSIDE THE HOUSE OF BAPTISTA, A WEALTHY NOBLEMAN Hortensio, a fop, Lucentio, a student, and Gremio, an elderly roué, serenade the beautiful Bianca, one of the nobleman's daughters. Their love songs are rudely interrupted by her sister, Katherine, who thinks herself just as beautiful. In addition, Baptista explains to the suitors that Kate, as the elder of the two, must be married first. Neighbors, awakened by the serenade and the rumpus, chase the thwarted lovers away.

ACT ONE, SCENE TWO: A TAVERN Here Petruchio, a gentleman of more generosity than means, is robbed of his last penny by two ladies of the streets. The suitors suggest that he, therefore, might be interested in the charms and fortune of Katherine. He readily agrees.

ACT ONE, SCENE THREE: INSIDE BAPTISTA'S HOUSE Bianca muses over her preferences among her three suitors. She is interrupted by a jealous outburst from Kate, a rowdy tomboy of a girl, who calls her a scheming flirt. This dispute is further interrupted by the arrival of Petruchio, who is accompanied by Bianca's suitors in disguise. Petruchio is none too favorably received by Kate. Alone with Bianca, the suitors throw off their disguises and continue their wooing in the form of singing, dancing, and music lessons. Bianca soon recognizes Lucentio as the most desirable.

Kate reacts violently against Petruchio's protestations of passion, thinking that they are a false mockery, but something in his manner convinces her, nevertheless, to accept his offer and they agree to get married.

ACT ONE, SCENE FOUR: A STREET   Here neighbors on their way to Kate's wedding treat the whole matter as a huge joke. The three suitors, now in high hopes that Bianca will soon be released to marry one of them, join them.

ACT ONE, SCENE FIVE: INSIDE BAPTISTA'S HOUSE   The guests have arrived. Kate in her bridal array is all expectant and waiting, but the bridegroom appears to have forgotten the day. When he does appear, in fantastic garb, Petruchio behaves very badly, ill-treating the priest and carrying off Kate before the wedding festivities have started.

ACT TWO, SCENE ONE: PETRUCHIO'S HOUSE   Kate is a fiery-tempered girl and Act Two shows what Petruchio aims to do about it. In the first scene he finds fault with the food and the girl has to go without her supper.

ACT TWO, SCENE TWO: A CARNIVAL   Meanwhile, in a scene at the carnival, two of Bianca's suitors, Gremio and Hortensio, encounter a masked and cloaked stranger. Both of them believing her to be Bianca are only too eager to take their marriage vows. Too late they discover that they have been duped and married to ladies of the street, who have been suitably briefed, bribed, and disguised by Lucentio.

ACT TWO, SCENE THREE: PETRUCHIO'S HOUSE   When Petruchio finds fault with the new clothes that he has ordered for Kate, her weary resistance finally crumbles and she capitulates, only to find that her master is a kinder, wittier husband than she thought possible.

ACT TWO, SCENE FOUR: ENROUTE TO BIANCA'S WEDDING   Petruchio indulges in more whims, fancies, and tricks, but Kate has learned her lesson and joins in the fun.

ACT TWO, SCENE FIVE: BAPTISTA'S HOUSE   At Bianca's wedding the action is all tied up. Gremio and Hortensio have found out that the joys of marriage are a mixed blessing, and even Lucentio has reason to fear that Bianca is not the angel that she appeared to be. Kate, on the other hand, and to everyone's astonishment, turns out to be the truest, most obedient, most loving of wives. Which goes to show that women are not always what they appear to be or, in other words, never judge a book by its cover.

TARANTELLA

Music by Louis Moreau Gottschalk, reconstructed and orchestrated by Hershy Kay. Choreography by George Balanchine. Costumes by Karinska.

*First presented by the New York City Ballet at the New York State Theatre,
January 7, 1964, with Patricia McBride and Edward Villella.*

This *pas de deux* is one of a long series of short ballets I have made for the
gifts of specific dancers. The music is for solo piano and orchestra, based on
the *Grande Tarantelle* of the New Orleans pianist-composer Louis Gottschalk
who dazzled Europe and the United States with his recitals a hundred years
ago. This work, which I asked Hershy Kay to orchestrate for us, is thought to
be the first work for piano and orchestra ever composed by an American. It is
a dazzling display piece, full of speed and high spirits. So, I hope, is the
dance, which is "Neopolitan" if you like and *"demi-caractère."* The costumes
are inspired by Italy, anyhow, and there are tambourines.

TCHAIKOVSKY CONCERTO NO. 2 (*see* BALLET IMPERIAL)

TCHAIKOVSKY PAS DE DEUX

*Music by Peter Ilyich Tchaikovsky. Choreography by George Balanchine.
Costumes by Karinska. First presented by the New York City Ballet at the
City Center, New York, March 29, 1960, with Violette Verdy and Conrad
Ludlow.*

When Tchaikovsky composed his ballet *Swan Lake,* some of the music did not
fit in with the plans of Petipa, his choreographer, and was discarded. When I
learned that this music had recently been discovered in the Bolshoi Theatre
archives, I was naturally interested to see what it was like. Upon receiving
the score through the Tchaikovsky Foundation, I decided at once that the
pieces would form an accompaniment to a *pas de deux* for two of our leading
dancers. As such, it is of course a display piece, based on the music and the
maximum gifts of virtuoso performers. Once, after a successful first performance of a similar display *pas de deux,* one of our dancers said that she did not
know if she would be able to do the piece again. Of course she did it again,
and again and again, and better! What had seemed at the beginning a
stretching of her capacities became easy second nature and she went on to
new achievements. Violette Verdy and Edward Villella have appeared frequently in this *pas de deux,* which is also in the repertory of the Royal Ballet
and other companies.

TCHAIKOVSKY SUITE NO. 2

Music by Peter Ilyich Tchaikovsky. Choreography by Jacques d'Amboise. Production designed by John Braden. Lighting by Ronald Bates. First presented by the New York City Ballet at the New York State Theatre, Lincoln Center, January 9, 1969, with Marnee Morris, John Prinz, Allegra Kent, Francisco Moncion, Linda Merrill, and John Clifford as principals. Conducted by Robert Irving.

The first of a series of Tchaikovsky suites in the New York City Ballet, this dance ballet is performed to music from the composer's *Suite No. 2* for orchestra. In keeping with Tchaikovsky's music, which is fascinating in its Russian references, the ballet makes gestures to Russian, Georgian, and Ukrainian folklore or costumes, but the dances may be said to take place in any time and place. If you do not know this music of Tchaikovsky's, and it is no doubt the least famous of the four suites for orchestra, I with pleasure recommend that you become acquainted with it.

Reviewing the ballet for the New York *Times*, the critic Clive Barnes wrote: "Mr. d'Amboise, a strong dancer himself, of course, creates gratefully for dancers. Here in the first movement he has precisely caught in the delightfully skittish quality of Marnee Morris, the special lilt of laughter in her dancing, and contrasted this with the pouncing, very virile quality of John Prinz. Both dancers responded happily.

"The deep-set mystery of Allegra Kent and the somber power of Francisco Moncion have inspired the softer-toned second movement. Miss Kent showed just the right misty poetry, while Mr. Moncion, filled with a kind of animal nobility, made her an ideal partner.

"For the third movement the ballet reverts to the lighter-hearted tone of the beginning, and here Linda Merrill (in her first major created assignment) and John Clifford fly around blithely and impressively."

TCHAIKOVSKY SUITE NO. 3

Music by Peter Ilyich Tchaikovsky. Choreography by George Balanchine. Scenery and costumes by Nicolas Benois. Lighting by Ronald Bates. First presented by the New York City Ballet at the Saratoga Performing Arts Center, Saratoga, New York, July 23, 1970, with Karin von Aroldingen and Anthony Blum, Kay Mazzo and Conrad Ludlow, Marnee Morris and John Clifford, Gelsey Kirkland and Edward Villella in the principal roles.

In 1947, for American Ballet Theatre, I did a ballet called *Theme and Varia-*

tions that used the last two movements of Tchaikovsky's *Suite No. 3 in G Minor*. The first three movements of this *Suite* I have always liked, too, and so I decided in 1970 to make dances for them. Putting all the dances together, plus *Theme and Variations*, we had a new work, *Tchaikovsky Suite No. 3*. It is interesting that when this *Suite*, not envisioned as a dance score, was first performed in St. Petersburg (1885), it was an enormous success, while his ballet score to *Swan Lake* (1877) was considered "too symphonic" and his music for *The Sleeping Beauty* (1890) was judged simply "very nice" by the Tsar.

1. The curtain rises on the *Élégie* after the orchestra has established a pensive, romantic mood. We are in an empty, dark space, behind a scrim, perhaps a ballroom. Ghosts are possible. A boy kneels left. Seven girls appear to him. He seems to seek another and then before we are aware of it he is dancing with one of the girls. She, like him, barefoot, dances with him in ecstatic abandonment. Both sense that this will not last long, that he is bound to lose her. She rests her head on his shoulder and acknowledges this. And soon she is one of seven girls again. She is the last to leave him as he kneels before her in the abandoned room.

2. *Valse Mélancolique:* A *pas de deux* for another couple, again with a mysterious atmosphere, behind the scrim. Nothing is permanent. She disappears, returns, goes again.

3. The *Scherzo* is danced by a girl and boy and eight supporting girls. Here the vitality of the score supports a flowing animation in the *pas de deux* and there is an impression of endless speed. Here in a brighter light, we make out chandeliers in the distance. As the music ends, the scrim rises and brilliant lighting illuminates a grand ballroom.

4. *Tema con Variazioni* begins in this space. See *Theme and Variations*, page 636.

TEXAS FOURTH

Music: traditional songs by Harvey Schmidt arranged by David Baker and orchestrated by Elizabeth Myers. Choreography by Agnes de Mille. Scenery by Oliver Smith. Costumes by A. Christina Gianini. Lighting by Nananne Porcher. First presented by the Agnes de Mille Heritage Dance Theatre at the North Carolina School of the Arts, 1973. First presented by American Ballet Theatre at the New York State Theatre, Lincoln Center, July 8, 1976, with Dennis Nahat, William Carter, Rebecca Wright, Eric Nesbitt, George de la Pena, Buddy Balough, and Ruth Mayer in principal roles.

A bicentennial celebration of memory and recollection, *Texas Fourth* reminds us what the Fourth of July was like in Texas back in 1936. It begins with four couples square-dancing on the plains while a fiddler calls the tune. A boy does a buck and wing. Next, we are in the midst of a razzmatazz Fourth in a small town. A vigorous batonist leads a troupe of drum majorettes and there is a girl who likes a boy. Everyone seems to be having a rousing, noisy great time when there is a time-stop. The girl sees the ghost of her mother and has a vision, too, of the people of *her* time, dancing and behaving in a quite different, decorous, polite, and genteel way. Texas was different then. But so is the girl, now! We are our ancestors but ourselves, too. Blessed by her mother, she rejoins the boy and the future begins.

After the first performance of *Texas Fourth* by American Ballet Theatre, Agnes de Mille was given the Handel Medallion, New York City's highest award for artistic achievement. She remarked in her acceptance speech that *Texas Fourth* is about "all those lovely, old-fashioned virtues." The action of the ballet takes place in Baird, Texas, her husband's birthplace, and the piece is dedicated to the memory of his grandmother, Roma Foy.

THEATRE

Music by Richard Strauss. Choreography by Eliot Feld. Costumes by Frank Thompson. Lighting by Jennifer Tipton. First presented by the American Ballet Company at the Brooklyn Academy of Music, New York, January 6, 1971, with Eliot Feld, Elizabeth Lee, and Edward Verso in the principal roles.

Theatre is a tragic *commedia dell'arte* ballet. Here we see the classical figures Pierrot, Columbine, and Harlequin in a new combination. The character of the ballet is prefigured by a note in the program quoting John Keats:

I asked to see what brings the hollow brain
Behind environed; what high tragedy
In the dark secret chambers of her skull
Was acting.

The score is the *Burlesque for Piano and Orchestra* of Richard Strauss.

The central figure in *Theatre* is Pierrot, whom we first see sitting making up backstage. Naked to the waist, he stares out at us, as if we were his mirror, examining his face. His countenance is a pasty mask and it is difficult to imagine its being amused at anything. A curtain comes down, lights come up, and suddenly we are on stage, with Columbine and Harlequin and other dancers. The two lovers dance together; alongside their convivial happiness Pierrot is rejected, tearful. Harlequin dances in a kind of triumph and Pierrot joins in to play ball with them. Here, too, he fails. Pulcinella doesn't help matters by introducing a bag of money into the situation. Nothing will cure Pierrot's misery. As he dances alone now his deep despair seems almost overwhelming. As if to crush and release him simultaneously a shower of colored balls falls on Pierrot from above. Now the dancers return and the sad figure of Pierrot leaves the scene.

Writing of *Theatre* in *Dance and Dancers* magazine, Patricia Barnes said that "Feld is quite exceptional in the role of Pierrot, deeply poignant yet never sentimental. It is a performance I shall treasure. As Harlequin, Edward Verso has just the right air of cool mischief. His dancing, quickly precise, helped to create a character, and Elizabeth Lee was equally successful with her sleekly feminine Columbine.

"Among the major assets of the ballet were the incredibly beautiful costumes by Frank Thompson, which must be among the most successful created for an American company in recent years. In their color, cut and conception they were ravishing. While placed within the world of *commedia dell'arte,* they were nevertheless freshly and brilliantly realized and once again Jennifer Tipton's lighting helped enormously. Throughout the season Christopher Keene produced playing from the orchestra of a consistent high standard. He is a young conductor of immense talent, and has been of enormous help to this company."

THEME AND VARIATIONS

Classic ballet. Music by Peter Ilyich Tchaikovsky. Choreography by George Balanchine. Scenery and costumes by Woodman Thompson. First presented by Ballet Theatre at the City Center, New York, November 26, 1947, with Alicia Alonso and Igor Youskevitch in the leading roles.

In addition to his ballet scores, Tchaikovsky composed a great deal of music ideal for dancing. This was perhaps natural for a man who had discovered in ballet a genuine inspiration. Between the time of his first ballet, *Swan Lake* (1877), and his second, *The Sleeping Beauty* (1890), Tchaikovsky wrote four orchestral suites. They were not composed for dancing, yet to listen to them is to think immediately of dancing. They remind us that it is a pity that the composer was not, during this period, a favorite of his contemporary choreographers.

In 1933 I arranged the ballet *Mozartiana* to the fourth of these orchestral suites. *Theme and Variations* is arranged to the final movement of the *Suite No. 3, in G.* This is a dance ballet; like *Ballet Imperial,* it evokes that great period in classical dancing when Russian ballet flourished with the aid of Tchaikovsky's music.

When the curtain rises, we see that the setting is formal: the scene is a great ballroom with huge, towering pillars decorated with vines, luxurious red draperies, and crystal chandeliers containing thousands of candles. A formal garden can be seen in the background. There is a *corps de ballet* of twelve girls arranged in two groups about the ballerina and the *premier danseur.* The girls are dressed in muted colors; the ballerina is in white with a coronol of white flowers. The *premier danseur* wears a blue costume and a blue beret embellished with a white plume.

The music begins, and the ballerina points her toe, dancing softly as the violins play the principal theme. Her steps are simple and graceful, like the melody, and with her feet she seems to point to the quiet charm of the music. Her partner similarly introduces the music and leaves the stage with the ballerina. The twelve girls move forward lightly. They dance a brief ensemble as the theme is repeated on insistent plucked strings to the accompaniment of flutes and clarinets.

Now the tempo increases. The ballerina returns and, surrounded by the *corps de ballet*, begins to display her virtuosity, whirling quickly and brightly in *fouettés* to a restatement of the theme which the strings treat like a *perpetuum mobile*.

The woodwinds announce the theme in a slower tempo; the *corps de ballet* of twelve girls divides into three close groups and describe shifting, flowing lines on the stage. The music becomes assertive again in the fourth variation. The full orchestra plays the theme with a flourish, and the *premier danseur* performs a graceful, yet animated, dance.

When the soloist has left the stage, the orchestra snaps the *corps de ballet* into movement with a sudden chord and plays a fast fugue to which the girls dance their first brilliant ensemble. Just as suddenly, the variation ends. The *premier danseur* now dances alone, describing diagonals across the stage with long, bold leaps. The music is staccato, the strings whirring in tarantella fashion to strong, persistent chords.

The seventh variation is a subdued and noble treatment of the theme. Four girls gather softly, hold hands, and move slowly on point. The ballerina enters. The girls cluster about her in a close semicircle. The English horn varies the theme, and the girls support the ballerina as she executes beautiful adagio movements.

The music trippingly accelerates. The ballerina separates herself from the *corps* and dances vigorously and joyously to the demanding rhythm, her pose changing with quick elegance to the beat of the music, her *pointes* stabbing at the floor in response to the sharp attack of the orchestra. She turns rapidly across the stage and pauses.

The *premier danseur* joins her. A solo violin sounds the melody, and a *pas de deux* begins. Its beginning is softly playful; but as a new variation sweeps the orchestra into a piercing, flowing melody, the dancing is noble and tender. To this theme of open joy and romance the ballerina, supported by her partner, executes slowly and perfectly movements—simple, yet also difficult—that display her full beauty.

When the two principals leave the stage, a drum roll sounds, followed by a bright fanfare on the horns. Eight boys enter with a flourish. The *corps de ballet* joins them, with the two principal dancers, as the orchestra announces with blaring pomp a regal polonaise. There are swift variations by the two principals—the ballerina accompanied by the girls; the *premier danseur*, by the boys—and rapid regroupings and shiftings of partners in the ensemble as the final variation increases in liveliness. The two principals, hand in hand, lead the dancers about the ballroom in a sweeping circle. There is vigorous dancing to the final crashes of music, and then, at the last chord, a tableau in which the ballerina is lifted high to her partner's shoulder while all her court salutes her.

THE THREE-CORNERED HAT

Dramatic ballet in one act. Music by Manuel de Falla. Choreography by Leonide Massine. Book by Gregorio Martínez Sierra. Scenery and costumes by Pablo Picasso. First presented by Diaghilev's Ballets Russes at the Alhambra Theatre, London, July 22, 1919, with Leonide Massine as the Miller, *Tamara Karsavina as the* Miller's Wife, *Leon Woizikowski as the* Corregidor, *and Stanislas Idzikowski as the* Dandy. *First presented in the United States by the Ballet Russe de Monte Carlo at the St. James Theatre, New York, March 9, 1934, with Leon Woizikowski as the* Miller *and Tamara Toumanova as the* Miller's Wife.

The Three-Cornered Hat tells a love story of Spain with humor and warmth. The scene is a small Spanish village. The Spanish tone of the ballet is established immediately by the music, by cries of *"Olé! Olé! Olé! Olé!"* from behind the curtain, and by the sound of rhythmic castanets, dancing feet, and hand clapping.

The curtain rises on the village scene. The village miller stands before his house, whistling to a black bird who sits in a cage. The bird will not sing as he wishes it to. The miller's wife comes out of the house and teases her husband. He chases her and they embrace.

The couple go to the well to draw water. While the miller is busy at the well, a dandy passes by and blows kisses to his wife, who responds flirtatiously. The miller looks up and sees this exchange and chases the dandy off. He is not angry with his wife. He is delighted that other men find her as beautiful as he does. They are very much in love.

Now the governor of the province, the corregidor, enters with an escort. A doddering old fool, he looks absurd in his finery among the simple folk of the village. He wears a three-cornered hat, symbol of his class and position.

Almost immediately the corregidor eyes the miller's wife and decides that she must be his. The miller's wife is polite to him, but no more. He passes on. Noting that his wife is getting all the attention, the miller decides he'd better give another girl some favor. He playfully flirts with one of the lovely girls of the village. Now that both husband and wife have cause to be jealous, they are amused at each other and embrace.

The miller goes into the house. His wife, remaining outside, dances a brilliant *fandango*. The corregidor has come back and secretly watches her. Soon he approaches her and tries to make advances. The woman eludes him cleverly and flees. The old man, however, pursues her.

The miller has watched this scene from inside the house and runs out to help his wife. The corregidor can run no more and falls to the ground, exhausted. The miller and his wife pick him up, dust him off, and try to act as if it were all an accident, but the corregidor, furious with them, suggests that this is only the beginning of what they may expect of him. The husband and wife dance together.

Evening falls. The village folk come to the miller's house to join in a festival with the happy couple. The miller gives them wine and then dances alone a *farruca*, which everyone applauds. The villagers hear the approach of marching soldiers. The escorts of the corregidor enter. The men arrest the miller and take him off. Abandoned by her friends, the miller's wife is alone.

But not for long. The corregidor is back again, seeking her favor now with real determination. The miller's wife throws him to the ground as he clumsily holds her. He rises with difficulty and pursues her to the village bridge, which crosses a running stream. On the bridge, the corregidor again attempts to embrace the girl. In the process of pushing him away, the miller's wife pushes him off the bridge into the stream. She laughs at him, but helps the corregidor out of the water. But the old fool takes up the chase again. The miller's wife takes a gun from the house and, threatening the corregidor with buckshot, flees over the bridge away from the village.

The corregidor stands in front of the miller's house, alone, his clothes still dripping from the dunking he got in the stream. He takes off his outer garments and his three-cornered hat, lays them out to dry, and goes into the house to sleep.

Dawn comes. The miller has escaped the corregidor's henchmen and returns home. In front of his house he sees the corregidor's clothes and the three-cornered hat! Then he observes the corregidor himself, walking around in one of his own nightshirts! The miller decides there's only one thing to do. He will pursue the corregidor's wife, who is also young and beautiful! On the walls of his house he draws a caricature of the corregidor and leaves.

Now the poor corregidor is attacked by his own soldiers, who don't recognize him in the miller's nightshirt. He curses them, and the village folk come to see what the trouble is. The miller and his wife, who have found each other outside the town, come in. Their friends are told what the corregidor has tried to do, and in anger all the people rise up against the governor and his cohorts. The intruders are routed, and all dance triumphantly, led by the miller and his wife. A dummy representing the defeated corregidor is thrown higher and higher into the air by the crowd.

NOTES   Although Leon Woizikowski first danced the miller at the American

première of *The Three-Cornered Hat,* Leonide Massine later danced the role
in the United States. The ballet was revived by Massine for Ballet Theatre in
1943 and for the Sadler's Wells Ballet in 1947.

Tania Massine, the choreographer's daughter, assisted by Yurek Lazowski,
staged a revival of *The Three-Cornered Hat* for the City Center Joffrey Ballet
in New York, September 25, 1969. Luis Fuente was the *Miller,* Barbara Rem-
ington the *Miller's wife,* Basil Thompson the *Corregidor,* Rebecca Wright the
Corregidor's wife, and Frank Bays the *Dandy.* The original Picasso designs
were reconstructed by William Pitkin.

THREE ESSAYS

*Music by Charles Ives. Choreography by Lar Lubovitch. First presented
by American Ballet Theatre at the City Center, New York, January 15,
1974, with Warren Conover, Christine Sarry, Clark Tippet, and Ian Horvath in leading roles.*

Like an earlier work by the dancer-choreographer Lar Lubovitch for the same
ensemble (see *Scherzo for Massah Jack*), this ballet is a period piece based on
its score. The American master Charles Ives was, of course, remarkable in his
many gifts, among them a memorable capacity to recollect the past, which is
what the ballet here also aims to do. The composer's notations for the three
parts of the music are embodied by the choreographer: "Elegy to Our Forefa-
thers"; "The Rockstrewn Hills Join in the People's Outdoor Meeting"; "From
Hanover Square North at the End of a Tragic Day (1915)."

What we see portrayed in dance terms is a commentary on these themes of
the composer, and an ironic one, relating to World War I, and all that conflict
meant, or seemed to mean, to Americans, together with its consequences.

Commenting in *Cue* magazine, the critic Robert Jacobson wrote: "Lubovitch's piece is marked by turbulence . . . and commands respect . . . His images are often memorable and he leaves you thinking."

THREE VIRGINS AND A DEVIL

*Music by Ottorino Respighi. Scenario by Ramon Reed. Choreography by
Agnes de Mille. Scenery and costumes by Motley. Setting designed by Arne
Lundborg. First presented by Ballet Theatre at the Majestic Theatre, New
York, February 11, 1941, with Agnes de Mille as the Priggish One, Lucia
Chase as the Greedy One, Annabelle Lyon as the Lustful One, Eugene
Loring as a Devil, and Jerome Robbins as a Youth.*

The critic Robert J. Pierce has called this ballet a burlesque in the form of a medieval morality play. Arranged to Respighi's *Ancient Dances and Airs for the Lute*, this *danse caractère* personifies three typical but differing young women and shows what happens to them under devilish circumstances.

After a short overture the curtain rises on a medieval landscape, a monastery gate at the right, with door shut; a grotto at the left, leading to a cave. Three girls come in. Their leader, a priggish lass, is trying to drag her friends to church. She displays maximum piety in this undertaking, trying to persuade the Greedy One, who is decked out in finery, to put her belongings in the alms box. Not to be overlooked, the Lustful One, a child of nature with a garland of flowers, sees the directions things are taking and decides to renounce her wreath. When a prancing Youth enters to find all the virgins swaying in prayer, he is clearly astonished at such unanimous piety. He cannot persuade any of the girls to join him.

Now a hermit enters, asking the Greedy One for money. The beggar is a peculiar sort of fellow, almost spastic in his movements as he seems to try to hide one of his feet under his cloak. The foot keeps trembling and bothering him. When he can bear it no longer, he throws off the cloak and reveals himself as a Devil, tail, horns, cloven foot, and all.

The virgins, in their uniform piety, are appalled, but when he brings out a sort of cello and starts to play, they all dance lustily to his tune. They get so carried away by their revels that when the Youth returns, again beckoning to the Lustful One, she jumps obligingly onto his back, whereupon he carries her swiftly into the grotto—a gate, of course, to hell.

The Devil tempts next the Greedy One, who responds to his offer of a bright jewel and follows her sister to the other world. The Priggish One, of course, is harder to tempt and the Devil has his own time of it getting from her the proper response. She mothers him and strikes terror into him by trying to get him into the monastery. Unable to bear such tactics any longer, he begins to chase her like a man possessed. In terror she flees, running from him in a wider and wider circle, but pursuing him, too, determined to have yet another convert. The widening circle of the chase leads to the grotto entrance, where the Devil stands aside and permits the lady to dash down to hell with her own momentum.

NOTES Agnes de Mille first produced a ballet to this theme in London, in 1934, at the Palace Theatre, in the musical comedy *Why Not Tonight?* Greta Nissen, Elizabeth Schooling, and M. Braithwaite were the Girls and Stanislas Idzikowski the Devil. The music was by Walford Hyden.

American Ballet Theatre revived *Three Virgins and a Devil* at the New York State Theatre, Lincoln Center, New York, July 25, 1973, with Sallie Wilson (now called the Fanatical One), Ruth Mayer, and Christine Sarry as the Virgins, Dennis Nahat as a Devil, and Daniel Levans as a Youth. The conductor was Akira Endo and the lighting was by Nananne Porcher.

TIL EULENSPIEGEL

*Ballet by Jean Babilée. Music by Richard Strauss. Choreography by Jean
Babilée. Scenery and costumes by Tom Keogh. First presented by Les Bal-
lets des Champs-Élysées, November 9, 1949, at the Théâtre des Champs-
Élysées, Paris, with Jean Babilée in the title role. First presented in the
United States by Ballet Theatre at the Metropolitan Opera House, New
York, September 25, 1951, with a cast headed by Jean Babilée and Ruth
Ann Koesun. Costumes by Helene Pons.*

Richard Strauss's score *Til Eulenspiegel's Merry Pranks* was not composed to
be danced, but the fact that the music has a plot and relates incidents in the
life of one of the most popular figures in European folklore has made it naturally attractive to choreographers. Til Eulenspiegel is the perennial prankster
who never seems to get his comeuppance. Although he may hurt people when
he tricks them, he really has no harmful intentions; he is a maker of fun motivated by his own innocent pleasure and not by cunning. Such a man sooner or
later runs into trouble with the law, for much as we may admire his artfulness
and daring, the law will be more impressed with the number of his mis-
demeanors.

This ballet shows us the roguery of Til—his inability to conform to convention and his contempt for the law. Here his pranks are so good-humored that
even the law is inclined to forgive him.

The curtain rises as the music begins. The scene is an improvised impression
of an ancient market place. Against a mottled gray background, five colorful
booths are arranged in a semicircle. The light is dim; spotlights shine down
on the brightly colored awnings over the booths. A girl enters. She is small,
has long blond hair, and wears a flowing dress. She dances across the market
place to the soft opening bars of the music and disappears.

Two by two, a group of ragamuffin merchants march out to stand behind
their booths and wait for customers. As soon as they are all stationed at their
jobs, they look in unison from right to left. A quiet, impudent theme is heard
in the orchestra, and the men sense that something is going on behind their
backs. They are right. Til Eulenspiegel dances in. His face is chalk-white beneath his orange hair, but this does not disguise his expression of impudence.
His dance is spontaneously graceful and grotesque at the same time; we imagine already that anything he does will be funny.

As he runs about the market place, Til almost collides with a young girl. Immediately he begins to make up to her. He kneels before her, begging for a
mere glance. The girl, dressed in formal medieval costume, will have none of
his impertinence and repulses him. This only encourages Til, who encircles her
in a tumbling dance that infuriates the girl. When he sees that she does not

like him, Til makes fun of her behind her back. The merchants are delighted. The girl orders him away. The exuberant Til complies and jumps up backward to sit on one of the booths. There he watches the girl with what seems to be an innocent eye. But the cymbals crash, the music bursts into a loud ruckus. At a sudden signal from Til, all the merchants jump out from behind their booths. They grab the girl and toss her in the air. She crawls off, disheveled, on all fours—no longer a charming young lady: Til's magic has turned her into a witch.

Til and the merchants go back to their booths. A courtly theme is heard, and a gentleman enters with his lady. Til is very amused at their formal ways and laughs at the flowing feather in the gentleman's cap. They try not to notice him, but Til forces himself between them and tries to engage the lady's attention. He jumps up and down in his excitement to please her. He pleads with her to notice him and to send her escort away so that they may dance together alone. The lady, however, is shocked by this behavior. Unfortunately her escort cannot assist her, for just as he flirts with the lady, Til is also trying to humiliate the gentleman. He runs out and returns quickly, dressed in a hat filled with variously colored long-flowing feathers. When he bows to the lady, these absurd feathers reach to the floor. She now thinks him ridiculous as well as rude and will never respond to his advances. Til must have his good-humored revenge. He throws down his hat with a flourish at the lady's feet and challenges her lover to a duel. The lady is aghast as the two men assume dueling stances before her. The merchants applaud the combat. The two duelists rush each other, turn each other upside down in a cartwheel of movement, and roll over and over together, their bodies joined in a tumbling hoop. The gentleman has clearly had enough by this time and, seizing his lady by the hand, dashes off.

No sooner have they departed than a group of ragged hunchbacks come into the market place, begging for alms. The lights dim, Til runs out, and the merchants hide behind their booths. Now Til is back again, but dressed in a long black cape and a high-peaked hat. He, too, is a hunchback all of a sudden; he joins the pilgrimage of the stricken men. The men accept him as their equal in misery and marvel when by a quick miracle he is cured: the hump on his back has vanished! They congratulate him on his cure and, to ensure a cure for themselves, do what Til anticipated: they give him all their money and walk out of the square, certain that this tribute to one of their former fellows will hasten their own recovery. The wealthy Til rids himself of cap and cloak and counts his fortune.

His girl, Nell, the blonde who appeared at the beginning of the ballet, comes into the square. In the soft light, she and Til dance together. Now completely happy, he swings her around and around in the air. A distant trumpet call is heard; Til cups his hand to his ear for a moment to listen, but then continues with the dance. He and Nell rush off into the night together.

The trumpet theme grows in the orchestra. Til runs back in and circles the stage in leaps timed to its open, joyous melody. The merchants jump out from behind their booths, tear down the awnings, and—using the awning poles for lances—surround him in a mock military drill. Til, in the center, jumps up and down in glee. The merchants form a parade and rush around the stage. At the theme's fullest crescendo, Til leaps onto their backs and rides high above them in triumph.

But the theme is cut short sharply. There is a menacing drum roll, the theme of the gallows, and ominous, plodding music changes Til's ebullience into fear. Six soldiers dash in and rush him. Til runs for one of the booths, but the soldiers jump up after him. Til escapes between their legs and hides underneath. Til's impudent theme, sounded by the clarinet, laughs at the loud, heavy theme of the law. The soldiers gang up on him again; again he escapes and the music ridicules them. Finally they grab him and hold him securely after a long tussle.

One of the soldiers runs off. He returns with a judge and a hangman. Til's legs run in the air as he is held motionless; he wraps his legs around one of the soldiers in his fright. The judge flourishes a scroll and begins to read the indictment against Til for all his crimes. The criminal is led forward, his head bowed. A soldier kneels down to form the chopping block, and Til is placed across it. The hangman aims the ax. The sonorous theme of authority is sounded firmly; Til's merry theme reaches a high shriek of terror and disintegrates as it descends the scale. There is a moment of silence. Still the ax is posed above Til, but the executioner does not move. Nell enters on the right. The judge, the executioner, the soldiers—all turn to look at her. They pardon Til because of the reality of his love for her and imagine that with Nell he will lead a less prankish life. His head still on the block, Til anxiously feels the back of his neck. He looks up carefully. When he sees that they don't intend to execute him, after all, he rushes over to Nell and kneels to her in gratitude. He touches her hands then, and they dance briefly.

Now that everything is back to normal, now that he still has his neck and his Nell, Til reverts instantly to his old ways: he runs over, assaults the judge, and berates him for treating him like a common criminal! Before the judge can retaliate, Til has run off after Nell.

Babilée's *Til Eulenspiegel* was the second ballet based on Richard Strauss's famous score. The first was by Vaslav Nijinsky, whose last ballet it was. Nijinsky's *Til* was presented for the first time by Diaghilev's Ballets Russes at the Manhattan Opera House, New York, October 23, 1916. The scenery and costumes were by Robert Edmond Jones. Carl Van Vechten wrote of this performance:

"*Til Eulenspiegel* is the only new ballet the Russians have produced in America. In selecting this work and in his arrangement of the action Nijinsky was moved, no doubt, by consideration for the limitations of the company as it existed. The scenery and costumes by Robert E. Jones, New York, were decidedly diverting—the best work this talented young man has done, I think. Over a deep, spreading background of ultramarine, the crazy turrets of medieval castles leaned dizzily to and fro. The costumes were exaggerations of the exaggerated fashions of the Middle Ages. Mr. Jones added feet of stature to the already elongated peaked headdresses of the period. The trains of the velvet robes, which might have extended three yards, were allowed to trail the full depth of the Manhattan Opera House stage. The colors were oranges, reds, greens, and blues, those indeed of Bakst's *Scheherazade*, but so differently disposed that they made an entirely dissimilar impression. The effect reminded one spectator of a Spanish omelet.

"In arranging the scenario, Nijinsky followed in almost every detail Wilhelm Klatte's description of the meaning of the music, which is printed in programme books whenever the tone-poem is performed, without Strauss' authority, but sometimes with his sanction. Nijinsky was quite justified in altering the end of the work, which hangs the rogue-hero, into another practical joke. His version of this episode fits the music and, in the original *Til Eulenspiegel*, Til is not hanged, but dies in bed. The keynote of Nijinsky's interpretation was gaiety. He is as utterly picaresque as the work itself; he reincarnated the spirit of Gil Blas; indeed, a new quality crept into stage expression through this characterization. Margaret Wycherly, one of the most active admirers of the dancer, told me after the first performance that she felt that he had for the first time leaped into the hearts of the great American public, whose appreciation of his subtler art as expressed in *Narcisse, Petrouchka,* and even *Scheherazade,* had been more moderate. There were those who protested that this was not the Til of the German legends, but any actor who attempts to give form to a folk or historical character, or even a character derived from fiction is forced to run counter to many an observer's preconceived ideas."

TILT

Music by Igor Stravinsky. Choreography by Hans van Manen. Decor and costumes by Jean-Paul Vroom. First presented by the Netherlands Dance Theatre, January 21, 1972, at the Circustheater, Scheveningen, Holland. First presented in the United States by the same ensemble at the Brooklyn Academy of Music, New York, April 7, 1972.

The choreographer, Hans van Manen, has described his own ballet: "Stravinsky's *Concerto in D for String Orchestra* [the same score Jerome Robbins used in 1951 for his ballet *The Cage*] is played in its entirety twice—the choreography being almost exactly the same for both versions. However, with the repeat of the music, as opposed to the first time it is played, the choreography for the six dancers is redistributed as follows:
  —the first variation for six dancers is divided into three *pas de deux*
  —the *pas de deux* is danced simultaneously by three couples
  —the male variation is performed by three girls.

In the section that follows the sexes are transposed—the girls dance the parts of the men and the men those of the girls.

"The next three *pas de deux* remain unchanged but are danced by different couples. The finale is repeated in mirror-image with a change in each of the two *pas de deux*. Movement alone has no meaning for me in itself; it takes its significance only from the context in which it is placed."

TIME PAST SUMMER

Music by Peter Ilyich Tchaikovsky. Choreography by Benjamin Harkarvy. First presented by the Pennsylvania Ballet at the Academy of Music, Philadelphia, February 14, 1974, with Alba Calzada, Joanne Danto, and Lawrence Rhodes in leading roles.

Eleven Tchaikovsky songs accompany this ballet, which looks back to the Russia of Chekhov and some of the characters in his memorable plays and stories. Writing in the *Dancing Times* the critic George Dorris said: "People at a Chekhovian garden party listen to two singers and think over their lives . . . An effective, moving ballet."

LE TOMBEAU DE COUPERIN

Music by Maurice Ravel. Choreography by George Balanchine. Lighting by Ronald Bates. First presented by the New York City Ballet at the Hommage à Ravel at the New York State Theatre, Lincoln Center, May 29, 1975. Conducted by Robert Irving.

Ravel said that, in style, *Le Tombeau* is not so much a homage to the great French composer François Couperin as a tribute to eighteenth-century French music in general. The music, orchestrated from an original piano suite dedicated to friends of Ravel who had died in World War I, is in six parts: *Prélude, Fugue, Forlane, Rigaudon, Menuet,* and *Toccata*. The ballet that I arranged to this music doesn't say anything beyond the combination of these particular dancers moving to Ravel's lovely score, his memorial to Couperin.

These particular dancers are sixteen in number, eight couples divided into two quadrilles. They are mid-twentieth-century dancers moving to the work of a man who, in 1919, wrote tributes to a composer who flourished at the court of Louis XIV.

The American composer Norman Lloyd has written in the Golden Encyclopedia of Music that Couperin "is one of the greatest composers of the Baroque period, and one of the subtlest and most musicianly minds France has produced." I wholeheartedly agree; one of the pleasures this particular piece gave me as we made so many ballets so swiftly for our homage to Ravel in 1975 was my recollection of this master's work.

TRACES

Music by Gustav Mahler. Choreography by John Cranko. Scenery and costumes by Jürgen Rose. First presented by the Stuttgart Ballet at the Württemberg State Theatre, Stuttgart, Germany, April 7, 1973. First presented in the United States by the Stuttgart Ballet at the Metropolitan Opera House, New York, May 30, 1973, with Marcia Haydée, Heinz Clauss, and Richard Cragun in the principal roles. Conducted by Stewart Kershaw.

Traces is a dramatic ballet about the past, as recalled in the present. The score is the *Adagio* from Mahler's *Tenth Symphony*. To its music a woman, released from obviously terrible captivity (a concentration camp?), adjusts to her new freedom while the past pulls at her memory.

The scene is an empty ballroom, with a sofa and chair. The woman enters. Her lover greets her, patient, understanding, warm. As they look together toward the back of the room, a group of dancers emerges. In the midst of their dance the woman sees a vision of a man in her past. He, a victim of persecution, head shaven, thin, in ragged clothes, draws her sympathy. In his spell her world seems to change completely. In the darkness the dead appear to waken. They rise slowly and crawl toward us. The man in her past stands out among them, leaping and springing in a kind of frantic agony. The woman joins him and comforts him when he collapses. Alternately drawn toward him and away from him, dreading yet cherishing the memory, the woman flings herself against the man. Now he leaves. She goes mad with grief. In the mass of prisoners he falls. They step over him—another victim, as they themselves shall likely be. The woman seeks refuge in her new lover's arms. She looks back at the prisoners, who turn suddenly and drop the rags from their backs to reveal numbers. They crouch down again and the ballroom dancers move among them. The woman dances with her new lover but is not to be comforted by his gentleness. Moving rigidly as in a trance, she walks slowly with him toward the back, toward a glowing circle of fire that might be the sun.

TRIAD

Music by Serge Prokofiev. Choreography by Kenneth MacMillan. Setting and costumes by Peter Unsworth. First presented by the Royal Ballet at the Royal Opera House, Covent Garden, London, January 19, 1972, with Antoinette Sibley, Anthony Dowell, and Wayne Eagling. First presented in the United States by the Royal Ballet at the Metropolitan Opera House, New York, in 1972.

The three principal dancers in *Triad* are a girl, a boy, and his brother. The two boys are devoted but from the start there is a problem. One of them is upset and cries. A girl comes to them and dances. One brother tries to shield the other from the effects of this dance of the girl's but the girl will not permit it. Now one of the boys dances for the girl, then she again for *him.* After a dance for all three, the girl tries to persuade one to come away with her. She goes but he stays. The two boys dance, one continuing to try to shield the other. But not for long. When three male "companions" enter, the stronger brother throws the weaker to them, only to rescue him at the last minute. After a passionate *pas de deux* between the stronger boy and the girl, the younger brother despairs. He leaves but returns, tries to separate them, fails, again despairs.

NOTES Writing in *Saturday Review* about *Triad,* the critic Walter Terry said that while the ballet "may seem to some to have homosexual overtones, I felt it to be rooted in something like the deep mystique of twins who are both dual and one. MacMillan captures this feeling tastefully but, what is more, imaginatively. The contours of his movements are generally balletic, but the dynamism is that of modern dance; that is, indeed, a striking integration of the elegance and dignity of classicism with the passionate, almost visceral, expressivity of free dance.

"In the cast I saw, Dowell and Wayne Eagling were most appealing as the brothers whose bond goes deeper than physicality, and Miss Sibley, as the girl, touched the heart with a portrayal involving need, desire, rejection. A most rewarding, adult ballet, rich in striking designs as well as in dramatic intensity."

TRINITY

Music by Alan Raph and Lee Holdridge. Choreography by Gerald Arpino. Lighting by Jennifer Tipton. Conductor: Walter Hagen. Rock Group: Virgin Wool. Organ: Hub Miller. Boys Choir: St. Luke's Chapel. First presented by the City Center Joffrey Ballet, October 9, 1969, with Christian Holder, Gary Chryst, Rebecca Wright, Dermot Burke, Donna Cowen, Starr Danias, and James Dunne in principal roles.

Named for its three parts, *Sunday, Summerland,* and *Saturday, Trinity* is a homage to youth, joyful and aspiring. It uses for music themes reminiscent of Gregorian chant and Baroque styles translated into rock, employing sections of the regular orchestra, a boy's choir, and a rock group, "Virgin Wool." There are two conductors, one for the orchestra and chorus, one who leads the rock group from the organ.

Thirteen dancers participate in *Sunday*, which is heralded by a brass chorale before the curtain rises. The dancers enter gradually until finally all are present to respond to the throb of the rock organ. This is a group dance, exuberant, demanding in its rhythm and pulse, persistent, rejoicing in companionship and celebratory of youth. There are a number of solos and small ensembles as the mixture of rock and Baroque mounts in intensity. At the end, all lie in a circle on the floor as lead boy leaves.

In the part called *Summerland*, the pulse of the score slows down. The dancers rise from the circle and in varied ensembles suggest the sweetness of young love. Couple after couple now take the stage, one of them dancing a protracted adagio of affection. The accent here is on high spirits, too, shown in the many remarkable lifts in which the boys reach the girls up to the skies. All six couples rejoin as chimes sound twice and the boys carry the girls off.

Saturday, standing for the ancient Sabbath, begins as two boys enter the darkened scene carrying candles. The entire group follows, each bearing a lighted candle. They leave then and a boy comes forward to perform a dance to the hymn/rock beat, a version of the *Ite, missa est* that concludes the Latin Mass. He is joined by other male soloists and we have an impression that there is nothing on earth like lifting your arms and responding to the swell of the mighty organ that dominates the music here. The score intensifies in cracking crescendos of sound. All of the dancers then re-enter, each putting a candle on stage. The music gradually diminishes and the lights diminish, too, so that all we see on stage is the presentation of the candles.

NOTES   Speaking of his ballet to Anna Kisselgoff of the New York *Times*, the choreographer of *Trinity*, Gerald Arpino, said, "I think I'm in tune with my time. . . . This is my Aquarius ballet. I wanted the classic idiom with its escape from gravity—for the highest reach man can assume. I don't want to sound corny, but this is a ballet about man seeking his inner self. When the kids leave the candles on the floor, it's not meant to suggest just the literal peace marches. In the end, each individual must express himself. All he can leave is the light of himself."

The critic Andrew Porter reviewed *Trinity* at the time of the City Center Joffrey Ballet's London debut in May, 1971: "Gerald Arpino's *Trinity* made a whizzing start. For here the company seemed to be the 20th century's answer to the Bolshoi Ballet: which is to say nothing prissy, and nothing pretentious, but tremendous vigour and soaring virtuosity; flashing, exhilarating achievement rather than refined niceties; punch rather than polish. But—unlike the Bolshoi—an imagery both on stage and from the players that belongs to the present day: thoroughly demotic images supercharged into a buoyant art.

"The score, for the company's own group The Virgin Wool, choirboys, electric organ and orchestra, strikes into plain chant and Palestrina, and turns them into rock—not self-consciously but exuberantly. The dancing strikes into classicism at times, and breaks it into modern movement. The whole is heady and joyful, a celebration of a youth that can effortlessly encompass and transform the past."

John T. Elson in *Time* magazine wrote that *Trinity* "represents a throbbing fusion of classic dance with the sound of now. It perfectly epitomizes the jaunty style and passionate, youthful temperament of the New York City Center's Joffrey Ballet."

Patricia Barnes, in *Dance and Dancers*, wrote: "*Trinity* is a hard ballet to describe for its vitality, sincerity and passion, its dynamic coloring, both choreographic and musical, must be seen. Nor can words alone convey the personality and power of dancers such as Gary Chryst, Christian Holder and Dermot Burke; these three did a great deal to make *Trinity* the success it was. However, the whole cast had a splendid exuberance that made the ballet a pleasure to watch."

In the *Village Voice*, writing of the work of choreographer Gerald Arpino, Deborah Jowitt said: "His new ballet, *Trinity*, never lets go of you, never stops pounding and hurling fast, smart-alecky movement at you. He ignores—or perhaps uses—several basic dichotomies with magnificent ease. The Joffrey dancers are young and phenomenal. The best of them may grow in artistry or sensitivity, but they will probably never be more indomitable. Although they are young, they already have a discipline that very few people their age possess. I think it is the combination of discipline and vigor that excites Arpino. The three-part *Trinity* is set to some very good rock music (written by Alan Raph and Lee Holdridge and played by Virgin Wool), and the whole dance seems a taut by-play between the freedom inherent in rock and the control necessary for ballet. The dancers progress from the flung *développés* of Broadway to perfectly centered pirouettes rendered dangerous and exciting by fast, off-balance head circles or contrary arm gestures. This gives the movement an odd duality; ballet with a loose, whizzing quality in one part of the body only.

"Rock is heavy, ballet light. In *Trinity*, the dancers skid and wiggle on top of the beat; they punch it, but rarely drop onto it. Another interesting paradox. The movement is, for the most part, fast and very intricate—except for a slow ritual with votive candles in the last section and a softer second movement that features those stunning one-arm lifts that drove the crowd wild."

THE TRIUMPH OF DEATH

Dance drama in ten scenes after Eugène Ionesco by Flemming Flindt. Music by Thomas Koppel. Scenery and costumes by Poul Arnt Thomsen. Lighting by Jorgen Mydtskov. Music recorded by The Savage Rose. First presented by the Royal Danish Ballet at the Royal Theatre, Copenhagen, Denmark,

February 19, 1972. First presented by the same ensemble at the Metropolitan Opera House, New York, May 27, 1976.

A harsh and direct statement of the ills of this and other times, set to a score by a Danish rock group, this ballet sets out to deliver a message against all the destructive forces in the modern world, from pollution to political tyranny and human corruption. In a universal protest designed to force audiences to open their eyes, Flindt shows a materialistic society destroyed by corruptive influences.

TROIS VALSES ROMANTIQUES

Music by Emmanuel Chabrier. Choreography by George Balanchine. Costumes by Karinska. First presented by the New York City Ballet at the New York State Theatre, April 6, 1967, with Melissa Hayden and Arthur Mitchell, Gloria Govrin and Frank Ohman, and Marnee Morris and Kent Stowell in the principal roles.

This is the third ballet I have done to music of Chabrier, a favorite composer of mine. I first heard music by this marvelous Frenchman soon after I left Russia and joined Diaghilev's Ballets Russes. In Paris I heard a concert of his music and liked it right away. I thought then that doing a ballet to Chabrier's music would be a pleasure and when the first opportunity presented itself some years later, I arranged *Cotillon*. The third of the *Trois Valses Romantiques* was included in that score. Then there was *Bourrée Fantasque.*

The ballet has no subject beyond the music and what it stands for to me. The first waltz is marked *Très vite et impétueusement,* the second *Mouvement modéré de valse* and the third *Animé.* The dances I arranged to these lovely pieces are simply expressive of the music as I see it, dances for a boy and a girl with two supporting couples, and a *corps de ballet* of six couples. The dances are about love and romance and what might happen.

TWICE

Music by Herbie Mann, Steve Miller Band, James Brown, and Santana. Choreography by Hans van Manen. Film visualization by Jean-Paul Vroom. Assistant film direction by Richard Brink. Costumes by Joop Stovkis. First presented by the Netherlands Dance Theatre at the Sadler's Wells Theatre, London, November 2, 1970. First presented in the United States by the same ensemble, April 2, 1972, at the Brooklyn Academy of Music.

Like *Mutations,* the signature work of the Netherlands Dance Theatre in the early 1970s, *Twice* relies on both live dances and dance on film. Hans van

Manen was responsible for the cine-choreography of *Mutations*, a technique he elaborates here. The title, originally *Sock It to Me*, applies to repeats in movement and to the mirroring of live movement in film.

Twice consists of four parts. The first, *Double*, to Herbie Mann's "Memphis Underground," is performed by an ensemble on stage whose movements are seen, too, on a movie screen high above the scene. The camera closes in on certain individuals and focuses the general attention on particular gestures and movement. In the second part, *Superimpositions*, a masked couple dance to the Steve Miller Band playing "Song for Our Ancestors." A flowing dance, the *pas de deux* yields to an ensemble, where other masked dancers pick up choreographic themes we have just seen.

Theme, the third part, is a solo for a boy to James Brown singing "Sex Machine." The dance begins slowly, builds to a frantic finish, and the scene blacks out. The finale, *Twice*, to music by Santana ("Savor"), gives the stage again to all twelve dancers, whose movements assume a brilliant staccato to the rhythm of strobe light.

THE TWO PIGEONS

An Allegory in two acts, based on the Fable by La Fontaine by Henry Regnier and Louis Mérante. Music by André Messager. Choreography by Louis Mérante. First presented at the Opéra, Paris, October 18, 1886. Presented by the Royal Ballet in a new version with choreography by Frederick Ashton at the Royal Opera House, Covent Garden, London, February 14, 1961. Scenery and costumes by Jacques Dupont. The principal roles were danced by Lynn Seymour, Christopher Gable, Elizabeth Anderson, and Johaar Mosaval. First presented in the United States by the Royal Ballet at the Metropolitan Opera House, New York, April 24, 1963, with Lynn Seymour, Alexander Grant, Georgina Parkinson, and Johaar Mosaval in the principal roles.

The historian and critic Ivor Guest has noted that the discovery at the Royal Opera House of the score used for a 1906 presentation in London of *The Two Pigeons* prompted Frederick Ashton to stage a new version of the ballet. For this he discarded the scenario of the old ballet in favor of an allegorical treatment of the fable of his own devising. The story the ballet depicts is based on the poem *Les Deux Pigeons* by La Fontaine. While the two birds love each other, one tires of home and longs to roam abroad. When his love protests the pigeon replies that she is not to worry; after all, he will be gone only three days and just think of the adventures he will be able to tell! After his trip is over, the pigeon gratefully returns to his true love and they live happily ever after.

The choreographer has situated the action in Paris, where a young painter and his love live in an attractive garret. The painter is restless, however, and

when a band of gypsies happens by, he is so enchanted by their free spirit—
and also so interested in one of the girls—that he goes off. As his girl looks
sadly after him from the balcony of the garret, a pigeon flies across the stage.

In the gypsy encampment, the boy learns that the transient life is not all
moonlight and roses. He also learns that his affection for the gypsy lady has
aroused the jealousy of her lover. There is much fiery gypsy dancing and appropriate displays of passion. The boy sees the gypsies have been kind to him
only as a trick, but before he can escape they have tied him up and given him
a rough time.

Meanwhile, back at the studio, his faithful love still sits on the balcony,
awaiting his return. When she sees him her arms touchingly imitate the happy
flapping of pigeon wings. They are reunited, dance ecstatically, and then rest
by a chair, where first one pigeon comes to rest, and then another.

TZADDIK

*Music by Aaron Copland. Choreography by Eliot Feld. "For My Grand-
mother Bessie." Setting and costumes by Boris Aronson. Lighting by Jennifer Tipton. First presented in 1974 by the Eliot Feld Ballet at the Newman
Theater, New York, with Eliot Feld in the leading role.*

There is a saying, Eliot Feld, the dancer and choreographer, reminds us: "A
Jew without learning is incomplete." His ballet is a dramatic dance about an
old rabbi and two students. The music is a trio, too: Copland's *Vitebsk*.

The students are two young men. Devoted to the master and anxious to do
what he wishes, what they do is never enough for him. They are younger, after
all, and represent the possibly dangerous and innovatively new. Amid the displayed exhortation it is easy to imagine the learned man's acquiring such
knowledge of the young men that they are forever in his power, for their own
good and the love of God. In the end, at his command, the sacred scrolls are
unraveled. The students and their master are wound up in them, wholly committed to the sacred text.

Writing about *Tzaddik* in *Dance and Dancers* magazine, the English critic
John Percival said: "This is an unusual theme for dancing, but it works, thanks
to the striking imagery Feld has discovered for its expression. The movement
is often hectic, small in scale and agitated. The impression is not of calm academic learning but an intense desire to convey beliefs deeply held . . . The
performance by Feld as the teacher is intense and impassioned."

TZIGANE

*Music by Maurice Ravel. Choreography by George Balanchine. Costumes
by Joe Eula. Lighting by Ronald Bates. Solo violin: Lamar Alsop. Con-*

ducted by Robert Irving. First presented by the New York City Ballet at the Hommage à Ravel at the New York State Theatre, Lincoln Center, May 29, 1975, with Suzanne Farrell and Peter Martins as principals.

The tziganes were Hungarian Gypsies who lived near Vienna. Haydn and Schubert, who summered nearby, both used elements of their music. Liszt, who was born in their midst, wrote that the tziganes played "as if suddenly given the power to express their pleasure, they flew to their violins and cymbals and began playing in a fury of excitement."

Ravel's music, for violin and piano originally (1924), was composed for the Hungarian violin virtuoso Yelly d'Aranyi. It was later orchestrated.

The ballet we made for our Hommage à Ravel to this exciting music tried to catch its atmosphere and dynamism. The first part is a solo for the ballet's heroine to the accompaniment of a long, pleading solo by the violin. A boy joins her. He and a small *corps de ballet* of eight dancers then gather for a cumulative dance of joy and exultation to the driving force of the music.

UNDERTOW

Ballet in one act with prologue and epilogue. Choreography by Antony Tudor. Music by William Schuman. Libretto by Antony Tudor, after a suggestion by John van Druten. Scenery and costumes by Raymond Breinin. First presented by Ballet Theatre at the Metropolitan Opera House, New York, April 10, 1945, with a cast headed by Hugh Laing as the Transgressor, Alicia Alonso as Ate, Diana Adams as Cybele, Nana Gollner as Medusa, Shirley Eckl as Volupia, Patricia Barker as Aganippe, and Lucia Chase as Polyhymnia.

Modern ballets are continually enlarging the subject matter of the dance. It might seem strange to us now, but not until 1936—when Antony Tudor produced *Lilac Garden*—did we ever see on the ballet stage people, who looked and acted somewhat like ourselves, in a dramatic ballet. The women in *Lilac Garden* wore long party dresses, not romantic *tutus;* the men were anxious lovers, not mechanical cavaliers. And the characters in the ballet were caught up in a dramatic situation that was dominated by their inner feelings.

Undertow represents another effort to extend the dramatic dance. It attempts to show us why a young man, called the transgressor, commits murder. It shows us where he was born, the people he grew up with, and the people who influenced his life. All the characters in the ballet, except the hero, have names derived from mythology. They are thus not particular personalities, but universal characters recognizable in the life of every man. The time is the present.

PROLOGUE: BIRTH AND INFANCY The light is dim. We make out Cybele, great mother of gods, in labor. She gives birth to a son, who creeps out from between her limbs and cries. The mother is revolted by the sight of her son and the agony she has suffered. She abandons him and seeks a lover—Pollux, the immortal youth who is born anew each day. Her son instinctively despises his mother and nurtures his grief. Even as a child, the transgressor discovers in the world no love.

THE CITY: ADOLESCENCE AND MANHOOD   The scene is a street in the slums of a huge city. We sense immediately the irony of the splendid statues that dominate the nearby square: great winged horses fly away from a place the inhabitants can never leave. Their life is so miserable that they cannot entertain the notion of accustoming themselves to anything else. A woman, made up hideously, stands pouting, waiting for someone to notice her. She is Volupia, here a bedraggled personification of sensual pleasure.

The transgressor, now a youth, enters with a pretty young girl. Her name is Aganippe and she is innocent inspiration. They appear to be having a good time together until the boy notices the streetwalker. He is fascinated by her and observes her with open curiosity. His girl abandons him. Volupia looks at the boy contemptuously and smartens up for a man who now struts onto the scene. He goes directly to her and follows, as she knowingly leads the way.

A rowdy bunch of boys race into the street. What seems to be playfulness on their part is genuinely mean and cruel. They are aware of nothing else in the world but the nuisance they may cause. The hero observes them. On the surface he has no reaction; underneath we suspect that he despises his life and is compelled to watch these people only because he seeks an explanation of their grossness.

Volupia, her first mission over, comes back looking for another man. An old man makes furtive advances toward her. He is so timid that the woman turns on him and ridicules him. He leaves the scene.

The youth's companion, Aganippe, comes back into the street. She is accompanied by another girl, Nemesis, with whom she is playing a private game. The man who has just recently finished his rendezvous with Volupia is attracted by Aganippe's beauty and innocence. He tries to strike up a conversation with her. The transgressor turns on him in a rage, orders him to leave the girl alone, and chases him off.

Polyhymnia, the muse of sacred music, enters as an overcheerful, pious busybody who is deluded into thinking she can change the lives of the people in this slum with the right word. She is recruiting an audience for a prayer meeting and invites all the passers-by to come. Several people join her: among them, Pollux, still the handsome youth, who is now courting the modest Pudicitia, and Ate, the hideous creature who would lead all men into evil. Ate's body is demure and innocent, her face and gestures grotesquely obscene. She accompanies the religious woman only out of malice and soon leaves.

Ate approaches the transgressor, but he is immune to her invitations and she seeks the company of Aganippe's discouraged admirer. In vivid contrast to this sordid couple, a bride and groom, Hymen and Hera, enter and—in a gay and tender dance—suggest to the young hero the true power of love. The transgressor watches them enviously, then disbelieves in their happiness to conceal his own misery.

Three lewd drunken women cavort about the scene noisily, braying and bawling Polyhymnia's call to prayer. Ate comes back to seek more mischief with the gang of dead-end kids. The transgressor and Aganippe watch her. She runs off with the gang, and the two innocents look at the ground in disgust. When Ate re-enters, this time alone, the youth goes directly to her and accosts her. He puts his hands around her neck and threatens to choke her to death. Aganippe flees. The transgressor proceeds to kill Ate, but stops, frightened, when the girl Nemesis comes in, guiding home one of the besotted women. Ate takes advantage of the youth's hesitation to elude him.

Still another kind of woman comes on the scene to disturb the hero. Medusa, true to her name, seems to be attractive, but her beauty is empowered to turn men to stone. She is so different, and yet so like the streetwalker and Ate, that the transgressor watches her with interest. She tries to take up with Pollux, but this youth has sense enough to repulse her. Medusa looks toward the transgressor: she must have someone. He is about to join her, when Polyhymnia begins to lead a revival meeting in the middle of the street. The youth participates in the meeting, hoping to escape. Medusa perceives this ruse and sends Polyhymnia and her crowd packing.

Now the transgressor is alone with a woman for the first time in his life. He is tense, expectant. The woman appears to control the youth as he responds to her advances. But gradually his true feelings become plain and we see that in reality he has control of the woman. Finally he can no longer conceal the hatred he has felt for women all his life. He becomes violent, and Medusa is afraid. The transgressor laughs. It is too late. He throws her to the ground, embraces her as she at first desired, and in the act, seizes her throat and chokes her viciously to death. The full orchestra is unleashed in a thundering, violent crescendo. The scene blacks out.

EPILOGUE: GUILT The hero is alone on the scene. In the back, the misty panorama of the city and the winged horses of the square gradually rise into the sky, as if the very scene of the crime would flee from the criminal. The transgressor moves as if recovering from a hideous nightmare, the dream that has been his life. Yet in remembering the end of the dream, he sees that he has destroyed his life. He wonders what else he could have done, what other ending such a dream could have had. He finds no answer. But perhaps no one knows what he has done! Perhaps he can escape!

Curious people come into the street to watch him. He ignores them. Surely, in every way, he is better than they. Then Aganippe comes in, playing with a balloon. She stops and stares at him. The transgressor recalls their early friendship, smiles at her, and walks toward her. But the girl knows. She points at him, and everyone watches as her forgotten balloon rises in the sky. His guilt reaffirmed by the one person in the world he respects, the hero walks away to meet his end.

UNFINISHED SYMPHONY

Music by Franz Schubert. Choreography by Peter Van Dyk. Costumes by Kalinowski. Lighting by Nananne Porcher. First presented in Paris, 1958. First presented in the United States by American Ballet Theatre at the New York State Theatre, July 1971, with Cynthia Gregory and Michael Denard.

A dance ballet to Schubert's great *Unfinished Symphony*, the choreographer has created here a dance for two persons. They are lovers but there is a sense of experience and apparent detached civilization in their approach to each other. There is no radical discontent but there is a continuing sense of potential drama about their relationship.

Writing in *Cue* magazine, the critic Greer Johnson wrote of the ballet: ". . . This is a full-bodied if serenely understated hymn to two mature lovers so responsive to one another that touch and gesture are transformed into literally metaphysical poetry. The work is quiet; it enfolds you; it flows and caresses to make its unhurried, knowingly sensual point."

Deborah Jowitt, writing of *Unfinished Symphony* in the *Village Voice*, found the ballet "a curiously hypnotic duet performed by Cynthia Gregory and Michael Denard. They're both in blue-gray, and the lighting creates a blue ambience, and they move quite slowly with a smooth, barely inflected dynamic. Everything they do looks thoughtful and deliberate; even the more abandoned poses are carefully charted. They might even be sleepwalkers. Once they look sharply at each other and then at one corner of the stage, and the contrast is startling. . . . The calm heroism of some of the poses at times suggests a dream battle in which they are both engaged—sometimes as colleagues, sometimes as antagonists. Both Gregory and Denard sustain the gliding, weightless choreography beautifully, and the Schubert music provides the plangent tension that keeps the somnambulism from being soporific."

UNION JACK

Music by Hershy Kay, adapted from traditional British music. Choreography by George Balanchine. Scenery and costumes by Rouben Ter-Arutunian. Lighting by Ronald Bates. Conducted by Robert Irving. First presented by the New York City Ballet at the New York State Theatre, Lincoln Center, New York, May 12, 1976, with Jacques d'Amboise, Helgi Tomasson, Sara

Leland, Peter Martins, Kay Mazzo, Karin von Aroldingen, Suzanne Farrell, Patricia McBride, and Jean-Pierre Bonnefous as principals.

It is no secret that I love England. Ever since I first went there, in the 1920s, soon after I left Russia and joined Diaghilev's great Ballets Russes, I liked London best of all the cities we visited. After Diaghilev died and I wanted to find the best place to make ballets, England was where I should have liked to remain. The immigration laws did not then permit such a step and when later Lincoln Kirstein came to see me and made it possible for me to come to America, I seized the independent alternative. I was lucky. Ever since, however, I have gone back to Britain whenever I could, and recall with affection the New York City Ballet's visits to London and Edinburgh and other cities. *Scotch Symphony* grew out of one of these visits and I shall never forget the long engagement the New York City Ballet had at Covent Garden in 1950. It was the longest period up to that time that we had had to dance on any one stage, and when we came back to the City Center the autumn of that year, everyone knew, I believe, that there was no stopping the objectives Lincoln Kirstein and I had set out to accomplish. So it is not only that I love Britain; we owe it a lot. When it was a question of what we as a ballet company should do to celebrate the American bicentennial, for me as for Lincoln Kirstein it was no question: we should celebrate as we could the English and what they have given us. We were helped in this ambition by many friends, from the composer Hershy Kay, our magnificent dancers, and the designer Rouben Ter-Arutunian, to our supporters, like Jacques d'Amboise's wonderful friends, the Leslie R. Samuelses. Making the ballet, for this time and place, was a pleasure.

As Lincoln Kirstein recalls, Americans and others in London at 11 A.M. precisely every morning may observe at Buckingham Palace the changing of the guard, a ritual of care that has its equivalent in Scotland and throughout the United Kingdom. It is a question of order and protection, perhaps only a symbol in these days of potential higher threats no guards could control, but for many of us it is the ultimate civilized gesture, as it has always been. My ballet is meant as a tribute to all that represents.

Our ballet is a three-part salute that acknowledges those ritual aspects of Britain as alive today in military ceremony and theatrical vitality as they have been for the past two centuries. It utilizes folk, military, naval, and music-hall themes for action as well as music. The music is composed by Hershy Kay on themes and variations drawn from the following sources, which by name and association give the best idea of associated action:

Part I: *Scottish Guards.* A procession of dancers to the music of "Keel Row," "Ye Banks and Braes o'Doon," "Caledonian Hunt's Delight," "A Hundred Pipers," "Dance wi' My Daddy," Regimental Tattoos: "Amazing Grace."

Part II: *Costermonger pas de deux* (Pearly King and Queen), a dance for the hero and heroine of the annual Cockney celebration for those born within the sound of the bells of St. Mary le Bow in the City of London, accompanied by: music-hall songs of London, 1890–1914, and "The Sunshine of Your Smile," "The Night the Floor Fell In," "Our Lodger's Such a Nice Young Man," "Following in Father's Footsteps," and "A Tavern in the Town."

Part III: *Horn Pipe,* with music based on "Rule, Britannia."

LES VAINQUEURS

Ceremony in five tableaux based on an idea of Richard Wagner's. Choreography by Maurice Béjart. Decor and costumes by Yahnele Toumelin. Lighting by Serge Apruzzese. First presented by the Ballet of the Twentieth Century, December 10, 1969, at the Théâtre de la Monnaie, Brussels. First presented in the United States by the same ensemble at the Brooklyn Academy of Music, New York, January 30, 1971.

Few persons are aware of the importance of Buddhism in the life and work of Richard Wagner. The choreographer of this ballet about love and renunciation, Maurice Béjart, has said: "It is curious to observe the little importance that biographers of Richard Wagner place both on his discovery of Buddhism and the influence that Buddhism had on his life and work beginning in 1855. Yet it is only in full awareness of this development that his two greatest works *Tristan* and *Parsifal* can be musically and intellectually understood. The theory of the leitmotif carried to its logical conclusion reflects the psychological concept of the states of consciousness of Buddhism and their constant mutations.

"It is interesting to note, too, that many scholars have found great similarities between the Celtic cosmogony and myths and the Indo-Tibetan Buddhist. And the two works of Richard Wagner, *Tristan* and *Parsifal,* in which Buddhist influence is strongly present, are in fact based on Celtic lore.

"'*Parsifal* is a Buddhist scion transplanted to a Christian soil and climate, or, even more exactly, an attempt to correlate and fuse Buddhism and Christianity, but then the word "attempt" does not sit well on Wagner, so let us say, rather, an aim fairly well accomplished, for the duality of the religious sources does not bother the spectator and has not much concerned the critics.' (G. Leprince: *The Presence of Wagner*)

"If *Les Vainqueurs* has not been published, the reason could very well be *Tristan.* It is hard to bring forth two great works at one time: one will always end up swallowing the other: the night of *Tristan* has darkened the light of *Les Vainqueurs.* And if no sketch has been found of a subject on which he worked for so long a time, it is simply that the passion of Isolde absorbed the musical material of the love of Ananda for the pure Savitri.

"What is the meaning of this 'ceremony'? The dance is a rite. A ballet which descends to the roots of its origins is always a ceremony. Every work of art has multiple meanings. This is more so the case in a dance work where the idea transcends the word and the limits of the word, for dance belongs wholly and integrally to the world of form. Consequently what the public discovers in it is a reflection of its own thought.

"If people see nothing but a magic universe of shapes and colors, they are pretty nearly right. Whether they read into it a wondrous fairy tale, a romantic and exotic love story, the psychoanalytic version of the Tristan myth, or the initiation voyage toward illumination, will depend upon their own bent of mind. Some, to be sure, will see the work as a sacrilege, others, I hope, as an act of love, a love which for Wagner transcends human love, as 'it is the road which leads to elimination of the individuality, abjuration of the urge to live, achievement of the peace of Nirvana.' It is this cosmic love that makes Isolde declare at the end of the work:

In the mass of waves
of this sea of delights
in the thunder, the clamor and the din
waves of perfume
breathing into ALL
by the breath of the world,
to sink, to drown, to lose consciousness,
joy supreme."

Béjart uses as a signature for the ballet verses from the Buddhist Mantra:

"Thou, the Victor, the Delivered, Deliver!
Arrived upon the other shore,
Cause the other there also to arrive."

The music of the ballet, as so often in the work of this choreographer, alternates in contrast, the one here between Wagner's score from *Tristan und Isolde* and Indo-Tibetan ragas.

A dramatic Buddha figure at the beginning of the ballet turns into a Tristan figure. He finds his love, there is a voyage, reminiscent of the action of the opera. The action then shifts to the contemporary, and there is a dance celebration by performers in jeans. Everything appears to be timeless.

Maurice Béjart has spoken of the libretto inspired by the life of Buddha that Wagner was writing at the same time he was working on *Tristan*. To a reporter for *The New Yorker*, Béjart said: "The libretto—which is also called *Les Vainqueurs*—exists, but nobody has ever discovered a note of the music. So I made a theory from my own experience as a choreographer. If you work on two ideas simultaneously and produce just one of them, the dominant work absorbs the ideas you prepared for the other one. I think that some of the music Wagner wrote for *Les Vainqueurs* ended up in *Tristan*, so I combined the two works. The final words of Isolde, when she says, 'I sought to dissolve myself in the ocean of life,' are very like a well-known Buddhist prayer."

VALENTINE

Music by Jacob Druckman. Choreography by Gerald Arpino. Lighting by Jennifer Tipton. Contrabass: Alvin Brehm. First presented by the City Center Joffrey Ballet at the City Center, New York, March 10, 1971, with Rebecca Wright and Christian Holder.

Valentine is a dance for a girl and a boy accompanied by a double bass. The composer Jacob Druckman has said of the music for *Valentine:* "The work is one of the most difficult ever written for the contrabass and demands that the player attack the instrument with bow, tympany stick, both hands alternating percussive tapping on the body of the instrument with pizzicato harmonics, while the voice sustains tones, sings counterpoints, and punctuates accents. All of this necessitates the player's assaulting the instrument with an almost de Sade-like concentration (hence the title)."

That is the way of the dance, too, for the dancers are dressed and behave like competing boxers in the ring. They shadowbox, spar, stand off, get together, and react to the ferocity of the score.

LA VALSE

Ballet in two parts. Music by Maurice Ravel. Choreography by George Bal-anchine. Costumes by Karinska. Lighting by Jean Rosenthal. First presented by the New York City Ballet at the City Center, New York, February 20, 1951, with Tanaquil LeClercq, Nicholas Magallanes, and Francisco Moncion in the principal roles.

Ravel called his composition *La Valse* a "choreographic poem." It was composed to be danced, "a sort of apotheosis of the Viennese waltz . . . the mad whirl of some fantastic and fateful carrousel." The ballet follows in outline the theatrical scheme Ravel imagined for his music: "At first the scene is dimmed by a kind of swirling mist, through which one discerns, vaguely and intermittently, the waltzing couples. Little by little the vapors disperse, the illumination grows brighter, revealing an immense ballroom filled with dancers . . ." Prior to this scene, the ballet makes use of another composition of Ravel's, *Valses Nobles et Sentimentales,* a group of eight short waltzes that introduces the ballroom scene and its principal dancers.

PART ONE: VALSES NOBLES ET SENTIMENTALES The first waltz serves as the overture. Percussion instruments underline the liveliness of the animated waltz rhythm. The curtain rises, and the second waltz begins.

Three girls stand before a blue net curtain in formal dress. They hold their white-gloved hands in a light, mannered pose. The music is soft and beguiling. The girls bow low and begin to dance, at first somewhat wistfully, then coyly, but always their movements are as formal as their long white gloves, which seem to accent every one of their gestures. Underneath their slate-colored costumes their full skirts are brilliant red, and as they separate and move more freely, the whirling dresses color their dance. Far behind the blue net curtain, in the obscure distance, hangs a cluster of dimly lighted chandeliers. The girls exit modestly, their white-gloved arms before their faces.

A handsome couple, holding hands, dance out gaily to the tinkling tune of the third waltz. Their lighthearted duet is marked by quick, sprightly steps. They dance together closely and separate only as they exit at opposite sides of the stage.

The next waltz is more open in its melody, and to its rapid rhythms another couple dance boldly and freely. They run past each other in high, joyful leaps. The fifth waltz begins with subdued, romantic contrast. The girl who dances it moves gracefully and deliberately. Her partner kisses her hand and kneels. The music becomes blithe, and the ballerina dances before the boy with close, lighthearted steps. The boy marvels at her beauty and reaches out to claim her. This girl dances alone to the sixth waltz, after which her partner rejoins her.

As this couple exit toward the right, they are met by two girls. The couple pause, then the ballerina leaves the stage and a third girl takes her place. These are the same three girls who danced the first waltz. The seventh waltz begins. They claim the boy, covering him with their arms. One girl breaks away to dance, then another. The boy joins them, lifts them high as the music races its tempestuous theme. The four stand together, and one of the girls falls back in the boy's arms. He kneels as the girls run off. The music hesitates in its momentum, and the girls and boys of the earlier waltzes rush in and out, over and about him. He rises, turns swiftly, and the three girls confront him. He dances with them again as the waltz theme returns, then leaps off into the wings.

The stage is empty as the sinuous, final waltz commences. A girl in white emerges. She steps forward, opening her arms slowly; her body recoils slightly as she moves forward. She walks over to the right; her arms mime the flow of the expectant music. A boy enters at the back. They do not see each other. They exchange positions, then each bends backward and recognizes the other. They approach, touch hands warily, and with formal, sophisticated movements of her arms, the ballerina gives her partner her hand. They separate, pass, and come together back-to-back in the center of the stage, where they turn together, their arms entwined. Now they separate again and repeat their introduction. The boy lifts the ballerina slowly; her white dress flows with the final measures of the waltz. He lifts her off into the wings.

PART TWO: LA VALSE   The lights dim, the blue net curtain is raised, the distant chandeliers brighten, the music to *La Valse* begins. The music throbs low and mysteriously; light catch-phrases from a waltz hover over a deep, foreboding background of sound. A spotlight picks up a boy, who runs onto the stage in search of a girl he cannot find. He looks for her helplessly in the dark ballroom. Another boy enters with his dancing partner. They appear to be lost. Suddenly, on the opposite side of the stage, the spotlight shines on three girls, whose white-gloved arms are held up before their faces like masks. The boy chooses one of the girls and starts to dance with her, but the girl falls back strangely in his arms as they move in a circle. They exit. Another couple moves across the scene hurriedly, and three girls and three boys run on and off seeking their partners. All the dancers seem to be waiting for the waltz to emerge through the weird music that holds it in abeyance. The waltz rhythm pulsates; a sparkling rush of sound from the harp heralds its full waltz melody. The ballroom brightens; eight couples fill the stage.

They dance joyously in a large circle; the color of the girls' skirts contrasts vividly with the black walls of the room. As the couples swirl past, we see that the chandeliers are hung with crepe. The black cloth hangs low into the room. The couples change partners in the center of the circle and continue their tempestuous dance. A loud fanfare in rapid waltz rhythm announces the arrival of two new groups of dancers, who cross the stage diagonally as the others stand back. Two couples dance before the group, then the boys gather in the center of the circle, where they choose partners. Now there are two girls for each boy.

The ballerina of the fifth waltz enters with her partner, and the fierce, pounding waltz abates to a soft, mellifluous volume and tempo as they dance softly. The boy exits; the ballerina dances with a group of girls as the couples stand and watch. The cymbals clash, the momentum increases, and the ballerina in white enters. She leaps toward the front, all the dancers gathering on each side of the stage to form wide, opening doors of movement to heighten the speed of her dazzling entry. The dancers move toward the center of the room, where one of the girls is lifted high above them all; the group circles about her. In back, the black crepe swirls as the dancers pass.

The ballerina in white dances happily with her partner; the waltz is quiet again. The couples stand aside and converse and do not notice them. Their dance is slow at first; the ballerina's movements are retarded and she seeks to move more freely as the waltz attempts to resume its previous intensity. But the music hesitates overlong; it unwinds with a snap of sound like a spring that has been wound up too tightly. Disintegrating patterns of waltz melody and tempo struggle helplessly against the orchestra. The once brilliant theme sounds with the pathetic intensity of a hurdy-gurdy. The girl turns with despairing speed to her partner's arms. A staccato trumpet heralds a pause; the weird, warning first bars of *La Valse* cause all to stand aside. They all look toward the back.

A figure in black emerges beneath the funereal chandeliers. His head is bowed as he walks forward slowly. About his neck hangs a heavy black medal on a black chain. The girls kneel before him; their partners turn their faces away. The ballerina in white turns away in terror. The black specter is followed by a page, who holds in his arms a mirror and a black gown. The music whirls frantically in anticipation.

The girl in white staggers toward the man unwillingly, as if hypnotized by his presence; she goes to him recognizing her own fears of his fatal attraction. He presents her with a splendid necklace and holds the mirror before her. He waits anxiously for her reaction. The girl turns away in horror: the mirror is cracked black glass. Her horror turns to fascination as the waltz attempts to penetrate the mystery of sound and sight. It races suddenly to a desperate loud statement, falters away again. The man offers the girl a pair of long black gloves. He holds them open, and she slides her arms into them as the music sounds a booming, relentless crescendo. Presented now with a black gown, the girl slips into it delightedly and covers her white costume. The stranger rewards her finally with a black bouquet. He kisses her hand, takes her about the waist, and begins to turn her about the room.

The crescendo has now receded, and the waltz attempts again to come to life. The girl is moved faster and faster by her partner as the waltz resumes its momentum. She throws down her bouquet and begins to fall limp in his arms. He turns her faster; she cannot break away. The waltz reaches the peak of driving, irrevocable rhythm; crashes of its beauty tear the air. The girl falls back, then rises to the close embrace of the grotesque black figure. She dies. The specter disappears. Her lover drags her off.

The couples return to their dancing, now rushing about the cold, dark ballroom in frantic pursuit of the pleasure the music will no longer allow them. The exhausted waltz is now heard only in a climactic struggle of instruments. The boy enters in the back, carrying the dead girl in his arms. The boys lift her away from him to their shoulders. Her head falls back, her arms hang loose. Her lover attempts to embrace her, but she is lifted high above him. All of the dancers close in. The girl's body is turned around and around. About the circling center, the group races in a fateful, fantastic carrousel.

Elena Bivona, in an essay on Patricia McBride in *Ballet Review* (Vol. 3, No. 3), wrote of a performance of *La Valse:* "From a ballet of delicate suggestion she has extracted religious horrors without leaving a smudge on the delicate framework. In one performance, her first waltz had marvelously slow-sharp inflections of arm and hand; the gestures clawed and sank at the same time, brittlely artificial and softly demanding. As Bruhn can in *Giselle*'s last act, she interfused tension with luxuriance to make a dream-ridden girl innocent of her own evil but evil nonetheless. And against the articulate arms she countered a tense neck, the tight muscles keeping her head alert, watching without object, waiting half-aware. Another performance made the same waltz the world of a woman a thousand years old in corruption, her movements still and stretching, her vitality at a controlled scream-pitch ready to devour new adventures, and there are obviously none left but the destruction she finally conjures up, to her astonishment, fear, and joy. On this night, the girl was no innocent; she was the hostess, her white dress an obscenity of wit, her physical youth a Dorian Gray monstrosity, her corruption radiating as if it were beauty, and she is so fascinating she must feed on the fascination she draws to herself. Vampira. A monster—or two monsters, three, a slightly different one each time to find out who this death-lover in her, in Balanchine, in us, is.

"She met Death once with a hypnotized, terrified blankness, tight neck muscles hardened to a vise for her staring face, and her body a Bunraku doll's manipulated by a puppet master: fluent in her upper body, simple and a little jerky from the waist down. She could abandon that possibility another night to make her softness an all-knowing perverted eroticism, her presence so strong Death himself makes no impact until the moment, when he seizes her for their first dance, that his strength overpowers hers; and that, perhaps only because she and Death are a single identity and the recognition itself is what claims her, is what lets loose the chaos of the ballet's finale. *La Valse* that night became a circle of evil seeking its own face for which Death holding his mirror was the perfect metaphor."*

VARIATIONS

Music by Igor Stravinsky. Choreography by George Balanchine. Lighting by Ronald Bates. First presented by the New York City Ballet at the New York State Theatre, March 31, 1966, with Karin von Aroldingen, Karen Batizi, Diane Bradshaw, Marjorie Breler, Elaine Comsudi, Rosemary Dunleavy, Susan Hendl, Ruth Ann King, Jennifer Nairn-Smith, Delia Peters, Donna Sackett, Lynne Stetson, Robert Maiorano, Paul Meija, Frank Ohman, John Prinz, David Richardson, Michael Steele, and Suzanne Farrell.

Stravinsky composed his *Variations for Orchestra* dedicated to the memory of Aldous Huxley in 1963–64. Soon afterwards I was able to see the score. I decided that as soon as possible I would like to do a ballet to the music. What kind of ballet it was to be, however, was not then clear. Stravinsky's work is concise, lasting only four minutes, forty-five seconds, which is not in the theatre a sufficient time to develop and hold the attention, not to mention the ears, of the audience. Stravinsky's music also demands to be heard not just once, but many times. I accordingly decided to have the music played three times for a set of three dances.

The curtain rises and twelve girls are seen on the stage. There is no setting. Stravinsky's piece was composed, he tells us, on a pitch series, a succession of

* Reprinted by permission of *Ballet Review,* Marcel Dekker, publisher.

twelve notes that came to his mind as a melody and was then seen as material for variations. As the music begins, the girls face the audience in two groups of six. There is a variation for twelve violins in the orchestra which is taken up in a different way by mixed strings, and later by twelve woodwinds. The dancers reflect these changes in the orchestra in different groupings and separations, each of the twelve dancing a little differently from the others. As the first part ends, the original two groups of six have become three groups of four. Stravinsky has said in a program note: "The halves . . . are unities as well as fragments, and are therefore divisible in turn, and invertible, reversible, mirror-invertible, mirror reversible."

The second playing of the music is danced by six boys, who stand at the beginning in two rows of three. They dance in various combinations, one of them at a certain point being singled out by the other five.

For the third playing, a girl dances on stage quickly. In yet another version of the same subject, she reflects the conciseness of Stravinsky's score.

VARIATIONS FOR FOUR

Music by Marguerite Keogh. Idea and choreography by Anton Dolin. Costumes by Tom Lingwood. First presented by Festival Ballet at Royal Festival Hall, London, September 1957. First presented in the United States by American Ballet Theatre at the Metropolitan Opera House, New York, September 25, 1958.

Many ballet-goers are familiar with Anton Dolin's re-creation of the great nineteenth-century ballet *Pas de Quatre*, in which the four leading ballerinas of the day appeared together for a single performance of display and polite competition. Dolin, renowned as a *danseur* since his debut with Diaghilev's Ballets Russes, conceived the idea of staging a similar showpiece for four outstanding male soloists. The result is a popular work both here and abroad, where it has been performed by gifted *premiers danseurs*.

The bright music that raises the curtain heralds a festive occasion. The four dancers enter to a stately theme, pose and dance together briefly, then separate to perform independently their special skills in a series of variations. These vary in tempo and energy, building to a brilliant display of speed and virtuosity for all four. There is also a sustained *adagio* for one of the soloists, to remind us of the *danseur*'s romantic role. All four participate in a rapid, flourishing finale.

NOTES After its revival by American Ballet Theatre at the New York State Theatre, July 12, 1972, Clive Barnes wrote in the New York *Times:*
"Let me confess to a prejudice. I love Anton Dolin's *Variations for Four*. In classic ballet women have so much of it their own way. For years the male

dancer has stood politely, sometimes sufferingly, behind his ballerina, flexing his muscles and practicing his humility. Dolin was one of the first great male dancers of the century—with Serge Lifar he was one of Diaghilev's last two premier danseurs, and he played a principal role in the development of both British and American ballet—and this pas de quatre is almost a charter of Men's Liberation in ballet. There are just four men dancing; brilliantly, competitively and with no apologies.

"Since the work was first created for London's Festival Ballet, a company Dolin himself formed, it has been in the repertory of many leading companies, including American Ballet Theatre. But on Wednesday night at the New York State Theatre the ballet had its first revival with the company since its original American production in 1958. It was exultantly danced.

"In some ways, rather like the Royal Danish Ballet, the male dancers of Ballet Theatre are more interesting than the women. Undeniably Ballet Theatre has gathered together a most unusual collection of men, and this *Variations for Four* can show some of them off in style. At the first performance it was danced by an immaculate Ted Kivitt, a forceful John Prinz, a gutsy Alexander Filipov and, in the final solo, Ballet Theatre's newest star, the Italian Paolo Bortoluzzi. Mr. Bortoluzzi needs to be careful of his fine Italian hands— he is at times too flamboyant for New York taste—but he is a magnificent dancer with a special pulse and arrogance of his own. He is like an Italian racing car—extravagant, different but powerful."

VARIATIONS POUR UNE PORTE ET UN SOUPIR

Sonority by Pierre Henry. Choreography by George Balanchine. Scenery and costumes by Rouben Ter-Arutunian. Lighting by Ronald Bates. First presented by the New York City Ballet at the New York State Theatre, Lincoln Center, January 17, 1974, with Karin von Aroldingen and John Clifford.

Variations for a Door and a Sigh has an interesting score, or sonority, as the French composer Pierre Henry calls it. I first heard work by the composer when I visited him some years ago in Paris, at the suggestion of Nicolas Nabokov, and decided then that I would like to do a ballet to this piece one day. Henry was the first "traditionally oriented" composer to interest himself in electro-acoustical techniques. This particular piece makes maximum use of the whole gamut of sounds that can be associated with sighs and the opening and closing of doors. I picked out fourteen of the twenty-five variations Henry wrote for the original concert version, and arranged to them a *pas de deux*, a duet for the female door and the male sigh. The ballet begins with a sigh.

It is dark and silent as the curtain rises. A spotlight reveals a male figure all in white responding to the sound of sighs. We hear then the sound of a creaking door and the woman is revealed, also in white, but with a black silken skirt attached to her waist that stretches like a wide train across the whole stage. In its center, like the central support for a tent that has yet to rise, she dances to the door sounds. Her limbs open and close, creaking and slamming, about an invisible hinge. She approaches the man and then he dances again. They continue to alternate dances as a relationship becomes more intense. Her enveloping skirt is agitated and rises and falls in waves of blackness that engulf the stage. She is all cool control, he white heat. He achieves an ultimate sigh as her inundating black skirt enfolds him. He disappears in its folds; she, too, bows beneath it.

A number of persons have called *Variations* "the male liberation ballet." I prefer to think of it as an every-man-for-himself ballet. Maybe it shows, in a way, man's weakness—how he strives to get involved but, once there, doesn't know how to get out.

In 1965, in Brussels, Maurice Béjart arranged his own cycle of Pierre Henry's variations for seven dancers in homage to the visual talent of the artist Arman: "Seven dancers enter the stage to create a ballet in which choreography has no place." The dancers improvised their movement according to suggestions from the sonorous structure; each time sequence was propelled by the dancers themselves.

In 1972, in Glasgow for the Scottish Theatre Ballet, Peter Darrell staged his ballet *Variations for a Door and a Sigh*. A program note stated that the work "explores the realms of sexual behavior and the conflicts of personal commitment." Peter Darrell also alluded to a quotation from Tolstoy as the starting point for his ballet: "Man survives earthquakes, epidemics, terrible illnesses and every kind of spiritual suffering, but always the most poignant tragedy was, is and ever will be the tragedy of the bedroom."

VESTRIS

Music by Genaidi Banschikov. Choreography by Leonid Jacobson. First presented at the International Ballet Competition, Moscow, June 1969, with Mikhail Baryshnikov. First presented in the United States by American Ballet Theatre at the Kennedy Center of the Performing Arts, Washington, May 20, 1975, with Baryshnikov. Costume by Marcos Paredes. Conductor: David Gilbert.

One of the greatest dancers of all time, Auguste Vestris appeared to be the natural subject for a ballet in which a young dancer might show, in a very short time, the complete range and versatility of his gifts, in dance and mime. The Soviet choreographer Leonid Jacobson accordingly responded to the young dancer Mikhail Baryshnikov and made for him a seven-minute display piece that sums up a forgotten but illustrious dancer in a forgotten time.

Vestris was born in Paris in 1760 and died there eighty-two years later. Famed for his elevation, pirouettes, and *batterie*, Vestris's performances enthralled Europe for many years, from his debut at age twelve until his retirement at fifty-six. Parliament recessed to watch him and his father, another virtuoso, in 1781. Vestris danced the first performances of great ballets by Noverre and later taught pupils who were to govern ballet in Europe: Didelot, Perrot, Auguste Bournonville, and Marie Taglioni. There are many lithographs and prints of Vestris in performance of many roles, all of which were studied by Jacobson and Baryshnikov as the ballet was being made.

The action is divided into seven brief sections and the basic idea is not to re-create Vestris historically so much as to give a notion of his time as another dancer displays a similar range of versatility. The seven parts are: "An Old Man Dancing a Minuet," "The Coquette Dance," "The Preacher-Prophet," "Classical Dance Variations," "Prayer," "Laughter," and "Dying Man."

In formal ballet dress fashioned after the eighteenth century, with white wig, white jacket and tights, the star dancer acts his age, relives youth and shows what he is made of.

Vestris was performed at Wolf Trap, near Washington, in 1976, filmed for television, and broadcast first by WNET, New York, on December 6, 1976.

Reviewing the ballet in the New York *Times,* the critic Clive Barnes said "the dance itself is a perfect joy—a cameo impression of a dancer, of a style, of a period and of a man. Within its brief compass it manages to convey a whole sheaf of dramatic and choreographic messages."

In the book *Baryshnikov at Work,* the dancer recalls the genesis of the ballet, which has been recorded there in marvelous pictures by Martha Swope.

VIOLIN CONCERTO

Music by Igor Stravinsky. Choreography by George Balanchine. First presented by the New York City Ballet at the Stravinsky Festival, at the New York State Theatre, Lincoln Center, June 18, 1972, with Karin von Aroldingen, Kay Mazzo, Peter Martins, and Jean-Pierre Bonnefous in the leading roles. Lighting by Ronald Bates. Conducted by Robert Irving. Violin soloist: Joseph Silverstein.

Stravinsky has written (see NOTES below) that he did not like the standard violin concertos. I myself have always preferred Stravinsky's. Some years ago, when the Original Ballet Russe happily gave me the opportunity, I made a ballet to this violin concerto of his. It was called *Balustrade,* largely after splendid scenery by the great artist Pavel Tchelitchew, who painted a décor that was dominated by a white balustrade in perspective in the background. *Balustrade* was first danced at the Fifty-first Street Theatre, New York, January 22, 1941, with Tamara Toumanova, Roman Jasinski, and Paul Petroff in the leading roles. I do not remember this ballet; but not, alas! What I did then was for *then*, and what I wanted to do to this same music for our Stravinsky Festival at the New York City Ballet represented more than thirty years' difference. The dancers were different and I liked the music even more.

The score is in four movements, the middle part being a center or core of two "Arias" enclosed by introductory Toccata and a final Capriccio.

And so is the ballet in four movements, the center being arranged as two *pas de deux* for different couples to accompany the Arias. The introductory Toccata introduces the principal dancers with a small *corps de ballet*. All four of the soloists participate in the Capriccio finale. The best guide to the character of these dances is a number of hearings of the music.

NOTES   In the book *Dialogues and a Diary*, Stravinsky recalled that "The *Violin Concerto* was not inspired by or modeled on any example. I do not like the standard violin concertos—not Mozart's, Beethoven's, Mendelssohn's or Brahms's. To my mind, the only masterpiece in the field is Schoenberg's, and that was written several years after mine. The titles of my movements, Toccata, Aria, Capriccio, suggest Bach, however, and so to some extent, does the musical substance. My favorite Bach solo concerto is the one for two violins, as the duet with a violin from the orchestra in the last movement of my concerto must show. But the *Violin Concerto* contains other duet combinations, too, and the texture of the music is more often chamber music in style than orchestral. I did not write a cadenza for the reason that I was not interested in violin virtuosity. Virtuosity for its own sake plays little part in my concerto, and the technical difficulties of the piece are, I think, relatively tame.

"The ballet *Balustrade* (1940) by George Balanchine and Pavel Tchelitchew, and with the music of my *Violin Concerto*, was one of the most satisfactory visualizations of any of my theatre works. Balanchine worked out the choreography as we played my recording together and I could actually watch him imagine gesture, movement, combination, composition. The result was a dance dialogue in perfect co-ordination with the dialogues of the music. The dancers were few in number, and the whole second Aria was performed—and beautifully performed—as a solo piece, by Toumanova. *Balustrade* was produced by Sol Hurok, that master judge of the *vox populi* (I imagine *Balustrade* must have been one of his few misjudgments in that sense). The set was a very simple white balustrade across the back of the dark stage."

Reviewing *Violin Concerto* in *The Nation*, Nancy Goldner wrote of the dance to the second Aria: "The duet for Kay Mazzo and Peter Martins is amazingly complex and dense, as is most of the ballet. It churns and seems to be a continuous process of knotting and unknotting. In their first phase, she faces him for a second, grabs his waist and slides to the floor, resting on her front haunch while her back leg is tensely stretched. He looks to the right. She looks to the left, her arm partly covering her face. There is discord here, which builds and builds as their sculptured and quickly changing poses become more multi-dimensional. Too, their relationship with the music becomes increasingly independent, until they finally seem to be in total counterpoint, though never in disharmony. Perhaps that is one reason why Mazzo's simple big movement to the one resounding chord in the score is such a shock. Another reason is that nothing is simple between this couple. But as soon as she has made that simple declaration the duet turns convoluted again. She collapses her knees inward and rotates away from Martins, who is grasping her ankles. The choreography is so innovative, intense and rich that detailed analysis of it, and clues as to why it seems to be a profound embodiment of inner turbulence, must await further performances. But first let me describe one luscious detail in it. Martins rolls Mazzo from one foot to another. In this little air voyage, she starts out with one foot pointed and the other flexed. With great deliberation and yet speed, she simultaneously points the flexed foot and flexes the pointed one. We can almost see each dot along the arced paths her feet trace. As the trip ends, she lands on one foot and whips her flexed foot along the floor into a point. This is an exclamation point to a juicy five-second game. Many choreographers have played with flexed feet in classical ballet, but Balanchine's version is now the definitive one."

VIVA VIVALDI!

Music by Antonio Vivaldi. Choreography by Gerald Arpino. First presented by the Robert Joffrey Ballet at the Delacorte Theatre, Central Park, New York, September 10, 1965, with Robert Blankshine, Jon Cristofori, Edwina Dingman, Luis Fuente, Ian Horvath, Margo Sappington, and Trinette Singleton in leading roles.

This lively dance ballet with a Spanish flavor is set to music by Vivaldi (*Violin Concerto in D major, P. 151,* arranged for guitar and orchestra). A display piece for fine dancers, who perform both allegro and adagio roles, there is no story, only the tempo and melody of the score and the expression of the dance accompaniment.

VOLUNTARIES

Music by Francis Poulenc. Choreography by Glen Tetley. Designed by Rouben Ter-Arutunian. Lighting by John B. Read, executed by Gilbert V. Hemsley, Jr. First presented by the Stuttgart Ballet at the Württemberg State Theatre, Stuttgart, December 22, 1973, with Marcia Haydée and Richard Cragun in the leading roles. First presented in the United States by the same ensemble at the Metropolitan Opera House, Lincoln Center, New York, June 4, 1975, with the same principals.

Lawrence Rhodes in *At Midnight*. Photo by Martha Swope.

Lydia Abarca and Derek Williams in *Agon*. Photo by Anthony Crickmay.

Paul Russell in *Le Corsaire*. Photo by Martha Swope.

Trinette Singleton and Dermot Burke in *Astarte*. Photo by Herbert Migdoll.

Starr Danias and Dennis Wayne in *Sacred Grove on Mount Tamalpais*. Photo by Herbert Migdoll.

Paolo Bortoluzzi and Jörg Lanner in *Nijinsky, Clown of God*. Photo by Rosemary Winckley.

Suzanne Farrell in *Nijinsky, Clown of God*. Photo by Rosemary Winckley.

Jorge Donn in *Nijinsky, Clown of God*. Photo by Rosemary Winckley.

Marcia Haydée and Richard Cragun in *Daphnis and Chloë*. Photo by Beverley Gallegos.

Created in memory of John Cranko, the Stuttgart Ballet's founder, *Voluntaries* is a dance tribute and valedictory by Glen Tetley. It was Tetley's first work for the company, of which he was appointed director in the winter of 1974 after Cranko's sudden death in the summer of 1973.

The choreographer's program note for the ballet tells us that, by musical definition, voluntaries are free-ranging organ or trumpet improvisations that are often played before, during, or after religious services. The Latin root of the word also connotes desire or flight. The choreographer says that the ballet is conceived as "a linked series of voluntaries." The music is Poulenc's *Concerto for Organ, Strings, and Percussion;* the soloists in New York were Calvin Hampton, organist, and Howard Van Hyning, timpanist.

The stage action is both a tribute and a dance celebration, a ritual of remembrance and rededication that looks forward rather than back. A stranger to the occasion would know only of the dance event itself and not of its sentimental pretext.

Voluntaries is danced before a painted backdrop of concentrated color and design that suggests liveliness, a kind of microscopic slide depicting continuity and no interruption. The stage action shows Cranko's principal dancers in combinations and permutations of movement that remember. They also look forward to the future!

Writing of the New York premiere, the critic Clive Barnes said in the New York *Times* that *Voluntaries* "is an outstanding amalgam of classic ballet and modern dance and, probably, Mr. Tetley's more purely beautiful and sinuous work to date . . . At the end the cheers for the company and Mr. Tetley engulfed the opera house."

WALK TO THE PARADISE GARDEN

Music by Frederick Delius. Choreography by Frederick Ashton. Setting by William Chappell. First presented by the Royal Ballet at the Royal Opera House, Covent Garden, November 15, 1972, with Merle Park, David Wall, and Derek Rencher.

Frederick Ashton has called this brief ballet a *Liebestod*—or love-death. The music is from Delius' great lyric opera, *A Village Romeo and Juliet,* and it serves as the prelude to the final scene of that work, where the two lovers kill themselves. Similarly, in the ballet, the lovers, after ultimate expressions of joy in each other, discover no other course but suicide to perpetuate the depth of their passion. They meet white-robed Death, submit, and rejoice again.

Writing in *The Times* of London after the premiere, the critic John Percival said that this was "the first big part Ashton has created for Merle Park, and he reveals in her a lyricism and natural warmth her usual bravura roles have hidden. She and David Wall play a pair of lovers, entirely absorbed in each other

. . . What they have to do includes some fantastically difficult things. Not only the familiar Bolshoi . . . tricks, like spinning the girl horizontally through the air and catching her again, but even a moment when she is held upside down high above his head. Yet Ashton sets these virtuoso tricks so smoothly into the dance, and they are so effortlessly done by this couple, that you hardly notice the difficulty, rather the rapture they express. Yet there is about the dance a sense of stolen time, an undertone of feeling that the moment cannot last, and at the end this manifests itself chillingly in the form of a stern angel all in stark white (Derek Rencher), who draws the lovers to him, parts them and allows them to be joined again only in death. Ashton has caught the mood of the Delius music perfectly, although seeing deeper into it than his audience perhaps expected. A handsome setting by William Chappell completes a small but perfectly-formed work."

In his authoritative biography of Frederick Ashton, David Vaughan describes the process of the ballet's creation in detail. He also remarks: "This dance was the most important role that Ashton ever choreographed for Merle Park, and as with so many other dancers he brought out reserves of passion that had been hidden until then."

WALPURGIS NIGHT

Music by Charles Gounod. Choreography by Leonid Lavrovsky. First presented by the Bolshoi Ballet at the Filial Theatre, Moscow, 1941. First presented in the United States by the Bolshoi Ballet at the Metropolitan Opera House, New York, April 23, 1959.

The Walpurgis Night scene in Gounod's opera *Faust* occurs at the beginning of the last act. Here Mephistopheles brings Faust to witness the revels that traditionally take place on the eve of May Day at Brocken, highest point of the Hartz Mountains. There Mephistopheles summons the shades of famous courtesans. The ballet freely depicts the height of the revels.

WATERMILL

Music by Teiji Ito. Choreography by Jerome Robbins. Costumes by Patricia Zipprodt. Lighting by Ronald Bates. Décor by Jerome Robbins in association with David Reppa. First presented by the New York City Ballet at the New York State Theatre, Lincoln Center, February 3, 1972, with Edward Villella, Penny Dudleston, Hermes Conde, Jean-Pierre Frohlich, Bart Cook, Tracy Bennett, Victor Castelli, Deni Lamont, Colleen Neary, and Robert Maiorano in the principal roles. Musicians: Dan Erkkila, Genji Ito, Teiji Ito, Kansuke Kawase, Mara Purl, and Terry White.

The score of *Watermill*, by the contemporary composer Teiji Ito, is radically
different from the music we customarily hear in the ballet theater: it is quiet,
full of pauses (what the composer calls "silent sounds") and stems mainly
from the religious ceremonial and theatrical music of the Orient. It employs
numerous percussion and wind instruments, including the Shakuhachi, a bam-
boo flute used in Japan in the thirteenth century. This flute was played mainly
by Zen Buddhist priests whose compositions for the instrument still survive.
These musical-religious works are usually contemplative evocations of nature
and the seasons. So also is this ballet—a contemplation on a man's life as seen
through the passage of the four seasons. However influenced by the music and
theater of the East, the ballet—its world, people and events—are not to be
taken as Oriental.

Writing of *Watermill*, Jacqueline Maskey in *High Fidelity/Musical America*
aptly described the theme: a ritual of remembering.

"The man recalls: himself as a youth, light and graceful, boneless as a leaping fish; the ritual games that test and harden him; the perfections of love in
which his partner seems woman, earth, moon-goddess; then the devils, irrational phantoms that tear and torment. Peasant figures—sowing, reaping, win-
nowing, gleaning—thread through his recollections. He recognizes, in a ceremony with grain stalks, nature and his oneness with it and, in a bent figure,
the inevitability of old age. As he gazes, boys release curious and buoyant
paper shapes which rise into nothingness as must his own dust, and the curtain
falls.

"*Watermill* is a particular view of human existence, expressed in terms of
the inexorable cycle of the seasons. Man matures and declines; the moon
waxes and wanes; the earth is fruitful, then fallow; snow follows sun."

The six musicians, all in Japanese costume, enter and sit on the right of the
stage. A framed scrim faces us. As the music begins with a plaintive sound, we
discern behind it gradually three high mysterious shapes that we can't quite
make out—they are not trees, for wasp-waisted, they spread out at the base,
too; they are not giants or windmills. They stand in a field filled with mist
under a crescent moon. As the mist lifts a bit, we see that they are high
sheaves of grain, the stalks gathered in tightly at the middle. There is a fence
in the distance, and before we know it, we see there is a man there, too, standing in the field in a long black cloak, his face hidden, a part of the natural
landscape, too. What we have gradually seen here and made out patiently in
the mist is characteristic of the voyage of recollection and discovery that now
begins for this man and for us.

Slowly, slowly, looking up for a moment at the sky, the man comes toward
us. He kneels, rises, leaving his cloak on the ground. He takes off his shoes
then, and his shirt and trousers. Standing now almost naked, he stretches out
his arms as figures bearing multicolored lanterns approach him. They come up
to him closely, their lanterns poised at the end of long wands, as if to illumine
his body fully, then go away. To a chanted song that rises from the music, the

man begins to dance. But not for long. He sits down and youths enter with kites, an umbrella, etc.

A boy runs as men in the background till the fields. The man notices the boy, reaches out his hand to him, but the boy sees another man in the distance and goes to him. Five boys trot across the field, five more, too, these carrying sticks. The man walks among them. They do warlike gymnastics, as if preparing for battle. But the man runs off. He returns as the youths stop and remain motionless.

A woman enters in a long green dress and turban. In the background, a group of young persons arrange a picnic on the grass behind one of the sheaves of grain. The woman puts down a rug on the grass. There is a longer period of waiting. She lets fall her outer garment and her long hair, which she combs slowly. The man watches her some distance away. We have the impression that he is both with her and is remembering her, their contact is so close. She lies down to sleep; so does he. Darkness falls. A boy—the man in his youth?—enters and goes to the woman. He pulls her body to his and she stretches around him; to the light of the moon they embrace closely. They roll and undulate together on the blanket and stop. The picnickers in the back rise and go; the moon keeps on descending.

The man awakens and lifts his arm. The boy on the blanket raises his arm simultaneously. The girl, too, hails the descending moon. The man and the boy rise together; the man goes to the girl as the boy backs out. The man takes the girl's hand, then lies with his head in her lap as, on the right, the boy of the first scene sleeps. The girl gets up, takes her rug, and leaves as the man and boy sleep.

There is a menacing atmosphere. A bearded creature enters; two black figures follow. The man wakes up the boy, and to howls it seems of dogs and the beat of percussion, there is an attack of some sort. The man watches; the boy runs off. The man stretches out now as if dead. Figures enter with baskets to gather pebbles. Leaves flutter down in the autumn air. The man glances up, then sits bowed over, head on knees. Rose petals fall. Peasants enter, take shafts of wheat and let them balance and fall within their fingers. The moon rises and is seen in eclipse. The man kneels and watches the peasants as ever so slowly they wave the stalks of wheat in the still air, then return them to the shaft. One girl remains and gives the man two wheat stalks. He holds them aloft, balancing them carefully; they seem to be balanced extensions of his arms. Snow falls gently. The man dances as it were with the stalks of wheat; they quiver in the evening air. The man kneels within a cross they have made of the stalks. A girl and boy come in with more wheat stalks as the snow thickens. The man moves, holding the stalks; they seem extensions of his arms and tremble at his every movement. Snow falls. He dances as it were with the stalks of quivering wheat, crossing them and kneeling as they cross. A girl and a boy enter with wheat tassles. They soon leave and the man rises as the boy returns; the girl does, too. The man lays down the cross of wheat and the boy who died. The snow has stopped. The man is alone. He takes up his cloak and leaves as an aged figure with a stick comes in. So, also, do men who carry on their shoulders heavy burdens. They cross the stage, slowly, at the back. Suddenly their burdens begin to lift off their shoulders and rise into the air. The curtain falls.

NOTES Nancy Goldner reviewed *Watermill* for *Dance News:* "Jerome Robbins's *Watermill* is one of the most perfect productions I have seen. It is beautiful, by all means—but it is more than that. It is exquisite. The details are the thing, although the work deals with large themes. The ballet is a meditation on nature. There is a meditator. His world is populated by seeders, tillers, harvesters, and phenomena of nature—the moon, wind, snow, stalks of wheat. Even the music, written by Teiji Ito and played by him and friends on the side of the stage, is as natural sounding as it is sounds of music. But it is always the details. Some boys wave small kites; each bobs at a different altitude. They also carry lanterns at different heights. This sensitivity to slight variation is exciting and moving. Four of the lanterns are large, in primary colors. Two of them are tiny and white. They look so fragile next to the larger ones. In addition to going through its phases, the moon ascends and descends. It seems to move when you're not looking. Its changing aspects are always something of a surprise. The wind which causes the wheat bundles to rustle is slight; it becomes a presence, like the moon. When fall comes, the leaves float onto the stage one by one. Even the snow seems to have been sprinkled over the land by a Haiku poet-god, so gentle is the fall and isolated the flakes. The list could go on. . . .

"The Orientalisms are not only in the music, props, and use of props. The entire spirit of *Watermill* is Orientally meditative. It unfolds slowly. With the exception of the dance of the spring/youth figure and the running sequence, which in itself is a rare-faction of the action—the boys and protagonist do a trot-like stylization of a run—the dancers move slowly, very slowly. Time becomes thick, sliceable. Edward Villella, the meditator-dreamer, has a quality here that suggests great power beneath the stillness. It is this suggestion of action that makes him so compelling, and maddening. Like the wind and moon, he becomes a presence. Unlike the moon, he does not mark the passing of time but seems to be a second of time stretched into forever. You either settle into his state of consciousness, or go insane. Maybe you can settle on a compromise by coughing and fidgeting. But you can't go to sleep. Robbins gets at some part of you.

"There are some obscure sections. Some actions are not definable by line and verse, but they do make emotional sense. Some things make such sense that they become permanent images in the mind. One such moment was the sound of wind before the nightmare. It struck to the core. It was one of the great moments in the theater. Oddly enough, though, the nightmare itself hit sideways. For me, the totality of the piece was not equal to some of the parts.

Not because the parts were unconnected to each other and to the larger theme; on the contrary, never have I seen a dance so perfectly interrelated. But because the ballet is not so much about nature, time, life cycles, and whatnot as it is 'about' a particular state of consciousness. And now I must confess that I was one of those who were going insane. The moments when I was thoroughly engrossed were the moments when I was most detached from the proceedings, when my attention was drawn away from the slow-moving dancers and from time. Only my aesthetic sense was engaged and heightened. Robbins wanted the whole being to be there. Those who find dwelling on a stalk of wheat exhilarating will find *Watermill* a masterpiece to end all masterpieces. I can only admire Robbins' essay."

Writing in *Dance and Dancers* magazine, Patricia Barnes said: "Every so often—but not that often—a ballet turns up which instantly convinces one of its place in dance history. It becomes a landmark. Such a one is Jerome Robbins's *Watermill*, a creation of such imagination, depth and profundity that no one seeing it can remain untouched in some way by it. The first night audience greeted it with a mixture of cheers and boos; some were clearly baffled by its newness and just sat looking stunned and perplexed. But it is not just that it is new and different: innovation alone does not make great art. *Watermill* is, in addition, a work of extraordinary beauty: a poetic and deeply felt work that seems to have been torn from the very soul of its creator. It has even been suggested that the ballet is part autobiographical, and certainly the title is the same as the island where Robbins has his country home.

"In 1964 Robbins studied the Noh technique, and clearly what he learned has been stirring in his mind ever since. *Watermill* incorporates much that can be traced to Noh—the deliberation, refinement and simplicity of movement, the stripping away of excessive gesture—but despite the influence of the music and theater of the East, this ballet's world, people and events, according to a program note, are universal and not to be construed as Oriental.

"Another influence on this particular world appears to be Robert Wilson, the fascinating and provocative young director who has forged a whole new theater style, and who recently performed in Paris with enormous success. But the creative genius of *Watermill* is Robbins alone. How incredible this choreographer is, never sitting back on the laurels of past successes, never choosing the easy way, but constantly challenged by new vistas and new ideas, a choreographer who can equally touch the heart and stimulate the intellect."

A WEDDING BOUQUET

Comic ballet in one act. Music by Lord Berners. Choreography by Frederick Ashton. Words by Gertrude Stein. Scenery and costumes by Lord Berners. First presented by the Vic-Wells Ballet at the Sadler's Wells Theatre, London, April 27, 1937, with Mary Honer as the Bride, Robert Helpmann as the Bridegroom, *Margot Fonteyn as* Julia, *June Brae as* Josephine, *Julia Far-ron as* Pépé, *and Ninette de Valois as* Webster. *First presented in the United States by the Sadler's Wells Ballet at the Metropolitan Opera House, New York, October 25, 1949, with Margaret Dale as the* Bride, *Robert Helpmann as the* Bridegroom, *Moira Shearer as* Julia, *June Brae as* Josephine, *Pauline Clayden as* Pépé, *and Palma Nye as* Webster.

When *A Wedding Bouquet* was first presented, one critic called it a *ballet bouffe*. That is exactly what it is: a comic work that achieves some of its funniest farce by exposing the absurdity of great dignity and seriousness. Its subject, a wedding in a provincial French town near the turn of the century, presents a set of conventions that must not be upset; and at the cost of many laughs, all the conventions are observed. They are observed in the determined, apparently senseless fashion with which people in René Clair movies observe their conventions: everything seems to combine against them, but in the end everything is all right. It is possible to watch *A Wedding Bouquet* and see it as a continental comic equivalent to the Edwardian pathos of such a ballet as *Lilac Garden*. Gertrude Stein's commentary on the action is spoken during the ballet by an observing orator.

The curtain rises on the garden of a farmhouse near Bellay. There is a long table set out for the wedding feast, and the ballet begins as people scurry about preparing the refreshments. Webster, the maid, is certain that things will not be ready by the time the bride and groom arrive. On the right, sitting apart from the scene, is the orator. He pours himself a glass of champagne.

As the guests begin to arrive, the orator speaks over the music to tell us about some of them. In addition to the peasant girls and boys and the usual gate crashers, there are Josephine ("She may be wearing a gown newly washed and pressed") and her two friends, Paul ("Pleasant, vivacious, and quarrelsome") and John ("An elder brother who regrets the illness of his father"). There is the aggressive young lady Violet ("Violet, oh will you ask him to marry you?"), who eagerly pursues a young man named Ernest ("May be the victim of himself"). Ernest eagerly repulses Violet's advances.

Now Julia enters. The orator tells us that she "Is known as forlorn," and forlorn she certainly is. She can hardly walk, she is so dejected. Apparently the trouble is that the fickle bridegroom of the day has abandoned her. Tagging along behind Julia is her dog, a Mexican terrier called Pépé ("Little dogs resemble little girls"). Julia directs all her affections to Pépé, and Pépé switches her tail like a little girl honored with a lollipop. One of the men tries to cheer Julia up, but Pépé protects her mistress. It appears that Josephine is terribly sorry for Julia. She tries to comfort her like a true friend, and Julia sulks with lunatic pleasure.

The bridal party approaches. First, the bride ("Charming! Charming! Charming!"). The bridesmaids dance together under her bridal veil. The bridegroom is clearly harassed. ("They all speak as if they expected him not to be charming.") As if the silly wedding weren't enough, he must now deal with the guests ("They incline to oblige only when they stare") and with Julia. The sight of this demented past indiscretion of his makes the bridegroom despair. Patiently he poses with the bridal party for a photograph of the wedding group. Then he tries to act as if nothing had happened.

Julia won't let him. She hangs on him like a cat. She won't give him up! The guests titter and chatter among themselves, guessing at the bridegroom's situation. Pépé tries to distract the bride, who begins to be suspicious. The bridegroom tries to push Julia off, and she throws herself at his feet. The bride despairs.

Now Josephine, too, is crying in her beer. She is so upset, because Julia is upset, that she drinks far too much. She starts to make the inevitable scene and is asked to leave. The groom, alone with Julia and all the other girls he's been intimate with, dances a bright tango. When he observes all these demanding women, he is lighthearted: marriage has set him free at last! Apparently his new bride sees how lucky she is.

Night begins to fall and the guests start to leave ("Thank you. Thank you."). The bridegroom goes to his bride, and the unhappy Julia is left alone. She still has Pépé, however. The dog tries to comfort her as Julia stupidly stares off into space.

WEEWIS

> Original commissioned score by Stanley Walden. Rock group: Virgin Wool. Choreography by Margo Sappington. Lighting by Jennifer Tipton. First presented by the Joffrey City Center Ballet at the City Center, New York, October 28, 1971, with Gary Chryst, James Dunne, Rebecca Wright, Christian Holder, Susan Magno, and Tony Catanzaro.

The name of this ballet is a small mystery: it is the name of the choreographer's cat. Weewis is a dance ballet, a series of duets, performed to the music of a rock group. Writing of the ballet in Time, the critic John T. Elson said that the three couples "appear to exemplify the varying moods of love (definitely profane)." The first dance is for two boys. The second is for a girl and boy and shows the sinuous variations possible in sophisticated lovemaking. The third dance is a fierce apache number for another girl and boy.

WESTERN SYMPHONY

> Ballet in three movements. Music by Hershy Kay. Choreography by George Balanchine. Scenery by John Boyt. Costumes by Karinska. First presented by the New York City Ballet at the New York City Center, September 7,

1954, with Diana Adams, Herbert Bliss, Janet Reed, Nicholas Magallanes, Patricia Wilde, Tanaquil LeClercq, Jacques d'Amboise, and others.

My idea in this ballet was to make a formal work that would derive its flavor from the informal American West, a ballet that would move within the framework of the classic school but in a new atmosphere. Earlier ballets on American folk themes (*Billy the Kid, Rodeo,* et al.) have been based on cowboy lore, but these have been story ballets. I wanted to do a ballet without a story in an unmistakably native American idiom. To accomplish that, I needed a new score and turned to the young composer Hershy Kay.

Western Symphony was a close collaboration between us. I was neither interested in local atmosphere nor narrative pantomime and told Kay that I wanted to try a symphonic American dance work which, by the impetus of indigenous melodies, would help me to use the universal language of the classic ballet in a fresh way. He liked the idea and wrote a symphony to order, a work in four movements, based on themes like "Red River Valley," "Old Taylor," "The Gal I Left Behind Me," "Rye Whiskey," "Golden Slippers," and others. To these movements I arranged a series of dance ensembles that I hope have some of the sentiment and candor of the time and places where those tunes were first sung.

I have crossed the United States by car some dozen times, have camped in the open air in New Mexico and Wyoming, in Montana and South Dakota. The vast sweep of the land, the impression of the Rockies and the plains, and the vision of the men who crossed the mountains and worked the plains, on foot and on horseback, cannot fail to move any newcomer, particularly one who has fresh memories of Europe, most of which is closely settled and where there have been few empty natural spaces for thousands of years.

Western Symphony was originally presented in practice clothes without a set. This was regrettable but we had no money at that time and had to wait for the following season for the designs of John Boyt and Karinska to materialize. The original four movements of the ballet have since been cut to three, omitting the third movement. In 1956, in Paris, during our third European tour, the United States Information Agency made a color film of the ballet with all its four movements.

THE WHIMS OF CUPID AND THE BALLET MASTER

Music by Jens Lolle. Choreography by Vincenzo Galeotti. First presented by the Royal Danish Ballet at the Royal Theatre, Copenhagen, October 31, 1786. First presented in the United States by the Royal Danish Ballet at the Metropolitan Opera House, New York, September 22, 1956. Scenery and costumes by Ove Christian Pedersen.

This is said to be the oldest ballet in the repertory. It has survived for almost two centuries at the Royal Theatre in Copenhagen and has never been omitted for such a length of time as to prevent several of the previous cast from assisting the new production, thus carrying on the original choreography by Galeotti in the proper spirit. Galeotti, who came to Denmark from Italy as early as 1775, is the first choreographer of importance to the Danish ballet.

The story is a comedy about lovers from many countries who come to pay tribute to the god Cupid. They dance before him the characteristic styles of their lands and then he plays a trick, blindfolding the couples. The curious matchmaking that results leads to hilarity and what the original program called a finale of "great confusion."

WHO CARES?

Music by George Gershwin, orchestrated by Hershy Kay. Choreography by George Balanchine. Costumes by Karinska. Lighting by Ronald Bates. Pianist: Gordon Boelzner. First presented by the New York City Ballet at the New York State Theatre, Lincoln Center, February 5, 1970, with Karin von Aroldingen, Patricia McBride, Marnee Morris, and Jacques d'Amboise as the principal dancers.

This ballet is a set of dances to some songs by George Gershwin that I have always liked very much. "Who Cares?" goes back to 1931 and *Of Thee I Sing*. In Europe in the late 1920s and 1930s, we all knew Gershwin's music and loved it; it is beautiful, very American, too. Before I came to America I saw the Gershwin musical *Funny Face* in London and admired it. I did some work in musical comedies in London after that and continued to make dances for them after I came to New York. I don't think I would have done that if it had not been for George Gershwin's music. There are popular songs and popular songs; Gershwin's are special.

I was lucky enough to know Gershwin, who asked me to Hollywood to do dances for the movie *Goldwyn Follies*. Gershwin gave me a book of his songs, arranged in the way he used to do them in concerts. One day at the piano I played one through and thought to myself, Beautiful, I'll make a *pas de deux*. Then I played another, it was just as beautiful and I thought, A variation! And then another and another and there was no end to how beautiful they were.

And so we had a new ballet. No story, just the songs. Here they are, with the dancers who first danced them: "Strike Up the Band" (1927), Ladies and Gentlemen; "Sweet and Low Down" (1925), Ensemble; "Somebody Loves Me" (1924), Deborah Flomine, Susan Hendl, Linda Merrill, Susan Pilarre, Bettijane Sills; "Bidin' My Time" (1930), Deni Lamont, Robert Maiorano, Frank Ohman, Richard Rapp, Earle Sieveling; "'S Wonderful" (1927), Susan Pilarre and Richard Rapp; "That Certain Feeling" (1925), Deborah Flomine and Deni Lamont, Bettijane Sills, and Earl Sieveling; "Do Do Do" (1926), Susan Hendl and Frank Ohman; "Lady Be Good" (1924), Linda Merrill and Robert Maiorano; "The Man I Love" (1924), Patricia McBride and Jacques d'Amboise; "I'll Build a Stairway to Paradise" (1922), Karin von Aroldingen; "Embraceable You" (1930), Marnee Morris and Jacques d'Amboise; "Fascinatin' Rhythm" (1924), Patricia McBride; "Who Cares?" (1931), Karin von Aroldingen and Jacques d'Amboise; "My One and Only" (1927), Marnee Morris; "Liza" (1929), Jacques d'Amboise; "Clap Yo' Hands" (1926), Karin von Aroldingen, Patricia McBride, Marnee Morris, Jacques d'Amboise; "I Got Rhythm" (1930), Entire Cast.

NOTES The first performance of *Who Cares?* had only an orchestral beginning ("Strike Up the Band") because the composer Hershy Kay, who was arranging the songs for us, was busy with a musical. Gordon Boelzner, the pianist, played all the other songs except for "Clap Yo' Hands," where we played a recording of Gershwin doing the piece himself. We still do.

We did not have much scenery for the ballet at the beginning. This was provided later by Jo Mielziner, November 21, 1970, who gave us a scrim with two layers of silhouetted skylines of New York in a kind of fan shape for the backdrop and, for the sides of the stage, skyscraper cliffs.

When *Who Cares?* was first done, Lincoln Kirstein wrote an extensive note for our program: "*Who Cares?* is both the name of a new ballet in the classical idiom by George Balanchine and an old song George and Ira Gershwin wrote in 1931 for *Of Thee I Sing*. The dictionary says *classic* means standard, leading, belonging to the highest rank of authority. Once it applied mainly to masterpieces from Greco-Roman antiquity; now we have boxing and horse racing classics, classic cocktail dresses and classic cocktails. Among classic American composers we number Stephen Foster, John Philip Sousa and George Gershwin (1898–1937). First heard fifty years ago, the best of the Gershwin songs maintain their classic freshness, as of an eternal martini—dry, frank, refreshing, tailor-made with an invisible kick from its slightest hint of citron. Nostalgia has not syruped their sentiment nor robbed them of immediate piquancy. We associate them with time past, but when well sung or played, or preferably both at once, they not only revive but transcend their epoch. Lovely in themselves they are by way of becoming art songs, which that beautiful singer Eva Gauthier long ago realized when she first sang them in concert well after they had become familiar hits. The Gershwins wrote hit songs which were art songs. Most art songs pretend to be love songs; the Gershwin genre seem to be about playmates more than lovers. It was not by accident the best dance team of the time, Fred and Adele Astaire, were brother and sister.

"To the musician George Gershwin, perhaps their most important element was their potential as piano pieces. He played energetically, long and magically at private parties and in public. His semi-improvisational style was taken seriously even by 'serious' critics. Gilbert Seldes, our first popularizer of what

we now call pop art (in painting as well as theater), indeed complained that
The Rhapsody in Blue was a masterpiece marred by Liszt-like extended
cadenzas; certainly Gershwin was a hypnotic virtuoso as well as a knowing
and generous analyst of the jazz style of which he was a master. This he traced
to the individual ragtimers at the turn of the century whose collective ingenui-
ties in piano playing built up a tradition which he inherited, and which he
used with a new articulate sophistication, flexibility and brilliance.

"But there is another serious aspect of the Gershwin songs which marks
their sturdy structure—words supporting the tunes, mainly by his brother Ira.
The wit, tact, invention, metaphor and metric of Ira's rhymes meant that you
not only left the theater whistling melodies, but singing words. His phrasing
was simple enough, his phrases sharp enough to impose themselves at one
hearing; once heard, they were almost infectiously memorable. Love & dove,
June & moon, true & you long comprised the pidgin English of Tin Pan Alley.
Ira Gershwin not only transubstantiated such base metal; with condescension
or parody he created a new prosody, a new means for lyric writing which in-
corporated the season's slang, references to local events, echoes of the vernacu-
lar rhythms of ordinary speech in a frame of casual thrown-away elegance
which was never false, insistent or self-conscious. He seemed to have stumbled
on what was right, fitting, appropriate, surprising and charming, as if such had
been coins tossed in his path. But such coinage is art, not accident, and Ira in-
cidentally was a poet and a master of mnemonics. He was also a satirist; there
had always been comic ballads, but it is odd to find in 'Strike Up the Band'
(1927), an ostensibly patriotic hit tune, its almost Brechtian tang. . . . Ira
Gershwin's lyric style involved his skill in manipulating repetition, shift of
breath, perfect punctuation, instinct for vulgarism in a mosaic of unusual context, plus a laconic polish. His vocabulary was small; both Noel Coward and
Cole Porter were more literary; Lorenz Hart's smashing pastiches depended on
a wide reading. These three derived from Gilbert and Sullivan, a more oper-
atic or light-operatic tradition. Ira was in the line of minstrelsy—the minstrel
show and the ancient descent from troubador soloists. All the songs sang 'I
love you,' but Ira's hummed it with a unique American, or rather Manhattan
(cocktail), simplicity and savor. Lyrics are to be sung, not enunciated like pat-
ter songs, or launched—like arias. In love songs, intense emotion is usually in
inverse proportion to the heartbreak clarity of words. George Gershwin's tunes
were not impassioned but playful. Their pretext was not profound feelings, but
sportive sex, flirtatious games, gallantry in a tennis tournament: love, set,
match. George Gershwin took forms and archetypes as he received them and
composed something unheard before out of formulae. He did not so much
write parodies of Negro spirituals, barroom ballads or cowboy songs; he appro-
priated familiar atmospheres and by his mastery whipped them into the strict
form of the hit song, as someone might break a green colt into a pacer. He al-
ternated tenderness with ironic narcissism, or contrasted a smashing climax
with the most delicate expression of loss or confusion. And Ira's lyrics were

indeed—lyric: personal, enthusiastic, eminently singable. The Gershwins were showmen; they gloried in hits, show stoppers, grand finales with everybody shouting in the aisles, but their brashest choirs never obscured the fragility of certain solos when George almost seemed to be singing to himself. Idiosyncratic serenades, at once self-deprecatory and wistful, they were as elegant, athletic and lonely as he was in life, which no one knew better than his brother.

"This faintly confessional residue of George Gershwin is a touching legacy. In 1930, for *Girl Crazy*, he and Ira wrote a deliberately paced number for a chorus of dubious cowboys, dude ranch gigolos leaning on the fence of a Reno divorce ranch. The wrangler of 1930 had already become a drugstore cowboy on his way to becoming a midnight cowboy; but forty years ago he was more the dandy than the hustler. And in Ira's deft quotation of the titles of four popular songs in his introduction, we have his compliments to colleagues in the song writing industry, a delicious in-joke of the era, as well as a not unjustified boast of the Gershwin superiority, as aristocrats of American lyricism, masters of music to the American electorate. The Gershwins' beautiful manners and high style, their instant melange of insouciance and shrewd innocence, their just estimation of the imaginative elasticity of an elite audience which they had developed, have left a body of words and music which lives, unblurred by vulgar rhetoric or machine-made sentiment. To combine an intensely personal attitude with a flagrantly popular language is a feat which few popular artists manage, and it is appropriate that Balanchine has used the songs not as facile recapitulation of a lost epoch, but simply as songs, or melodies for classic, un-deformed, traditional academic dances, which in their equivalence of phrasing, dynamics and emotion, find their brotherly parallel."

Soon after the first performances, Arlene Croce, editor of *Ballet Review*, wrote about the ballet in the *Dancing Times:* "The title of Balanchine's Gershwin ballet, *Who Cares?*, has a double significance. It means, Who Cares what we call it ('as long as I care for you and you care for me'), and it suggests that the piece is an elegant throwaway. That's how it looks, too—like nothing much. The curtain goes up while the orchestra is playing 'Strike Up the Band' and we see a double exposure of Manhattan skylines projected in a pinkish haze on the backcloth. An excellent idea, but it stops there. The rest of the stage looks bleak. The girls wear their very well-cut Karinska tutus, this time in turquoise and lemon-yellow. The skirts have pleats and look 1920s and mini-mod at the same time. So do the boys' black bellbottom slacks. Like the title and the sky-line, everything has a double impact, with one effect or style superimposed on another—Now on Then, ballet dancing on show tunes. The two planes of meaning are so shuffled that we're never completely in one world or the other, we're in both at once. Or rather, we're in four worlds since *Who Cares?* scram-bles two elements, classical dancing and show dancing, and two eras, the Twenties and the Seventies, with equal paronomasiac facility. And since the Twenties was itself a period of classical revival, the play of references can grow almost infinitely complex. When Balanchine has five boys do double air

turns (one boy at a time) in 'Bidin' My Time,' we're pleased with ourselves for
thinking of the boys' variation in *Raymonda*, Act Three (the metrical swing of
the music is pretty much the same), and even more pleased when we remember the masculine ensemble that made the song famous in *Girl Crazy*.
That's simple enough. But when toward the end of the ballet his four stars fly
across the stage to 'Clap Yo' Hands' in what is unmistakably a series of quotations from *Apollo*, we catch an unframeable glimpse of the multiple precedents
Who Cares? is made of. It's then that we see, for just the flash of the moment
that he gives us to see it, how comradely the links are between the Gershwin
of *Lady Be Good!, Tip Toes, Oh, Kay!* and *Funny Face*, and the syncopated
Stravinsky of *Apollon Musagete*. We notice that the dancers in the ballet wear
necktie-belts in homage not only to Astaire but to the Chanel who in 1928
knotted men's striped cravats around the waists of Apollo's muses. But the allusion to 1928 isn't endstopped; it reverberates with *Apollo*'s own recapit-
ulations of the Nineties and Marius Petipa—high noon at the Maryinsky—and
so we are borne back ceaselessly into the past. To the question 'What is classicism?' Balanchine responds with a blithe shrug and a popular song. Classicism is the Hall of Fame viewed as a hall of mirrors. The Fun House. . . .

"The ballet suddenly . . . finds its own life—when the boys and girls start
dancing out in pairs to ''S Wonderful,' 'That Certain Feeling,' 'Do Do Do,' and
'Lady Be Good'; the dance invention tumbles forth, so does the applause, and
we realize that what we're going to see is not a clever foreigner's half-infat-
uated, half-skeptical view of a popular American art form, we're going to see
the art form itself, re-energized. But this spectacle we see isn't like a musical
comedy, it's more like a lieder recital with a few social mannerisms mostly in
the pleasant, sappy, ingenue style of Old Broadway. Just when you think that
maybe the dancers do represent a musical comedy chorus full of stock types
(with Linda Merrill as the company's inevitable redhead), they vanish and another ballet, or musical, or recital begins.

"The second half of *Who Cares?* has an *Apollo*-type cast—one boy (Jacques
d'Amboise) and three girls (Patricia McBride, Marnee Morris, and Karin von
Aroldingen). Each girl dances once with the boy and once by herself and then
the boy dances alone. They are all four together in the Apollonian coda. The
music is the same parade of Gershwin hits that has been going on since the beginning, only now, with the lights blue and the stars out, we listen more intently. If this is a musical comedy world, it's the most beautiful one ever imagined. In 'Fascinatin' Rhythm,' Patricia McBride holds a high extension in
second and then in two or three lightning shifts of weight refocuses the whole
silhouette while keeping on top of the original pose. It's so charming to see in
relation to that unexpected stutter in the music which unexpectedly recurs,
that it hits the audience like a joke, but that's fascinating rhythm, and that's
Who Cares? Classical syntax, jazz punctuation. I couldn't begin to say what
d'Amboise's solo to 'Liza' is composed of, though—it suggests soft-shoe virtuoso
tap and classical lift and amplitude all at once, and d'Amboise, whose style in

classical ballet has characteristically a casual, crooning softness played against sudden monkey-like accelerandos and sharp bursts of detail, dances it in total splendor. Everywhere the tight choreography sustains an almost unbelievable musical interest.

"As if it weren't enough for Balanchine to give us dances of extreme tension and wit and elegance, he also gives us back the songs unadorned by their usual stagey associations. 'Stairway to Paradise' isn't a big production number; it's one girl (von Aroldingen) covering ground in powerful colt-like jumps and turns. And in the duets, the emotion is more serious (the sense of receding hopes, for example, in 'The Man I Love') for not being acted out. It isn't emotion that dominates the stage so much as a musical faith that the choreography keeps, and that's what convinces us that the songs are good for more than getting drunk at the St. Regis by—that they have theatrical momentousness and contemporary savor. Gershwin in 1970, in the age of Burt Bacharach, has no trouble sounding classical, and that is how Balanchine hears him.

"I am also persuaded that Balanchine hears Gershwin the way Gershwin composed, i.e. pianistically, and this brings up the subject of orchestration and Hershy Kay. Kay had been set the task of orchestrating sixteen of the seventeen songs that Balanchine uses in *Who Cares?* (one number, 'Clap Yo' Hands,' is a recording made by Gershwin himself at the piano), but because of commitments to the Broadway show *Coco*, Kay has so far orchestrated only the opening ('Strike Up the Band') and closing ('I Got Rhythm') songs. The remaining fourteen songs were played for the three performances of *Who Cares?* that were given this season, with his customary sensitivity and attack, by Gordon Boelzner, from Gershwin's own concert arrangements. These piano arrangements were unvaryingly simple: verse followed by chorus followed (sometimes twice) by chorus repeat. But they are also beautiful examples of Gershwin's highly developed keyboard technique. Gershwin's pianism was comparable in its own time to Gottschalk's, and I hope Kay's further orchestrations of Gershwin are as good as the ones he did for the Gottschalk ballet *Cakewalk*, by far his best orchestration for the ballet theater. To my disappointed ear, his 'Strike Up the Band' and 'I Got Rhythm' were in the vulgarized idiom of his 'Stars and Stripes'-hotcha added to heat; and while the musical format of *Who Cares?* precludes his 'symphonizing' in the style of *Western Symphony*, orchestral thickening could destroy the bone-dry delicacy, the tonal transparency of this music and should be avoided like temptation. The more so as Balanchine has taken such evident delight in choreographing the countermelodies, cross-rhythms and abrupt syncopations out of which Gershwin built his compositions—it isn't all razz-ma-tazz—and not since the heyday of Fred Astaire have such felicities been observed.

"Fred and Ginger, Fred and Adele, George and Ira, George and Igor . . . it's easy to be seduced by the nostalgia of it all, but the remarkable thing about *Who Cares?* is how infrequently it appeals to that nostalgia. It certainly makes no appeal on the basis of period glamor or period Camp. The multiple images, the visual punning, the sense of a classical perspective—all of that sweeps by with a strength of evocation more powerful than any individual moment of recognition. It's mysterious, the mythological intensity built up by a ballet that doesn't seem to have a thought in its airy head. No single cultural myth seems to be at the core of it. Manhattan in the Golden Twenties, penthouse parties, where composers of brilliance entertained at the baby grand until dawn, are lovely to think about but aren't the subject of *Who Cares?* any more than a rainbow on a wet afternoon is. To put it as simply as I can, this wonderful ballet enriches our fantasy life immeasurably, as works of art are meant to do. It's tonic, medicinal, too. Its fresh unclouded feeling seems to strike with special directness at the city's depressed spirits. Just before the première (on February 5), Balanchine received New York City's biggest award for cultural achievement, the Handel medallion, on the stage of the State Theatre. He made a number of jokes in the disreputable manner of his hero on such occasions, Bob Hope, had what they call in show business a 'good roll,' and then rang up the curtain on a Gershwin march. The Higher Seriousness didn't have a chance, but who cares?—the ballet was a beaut."

The critic Robert Sealy has also written at length of his impressions of the first performances of *Who Cares?* (in *Ballet Review*, Vol. 3, No. 3).

"*Who Cares?* is a brilliant high wire act: a classical ballet to Gershwin show tunes. It must have been difficult to get it all set, balanced and in focus, to keep it from becoming what it most definitely is *not:* nostalgia, show biz, Broadway, dear old Busby or anything, for that matter, to do with the past. It is to be danced at the moment, in the now of things. What it's really about is the inherent joy of being a man or a woman with a healthy body and the ability to *dance, dance, dance.* As usual, Balanchine has walked the wire over the falls.

"Like all strong, self-assured artists, Balanchine makes his intention clear right at the beginning; he puts his hands on your head and *makes* you see it his way. The principals do not appear in the *Raymonda* part. To emphasize that *Who Cares?* is a classical ballet, eight songs ('Strike Up the Band,' 'Sweet and Low Down,' 'Somebody Loves Me,' 'Bidin' My Time,' ''S Wonderful,' 'That Certain Feeling,' 'Do Do Do,' 'Lady Be Good') have been made into a suite of classical dances, by turns dainty, humorous, robust and romantic, and given to the ensemble. Many people squirm in their seats (as they would through the prologue to *The Sleeping Beauty* or the first act of *Swan Lake*) waiting for the stars; they object to this 'Eat your greens before dessert' attitude—but I think the greens are delicious. 'Somebody Loves Me,' the second number after the 'icebreaker,' is rather daring in that it is a *very* long pas de cinq. Four little girls who might be on the field hockey scrub team, led by Captain Bettijane Sills, twirl and kick over and over, so sweetly, so demurely, the sort of thing the swan girls do while waiting for Odette. It is very appealing, but it makes the audience rather cross. This is exactly the sort of thing in NYCB repertory where proper setting and lighting would help (a hockey field in Riverside Park just before spring dusk, for example). As it is, it must flounder about by itself and get crushed by the big kids. In the first 'act,' 'Bidin' My Time' is the crucial support of the piece, the stem of the flower: heavily masculine quotes from *Raymonda* danced by five men. Unfortunately, the boys are too willowy and not up to it. What is wanted is the easy coordination of a basketball team warming up, easily, almost languidly, the tension is ahead. The last four songs are one long dance with a fresh use of strutaways and rapid turns, especially in the breathless pas de quatre, 'That Certain Feeling.'

"A Gershwin *Apollon Musagéte*—behind the Metropolitan Museum certainly. This memorable quartet dances to eight songs: 'The Man I Love' (Apollo, Terpsichore); 'I'll Build a Stairway to Paradise' (Calliope); 'Embraceable You' (Apollo, Polyhymnia); 'Fascinating Rhythm' (Terpsichore); 'Who Cares?' (Apollo, Calliope); 'My One and Only' (Polyhymnia); 'Liza' (Apollo) and 'Clap Yo' Hands' (the fingers-to-chin, muscled roundabout, Apollo-and-the-muses-at-play part, before the call to Mount Olympus). I am afraid I must call it an affair of sentiment, retire before it and pass out. Never in a theater have I wanted so much to jump the moat and join in. It is pure, unmitigated, uncut joy, an open, palpitating, vulnerable heart on the sleeve. Patricia McBride as Terpsichore clears the high Petipa hurdles of 'Fascinating Rhythm' with room to spare; Jacques d'Amboise (who else?) as Apollo does the big solo leaps in yellow shoes and has a finish of arms-raised ecstasy; and the two of them in 'The Man I Love,' angular, cat-wary, in and out of each other's arms, alternately aloof and impassioned, alert to the rising and falling sounds from the piano, have the memory-burning dance of a lifetime. It is finally Gershwin's music itself, with its slight pretentiousness, its striving after The Better Things (this uniquely New York thing that makes 'Rhapsody in Blue' and *Porgy and Bess* rise above derivation, surpass eclecticism and become great light music) that jells the ballet, preserves Balanchine's fast-stepping, high-breasted, cheeky, slightly put-on attitudes and keeps the whole thing from becoming a dance cavalcade of evergreens."*

WILLIAM TELL VARIATIONS

Music by Gioacchino Rossini. Choreography by Auguste Bournonville. Staged by Hans Brenaa. Lighting by Thomas Skelton. First presented in the United States by the City Center Joffrey Ballet at City Center, New York, March 23, 1969, with Charthel Arthur and Luis Fuente as principals.

This dance ballet by the great Danish ballet master has an interesting history. There are several versions of it, one claiming that the ballet originated in an-

---

* Reprinted by permission of *Ballet Review*, Marcel Dekker, publisher.

other form as a *divertissement* in the first production of Rossini's *William Tell* at the Paris Opéra, August 3, 1829, another that it derives from Bournonville's *Tyrolerne,* an idyllic one-act ballet with music by J. F. Frohlich first performed March 3, 1835. *Tyrolerne,* according to Clive Barnes, who knows the Danish ballet and its history extremely well, also had music by Rossini; it is his theory that Bournonville later expanded the Rossini score with music from *William Tell.* The ballerina Marie Taglioni danced a famed *Tyrolienne* at the first performance of Rossini's opera but the choreography for her dance was by Aumer, not Bournonville.

In any case, Bournonville's ballet is a treasure of the Danish tradition and was taught to Hans Brenaa, who staged the work, when he was a young student at the Royal Danish Ballet School.

It is a dance ballet for a girl and a boy and two supporting couples, an entertainment for the eye and ear to glorious music by Rossini.

THE WIND IN THE MOUNTAINS

A Country Calendar. Music by Laurence Rosenthal. Choreography by Agnes de Mille. Costumes by Stanley Simmons. Lighting by Jean Rosenthal. First presented by the American Ballet Theatre at the New York State Theatre, March 17, 1965, with Joseph Carow, Karen Krych, Gayle Young, Judith Lerner, and William Glassman in the principal roles.

To a score based largely on early American songs and folk tunes, this dance narrative traces the progress of the seasons in the country—"Traveling Weather," "Wind," "Ice," "Rain," "Natural Catastrophe," "All Clear," "Apotheosis." It begins with a cowboy shouting out to the mountains and the world, "Hello, there," and his words echo back from the hills. A pathfinder enters, then a young couple in love dance with their friends. A lady in red tries to lure the boy away, he follows her and his girl laments. Another suitor tries to cheer her up but she falls on the ice and is undone. Then in the rain she is alone and sad when she sees her lover. A man prays and the rain stops. A train is heard in the distance and in comes a stranger, a Wild West traveling salesman who delights the whole town. The ladies fall at his feet, except the girl, who remains faithful to the memory of the boy. The boy comes back. A square dance is called and around and around in a big circle to a hymnal tune the friends and neighbors go.

WITCH BOY

Music by Leonard Salzedo. Libretto and choreography by Jack Carter. Scenery and costumes by Norman McDowell. First presented by the Ballet

der Lage Landen, Amsterdam, May 24, 1956, with Norman McDowell in
the title role. First presented in the United States by the National Ballet
at the Lisner Auditorium, Washington, D.C., March 29, 1971, with Gerard
Sibbritt in the title role.

Based on the American folk ballad of Barbara Allan and set in the Smoky
Mountains about the turn of the century, *Witch Boy* is the work of British
choreographer and dancer Jack Carter. Carter has said that the theme of the
ballet "is that very nice, ordinary people can, by force of circumstances, be
turned into a mob." *Witch Boy's* story, of frontier days, tells of the unwelcome
advances a Preacher makes to Barbara Allan, who flees to the mountains to escape him. There on the mountainside, she meets the Witch Boy, a possessed,
handsome youth, child of the Conjureman. They fall in love.

Bringing the Witch Boy back to her home town, Barbara Allan finds that
things are not so simple. Though the two join in the dancing they find there,
her friends and relatives clearly think the Witch Boy an odd choice for her
to make, particularly when the Preacher loves her. In addition to his quaint
mountain garb, the Witch Boy behaves in a manic way that visibly makes all
the townsfolk nervous. The Preacher, seizing the chance to put down the competition, craftily suggests to his parishioners that the boy is guilty of witchcraft. Their response is instantaneous and violent: they beat the boy and lynch
him. As he hangs from a tree, the Conjureman returns, mourns, and by the
magic he possesses, a new Witch Boy appears, born afresh to haunt the community and future Barbara Allans.

NOTES *Witch Boy* was an important vehicle for the English *premier dan-*
seur John Gilpin, whose dramatic interpretation was much applauded. He first
danced the part in the London Festival Ballet's production of November 27,
1957, with Anita Landa as Barbara Allan.

Talking with critic Jean Battey Lewis of the Washington *Post* at the time of
Witch Boy's American premier, in 1971, Jack Carter spoke of the power of
classical ballet: "Putting on a ballet in sneakers and jeans doesn't make it original. And I don't think you need bare feet and dirty soles to show emotion. I
think classical ballet technique is so strong it can absorb new discoveries in
movement. I'm interested in movement to say something. Antony Tudor
started me off. In *Lilac Garden* you can see people think through movement.
I'm interested in people and the human relationship."

Reviewing the National Ballet's production, Clive Barnes wrote in the New
York *Times* that *Witch Boy* "is a sensationally theatrical ballet, with a couple
of parthenogenetic births, a hell-fire preacher and a lynch party. It is a very
strong dramatic work with a wonderful part for the Witch Boy. Gerard
Sibbritt danced with great dramatic strength, providing the role with febrile

agony, and that animalistically evil quality, ill-defined but menacing, that the Witch Boy must possess." The part of the Preacher has been notably danced in England by Anton Dolin and by Frederic Franklin in the United States. Lydia Diaz-Cruz danced Barbara Allan in the National Ballet's production.

PART TWO

How to Enjoy Ballet

It is strange that many people think ballet is a difficult thing to enjoy. Ballet isn't any harder to enjoy than a novel, a play, or a poem—it's as simple to like as a baseball game.

Yet imagine a person who goes to a baseball game for the first time. He hasn't played the game, he doesn't know the rules, and he gets confused trying to watch everything at once. He feels out of place and annoyed because he isn't sure why everyone else is so excited.

If he had played baseball himself, he wouldn't have this problem. But he doesn't have to play to enjoy. Once he knows what it's all about, once he understands why the players run and slide and leap and catch as they do, he begins to appreciate the game. He becomes familiar with its elements, he enjoys it. The same thing is true of ballet.

Dancing is very popular here in America. Most of us learn to dance when we are young. And I don't mean ballet dancing. We hear music just about everywhere we go; we have a response to its rhythm and melody and want to express this response in a natural way, so we begin to dance. Ballet dancing is an entirely different thing from ballroom dancing, the dancing most familiar to us, though that, too, requires skill. Ballet also began in the ballroom, in the courts of Italy and France, but over the years it has been elevated to the stage and has become an art. This art is based on something natural to us, response to music, but it expresses this response in a specific, formalized way. Over the past four hundred years, dancers and ballet masters have built up a grammar of movement, a synthesis of what is anatomically possible and pleasing. This is the basic vocabulary of the dancer and the people who make ballets. They have to learn it like a language, from the elementary forms and words. The choreographer chooses certain elements he wants from ballet's extensive vocabulary, makes some new ones, and arranges all these in a new pattern to a meter he derives from music. But we don't have to understand this language in detail to enjoy ballet, any more than we have to know about the pigments of the painter or the complex meters of the poet.

Ballet takes our natural impulse to move, to make signs, to make ourselves as attractive and graceful as possible, and turns it into something new, something entirely different. Perhaps what we see the first time we go to the ballet we don't like at all. Dancers in strange costumes do nothing but move to a piece of music we're unfamiliar with; people who represent characters in an ancient Greek myth, for example, dance a story we don't remember much about; or characters in a modern story-ballet behave quite differently from the people next door. We come away saying that ballet's unnatural.

This is exactly true: ballet is unnatural, it has nothing to do with our daily lives in an immediate sense. What ballet does is to take movements we're all familiar with—running and jumping, turning and balancing, lifting and holding —and mold attitudes that underlie these actions into a spectacle that entertains. The melodies we hear in music are very different from the natural noises we hear in the everyday world: the slamming of doors, running brooks, the sound of wind in the trees. Melody is artificial, it is made by man. Ballet is artificial in this same sense: its roots are in everyday life, but it is created by artists. What ballet takes from life it transforms.

Broadway at Times Square, for example, is certainly a kind of spectacle, but it doesn't always entertain. It depends on how good we are at seeing. A talented choreographer can see superbly: he can watch this same scene and, by showing us special patterns of movement and behavior, entertain us with a character ballet, make us laugh or make us sad. He makes order out of what seems to us crowded and chaotic, makes what is fleeting and transitory permanently interesting.

The choreographer can do this in a number of ways: in ballets with stories, in ballets that aim to create a certain mood, or simply in dance ballets, where the music provides the plot the dancers move to. I think it's important to understand these distinctions.

Story ballets are entirely different from the stories we read in books: or they should be. In a story depicted on the ballet stage, we *see* what happens, it can't be explained. The plot is simple, the characters easily identifiable, and what happens to them is luminously clear.

What I've called "mood" ballets don't necessarily tell any kind of story; usually, as in *La Valse*, they are ballets in which an outside force, like destiny, seems to control the movement of the dancers.

In dance ballets there is no story, no outside force, only the music. The choreographer works with the music he has chosen much as the poet works with his meters. Most ballets, indeed, are like dramatic or lyric poems: they are created in relation to music and sometimes set within a fable or story. In ballet, the clumsy becomes graceful, the hesitant, inarticulate thought is expressed in direct, eloquent gesture, and nothing appears impossible; love can triumph over everything. In many great ballets, love does.

If you say that all this is fantasy, all imagination, you are right. Some people try to persuade us that poetry and painting and music and dancing are like what we see and do every day. In order to convince us that art is interesting, they tell us that the rumble of drums and the loud crash of cymbals in a piece of music represents Fate, for example, or that a certain portrait painter has depicted a girl's coloring just as it was in real life.

These people, well intentioned as they often are, actually put a stumbling block in our path. They make art easy in the wrong way. If we're told a great deal about a moment of history represented in a painting, for instance, and learn the background of the historical event, our appreciation is severely limited. Our appreciation is intellectual, based on something besides the picture. We could much more profitably spend our time just *looking* at the picture.

Some works of art can be appreciated intellectually, but not many good ones. To enjoy the good ones, we must have an openness of mind in addition to information or their beauty will forever escape us. First of all, we must suspend our prejudices.

As adults, we are well informed about certain things and we have definite ideas on many subjects. But in a sense we are all prejudiced. The older most of us get, the more we have to unlearn in order to learn something new. For instance, many of us were introduced in school to only certain types of music, only certain forms of poetry, and only particular schools of painting. As a result we have a tendency to resist anything new, as well as innovations in something we have become fond of. Children don't have this problem. You can play a Bach suite or a Mozart serenade to a child, and she may very well dance to it. It doesn't occur to her that these composers are old and "classical" or dull and cold or different from what she hears over the radio. She realizes instinctively that the exciting thing about all the arts is that they don't confirm what we already know, so much as they inform us of something new. They contain, in words, in music, in movement, new visions of the world.

Just as a child has her ears open, she keeps her eyes open if you take her to the ballet. Don't be afraid that she will be bored—with no trouble at all she'll become part of the magical world ballet is portraying and she'll not resist its impact. She is not afraid of being afraid (she even enjoys it a little when a wicked fairy appears), she is capable of being moved by love, by the attitudes people have toward one another on the stage. She will sense instantly that a boy partnering a girl well is gentle, respectful, eager for the girl to be as beautiful as possible and that a boy who is a bit of a show-off is not right in his part. She is apt to know, in short, much more than we do.

In order to place ourselves in her position and learn what she knows instinctively, we must go to the ballet with an open mind. If we go often, if we learn gradually that we can't see everything on the stage at once, if we learn to identify dancers and see different dancers in the same part, we'll establish a familiarity with the art and begin to enjoy it. There's no sense in being like the man who says he doesn't know anything about dancing, but he knows what he likes. By saying this, he cheats himself, protects his prejudices from exposure, nurses his own stubbornness. He's not only unwilling to learn anything, he would be embarrassed to learn anything.

Where ballet is concerned, learning by doing is impossible for most of us. We can learn, however, by seeing and by listening; we can learn nothing if we don't go see the ballet, and our appreciation of it will be severely limited if we do not have an awareness of the music that is played there. For ballet is not dancing alone: it is a composite of music and dancing. The relation of dancing to music is not a literal one. It is not a matter of plotless interpretation, a note-by-note, bar-by-bar rhythmic picture of music. On the contrary, it is a complement to the music, something added that is in the mood and spirit of the music as a choreographer sees it. We all have certain emotions when we hear a piece of music. So does a choreographer. He expresses and orders his emotions by placing people on the stage in a particular fashion and arranging their movements so that they have a certain quality: they may be sad, for example, though there isn't always a story to give them a reason for this. The music is sometimes the story. If the choreographer has chosen his music well, we will appreciate the complement the dance makes to its sound: the music will be, as it were, the floor on which the dancer moves. It will not be an excuse for the imposition of literary ideas foreign to music.

But frequently a too sensitive awareness of music can be a disadvantage to the inexperienced balletgoer. Some music lovers are very stubborn, they know what they like, they hold certain things sacred and won't even entertain the notion that they might enrich their musical experience. Their ears are open to only a few pieces, or they think dance "violates" the pieces they love. It may be difficult in such cases to expect a music lover to keep both ears *and* eyes open. I know an intelligent young lady, for example, who walked out on a performance of *The Sleeping Beauty* because she didn't like Tchaikovsky; and a young man who said he loved Bach so much that he could not watch *Concerto Barocco*. Both these people missed a chance, I think, to see in ballet things that might have changed their minds. Love of music can be so intense with some of us that it is acutely private and we resent any intrusion on that privacy.

Ballet in many cases can show us how to appreciate music. The structure of a symphony, how a piece of music is put together, may be something we have no interest in now, but continual attendance at the ballet will cause us to think differently. Dancing is always pointing to music, showing it, making it visually interesting. If our eyes are entertained, we begin to listen in a new way.

Reading about the ballet can be of help to the balletgoer. The numerous story-ballets with complicated plots are not always intelligible when we see them the first time, and it is advisable to know what happens. After our appreciation has matured somewhat, we will find other books—histories and criticism —interesting. Some two or three books of criticism on dancing, such as Noverre's *Letters* and Gautier's ballet reviews, are among the finest works of art appreciation.

But until we have *seen*, no amount of reading will help us. There is no short cut to seeing. *What* you see is not important. Good ballet can be seen frequently throughout the United States. Ballet companies may not visit your community with any regularity, but many of the large cities have their own permanent ballet organizations. Nor does it matter which you see. You cannot tell who is or who is not a good dancer if you don't know anything about the subject, and it is absurd to let anyone tell you. He may very well be wrong, and you'll miss a great deal, perhaps never go back to the ballet because you thought he was right. Much antagonism toward ballet is often created by someone who tells us that so-and-so is the world's greatest dancer in such-and-such a ballet. The inexperienced balletgoer sees the ballerina, doesn't like her, and never goes again.

Certain people don't like "cold" dancers. They use this word as if it meant something bad, something negative. The strange thing is that this quality of "coldness," which some regard negatively, often achieves positive results. I think you will find that people who say they prefer "hot," fiery dancers tend to create their own image of what they want to see, instead of watching the stage and seeing that the dance has its own quality—which might be cool and clear as crystal or, like a diamond seen in different lights, first cold, then hot.

What is it, then, that we should appreciate about a dancer? What things should we watch for the first time we go?

You will often hear people talk about the technical accuracies of dancers. They will say, "It's not important how many *fouettés* a girl can do, it's important that her supporting foot remain in place" and "Male dancers must always point their toes while doing *entrechats*." These things are quite true, there are many other such things, many finer points of technique, and we learn them as we watch, but all these criticisms are only part of a general appearance and manner that we must watch for first.

We should be ready, too, to enjoy the artist who perhaps has not yet achieved great success. We may discover later on that we saw the first of many dances that made her eventually a ballerina. That will be exciting. However, the good dancer will not in performance remind us of this kind of success. Watching her dancing over the years, we will see and appreciate the movement, the victory she appears to achieve in executing effortlessly a particular step or gesture at a specific time in a specific place. Her dancing will refract and amplify and make spacious, as music does, the emotion a particular dance intends. She is not someone we are in love with, or someone we should like to love, though some of her dancing reminds us of the happiness, the understanding, the playfulness and tenderness love has.

Only the professional dancer can analyze a performance and tell us that a certain dancer missed something. Dancers are not automatons. Every performance is different. Dancers must adjust themselves at almost every performance to a new pair of shoes, just as the tennis champion adjusts his hand to a new racket and the violinist adjusts to a new bow. Moreover, the condition of the stage floor is crucial to all dancers. No dancer dances well on a stage with a bad floor. If you have been to ballet performances where famous ballerinas seemed to be holding something back, where all the members of the *corps de ballet* danced hesitantly, refusing to commit themselves wholly to the dance, it was probably because they were risking their professional lives on the floor they were dancing on. The ideal stage for dancing is unfinished pine, smoothed over: it is not glossy linoleum or highly polished hardwood or the shiny plastic distances we see in the movies, or wood laid over cement or linoleum. When the nineteenth-century French critic Gautier remarked that an

Italian dancer's feet were "like two steel arrows rebounding from a marble pavement," he was able to make the simile because she was dancing on a wooden stage. The dancer feels most secure when she knows that her ballet slippers are in real contact with the floor when she wants them to be; when she can feel the friction of the floor as she turns in pirouettes; when she can descend from a jump without fear of sliding.

Some stages, too, are precariously raked, or pitched: the back of the stage is higher than the front. The designers of such stages had more consideration for the audience's ability to see than for the perfection of the performance that entertains the audience. The degree of rake differs from stage to stage in old theatres, and it is naturally extremely hard for dancers to adjust their balance to them. These are not excuses; they are the conditions under which every dancer works, and no dancer should be punished for them. In one recital a pianist plays millions of notes; if you aren't a pianist yourself, you won't know the ones he missed. The great pianist Anton Rubinstein once said that if he'd been paid a penny for every note he missed, he'd be a very rich man.

Ballet is now so advanced in the United States that very seldom do we see incompetence on the stage. Bad dancers appear less and less. Our dancers are professionals. Like professional ball players, they must possess a technique. Usually their technique is so great that however tired they are (and tired they often are, with eight performances a week), their exhaustion is invisible to the audience. Only the professional can see it.

The audience must watch technique as part of a performance, not as a separate thing. The stage illusion and the atmosphere created by the dancing are destroyed if you sit in your seat and count turns or stop-watch changes of position. We take it for granted that flowers are beautiful; we don't have to take them apart to see this. We take them as they are. The taking apart is the job of the botanist, just as the technical analysis of a performance is the job of the professional dancer.

Great technical ability is only part of being a great dancer. At first we might find ourselves applauding a feat that seems astonishing, and six months later, when we've seen dozens of dancers do the same thing with an equal amount of facility, we might applaud less. We have to see to know better. We have to compare. But what we will all like at the beginning and what will make us want to go again soon is a dancer who interests us in an extremely simple way: we will remember afterward what her dance looked like. We will remember the girl, but only because of the dance she showed us. No doubt she was attractive, but she didn't play on that and make us think of it. No doubt she did some steps that seemed incredibly hard, but she didn't stress this, she didn't try to hit us between the eyes with her skill as if to say, "Look! *This* is good." Instead, the big moments of the dance came with the same lack of effort and stress as the small ones. She will quietly and effortlessly seem to conquer the stage space in which she moves to the time of the music.

Where the dancing of dramatic roles is concerned, we must beware of standard images. Some people think that the heroine in *Swan Lake* must always be very slender, short, have black hair parted in the middle, and dance like a bird, with lyrical feeling. Actually, what they mean by lyricism is often lethargy. I have seen dozens of Swan Queens. Some of them looked like birds, others did not, and all gave fine performances. Great ballets were not devised for one type of dancer. Sometimes I hear people say, "But so-and-so wasn't like Pavlova." They forget that if Pavlova and other great dancers of the more distant past were here today, they would not be so sentimental. They were professionals. They would appreciate the greater technical difficulties of modern classical choreography and admire our dancers with an affectionate, professional understanding. If they were dancing today, they know, they would be trying to do the same things our dancers do.

Seeing great classical ballets of the past is like seeing great plays: we are so familiar with *Hamlet* and *Romeo and Juliet,* know the lines so well that we think we can say them with more understanding than any actor. We may see these plays many times and come away disappointed, but one day we experience an extraordinary thing. We hear an actor say the words that are so familiar to us, and suddenly they are no longer private quotations to us. The play becomes new and moving. The same thing happens at the ballet.

Like all the arts, ballet is many things to many people. It is high-brow and something to make fun of to some people because they are afraid to understand it. Others have no wish to understand it and go to the ballet merely to show off their clothes, to see their friends or to make new ones. Still others seek the fashionable and go to the theatre because a particular dance or dancer has been praised extravagantly. Finally, there are those who enjoy the ballet with no pretension at all. They are able to do this because they understand what ballet is as a particular form of entertainment, because they are not frightened by other people telling them that ballet is "important" and "significant." Ballet is important and significant, but first of all it is a pleasure.

When we first start going to the ballet, it is no more significant or important than most of the other things we enjoy watching. It may become significant later, after we have enjoyed it and been entertained by it, after it has become important to us in a personal way. But at first we should simply watch it, as we watch our friends swimming or ice-skating, or playing baseball or tennis. Music, we all know, is an aural perception: reading notes is not sufficient, we must hear them. Ballet is a visual art, like painting or architecture. But unlike painting or architecture, ballet is a visual spectacle that moves: it is not static. We can always see famous paintings by going to museums or famous buildings. Ballet, by comparison, is transitory. We no sooner take in a particular movement in a ballet than it has become another movement. The movements accumulate rapidly, and if we don't watch carefully, we are lost. We must train ourselves to see.

I think we must do this for the same reason and in the same way that we train ourselves to enjoy any of the other arts. To read a book—and we all have experience with this—is not necessarily to understand it. Similarly, to listen is not always to *hear*, and to look not always to *see*. Often, when we want to say that we understand something, we say that we "see" it. Ballet, with application and attention, can be seen and not merely watched.

We go to the theatre to see ballet and watch dancers—people like ourselves, with bodies and heads and arms and legs, running and jumping and lifting to a piece of music. We ask ourselves, why should they do this? The answer is that ballet displays the most beautiful movement of which the human body is capable. The human body, of course, has its limitations. We can bend it and stretch it and lift it, but only to a certain degree. We can, however, decrease the body's limitations with practice. After we have learned to walk, we can run; after we have lifted light objects, we are able to lift heavy ones. The dancer's concern is to fulfill the maximum of what the body can do in a beautiful way.

But the skill of dancers is useless unless it is displayed in a certain form. No one would enjoy watching a group of dancers jump about the stage aimlessly, no matter how well they jumped. Ballet asks the body to move in time. Ballet uses music to indicate time.

Not only in its movement and transitory nature, then, is ballet different from other visual arts. It is two things at once: a composition, a unification of music and dancing. We must hear and see at the same time. This process is something like reading a poem or watching a movie. A poem says something to us, but it speaks in a certain rhythm, a certain time scheme, a certain music. In a movie, the continuous pictures the camera shows us are controlled in sequence and length by what the script specifies. Music is ballet's timekeeper.

To show dancers moving with ideal strength and grace requires beautiful people. Few dancers are beautiful when they begin to study, but when they dance well, they become beautiful. Beautiful dancers are easily associated with ideal characters in stories, with kings and queens and princesses, with love, victory over evil, and death. Many ballets have stories with such heroes and heroines. But sometimes there is no literal story at all in ballet, no narrative. Just as people in real life make different gestures and stand in different positions when they are in different moods, so do dancers in a ballet. A *pas de deux*, for example, is simply a dance for two people, a man and a woman; and even when it is performed on a bare stage with no surrounding story, a *pas de deux* is always a kind of romance. The man is tender and admiring as he lifts the woman and supports her in order to display her beauty, while she, in her reliance on his strength and assurance, admires him in return. This quality in the *pas de deux* may not be apparent to the newcomer to ballet, but the more often this kind of dance is seen, the clearer become its romance and tenderness.

Program music is very easy for most of us to understand. When a composer tells us that his symphony is about a thunderstorm, we immediately have something to compare it with. Some ballets are like program music. These ballets require program notes to tell us what the ballet is really about. Some things, of course, are impossible to represent clearly on stage without the spoken word, but the central idea of every dramatic ballet is clear the first time we see it.

Many ballets are like symphonies that only have identifying numbers. A *pas de deux* or a dance ballet may have to be seen a number of times before we begin to enjoy it. Then passages we were able to like at the beginning become connected with other passages we appreciate later; we soon retain in our minds all the different passages and detect their connections.

Here are a few final suggestions which I hope will enhance your enjoyment of this great art. All ballets are accompanied by music, but because it is hard to listen to music and watch dancers at the same time, play the music over before you go to the ballet or listen to it on records. This is particularly important, naturally, in ballets that do not have conventional stories, where the ballet is based on the music.

Many ballets have plots. There are stories taken from fairy tales (*The Sleeping Beauty*), from ancient myths (*Orpheus*), from the Bible (*Prodigal Son*), from poems (*Illuminations*), and from stories devised especially for particular ballets. Not all of these stories are simple, and brief program notes are often insufficient. As I have said, ideally the best stories for ballets are those that can be *shown*, stories that require no elucidation at all in the written word. But stories inevitably have their complications. These complications were cleared up in the old ballets by pantomime. People could understand this when these ballets were created, for they were familiar with the mime vocabulary, but today, when that vocabulary has gone out of fashion, miming on the stage is often obscure to us and we aren't sure what is happening. Read the stories through, then, and in the theatre you will not be looking down constantly at an incomplete program note. You will be watching the stage.

Many people who go to the ballet, and not only newcomers, feel there is something suspect about ballets without stories—about dance ballets pure and simple. They think there is a hidden meaning they don't grasp. The real point is that they are trying to appreciate ballet intellectually. They expect ballet always to be like the theatre or literature or the movies, which, quite naturally, it is not. Ballet is like nothing so much as dancing. To appreciate it you have to watch it, not think about it. If you only think about it, you'll probably miss the next step and miss something you might have liked very much.

Don't hesitate to go to see ballet companies that you don't think are first-class. Only by seeing *all* the companies can you compare, analyze, and discover what you prefer.

Another thing I'd like to mention is this. Many of us are interested in reading ballet criticism in newspapers and magazines. This criticism can be informative and revealing but I think it is important for us, if we read critics, to read *all* of them, and then go to the ballet and see for ourselves. You will often find that critics radically disagree. How can you discover which one is right unless you see the ballet in question? It also happens very often that dance critics change their minds. Dance critics, like music critics, review the same pieces year after year; what they disliked one year they sometimes like another. If you have read a particular dance critic or music critic over the years, you will discover this to be true.

And, finally, no one can enjoy the ballet if he decides he will go only a certain number of times. If you go only occasionally, once or twice every few years, say, you will never be fully entertained. You must go as many times as possible, as often as you read a novel, as often as you go to the movies or the theatre, as often as you look at paintings or listen to a concert or an opera. We come to enjoy all of these arts through persistent exposure to what each has to teach us about the pleasures that life contains. If we neglect the ballet, we are depriving ourselves of one of the greatest of these pleasures. Naturally, we can live without art: we can eat and sleep and live by our senses alone. But throughout history man has never been satisfied with the necessities of life. He has sought entertainment and enlightenment through art and has become a happier being.

PART THREE

A Brief History of the Ballet

Our word *ballet* comes from the Italian *ballare,* to dance, and it is to the courts of Italy at the height of the Renaissance that we trace the beginning of ballet as we know it today. Dancing as primitive ritual—as a form of hero worship and worship of gods, as glorification of the dead, as a means of celebrating the seasons and the elements—is fundamental in history. Dancing as a popular skill embodied in folk dances is familiar in every country. Dancing as a skill, as a refined human discipline, was developed in religious rites of Mediterranean countries and in the ancient Orient, where chosen persons were taught godlike gestures and movement in order to emulate and celebrate for the populace the drama of their common deities. In the choral dance of Greece, dancing as an art designed for entertainment grew out of the native ritualistic dance. Now the trained performer of a common ritual became the dedicated dancer who aimed to give pleasure to a nondancing audience.

Greek drama began with group or choral dances interrupted and embellished with storytelling. As the chorus of dancers began to sing and to participate in the action of the stories devised by poets, pantomime and meaningful movement evolved. The masks worn by the Greek chorus were a feature of the theatrical dance till late in the eighteenth century. The poet Aeschylus, whose plays were performed by two principal actors and a chorus, rehearsed his choruses in the postures, movements, and gestures proper to the dramatic situation. With his successors, Sophocles and Euripides, the importance of the chorus was proportionately reduced with introduction of a larger cast of characters, but a basic vocabulary of theatrically effective mimicry, attitude, and movement had been established.

What the Greeks achieved was extended by the Romans, who exploited the comic possibilities of mime and dance. The Romans combined the two with acrobatics and circus routines and used them to illustrate popular fables. Tumblers, jesters, and buffoons so humanized dancing that the ritualistic base of Greek tragedy was wholly forgotten.

The comic art of the Romans was reborn in sixteenth-century Italy by traveling players who embodied the *commedia dell'arte:* skilled popular comedians who improvised variations on stock characters—Pulcinella, Punch, Columbine, Pierrot, Harlequin, and others—in stock plots. The gestures, costumes, and characterization of these actors became comic archetypes for all of Europe, influencing many others—the dancers of Paris, the plays of Molière, the carnival puppet shows (*Punch and Judy, Petrouchka*) of the Western world.

While these troupes entertained the provinces of Italy and southern France, the capitals of the Renaissance saw splendid revivals of Roman opulence in the form of pageants and staged celebrations. The rulers of these capitals used every happy event—engagements, marriages, visits of notable persons, military victories—as an excuse for spectacular entertainment in poetry, painting, dance, song, and theatrical mechanics. Appropriate myths inherited from Rome were adapted for the particular occasion, depicted by artists, and danced by the masked members of the court. Interludes of dancing were performed at pageants between recitations and songs, between courses at banquets, and to accompany with appropriate representation the serving of rare dishes at great feasts.

Like the popular art of the *commedia dell'arte,* court dances also had special forms. The folk dances that the courts had sophisticated were further refined into precise floor patterns, simple set steps that required set preparations, and endings performed with elegant bows and flourishes. Popular court dances of this time were called *balletti* (diminutive of *ballo;* hence *ballet*); they were similar to the English morris dance. Castiglione, master of Renaissance manners, wrote in *The Courtier:*

"There are certain other exercises that can be practiced in public and in private, like dancing; and in this I think the Courtier ought to have care, for when dancing in the presence of many and in a place full of people, it seems to me that he should preserve a certain dignity, albeit tempered with a lithe and airy grace of movement; and although he may feel himself to be very nimble and a master of time and measure, let him not attempt those agilities of foot and double steps which we find very becoming in our friend Barletti, but which perhaps would be little suited to a gentleman. Yet in a room privately, as we are now, I think he may try both, and may dance morris-dances and brawls; but not in public unless he be masked, when it is not displeasing even though he be recognized by all." Within the aristocracy of the court a new aristocracy developed—the aristocracy of the best dancer.

Catherine de Médicis introduced the new Italian pageantry to France. Under her influence, Italian musicians and dancing masters came to Paris and staged for the court spectacles consisting of vocal and instrumental music, spoken dialogue, pantomime, dancing, and mechanical effects. The combination of these elements produced the *ballet de cour,* or court ballet, the European model for costly entertainment. With the assistance of their ladies, gentlemen of the court performed *masques*—allegorical plays with poetry and dancing—and *mummings*—colorful dances performed by masked figures among dancers at court balls.

Toward the end of the sixteenth century, Catherine de Médicis, with the assistance of an Italian musician turned dancing master, produced at her court an entertainment that superseded in extravagance and purpose all those previously seen in Europe. This work was called the *Ballet Comique de la Reine.* It employed all the familiar elements of the *ballet de cour* and Italian opera—music, singing, dancing, royal processions, declamation of verse, elaborate scenery and mechanical effects—but for the first time these elements were fused in a dramatic whole that made sense to the spectators: the disparate parts were not mere diversions at a court function, they represented a conscious design to entertain an audience with a unity of comedy, dance, music, and spectacle. The performance cost 3,600,000 francs, lasted for five hours, and was witnessed by some ten thousand people. Its success assured the future of dancing as a necessary part of regal entertainment. It was, in effect, the first ballet as we recognize the term today—a combination of music, dancing, plot, and design.

Seven years later there appeared in France a book that provided the first foundation for the establishment of dancing as a profession. Arbeau's *Orchésographie* (*The Writing of Dancing*) illustrated and gave directions for executing the popular court dances of the time. Arbeau also indicated the principles for the five basic positions of the feet that were to become the foundation of the classic dance. In an effort to teach the dances that had become so popular, it was necessary to arrive at principles upon which all teaching could be based: the limitations of the human body, how and in what directions it could move, and the fundamental steps that best prepared it for movement.

The popular dances of the continent had meanwhile become the courtly habit in England, where Queen Elizabeth appointed a gentleman to the post of Lord Chancellor because "he wore green bows on his shoes and danced the *pavane* to perfection." The poets Ben Jonson, Milton, and Campion, and the great designer Inigo Jones developed masques in imitation of the *ballet de cour*. The masques featured dancing by members of the court, but the real contribution England made to the development of ballet was in the antimasque, a pure dance that preceded the performance of the masque proper, danced by professionals. Ben Jonson thus addressed Queen Elizabeth in 1609:

"And because Her Majesty (best knowing that a principal part of life in these spectacles lay in their variety) had commanded me to think on some dance, or show, that might precede hers, and have the place of a foil, or false masque: It was careful to decline, not only from others, but mine own steps in that kind, since the last year, I had an *antimasque* of boys; and therefore now devised that twelve women, in the habit of hags or witches, sustaining the persons of Ignorance, Suspicion, Credulity, etc., the opposites to good Fame, should fill that part, not as a masque, but a spectacle of strangeness, producing multiplicity of gesture."

In France, dancing flourished at the court of Louis XIV, himself an accomplished dancer. In 1661 Louis XIV founded the first dancing academy in the world, an institution for the instruction of dancing that has continued down to the present day at the Paris Opéra. Under the direction of Beauchamp, the king's dancing master, and the Italian musician and dancer Jean Baptiste Lully, students were taught professionally, to perform on a stage. The great dramatists Molière and Corneille collaborated with Lully in the production of comedy and tragedy ballets that secured the admiration of court and public.

The excellence of stage performance gradually superseded the court dances; the larger, freer movements possible in the theatre replaced the confined gestures of the ballroom. Louis Pécourt became the first *premier danseur,* the first dancer to excel in performances in a theatre. Soon women appeared as professional dancers for the first time.

Beauchamp specified the Five Positions of the classic dance, positions of the feet that became the prerequisite for a dancer's training at the French Academy and the instinctive basis for all performance. The positions are still the basis of ballet today. These positions are absolute in their anatomical authority: the ease with which they are taught to young students, the ease and security they allow the dancer on stage, and, most important of all, the variety of movement made possible by their use. They are as essential to ballet as fundamental techniques of sound structure are to architecture. The Five Positions, with their embodiment of the turned-out leg, distinguished ballet from all other forms of theatrical dance. Ballet dancing had now become a profession, one that could be taught and learned and mastered.

Now that there was fundamental agreement on the basis of the classic dance, there were quarrels about innovations of technique. While Lully in his years at the French Academy had devised dances that were complex in pattern and floor design, he had not considered dancing off the floor, dancing that aimed at elevation, at flight. His successor, Rameau, thought differently and encouraged his dancers to turn in the air and perform steps high off the floor. In Lully's time, when dancing was moved from the ballroom to the stage, it was quite natural for ballet to imitate the technique of dancing in a ballroom—where performers and spectators stood on the same level—but Rameau realized that on a raised stage the dancers were seen from an entirely different perspective by the spectators, that the dancers' feet were clearly visible for the first time, and, accordingly, that the dance must make an adjustment of technique to hold its audience. The conservative adherents of Lully, those who advocated a "horizontal" dance, contested the theories of the new, rebel "verticalists" of Rameau.

This contest between the Lullists and the Rameauists contained the basic argument that runs throughout the history of ballet down to the present: the argument between "tradition" and innovation, between strict classicism and expressiveness, between pure dance and "literary" ballets, between ballet and modern dance. This argument was embodied in two popular dancers of the time: Marie Camargo and Marie Sallé. Camargo, champion of the new *danse verticale,* was a brilliant technician, praised for her airiness and strength. She was the first *danseuse* to perform the *entrechat-quatre,* to execute high *cabrioles* and jumps. To display her skill, Camargo shortened the conventional cumbersome ballet dress so that her agile steps might be seen. A great innovator, Camargo was also a traditionalist, interested in technique rather than the human and dramatic elements of the dance.

Camargo's rival, Marie Sallé, "muse of gracious, modest gesture," exemplified in her refined and gracious dancing a spiritual rather than technical elevation. Here the accent was on nobility of posture and deportment and on characterization of a particular part for dramatic effect. Sallé did not dance simply for the sake of dancing. Her most famous role, that of the statue beloved by Pygmalion, she devised for herself. Called a *ballet-pantomime* in opposition to the rigid and formal opera-ballets of the Paris Opéra, Sallé's dancing in this work was faithful to the Greek style of its story. Effecting another innovation in costume, Sallé let her hair down and over her corset and petticoat wore only a muslin dress "draped about her in the manner of a Greek statue."

Rameau's ballets at the Paris Opéra accommodated both the new technique and dramatic expression within the frame of the opera-ballet, a series of danced *entrées* connected by a threadlike plot. The *entrées* depicted dances in various countries—Turkey, Peru, Persia, America—which allowed for spectacle as well as for occasional dramatic interest in stories imposed upon the natives. With their great geographical variety and concern for imitation of native dances throughout the world, Rameau's ballets brought down to earth the mythological characters with which the dance had been preoccupied since the Renaissance.

Another dancer wanted ballet to go still further. After Rameau's death, ballet at the Paris Opéra degenerated to the point where each of its elements— dancing, music, story, and spectacle—seemed to exist for its own sake. The dancers' technical proficiency was displayed, with marked contempt for music, in ridiculous dramas. Jean Georges Noverre, a student of Louis Dupré, a great admirer of Marie Sallé and of the English actor David Garrick, wanted to unify the elements of ballet into a dramatic whole. He wrote, in ballet's first critical text, *Letters on the Dance and Ballets,* that poetry, painting, and dancing should be a "faithful likeness of beautiful nature," that dancing should be united with pantomime to ensure dramatic expression, and that such expression must be related directly to music. Working with such musicians as Christoph Willibald Gluck, whose reforms in opera were closely allied to Noverre's in ballet; with such dancers as Gaetan Vestris, first great classical dancer in Europe; with Marie Allard and Madeleine Guimard, superb mimes as well as dancers; and with the patronage of such notable persons as Marie Antoinette— Noverre successfully initiated reforms in ballets that were seen and applauded all over Europe. His ballets were danced in London, Vienna, Paris, Milan, and St. Petersburg. All of Europe delighted in the new *ballet d'action*—works in which dancers reflected in their movement and gesture the dramatic intention of plot and music. Among Noverre's students were Vincenzo Galeotti, who became ballet master at the Royal Theatre, Copenhagen; Charles Didelot, the Frenchman who became "the father of Russian ballet" at the Imperial Theatre in St. Petersburg; and Jean Dauberval, who, in *La Fille Mal Gardée,* created what was perhaps the first comic ballet.

One of Dauberval's pupils, Salvatore Vigano, extended Noverre's reforms in spectacular ballets produced in his native Italy. At La Scala, Milan, Vigano mounted works that unified music, dancing, and mime as Noverre had never been able to do. Mime, Vigano regarded as the expression of the "movement of the soul: it is the language of all peoples, of all ages and times. It depicts better than words extremes of joy and sorrow . . . It is not sufficient for me to please the eyes. I wish to involve the heart." Indeed, he regarded mime with such importance that the composer Rossini remarked to Stendhal, the choreographer's great admirer, that Vigano's ballets had too much pantomime and not enough dancing. Vigano's idea was the *choreodrame*, ballets in which Noverre's principle of dramatically expressive embodiment was seen in every dancer on stage, in the *corps de ballet* as well as in the performances of principal dancers. Within particular settings and plots, Vigano worked tirelessly to arrange dances appropriate to drama and score. Under his direction, La Scala became the greatest ballet theatre in all of Europe.

This pre-eminence of Italian ballet was sustained by the dancer, choreographer, and teacher Carlo Blasis, student of Dauberval, who wrote—in his *Elementary Treatise upon the Theory and Practice of the Art of Dancing* (1820) and in the *Code of Terpsichore* (1829)—the first lexicons of the classic dance. Here the basic theories of all the great dancers and choreographers who preceded Blasis were tacitly assumed in general instructions to pupils and ballet masters and were embodied in detailed, illustrated instruction on practice: the proper execution of positions, poses, movements, and steps of elevation—all the resources known to the classic dancer. Blasis' work has been the foundation of all instruction in the classic dance ever since. The classic disciplines he insisted upon in his teaching at La Scala were precursors of the instruction that later dominated the Russian Imperial School at St. Petersburg and ballet everywhere.

Vincenzo Galeotti produced in 1786 in Copenhagen a ballet still in the current repertory, *The Whims of Cupid and the Ballet Master*. His most distinguished student, August Bournonville, who studied also in Paris under Vestris, advanced Galeotti's commitment to dramatic expression in ballet. Audiences at performances of the Royal Danish Ballet today recognize the importance of pantomime and drama that Bournonville introduced in the more than fifty ballets he choreographed for that company. They recognize, too, a vigorous dance style that Bournonville established and taught to Christian Johansson, the Swedish dancer who became in St. Petersburg the most celebrated *premier danseur* of his time. From 1860 until his death in 1903, Johansson taught in St. Petersburg all of the great dancers of the Russian ballet.

Founded in 1735 to teach court cadets the fashionable dances of Europe, the Russian Imperial School, adjunct of the Imperial Theatre, was directed by a series of French and Italian ballet masters, who produced in St. Petersburg the work of European choreographers and invited to the Russian capital foreign dancers to star in these works. The Frenchman Charles Didelot was the first to establish the Russian school and theatre on a firm base. Didelot, student of Noverre, Dauberval, and the *premier danseur* Auguste Vestris, was appointed ballet master at St. Petersburg in 1816. He established at the Imperial School a consistent foundation of classical instruction and mounted such excellent ballets at the Imperial Theatre that the poet Pushkin was moved to say that in Didelot's ballets there was more poetry than in all the French literature of that time. After Didelot's death (1837) the Russian Theatre continued to flourish, but principally as an opulent setting not for Russian, but for the finest ballets and dancers of Western Europe.

In Western Europe of the 1830s, the supremacy of Italian dance technique combined with the Romanticism that dominated the other arts of the time to produce a new kind of ballet. Romanticism in ballet, as in the other arts, was a rebellion against classical subject matter, classical technique, and classical attitudes. The Romantic ballet extended the classical dance technique with daring innovations: girls danced on their toes for the first time, and new steps of elevation were devised to display voluptuous real-life heroines who by theatrical magic became idealized, unattainable creatures of wood and glade. Heroines of ballets were no longer characters from classical mythology: wronged peasant girls and sylphs displaced the Medeas, the Junos, the Aphrodites. Audiences rejoiced in the theatrical display of the beauty of the broken heart. Paris, again, and London were the ballet capitals of the world.

Marie Taglioni, creator of the wistful *La Sylphide*, became the first famous dancer Europe had ever known. The ballet *Giselle*, inspired by the Romantic poet Gautier, superseded Taglioni's vehicle in excellence of plot and dance, and enthralled audiences from St. Petersburg to Boston. Taglioni's contemporaries—Carlotta Grisi, the first dancer of *Giselle;* the Danish ballerina Lucile Grahn; the lively Fanny Cerrito—appeared in a score of ballets on romantic themes, while the great Fanny Elssler, Taglioni's archrival, was so secure in her reputation that she could abandon the opera houses of Europe for two years and dance on tour throughout the United States. Elssler's phenomenal success in America in 1840–42 was typified by the reception tendered her by President Van Buren and his Cabinet at Washington and by the banquet given by members of Congress in her honor at the Capitol. In 1845 Jules Perrot, the Romantic ballet's finest choreographer and the one male dancer who managed to hold his own in this age of romanticism, staged in London a special dance for Taglioni and three of her rivals—Grisi, Cerrito, and Grahn. The success of this *Pas de Quatre* obliged *The Times* to call the ballet "the greatest Terpsichorean exhibition that ever was known in Europe."

While the triumphs of these first great ballet stars increased the popularity of the art, the art itself began to suffer. Interest in all performances was centered on the stars and what they danced; people cared less and less about the music they danced to, the plots they acted, or the productions that displayed them. Taglioni or Elssler, alone, was enough. Prospective dancers and choreographers therefore saw little profit in remaining in Paris and London. In Russia, they knew, the Tsar's court required spectacular entertainment. And it could support it by the most bountiful treasury in Europe.

In the year Taglioni retired (1847), a young Frenchman, Marius Petipa, was engaged as a dancer at the Russian Imperial Theatre. Petipa was successful as a dancer in St. Petersburg; there he watched the work of the French ballet masters Jules Perrot and Arthur Saint-Léon as they entertained a new avid audience of aristocratic balletomanes. Then suddenly there was an opportunity to create a ballet of his own. In 1860 he had restaged the Perrot-Coralli *Giselle*, the romantic ballet that seemed certain to remain a permanent fixture in the Russian repertory. But ballet by this time required a new impetus, which Petipa discovered in a reawakened classicism. He devised for his ballet a mass dance on a tremendous scale, with spectacular stage effects. Beginning in 1862, with his first great success, a four-act dance extravaganza set in the desert, with pyramids and colossal palaces of ancient Egypt, Petipa succeeded Jules Perrot as ballet master to the Imperial Theatre. His influence was to dominate the Russian ballet almost up to the time of his death fifty years later. His supremacy survived the reigns of four Tsars, who delighted in the entertainment he provided their courts and in the universal model of excellence he caused the Russian ballet to become. Petipa created fifty-seven full-length, evening-long ballets, devised countless shorter *divertissements*, restaged seventeen ballets by other choreographers, and mounted ballets in thirty-four operas during his years at the Imperial Theatre.

St. Petersburg was now the ballet capital of the world. The French ballet master Petipa welcomed to Russia dancers and teachers from Italy, France, Germany, and Scandinavia; with their assistance he made the Imperial Ballet School the greatest in the world. Petipa's school provided the standard for the dancer's training, as his theatre was the exemplar for the dancer's performance. Foreign dancers who came to Russia for guest engagements introduced diverse technical elements from all of Europe: brilliant classicists, who had been trained in Italy under the disciplines founded by Blasis, contributed to the growth of a new style. This style was not so much Russian as polygenous. It was historic in its all-inclusiveness, in its gigantic assimilation of classic dance techniques as they were practiced in all of Europe. It produced, toward the end of the nineteenth century, great Russian dancers, who danced in such ballets as *Swan Lake* and *The Nutcracker*, works by the Russian choreographer Lev Ivanov, who produced them under Petipa's direction, and Peter Ilyich Tchaikovsky. Tchaikovsky was commissioned by Petipa to write the score for the ballet that turned out to be the masterpiece of both men. *The Sleeping Beauty*, Russian ballet music, as well as Russian ballet and Russian dancers, was the accepted standard throughout the Western World.

Petipa died in 1910. Some years before his death, the classical ballet he had perfected had passed its zenith; it began to disintegrate as its elements became disassociated. A young dancer and choreographer, Michel Fokine, who in 1905 created for the ballerina Anna Pavlova the short lyric dance *The Dying Swan*,

rebelled against the omnipotence of "tradition." Like Sallé, Noverre, and
Vigano before him, Fokine aimed at unification of dancing, music, and design.
He asserted that dancing was interpretative, expressive. "The ballet must no
longer be made up of *numbers, entries,* and so on. It must show artistic unity
of conception . . . Ballet must have complete unity of expression, a unity
which is made up of harmonious blending of the three elements—music, painting, and plastic art." Fokine's suggested reforms were rejected by his superiors
at the Imperial Theatre. They were championed by a man who understood
music, painting, and dancing: Serge Diaghilev.

Diaghilev wished to take the Russian ballet to Paris. In 1907 he had
presented Russian music to Western Europe for the first time, and he now
wished Europeans to admire what he knew to be the finest dancing in the
world. He chose Fokine as choreographer to a company to be known as
Diaghilev's Ballets Russes. Anna Pavlova, Tamara Karsavina, and Vaslav Nijinsky secured leave from the Imperial Theatre to be his principal dancers. His
dancers, his designers, his musicians, were the finest in Russia.

On May 18, 1909, Diaghilev's Ballets Russes opened their first season in
Paris. In the new ballets of Fokine, ballets like *Prince Igor* and *Les Sylphides,*
and in the quality of the dancing, the music, and theatrical design, the season
was an unprecedented success. This pattern of success continued the next year,
with the Stravinsky-Fokine *Firebird,* and the next, with the Stravinsky-Fokine
Petrouchka, and the next, with the Debussy-Nijinsky *The Afternoon of a Faun*
and the Fokine-Weber *Le Spectre de la Rose,* and so on, season after season,
year after year, for twenty years of dance entertainment based on an inviolable
rule of uniform excellence in choreography, music, decor, and performance.

Paris was again the world capital of dance. Diaghilev's Ballets Russes provided a center of artistic endeavor such as Europe had not known since the
Medici courts of the Renaissance. And Diaghilev, like the Renaissance princes,
not only perpetuated established talent, he discovered, encouraged, and developed talent. He numbered among his principal female dancers Pavlova, Karsavina, Lopokova, Spessivtzeva, Dubrovska, Nemtchinova, Sokolova, Tchernicheva, Egorova, Nijinska, Danilova, and Markova; among the men, Nijinsky,
Fokine, Vladimiroff, Bolm, Mordkin, Novikoff, Volinine, Cecchetti, Massine,
Woicikowski, Idzikowski, Dolin, and Lifar. Among his composers were Stravinsky, Debussy, Ravel, Richard Strauss, Fauré, Satie, Respighi, De Falla,
Prokofiev, Poulenc, Auric, Milhaud, Dukelsky, Rieti, Lambert, Berners, Sau-
guet, and Nabokov. His designers were such painters as Benois, Roerich,
Bakst, Soudeikine, Doboujinsky, Larionov, Picasso, Derain, Matisse, Braque,
Gris, Utrillo, Miró, Tchelitchew, Di Chirico and Rouault. His choreographers
were Fokine, Nijinsky, Massine, Nijinska, and myself.

Since the disbandment of Diaghilev's company following his death in 1929,
his dancers and choreographers have influenced ballet throughout the world.
Serge Lifar has been for many years ballet master at the Paris Opéra, which,
with the Royal Danish Ballet at Copenhagen, continues the oldest traditions of

teaching and performance in the free world. Ninette de Valois, a soloist with the Diaghilev company, founded a ballet company and an associated school in London which became in time the Royal Ballet, the national company of Great Britain. Massine and I were the first choreographers of the Ballet Russe de Monte Carlo, founded in Europe in 1932. In America, I founded with Lincoln Kirstein the American Ballet, precursor of the present New York City Ballet. The American Ballet's complementary group, Kirstein's Ballet Caravan, produced, in addition to classical works, ballets based on native American material—*Filling Station, Billy the Kid, Yankee Clipper,* etc.—with choreography by such American dancers as Lew Christensen, Eugene Loring, and William Dollar and with music by American composers. The New York City Ballet, with its associated school, the School of American Ballet, represents the result of many years of work toward the achievement of excellence in classical performance.

The Ballet Theatre, now the American Ballet Theatre, founded by Lucia Chase and Richard Pleasant, grew out of the New York ballet school of Mikhail Mordkin. Fokine, who had staged many of his own works for many ballet companies, supervised productions of his ballets by the Ballet Theatre and created his last ballet for this company in 1941. The English choreographer Antony Tudor, who—like Frederick Ashton, principal choreographer to the Sadler's Wells Ballet—had been a student in London of Marie Rambert, joined the Ballet Theatre at its inception. This company has produced many works by native American choreographers.

Many other companies have appeared since. The City Center Joffrey Ballet in New York, the Pennsylvania Ballet in Philadelphia, the Boston Ballet, the Dance Theatre of Harlem, the Eliot Feld Ballet are representative of the tremendous growth in the number and talent of our dance ensembles. In Canada, the National Ballet of Canada and the Royal Winnipeg Ballet have concurrently set high standards for performance. Companies from England, Denmark, Germany, Russia, France, Holland, Belgium, Australia, and other countries that visit North America regularly bring us new repertories. It is possible to compare.

Our schools for the teaching of ballet have established new criteria for excellence. You cannot really have a ballet company without a school to train the talent you require. Dancers from all over the world come to work at our schools when they visit us, just as we go to theirs. Ballet is a truly international art; everyone understands.

Nancy Hanks, chairman of the National Endowment for the Arts, acknowledged in 1976 that dance is "the fastest growing art in the nation." In New York it used to be that the summer was the doldrums and no ballet companies would appear. Now, it is almost impossible to find enough theatres for the companies who wish to perform here in the summer. The dance season is now a year-round affair that never stops.

Writing in the New York *Times* about ballet's soaring popularity, the critic

Anna Kisselgoff noted: "In 1965, the report of the Rockefeller Panel on the Arts placed dance attendance in the United States at one million. For 1975, it was fifteen million, according to the Association of American Dance Companies . . . These are not fanciful figures. One has only to compute the number of seats and performances among the array of dance companies scheduled in New York between April and September 1976 to realize that close to one and a half million people will attend dance performances in this city in just the next four months."

With more persons watching dance performances regularly, knowledge of and concern for ballet have grown, too. Many companies, like the New York City Ballet, have wonderful subscribers—interested persons who have come to know what we represent, wish to keep up with it and to see more, regularly. Their support, needless to say, is vital to us. And I do not mean in terms of financial support, valuable as that is; I mean in terms of interest and response. They simply *know* more than those who come only occasionally and they are a most rewarding and perceptive audience. The more companies fortunate enough to have that kind of support, the better for all of dance. Ballet has come a long way from its beginnings at the court of Catherine de Médicis in the sixteenth century.

PART FOUR

*Chronology of Significant Events
in the History of Ballet*

Ballet, we have seen, is an art without nationality; it has a family history. The new ballets we see on the stage today come at the end of a long line of descent from the past. Dance has a living past in the dancers of today; its traditional theory of basic steps and movements is the foundation of its current practice. No one can learn to dance without a teacher, and that teacher was the student of an earlier master. In the eighteenth century, the Frenchman Noverre and the Italian Galeotti taught the Dane Antoine Bournonville, whose son Auguste was the master of the Swede Johansson, teacher of the Russians Pavlova and Fokine.

The dancers, teachers, and choreographers we are familiar with today are thus offshoots of a great international family tree—living embodiments of a precise tradition. Ballet's history is a record of teachers and students: what the teacher handed down, what the student learned, what he carried forward and extended, what he rejected, what he changed. In the gradual unfolding of this story, we see how the contributions of different individuals in different countries move forward, seem to falter, then converge in the ballet we know today.

1469   Lorenzo de' Medici, great patron of the arts, succeeds to the rule of Florence. His marriage to Clarice Orsini: grand procession, tournament; allegorical masque, executed by the foremost painters, poets, and sculptors of the time, depicts in song and spectacle the glories of antiquity.

1475   Grand tournament of Giuliano de' Medici is held at Florence: scene, costumes, and dance figures commemorated in the *Birth of Venus, Mars and Venus,* and *Primavera* of Botticelli.

c.1500   Development in Italy and southern France of the popular court dance form the *ballo,* social dances performed in a ballroom or in the open air. The *ballo* is freer, more animated, than the other variety of dance popular at this time, the *basse danse* (low dance). Originally Italian, the *basse danse* was a carefully prescribed court dance, the ancestor of the minuet. *Balletti* is the diminutive of *ballo,* and it is from this word that we derive *ballet.*

1512   The *masque,* variation of princely Italian masquerades, is introduced in England, at the court of Henry VIII. Social, rather than theatrical or dramatic, at first, the *masque* later includes songs, speeches, introductory dance, general dance, and finale of speech and chorus.

1523   Robert Copland's *The Manner of Dancing Basse Dances After the Use of France* appears in England.

1533   Catherine de Médicis arrives in France. Her marriage to Henry of Orleans (later Henry II) takes place: introduction of Italian pageantry to France.

c.1555   Baldassarino de Belgiojoso (Balthazar de Beaujoyeulx), Italian violinist, immigrates to France and becomes a member of the French Court: later develops French and Italian elements into the first modern ballet.

1558   Royal fete and ball is held on April 24 for the marriage of Francis, eldest son of Catherine de Médicis, and Mary Queen of Scots: spectacle with *"masques* and *mummeries,"* beginning of the *ballet de cour,* costly court entertainments consisting of vocal and instrumental music, spoken dialogue, pantomime, dancing, and mechanical effects. All dancers in these ballets wear masks. Ladies of the court participate, but principal roles are taken by men.

1570   Jean Antoine de Baïf, French poet, and Joachim Thibault de Courville, French musician, found the Academy of St. Cecilia in Paris to encourage the fusion of poetry, music, and movement after the manner of the ancients. Dancing to be in accord with music and song.

1571   Troupe of Italian comedians popularize in Paris the *commedia dell'arte* (Columbine, Harlequin, et al.), traditional native farces of Italy.

c.1575 Giovanni da Bologna's *Mercury*—inspiration for the *attitude,* basic prose of classic ballet. "On one occasion, performing the part of Mercury, I took, as I turned in my pirouette, the attitude of the statue of Mercury by Bologna." —Carlo Blasis, 1830.

1580   The history of ballet as we know it today begins on October 15, when Beaujoyeulx presents *Ballet Comique de la Reine* at the court of Catherine de Médicis on the occasion of the marriage of Marguerite of Lorraine, the Queen's sister, to the Duc de Joyeuse: assimilation of French and Italian elements of dance, music, and spectacle into a coherent dramatic whole. To its creator, this work was called a *ballet* because it presents "a geometrical arrangement of numerous people dancing together under a diverse harmony of many instruments"; it is *comique* "for the lovely, tranquil, and happy conclusion by which it ends, by the quality of the personages involved, who are almost all gods and goddesses." Beaujoyeulx's musico-dramatic synthesis of Italian opera and French *ballet de cour* originates the school of French ballet and opera that is to serve as the model in Europe for two centuries.

1588   Jehan Tabourot, priest of Langre, publishes—under the pseudonym Thoinot Arbeau—*Orchésographie* (writing of dancing), *treatise in the form of a dialogue whereby all manner of persons may easily acquire and practice the honorable exercise of dancing:* illustrations and directions on the proper execution of dances of the time (pavane, galliard, gavotte, etc.), and establishment of principles for the five absolute positions of the classic dance (*see* Glossary). Arbeau's work provides the potential technical base for instruction in dancing and assures French supremacy in the initial development of ballet.

1597   Thomas Morley's *Plaine and Easie Introduction to Practical Musick* details the differences between types of music for dancing, calling the pavane "a kind of staid musick ordained for grave dancing" and the galliard "a lighter and more stirring kind of dance." The pavane, galliard, allemande, sarabande, polonaise, minuet, jig, gavotte, etc., were originally dance tunes that originated among the peoples of Italy, France, Germany, Spain, and Poland in the sixteenth century or before. These popular or courtly dances soon gave rise to a new form in music, as composers stylized the contrasting moods of the dances in the writing of *suites.*

1605   Ben Jonson, English poet and dramatist, and the architect Inigo Jones collaborate on the production of the *Twelfth Night Masque:* unrivaled scenic and dramatic effect.

1607   *Orfeo,* opera by Monteverdi, is performed on February 24 at the Academia degl'Invaghiti, Mantua: development of principles of *ballet comique* in musical work; first opera to use accompaniment of full orchestra.

1608   First antimasque, in *The Hue and Cry after Cupid,* Jonson-Jones, surrounds heroic figures with sportive dancers to amuse spectators with "antic faces" and "ridiculous gesture."

1625   Ballet in France regresses to nondramatic dances introduced by poems or songs.

1632   Jean Baptiste Lully (Giovanni Battista Lulli), musician and dancer, is born in Italy on November 29.

1634   First performance of *Comus,* masque by John Milton.

1641   *Prosperity of the Arms of France,* ballet by Cardinal Richelieu, performed.

1645   Cardinal Mazarin, successor to Richelieu as Prime Minister, introduces Italian grand opera to Paris: France absorbs Italian mechanical stage devices to increase the spectacle of ballet.

1645   Louis XIV, at age seven, first dances publicly.

1653   Louis XIV appears as *Le Roi Soleil* (the Sun King) in the *Ballet de la Nuit,* composed partly by Lully.

1658   "Tragedy and ballet are two species of painting in which what is most illustrious in the world is placed on view," writes Abbé Michel de Pure in *Idée des Spectacles.*

1661   Académie de Danse is founded by Louis XIV in a room in the Louvre, Paris: "Although the art of dancing has always been recognized as one of the most honorable, and the most necessary for the training of the body, to give it the first and most natural foundations for all kinds of exercises and amongst others for those of arms; and as it is . . . many ignorant people have tried to disfigure the dance and to spoil it . . . we deemed it opportune to establish in our good town of Paris a Royal Academy of Dancing." On June 28, 1669, Louis XIV of France grants royal letters patent for the establishment of a theatre in which to present opera and drama with music: L'Académie de Musique et de Danse, the institution we know today as the Paris Opéra. Although the name of this institution has changed with different French regimes and it has occupied numerous buildings, the name on the Théâtre de l'Opéra in Paris is L'Académie de Musique et de Danse, representing almost three hundred years of uninterrupted history in teaching and performance.

1664   On January 29, in *Le Mariage Forcé,* Italian composer and dancer Lully begins collaboration with the French poet-playwright Molière; *commedia dell'arte* combined with the tradition of French court dancing in the creation of comedy ballets to incidental music. Louis XIV, Lully, and Pierre Beauchamp, first great French dancer, participate in performance.

1670   *Les Amants Magnifiques* is presented: comedy ballet by Molière and Lully in which the performers "by their steps, gestures, and movements, visibly expressed all things." On October 23 there is presented *Le Bourgeois Gentilhomme,* last collaboration between Molière and Lully: play includes overture, ten musical numbers, dialogue for soprano and contralto, a ballet in

Act One (*Ballet des Nations*), and finale for solo and chorus. Lully dances at the first performance. Excerpt from the play: "All the ills of mankind, all the tragic misfortunes that fill the history books, all political blunders, all the failures of great commanders, have arisen merely from lack of skill in dancing . . . When a man has been guilty of a mistake, either in ordering his own affairs, or in directing those of the State, or in commanding an army, do we not always say: so-and-so has made a false step . . . ?"

1671   *Psyche,* tragedy ballet by Molière, Corneille, Lully, and Quinault, presented on January 17.

1671   The Paris Académie opens on March 19 with *Pomone,* a *pastorale* with music by Cambert, dances by Beauchamp, and text by the Abbé Perrin, director of the Académie.

1671   Pierre Beauchamp, dancing master to the King, becomes first ballet master of the Académie. Dancing begins to be a profession, rather than a court pastime.

1672   Lully succeeds to the directorship of the Académie as composer, conductor, and manager; dancing school inaugurated under Beauchamp. Under Lully's direction, formal court dance is adjusted to the stage: larger, more open movements of the theatre replace small, confined gestures of the ballroom.

1672   Louis Pécourt, pupil of Beauchamp, makes his debut at the Académie, becomes *premier danseur,* dancing principal roles in ballets by Lully and Beauchamp. He was "handsome and well made," danced "with all possible noblesse," appeared always "with grace, justness, and activity," and was "so agreeable in conversation that the greatest lords took pleasure in his company."

1681   *The Triumph of Love* (Lully) presented on January 21 at St. Germaine en Laye, the first ballet in which women appeared as professional dancers. Ladies of the French court dance the first performance on this work (but it was later danced at L'Académie Royale, when Mademoiselle Lafontaine, first *première danseuse* in the history of ballet, made her debut).

1682   Père Claude François Menestrier's *Ballets Ancient and Modern* becomes the first published history of dancing.

1684   *An Arrow against Profane and Promiscuous Dancing Drawn Out of the Quiver of the Scriptures,* by Increase Mather, is published in Boston.

1687   Lully dies on March 22. In the fifteen years he superintended the Académie, Lully produced twenty grand operas in addition to other works and firmly established the new school of opera-ballet, in which music and dancing shared equally in the drama. Italian grand operas of this time give dancing a secondary place and include ballets only as *divertissements.* Lully, violinist and dancer, leaves French lyric drama so successfully formulated that Paris is the theatre capital of the world, a universally accepted model of teaching and execution.

1687   Beauchamp retires as ballet master; he is succeeded by Louis Pécourt.

1689   *Dido and Aeneas,* opera by Purcell, is performed by Josias Priest's Singing and Dancing Academy in London.

1697   Birth of Louis Dupré, *Le Grand Dupré,* great French dancer: a "rare harmony in movement earned for the celebrated Dupré the glorious title of '*Dieu de la Danse*': and in fact this excellent dancer seemed a divinity rather than a man: the calm and flowing continuity of his every movement and the perfect coordination and control of every muscle made for a perfect ensemble."—Noverre.

c.1700   Pierre Beauchamp names the five basic positions of the classic dance (*see* Glossary). As a dancer, Beauchamp had also been a model for future technique in dancing; he was a virtuoso executant of *pirouettes* and *tours en l'air*.

1701   *Choreography, or the Art of Writing Dancing* is published in Paris. This early work on dance notation was edited by Raoul Ager Feuillet; it has been attributed to Louis Pécourt.

1705   Françoise Prévost succeeds Mademoiselle Lafontaine as *première danseuse* at the Académie. Rameau wrote that Prévost "put into one single dance all the rules we are able to give in our art and she puts them into practice with such grace, justness, and activity that she may be looked upon as a prodigy of her kind."

1707   Birth of Marie Sallé. Niece of the famous harlequin Francisque Moylin, and daughter of a tumbler, she is to endow her dancing with dramatic gesture and mimed expression and become a great *danseuse* of the century.

1708   At the Château of the Duchesse du Maine, two celebrated dancers from the Opéra, Françoise Prévost and Jean Balon, perform the final scene of Act Four of Corneille's *Horace* as a pantomime. The scene is acted in silence, "through gestures and bodily movements, among which was not a single all-too-pronounced dance step": early introduction of dramatic mime into ballet.

1710   Marie-Anne Cupis de Camargo, celebrated French dancer of Spanish descent, is born on April 15; she becomes the principal rival of Sallé.

1712   *Manual*, by John Rich, provides a series of exercises for facility in dancing based on the five basic positions indicated by Arbeau (1588) and specified by Beauchamp (c. 1700): beginning of a systematic foundation for the ideal execution of the classic dance.

1714   Birth of Christoph Willibald Gluck, German composer, the founder of modern opera.

1717   On March 2, John Weaver, English dancer and ballet master at the Drury Lane Theatre, London, presents a "new dramatic pantomime, after the manner of the ancient pantomimes," *The Loves of Mars and Venus*. This pantomime ballet with a plot is the first *ballet d'action* on record. Wrote Colley Cibber: "The fable of Mars and Venus was formed into a connected presentation of dances in character, wherein the passions were so happily expressed, and the whole story was so intelligibly told, by a mute narration of gesture only, that even thinking spectators allowed it both a pleasing and rational entertainment."

1721   *Anatomical and Mechanical Lectures upon Dancing*, by John Weaver, is published: establishment of an anatomical base for proper dance instruction. "Dancing is an elegant and regular movement, harmoniously composed of beautiful *Attitudes*, and contrasted graceful postures of the Body, and parts thereof."

1725   *The Dancing Master*, by Pierre Rameau, is published: descriptions of dances of the time and detailed instructions on the five absolute positions. "Dancing adds graces to the gifts which nature has bestowed upon us, by regulating the movements of the body and setting it in its proper positions. And, if we do not completely eradicate the defects with which we are born, it mitigates or conceals them. This single instance will suffice to explain its utility and to excite a desire to be skilled in it."

1725   Marie Sallé appears at John Rich's Lincoln's Inn Fields Theatre, London, in ballet-pantomimes. It was in England, rather than in the set, conventional pattern of ballet at the Paris Opéra, that Sallé could use freely the gestural dance that interested her. She was so popular, however, that the Opéra continually asked her to return. When she did so, the Opéra was obliged to produce the *ballets d'action* that she acted and danced with such expression. Thus popularity and intelligence combined to introduce a new kind of ballet to Europe.

1726   Marie Camargo makes her debut at the Opéra on May 5.

1726   First French dancing master is appointed to the Court of Denmark.

1727   Jean Georges Noverre is born on April 29.

1729   Gaetan Vestris is born in April, in Florence. He becomes the first *danseur* of his time, the first great classical dancer in Europe, a choreographer, mime, and ballet master; he is student of Louis Dupré.

c.1730   The *danse haute* (high dance) begins to replace the *danse terre à terre* (dance close to earth). The old court spectacles had been performed in rooms, with the audiences grouped about the dance area on raised platforms. In the theatre, the stage itself was raised and the audience watched from below. Lully's ballets, though making certain concessions to the theatre, still remained horizontal, describing dances on the horizontal plane of the stage floor as if it were still the ballroom and audiences were looking down on it. Rameau aimed at a vertical dance, where a theatre audience could be entertained by dancers who jumped and leaped. In the fierce controversy that raged between the Lullists and Rameauists, the latter found great support in the popularity of the spectacular *danse haute* of Marie Camargo, who about this time shortened the traditional ballet dress in order that the audience might see the *entrechat* and other remarkable steps of elevation. Camargo is credited with introducing the ninety-degree turnout for dancers and the *entrechat-quatre* (*see* Glossary).

1734   Marie Sallé creates in London the ballet-pantomime *Pygmalion*. "She has dared to appear in this *entrée* without pannier, skirt, or bodice, and with her hair down; she did not wear a single ornament on her head. Apart from her corset and petticoat she wore only a simple dress of muslin draped about her in the manner of a Greek statue."

1735   Opening of the Imperial Dancing Academy in St. Petersburg, Russia, as the Empress Anna Ivanovna orders that all cadets be taught to dance in order to replace foreign artists at the Russian court. A Frenchman, Lande, is appointed director and an Italian, Francesco Araya, is engaged to teach the cadets Italian dances.

1735   *Les Indes Galantes*, opera-ballet by J. P. Rameau, is presented at the Opéra on August 23 with Dupré, Camargo, and Sallé.

c.1737   The works of Jean Philippe Rameau begin to replace those of Lully at the

Académie. At this time, the original thirty-seven members of the company have increased to one hundred and forty-nine.

1738 Imperial St. Petersburg Theatrical Academy (now the Leningrad Choreographic Academy) is founded.

1743 Jean Georges Noverre, pupil of Dupré, makes his debut at the Opéra Comique, Paris.

1745 *The Princess of Navarre*, lyric comedy ballet by Rameau, libretto by Voltaire, is produced.

1745 On December 29, Jean Barthélemy produces in Berlin his recollection of Marie Sallé's *Pygmalion*. The statue is danced by La Barberina (Barberina Campanini), Italian *danseuse* who popularizes the Italian pantomime in European dance. She appeared at the Opéra, where Rameau arranged dances for her, and in London at John Rich's theatre, where she acquired knowledge of English pantomime. C. H. Graun composes for this production of *Pygmalion* music that substitutes for the conventional dance numbers a free score related directly to the action: the first score of this kind. Among the dancers in this production is Jean Georges Noverre.

1746 "It is up to poetry, music, and dance to present to us the image of human actions and passions," writes Charles Batteux, *Les Beaux Arts reduit à un même principe*.

1748 The Royal Theatre, home of the Royal Danish Ballet, opens in Copenhagen.

1750 Noverre partners Camargo at Lyon.

c.1751 Noverre stages his first ballet, *Les Fêtes Chinoises* (*The Chinese Festivals*).

1751 Gaetan Vestris succeeds Louis Dupré as *premier danseur* at the Opéra.

1755 On February 5, Noverre signs contract with David Garrick to arrange dances at the Drury Lane Theatre, London. To Garrick, Noverre is "the Shakespeare of the Dance." To Noverre, Garrick is "the most handsome, the most perfect, and the most worthy of admiration of all actors; he may be regarded as the Proteus of our time, because he understood all styles and presented them with a perfection and truth which aroused not only the applause and praise of his countrymen, but also excited the admiration and encomiums of all foreigners. He was so natural, his expression was so lifelike, his gestures, features, glances were so eloquent and convincing, that he made the action clear even to those who did not understand a word of English."

1756 Marie Sallé dies. Writes her friend Noverre: "Mademoiselle Sallé . . . replaced tinsel glitter by simple and touching graces. Her physiognomy was noble, sensitive, and expressive. Her voluptuous dancing was written with as much finesse as lightness; it was not by leaps and frolics that she went to your heart."

c.1757 Gallini sees "the celebrated Dupré, at near the age of sixty, dance at Paris with all the agility and sprightliness of youth, and with such power of pleasing as if the graces in him had braved superannuation."

1757 "The dance still awaits a man of genius. It is in a bad state everywhere, for hardly anyone suspects the essence of it to be a kind of imitation . . . A dance is a poem. This poem should have its independent representation. It is an 'imitation' by virtue of the movements, an imitation which presupposes

the collaboration of poet, painter, musicians, and pantomime-dancer."—Denis
Diderot.

1760 On March 1, Noverre at Stuttgart, ballet master to the court of the Duke of
Württemberg, begins reforms in the direction of the *ballet d'action,* pantomime ballet with definite plot, where dance is integrated with the action of
the story.

1760 Auguste Vestris, great French dancer, son of Gaetan Vestris and the *danseuse* Marie Allard is born on March 27. Said his father, Gaetan: "Auguste
is more skillful than I and the explanation is simple: Gaetan is his father—an
advantage nature denied me." Auguste Vestris is credited with introducing
the *entrechat-huit* and multiple pirouettes. He was the teacher of Charles
Didelot, Jules Perrot, Carlotta Grisi, and Fanny Elssler, among others.

1760 Marie Allard makes her debut in June at the Opéra, Paris. Allard soon becomes a ballerina. She is a student of Gaetan Vestris.

1760 Noverre's *Letters on the Dance and Ballets* published in December in Lyon
and Stuttgart: "Children of Terpsichore, renounce *caprioles, entrechats,* and
overcomplicated steps; abandon grimaces to study sentiments . . . study
how to make your gestures noble, never forget that is the lifeblood of dancing; put judgment and sense into your *pas de deux* . . . away with those
lifeless masks, but feeble copies of nature; they hide your features, they
stifle, so to speak, your emotions and thus deprive you of your most important means of expression; take off those enormous wigs and those gigantic
headdresses . . . discard the use of those stiff and cumbersome hoops, which
disfigure the elegance of your attitudes . . . Lully's dance music is cold, tedious, and devoid of character . . . What was compatible then is no longer
so . . . A well-composed ballet is a living picture of the passions, manners,
habits, ceremonies, and customs of all nations of the globe, consequently it
must be expressive in all its details and speak to the soul through the eyes; if
it be devoid of expression, of striking pictures, of strong situations, it becomes a cold and dreary spectacle. This form of art will not admit of
mediocrity."

1761 On June 12 there takes place at the Opéra the debut of Dauberval, afterward *premier danseur* and choreographer of the first comic ballet; he was a
student of Noverre.

1761 *Don Juan,* "pantomime ballet in the manner of the ancients," with music by
Gluck and choreography by Gasparo Angiolini (1723–96), is presented on
October 17. This work, created independently of Noverre, claims to be the
first of its kind. Its music and dancing are subordinate to a plot; Gluck's
score is composed in terms of stage action.

1762 The *première* of Gluck's *Orpheus and Eurydice* takes place on October 5 at
the Burg Theatre, Vienna. This opera epitomizes for music what the new
ballet d'action of Noverre accomplished for dancing. Just as Noverre wished
to replace the virtuoso dancer with action and meaningful gesture, Gluck in
Orpheus broke the tyranny of the virtuoso singer and replaced casually connected solos with musical drama. The first production of *Orpheus* has ballets
by Angiolini; a later production, ballets by Noverre.

1763 *Jason and Medea, ballet d'action* by Noverre, to music by Rodolphe, is produced on February 11 at Stuttgart with Gaetan Vestris as Jason.

1766   Double pirouettes are introduced in Paris by the German ballerina Anna Heinel.

1767   Noverre is appointed ballet master to the Imperial Theatres in Vienna, dancing master to Empress Maria Theresa and her family, and teacher of her daughter, Marie Antoinette; this is the beginning of his collaboration with Gluck.

1767   Birth of Charles Louis Didelot, French dancer, choreographer, ballet master, "father of the Russian ballet."

1767   The first performance of *Alcestis*, opera by Gluck with ballet by Noverre, takes place on December 26 at the Burg Theatre, Vienna. In his dedication of the opera, Gluck applies Noverre's doctrine to opera: "I shall try to reduce music to its real function, that of seconding poetry by intensifying the expression of sentiments and the interest of situations without interrupting the action by needless ornament. I have accordingly taken care not to interrupt the singer in the heat of dialogue to wait for a tedious *ritournel*, nor do I allow him to stop on a sonorous vowel, in the middle of a phrase, in order to show the nimbleness of a beautiful voice in a long cadenza."

1768   John Durang, first American to become famous as a dancer, is born on January 6.

1769   Salvatore Vigano, Italian dancer, choreographer, teacher, and ballet master—student of Dauberval—is born on March 25. "It is not enough for me to please the eye; I wish to interest the heart."

1770   Gaetan Vestris revives Noverre's *Jason and Medea* on December 11 at the Opéra, Paris, with Marie Allard. Vestris discards the mask customarily worn by dancers, freeing the features for expressive mime and the dramatic expression essential to Noverre's *ballet d'action*. A member of the audience later wrote of Vestris' performance: "The particular merit of Vestris was his grace, his elegance, his delicacy. All his *pas* had a purity, a finish of which one can have no idea today, and it was not without reason that they compare his talent to that of Racine."

1771   Noverre produces on October 17 a second version of his ballet *Les Jalousies ou Les Fêtes du Serail* at the Teatro Regio Ducal, Milan, to music by Mozart. The ballet performed between the two acts of Mozart's festival production is *Ascanio in Alba*.

c.1772 "Ballet is an action explained by a dance" appears in the *Encyclopedia* of Diderot and D'Alembert.

1773   Maximilien Gardel, *premier danseur*, discards his mask in performances at the Opéra.

1774   Noverre becomes ballet master at Milan.

1775   Royal Theatre, Copenhagen, engages Vincenzo Galeotti as ballet master, choreographer, and *premier danseur*. A student of Noverre, Galeotti remained active in Denmark until 1816. He built up a repertory of some fifty ballets which have been performed more than two thousand times.

1776   Gaetan Vestris becomes ballet master at the Paris Opéra.

1776   Revival of Noverre's *Les Caprices de Galathée* in November at the Opéra, Paris, with Madeleine Guimard, Marie Allard, and Le Picq.

1776   Ernest Theodor Amadeus Hoffmann, German writer, composer, lawyer, and masterful writer of romances, is born on January 24. Hoffmann wrote many imaginative and supernatural stories, of which only a few are contained in Offenbach's opera *Tales of Hoffmann*. The ballets *Coppélia* and *The Nutcracker* are based on two of Hoffmann's stories.

1776   Noverre succeeds Gaetan Vestris as ballet master at the Opéra in August; appointed by his former pupil, Marie Antoinette, now Queen of France.

1778   First performance of *Les Petits Riens* (Mozart-Noverre) at the Opéra, Paris, on June 11.

1778   August 3: Teatro alla Scala opens in Milan. Five ballets are produced the first year.

1779   *Mirza, ballet d'action* by Maximilien Gardel, with Gardel, Dauberval, A. Vestris, Guimard, and Allard, is presented in Paris. Act Three of this work takes place in America; it is the first ballet with an American scene.

1779   On May 18, Gluck and Noverre produce *Iphigenia in Tauris* in collaboration.

1780   Noverre becomes ballet master at the King's Theatre, London.

1781   On October 13, Mozart, writing on opera in a letter to his father, reaffirms Noverre's principles: "Why do Italian comic operas please everywhere—in spite of their miserable libretti? . . . Just because in them music reigns supreme, and when one listens to it all else is forgotten. Why, an opera is sure of success when the plot is well worked out, the words written solely for the music and not shoved in here and there to suit some miserable rhyme (which, God knows, never enhances the value of any theatrical performance, be it what it may, but rather detracts from it) . . ."

1783   First English translation of Noverre's *Letters* is published.

1783   The Bolshoi Theatre, until 1889 the center of Russian ballet, opens in St. Petersburg on October 5.*

1786   *La Fille Mal Gardée* (Dauberval-Hertel), probably the first comic ballet, is presented.

1786   *Les Caprices du Cupidon et le Maître du Ballet* (Galeotti) is produced on October 31 at the Royal Theatre, Copenhagen. This ballet has been in the repertory of the Royal Danish Ballet since its first performance; it is the oldest ballet in existence with its original choreography intact. Harald Lander revived the ballet for the Paris Opéra on February 27, 1952.

1792   Alexander Placide and his wife dance a ballet, *The Bird Catcher*, on January 25 in New York. John Durang, first professional American dancer, is in the cast.

1795   *Jason and Medea*, great *ballet d'action* by Noverre, is produced in St. Petersburg by his student Le Picq.

1796   *Flore and Zéphire*, ballet by Didelot, is produced on July 7 in London: the first ballet in which a dancer is suspended on wire to simulate flight.

1796   *Danse*, by M. L. E. Moreau de Saint-Méry, is published in Philadelphia. Probably the first book on dancing published in the United States, *Danse* was freely quoted by Blasis thirty-four years later. Saint-Méry expressed the opinion that the principal object of the dance is "the same as that of music,

---

* New Russian calendar dates are used throughout this book. Exceptions are those few instances where tradition or the preference of living persons dictates the use of the Old Style. Both Old and New Style dates are used in these few cases.

the expression of sentiment and passions. A gesture is beautiful only when it depicts sadness, tenderness, pride—in a word, the soul."

1801 Charles Didelot becomes choreographer at the Imperial Russian Theatre. Pushkin, the great Russian poet, expresses the opinion that in Didelot's ballets there is more poetry than in all the French literature of the period. Didelot believed that ballet must have a plot; that dancers, in accordance with the action, must be able to solve their own problems, reconstruct the characters themselves: "A true dancer must be also a good actor and a poet at heart." His teachers were Auguste Vestris, Noverre, and Dauberval. Didelot is known as the "father of the Russian ballet."

1801 *The Creatures of Prometheus* (Beethoven-Vigano) is produced on March 28 at the Court Theatre, Vienna.

1803 Noverre's *Letters* is translated into Russian and Danish.

1804 Marie Taglioni, great ballerina of the Romantic era, is born on April 23.

1805 Hans Christian Andersen, Danish poet and fabulist, balletomane, is born on April 2. Andersen's fairy stories provide plots for many ballets.

1808 Gaetan Vestris dies on September 23.

1810 Noverre dies on October 19.

1810 Fanny Elssler, Romantic ballerina, is born on June 23.

1810 Jules Perrot, great *danseur* of the Romantic ballet and its finest choreographer, is born on August 18; creator, with Jean Coralli, of *Giselle, Pas de Quatre,* etc. In Perrot's view, ballet must be filled with dramatic action and presented as a realistic reflection of life. He was responsible for the integration of dance and pantomime that made possible the dramatic ballet as we know it today. His teachers were Auguste Vestris and Salvatore Vigano.

1811 Théophile Gautier, poet, novelist, critic, guiding spirit of the Romantic ballet, is born on August 31.

1812 The celebrated dancer and student of Dauberval, Salvatore Vigano, becomes ballet master at La Scala, Milan, and progress in the development of ballet shifts from France to Italy. Vigano's contribution was the *choreodrame,* or dance drama, a more complete development of Noverre's *ballet d'action* than had been realized in France. This was a dramatic spectacle that integrated principals, moving masses of dancers, and authentic backgrounds with music. His work anticipated Fokine's reforms and the mass spectacles of D. W. Griffith by a hundred years.

1815 Birth of Arthur Michel Saint-Léon, French dancer, choreographer, musician, and ballet master.

1816 Charles Didelot becomes first ballet master at the Imperial Russian Theatre. He remains in Russia until his death in 1837. In addition to the many excellent ballets Didelot produces in Russia, he establishes in the Imperial School the teaching methods and techniques that are afterward to make it famous.

1816 Antoine Bournonville, pupil of Noverre, succeeds Galeotti as ballet master and choreographer at the Royal Theatre, Copenhagen.

1819 Birth of Carlotta Grisi, ballerina of the Romantic era, creator of *Giselle.*

1820 Carlo Blasis' *Elementary Treatise on the Theory and Practice of the Art of Dancing* is published in Milan. The first complete work on dance technique, this book is still the primary text of classical dancing today.

1820 This is the approximate beginning of the Romantic ballet.

1821   Fanny Cerrito, Romantic ballerina, is born.

1821   Lucile Grahn, Danish ballerina of the Romantic era, is born on June 30.

1821   Salvatore Vigano dies on August 10.

1821   Date of the first known print depicting a dancer *sur les pointes* (on toe). Dancing on *pointes* is the outstanding innovation in technique of the Romantic ballet.

1822   On February 6, gas lighting is first used at the Paris Opéra. The soft, misty quality of this lighting did much to support the ethereal scenes of the Romantic ballet.

1822   Marius Petipa, great choreographer and ballet master, the founder of Russian classicism, is born on March 24.

1822   Marie Taglioni makes her debut on June 10 at the Hoftheatre, Vienna, in a ballet created especially for her by her father, Philippe Taglioni: *The Reception of a Young Nymph at the Court of Terpsichore.* Another young dancer in the ballet who was also making her debut: Fanny Elssler.

1825   Birth of Augusta Maywood, first American ballerina to become internationally famous.

1825   The Bolshoi Theatre, Moscow, opens on January 18. The Moscow Ballet alone danced in this theatre until 1939, when it became the principal Soviet ballet theatre.

1826   Auguste Vestris gives his farewell performance at the Opéra.

1829   Auguste Bournonville succeeds his father, Antoine, as ballet master, choreographer, and *premier danseur* at the Royal Theatre, Copenhagen. Until his death, in 1879, Bournonville worked almost uninterruptedly in Denmark. He was the Royal Danish Ballet's greatest choreographic genius and also its finest organizer. He made ballet equivalent to opera and drama in importance at the Royal Theatre, developed Danish dancers, and enriched the Danish repertory with more than fifty original ballets. These works were not only romantic, in conformance with their time, but bright, comic ballets that depicted the life of the people. *Napoli,* his presentation of Italian life, is perhaps the finest of the ten ballets by Bournonville still performed in Copenhagen. A great dancer himself, the pupil of his father's friend Auguste Vestris and of Galeotti, Bournonville choreographed—in opposition to the French *ballet blanc*—for men as much as for women. Wrote Hans Christian Andersen: "When the Italian Galeotti died in Denmark, Terpsichore wept. Who was there that could supply his place as ballet composer? No one took his place; but a new one was born, who, like every true genius, made his own way—and that is Bournonville."

1829   Carlo Blasis' *Code of Terpsichore,* primary text for dancers, establishes fundamentals of the modern classic dance.

1830   The sylphide costume first appears, in Paris. This long, diaphanous ballet dress that reaches well below the knee, almost to the ankle, was named *post facto* for *La Sylphide,* the famous ballet created by Marie Taglioni in 1832. In its guise appeared many heroines of the Romantic ballet; the costume is still familiar in the second act of *Giselle,* in *Swan Lake,* and in *Les Sylphides.*

1830   Jules Perrot makes his debut at the Opéra.

1830   *Le Dieu et la Bayadère* (P. Taglioni-Auber-Scribe) is presented at the Opéra on October 13 with Marie Taglioni.

1831   Jean Coralli becomes ballet master at the Opéra.

1831   This is the probable date of the first *ballet blanc*, or white ballet, familiar today in *Giselle* (Act Two), *Les Sylphides*, et al., at the Paris Opéra.

1832   Marie Taglioni dances the title role in *La Sylphide* on March 12.

1832   *La Sylphide* is presented in London on July 26 at the Theatre Royal, Covent Garden, with Marie and Paul Taglioni.

1834   Birth of Lev Ivanov, first great Russian choreographer (*Swan Lake*, etc.).

1834   Edgar Degas, French painter of the ballet, is born on July 19.

1834   Fanny Elssler makes her debut at the Paris Opéra in September, in *La Tempête* (Coralli). Elssler's immediate and brilliant success begins at this point to challenge the supremacy of Marie Taglioni, whose rival she never ceased to be.

1835   Auguste Vestris, age seventy-five, partners Marie Taglioni in a minuet at a special performance at the Opéra on April 8.

1835   The first American performance of *La Sylphide,* by Céleste, takes place on April 15.

1835   Fanny Cerrito makes her debut at the San Carlo Theatre, Naples. "There must be youth, and that I found in Cerrito! It was something incomparably beautiful, it was a swallow flight in the dance, a sport of Psyche," writes Hans Christian Andersen.

1835   The first book of Hans Christian Andersen's *Fairy Tales* (*Eventyr*) is published in Copenhagen.

1836   Clément Philibert Léo Delibes, French composer, is born on February 21.

1836   Carlotta Grisi makes her London debut on April 12 in a *pas de deux* with her husband, Jules Perrot.

1836   Fanny Elssler appears in *Le Diable Boiteux* (*The Devil on Two Sticks*), ballet by Jean Coralli, at the Paris Opéra, on June 1.

1836   Auguste Bournonville stages *La Sylphide* for Lucile Grahn at the Royal Theatre, Copenhagen. This version, which had new music by the Danish composer Herman Løvenskjold, has been in the repertory of the Royal Danish Ballet since it was first produced.

1836   Théophile Gautier begins to write art and theatre criticism for *La Presse* in Paris.

1837   Carlo Blasis is appointed director of the Imperial Academy of Dancing and Pantomime at La Scala, Milan.

1837   Marie Taglioni makes her St. Petersburg debut on September 30, in *La Sylphide*. Taglioni remains in Russia until 1841.

1837   Augusta Maywood and Mary Ann Lee make their debuts in *The Maid of Cashmere* (*Le Dieu et la Bayadère*) on December 30 at the Chestnut Street Theatre, Philadelphia.

1838   Lucile Grahn makes her Paris debut.

1838   *La Sylphide* with Augusta Maywood in the title role and Mary Ann Lee as Flora is presented on March 17, at the Chestnut Street Theatre, Philadelphia.

c.1838   George Washington Smith, first American *danseur noble,* makes his debut at the Chestnut Street Theatre. Smith partners the American ballerinas Lee and

Maywood, and Fanny Elssler. His popularity is such that he receives equal billing with all of his famous partners.

1839   Marius Petipa visits the United States with his father, Jean Antoine Petipa, in the ballet company of Madame Lacomte.

1839   La Sylphide, with Paul Taglioni and his wife Marie is presented on May 21, at the Park Theatre, New York.

1839   The American ballerina Augusta Maywood makes her debut on November 11 at the Paris Opéra.

1840   Carlotta Grisi makes her debut in Paris on February 28.

1840   Peter Ilyich Tchaikovsky is born on May 7/19.

1840   Fanny Elssler makes her American debut on May 14 at the Park Theatre, New York, in La Tarentule (Coralli) and a solo, La Cracovienne. Elssler's success is greater than that accorded any other European artist up to this time; she is received by President Van Buren, feted by Congress, and becomes the adored idol of millions.

1840   Fanny Elssler dances La Sylphide in New York on June 1.

1840   Marius Petipa first dances in Paris, at the Comédie Française, with Carlotta Grisi.

1841   In June, Fanny Cerrito dances La Sylphide in London.

1841   Christian Johansson, brilliant pupil of Auguste Bournonville, makes his debut at the Imperial Russian Theatre, on June 24, in a pas de deux with the ballerina Andreyanova. Johansson later becomes premier danseur.

1841   First performance of Giselle (Adam-Perrot-Coralli), greatest of all the Romantic ballets, takes place on June 28, with Carlotta Grisi and Lucien Petipa, at the Paris Opéra. Writes Théophile Gautier: "Carlotta danced with a perfection, a lightness, boldness and chaste and delicate voluptuousness which place her in the first rank between Taglioni and Elssler; as for pantomime she exceeded all expectations; not a conventional gesture, not a false movement; she was nature and artlessness personified. True, she has Perrot the Aerial for husband and teacher."

1842   Perrot is in London as dancer, choreographer, and ballet master; active there until 1848.

1842   Fanny Elssler dances La Fille Mal Gardée on July 1, during her last performance in the United States. The visit that had been scheduled to last only for a few months has been extended to more than two years.

1842   Marie Taglioni's farewell performance in St. Petersburg takes place on March 30.

1842   Napoli, masterpiece by Auguste Bournonville, is presented on March 29 by the Royal Danish Ballet. This ballet has been in the active repertory of this company ever since it was first produced.

1842   Auguste Vestris dies on December 5.

1843   Lucile Grahn makes her St. Petersburg debut in January, in Giselle.

1844   Les Trois Graces (The Three Graces), famous Romantic ballet print by Eugene Lejeune, is published in London on June 1. This lithograph is unique in its portrayal of three great dancers of the Romantic period: Taglioni as La Sylphide, Fanny Elssler as Florinda in Le Diable Boiteux, and Carlotta Grisi as Beatrix-Diane in La Jolie Fille de Gand. Elssler is the center and pre-eminent figure in the print—an acknowledgment of her supremacy over the older Taglioni and the younger Grisi. The identity of the designer and the accurate identity of all three Graces—overlooked for a hundred years—was not established until 1944 by George Chaffée, who related his findings in *Dance Index* (Vol. 3, Nos. 9–11).

1844 The American dancer Mary Ann Lee studies with Jean Coralli at the Paris Opéra.

1845 Taglioni, Grisi, Cerrito, and Grahn dance Jules Perrot's *Pas de Quatre* at Her Majesty's Theatre, London, on July 12.

1845 The Russian ballerina Andreyanova appears in Paris. Andreyanova studied with Taglioni when the latter visited Russia and in 1842 danced a version of *Giselle* in St. Petersburg. She was probably the first Russian dancer to appear in Paris.

1846 Taglioni, Grahn, and Cerrito appear as the Goddesses, Perrot as Mercury and Saint-Léon as Paris, in *The Judgment of Paris* (Perrot-Pugni) at Her Majesty's Theatre, London, on July 23.

1846 *Giselle* is presented for the first time in America on January 1, with Mary Ann Lee and George Washington Smith, at the Howard Atheneum, Boston.

1847 Marie Taglioni retires.

1847 Mazilier succeeds Coralli as ballet master at the Opéra.

1847 Marius Petipa arrives in St. Petersburg as *premier danseur* at the Imperial Theatre.

1848 *Première* of *Faust*, fantastic ballet in seven scenes, ballet by Jules Perrot, is held on February 12 at La Scala, Milan. Fanny Elssler dances the first performance of this ballet; the American ballerina Augusta Maywood, the second. Maywood, who is to remain in Europe and found her ballet company, shares with Elssler the highest title a dancer can have in Italy: *prima ballerina e prima mima assoluta*.

1848 Fanny Elssler makes her Russian debut on October 22, in *Giselle*.

1848 Jules Perrot dances for the first time at the Imperial Russian Theatre on October 31. Perrot was ballet master at the Imperial Theatre from 1851–59.

1850 Enrico Cecchetti, dancer and teacher, is born on June 21.

1850 Lev Ivanov becomes a dancer at the Imperial Russian Theatre on March 2. Dancer, musician, and choreographer, Ivanov becomes second ballet master at the Imperial Theatre in 1855; as such he is chief assistant to Marius Petipa, who entrusts to him the choreography of *The Nutcracker* and almost the whole of *Swan Lake*.

1851 Carlotta Grisi makes her Russian debut on October 20, in *Giselle;* she remains in Russia until 1853.

1851 Last appearance of Fanny Elssler, in Jules Perrot's ballet *Faust*, on June 21, in Vienna.

1851 Cesare Pugni, Italian composer, is appointed official ballet composer at the Imperial Russian Theatre. In his many years in St. Petersburg, Pugni turns out music for more than three hundred ballets. This music is completely subservient to dance and possesses little dramatic interest. Only with the ballet scores of Delibes and Tchaikovsky does ballet become a coherent musical and choreographic whole.

c,1854 Carlotta Grisi retires.

1855 Fanny Cerrito makes her St. Petersburg debut.

1857   Enrico Cecchetti, age seven, appears with his family in the Ronzani Ballet at the opening of the Academy of Music in Philadelphia.

1858   The Royal Opera House, Covent Garden, London, first opens in its present form. Since its reopening after World War II, Covent Garden has maintained two state-supported institutions: the Covent Garden Opera and the Royal Ballet. Ballet was not regularly performed at Covent Garden until 1946.

1859   Arthur Michel Saint-Léon makes his debut at the Imperial Theatre, St. Petersburg, on October 19. Saint-Léon becomes ballet master and remains in Russia until 1867, when he is appointed ballet master at the Paris Opéra.

1860   The Maryinsky Theatre in St. Petersburg opens on October 14. This famous Russian theatre, today the Kirov State Academic Theatre of Opera and Ballet in Leningrad, was the home of the Imperial Russian Ballet from 1889 to 1939. Since the Bolshevik Revolution, the center of Soviet ballet has gradually shifted to Moscow and the Bolshoi Theatre, Moscow.

1860   Marius Petipa restages *Giselle* at the Imperial Russian Theatre, St. Petersburg, on October 20.

1860   Christian Johansson begins to teach at the Russian Imperial School. Johansson's fame as a teacher exceeds his fame as a dancer; what Petipa is to the theatre, Johansson is to the classroom. From 1860 until his retirement, soon after the turn of the century, Johansson is the master of all the great Russian dancers of this period. Pavlova and Fokine were but a few of his pupils.

1862   *The Daughter of Pharaoh* (Petipa-Pugni), first great success in Russia of Marius Petipa, is presented on January 30. This monumental spectacle, with scenes set in the desert, in pyramids, and in colossal palaces, introduces the mass dance on a large scale. Petipa stages the work in six weeks. With its success he becomes ballet master to the Imperial Theatre and begins that reign over Russian ballet that was to last almost until his death, nearly fifty years later.

1864   *The Humpbacked Horse* (Pugni/Saint-Léon), first ballet with a Russian theme, is produced by the Frenchman Saint-Léon in St. Petersburg on December 27.

1865   Lucien Petipa becomes ballet master at the Paris Opéra.

1866   Paul Gerdt becomes *premier danseur* at the Imperial Russian Theatre. He is twenty-two years old. Gerdt remains a first dancer in St. Petersburg for fifty years, until his retirement in 1916. He is Franz in Petipa's revival of *Coppélia* (1884) and the prince in the first productions of *The Sleeping Beauty* (1890) and *The Nutcracker* (1892). In 1907 he appears as a young man in *Le Pavillon d'Armide* (Fokine-Tcherepnine-Benois) with two of his famous pupils, Anna Pavlova and Vaslav Nijinsky. As classical dancer, partner, and mime, he is regarded by many as the finest *danseur noble* ever to appear on the Russian stage. As a teacher, he is in large part responsible for the excellence of the Imperial School in classes for mime and supported adagio. Among his pupils: Pavlova, Fokine, and Balanchine.

1866   *The Black Crook* is presented on September 12 at Niblo's Garden, New York City. Marie Bonfanti and Rita Sangalli, both students of Carlo Blasis, are among the dancers who appear in this popular musical extravaganza, which runs for 475 nights.

1867 Saint-Léon becomes ballet master at the Paris Opéra.

1869 Nicholas Legat, dancer, teacher, and choreographer, is born on December 27 in Moscow. Although he is a fine dancer, Legat becomes important principally as an excellent teacher. At the Imperial Ballet School and, later, in Europe, he trains many dancers who afterward become famous. Legat teaches in London after leaving Russia in 1914; the school he starts there is continued by his wife.

1870 The *première* of *Coppélia* (Saint-Léon/Delibes) takes place on May 25 at the Paris Opéra.

1870 Enrico Cecchetti makes his debut at La Scala, Milan.

1871 Birth of Carlotta Zambelli, ballerina, great teacher at the Paris Opéra.

1872 Serge Diaghilev is born on March 31.

1872 Théophile Gautier dies on October 23.

1875 The opening of the present Paris Opéra takes place on January 5. From the time of its founding in 1669, the Académie de Musique et de Danse has produced opera and ballet in twelve different buildings; this is its permanent home.

1876 *Sylvia, or The Nymph of Diana* (Mérante-Delibes) is first presented on June 14 at the Paris Opéra, with Rita Sangalli and Mérante.

1877 The first production of *Swan Lake* (Reisinger-Tchaikovsky) is presented on March 4 at the Bolshoi Theatre, Moscow.

1878 Isadora Duncan, American dancer, is born on May 27. "Man must speak, then sing, then dance. But the speaking is the brain, the thinking man. The singing is the emotion. The dancing is the Dionysian ecstasy which carries all away. It is impossible to mix in any way, one with the other."

1880 Michel Fokine, Russian dancer, choreographer and ballet master is born on May 8. "As a reformer, he is to the twentieth century what Noverre was to the eighteenth, for he has exerted a profound and beneficial influence in every branch of the art of ballet."—C. W. Beaumont.

1881 Anna Pavlova is born on January 15.

1882 Igor Stravinsky is born on June 17/29.

1882 Lev Ivanov is appointed *régisseur* of the Imperial Russian Ballet.

1883 The Metropolitan Opera House, New York, opens on October 22.

1884 Marie Taglioni dies in Marseille on April 23.

1884 Fanny Elssler dies on November 27.

1885 The Italian ballerina Virginia Zucchi, pupil of Carlo Blasis, first appears in Russia. Zucchi's dazzling technique compels the Imperial Ballet School to balance the softer French style of dancing with the brilliant grace of the more vigorous Italian style in its instruction.

1885 Paul Gerdt celebrates his twenty-fifth anniversary on the Russian Imperial stage, in *La Fille Mal Gardée*.

1885 Lev Ivanov is appointed second ballet master of the Imperial Russian Ballet.

1885 Birth of Tamara Karsavina.

1887 Enrico Cecchetti, Italian dancer, is engaged by the Imperial Theatre in St. Petersburg on November 23. As a dancer, as one of the second ballet masters (1890), and, most importantly, as a teacher at the Imperial School (1892–1902), in Diaghilev's Ballets Russes (1909), and at his own school in London (1918), Cecchetti instructs and influences many great dancers: Pavlova, Karsavina, Nijinsky, et al.

1889 On April 25, the Maryinsky Theatre, St. Petersburg, becomes the center of the Imperial Russian Ballet. This famous theatre (now the Kirov State Academic Theatre of Opera and Ballet) remains the official home of Russian ballet until 1939.

1889 Olga Preobrajenska is graduated from the Russian Imperial Academy. She is ballerina at the Maryinsky Theatre for many years, until 1917, and teacher, in Paris, of Irina Baronova, Tamara Toumanova, Tatiana Riabouchinska, and many others.

1890 The first performance of *The Sleeping Beauty* (Petipa-Tchaikovsky) takes place on January 27 at the Maryinsky Theatre, St. Petersburg.

1891 Léo Delibes dies on January 16.

1892 Jules Perrot dies on August 29.

1893 Peter Ilyich Tchaikovsky dies on November 6/17.

1894 Hans Beck becomes ballet master at the Royal Theatre, Copenhagen.

1895 The first presentation of the complete *Swan Lake*, with choreography by Lev Ivanov and Marius Petipa, is given on February 8 at the Maryinsky Theatre, St. Petersburg, for the benefit of the Italian ballerina Píerina Legnani.

1895 A "class in perfection" is introduced at the Russian Imperial School for dancers who have been graduated and are dancing regularly at the Maryinsky Theatre. Christian Johansson is the first teacher of this class, which is taken later by Nicholas Legat.

1898 Michel Fokine makes his debut on May 8 at the Imperial Theatre.

1899 Carlotta Grisi dies on May 22.

1899 Anna Pavlova makes her debut on June 25 at the Maryinsky Theatre.

1899 Isadora Duncan makes her debut in Chicago. This recital is not a success, and it is not until the following year, when she first dances in Paris, that Duncan's innovations are appreciated.

1899 The magazine *World of Art* first appears in St. Petersburg. Founded by Serge Diaghilev, Léon Bakst, and Alexandre Benois, this magazine gives first expression to those ideas of modern art that are to dominate Diaghilev's Ballets Russes.

1900 Vaslav Nijinsky enters the Imperial Dancing Academy in St. Petersburg on September 1.

1901 Lev Ivanov dies; he was a Russian ballet master, dancer, and choreographer, the choreographer of *The Nutcracker* and *Swan Lake* (except for Act One and Act Three, which are the work of Petipa). Associated with the Imperial Russian Theatre from the time of his graduation from the Imperial School in 1852 for almost fifty years, Ivanov remained inconspicuous because of jealousies and theatre intrigue.

1902 Tamara Karsavina makes her debut on May 13 at the Imperial Theatre.

1903 Anna Pavlova dances *Giselle* in St. Petersburg.

1904 Michel Fokine submits suggestions for reforms to the director of the Imperial Theatre: "Dancing should be interpretative. It should not degenerate into mere gymnastics. The dance should explain the spirit of the actors in the spectacle . . . it should express the whole epoch to which the subject of the ballet belongs. For such interpretative dancing, the music must be equally inspired. In place of the old-time waltzes, polkas, pizzicati and galops, it is necessary to create a form of music which expresses the same emotion as that which inspires the movements of the dancer. The ballet must no longer be made up of 'numbers,' 'entries,' and so on. It must show artistic unity of conception. The action of the ballet must never be interrupted to allow the *danseuse* to respond to the applause of the public . . . Ballet must have complete unity of expression, a unity which is made up of a harmonious blending of the three elements—music, painting, and plastic art." These suggestions are rejected.

1905 Michel Fokine creates the *pas seul Le Cygne* (*The Dying Swan*) for Anna Pavlova in St. Petersburg; this becomes the best known of all Pavlova's dances.

1905 Isadora Duncan makes her first appearance in Russia; her reforms in the dance, her dedication to music, and her contempt for the close-fitting costume and the ballet slipper in her improvised dances, are approved by those who seek reform at the Imperial Theatre—among them, Michel Fokine.

1906 Anna Pavlova becomes *prima ballerina* after a performance of *Swan Lake* at the Maryinsky Theatre.

1907 Death of Lucile Grahn.

1907 Serge Diaghilev organizes a series of Russian concerts in Paris with the assistance of Rimsky-Korsakov, Scriabin, Rachmaninoff, and Chaliapin.

1907 Fokine produces, for a charity performance on March 8 at the Maryinsky Theatre, the ballet *Eunice,* dances in the manner of stylized movement depicted on ancient Greek vases; the dancers appear in flowing tunics, barefoot.

1907 *Le Pavillon d'Armide* (Fokine-Tcherepnine-Benois), is presented on December 8 at the Maryinsky Theatre, with Pavlova, Nijinsky, and Paul Gerdt.

1908 *Chopiniana,* Fokine's first version of *Les Sylphides,* is presented on March 21, with Pavlova and Oboukoff.

1908 Vaslav Nijinsky is graduated from the Imperial Ballet School in May; he appears with Ludmilla Shollar in Fokine's dances in *Don Giovanni.*

1909 Diaghilev's Ballets Russes makes its first appearance, at the Théâtre du Châtelet, Paris, on May 18: *Le Pavillon d'Armide* and *Prince Igor* (Fokine-Borodin-Roerich) create one of the most successful *premières* in history. This is the beginning of a new era in ballet, as Diaghilev makes possible the complete realization of Fokine's reforms and founds a ballet company dedicated to Fokine's ideal: unification of the three elements—music, painting, and dancing. Fokine is choreographer to Diaghilev.

1909 Diaghilev's Ballets Russes presents *Les Sylphides* on June 2, with Pavlova, Karsavina, and Nijinsky, at the Théâtre du Châtelet.

1909 Diaghilev appoints Enrico Cecchetti instructor to his Ballets Russes.

1910 Anna Pavlova and Mikhail Mordkin make their United States debut on February 28 in *Coppélia,* at the Metropolitan Opera House. "Her technique is of a sort to dazzle the eye. The most difficult tricks of the art of the dancer she executed with supreme ease . . . Grace, a certain sensuous charm, and a decided sense of humor are other qualities that she possesses. In fact, it would be difficult to conceive a dancer who so nearly realizes the ideal of this sort of dancing."—Carl Van Vechten in the New York *Times*.

1910   *Swan Lake* is performed in England for the first time, in May, at the London Hippodrome, with Olga Preobrajenska as Odette and George Kyaksht as Prince Siegfried.

1910   *Firebird* (Fokine-Stravinsky) is presented by Diaghilev's Ballets Russes on June 25.

1910   Pavlova and Mordkin dance *Giselle* on October 15 at the Metropolitan Opera House. "Grisi is said to have been gently melancholy in it, but Pavlova was probably more than that. Her poetic conception of the betrothed girl's madness when she finds that her lover has deceived her, and her death, come very close to being tragic. It is almost impossible to describe the poetry of her dancing in the second act, where as one of the *Wilis* she engages in the wildest sort of measures under the forest trees."— Carl Van Vechten in the New York *Times*.

1910   Tamara Karsavina succeeds Anna Pavlova as ballerina at the Imperial Theatre, St. Petersburg.

1910   Marius Petipa dies on July 14.

1911   Saison Russe is presented by Gertrude Hoffman in New York. Repertory includes first United States productions of *Les Sylphides* and *Scheherazade*. Gertrude Hoffman and Lydia Lopokova are the principal dancers. These versions of Fokine's ballets were not authorized by him.

1911   *Petrouchka* (Fokine-Stravinsky-Benois) is presented on June 13 in Paris by Diaghilev, with Karsavina, Nijinsky, Orlov, and Cecchetti.

1911   Diaghilev's Ballets Russes first appear in London on June 21.

1911   *Swan Lake* is presented in four acts on December 20 at the Metropolitan Opera House, with Catherine Geltzer, first dancer of the Moscow Imperial Opera, and Mikhail Mordkin.

1912   Nijinsky's *The Afternoon of a Faun* (Debussy) is presented by Diaghilev, Paris, on May 29.

1913   Anna Pavlova resigns from the Maryinsky Theatre; she never returns to Russia.

1914   In a letter to *The Times*, London, July 6, Fokine states the five principles of the New Ballet: (1) "Not to form combinations of ready-made and established dance steps, but to create in each case a new form corresponding to the subject, the most expressive form possible for the representation of the period and the character of the nation represented." (2) ". . . Dancing and mimetic gesture have no meaning in a ballet unless they serve as an expression of its dramatic action, and they must not be used as a mere *divertissement* or entertainment . . ." (3) "The new ballet admits the use of conventional gesture only when it is required by the style of the ballet, and in all other cases endeavors to replace gestures of the hands by mimetic of the whole body. Man can be and should be expressed from head to foot." (4) ". . . Expressiveness of groups and of ensemble dancing. In the older ballets the dancers were ranged in groups only for the purpose of ornament, and the ballet master was not concerned with the expression of any sentiment in groups of characters or in ensemble dances. The new ballet, on the other hand . . . advances from the expressiveness of the face to the expressiveness of the whole body, and from the expressiveness of the individual body to the expressiveness of a group of bodies and the expressiveness of the combined dancing of a crowd." (5) "Alliance of dancing with the other arts. The new ballet . . . does not demand 'ballet music' of the composer as an accompaniment to dancing; it accepts music of every kind, provided it is good and expressive. It does not demand of the scenic artist that he should array the ballerinas in short skirts and pink slippers. It does not impose any specific 'ballet' conditions . . . but gives complete liberty to their creative powers."

1915 Massine becomes choreographer to Diaghilev.

1916 The first American appearance of Diaghilev's Ballets Russes takes place at the Century Theatre, New York. The principal dancers are Pfanz, Bolm, Massine, Sokolova, Tchernicheva, Fedorova, and Cecchetti.

1916 Vaslav Nijinsky dances for the first time in the United States, in *Le Spectre de la Rose* and *Petrouchka*, with Diaghilev's Ballets Russes, on April 12 at the Metropolitan Opera House.

1916 The second New York season of Diaghilev's Ballets Russes opens on October 16 at the Manhattan Opera House with Nijinsky's *Til Eulenspiegel*. An American tour follows.

1917 *Parade* (Massine-Satie-Cocteau-Picasso) is presented by Diaghilev's Ballets Russes on May 18 at the Théâtre du Châtelet, Paris.

1917 *The Good-Humored Ladies* (Massine-Scarlatti-Bakst) is presented on April 12 by Diaghilev's Ballets Russes: the first major ballet by Massine.

1918 Enrico Cecchetti opens the Academy of Dancing in London.

1919 Nijinsky retires.

1920 The Royal Academy of Dancing is founded in London.

1921 The Fokine School opens in New York on January 1.

1921 Isadora Duncan is invited by the Soviet Government to open a school in Moscow.

1921 Diaghilev revives *The Sleeping Beauty* at the Alhambra Theatre, London, on November 2. Spessivtzeva, Lopokova, Egorova, and Trefilova alternate in the part of Princess Aurora. Pierre Vladimiroff is the Prince. Lopokova and Nijinska alternate as the Lilac Fairy. Parts of the fairies are taken by Dubrovska, Sokolova, Nemtchinova, Tchernicheva, Egorova, and Nijinska. Carlotta Brianza, the Princess Aurora of the original production of this ballet, is Carabosse. Stanislas Idzikowski and Lopokova dance the Bluebird *pas de deux* at the first performance. Ludmilla Shollar, Leon Woicikowski, and Anatole Vilzak are in the cast. This reaffirmation of the permanence of the classic dance fails with the ballet audience, which is accustomed to two or three ballets an evening, in the fashion made popular by Diaghilev himself.

1921 Bronislava Nijinska becomes choreographer to Diaghilev.

1922 On January 5, Enrico Cecchetti celebrates his fiftieth anniversary on the ballet stage by taking the part of Carabosse in Diaghilev's revival of *The Sleeping Beauty*.

1922 *A Manual of Classical Theatrical Dancing* (*Cecchetti Method*), by C. W. Beaumont and Stanislas Idzikowski, is published in London.

1923 "Dancing has forever been in existence as a spontaneous custom, a social discipline. Thus it is finally that dancing meets us not only as love, as religion, as art, but also as morals."—Havelock Ellis, *The Dance of Life*.

1923 *L'Âme et la Danse* (*Dance and the Soul*), dialogue by Paul Valéry, is published in Paris.

1924 Balanchine becomes choreographer to Diaghilev.

1924–25 Anna Pavlova and her company make their last American tour.

1925 *Petrouchka* is staged by Fokine for the Royal Danish Ballet on October 21 at the Royal Theatre, Copenhagen. With their careful attention to detail, respect for a choreographer's direction, and their scrupulous maintenance of tradition, the Royal Danish Ballet's production of this famous ballet is generally acknowledged to be the best in existence.

1925–26 Mikhail Mordkin and his Russian Ballet Company tour America.

1926 Martha Graham, dancer and choreographer, gives her first independent dance recital at the Forty-eighth Street Theatre, New York, on April 18. Like Isadora Duncan before her, Martha Graham has greatly influenced the theatrical dancing of her time, but more than Duncan—whose art was personal and inimitable—Martha Graham has developed in addition to a stage personality a new, nonballetic dance vocabulary expressive of inner tensions. This new system of dance can be imparted to others, can be taught with the same rigor as the classic ballet, and has become, under Martha Graham's tutelage, not only a contemporary contribution, but a lasting discipline.

1926 Ninette de Valois, former member of Diaghilev's Ballets Russes, establishes ballet school in London in May.

1926 Ballet Club (now Ballet Rambert), first permanent English company, presents at its first performance, on June 15, *A Tragedy of Fashion*, ballet by Frederick Ashton. Marie Rambert, the director of this company and its accompanying ballet school, was a student of Émile Jaques-Dalcroze and Cecchetti. Ashton, Tudor, De Mille, and Andrée Howard are a few of the celebrated choreographers who have studied under her direction.

1927 Isadora Duncan gives her last concert at the Théâtre Mogadon, Paris, on July 8.

1927 Isadora Duncan dies on September 14.

1928 *Apollo, Leader of the Muses* (Balanchine-Stravinsky-Bauchant) is presented by Diaghilev on June 12.

1928 Enrico Cecchetti dies on November 13.

1928 Ninette de Valois' Academy of Choreographic Art presents *Les Petits Riens* (De Valois-Mozart), on December 13, at the Old Vic Theatre, London.

1929 Atlanta Civic Ballet, oldest organization of its kind in the United States, founded as the Dorothy Alexander Concert Group.

1929 Serge Diaghilev in a letter to *The Times*, London, July 13, defends his Ballets Russes from charges that their dances are "extravagant, repellent, athletic, acrobatic": "The classical dance has never been and is not today the Russian Ballet. Its birthplace was France; it grew up in Italy, and has only been conserved in Russia. Side by side with the classical dance there has always existed the national or character dance, which has given the evolution of the Russian Ballet. I do not know of a single classical movement that was born of the Russian folk dance. Why have we got to take our inspiration from the minuet of the French Court and not from the Russian village festival? That which appears to you acrobatic is dilettante terminology for our national dance step. The mistake really, in fact, goes much deeper, because it is undoubtedly the Italian classical school which has introduced into ballet the acrobatic elements . . ."

1929 The last performance of Diaghilev's Ballets Russes takes place at Covent Garden, London, on July 26. The program includes: *Le Bal* (Balanchine-Rieti-Chirico), with Danilova and Dolin; *Prodigal Son* (Balanchine-Prokofiev-Rouault), with Lifar and Dubrovska; *Aurora's Wedding* (Petipa-Tchaikovsky-Bakst), with Danilova as Aurora, Lifar as the prince, and Markova and Dolin as the bluebirds.

1929 Serge Diaghilev dies in Venice on August 19.

1930 *Capriol Suite* (Ashton-Warlock-Chappell), ballet based on dances described in Arbeau's *Orchésographie* (1588), is presented by Marie Rambert Dancers in London.

1930 The American *première* of Massine's ballet to Stravinsky's *The Rite of Spring* is presented on April 11 at the Academy of Music, Philadelphia. Martha Graham dances the leading role. The music is performed by the Philadelphia Orchestra under Leopold Stokowski.

1930 Anna Pavlova makes her last public appearance on December 13 in *Giselle*, with Pierre Vladimiroff, London.

1931 Anna Pavlova dies at The Hague on January 23.

1931 Ninette de Valois opens a ballet school at the Sadler's Wells Theatre, London, on January 31. The Sadler's Wells Theatre at the time is under the direction of Lilian Baylis, director of the Old Vic Theatre.

1931 The Vic-Wells Ballet gives its first performance on May 5 at the Old Vic Theatre, London, under the direction of Ninette de Valois. Other performances are given at the Sadler's Wells Theatre, and the history of the Sadler's Wells Ballet begins.

1932 René Blum and Colonel W. de Basil found the Ballet Russe de Monte Carlo; its choreographers are Balanchine and Massine.

1932 Harald Lander becomes ballet master to the Royal Danish Ballet.

1932 Constant Lambert, English composer and conductor, becomes musical director of the Vic-Wells Ballet and begins to conduct ballet performances at the Sadler's Wells Theatre.

1933 The first performance of *Les Présages* (Massine-Tchaikovsky-Masson), at Monte Carlo on April 13. This "choreographic symphony" to Tchaikovsky's Fifth Symphony portrays man's battle with fate; it is the first ballet to a full symphony.

1933 The Jooss Ballet makes its first United States appearance.

1933 The first performance of Les Ballets 1933 (under the direction of George Balanchine) takes place in June at the Théâtre des Champs-Élysées, Paris.

1933 The Ballet Russe de Monte Carlo gives its first Paris performance in June at the Théâtre du Châtelet.

1933 Serge Lifar and his Russian Ballets appear in the United States.

1933 The School of American Ballet is founded in October by Lincoln Kirstein, George Balanchine, Edward M. M. Warburg, and Vladimir Dimitriev.

1933   First performance in the United States of the Ballet Russe de Monte Carlo on December 22 at the St. James Theatre, New York. The program: *La Concurrence* (Balanchine-Auric-Derain), *Les Présages* (Massine-Tchaikovsky-Masson), and *Le Beau Danube* (Massine-Strauss-Polunin). Among the dancers are Alexandra Danilova, Leonide Massine, Tamara Toumanova, Tatiana Riabouchinska, Irina Baronova, Leon Woicikowski, David Lichine, Yurek Shabelevsky, and André Eglevsky.

1934   The first all-English production of *Giselle* is presented on January 1 at the Old Vic Theatre, London, by the Vic-Wells Ballet, with Alicia Markova.

1934   The School of American Ballet opens on January 2 in New York.

1934   *Fundamentals of the Classic Dance*, by Agrippina Vaganova (1879–1951), is published in Russia. This is the crucial text of present-day Russian ballet technique (translated into English by Anatole Chujoy, 1946).

1934   Ruth Page is appointed ballet director and *première danseuse* of the Chicago Grand Opera Company.

1934   Vic-Wells Ballet produces the first complete *Swan Lake* staged in England, with Alicia Markova, on November 20.

1934   The School of American Ballet presents Balanchine's *Mozartiana, Serenade, Alma Mater,* and *Transcendence* on December 6 at the Avery Memorial Theatre, Hartford, Connecticut.

1935   In March, the American Ballet, founded by Lincoln Kirstein and Edward M. M. Warburg, opens a two-week season at the Adelphi Theatre, New York, with a repertory of ballets by George Balanchine. Tamara Geva and Paul Haakon are guest artists in a company that includes Ruthanna Boris, Gisella Caccialanza, William Dollar, Charles Laskey, Eugene Loring, Annabelle Lyon, and Elise Reiman, among others.

1935   The Littlefield Ballet is organized in Philadelphia by Catherine Littlefield (1904–1951): the first ballet company with an American director and American dancers. The following year this company becomes the Philadelphia Ballet. For this company, Catherine Littlefield choreographs a complete version of Tchaikovsky's *The Sleeping Beauty.*

1935   The American Ballet, under the direction of George Balanchine, becomes the resident ballet company at the Metropolitan Opera. Anatole Vilzak, Ruby Asquith, Harold and Lew Christensen, Erick Hawkins, Lillian Moore, and others join the company.

1935   *Dance: a Short History of Classic Theatrical Dancing*, by Lincoln Kirstein, is published in New York.

1936   *Lilac Garden* (Tudor-Chausson) is presented by the Ballet Club on January 26 at the Mercury Theatre, London.

1936   Ruth Page Ballets make their first appearance in New York on March 1.

1936   *Orpheus* (Balanchine-Gluck) is performed by the American Ballet on May 22 at the Metropolitan Opera House, with scenery and costumes by Pavel Tchelitchew.

1936   Ballet Caravan is organized in May by Lincoln Kirstein to provide opportunity for American dancers, choreographers, composers, and designers. Ballet Caravan tours the United States during three years, mounting new works by Lew Christensen, William Dollar, Erick Hawkins, and Eugene Loring to new music by Elliott Carter, Jr., Aaron Copland, Paul Bowles, etc. All the dancers, like those in the American Ballet, are students or graduates of the School of American Ballet; among them are Christensen, Marie-Jeanne, Caccialanza, Loring, and Danieli.

1936 *A Bibliography of Dancing* (Paul Magriel) is published in New York on August 2.

1937 The American Ballet stages a Stravinsky Festival on April 27 at the Metropolitan Opera House: *Apollo, Leader of the Muses; Card Game;* and *The Fairy's Kiss*—all with music by Stravinsky and choreography by Balanchine.

1937 The Philadelphia Ballet has a season at the Théâtre des Champs-Élysées, Paris, during the International Exposition: it is the first American ballet company to visit Europe.

1937 The San Francisco Ballet, with associated ballet school, is organized by William Christensen.

1938 *Billy the Kid* (Loring-Copland-Kirstein-French) is presented on October 16 by Ballet Caravan at the Chicago Opera House: the first successful ballet with an American subject portrayed in an American dance idiom.

1938 *Ballerina* (original title *La Mort du Cygne*), the first movie to deal in detail with ballet, is filmed in France, with Mia Slavenska and Yvette Chauviré. Many of the young students who appear in this film later become noted dancers.

1939 Nicholas Sergeyev's production of *The Sleeping Beauty* is presented by the Sadler's Wells Ballet on February 2 at the Sadler's Wells Theatre, London, with Margot Fonteyn, June Brae, and Robert Helpmann.

1939 Royal Winnipeg Ballet of Canada founded.

1940 Ballet Theatre's first performance takes place on January 11, at the Center Theatre, New York: *Les Sylphides, The Great American Goof* (Loring-Brant-Saroyan-Aronson), *Voices of Spring* (Mordkin-Strauss-Simonson). Among the dancers are Adolph Bolm, Patricia Bowman, Edward Caton, Lucia Chase, Karen Conrad, Leon Danielian, Agnes de Mille, Anton Dolin, William Dollar, Viola Essen, Nora Kaye, Andrée Howard, Hugh Laing, Eugene Loring, Annabelle Lyon, Dimitri Romanov, Nina Stroganova, Yurek Shabelevsky, and Antony Tudor. During its first season, Ballet Theatre presents eighteen ballets. Fokine stages his own ballets for the company.

1940 The Dance Notation Bureau is founded in New York for the purpose of recording ballets and dances in an intelligible dance notation.

1941 The American Ballet makes a South American tour. In its repertory are *Ballet Imperial, Concerto Barocco, The Bat, Billy the Kid, Time Table, Filling Station, Errante, Serenade, Apollo, Charade,* and *Pastorela.* Among the dancers are Marie-Jeanne, Lew Christensen, William Dollar, Nicholas Magallanes, Beatrice Tompkins, and Mary Jane Shea.

1941 Ballet Theatre makes its first transcontinental tour; Alonso, Baronova, Hightower, Markova, Osato, Robbins, and Skibine join the company.

1941 International Ballet is founded in England by Mona Inglesby. The repertory of this company includes the reproductions by Sergeyev of *Giselle, Coppélia, Swan Lake,* and *The Sleeping Beauty.*

1942 *Pillar of Fire* (Tudor-Schoenberg-Mielziner) is presented by Ballet Theatre on April 8 at the Metropolitan Opera House, with Nora Kaye, Hugh Laing, and Antony Tudor.

1942   Fokine dies on August 22.

1942   The first performance of *Rodeo* (De Mille-Copland-Smith) is presented by the Ballet Russe de Monte Carlo on October 16 at the Metropolitan Opera House, New York.

1944   The first American tour of the Mia Slavenska Company begins on January 3.

1944   *Fancy Free* (Robbins-Bernstein-Smith) is presented by Ballet Theatre on April 18 at the Metropolitan Opera House, New York.

1944   The first performance of Ballet International takes place on October 30 at the International Theatre, New York. The principal dancers are Viola Essen, Marie-Jeanne, André Eglevsky, and William Dollar. This company gives its last performance on December 23, 1944. Its founder, the Marquis George de Cuevas, established the Grand Ballet de Monte Carlo in Europe in 1947. This new company, which features many American dancers, returned to the United States for a four-week engagement at the Century Theatre, New York, November 1949, as the Marquis de Cuevas' Grand Ballet. The principal dancers are Rosella Hightower, André Eglevsky, Marjorie Tallchief, and George Skibine. This company returned to Europe in 1950.

1945   The first season of Les Ballets des Champs-Élysées, in Paris. Its managing director is Roger Eudes; artistic director, Boris Kochno; ballet master and choreographer, Roland Petit.

1946   In London, the Sadler's Wells Ballet reopens the Royal Opera House, Covent Garden (closed as a theatre during the war), on February 20, with a performance of *The Sleeping Beauty:* Sadler's Wells Ballet, as the first permanent resident company at Covent Garden, becomes the national ballet of Britain.

1946   The first full evening of ballet by the Sadler's Wells Theatre Ballet is given on April 8 at the Sadler's Wells Theatre, London. It consists of *Promenade* (De Valois-Haydn), *Assembly Ball* (Howard-Bizet), and *The Nutcracker.*

1946   Ballet Society, a "non-profit organization for the advancement of the lyric theatre by production of new works," is founded in New York in July for private, subscription audience. Musical Director, Leon Barzin; Secretary, Lincoln Kirstein; Executive Manager, Frances Hawkins; Technical Director, Jean Rosenthal; Artistic Director, George Balanchine.

1946   Ballet Theatre opens its first overseas engagement on July 4 at the Royal Opera House, Covent Garden, London, with *Les Sylphides, Fancy Free, Black Swan pas de deux,* and *Bluebeard.*

1946   Ballet Society gives its first performance in New York on November 20. The program: *The Four Temperaments* and *The Spellbound Child.* Among the dancers are Mary Ellen Moylan, Tanaquil LeClercq, Beatrice Tompkins, Elise Reiman, Fred Danieli, Nicholas Magallanes, Todd Bolender, Francisco Moncion, and Herbert Bliss.

1948   Alicia Markova, Anton Dolin, and Mia Slavenska join the Ballet Russe de Monte Carlo on September 16 as guest artists for a season at the Metropolitan Opera House.

1948   The first performance of *Orpheus* (Balanchine-Stravinsky-Noguchi) is given on April 28, with Nicholas Magallanes, Maria Tallchief, and Francisco Moncion, by Ballet Society, at the New York City Center.

1948   The first public performance of Ballet Society takes place on April 29 at the New York City Center: *Renard, Élégie, Orpheus, Symphonie Concertante.*

1948   The first performance of Les Ballets de Paris de Roland Petit, at the Théâtre Marigny, Paris, on May 22.

1948   The Paris Opéra Ballet opens its season at the New York City Center on September 21.

1948   The first performance of the New York City Ballet, on October 11, as Ballet Society becomes the resident company at the New York City Center of Music and Drama. The program consists of *Concerto Barocco, Orpheus,* and *Symphony in C.* The Musical Director is Leon Barzin; General Director, Lincoln Kirstein; Lighting by Jean Rosenthal; principal dancers, Maria Tallchief, Marie-Jeanne, Tanaquil LeClercq, Beatrice Tompkins, Nicholas Magallanes, Francisco Moncion, and Herbert Bliss; Artistic Director, George Balanchine.

1948   *Cinderella* (Ashton-Prokofiev-Malclès), first full-scale, three-act English ballet, is presented by the Sadler's Wells Ballet in London on December 23.

1949   *The Dance Encyclopedia,* compiled and edited by Anatole Chujoy, is published in New York on March 21.

1949   The Sadler's Wells Ballet makes its first appearance in the United States on October 11 at the Metropolitan Opera House, New York.

1949   Jerome Robbins becomes associate artistic director of the New York City Ballet in November.

1949   *Firebird* (Balanchine-Stravinsky-Chagall) is given its first performance, with Maria Tallchief and Francisco Moncion, by the New York City Ballet at the City Center, New York, on November 27.

1950   Vaslav Nijinsky dies in London on April 8.

1950   The Sadler's Wells Ballet observes its twenty-first birthday in a gala performance at the Sadler's Wells Theatre, London, on May 15. At this performance, Ninette de Valois, director, dances the part of Webster, the maid, in *A Wedding Bouquet* (Ashton-Berners-Stein) and Margot Fonteyn takes the part in which she first appeared as a soloist, on December 4, 1934: Young Treginnis, in *The Haunted Ballroom.*

1950   The New York City Ballet opens its first overseas engagement at the Royal Opera House, Covent Garden, London, on July 10 with *Serenade, The Age of Anxiety,* and *Symphony in C.*

1950   Ballet Theatre begins its first European tour, in August, at Frankfurt, Germany.

1950   The first season of Festival Ballet opens in London on October 24, with Alicia Markova and Anton Dolin.

1951   Nora Kaye and André Eglevsky join the New York City Ballet in January.

1951   Jean Babilée and Nathalie Philippart are guest artists with Ballet Theatre at the Metropolitan Opera House, New York.

1951   Ballet Theatre opens its first South American tour on May 21, in Rio de Janeiro.

1951   Ballet Rambert celebrates its twenty-fifth anniversary in London on July 29. This company, under the direction of Madame Marie Rambert, has been in continuous existence longer than any other English company.

1951   American Ballet Theatre School opens in New York on September 17.
1951   Sadler's Wells Theatre Ballet begins its first tour of Canada and the United States on October 5 at Quebec City, Canada.
1952   *The Classic Ballet* (Stuart-Dyer-Kirstein) is published in New York.
1952   The National Ballet of Canada is founded in Toronto.
1952   First European tour of the New York City Ballet opens in Barcelona, Spain, on April 15.
1953   The New York City Ballet ends a three-month engagement at the City Center, New York, on January 25: the longest run of any ballet company in the United States.
1953   First appearance outside Denmark of the Royal Danish Ballet—at the Royal Opera House, Covent Garden, London.
1953   Agnes de Mille Dance Theatre begins first tour of the United States.
1956   First tour of the United States by the Robert Joffrey Ballet.
1956   Royal Danish Ballet begins first United States tour at the Metropolitan Opera House, New York, September 16.
1956   First American Regional Ballet Festival takes place in Atlanta, Georgia.
1957   First overseas tour of the San Francisco Ballet.
1957   The Bolshoi Ballet begins first United States and Canadian tour.
1958   Les Grands Ballets Canedien founded in Montreal.
1960   American Ballet Theatre tours the U.S.S.R. for the first time.
1961   First United States and Canadian tour of the Leningrad Kirov Ballet.
1962   The New York City Ballet tours the U.S.S.R.
1963   First performances in Washington, D.C., of the National Ballet.
1963   The Robert Joffrey Ballet tours the U.S.S.R.
1963   Ford Foundation announces ten-year program for the long-range professional development of ballet in the United States.
1964   Opening of the New York State Theatre, designed by Philip Johnson for dance.
1965   Debut of the Harkness Ballet at Cannes, France.
1965   First United States government grants to dance.
1965   *Ballet Review* founded in New York by Arlene Croce.
1966   Robert Joffrey Ballet becomes City Center Joffrey Ballet.
1967   Association of American Dance Companies founded.
1969   First U.S. appearances of the Stuttgart Ballet.
1970   Eliot Feld forms a ballet company.
1971   First U.S. appearances of the Australian Ballet.
1972   Second Soviet tour of the New York City Ballet.
1973   First U.S. appearances of the National Ballet of Canada.
1976   American Ballet Theatre, City Center Joffrey Ballet, Alvin Ailey Dance Theatre, and the Eliot Feld Ballet assume control of the City Center Theatre, New York.
1976   Fiftieth anniversary of Martha Graham's first independent dance recital in New York, April 18.
1976   New York City Ballet, the Royal Ballet, the Royal Danish Ballet, American Ballet Theatre, and the Soviet folk-dance company appear at Lincoln Center, New York, in the spring and summer months.

The chronology of important events in the history of theatrical dance to be found in *Dance,* by Lincoln Kirstein (1935), is the master list upon which any chronology of the history of ballet must naturally be based, and I acknowledge my great indebtedness to it, as well as to the text of that monumental work. I am also indebted to numerous other sources, principal among which are: *The Dance Encyclopedia,* compiled and edited by Anatole Chujoy, the largest single collection of data on ballet in English; various contributors of articles to *Dance Index,* especially Lillian Moore, George Chaffée, Anatole Chujoy, and the late Dr. Artur Michel; numerous historical articles published in the indispensable magazine *Ballet,* which has unfortunately ceased publication; and the pioneer researches of C. W. Beaumont.

The scrupulous historical essays that appeared in *Dance Index* during that magazine's brief existence eloquently demonstrated that many writers on ballet have a cavalier tradition of carelessness and indifference to the accuracy of dates, names, places, and events. Insofar as possible, I have tried not to parrot previous errors and earnestly hope that, in the interest of accuracy, any readers who discern mistakes will be good enough to inform me of them in care of the publishers.

PART FIVE

*How I Became a Dancer
and Choreographer*

A dancer's history usually begins at the age of eight or nine. I myself began to study dancing, in Russia, when I was nine. In my case, this was almost accidental. My father was a musician, a composer, and we were naturally a musical family. My brother played the piano, my sister played the violin, and from the time I was five years old, I, too, studied the piano. There was no idea that I should be a musician; I only studied music because my parents felt I should be missing something important in life if I knew nothing about it.

Many men in my mother's family had been in the army, and for a while it was thought that I would become one of the Tsar's cadets. But one day my mother happened to be visiting the Imperial Ballet School in St. Petersburg. She had always loved dancing, and when one of the governors of the school suggested that she try to enter me, she agreed. After all, I could always go into the army if I didn't turn out to be good.

That was in 1914. In August of that year the Imperial School held its regular auditions for new pupils in St. Petersburg. These were auditions for the eight-year course in ballet, drama, and music. The final choice of which art the student would permanently pursue was made after he had learned something about each one. But these were not auditions in any real sense; we had never danced before, and there was very little they could tell. First, a doctor examined us briefly. He felt our muscles, listened to our hearts and our breathing, and sent us to the large auditioning room of the school. There were about a hundred and fifty boys seeking admittance and more than two hundred girls. In small groups, the boys and girls separately, we went in before the judges, who were seated at a table down at the end of the auditioning room. Karsavina was there, I remember. Even then I knew what a great ballerina Karsavina was and I was a little afraid. I thought I looked awkward.

The judges asked us to walk and observed our posture, our carriage. We knew absolutely no dancing and could not have executed a step if we'd been asked. The judges picked a few boys out of each group that came before them. I was picked out, but from the judges' manner I couldn't tell if this was because I was good or bad. We were told to go to another room, and after a long wait we were asked to come back. The judges watched us again, then divided the group, sending some of us to one side of the room. Again we waited. We had no idea who had been chosen or who had been eliminated. At the end of the day, they announced the names of those who had been selected as new students. I was one of seven or eight boys.

Until I actually entered the school, I didn't know whether to be pleased or not. Once in the Imperial School itself, I was decidedly displeased. I didn't like it. I was homesick, and the army seemed to me a much better idea than ballet.

The first year, we were all on trial at the school. Only if we passed that first year successfully would we be admitted as permanent students. I didn't care. All of us lived at the school, in Theatre Street, in St. Petersburg. We could go home only at Easter, Christmas, and during the summer; our parents could not visit us. The discipline was very strict: we all got up at the same time, washed at the same time (always in cold water, except on Friday before dinner), ate on a strict schedule, went to the same classes, and were sent to bed promptly at nine o'clock. We wore blue uniforms, with silver lyres on the stiff collar and on the cap.

And I did not like it. My fellow students knew this because I sulked so much. They didn't help matters by calling me "Rat" all the time. When I thought I couldn't stand it any more, I ran away. I knew my parents would be very angry, so I went to the home of an aunt who lived in St. Petersburg. She was understanding, but also she was firm with me. She took me back.

Still I hated the school. I was certain I had no aptitude for dancing and was wasting my time and the Tsar's money. The only people who thought differently then were Olga Preobrajenska, the great *prima ballerina* at the Maryinsky Theatre, who was very kind to me, and my favorite teacher, S. M. Andreanov, who instructed me in classic technique.

Every day at the Imperial School we had the same schedule: ballet class, lessons in character dancing, classes in Russian literature, French, arithmetic, music (we all had to play some instrument), and religion. We also took fencing lessons. This was a curriculum similar to that of any fine European school, except for the ballet classes. I liked the classes in religion and music best, but still, even though I was admitted as a permanent student after the first year, I thought I was in the wrong place. I remembered that there were other departments at the Imperial School—drama and music—and thought that I might be better off there.

Then everything changed. What happened was very simple. In the first year at the school, we went only to classes; we were not associated with the Imperial Theatre, the Maryinsky, in any way. The second year, as was customary, we became a part of the theatre, dancing in large groups with the *corps de ballet*. I first danced on the stage of the Maryinsky in the garland dance in *The Sleeping Beauty*: the waltz in the first act. I also appeared as a cupid on one of the carriages in the final act. The Maryinsky was a beautiful theatre, all blue and gold, and as children we were very excited about dancing on its stage, where almost any magical effect could be made: real waves, scores of swimming swans, fire, and great cascading fountains banked in tiers. We learned very early what it was to be a part of a theatre; the theatre became a home to us, a natural place to be.

The garland dance in *The Sleeping Beauty* was performed by scores of people in the regular *corps de ballet* of the Maryinsky, and we children were nat-

urally unimportant, but that evening nevertheless changed my whole life. At
that moment I saw that others had been right about what was good for me. I
saw then what ballet was in terms of a theatre.

The Maryinsky production of *The Sleeping Beauty* was wonderfully elaborate, a real spectacle, the kind of thing Hollywood tries to achieve in its huge
productions. Only here there was more magic. The Tsar's treasury could afford
it! There were about two hundred and fifty dancers in the company; all were
professionals. The first act of *The Sleeping Beauty* was marvelous in scenic
effect: a huge garden with cascading fountains. When the wicked fairy
Carabosse appeared in the prologue, her great coach was drawn by a dozen
mice. Later, when she appeared in disguise and tricked the princess into prick-
ing her finger, her appearance changed completely. She turned to the king and
queen and said that the princess would die, and then, miraculously, her disguise disappeared into the floor and they saw before them the wicked fairy
they had forgotten to invite to their daughter's christening. It was fantastic—
there she was, a bent old lady, harmless, and the next moment her disguise
had fallen through the floor and she was black and shiny, the wicked fairy.
Fire came up all over the stage and everyone despaired. Of course, the Lilac
Fairy then intervened and predicted that the princess would wake up in a
hundred years. Then the whole palace went to sleep. From the stage floor,
great trees and shrubbery arose and climbed higher and higher, vines entwined about the colonnades of the garden, so that the whole palace was
overgrown and it was quiet, asleep.

Later, when the Lilac Fairy took the prince to the palace, there was a wonderful panorama scene, not an interval with music, as this part of the ballet is
performed nowadays. The music was played slowly, as it should be, and the
Lilac Fairy guided her boat across the stage. The scenery moved from left to
right so that the boat really seemed to be moving over a lake in an enchanted
forest. Then, in the finale, where the Princess Aurora is married, there was a
spectacular apotheosis: the stage was deep and high, and from high up in the
back down to the center of the stage there was a great flight of steps. On either side of the steps there was a flight of fountains, which spilled over, one
into the other, so that there was a continuous waterfall. All the fairies were
grouped on the stairs with their cavaliers, and they and all the court bowed in
tribute to the princess. It was beautiful.

And so I began to like dancing very much. I started to work very hard. I
wanted to dance more on the stage, and to do that I knew I had to be good,
very good. I was only ten, but I was experiencing with ballet the same kind of
lesson I had learned with music.

When I first took piano lessons, I hated them, too. For two years the only
thing that would make me practice was the thought of being sent to bed without my supper. Then, when I was seven, I learned a part of a Beethoven sonata. I didn't play it well at first, but well enough to hear how lovely it

sounded. I loved it and wanted to play it well, so then it would sound even more beautiful. And now I was learning the same thing about dancing: it took work, but when you saw what the work could produce, you wanted to work very badly.

Ballet performances at the Maryinsky in St. Petersburg were given only twice a week, on Wednesdays and Saturdays. The rest of the week, the theatre was devoted to opera. All of us looked forward to the ballet evenings, when the official court carriages would come to the school and take us to the theatre for our appearances. Only when we were brought back to the school, at midnight, did we have our supper. We were so excited about going on stage at the theatre that, young as we were, we were not hungry until it was all over.

As a child, I danced in all the ballets in the Maryinsky repertory that required a large male *corps de ballet:* in the first real Russian ballet, *The Humpbacked Horse;* in the Petipa classics *Paquita* and *Don Quixote;* in *The Nutcracker,* where I began as one of the toy soldiers and gradually danced bigger parts—the king of mice, the nutcracker prince, and dance parts in the *grand divertissement.*

In 1954 I finally arranged our own production of *The Nutcracker.* At the Maryinsky, the first act of this ballet was not merely a small family party with a miniature Christmas tree. There was an enormous Christmas tree with hundreds of presents under it. When the children had been sent to bed and little Clara tiptoed downstairs to rescue the nutcracker, her favorite gift, the stage picture changed completely. At the stroke of midnight, the toys under the tree came to life. The chief toy soldier became a general, challenging intruders. Mice invaded the room, and there on stage a great pitched battle between the soldiers and the rats took place. They fired muskets and shot off cannon balls of candy. Clara tried to help the soldiers, but only when her beloved nutcracker was transformed into a brave, handsome prince was the battle won. This kind of thing we do not see nowadays in revivals of *The Nutcracker.* People think of *The Nutcracker* as a "suite" rather than a ballet. First it was a ballet.

In the Maryinsky *Swan Lake,* too, there were marvelous stage effects. At the beginning of Act Two there was not just one swan swimming across the lake, as we see so often today: there were two dozen swans, gliding across what appeared to be real, rippling waves. Actually, each swan was secured to a long stick, which members of the Tsar's Finnish regiment maneuvered underneath the stage between the rippling canvas waves. Later, when the twenty-four swan maidens appeared on stage, the audience didn't have to guess who they were: they had already seen them.

In another Maryinsky production, Mazilier's famous ballet *Le Corsaire,* there was a real shipwreck. A gigantic ship was tossed high on the waves and completely demolished. The Tsar's Finnish regiment worked again here, moving large sheets of canvas so that they undulated like storm waves. After the ballet was over, the soldiers formed ranks and drilled out of the theatre with impeccable military style, as if their regiment had just won honors at a parade.

I've gone into some detail here about the Maryinsky production for two reasons: first, to give some idea of the natural excitement these ballets had for all of us at the Imperial Ballet School; and second, because I find that people in general are very curious about what they call "Russian ballet." There used to be a time, until very recently, in fact, when people thought that *Russian* ballet was all there was. That was wrong, of course. Only because the Tsar's treasury could afford it, only because the courts of the Tsar in the nineteenth century required opulent entertainment, and because schools had been provided to train people to provide it, did it happen that in Russia there was a great period in ballet. The Tsar's wealth created great theatres, schools were started to supply these theatres with dancers, and from all over Europe—the Frenchmen Didelot, Perrot, and Petipa; the Italian Cecchetti; the Swede Johansson—ballet masters and teachers, dancers and musicians all came to embellish the Imperial courtly entertainment.

Contrary to the general belief, ballet was not taken very seriously by the Russian public. It was an entertainment almost exclusively for the aristocracy, among whom there were perhaps only a few gentlemen who were not primarily interested in what the ballerinas were doing after the performance. After the first performance of *The Sleeping Beauty*, Tsar Nicholas I said condescendingly to Tchaikovsky, "Very nice." The Tsar was familiar with every ballet in the repertory of his theatre and yet he had no idea that he had just heard the greatest ballet score the Russian theatre has ever produced. Like the rest of the Russian audience, he had a dilettante attitude toward ballet.

The Russians, as I have said, established ballet schools, and in these institutions the best teachers in Europe made great Russian dancers. All the influences—the French, the Italian, the Scandinavian—all the talent commingled to form in the nineteenth century in Russia the finest dancing academy in all the world.

By the time I first saw ballet at the Maryinsky Theatre, both Pavlova and Nijinsky had left Russia, never to return. But there were still in St. Petersburg many great dancers. Principal among these were Tamara Karsavina, our ballerina, and Pierre Vladimiroff, who had succeeded Nijinsky as *premier danseur*. We idolized these dancers and strove to perfect ourselves.

I worked very hard at the school, appeared in my first character role, a Spanish dance in Fokine's *Jota Aragonese*, in January 1916, and acted also on the stage of the Alexandrinsky, the Tsar's dramatic theatre. At the ballet school we were trained in acting, too, and mime, where we learned the importance of stage gesture. We learned how different stage appearance was from ordinary life, how to work within theatrical disciplines to create illusion. One of my teachers, Paul Gerdt, appeared as a young man in Fokine's *Pavillon d'Armide* with two of his students, Pavlova and Nijinsky. Gerdt was then sixty-three years old, but from his stage presence he appeared as young as his students.

At the Alexandrinsky Theatre, I acted the part of the young student in Andreyev's *Professor Storitsyn,* among other roles, and at the Mikhailovsky, the Imperial Theatre for opéra-comique, I danced and acted in A *Midsummer Night's Dream* to Mendelssohn's music and danced one of the Furies in the Meyerhold-Fokine *Orpheus.* Like all other students at the school, I was almost oblivious to what was going on in the world outside. Few of us knew there was a war.

When Tsar Nicholas II abdicated in March 1917, the Imperial Ballet School was closed down. I lived at my aunt's in St. Petersburg, waiting for the school to open again. I worked as a bank messenger, as a saddler's apprentice, and at nights played the piano for silent movies in neighborhood theatres. During the October Bolshevik Revolution later that same year, Lenin selected the balcony of the *prima ballerina assoluta* of the Imperial Theatre, Mathilda Kschessinska, from which to address the people. I remember hearing him that night. I had gone, with a group of my fellow students from the school, to see what was attracting the huge crowd. All of us thought the man on the balcony must be a lunatic. Then we were young; we did not understand the Revolution.

The Bolsheviks did not wish to reopen the Imperial Theatres: the theatres were, after all, aristocratic and "bourgeois" institutions. But Lunacharsky, the new Bolshevik Minister of Education, was a balletomane. He persuaded the Bolsheviks to use the Tsar's old theatres for party meetings and for speeches to the public. Party members and the public were compelled to attend. In 1918 Lunacharsky further persuaded the Bolsheviks to allow the old Imperial Ballet Company and students of the school to perform *divertissements* in the old Maryinsky after these official functions were over. And so we danced again, this time in a "state" theatre, though it was the same Maryinsky, and the school was reopened. There was no heat, either in the theatre or at the school, and food and clothing were very scarce. On stage, in flimsy costumes, we could see our breath almost freeze; in the audience, people wore fur coats. At the school, we burned the polished parquet floors to keep warm and made trousers out of the draperies. The Tsar's carriages, which had previously driven us to the theatre, were not available, and we had to walk to and from our performances.

We worked hard at taking up our studies again. A new course in Marxian history at the school seemed a small sacrifice for the resumption of training for our chosen profession. We were not paid, we were undernourished and ill-clothed, but still we studied and danced. When Lunacharsky came to take us to see Griffith's movie *Intolerance* in 1920, we still wore the remnants of our Imperial uniforms.

In 1921 I was graduated from what had become the Academy of Opera and Ballet (now the Kirov Academy of Opera and Ballet). I had been a government charge since I was ten years old, and the Bolsheviks, like the Tsar before them, expected all graduates of state schools to remain in state theatres until they were pensioned. As an honor graduate, I secured good roles in the theatre's repertory.

This same year, 1921, I entered the Conservatory of Music in St. Petersburg. The famous composer Glazunov was then director of the conservatory. My interest in music had not diminished during the years I had spent learning the theatrical arts; rather, it had greatly increased. I had played the piano regularly at the school and on vacations, and it now seemed to me time to learn even more about music. For three years at the Conservatory of Music I studied theory, composition, and piano while I continued to dance in the state ballet company at the old Maryinsky. I wanted to be a fine pianist as well as a good dancer.

Meanwhile I had become interested in choreography. I do not know how to explain this interest. I had learned to dance, to move, I loved music, and suddenly I wanted to move people to music, to arrange dances. In 1920 I had arranged my first ballet, a short ballet in the Fokine style, to the music from Rubinstein's *La Nuit*, which was danced by my fellow students at the school. The boys and girls who were in my ballet liked it very much, though its quality of movement was new to them. Our teachers did not like it at all. I saw immediately that I should never be able to convince the management of the state theatre to become interested in my work. I would have to present it myself.

This I did, in St. Petersburg, in 1923, in a program called "Evenings of the Young Ballet," which I organized with Vladimir Dimitriev, who has remained in Russia as a designer. In this program I was responsible for all the choreography. I tried to show the evolution of ballet in Russia from Petipa's classicism through Fokine's reforms to my own ideas of movement. The dancers were members of the state company who had been graduated with me. We had a hard time finding a place to put on this program, which was finally presented in the amphitheatre formerly occupied by the Tsar's State Duma (Parliament).

The "Evenings of the Young Ballet" were popular with the dancers who performed them and with the young people in the audience, but they were not liked by the directorate of the state theatre. The director informed my dancers that they could not appear in my ballets and continue as members of the state company. We were therefore compelled to stop our performances, and I was obliged to arrange dances elsewhere.

At the Mikhailovsky Theatre I arranged the dances for Ernst Toller's *Broken-Brow*, devised pantomime ballets to the Milhaud-Cocteau *Le Boeuf sur le toit* and to Alexander Blok's poem *The Twelve*, and began work on a ballet set to Stravinsky's *Pulcinella*, which had already been staged in Western Europe by Diaghilev's Ballets Russes. I also arranged a dance scene for a production of Bernard Shaw's *Caesar and Cleopatra* at the Mikhailovsky. (This was the opening scene, which I depicted as a cabaret. Later, when I knew English and could read Shaw in his own language, I saw what nonsense this was!)

All this time, I was still dancing at the old Maryinsky as a member of the state company. The modern ballets of the Diaghilev repertory were becoming a part of the traditional Russian repertory. These ballets excited me enormously: I loved their music and choreography and marveled at the imagination of a man like Serge Diaghilev, whose Russian company in France could produce so many masterpieces so consistently. Needless to say, no equivalent creativeness existed in the theatre at St. Petersburg.

In 1924 I thought it would be a good idea to take a small group of Russian dancers to Western Europe. We had some difficulty with the Soviet authorities, but in those days it was actually possible to leave Russia and the authorities thought the tour might well have propagandistic value. They consented, provided that we went to Europe on our summer vacation from the state theatre. We were called the "Soviet State Dancers." There were actually very few dancers—Alexandra Danilova, Tamara Geva, Nicholas Efimov, and myself. I was then twenty, the oldest of all. I arranged a number of ballets, among them pieces to the "Oriental Dance" from Mussorgsky's *Khovantchina* and a waltz of Kreisler's. We learned these dances perfectly and in June 1924 sailed from St. Petersburg (it had become Leningrad) on a German boat. We were bound for Berlin, where we had secured our first engagement.

In Berlin we danced with some success, then went on to perform in German watering places and at Mannheim. Then we accepted an invitation to dance at the Empire Theatre in London. From London we went to Paris. There we were fortunate enough to secure an audition with Serge Diaghilev, the genius impresario who had brought the Russian ballet to Europe fifteen years before and had caused the ballet capital of the world to shift from St. Petersburg back to Paris. Diaghilev had seen one of our performances; he liked our dancing and our dances. He invited us to join his Ballets Russes.

When I became ballet master to Diaghilev's Ballets Russes, I was twenty-one years old. I was humble in this position in the most famous ballet company in the world and sought to learn everything possible from Diaghilev, the man who had fostered Fokine and Nijinsky and commissioned from Igor Stravinsky that great composer's first ballet scores, *Firebird* and *Petrouchka*. I had just arrived in Europe and, though I had learned European languages at the ballet school in St. Petersburg and knew the culture of Europe in general, I had much to learn.

Several years ago Anatole Chujoy's *Dance News* published an article of mine on Diaghilev to commemorate the twentieth anniversary of his death. What I said then seems just as true to me now:

"Perhaps it is only today, almost twenty-five years after his death, that all contemporary choreographers begin to realize the true proportions of the enormous artistic debt we all owe to Serge Diaghilev. If we analyze the work we have done since his death in 1929, we see that we are still following in his footsteps, still adhering to the principles laid down by him during the twenty years he guided the fortunes of his unique Ballets Russes. Were he alive today, Diaghilev would probably find a new direction in his beloved art form, a new approach to the creation and presentation of ballet. He was always twenty-five years ahead of his time.

"Diaghilev had the capacity to see not only the potentialities inherent in an artist, be he choreographer, composer, designer or dancer, he also knew what work, what style, what period, suited that artist best. Great though it was, his genius for discovery would not have been so overwhelming had he not had that innate and cultivated taste which alone distinguishes true artistic quality from a sense for novelty and craftsmanship.

"If I were to describe Diaghilev simply, I should say that he was a man of high culture. It so happened that he was a great ballet impresario, a patron of the arts, but he could just as easily have been a statesman, an ambassador: he could have held any post that required knowledge, intelligence, culture, taste. He was at home in world literature, music, painting and sculpture. He spoke three languages with the fluency and in the idiom of the native. Never a professional musician, he could read a musical score as one reads a book.

"Stravinsky has described Diaghilev's intimate musical knowledge in his *Autobiography* and Nicolas Nabokov, who also composed his first ballet for the Ballets Russes, has written of Diaghilev's great understanding of music in his book *Old Friends and New Music*. Never a choreographer or a dancer, Diaghilev knew what was exactly right and what was wrong about a particular ballet or in any portion of it. Never a painter, he possessed an unerring and intimate knowledge of art.

"These qualities made Diaghilev a creator, a real producer. He was not just the director or manager of a ballet company who guessed what the public would accept and what it would reject. He did not follow the public; the public followed him. He did not really care very much whether people agreed with him or not. What mattered to him was the work done by the best and most suitable choreographer, musician, designer and dancers. If they succeeded, their work was a success. Diaghilev so inspired the artists who worked under his direction that it is not too much to say that any ballet created for his company bore his personal stamp as well as that of the composer, painter and choreographer.

"Strangely enough, he did not interfere with work in progress. Before work began, he discussed projected ballets with their creators in great detail. We argued and recognized each other's points. Diaghilev had great respect for artistic integrity. By the time actual work began on ballets, every phase of their production represented a collaboration between artists and their producer.

"Even if we discount for the moment the fact that companies the world over are still using ballets created for the Diaghilev company (*Petrouchka, Les Sylphides,* etc.) and that much of what else there is in ballet today stems from the Diaghilev roots, we cannot escape the fact that it was Diaghilev who invented the formula of presenting three short ballets in one evening and thus made possible the presentation of ballet not only by big resident companies in the few opera houses of European capitals, but also by touring companies in big and small cities and towns in America and Europe.

"If it can be said at all that one man took ballet from the thin aristocratic stratum of society and gave it to the people at large, Diaghilev was the man who did it. To Diaghilev's additional credit, one is reminded that he never attempted to lower the artistic standard of ballet to the level of those who had no prior knowledge, taste or appreciation of the art form. On the contrary, by constant and painstaking work to present ballet of the highest calibre to the people to whom ballet was new, he succeeded in elevating the people to the appreciation of ballet, in developing their taste and increasing their enjoyment.

"Personally, I owe to Diaghilev my growth and development during the second period of my artistic life. The first part of it I owe to the Russian Imperial Theatre where I was brought up, to its strict discipline, to its classicism, the basis of all ballet, to its two-hundred-year-old tradition which instilled in me a love for ballet and a respect for its history and artistic principles.

"The second period of my artistic life began in the Diaghilev company, where I learned to recognize what was great and valid in art, where I acquired the ability and strength to analyze a work of art on its true merits and where, finally, I learned to be on my own, to do what my artistic sense prompted me to do—in short, to be an artist. All this I owe to Diaghilev without any reservation."

For Diaghilev's company, beginning in 1925, I rehearsed the repertory and danced with the company in addition to creating ten new ballets. I don't think there's any question that *Apollo* (1928) was the most important of these, certainly the most important for me personally, for I regard this ballet as the crucial turning point in my artistic life. In the first ballets I choreographed for Diaghilev I had been successful, I think, but for the wrong reasons. *Pastorale*, for instance, which I arranged to music by Georges Auric in 1925, contained diverse types of movement—at least ten different types—whereas only one type was sufficient for the piece: the others should have been set aside and the one proper type developed. Stravinsky's score for *Apollo* taught me that a ballet, like his music, must have a restraint and discipline. Stravinsky's music had a wonderful clarity and unity of tone, and I saw that gestures, the basic material of the choreographer, have family relations, like different shades in painting and different tones in music. Some are incompatible with others: one must work within a given frame, consciously, and not dissipate the effect of a ballet with inspirations foreign to the tone or mood one understands it must possess. *Apollo* depicted Stravinsky's music visibly.

Prodigal Son and *Le Bal* (with Danilova, Nikitina, Dolin, and Lifar) were my last ballets for Diaghilev. A few months after the first performance of *Le Bal*, Diaghilev died in Venice. His company disbanded: there then came to an end the most important and entertaining twenty years of creativity in music and painting and dancing that Europe had seen since the Renaissance.

After some months had passed, I accepted an engagement as ballet master at the Royal Theatre, Copenhagen, with the Royal Danish Ballet, which, with the Paris Opéra, has the oldest continuous tradition of instruction and performance in the world. After this, I worked in London on my first musical comedy and in France helped to organize the Ballet Russe de Monte Carlo and staged for them their first new ballets: *La Concurrence, Cotillon,* and *Le Bourgeois Gentilhomme.*

My own company, Les Ballets 1933, was formed soon after this. This company performed in Paris and in London. It was during performances of Les Ballets 1933 that the painter Pavel Tchelitchew introduced me to the young American Lincoln Kirstein, who with Edward M. M. Warburg invited me to come to the United States to found the ballet school he knew was necessary if the classic dance was ever to flourish in America. We opened the School of American Ballet in New York on January 2, 1934, in studios that had been used in years past by Isadora Duncan. The school has become, over the years, the largest institution for the training of professional dancers outside the European state schools. Students from this school have danced in every American ballet company and in many companies in Europe. More specifically, they have been the basis for the founding of ballet companies that Lincoln Kirstein and I have directed. These companies have evolved and matured in the New York City Ballet. Morton Baum, Chairman of the Executive Committee of the New York City Center of Music and Drama, and the directors of that corporation invited Kirstein and me to found in 1948 this permanent, resident ballet company at the New York City Center. It is not for me to comment on the New York City Ballet: this would be like a father telling you about his own children. I can only invite you to come and see it, as I urge you again to see all ballet companies in New York and on tour throughout America.

Writing about ballet is difficult for me, even talking about ballet is difficult for me; if I were naturally a writer or a lecturer, and expressed myself well in writing and speaking, I should not be a choreographer. But I have tried to make clear a number of things in this book that will be of help to the audience and to the potential dancer. This book, however, as I have said elsewhere, is no substitute for the ballet you can see on the stage. Only by seeing ballet repeatedly in the theatre can you understand why it has entertained audiences for three hundred years and how it has given some of us happiness because we have been able to provide some of that pleasure.

PART SIX

Ballet for Your Children

People often come to me and ask questions about dancing. They want to know if they should send their sons and daughters to ballet school, when to send them, how long it will take them to become dancers, and what chances they have for a career in ballet. Others ask about choreography: how I work, what I think of first when I am about to produce a ballet, whether choreography can be taught. In this and the following two sections I have answered these questions and many others that seemed to me important for students, dancers, parents of dance students, and—last but not least—the ballet audience.

Ballet must be seen to be enjoyed, but many of us are more easily entertained if we have in advance some information about an art that happens to be strange to us. Most people may want to relax and make no effort when they go to the theatre, but I think the answers to questions about a dancer's training, for instance, might help convince them that all art requires a certain amount of effort and ability on the part of the audience, too.

To ensure maximum clarity, I have arranged my views on ballet for your children, on dancers and choreography, in the form of particular questions and answers.

QUESTION What ballets should children be taken to see?
ANSWER Some people think that only ballets about puppets, such as *Petrouchka* and *Coppélia,* are good for children. They are, of course, but I think you will find that children enjoy almost all good ballet. A friend of mine, I remember, thought that a full program of four ballets would be too much for her five-year-old nephew to sit through; she thought the child would get bored and squirm. She decided that they would see only the first two ballets and then leave. But the child didn't want to go. He saw that all the other people weren't leaving and that there was obviously going to be more. He stayed for all the ballets and loved every minute of it.

Children enjoy ballets without stories as much as narrative ballets. If the ballet company is a good one and the orchestra good, they will love these musical ballets. We must understand that children are flexible; they have more imagination, more feeling for fantasy, than grownups. Grown-ups analyze. They come into the theatre and say sometimes, "This bores me, it's taking up my time"; or they compare, "My wife is better-looking than that girl"; or they complain that they see nothing on stage similar to everyday life. Children are open, freer, not so prejudiced. They have a natural ability to imagine things that ballet sometimes releases. The fascination life has for them is based on enjoying movement and change;

ballet, in its idealization of movement, fascinates them. A storyless ballet, simply movement to music, they like almost instinctively. They will certainly like anything that is good, if we only give them the chance.

QUESTION   When should a child begin ballet training?

ANSWER   Children should begin to study when they are eight, nine, or ten years old—certainly not before they are eight. All you can really do with children before the age of eight is permit them to run around, dance a little, and sing songs. This, of course, is recreation and produces no real result. Before the age of eight, ballet training can actually be harmful. It is serious training and it is hard work physically. In ballet class the first thing we teach the children are the basic ballet positions, positions that are unnatural to them. Their hips, knees, and feet have to be turned out in certain directions. Because the bones and joints are still soft at this early age, we never force children into the basic ballet positions. If they can't do them perfectly, we wait. If you overtrain the small, undeveloped muscles of children, the muscles become hard and don't develop properly with the body and the child is apt to become deformed. So even when a child begins at eight, we are very careful. Very often a mother will come to me and say, "My child dances very well and she is musical too. I think she is another Pavlova." The child is perhaps four years old! In all probability someone has advised the mother that the child should study ballet, someone who wants to make money and naturally doesn't care what happens to the child afterward. If you take a child of four in a ballet class and train her seriously, you may please her parents but you will seriously harm the child. However, when a child is eight or nine years old, she can take a certain amount of direction and you can really begin to teach her.

QUESTION   What is the age limit for starting ballet training?

ANSWER   This really depends on the individual case—on the person's build and on the softness of his joints. Generally speaking, beginning students with professional theatre careers in mind should certainly start before they are fifteen years old—preferably earlier. If they start to study at fifteen, they will probably not be ready for the stage until they are over twenty, by which time most dancers have been professionals for some years. But I repeat, it depends on the individual case. Usually, after the age of twenty-two no satisfactory results can be obtained.

QUESTION   If you want your child to be a dancer, what is the best preparation before the child begins to attend ballet class?

ANSWER   I would suggest reading the child fairy stories—Grimm, La Fontaine, Gozzi, and many others—read them stories from Greek mythology and the stories of E. T. A. Hoffmann. Most people know Hoffmann's stories from the operetta by Offenbach, *Tales of Hoffmann,* but he wrote a great many other wonderful stories. The story of the ballet *The Nutcracker* is just one of them. And by all means read the stories of the great Hans Christian Andersen. And I don't mean Andersen's stories,

Marianna Tcherkassky and Ivan Nagy in *Giselle*. Photo by Martha Swope.

Mikhail Baryshnikov and Marianna Tcherkassky in *Le Spectre de la Rose*. Photo by Martha Swope.

Gelsey Kirkland in *La Sylphide*. Photo by Louis Péres.

Mikhail Baryshnikov and Natalia Makarova in *Don Quixote*. Photo by Rosemary Winckley.

Gelsey Kirkland and Jonas Kage in *The Leaves Are Fading*. Photo by Martha Swope.

Rudolf Nureyev in *Le Corsaire*. Photo by Louis Péres.

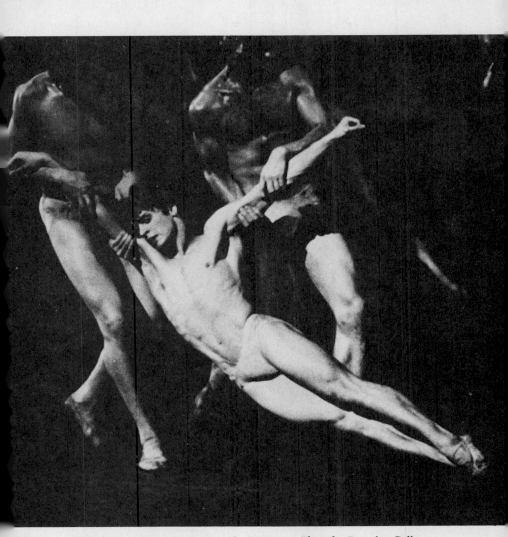

Mikhail Baryshnikov in *Le Sacre du Printemps*. Photo by Beverley Gallegos.

Gelsey Kirkland and Mikhail Baryshnikov in *La Sylphide*. Photo by Beverley Gallegos.

or any others, as they are watered down, especially translated and condensed for children. Good fairy stories were always written for intelligent people. Children are more intelligent than many of us think. Mickey Mouse will interest a child for only a short time; you should move on to fairy tales. It is well to remember that if a child continues to be interested only in Mickey Mouse, it is probably because you have not introduced him to something new. Children like to move on to new, more complicated things. They don't like to be talked down to; they like it very much if you respect their capacity for new experience.

You should also play music for your child. If you don't play an instrument yourself, play records at home. Play them all the time; make music a regular thing around the house, like bathing and brushing teeth. Don't bother with jazz or swing or popular records; the air is filled with it from morning to night, and children will hear enough of it. Play anything good. Don't bother to tell the children what you are playing; soon they will remember, hum the music, and whistle it. They won't care what it is especially, but they will surprise you when they recognize it. Then go on to play other things.

Don't expect children to like the music you play at once, don't coax them, don't even ask their opinion, just play it. If you think Mozart bores children, you may find out that Mozart is just boring you. Children are not so prejudiced: they don't have the barriers to enjoyment that so many of us grownups have. Children are more aware, more teachable, more vulnerable to entertainment. They have their ears open.

QUESTION Where are the best ballet schools in the United States?

ANSWER Excellent schools with fine teachers are to be found all over America —in New York, California, Chicago, everywhere—not only in the big cities, but in smaller communities. New York is the center of dance activity in the United States—in spite of the impressive growth of dance in cities throughout the country—and sooner or later, almost all dancers find themselves studying or working in New York, as all actors do. It often happens that dancers do not begin to study in New York until they have established some sort of reputation for themselves elsewhere and only continue their study in New York because it is convenient for their work.

QUESTION If you had a son, would you send him to ballet school?

ANSWER Yes. The people who ask me this question say they hesitate to send their boys to ballet school because they are afraid the boys will become "sissified" or perhaps will not develop strong, muscular bodies as they might in another activity. That isn't true. Male dancers must be very strong, not only for their own work but for partnering; their bodies must be flexible and they must have a great deal of endurance. This is the reason why many of our best dancers were good soldiers during the war. Of course, you can be strong and a "sissy" at the same time, but this has nothing to do with ballet: it is the person himself. We do not give ballet classes for boys and girls separately. They are together in class from the beginning. Perhaps if boys started to take dancing lessons early, they would appreciate the companionship and charm of girls even sooner than they ordinarily do!

QUESTION How is a child selected for admittance to a ballet school?

ANSWER About the only things you can judge a child on when she is eight or nine years old are her general appearance and her health. We can only tell whether a child's insteps are good, whether her limbs are in the right proportion, and whether they are flexible. We must be able to watch her in class, two lessons a week, for perhaps six months to come to a real decision. Also, at the beginning, talent is not always the first thing that a child shows. That might come much later, when she has learned to dance well enough to demonstrate talent. Some girls and boys at the beginning seem to be very good, but as time goes on it often happens that they just do not show progress or development. If they are satisfactory at the beginning and develop badly, we advise them not to continue.

It is good if a child is musical, if she knows how to keep time to music and reacts to it. But it often happens that it is impossible to make any judgment about this, too, until after some time has elapsed in training.

QUESTION What is a child taught first at a ballet school?

ANSWER At the beginning, each of the five ballet positions (see Glossary) is shown to the children and explained very simply and plainly. Then the children are placed facing the wall with both hands on the bar, so that their weight is evenly supported by both hands. Standing this way, they must first learn to stand in each of the Five Positions until they become completely familiar with them and can adopt one or another at will, but as yet without any connecting exercises. These first classes are taken slowly; children do these same exercises for a month or so and then they get used to it. Actually, an exercise is a memory of something, a spontaneous memory. Soon it becomes a part of your existence, of your body, and if you are trained well at the beginning, after a while you can move from one place to another in the right way without even thinking about it. The unnatural position, in other words, becomes natural. It's like reciting something. If you want to recite Shakespeare, you have to memorize. You repeat it for a hundred times perhaps, and then something happens in your brain. You can recite spontaneously.

The children's attention is drawn to correct posture at the beginning; they are taught to keep their backs straight, their shoulders down. Next they are taught to do *demi-pliés* (see Glossary, *Plié*) very slowly in each of the five positions, always paying strict attention to posture.

The training of children requires a long time, and trying to shorten it by hurrying the child does no good whatever. Children must be watched to see when they have had enough of each exercise. It is important never to strain them in order to speed their progress.

When the children are familiar with the Five Positions, they must learn how to change from one position to another by means of connecting movements. Next they learn *battements tendus* (*see* Glossary), beginning with the simplest: from first position to second position and back. They should be taught *battements* only in front, then only sideways, then in back, separately. All these exercises should be taught first with both hands on the bar, then with only one hand on the bar. At this point the children learn how the hand and fingers should be held. Then, away from the bar, in the center of the room, they are taught the arm positions.

QUESTION Should parents watch their children in class?

ANSWER No, or if they must, only very seldom, for it confuses things. The child's respect for his parent and his respect for his teacher are entirely different things, and until the child learns to dance well, I think it's a mistake to confuse the child with two kinds of authority. He will learn to respect his teacher and learn to dance much faster if parental concern is suspended during ballet class. At the School of American Ballet during a child's first two years, parents visit classes only once a month. We can all understand that parents are vitally interested in their children's progress, but when they have chosen a school and a teacher, they should trust their own judgment and have faith in the teacher.

QUESTION How soon should girls studying ballet begin to dance on toe?

ANSWER Children should not be allowed to dance on point until their fourth year of study—after they have completed three years of training. That is, if a child enters a school and begins regular training when she is eight years old, she is eleven before taking toe exercises. This period of preparation is vitally necessary because many foot and leg muscles must be developed properly before a child can dance on toe without injuring herself seriously. The child's soft bone structure may be irreparably harmed if she begins dancing on toe before she is ten or eleven. If a child of eight enters a school and takes daily lessons, two years of training will give her the proper preparation. No profit can come from permitting a child to dance on point before she is prepared. Her dancing future will be short and she will be harmed physically. Only competent teachers are in a position to judge exceptions to these rules.

QUESTION Is toe dancing painful?

ANSWER No, not if the proper muscles are trained well first. In good ballet schools we are always careful to do this. Naturally, at first the muscles ache from the unfamiliar movement, but to a dancer an aching muscle is a discovery: she knows that she is conquering something new.

If you have been to the ballet and seen dancers remain on stage for long periods of time in a difficult ballet, you have probably wondered at their physical endurance. Dancing, however, trains their muscles so that they are controlled or relaxed almost unconsciously. In a dancer's body there is no constant tension. Muscles must be relaxed until they are used.

In modern choreography there are steps so fast that some muscles have to be relaxed instantly or the dancer will tire in a few minutes.

QUESTION   Can knock-knees and other defects be corrected at ballet school?

ANSWER   Some children are knock-kneed when they're very young, but by the time they are ten, their structure changes completely and they aren't as knock-kneed as you thought they would be. Then they can go on with their lessons, for we can control the appearance of the knees slightly. If the child continues to be very knock-kneed, it is best to give up the lessons. The parents of one little girl we had at our school were different sizes: the father was very, very tall and the mother very, very short. I guessed correctly that when the girl grew up, she would have very short legs and a very long torso. But she wanted to continue studying and did so until it was apparent that she had grown the wrong way. You can't do anything about a structural defect like this. You just have to wait, to hope, that the young children who start lessons when they are eight or nine will still be well proportioned when they grow up. I'm sure some parents think this is too big a chance to take, spending all that money when they can't be sure their children will develop correctly for a professional career. But this chance must be taken, for if the child does not start lessons soon enough, it will be difficult—if not impossible—for her to become a fine professional dancer.

QUESTION   How is discipline maintained in a ballet class?

ANSWER   This is a question parents often ask, and they are quite right to be interested in it. When children go to a strange ballet class with a new teacher, they are a little in awe of the instructor, quite naturally. But actually this makes them more anxious to follow directions, to repeat the positions and steps that the teacher shows them. If their parents directed them at home in this way, they would probably say, "No, I won't, I don't want to." Parents naturally don't want to force things; they think their children really don't want to and that they might cry. But the teacher doesn't care, even if the children do cry. He simply directs them, politely and firmly.

The teacher must direct his young pupils quietly: you can't scream and correct children all the time. You can scream once, twice, maybe three times, and the children will be scared and obey you; but if you yell at them any more, they won't be frightened. They'll get used to your yelling, and you'll find that you have to pretend not to see them misbehaving—so that you won't scream any more and embarrass your authority.

Children see everything. They certainly see how you react when you turn around suddenly and catch them misbehaving. They know you will think ill of them. But if you don't notice, they'll say to themselves, "He doesn't care, he looks straight at us when we're horsing around, we can do anything we want to!"

But to a certain extent with children in ballet class you can't notice everything. You have to pretend not to see some of their little tricks, because for a whole hour it's very hard to hold their attention. You can hold their attention by noticing their tricks only once in a while. Then be firm with them, and they will behave for a little while. The next week they are quieter and behave for longer periods of time. By the end of the first year they respect you. They behave like soldiers: they come on time, they know when to start, wait obediently for your directions, and, finally, when you tell them that the lesson is over and say, "Thank you," they acknowledge this with a bow which will be so important to them later when they bow gracefully on the stage. They become such good soldiers that they don't leave the class unless you do say, "Thank you."

You can't expect all children to like ballet classes. I certainly did not like them at first, and I think this is more or less true of most young pupils. Only gradually do they learn to like it. After some time has elapsed, they enjoy bring able to do what they are told in class. They like the music the pianist plays for them to move to. First he plays music just for the sound, for rhythm and keeping time, but after a while he plays them little pieces. To look at the children, you'd think that they didn't know the difference, but they remember, they notice everything, they memorize music. Slowly they become trained to move well and to listen, and from a few steps and exercises they are able to do simple dance sequences. They watch grown-up dancers in other classes, admire them, and want to move beautifully too, by imitating with the little technique they have.

I think all children like the idea of dancing. If you tell them they're taking lessons to become something they don't know about, they don't listen to you. But dancing is different: they like it and somehow suffer through the lessons at first. It's like holding up a candy bar and saying to a child, "No, not yet, you must wait." They will wait, they will endure the lessons so that they can move brilliantly and beautifully. It is a natural thing for children to want to move well, to move well in time, to catch a baseball at the right moment, to hate to drop things. Dancing is a discipline that perfects this natural inclination: it gives us control over our bodies so that we are in a position to conquer space, so to speak, in given periods of time. Some music is very rapid, very complicated, and to move to it well is difficult, but the dancer is able to conquer the complicated time element of the music, she is able to move freely within the discipline of time.

Once we had at our school a child whose mother was a psychiatrist. The mother came to the school and wanted to know how the classes were run, how the children were made to behave, because at home she could do nothing with her own child. The mother watched her child in class, and this little girl—the little brat who at home was always doing the wrong thing—she was perfect! Like all the other pupils, she did exactly what the teacher said and enjoyed it. Afterward the mother wanted to know how this could happen. She said, "In my job I advise parents about their children. I'm supposed to know all about child psychology." She was told that it is a matter of knowing how to teach, when to notice things and when not to notice, and that children have a certain respect for what the teacher represents. For the child, the teacher is connected with a strange thing called the art of dancing, and the child knows that what she can learn from him is wonderful.

The respect that a child has for his teacher and the good manners she learns in ballet class are a very important part of the tradition of ballet, which is an aristocratic tradition. I use the word aristocratic here seriously, not because ballet is open only to an exclusive class of people, but because it is an exclusive art, practiced and completely understood only by those who are willing to spend a great deal of time and effort on it. The Greek word for aristocracy means the rule of the best, not the rule of an exclusive class. Ballet in this sense is a democratic art, open to all who are willing to work and to learn.

QUESTION   How many different classes are there in ballet schools?

ANSWER   Most schools are divided into different sections for beginners, intermediate, advanced, and professional classes, or classes equivalent to these distinctions. Classes for children are given separately. When a student has finished all the children's classes, she moves on to the regular classes. Students who have had previous study or experience are placed in the proper class after auditions.

QUESTION   Do students receive grades at ballet school?

ANSWER   Some schools give their children grades, but many promote students simply on the basis of their progress and ability in acquiring technique. Age has nothing to do with promotion, nor has the length of time spent in previous study. Promotion, in other words, is not automatic. It depends on the student's development. If a child has studied for some time and shows no aptitude for dancing, her parents should be so advised.

QUESTION   Should children practice ballet at home?

ANSWER   While practicing at home is not generally harmful, it actually does very little good; children should certainly not be made to do it. At home there is no teacher to watch and correct them; only in a class can they practice with real profit. It seems to me better if at home they think occasionally about their lessons and practice only the fine points they want to improve—hand movements and mime, for example.

QUESTION   Is it necessary for a student to continue her practice during long vacations?

ANSWER   It is not only unnecessary, it is inadvisable. If a serious student has been scrupulous about attending classes daily for nine or ten months of the year, rest and relaxation are recommended.

QUESTION   How many years of training are necessary before a beginner is graduated from a ballet school?

ANSWER Usually, five or six years. The period is longer if the student has not attended class daily (Monday through Saturday for a minimum of nine months each year), shorter if his ability is exceptional. Because few students are likely to make their professional debuts when they are fourteen years old, this is an additional reason for not beginning to study until after the age of eight. It must be stressed, however, that few schools have any graduating system. No dancer really finishes going to school. Even if she is a ballerina in a ballet company, she still takes classes.

QUESTION Is the public admitted to ballet classes?

ANSWER No. Many schools allow visitors in class, and there is nothing wrong with this, particularly when the dancers have reached the professional point and are appearing frequently on the stage. But when the dancers are younger, it isn't such a good idea. Visitors distract the teacher and, most important, distract the students, who will naturally play to such an audience and are tempted to show off. Actually, visitors should be respectful and considerate and just ask politely if they may come, just as they would if they wanted to visit a class in a public high school.

QUESTION Can students at a ballet school watch classes other than their own?

ANSWER Yes, certainly. In fact they should be encouraged to do so. Most children who come to ballet class like to spend time afterward looking in on other classes. A young student who watches a professional class sees there the technique she is aiming for. This reinforces her ambition and makes her more eager to learn.

QUESTION How do you tell whether or not a teacher is good?

ANSWER This is certainly a problem that confronts parents as well as prospective students. It sometimes seems to me that there are more bad teachers of dancing than of any other art. There is a great tendency to take advantage of people's ignorance, for it is impossible to make a judgment about a teacher unless you know something about dancing. You can visit a ballet class, perhaps, and like what you see, but you can hardly tell if the teacher is training the children properly. Over the years bad teachers have devised many so-called methods, short cuts to fame; they invent nonsense about muscular knowledge to confuse and exploit those interested in ballet training. In engineering and medicine it's hard to fool people in this way, and there are laws to protect the public from collapsing bridges and quack doctors. In ballet training, however, where there is no great physical danger, there are no laws to protect you from fake teachers.

There are no short cuts, no new "methods" to become a good ballet dancer. There is only one way, instruction in the classic dance as it has been codified over a period of three hundred years. All able instructors teach ballet in terms of this universal tradition.

I think the best thing to do in seeking a good teacher is to ask the advice of a well-known professional, an experienced dancer. If you admire a dancer, find out where she studied from *The Dance Encyclopedia* or write to her. There are many fine schools, many wonderful teachers.

QUESTION   Are all ballet classes taught by the same instructor in a ballet school?

ANSWER   In smaller schools, yes, because it is necessary, but in the larger schools this is never the case. Teachers' schedules change throughout the year, and most students have a chance to benefit from the special knowledge and experience that each teacher naturally possesses. Such a system exposes the young student to varied direction and tends to prevent him from unconsciously imitating one teacher.

QUESTION   Should dancers have stage experience while they are still studying?

ANSWER   Not until they have reached a stage of professional competence. Children who appear on the stages of state theatres in Europe are called upon to do only very minor roles: they are not allowed to take roles for which their learning and talent have not qualified them.

QUESTION   Do ballet schools provide room and board for students?

ANSWER   No, not unless these schools are attached to higher educational institutions such as colleges and universities.

QUESTION   Do some schools accept only professional dancers?

ANSWER   Most are open to all. Some schools, like the School of American Ballet in New York, are interested primarily in students who wish to become professionals; but this school also accepts serious students who do not have professional careers in mind. The state schools in Europe, of course, accept only those students who may graduate onto the stages of state theatres.

QUESTION   How do ballet schools in the United States differ from those in Europe?

ANSWER   There are private schools in Europe, but most of the famous schools are state-supported institutions associated with a state theatre. This is true in France, which has the oldest dancing academy in the world, in Denmark, and in Milan at La Scala; recently it has become the case in England. In Russia, the schools formerly supported by the Tsars are supported by the Soviet regime. Each of these schools is attached to a ballet company financed by the state—the ballet of the Paris Opéra, the Royal Danish Ballet; and England's Royal Ballet, the ballet of the Bolshoi and Kirov state theatres, etc. Students are selected on a competitive basis, the government pays their way, and, after graduation, the student is obliged to spend a certain period dancing only with the state ballet company. It is axiomatic that if a student successfully completes the course, she will graduate onto the stage of the state theatre and become a permanent member of the state ballet company. Because these schools are state-supported, no foreign students are admitted except under extraordinary circumstances.

Since students in the state-supported European schools are chosen at a very early age, the curriculum consists not only of dancing in many cases, but includes also courses that students would be expected to take in ordinary schools—languages, literature, history, science, geography, and courses related to the other arts.

Students begin in these schools when they are about nine years old. In France, at the Opéra, the oldest ballet school in the world, the young students remain in the *classes supplémentaires,* first and second, for five years, then move on to the *classes des quadrilles.* The *corps de ballet* of the ballet company at the Opéra is selected from these groups.

The Paris Opéra ballet itself is divided rigidly into classes: *élèves* (apprentices), the first *quadrilles* (equivalent to *corps de ballet*), *quadrilles secondes coryphées* (dancers who perform in smaller groups than the *corps de ballet,* but who are not yet soloists), *petits sujets* (minor soloists), *grand sujets, premières danseuses* and *premiers danseurs* and, finally, *étoiles* (prima ballerinas and leading male dancers). Dancers remain in these divisions until they are promoted by the examinations that are given every member of the company every year. It is the usual practice for all dancers to perform two variations specified in advance by the directorate. The *étoiles* and *premières danseuses* and *danseurs* do not take part in the examinations. The examinations are judged by a jury of administrators, dancers, and teachers, which changes from year to year.

All the ballet schools in the United States are private. This is, of course, also true of our ballet companies. A number of our ballet companies, however, have their own ballet schools, where the members of the companies take class scholarships alongside regular students. Here, of course, it is not axiomatic that successful completion of a course gives the dancer a job with the company associated with the school.

PART SEVEN

Careers in Ballet

QUESTION How are dancers selected for ballet companies?

ANSWER By audition. The ballet master and other interested people in our ballet companies usually have these auditions when they need to replace some of their dancers or want additions to their companies. These auditions are held in New York and all over the country; the latter is particularly true of those ballet companies that travel.

Often, at an audition, the ballet master will ask the dancer to perform a variation that is familiar to her; then he may show her a dance she doesn't know and see how she performs it, because the one thing that the dancer may know very well is not the best clue to her real talent. Previous experience is good to have, but every year all our ballet companies take in new girls and boys whose familiarity with the stage is meager indeed.

Many of our American companies, in New York and throughout the country, today have their own schools, and it is mostly from these schools that new members of the companies are selected. This would be the ideal situation for every ballet company, for in this way—with a definite idea of what kind of dancer they desire—companies can train students within their own requirements. The advantage of this is obvious, of course—even before a student dances on the stage, she will have had, in class, a real idea of the company's style and artistic demands.

QUESTION How tall should a dancer be?

ANSWER Between five feet and five-feet-six inches for a grown-up girl. Grown-up boys can be taller, of course, between five-feet-six and six feet, but not over six feet. There are exceptions, but not many. If a girl is five-feet-eight, on toe she will be way over six feet tall and will look silly with any partner she dances with. Dancers who intend to be only soloists can naturally afford to be taller, because their greater height will not be distracting or ludicrous as they will not be with girls or boys of average height in the *corps de ballet*. I must point out, however, that tall or short dancers with distinctive personalities and abilities can certainly achieve success.

QUESTION Should all dancers be musical?

ANSWER It would be wonderful if they were. At some time in her life a dancer should play a musical instrument—the piano, violin, flute, any musical instrument. She may not have talent and may play badly, but this experience will make her participate in music: she will not always be passive in relation to it. She will understand something about what music is. That, like dancing, music is hard to perform well. If it isn't possible for her to play an instrument, she should at least know solfeggio: how to sing scales (*do, re, mi, fa* . . . etc.), how to read a little music and be able to sing from the notes.

But being musical, of course, is not just being able to play an instrument, even if you play it well. There are, for instance, many unmusical singers who can sing the proper notes, but who haven't the least idea what the song is all about. The dancer's relation to music is very similar to the singer's: an orchestra is accompanying what she does; she is always moving with the music. She can move to the music automatically, count to herself all the time, and never really listen. Afterward she won't remember the music, only the sequence of steps. Counting is necessary, particularly in learning a new ballet, where you are anxious to remember the precise moment for entrances, exits, and particular steps; but after these simple things are grasped, the dancer should not only count but should also listen very carefully. After all, there's no reason why the public should be obliged to sit and watch a dancer move to music that she thinks is dull. They will think it is dull, too. Perhaps being musical is something a dancer is born with—either she reacts to it or she doesn't—but I think that, with intelligent application, any student can develop certain sensitivities to music that will improve the quality of her dancing immeasurably. No advice will help her as much as going to concerts and recitals frequently and listening to as much music as possible.

If your children take piano lessons or learn to play some other musical instrument, it is proper to enforce a certain discipline about it for some time; but if after a few years a child shows no aptitude for the instrument, it is foolish to compel her to continue. She will begin to hate music and undo all your work. If she has studied for some time, acquired a certain skill and been exposed to what music is, and doesn't wish to go on with her studies, allow her to stop. If she really loves music, she will go back to it; if she doesn't like it, you will have done her no harm.

QUESTION   Should dancers go to college?

ANSWER   It would be nice if they could, but since students who wish to become *professionals* should be studying dancing every day, it becomes difficult. Serious dance students have—in addition to their regular ballet classes—classes in character dancing, modern dance, supported adagio, and so forth. This means that unless dance students go to college at night, or between their classes at ballet school, when they are no doubt tired from their work at dancing, they can't go at all.

There are many people who say that all dancers are stupid, and some give as a reason for this the fact that dancers are not properly educated. It would be nice if we could have complete dancing academies in America, where students could be taught an academic curriculum, music, and the other arts to complement their study of dancing; but we have no such institutions, and besides, I don't think it is true at all that dancers are stupid. My experience has been that they are, on the contrary, apt to be very intelligent. It is also my experience that there are many stupid college graduates. Intelligence is not entirely a matter of education.

QUESTION   Must all dancers first be members of the *corps de ballet?*

ANSWER   Usually this is the case. Directors of a ballet company who have not seen a young professional in school do not know how talented she may be until she has had a chance to display her gifts, and most young dancers are therefore engaged first for the *corps de ballet*. Many of them, also, are too young to be placed in anything else. If they evidence talent in the *corps,* they will soon be given larger roles. But it is only seldom that a member of the *corps de ballet* becomes a ranking soloist overnight. Ballet companies that are directly associated with their own ballet schools can watch students from day to day and discover soloists among them; these students need not be tried out in the *corps de ballet*. Most of the great Russian dancers became important soloists as soon as they were graduated, some before they were graduated. Tanaquil LeClercq, a ballerina of the New York City Ballet, began as a soloist and leading performer. But it is by no means "once in the *corps de ballet,* always in the *corps de ballet.*" We must remember that André Eglevsky, *premier danseur,* joined the Ballet Russe de Monte Carlo when he was fourteen and was dancing leading roles six months later; that Alexandra Danilova began in the *corps de ballet* of the Maryinsky Theatre, advanced to soloist, and became a ballerina in Diaghilev's great Ballets Russes; that Alicia Markova took soloist roles in Diaghilev's company soon after she joined it at the age of fourteen; that Maria Tallchief joined the Ballet Russe de Monte Carlo as a member of the *corps* to become a soloist and a ballerina.

QUESTION   Is a dancing career incompatible with marriage?

ANSWER   By no means. Very often dancers retire when they marry, perhaps because they go to live with their husbands in places where there is little dancing or because they want to have large families, but many successful dancers continue their careers after marriage and their careers continue to be successful.

QUESTION   Must ballet dancers belong to a union?

ANSWER   There are several unions which a ballet dancer might conceivably join, depending on where the ballet company is performing. If the ballet company performs in a legitimate theatre or opera house, in all probability the dancer would join the American Guild of Musical Artists, because AGMA has agreements with virtually all companies who perform in these theatres.

QUESTION   How much are ballet dancers paid?

ANSWER   The minimum in 1977 was $200 a week for dancers in our *corps de ballet* at the New York City Ballet. In 1942 the minimum was $41.50, and it can be seen that the dancer's pay has risen with the times; it will certainly continue to do so. Soloists and leading dancers are naturally paid much more than the minimum, but there is no established rule for their wages; it is a matter decided by the individual companies and the individual dancers. Still, it is obvious that no one ever pursued a dancing career to make a great deal of money. Leading singers and actors receive a great deal more money for their services than leading dancers. It's strange that this should be the case, for when actors and singers aren't regularly employed they can work at outside jobs and keep in practice by private study at night. The unemployed dancer, however, must attend ballet class during the day and work at her art constantly to keep in perfect condition. She seldom has either time or energy left for an outside job. The dancer between engagements is thus apt to be very poor. Even when they are working, I think it is safe to say that all dancers are underpaid or overworked, or both.

QUESTION   How long does a dancer's career last?

ANSWER   This is not an easy question to answer. Usually, nowadays, dancers appear on the stage by their late teens, often when they are sixteen or seventeen. It is even possible for dancers to become very famous before they are twenty. Some years ago, when I brought Irina Baronova, Tatiana Riabouchinska, and Tamara Toumanova to the Ballet Russe de Monte Carlo, they were all under sixteen. They were the "baby ballerinas" and became famous overnight.

By the time they are thirty, dancers have more or less reached their peak: they have acquired just about all the technique that is possible for them. But after they are thirty they can, of course, develop what they have learned and become greater artists still. The great dancers of the past—Pavlova, Karsavina, Spessivtzeva—we remember not as young girls, but as mature women, beautiful and gracious. Pavlova never retired; she was fifty when she died. Karsavina danced in public for the last time when she was forty-seven. It's up to the individual dancer. They can dance only occasionally when they grow older, and only gradually will audiences detect a change in them. Naturally, it is a happier thing if dancers retire before their audiences compel them to.

QUESTION   Should dancers have children?

ANSWER   Certainly. It does no harm whatever. Many dancers have children. Many dancers are also naturally unwilling to sacrifice a year out of their careers in order to have them. It depends on the individual.

QUESTION   Are sports good for dancers?

ANSWER   Only as an occasional pleasure. Dancers must take good care of their bodies. I would say that it is dangerous to skate, for instance. In skating, the knees bend a different way and the ankles are used differently. Playing football would be particularly hazardous. In fact, any game in which you would have to kick a ball would not be good. If a toe is injured, a dancer may have to give up dancing and all those years of study will be wasted. Tennis is all right, I suppose, for a little pleasure and if not pursued too strenuously. Actually, too much athletic activity destroys the finesse of a dancer's gesture. The truth is, of course, that dancers are so busy working at their art and are usually so tired from their studies that they seldom have the time or energy for sports.

Nathan Milstein, the great violinist, doesn't like to carry his violin because of the weight of the case. He must curve his fingers around the handle, and he feels that this strains them. It doesn't, of course, strain them seriously, and he would naturally be able to play well in any case; but he has some fine reaction in his hand that makes him think he won't be able to play with complete refinement. Horowitz, too, cares for his hands, as do all great instrumentalists. The principal instruments of a dancer are, of course, her legs, and she must respect them.

QUESTION How is ballet training beneficial to those who do not intend to pursue professional careers?

ANSWER Training in ballet strengthens the general physical condition of the body and develops the muscular system. It also gives complete control—poise, grace, and balance—to the body. Many people do not know how to enter a room gracefully; dancers do. Notice sometime that most people, when they are in a room with other people, often unconsciously turn around to look over their shoulders. Actually, they are self-conscious, ill at ease with their own bodies. They hesitate to turn their backs. These people control their faces well enough and imagine that grace consists largely of facial beauty. Dancers don't worry about people watching them from behind. They move unself-consciously; their grace is confident, an attribute of the whole body. For this reason, ballet training is beneficial not only to those who intend to pursue professional careers, but to all people.

QUESTION What careers are open to dancers after they retire?

ANSWER Many of them become teachers. Certainly, experienced dancers who have appeared for many years on the stage are the best-equipped teachers. Many former dancers become ballet masters in our ballet companies. There they rehearse ballets, give classes, and preserve the artistic disciplines. Such a person must not only be an exceptional teacher, he must also have a good visual memory and be very musical. Others with talent become choreographers; perhaps they began to create ballets while they were still dancing. Still others continue to work in the theatre as character dancers and mimes. In this country we regard this as something of a comedown, but we really shouldn't. In the Royal Danish Ballet, for example, the dancers stay on in the company and are much respected. It is a wonderful thing to see a dancer who was once a ballerina doing a part such as the mother in *Giselle*. This sort of dancer is very familiar with the ballet and knows that the part is important. It is she and other dancers like her who hand down to younger people the old traditions, and not just in a gossipy way: they watch them rehearse, correct them tirelessly, make sure of every detail. In this way the original choreographer's intention is preserved, along with the steps he planned, and very old ballets survive intact. That is an exciting way for a dancer to pay her debt to her profession.

PART EIGHT

*Notes and Comments on Dancers,
Dancing and Choreography*

QUESTION What country produces the finest classical dancers?

ANSWER Classical dancing isn't a nationalistic question, and for a very simple reason: it isn't nationalistic dancing. Native character or folklore has nothing to do with it. The ability to "turn out" properly, for example, has nothing to do with the country from which a dancer comes. Americans have a great deal of ability because their bodies are strong and also because they are a very musical people. Maybe it's because we hear music, all kinds of it, everywhere here. Children respond to this rhythmical music. They clap, dance, and develop rhythmical sense almost by nature. This sense of rhythm needs schooling, very good schooling; but with such a background in your students, you can develop very great dancers. In France there are also lots of strong, well-built dancers who are musical, and certainly the same is true of England, Italy, and other countries. In other words, people of all nationalities make wonderful classical dancers. The problem really narrows down to where the best schools are. Where you have the best teachers, you have the best dancers, no matter what their nationality.

QUESTION Is there such a thing as purely American ballet?

ANSWER In answer to this question and the two that follow, I'd like to paraphrase the comment that I made on these subjects in Serge Lido's *Ballet 2*, some years ago.

From the time ballet began, it has been influenced by *all* the countries where it developed, from Italy, to France, to Scandinavia, and it has adapted itself to the physical abilities of the different countries. The historical development of the art has been traced in another part of this book. I hope I have successfully shown that the classic dance is a fully developed art form, which has now become universal. It has a body of classified and organized techniques which will remain as the basis of the vocabulary of classical dance until such time as ballet is replaced by some other form of theatrical entertainment.

I think that if there is such a thing as purely American ballet, it is reflected not in style but in subject matter. For example, a ballet about cowboys might be called American, as a ballet about Sherlock Holmes might be called English, or the cancan might be called French. The latter case, however, is a question of national rather than classical dance.

QUESTION Are there different styles of classical dancing for each country?

ANSWER As for style of dancing for different countries, there are naturally some small differences in execution, but they are mainly differences of personality. For example, there may be ten different interpretations of *Swan Lake* or *Giselle* in England, France, Denmark, Italy, and the United States—all equally valid. Some people, whose taste is inclined toward the obvious, have come to expect certain stylistic clichés from dancers—as, for example, that the dancer should be warm and passionate—but a dancer does not necessarily have to be warm or passionate. Some people are readily inclined to look for the obvious on stage. There are two types of personalities, for example, which seem to be universally pleasing to audiences: one is the vampire, almost like a female Mephistopheles; the other personality is like the lyrical or the poetic one, often almost lethargic. Yet some very good dancers that I have seen in my life were beautifully cold, like birds with no warmth at all. Others were like Oriental queens; others, again, were like pure crystal. The technique of classical dance necessarily creates a certain uniformity in dancers, which has little or nothing to do with nationality, but which is certainly modified by the personality of the dancer. I am, of course, talking about dancers with talent. Talent is God-given: it is not given by a nation or a passport. A dancer must certainly have this gift, but the gift can manifest itself in forms as various as the universe. One cannot say that sunshine is better than shade, or that a glass of cold water is worse than a flaming chimney.

There are many so-called connoisseurs who try to dictate a certain style of ballet dancing, and they talk about a tradition that they never knew. Fortunately, this does not endanger the progress or development of ballet, because the real public—the people who sit in galleries, at a small admission price which most of them can ill afford—can distinguish good dancing from an inferior imitation of a style which was interesting a hundred years ago. Every performance demonstrates that this is the true ballet public, without prejudice or fake balletomanism.

I was brought up in St. Petersburg. The style of dancing there was very strict and precise. At the same time, in Moscow, six hundred kilometers away, the style of dancing was close to that of a circus performance. The Muscovites accused us in St. Petersburg of being cold, and we accused them of bad taste. History shows that the dancers and choreographers who later influenced ballet as a whole came mainly from St. Petersburg.

QUESTION   What is the future of ballet in America?

ANSWER   The future of ballet in America, as well as in the other countries, depends on the rise of new choreographers capable of furthering its development. A school of dancing is not enough. A school naturally perpetuates the technique, but it cannot lead to a new style in the ballet; nor can a new style of ballet be invented. Progress in any art is a slow and complex process, and therefore it cannot be generated by one person only. Many people are necessarily involved. In the field of ballet, it is not only the personality of the dancer and the art of the choreographer which achieve or create a style—one should not forget the composers. Delibes and Tchaikovsky are, I believe, as responsible for what is now traditionally known as classic ballet as its choreographers and dancers.

Any good company needs a professional choreographer, just as any good restaurant needs a good chef. If a ballet company does not develop successfully, the blame must be laid at the feet of its choreographer. If he was given all possibilities of choosing the best dancers, and if he was given the liberty to do what he wanted, he should not have failed in his task of achieving adequate results.

QUESTION   How does a choreographer originate his ballets?

ANSWER   This is a question I can only answer by telling you how I go about creating a new ballet, because, of course, different choreographers have different ways of proceeding with their work. When I am about to produce a ballet, I begin in one of two ways: either I begin with the idea and then look for suitable music, or I hear a certain piece of music which inspires me with an idea.

This idea need not be explicitly dramatic, as in a narrative ballet such as *Prodigal Son* or *Orpheus;* it need not have a written libretto. On the contrary, the idea might consist only in a *location,* a place, where I might wish dancing to take place, the particular people I want to dance there, and a special mood. *La Valse,* for instance, doesn't have a plot, but it is dramatic in its casting, its dancing, and the mood which action and music evoke.

If I begin with an idea, I much prefer to have the music specially written for me and to be in constant touch with the composer while he is writing it. I try to tell him exactly what I want, and together we conceive the general mood and we time some of the dance sequences. I have found that most ballet composers like to have a definite timing for a ballet: they like to know when such-and-such occurs and how long it will last, whether a sequence is a dance sequence or a *pas d'action,* and so forth. Like novelists, they are interested in structure first. In this way, they can start to compose at any point in the ballet and not begin at the beginning. Working on the story ballets *Prodigal Son* and *Orpheus* was a collaboration between the composers, Prokofiev and Stravinsky, and myself.

If I begin with the music, I familiarize myself with the score thoroughly and try to understand what the composer had in mind musically when writing it. When he wrote his *Concerto in D minor for Two Violins,* Bach had no idea of composing music for a ballet; but in listening to this music, it is possible to conceive of movement that harmonizes with the score. Actually, it seems to me that the music of Bach and Mozart is always very close to dancing. It would be wrong to say that all music should be danced, but I think the greatest music is never far from dancing. I agree with the poet who said that music rots when it is too far removed from the dance, just as poetry rots when it departs too far from music.

To familiarize myself thoroughly with a piece of music, I study the score and listen to it. If a piano transcription of the score exists, I play the piece over and over on the piano; if it does not exist, I make a transcription myself. Often I spend much more time learning a score than I do working out a ballet. The Mozart score for *Caracole*, for instance, I had in mind for three years, whereas setting the steps took only seven days.

There is always music that I wish to arrange dances to. Sometimes I make the ballets right away, if this is possible. One night, some years ago, the composer Alexei Haieff played me some pieces of his on the piano. I liked the music, but I didn't think of producing a ballet. Several days later, when this music kept running through my head, I wanted very badly to make dances to it. The result was *Divertimento*. If I were a poet, I'd probably have written a poem about what this music sounded like and looked like; but I am a choreographer, a dancer, and only in dancing do I express myself naturally. In other cases, I have known the music for many years and have kept it for the right moment. This was the case with *Symphonie Concertante*, music which has always seemed to me Mozart at his most beautiful; it was also true of *Symphony in C, Bourrée Fantasque*, and many other ballets.

Before beginning rehearsals, then, I have an idea of what the general scheme of a ballet will be. I never arrange any of the dances or movements until I actually rehearse the dancers. I discuss scenery and costumes with the designer, so that they will be in accord with the idea. I discuss the lighting, and I discuss the music with the composer and the conductor, but I don't discuss the ballet with my dancers unless we are doing a story ballet.

If the ballet has no story, there is no need to discuss their parts with the dancers in any detail; these parts the dancers work out by themselves, in individual practice. But in the case of a story ballet, I tell them what characters they are playing and what their relation is to the other characters.

Other choreographers, naturally, work differently. In working on story ballets, some choreographers spend lots of time talking to the dancers, explaining the story to them: the time the story took place, the history of that era, and so forth.

I have no fixed procedure. I don't come to rehearsals with any idea so definite and fixed that it can't be changed on the spot. I never write anything down. Often I try a step, or a series of movements, on a particular dancer and then I change it to something else. I indicate the steps first, and then the dancers repeat after me. It is very simple to mount a ballet

using dancers you have worked with: they understand your smallest gesture and know what you want almost instinctively.

Sometimes I arrange the end of a ballet first; sometimes I commence in
the middle. Rehearsal time is limited, and I can't always indulge in the
extravagance of following the order of the music. If I have plenty of time,
I work with each dancer until he or she is absolutely perfect; but the natural thing is for the dancers to want to practice the steps alone and perfect themselves. This they automatically do when there is little time, as in
the case of *Prodigal Son,* which was produced in ten days in 1929, and
with *Firebird,* which was produced in a week in 1949.

It has been my experience that dancers drop naturally into their parts;
they gradually come to live them. Every detail is given: I show them
every precise movement and the smallest mimed gesture and action.

QUESTION   Is it proper for the old classical ballets to be revived and revised by
present-day choreographers?

ANSWER   Yes, I don't see why not, if the choreographers have respect for the
original music and for the intention of the work as it has come down to
us. This is a question that many people ask very seriously, as if it meant
the life or death of ballet. They talk about tradition as a matter of remembering old steps accurately and reproducing them on the modern stage.
The trouble is that no one can possibly remember all the steps of the
ballets he saw years ago. A consistent form of accurate, intelligible dance
notation has only recently been perfected—in 1940.

What, then, do these people mean when they talk of preserving the
classics in their original state? They mean, very simply, nothing at all.
They don't know, nor does anyone else, exactly what those ballets were
like. They just take the word of so-and-so that the old ballets, in fact,
looked like such-and-such. But this is just one man's impression, and
surely a faulty one: our memories are not as accurate as the movie camera.

We can naturally accept this man's word in part if the revivals he produces entertain us, but there is no use in deceiving ourselves into thinking
that now, in the middle of the twentieth century, we are watching dancing and acting precisely as they were done in the nineteenth century.
Those ballets—and their music—were changed radically and materially by
dancers, conductors, ballet masters, and choreographers within the lifetime of their original creators.

It doesn't make sense to ask for the original, in short, if you have no
idea of what the original was. People who always talk about tradition in a
narrow, limited sense remind me of the story of the young Russian tenor
who was to sing a leading part in a revival of an opera. During rehearsals,
he was instructed to interrupt the dramatic action of one of his scenes and
almost conceal himself at the back of the stage before he began to sing a
difficult aria. The young tenor thought this was senseless and complained
about it. But he was told that Mr. X, who had been very famous in this

role, used always to interrupt the action in this manner and that he, too, must do so. The singer did as he was told, though he thought it was very foolish indeed. Some time later he asked the famous old tenor why he had changed the action of the opera. The old tenor was surprised and amused; he said, "Well, confidentially, I found that aria very difficult and I always needed to spit before I started to sing it, so I walked upstage a little and no one saw me."

QUESTION   Can anyone be taught to be a choreographer?

ANSWER   No. To be a choreographer, it is first of all necessary to be a dancer, a good one. This was true of choreographers in the past, as it is today; all our distinguished choreographers have been dancers of real quality. To become a good dancer, you must study at a ballet school for some years. Then you join a ballet company. This ballet company will dance good and important things, old ones and new ones, and there you will associate with conductors, musicians, and designers—as well as dancers. They advise you and you begin to learn. It's not, in other words, a matter of just learning how to dance and then starting to choreograph. You have to go through a period of preparation. If I told fifty well-trained dancers to move, to dance, to entertain me, they would not know what to do.

You must go through tradition, absorb it, and become in a way a reincarnation of all the artistic periods that have come before you. For instance, you must be able to know and feel how people acted and moved in Molière's plays, what sense of humor those people had, what their stage looked like. If you are going to do an Italian ballet set in a certain period, you try to go to Italy and become a part of that world. Then you put everything together—your dancing technique, your preparation in tradition, your knowledge of music, your ability—and something happens. A ballet is born.

Sometimes nothing happens. Then, I'm afraid, nothing can be done. There is no school where you can learn to be a choreographer. People can be advised about technique, they can be told to do this or that differently, but you cannot advise a person to be talented. He is born talented. It is a strange thing: your life is made somewhere, you are pushed in a certain direction, and you move that way.

There's no school that can teach choreography, just as there is no school where you can learn to be a novelist or a poet. Schools can give you technique, but from that point on you are on your own. At ballet school you can learn to dance, just as you can learn to write correct English and poetic meters in other schools, but that is only the beginning. Nothing really helps but the person himself, what inclination he has, what talent. We ought to remember the story of the famous English novelist who wanted to bring his son up to be a novelist, too. He worked with the boy, made him notice details in the way people acted, tried to teach him all the things he had learned with so much difficulty. He was deadly earnest about all this. His son turned out to be not a novelist, but a sheep farmer in Australia.

A choreographer must also be a teacher. I learned this myself when I did my first ballet, a composition in the Fokine style. I was fifteen years old and I taught this little ballet to eight boys in my class at the Imperial Ballet School in St. Petersburg. They were very good dancers. To make them stretch and extend themselves the way I wanted, I had to show them how to execute movements altogether new to them.

Choreographic movement is used to produce visual sensations. It is quite different from the practical movement of everyday life, when we walk, lift things, stand up, and sit down. Movement in choreography is an end in itself: its only purpose is to create the impression of intensity and beauty. No one intends to produce beautiful movements when rolling barrels or handling trains or elevators. But in all these everyday movements there are important visual dynamics if you look for them. Choreographic movements are the basic movements that underlie all gesture and action, and the choreographer must train himself to discover them. It's only natural that these basic movements will seem at first affected and artificial to the body that is accustomed only to the practical movements of everyday life. The object of the dancer's technical training is to enable him to perform—with perfect ease—choreographic movements, movements not limited by considerations of practical, daily life.

People in love all over the world have a certain attitude of sweetness and tenderness in the way they look and talk and touch. A choreographer notices this and finds movements to portray not the romance of A and B, but romance in general. A choreographer must see things that other people don't notice, to cultivate his visual sense. He must understand the stage space in a particular setting and how to fill that space with interesting movement; and to do this well, he must know music—know how to play it, preferably, and how to read it. For ballet is all a matter of space and time—the space on the stage, the time of the music to which the dancer moves.

The structure of a ballet must be tight, compact, like the structure of a building; good ballets move in measured space and time, like the planets.

The choreographer frees his mind from the limitations of practical time in much the same way that the dancer has freed his body. He turns not away from life, but to its source. He uses his technical proficiency to express in movement his essential knowledge. Talent, inspiration, and personality are not sources which come to an artist in a flash and go away; they are the accumulated results of all he has felt, thought, seen, and done—the stories he heard as a child, the art he has enjoyed, his education, and his everyday life—and are always with him, capable of being reached by his technical ability and transformed into dynamic designs of the utmost intensity.

If movement is the main means, possibly the only way, of presenting the art of dancing in its fullest significance, it is easy to understand the importance of connecting movements to each other with subtle care, yet at the same time emphasizing, by contrast, their continuity. For example, very brief and small movements to a fast or slow tempo—in every angle or degree of angle—are developed in relation to subsequent broad, large movements in the identical tempo, and increased from their use by one dancer to their use by many dancers. A kaleidoscope of such movements lives within the choreographer's brain, not yet, of course, set to any tempo. They are as yet only abstract memories of form. Of these, silence, placidity, and immobility are perhaps the most powerful forces. They are as impressive, even more so, as rage, delirium or ecstasy. When the body remains transfixed and immobile, every part of it should be invisibly tense, and even in relaxation there should be an inner muscular control.

The steps which a dancer has learned (and after he has studied about ten years with good teachers, he should have an impressive vocabulary of movements) are, when separate, devoid of meaning; but they acquire value when they are co-ordinated in time and space, as parts of the continual, rhythmic flow of the whole.

The student choreographer should at first work out simple technical exercises: for example, fitting eight bars of movement to eight bars of music. Many different interpretations may be given to music; there is no single meaning behind it which the listener must discover, and the choreographic student can fit any number of combinations of movements to the same eight bars of music. On the other hand, he can fit the same combination of movements to several different pieces of music. Or he can fit bars of movement to silence, which has a tempo of its own. But if he uses music, he must be sure to fit the movements to it completely.

There is a lot of talk about counterpoint in dancing. It is generally believed that counterpoint is based on contrasts. Actually, counterpoint is an accompaniment to a main theme which it serves to enhance, but from whose unity it must not detract. The only kind of counterpoint that I can see in dancing is the movements of arms, head, and feet which are contrapuntal to the static—or vertical—position of the body. For instance, in the *croisé* position the body is vertical—but one arm is raised, the other horizontal; one foot points forward, while the other supports the body; and the head is inclined toward one of the shoulders. All this is an accompaniment to the main theme, which is the vertical position of the body. In dancing one should not strive to achieve counterpoint by contrasting the movements of two dancers or two groups of dancers on the stage. This results not in counterpoint, but in disunity. (There is no need to apply musical terms to the dance; but if it is done, their meaning must be clearly understood.)

The eye can focus perfectly only on objects which are in the center of its field of vision. Those objects which are not head-on are seen clearly only because the observer knows and imagines what they are, while he focuses on the center object. If some new or different form is placed in the secondary part of a composition, the eye instinctively changes its focus and convinces itself of the identity of each individual form. And as vision is the channel through which the art of choreography reaches its audience, this inevitably results in confusion and a loss of attention to the main theme. But the eye can follow the movements of a large group of dancers if these form a harmonious pattern within its central field of vision.

It is impossible for choreographers to work very satisfactorily unless they are associated with a ballet company. You can compose music without an orchestra, but you cannot create a ballet without working directly with dancers.

In ballet companies, too, you learn many other things. When I was new in the Diaghilev company, I didn't know anything about Italian painting. I had just left Russia. Diaghilev took me to see pictures all over Italy. At first I was bored, but soon I became very interested: I saw that these pictures had a relation to other traditions I had absorbed, and I began to love them.

Choreography, finally, becomes a profession. In making ballets, you cannot sit and wait for the Muse. Union time hardly allows it, anyhow. You must be able to be inventive at any time. You can't be like the cook who can cook only two dishes: you must be able to cook them all.

PART NINE

Familiarity with ballet terms is not really necessary when we first start going to the ballet. In fact, if we know too much about the terms, we'll be watching to see what they mean in action and we'll miss most of the performance—it would be like knowing the meters of poetry before enjoying a poem. But while familiarity with ballet phrases is not important at the outset, it becomes important later on, after we have seen something of dancing. When we go to the ballet often, we begin to remember different steps and poses and want to know their names. That is only natural.

The most fundamental steps and positions—from the point of view of the spectator—are described below; a number of additional terms, an understanding of which will increase the knowledge of inexperienced members of the audience, are also discussed briefly. Because ballet as we know it was born in France, French is the language of the vocabulary of the classic dance. As such, it is ballet's international language, just as English is the universal language of sport and Latin the universal language of medicine.

BASIC POSITIONS

The five fundamental positions of the feet are learned by the ballet student just as we all learn the alphabet. These positions constitute the basis for all steps in the vocabulary of the classic dance and are learned by the student at the very beginning, so that they become instinctive. These basic positions were indicated by Thoinot Arbeau (1588), formally established by Pierre Beauchamp, first ballet master at the Paris Opéra (c.1700), and set down in writing by Pierre Rameau in *The Dancing Master* (1725). They have been in constant use ever since, as the ideal foundation for exercises and performance. Each of the positions features the characteristic that distinguishes the classic dance from all other forms of theatrical dance—the turned-out leg. In ballet, each leg is turned out from the hip at an angle of ninety degrees, so that the feet form a single straight line on the floor. The five absolute positions are performed with the feet flat on the floor, high on the ball of the foot (*sur les demi-pointes*) or on the toes (*sur les pointes*).

FIRST POSITION: Heels are together; feet are turned out to make a single straight line.

SECOND POSITION

FIRST POSITION

SECOND POSITION: Feet are turned out to form a straight line; heels are separated by a distance equivalent to one of the feet.

THIRD POSITION: Both feet are turned outward as in First Position; one foot is placed in front of the other, each heel touching the middle of the opposite foot.

THIRD POSITION (LEFT)
AND TRANSITION INTO
FOURTH POSITION (RIGHT)

FOURTH POSITION: Feet are turned outward; one foot is placed in front of and parallel to the other at a distance of one foot. The toe of one foot is in line with the heel of the other.

FOURTH POSITION
FRONT VIEW (LEFT) AND
SIDE VIEW (RIGHT)

FOURTH POSITION
CROISÉ

FOURTH POSITION
EFFACÉ

FOURTH POSITION
LEFT FOOT SUR LE POINTE

FIFTH POSITION: Feet are turned outward; one foot is placed in front of the other, the heels and toes touching so that the big toe of neither foot projects: the feet are boxed in.

FIFTH POSITION

ADAGIO As in music, a slow tempo: a dance in a slow tempo. The word is derived from the Italian *ad agio,* meaning at ease or in a leisurely manner. Adagios are danced by ballerinas and their partners. Adagios may occur in a ballet when the drama of the piece so dictates (*Swan Lake,* Act Two), as the central portion of a *grand pas de deux* (*Swan Lake,* Act Three), or simply as the music demands (*Symphony in C,* second movement). In adagio, the ballerina displays her beauty in slow, unfolding movements and sustained graceful poses. The principal quality of adagio is control.

  Adagio is also the name for a section of any ballet class. Here the dancers practice—in the center of the room—slow, sustained exercises designed to give ease in the performance of dances that require balance, perfect line, and unquestionable authority in those who execute them.

  The great Italian ballet master Carlo Blasis regarded the correct execution of adagio as the "touchstone of the dancer."

ALLEGRO Dancing that is lively and fast, in comparison to adagio. All steps of elevation—jumps, *entrechats,* turns in the air, etc., are forms of allegro. An important quality of allegro is *ballon,* the ease with which a dancer remains in the air during a step in elevation and the ease with which he takes off and lands from a jump.

ARABESQUE Set pose. In the most common form of arabesque, the dancer stands on one leg, with the other leg raised behind her and extended fully. The height of the raised leg is variable, as is the position of the arms.

BASIC ARABESQUE AND ARABESQUE PENCHÉ

ASSEMBLÉ Literally, together. A step in which the dancer rises low off the floor, straightens both legs in the air, and returns to Fifth Position.

À TERRE On the ground. *Par terre* is synonymous. Some dancers are called *terre à terre* dancers because they succeed best in steps that require no elevation, steps performed on the stage.

ATTITUDE Basic pose of the classic dance, first described by Carlo Blasis (1829), who modeled it after the famous statue of Mercury by Bologna. In the basic attitude, the dancer stands on one leg and brings the other leg up behind at an angle of ninety degrees, with the knee bent.

BALLERINA A leading female dancer of a ballet company. If the company is a large one, one or more principal ballerinas (*prima ballerinas*) stand at the top of the company's list of soloists. A dancer earns the title ballerina through years of hard work and by great dancing over the years in great roles. No matter what the standards of particular ballet companies, the dancer's lasting right to the title depends on continuous excellence in performance over a period of many years: we think of the great ballerinas of the past—Taglioni, Pavlova, Karsavina, Spessivtzeva—not as young girls, but as mature women. Few dancers possess the title ballerina with any secure permanence until they are thirty years old, at which time their native talent and artistry have usually been developed to the maxi-

THREE VIEWS OF AN ATTITUDE

mum. A ballerina is almost always associated with a particular role in a ballet—a role that has been created especially for her or a role in an accepted classic.

In the famous European ballet companies, which are state-supported and have their own ballet schools, the title ballerina (in France, *première danseuse*) stands at the top of a rigorous hierarchy. Beneath this pinnacle are arranged major and minor soloists, *coryphées* (dancers who perform in small groups), and the numerous members of the *corps de ballet*. Above the rank of *prima ballerina* there sometimes reigns the *prima ballerina assoluta*. It is interesting that in the history of the Russian Imperial Theatre this title was used only twice: by Pierina Legnani, the Italian ballerina who created the leading role in the Petipa-Ivanov *Swan Lake* (1895), and by Mathilda Kschessinska, who succeeded to the title after Legnani left Russia in 1901. In the early years of this century, Olga Preobrajenska, Anna Pavlova, Vera Trefilova, Lubov Egorova, and Tamara Karsavina were all ballerinas at the Maryinsky Theatre in St. Petersburg; Kschessinska was the only *prima ballerina assoluta*. This did not mean that Kschessinska was a better dancer than all the others; it meant simply that she was a maturer artist, with years of experience and excellent performance. The hierarchies in the European state theatres were developed as a means of periodic appraisal of personnel, as a way of adjusting salaries. Dancing in these theatres is like the civil service: you are promoted according to your ability and your experience, and seniority is naturally important.

In America, where we have no such system, there really seems little need to use the Italian words *ballerina, prima ballerina,* etc., to indicate ranks we don't have. Moreover, so many inexperienced and unimportant dancers call themselves ballerinas in America that the term has little meaning. All our fine dancers are stars of our ballet companies; when the word *star* is used, we have a better idea of something special. The male equivalent of the rank of ballerina is *premier danseur*.

BALLET   From the Italian *ballare*, to dance, via *balleti*, the diminutive form of *balle*, a dance-song.

BALLET BLANC (white ballet)   Ballet in which girls wear long white gossamer costumes: *Les Sylphides*, *Giselle* (Act Two), etc.

BALLET D'ACTION   Literally, a ballet in which something happens: a ballet with a plot.

BALLET MASTER   In the early days of ballet, the ballet master was a choreographer, a man who designed or composed dances for a ballet company. In France and in Russia today, this is still the case. In England and America, the ballet master (or ballet mistress) is the person responsible for company instruction and discipline, the person who gives classes to all the company dancers, rehearses them in all ballets in the repertory, and assigns parts. He may or may not be a choreographer as well, though this is often the case. The name artistic director combines the jobs of ballet master and choreographer. In Diaghilev's Ballets Russes, the company choreographer was ballet master and the company instructor-disciplinarian was the *régisseur*.

BALLETOMANE   A ballet enthusiast: a person who attends the ballet regularly, has decided opinions about dancers, and is partisan about the type of ballet, music, etc., to be preferred above all others. In the ideal sense, the balletomane is one whose great love for ballet as an art transcends partisanship for the individual dancer and choreographer. It is to be regretted that the loud and long demonstrations of some balletomanes are sufficient to drive the newcomer from the theatre. Marian Eames has written: "Exactly who coined the word *balletomane* is not known. It would seem reasonable to assume that the behavior of the dance enthusiast was to blame for the selection of the ending *mane* rather than *phile*. Indeed, the dance enthusiast appears to have been frenzied to a degree in his devotion and often absurd. Yet his frenetic outbursts lacked the embarrassing hollowness of contemporary movie madness, for the idolatry lavished upon individual dancers was not born of a mere susceptibility to physical 'allure.' The adorer was moved by qualities and style which he could analyze and discuss; furthermore, his obsession with the art itself should not be confused with the easily bought allegiance of zealots who are beguiled less by the avowed object of their enthusiasm than by the glorious trappings which surround it."*

BALLON   A characteristic of *elevation* (dance in the air). The ease with which a dancer maintains in the air a position he normally holds on the ground; the ability to ascend lightly into the air and to land softly and smoothly. *Ballon* is the French word for *hand ball* and *balloon;* literally, it means *bouncing*. It is said that the term ballon was named after the French *danseur* Balon (active 1695), who possessed its qualities to a remarkable degree.

BARRE (or bar)   The round horizontal bar secured around the walls of a ballet classroom or rehearsal hall at a height of about three-and-a-half feet. The bar is usually placed opposite the long mirrors in which the dancer can watch what he

* Foreword to "Russian Balletomania" by Anatole Chujoy, *Dance Index,* Vol. VII, No. 3.

is doing. Every ballet class begins with exercises at the bar, the dancer holding the bar for support as the daily elementary and constantly repeated exercises are performed; the lesson continues with exercises in the center of the room.

BATTEMENT A nickname for an action of the leg. For example, the *battement tendu* (stretched beating), where the dancer—in the simplest form of this exercise —stands at the bar and extends her foot in front of her on the floor, or sideways, or back.

BATTERIE The master term that applies to all movements in ballet in which one foot beats against the other, or in which the two feet beat together. Two types of this movement are distinguished: *grande batterie* (large, high beating steps) and *petite batterie* (small beating steps executed at a lower elevation).

BRISÉ Literally, a broken movement. A beating step of elevation in which the dancer rises from the floor, beats one leg against the other, and returns to the same Fifth Position—distinguishable from the *entrechat* in that only one leg beats.

CABRIOLE A movement of *grande batterie*. The cabriole develops the *battement*—in which one leg moves away from the supporting leg and returns—into a brilliant step of elevation: here both legs beat together in the air. One leg swings up to an angle of ninety degrees, the other leg rises, meets it, and both calves are beaten together (the feet do not cross); the legs are fully extended, knees straight, toes pointed. Cabrioles are also executed at an angle of forty-five degrees from the floor; they can be performed in any direction—front, back, and to the side.

CARACTÈRE The character dancer, or the dancer *en caractère,* performs national or folk dances—mazurkas, polkas, etc.—dances that are not performed on point. The dancer *en demi-caractère* performs popular dances such as the cancan, but may dance these on point; these are comic or semiserious dances, in other words, performed with some classical technique.

CHANGEMENT DE PIEDS (changing of the feet) Small jump from Fifth Position in which the dancer changes the position of both feet in the air.

CHASSÉ Literally, chased. A sliding step: the dancer jumps low off the floor, lands, and the working foot chases the landing foot out of position. A *chassé* embodies the same mechanical principle we see when we watch a horse canter. There the hind legs, moving together, displace the front legs.

CHOREOGRAPHER Someone who makes dances. The word means, etymologically, someone who records dances. It has come to mean simply the person responsible for the design of movement in a ballet. It is inaccurate to say that a choreographer "writes" a new ballet—for no choreographer sets down on paper what he wishes dancers to do from one moment to the next—but this is sometimes said.

All good choreographers have been good dancers. But to be a good dancer, of course, is not necessarily to be a choreographer. The dancer wishes *to be moved,* the choreographer wishes *to move.* To combine the two inclinations successfully is rare, but rare indeed are great choreographers. The choreographer is best compared to the poet: he is a man who uses the material of the classic dance that has been developed over hundreds of years, just as the poet uses the language he writes in. Like the poet, the choreographer finds new ways of saying things.

CLASSIC The word classic when applied to ballet is not the contrary of romantic. It applies to a rigorous basic vocabulary of steps and movements capable of infinite variation and a system of instruction that makes such variation possible for individual dancers. Classic ballets can be romantic, realistic, or mythological in sub-ject matter. The classic dance is the dictionary of ballet and, as a method of in-struction, it is also its grammar: basic steps and movements that must be learned and mastered if the student is to become an instrument of its possibilities. The classic dance is the fundamental material out of which new ballets are made; it constitutes the basic, instinctive knowledge that permits the dancer to perform them. As a system of instruction, the classic dance has been perfected through centuries of innovation and experiment. We know what is anatomically sound and physically possible. We know what must be taught first, how that must be learned so well that it becomes instinctive, what to teach next. We learn all this in schools, as dancers and teachers before us have learned it. Properly speaking, what we call the classic dance might be more easily understood if it were called the academic dance, after the academies in which it was evolved; but the word *classic* has come down to us, along with the tradition of the developed academic dance, and is now universally accepted. When we go to the ballet and see a ballet described as *classic* in the program, we know that the word doesn't imply something that is serious and perhaps not entertaining: classicism in dance is the basis for the finest entertainment.

CORPS DE BALLET Dancers who appear only in large groups: the chorus, the backbone of every ballet company. Jean Georges Noverre (1759) advised the ballet master to "make your *corps de ballet* dance, but when it does so, let each

DÉVELOPPÉ À LA SECONDE

member of it express an emotion or contribute to form a picture; let them mime while dancing so that the sentiments with which they are imbued might cause their sentiment to be changed at every moment." Until the present century, the function of the *corps de ballet* was merely decorative: as a group they embellished with their poses and did not distract from the performances of principal dancers. In dramatic ballets, they reacted with appropriate emotion to the dramatic situation (the death of Giselle, the huntsmen in *Swan Lake*).

The New Ballet of Michel Fokine, as he himself expressed it in 1914, "in developing the principle of expressiveness, advances from the expressiveness of face to the expressiveness of the whole body, and from the expressiveness of the individual body to the expressiveness of a group of bodies and the expressiveness of the combined dancing of a crowd." Every dancer in the crowd scene in the original production of *Petrouchka* (1911) had something to do at every moment, and each dancer was related in both action and reaction to the principals on stage. Ballet prior to Fokine was essentially linear: the stage was divided into parts where the *corps de ballet* danced, where the soloists danced, where the ballerinas danced, and these established patterns were seldom violated. With Fokine, movement on stage became orchestrated: each dancer on stage was an instrument contributing vitally to the general impression. Formerly it was only possible for a soloist to dance diagonally across the stage; now this is done by large groups of dancers: every dancer in such a group must be a soloist. Although every *corps de ballet* contains dancers of great talent who may eventually become principal dancers, and although it is wise for every soloist to have had experience in a *corps de ballet*, it is always possible in large state schools to discover talent early and not to permit it to idle long in the *corps*. This is the practice today with our ballet companies that are attached to schools. Talent is discovered early and used as soon as possible in appropriate roles. In ballet companies where the directors must first observe their new dancers in the *corps de ballet*, the *corps* itself becomes a kind of school, a testing ground, where talent is discovered. Experience in a *corps de ballet* gives a dancer invaluable lessons which are difficult to learn in any other way. Here she learns timing and precision; she learns also her relation to other dancers and other groupings of dancers on the stage. She learns, in fact, all the things that she must know to become a star.

DANCE (and danse) From the old high-German *danson*, meaning to drag or stretch.

DANSE D'ÉCOLE Literally, dance of the school. The classic dance, the academic dance based on the Five Positions and turnout (*see* Classic).

DANSEUR NOBLE A classical male dancer; partner of the ballerina in classical roles (Albrecht in *Giselle*, Siegfried in *Swan Lake*, etc.).

DÉVELOPPÉ From the French word that means, literally, to develop or to unfold. A gradual unfolding of the leg as it rises from the floor and is extended fully in the air. As it is raised toward complete extension, the foot of the working leg passes (*passé*) the knee of the supporting leg.

DIVERTISSEMENT A dance or a series of dances for simple diversion and pleasure. A *divertissement* may be a whole number, like *Aurora's Wedding*, which contains plotless dance excerpts from *The Sleeping Beauty*, or it may be part of a whole ballet, like the folk dances that celebrate Prince Siegfried's birthday in the third act of *Swan Lake* or the series of character dances that come in the last act of *Coppélia*. A *grand pas de deux* taken out of a ballet and performed alone without its surrounding plot is a *divertissement*.

ÉCHAPPÉ (from échapper, to escape or slip)   Step in which the dancer's feet escape from a closed position to an open position as she jumps upward. The movement is brisk and vigorous.

ELEVATION   The ability with which a dancer rises from the floor to perform jumps, and the capacity to remain in the air in the midst of these movements. The *danse d'élévation* was first popularized by Marie Taglioni (active 1822–48); within living memory, Vaslav Nijinsky (active 1908–19) still serves as a model conqueror of the air.

EN ARRIÈRE   Backward.

EN AVANT   Forward.

EN DEDANS   Inward.

EN DEHORS   Outward.

ENTRECHAT   Probably derived from the Italian *intrecciare*, to weave or braid. A beating step of elevation in which the dancer jumps straight into the air from *plié* and crosses his feet a number of times, making a weaving motion in the air. The term *entrechat* is compounded with numerals to indicate the number of movements of the legs: *entrechat-trois, entrechat-quatre, entrechat-cinq, entrechat-six, entrechat-sept, entrechat-huit*. Each leg moves once in a crossing: hence the term *entrechat-six* means six movements—counting both legs—or three crossings. *En-*

ENTRECHAT a, b

ENTRECHAT c, d, e

trechats up to *entrechat-six* are movements of *petite batterie,* small beatings; *entrechat-six* and above are movements of *grande batterie,* large beatings.

FOUETTÉ (from fouetter, to whip) In *fouetté en tournant* (see illustration), a whipping motion of the free leg which propels the dancer around the supporting leg.

FOUETTÉ EN TOURNANT I, II (FROM RIGHT TO LEFT)

GLISSADE (glide) A gliding movement from Fifth Position to an open position and back to fifth position—usually seen as a preparatory step for jumps.

JETÉ (from jeter, to throw) The word is derived from *jeter* rather than *sauter* (the French word for jump) because in this movement, the dancer *throws* one leg away and up in the air. This is a jump in which the weight of the body is thrown from one foot to the other. There are small jumps in ballet (*assemblés, changements, échappés,* etc.), but these are all preparations for the large aerial jumps in which the dancer's body describes a swift, high trajectory in the air. In *grand jeté* the dancer pushes off from the floor with one foot in a variety of preparatory positions, holds a fleeting pose in flight, and lands softly on the other foot. It is sometimes supposed by people who do not know French that the word *j'ter* (which in English sounds like *shtay*) applies to a movement different from *jeter.* This is not the case. *J'ter,* of course, is simply a contraction which French-speaking people make of *jeter*—a contraction they make quite naturally.

LIBRETTO The story line of a ballet; in a ballet without a plot, the idea on which the ballet is based. The ideal ballet story can be seen plainly and requires no extraneous explanation. The story of the *Prodigal Son* is a good example: once there was a boy who had everything, then he had nothing, then again he had everything.

NOTATION The writing down of dances in a form sufficiently intelligible for their accurate reproduction. Dances were written down as early as the fifteenth cen-

GRAND JETÉ

tury, but it is only recently—by the system devised by Rudolf von Laban—that the recording of dances and ballets has become universal (rather than arbitrary), accurate, and capable of the precision that permits them to be reproduced without the presence of the choreographer. The Dance Notation Bureau (founded in New York, 1940) has recorded many dances and ballets that have been faithfully reproduced on the basis of notation, and for the first time in dance history the copyrighting of choreography seems imminently possible.

PANTOMIME (from the Greek)   Literally, all-imitating *pantomimos*. A dumb show of significant gesture, ballet's way of indicating intricacies of plot. The players in the original Roman pantomimes wore masks and could express themselves only with their bodies. These pantomimes portrayed mythic characters, gods and goddesses. The *commedia dell'arte* of Italy reduced these formal theatrical pantomimes into a popular burlesque with a permanent set of characters—Harlequin, Columbine, Pierrot, etc.—what has come down to us as the Punch and Judy show. The vocabulary of mime was gradually absorbed into ballet, as traveling Italian comedians visited France and as dancers and ballet masters required the dance to express human emotions and situations. While it was said of Camargo (active 1726–35) that "she danced to dance, not to stir emotion," it was said of her rival, Marie Sallé (active 1718–40), that she "replaced tinsel glitter by simple and touching graces. Her physiognomy was noble, sensitive and expressive." The acting and miming of David Garrick was an inspiration to the French ballet master Noverre, the "Shakespeare of the dance." The mime vocabulary is now unknown to most of us because it is no longer taught as it used to be. It is rarely used in modern ballets, but in the older ballets (*Giselle, Coppélia, Swan Lake, Sleeping Beauty*) mime was essential; as we watch the older ballets, a knowledge of some of its elements is essential for us.

Mime is limited. There are some things it is foolish to try to indicate in a ballet: you cannot indicate your mother-in-law and be readily understood. But within the limits of pantomime, much can be expressed. Noverre wrote: "Gesture is the countenance of the soul, its effect must be immediate and it cannot fail to achieve its effect if it is true. . . . Dancers, like actors, should devote themselves to depict and feel: they have the same object to attain." Here are a few important mime expressions seen in ballet:

YOU: Point to person with open hand (with pointed finger when angry).

BEAUTIFUL (or GIRL): Circle the face gently with the back of the hand, letting the back of the middle finger outline the face.

PRINCESS: Lift arms and hold hands just over top of head, as if enclosing a crown.

DANCE: Circle the hands around each other above the head.

KISS: Touch lips with finger.

LOVE: Hold both hands over the heart.

MARRY: Point to wedding-ring finger with index finger of right hand.

ME: Point toward self with middle fingers of both hands simultaneously.

KING: With a flourishing gesture raise the right hand above the head, indicating the feather commonly worn in the hats of the nobility.

QUEEN: Let index finger of right hand touch top of forehead at points where crown touches.

STOP: Hold up hand, palm out.

ANGRY: Raise arms above the head, elbows front, and shake fists.

SAD: Let fingers trace tears as they fall down the face.

WEEP: Hide face in both hands, or rub eyes with clenched fists.

BEG MERCY: Hold arms out, palms together, as if praying.

NO: Hold arms at the side, then cross them before the body in a definite gesture as the head shakes.

OBEY: Point to floor with decided gesture.

FORGET: Hold out hands loosely, palms up, and shake the head slightly.

REMEMBER: Touch the temple with the index finger.

FRIENDS: Clasp hands together on a level with the waist.

BLESS: With the hand, touch the head of the person blessed.

DIE: Bring arms up to the side of the head, then bring them down quickly so that the hands, fists clenched, are crossed in front of the body.

SLEEP: Incline the head against the back of the hands.

CHILD: With both palms down, raise the hands in three steps, as if measuring the height of a growing child.

THANK YOU: Inclining the head simply, bring one hand down from the chest, extending it toward the person thanked.

PAS   A pace, a formalized or measured step. The dancer's step, or *pas*, is very different from the ordinary step we take when walking: it is closer to the pace, which we take when we measure or consider something. A *pas* is a gesture of the whole body.

PAS D'ACTION   Action in dancing—that part of a dramatic ballet, for example, where the relation of the characters is clarified. A *pas d'action* is not pure dancing and not pure mime, but a combination of the two, an integral part of the ballet spectacle. It's similar to many moments in opera where characters—after suspending the action for a while and singing a quintet—turn again to each other and resume their dramatic relation.

PAS DE DEUX   A dance for two people. Although a *pas de deux* is any dance for two people, the usual, standard *pas de deux* consists of five parts: the *entrée*, in which the ballerina and the *premier danseur* make their appearance; the adagio, in which the *danseur* supports the ballerina in a slow, graceful dance; a variation of the ballerina; a variation of the *danseur*; and the coda, a concluding passage for both ballerina and *danseur* in which the dance is brought to a felicitous conclusion.

PAS DE TROIS   A dance for three people. *Pas de quatre* is a dance for four people; *pas de cinq*, a dance for five; *pas de six*, for six; and so forth.

PIROUETTE   A complete turn of the body on one foot. *Pirouette* used to be applied only to turns by men, while the term *tour* was reserved for turns by women. The terms are synonymous. Girls turn in pirouettes on *pointe*, boys on *demi-pointe*. Ideally, the body is vertical in pirouettes; the foot of the supporting leg remains in one place. The free leg can be lifted slightly off the floor, the knee bent, as in the most common form of pirouette; it can be raised in back, the knee straight, as in *pirouettes en arabesque;* or it can be raised in back, the knee bent, as in *pirouettes en attitude;* and so forth. Pirouettes have dazzled audiences since the history of ballet began, but multiple pirouettes were not introduced until 1766. At

PIROUETTE I, II (FROM RIGHT TO LEFT)

that time, three turns by a boy and two by a girl were considered spectacular. Turns performed off the floor are called *tours en l'air*.

PLIÉ (from plier, to bend) In the classic dance, this is a bending of the knees, the knees wide open, the feet turned outward. The function of the *plié* in the dancer's body is like the function of springs in an automobile: it is necessary for the development of elasticity. *Demi-plié* is a half, or small, bending; *grand plié* is a deep bending of the knees.

POINTE The dancer *sur les pointes* dances on her toes. This innovation of the Romantic ballet (c.1820) is now universally used by female dancers in ballet: men stand on their toes only in certain Russian folk dances. If the dancer has been properly trained, dancing on point is neither painful nor uncomfortable nor damaging. Although the classic ballet is the only form of dance that uses toe dancing consistently, ballet existed long before toe steps were introduced; dancing on *pointes* cannot be called the single hallmark of ballet. Dancing on *pointes* is actually an extension of a basic feature of the classic dance: the straight line formed by the stretched leg and the pointing foot when the free leg moves from the floor. The ballet slippers of Marie Taglioni, who popularized toe dancing, were unblocked. The toes of ballet slippers were later blocked with glue, as they are today, to give the dancer additional support. Every dancer darns the exterior of the toe of her ballet slipper—not for support, but to provide security of position while she dances and to prevent slipping. Dancing *sur la demi-pointe* is on the half-toe, where the dancer is supported high on the ball of the foot and under the toes.

PORT DE BRAS   Movement or carriage of the arms.

RELEVÉ (from relever, to lift again)   In ballet, the raising of the body onto *pointe* or *demi-pointe*.

RÉVÉRENCE   A deep bow.

ROMANTIC   Ballets that we call Romantic are a *kind* of classical ballet. *La Sylphide* (1832), which epitomized—until the masterpiece *Giselle* (1841)—what we recognize as Romanticism in ballet, was romantic in subject, temper, and mood; but both ballets expressed this, with innovations, in the vocabulary of the *classic* dance. Similarly, *Les Sylphides* (1909)—which embodies Romanticism in name, substance, and music—consists of classical steps and movements. What is classic in ballet is what has been developed over the years; what is romantic is a period through which that development passed. Romanticism in ballet, in other words, is not the opposite of classicism.

Romanticism was responsible for revolutionary innovations in classic technique and in the subject matter of ballets. Its desire for ethereal creatures caused dancers for the first time to rise on their toes, introduced the white ballet costume so familiar to us in *Giselle, Swan Lake,* and *Les Sylphides,* and caused the expansion of the dance vocabulary to meet the expressive requirements of elfin, unattainable heroines and heroes who aimed at—and so seldom secured—permanent happiness. As it contrasted real life with fantasy, the Romantic Ballet naturalized the pastoral theme that dominated earlier ballet. Where previously nymphs and shepherds were potential gods and goddesses, these pastoral characters now became realistic, only to escape later from realism's cruelty to supernatural kingdoms (Act Two of *La Sylphide* and *Giselle*).

The heroes of the Romantic movement in ballet are: Théophile Gautier (1811–1872), French poet, critic, and novelist, the librettist of *Giselle;* Jules Perrot (1810–1892), dancer and choreographer, collaborator on *Giselle* and creator of the *Pas de Quatre.* Its heroine is its great ballerina Marie Taglioni (1804–1884), creator of *La Sylphide.* The Romantic Ballet dominated the classic dance from about 1820 to 1870.

After this time, what we recognize as the great classical ballets—*Swan Lake, The Sleeping Beauty,* etc.—were created on the basis of a new uncovered, unconcealed technique and a more exacting dance discipline. Thus, unlike literature, music, and the other arts, ballet's great period of classicism came *after* the development of Romanticism.

ROND DE JAMBE   A rotary movement of the leg; the dancer describes circles in the air, or on the floor, with the pointed toe of the working foot. The *rond de jambe* is a basic exercise in the ballet class and a ballet step seen frequently on stage. The *rond de jambe en l'air* is executed away from the floor.

SAUTÉ (from sauter, to jump)   The word is used as a modifier to explain that a jump is involved in a step or pose: *sauté en arabesque, échappé sauté,* and so forth.

TOUR   *See* Pirouette.

TOUR EN L'AIR   A turn in the air. The dancer, standing in Fifth Position, rises from the floor from a *demi-plié,* executes a complete turn, and returns to original position. *Tours* may be doubled or tripled for spectacular effect, but three complete turns in the air is the maximum.

TURNOUT   The distinguishing characteristic of the classic dance: knees that face frontward in a normal standing position are turned out from the hip at an angle of ninety degrees (*see* Basic Positions). Because dancers wore heels on their shoes at the time the five absolute positions were established, the complete ninety-degree turnout was not perfected until some time later. Complete turnout is not forced in beginning students.

TOUR EN L'AIR I, II (FROM RIGHT TO LEFT)

TUTU   Ballet skirt; a nickname for *tunique,* tunic. The so-called Romantic tutu, which reaches to about twelve inches above the floor, was made famous by Marie Taglioni in the first famous Romantic ballet, *La Sylphide;* it is still familiar to us in *Giselle* (Act Two) and *Les Sylphides.* Gradually, however, with the perfection of dance technique, the tutu has been shortened to make the whole leg visible.

VARIATION   A solo, a dance for one person. Synonym: *pas seul.*

INDEX